The publisher gratefully acknowledges the generous support of the Music in America Endowment Fund of the University of California Press Foundation, which was established by a major gift from Sukey and Gil Garcetti, Michael P. Roth, and the Roth Family Foundation.

The publisher also gratefully acknowledges the generous suport of the Constance and William Withey Endowment Fund for History and Music of the UC Press Foundation.

Norman Granz

Norman Granz

The Man Who Used Jazz for Justice

Tad Hershorn

Foreword by Oscar Peterson

UNIVERSITY OF CALIFORNIA PRESS

Berkeley · Los Angeles · London

University of California Press, one of the most
distinguished university presses in the United States,
enriches lives around the world by advancing
scholarship in the humanities, social sciences, and
natural sciences. Its activities are supported by the UC
Press Foundation and by philanthropic contributions
from individuals and institutions. For more
information, visit www.ucpress.edu.

University of California Press
Berkeley and Los Angeles, California

University of California Press, Ltd.
London, England

Library of Congress Cataloging-in-Publication Data

Hershorn, Tad.
    Norman Granz : the man who used jazz for justice /
Tad Hershorn ; foreword by Oscar Peterson.
        p.   cm.
    Includes bibliographical references and index.
    ISBN 978-0-520-26782-4 (cloth : alk. paper)
    1. Granz, Norman, 1918–2001.   2. Impresarios—
United States—Biography.   3. Jazz—History and
criticism.   I. Title.
    ML429.G696H47   2011
    781.65092—dc22
    [B]

                                    2011011292

Manufactured in the United States of America

19   18   17   16   15   14   13   12   11   10
10   9   8   7   6   5   4   3   2   1

In keeping with a commitment to support
environmentally responsible and sustainable printing
practices, UC Press has printed this book on Rolland
Enviro100, a 100% post-consumer fiber paper that
is FSC certified, deinked, processed chlorine-free, and
manufactured with renewable biogas energy. It is acid-
free and EcoLogo certified.

Contents

Illustrations

Foreword

I have a boundless love for and enduring remembrance of Norman Granz. I grieve to this day because of his absence from all of us, and most importantly (and selfishly) from me.

Norman Granz represents a truly unbridled and honest love for jazz. The world benefited tremendously from his recordings and concerts. But Norman should be noted not only for his great contribution to the jazz world musically but also for his unbiased treatment of the players, regardless of their racial background. He sanctioned his musical belief in jazz by hiring the people whose playing he admired, regardless of their race.

One of my foremost memories of this man I so revere was his fearless presentation of what he believed to be true jazz. He mixed everything from Italy to Africa to Jerusalem to Canada. His musical legacy to the world is the unbiased truth with which he presented truly talented jazz players, some of whom would not have reached the top of the mountain without his belief and help. His integrity, personally and musically, never wavered. He remained true always to jazz and would never compromise in his presentation of the best. He presented musicians and made recordings knowing that even though they would never bring financial gain, they were important *musically*.

To this day I also don't believe that Norman has been and is truly recognized for the great influence he had racially on people of that era. His dedication to and belief in equality caused him many moments of confrontation. He never wavered in standing up for his strong beliefs, even in the face of danger to himself.

I would like people to remember him as the most honest and musically upright impresario ever in the jazz field. He could not be bought or sidelined in his belief not only in musical elegance but also in racial equality. I shall always love him and respect him for the man he was and is, and for his truth, integrity, and deep friendship. God bless him, and may the world learn a lesson from him in truth and tolerance.

Oscar Peterson
August 2007

Prologue: "I Made Things Work"

The chartered bus carrying impresario Norman Granz and his Jazz at the Philharmonic troupe pulled into the parking lot of the Regent Restaurant in Jackson, Michigan, about sixty-five miles west of Detroit, with a couple of hours to spare before their appearance at the Jackson County Auditorium on Monday, October 6, 1947. Granz and JATP, as the national concert tours were already known by legions of fans, had been building a reputation for fiery jam sessions of all-star musicians in integrated settings since the concerts had begun in his hometown of Los Angeles in July 1944. The bus that night carried Granz, who emceed his shows, and a lineup including tenor saxophonists Coleman Hawkins and Flip Phillips, trumpeter Howard McGhee, trombonist Bill Harris, pianist Hank Jones, drummer J. C. Heard, and bassist Ray Brown—all dressed in tuxedos—as well as the equally resplendent former Count Basie singer Helen Humes.

What unfolded at the diner was vintage Granz. An increasingly vocal provocateur on the subject of racism, he had begun campaigning in 1947 for antisegregation contracts across the touring band circuit and without blinking had turned down $100,000 in bookings by promoters who could not abide his terms. As always, it was a headache (though one he gladly bore) finding hotels and restaurants that would accommodate the racially mixed group. Granz and company often operated from Detroit's black Gotham Hotel as a temporary hub for concerts in neighboring cities as he strung together smaller dates across the country in between big paydays in the major cities.

"Helen and I got off first," Granz recalled in 2000. "The musicians wanted to put their instruments away. We went into the restaurant about 6:30. It was totally empty. The woman, wearing a typical black taffeta dress, rushed over and said, 'What can I do for you?'"

"We came in to eat."

"Do you have a reservation?"

"You have reservations here?"

"Yes, and if you don't have a reservation . . . "

"But you're empty!"

"I'm sorry, you have to have a reservation."

They were still arguing when a white couple walked in. Granz asked them if *they* had a reservation. "No, this restaurant doesn't give reservations."

"Now will you give us a table?"

"No, you don't have a reservation," she said, showing the couple to a table.

Granz called the rest of the musicians in, and they made their way to the counter. "Then I said, 'Now you've got to serve us, because we don't need a reservation for the counter.'"

After telling them it might take as long as four hours to be served at the counter, the waitress had had her fill of Norman Granz and called the police. When the officer arrived, Granz buttonholed him: "I'm so glad you're here. I want your badge number. We've got a problem. These people won't serve us. No one is drunk, and we have a concert. We're advertised in the newspaper."

The policeman said, "Listen, between you and me, yes, you're right. And I can take you to a very nice restaurant not far that serves blacks."

"I don't want to go to a black restaurant," Granz countered. "I want to go to *a* restaurant. We're all Americans, and I want to sit wherever we choose to and pay whatever the tab is. So we're not going to do it. In fact, we're going to sue them, and you're going to be *our* witness."

The restaurant began filling up with people, many of them headed to the concert. Granz and the musicians occupied the counter until around 9:30. The concert was by then an hour late in starting, and he finally decided it would be unfair to make the audience wait any longer, so the musicians departed for their venue.

The concert began as always. "We had a routine with Jazz at the Philharmonic," Granz said. "Everywhere, we started with 'The Star Spangled Banner.' I did that for two reasons. One, it settled the people, because there are always people rushing in with their overcoats and stumbling over people or in case a member of our group was late."

Granz had more on his mind than introducing the musicians when, following this patriotic salutation, he stepped to the microphone. "Ladies and gentlemen, we are happy to be here. Now I want to apologize for not having begun the concert as advertised. But let me tell you a story." He named the restaurant and recounted the tawdry story of what had just occurred. "This is supposed to be America and American freedom," he concluded. The result, as he recounted later, was that "everybody clapped. We did the concert and went back to Detroit." Granz called his attorney in New York the following morning, and he, Humes, McGhee, Jones, Phillips, and Heard filed suit under Michigan's civil rights law. Ultimately, the restaurant owner preferred to maintain his policy and paid the fines.[1]

"I don't care about posterity. I don't care about what I accomplished, if anything," Norman Granz said in his Geneva apartment in a final interview for this book. His voice was hollowed out with the cancer that would kill him six months later, on November 22, 2001. Granz, at eighty-two, crankily dismissed the music business he had had such a hand in shaping. But history's spotlight illuminates him, along with his contemporaries George Wein and John Hammond, as one of the most influential nonmusicians in jazz history. In his early twenties Granz had fallen in love with jazz after hearing Coleman Hawkins's 1939 classic "Body and Soul" and had started hanging out with black jazz artists in Los Angeles and absorbing their music. He eventually became a leading promoter of jazz in concerts and on records, using his forum to present great artistry and, with equal force, to campaign relentlessly against racial segregation in the music business and in society at large.

Recent books tell the stories of Hammond and Wein; this volume, by telling the story of Granz, the most independent of the three, completes the narrative of how jazz reached a mass audience in the heyday of the music. John McDonough's observations on Wein apply equally to Granz. McDonough reserves a special place in the jazz pantheon for the handful of truly great impresarios, promoters, and record producers who presented the music to the public and helped make jazz a viable living for its practitioners. The "musician-centered view of jazz has driven many chronicles of jazz history. . . . But turning jazz history into a string of musicians' bios is like telling American history through the presidents. It may be basic, but it's hardly the whole story."[2]

Until his final retirement in the late 1980s, Granz was a pioneer in making live recordings, doing worldwide jazz concert tours, and radically coupling his popular jam session concerts with his voluminous and artfully packaged records of the performing artists. The first of his legendary touring jam session concerts, known as Jazz at the Philharmonic, got under way in Los Angeles in July 1944 and quickly became a national phenomenon. He rode the wave of popularity to an enviable and solitary niche in the music business in the 1940s and 1950s. By 1953 half a million people a year attended his concerts in the United States, Europe, and Japan, and he was producing half the jazz records in America. His loyalty to the generation of musicians with whom he came of age impelled him to return to active recording with Pablo Records in 1973, long after his relocation to Switzerland in 1959, for the simple reason that many of his favorites were no longer being recorded. They deserved better.

Granz was unique as a white promoter for his ties to the black community, including its powerful press. Black newspapers early on recognized him as an uncompromising artistic and social maverick, and they covered his events widely. Granz's philosophy of jazz rested on his belief in a race-blind democracy of talent as vetted by the jam session, which he upheld throughout his life as the most personally and musically challenging proving ground for jazz musicians. This belief squared perfectly with his confident, risk-taking, hard-driving, and competitive nature.

Granz was one of the few mid-twentieth-century progressives to make capitalism simultaneously serve his adventurous artistic aspirations and a then-radical social agenda of racial and economic justice, integration, and equality. He resolved that jazz artists who worked for him would enjoy respect, financial rewards, top-drawer working conditions, and recording and promotional opportunities. "I insisted that my musicians were to be treated with the same respect as Leonard Bernstein or Jascha Heifetz because they were just as good, both as men and musicians," he once said.[3] Granz's cachet as manager and recording producer made Ella Fitzgerald and Oscar Peterson, and later guitarist Joe Pass, top international stars throughout their lengthy careers without their ever having signed formal contracts with him. Decades after Jazz at the Philharmonic ceased touring in the United States in 1957, his stamp is evident to anyone who has waded into the jazz section of a record store and discovered his vast output: on Verve from the 1940s to 1960; on Pablo Records, which he operated from 1973 until 1986; in a massive reissue of award-winning Granz-produced albums for Clef, Norgran, and Down Home (which Granz had consolidated into Verve) undertaken by PolyGram and later Universal Music, subsequent owners of Verve; and in similar reissues from Pablo, acquired from Granz by Fantasy Records and then sold in 2004 to Concord Music Group under the ownership of another Norman—Norman Lear, the groundbreaking television producer and political activist.

Gene Lees, jazz historian and biographer of Oscar Peterson, has compared the breadth and quality of Norman Granz's recorded output to the printed music of Franz Schubert: the comprehensive Art Tatum recordings from the mid-1950s, the Ella Fitzgerald songbooks, three hundred pages of discographic listings by Oscar Peterson, and a blitz of recordings by the likes of Count Basie, Duke Ellington, Louis Armstrong, Benny Carter, Charlie Parker, Dizzy Gillespie, Lester Young, Coleman Hawkins, Joe Pass, Ben Webster, Roy Eldridge, and Buddy Rich, to name a few. His output was so prolific that it yielded ten compact discs of the work of Billie Holiday alone. "He made music so available, so hugely accessible, in both concerts and on records that people carped about it: this album wasn't as good as that one, and so on," wrote Lees, who praised Granz despite his personal dislike for the man. "The collective work of Norman Granz can be seen now, for those who care to reevaluate it, as being among the most important musical canons of the twentieth century. . . . No one else created anything remotely resembling the collected body of his work. And let us note in passing, nobody else created so much work for so many musicians."[4]

To tell the Granz story, I have explored how he fulfilled the three oft-repeated aims on which he founded his reputation: presenting good jazz, challenging segregation, and showing that good money could be made by bringing the two together. Granz's brilliance and toughness, along with the era in which he emerged—a confluence of circumstances never to be repeated—made him successful in all three aims and shaped the music business that came after him.

Granz presented and recorded jazz from Cole to Coltrane. He intuitively grasped the opportunity to transcend parochial arguments between jazz purists in the swing and bop fiefdoms of the 1940s, gathering the best talent from both schools of jazz and creating an intriguing mixture of top figures that no other promoter dared put together on one stage. Nat Cole and Lester Young represented the style of jazz he discovered in the early 1940s in Los Angeles and championed throughout his career in music. John Coltrane and others included in his European tours in the 1960s may have marked the outermost limits of his musical sensibilities, but his personal tastes did not dull his pragmatism in recognizing what contemporary audiences wanted to hear a generation later.

Granz never faltered in his commitment to civil rights. Born in 1918, the first-generation American son of impoverished Russian Jewish immigrant parents, he held his country accountable to its basic creed of equality. The first JATP concert in 1944, a fund-raiser for the Latino defendants in the notorious Sleepy Lagoon murder case, was a preview of Granz's dedication of jazz to the cause of racial justice, a position that gained economic clout when in 1949 Ella Fitzgerald joined JATP. Time and again, Granz exhibited quick wits, physical and moral courage, and an unbending force of will to open accommodations for his African American musicians. Challenging segregation policies in hotels, restaurants, and transportation was even more important to him than playing in the country's most prestigious concert halls. He was truly in the vanguard of the modern civil rights movement that emerged from World War II, embracing tactics the movement would not adopt on a wider scale for another decade. His strategies were rooted in the philosophy of A. Philip Randolph, president of the all-black Brotherhood of Sleeping Car Porters, and the founders of such militant new organizations as the Congress of Racial Equality (CORE), established in 1942, who understood that economic opportunity, direct action, and political freedom were inseparable components of full equality for blacks. Granz's brief flirtation with the organized Left—he joined the Musicians Section of the Los Angeles County Communist Party between 1945 and 1947, for which he would be questioned by the FBI a decade later—was motivated by the party's bold stand on race relations.

Granz built up national and international constituencies for his artists, concerts, and recordings as part of his dual mission of making money on jazz and raising its status as an art form. Jazz concerts, intermittent until Granz came along, were packaged as seasonal fare with a strong band name identity in much the same way that classical music had long been handled. In the hands of Granz and others who followed in his wake, these concerts became commercial juggernauts. But it was Granz alone who possessed the concert mechanism—some of the best talent in jazz, the financial resources, and the vision—that permitted him to maintain a near-monopolistic status in hiring, concert presentation, and recordings for a decade beginning in the late 1940s. He used that financial leeway to release volumes of JATP records, along with art pieces such as *The Jazz Scene* and *The Astaire Story,* precursors to the Ella Fitzgerald songbooks. *New York Times* jazz critic Peter Watrous, writing in 1994, said that his "particular genius was to make show business subservient to jazz."[5]

Granz brought a benevolent order to what previously had been a poorly governed and especially venal sector of the music business, where musicians were all too frequently the biggest losers. His money was about as clean as it gets in show business, especially because of his unstinting personal and financial generosity toward musicians who were in his tours at the time—and often much, much later. He proved that jazz could put bread on musicians' tables and provide him with a livelihood as well. The record of his business conduct is virtually unblemished, despite the dubious assumption that any promoter who made money on jazz was ransacking others' talent. This book discloses few surprises or unreported scandals regarding his business affairs to contradict the consensus that Granz, although tough and shrewd, was entirely aboveboard in his dealings. To be sure, his legendary brusqueness, which often carried with it a naive, blunt honesty, put off many natural allies. But he combined his entrepreneurial ambition with self-discipline, love for the music, devotion to its most visible and important artists, and a sense of fairness.

Jazz at the Philharmonic's financial success, which Granz had built up for his concert and recording empires, showed the way to such generational successors as Newport Jazz Festival impresario George Wein and later Wynton Marsalis, artistic director for Jazz at Lincoln Center. Like Granz, they captured the biggest stages for presenting (and defining) jazz in their day, although Granz was the only truly financially independent operator. For their labors as well, some critics denigrated their views of jazz and its direction and meaning and questioned the commercialism of their efforts. But they too secured large, grateful audiences and helped make jazz a viable living.

Granz's saga is far more than just an industry story or the biography of a figure on the music's sidelines. His bold interaction with culture and ideas over decades gives his life the dimensions of a great American story. If history is late in getting to that story, it is partly a measure of the conflicted emotions with which Granz viewed the prospect of such a work. It may be due as well to the broad and layered scope of the story, the fact that the world of this well-known international impresario was populated by giants within music and beyond. Whatever the reasons,

Granz became embittered, feeling that America was usually "a little late" to honor her cultural contributors. Yet he did little to cultivate his own fame. He had always labored behind the scenes and preferred to leave it that way. "I made things work," Granz said late in life.[6] Like A. Philip Randolph and Bayard Rustin, organizers of the 1963 March on Washington, which bestowed immortality on Martin Luther King, Granz was not on the same public plane as his artists. In fact, though he emceed his shows, he rarely if ever even introduced himself.

The delay in honoring Granz may also stem from the fact that he did not endear himself to writers and others in and beyond the music business. He did not—to put it mildly—glad-hand his way through life. His humanistic values existed in tension with a keen intelligence that deterred fools and discouraged the well-intentioned and well-informed as well. "He could offend a thousand people as easily as he could offend one person," said his longtime friend Archie Green. "Norman didn't tolerate fools. I knew that. But so what? I accepted that. He was moral and straight and honest, but he remains an enigma."[7] In a reevaluation of Granz, Gene Lees asked whether he had alienated writers who otherwise might have told his story. "If Norman Granz is not given his due in the history of jazz, it is to some extent his own fault," he wrote.[8] His friend Benny Green put it another way when he said that "Norman hasn't got the slightest interest in his reputation. He doesn't care about people's opinions, only the musicians. He looks upon himself as a kind of conduit down which the music has flowed, that's all. In that sense, he has no ego at all."[9] Granz was a blunt instrument, a battle-hardened free agent, wealthy beyond retribution, who felt he had met his obligations to posterity by providing a creative atmosphere for musicians in concert and in the studio and by satisfying the multitudes who came to his shows and bought his records.

Granz addressed the issue of legacy, although in a different context, when Duke Ellington declined to cooperate in a biographical film of the bandleader that Granz had optioned in the mid-1960s and in which he had given Ellington half-interest. Granz hoped that a more thorough autobiography than the one that eventually appeared in 1973 might emerge as a result. It is useful to consider his frustration, self-revelatory in some respects, concerning Ellington's diffidence about revealing himself and the loss to history Granz believed would result. "All I can think of is that, to the very end, he made sure he left nothing behind that would let people know the real Duke Ellington. That's the only conclusion you can come to. He really worked out a theory: let my music speak for me." Ellington further obscured the trail, Granz observed, by his rhetorical caginess with interviewers—an evasiveness that found its counterpart in Granz's own refusal even to grant many such opportunities. "He really missed his last act."[10]

Did Norman Granz willfully court a self-defeating "last act" himself, or did he just not care about his legacy? His disillusionment, disdain, and combativeness suggest both. Once in the 1970s, when he considered writing an autobiography, Granz traveled to Chicago to dig through past issues of *Down Beat* magazine. He came away with a lengthy list of articles chronicling his career over twenty years, from his earliest days of organizing freelance jam sessions in Los Angeles nightclubs to the first Jazz at the Philharmonic concert through the sale of Verve Records in 1960. He even started writing about his hardscrabble upbringing before setting the manuscript aside, reluctant, like many self-made people, to publicly revisit where he had come from.

Despite this quickly aborted effort, for decades Granz had vowed that he would not write an autobiography. The first glimpse of his reticence came during a November 1963 interview with the British journalist Sinclair Traill. "I am unhappy to say that he informed me he was not interested [in writing an autobiography]," Traill wrote. "Yet here is a man who by his own work has been in close harmony with so many famous musicians that he must have a story to tell—a story that should not be lost."[11] But Granz did not see his life, he often stated, as a string of anecdotes about "what Billie Holiday ate for breakfast," whatever clarity and liveliness such details might add to the bigger picture. He challenged potential biographers to understand the premise of any work that might engage his cooperation: the raison d'être of his career was fighting racial segregation in the United States, using jazz as his medium.

Although Granz declined to set down his memories for posterity, he could get thoroughly riled when he thought mistakes or misrepresentations about his life had found their way into print. He scoffed at a 1999 interview with Illinois Jacquet in which the saxophonist claimed credit for insisting that an integration clause be included in the contract for a Houston JATP concert in October 1955 as the troupe prepared to play on his musical home turf. That provision had been a standard feature of Granz's contracts for nearly a decade.

Granz compounded his reclusive ways with a sparse paper trail hardly worthy of his many deep and lengthy involvements. This neglect contrasts sharply with George Wein's collection, in a Manhattan storage facility, of hundreds of boxes of historic business records, documents, correspondence, and memorabilia that date back to the Newport Jazz Festival's early days over half a century ago—a personal archive Wein consulted frequently in writing his 2003 autobiography. The first major loss of Granz's papers came as he was wrapping up his affairs after selling Pablo Records to Fantasy in late 1986. He disposed of about seventy boxes of files probably dating from the late 1940s or early 1950s, a veritable treasure, stored in a back room of his Beverly Hills offices. Granz was especially sensitive about protecting the privacy of salary and other business and financial transactions, including his art trading. He made a more selective decision in the months before his death when he disposed of several plastic garbage bags containing papers, tapes, and other material to make sure they remained forever private. (He took it with him.) The most exciting extant records are some papers, photographs, and other items still held by his widow, Grete.

The loss of extensive documentation, along with the inevitable thinning of the ranks of firsthand observers, puts out of reach much knowledge regarding Granz, his operations, and musicians, many of whom shared long relationships with him. It underscores the biographer's difficulties in venturing to reconstruct a whole from fragments of the past. In the case of Norman Granz, many missing links are filled in by decades of coverage of his activities in the press and in books, new sources uncovered in researching this book, and the myriad recordings to his credit. Some events, absent conclusive evidence, lead to the use of more *likely*s, *probably*s, or *might*s than I prefer, but these are labeled as qualified, reasonable assumptions. Given that Granz was a man whose personality could switch gears unpredictably, he nonetheless exhibited a consistency and confidence seen first by his peers at Roosevelt High School and later by those who came to appreciate the energy he applied to solidifying his place in the world of jazz and pursuing other endeavors in his equally eventful and satisfying private life.

The beginnings of this book date back to 1975, when my late mother, Connie Hershorn, an entertainment writer for the *Dallas Morning News,* began sending me the earliest Pablo Records with the understanding that I would review them under her column heading. During this time, I began photographing some of Granz's artists, "Pablovians" (as Gary Giddins once called them), beginning with an August 1976 solo concert by Joe Pass at San Francisco's Great American Music Hall. In subsequent years I took enough pictures of Ella Fitzgerald, Oscar Peterson, Count Basie, Pass, Clark Terry, and others to show to Granz in Dallas personally in March 1980, encouraging him to use them on record covers, as he did beginning the following year. That same week, I met Fitzgerald's manager and longtime Granz employee Pete Cavello, who sparked my interest in Granz's multifaceted life and career.

Granz's early commitment to racial justice resonated with me. The civil rights era of the 1960s was very much a presence in the household in which I had grown up because of my father Shel Hershorn's work as a freelance photojournalist covering the movement for national magazines and my mother's progressive views on the subject of race. When I first contacted Granz about writing his biography in 1981, I had great enthusiasm but no credentials to speak of. His reputation and my brief firsthand experience confirmed that he was no pushover—unless it was you he had pushed over. After all, when I had showed him the portfolio of my photographs of Pablo musicians, his reaction had been, "My records are so esoteric, people would buy them if they were in grocery bags." The second time I asked Granz about writing his biography, at his office in Beverly Hills two blocks from Rodeo Drive in July 1987, he said he was not interested because he thought most writers would miss the centrality of civil rights in shaping his story.

The long march toward this book began in earnest when, after seventeen years as a newspaperman for smaller Texas papers, I began the first of two master's degrees in the 1990s and wrote a thesis on Granz as part of a history degree at George Mason University. The greatest surprise in my initial research came with the discovery that there was no previous master's thesis or doctoral dissertation on him. Granz, who predictably ignored my requests to interview him, received a copy of my finished thesis shortly after it was submitted in June 1996. On August 7, he called me out of the blue in Houston to say that he had finished reading it the day before, his seventy-eighth birthday, and I "pretty much had the story straight," despite some factual errors we could discuss later. But getting his attention was easier than maintaining it while collaborating on an undertaking for which he had long expressed antipathy. That said, we began a series of conversations that lasted over the final five years of his life.

A few other comments on my approach to the subject are relevant here. Few biographers are invited into their subjects' lives to participate in a project that, for good or ill, may come to define that person's memory, and many authorized accounts may be suspect because of possible compromises made in exchange for access to the subject or to private papers. Consequently, there is a question of whether writers pull their punches in accounts of people of Granz's stature and accomplishment.

I did not approach this task with any overriding opinion regarding Granz's legacy and was prepared to learn anew from the avalanche of existing and fresh sources in building the story. Although Granz and I had many conversations from 1996 onward, I did not get to know him personally. As far as this biography's being "authorized," that was a sometime thing and largely undefined.

Our relationship culminated in a series of interviews from May 18 to 25, 2001, after Granz graciously invited me to Geneva at what was probably the last time his health would have permitted such a visit. He called on Tuesday, May 7, and said to be prepared to come the following week. He called a week later to ask me to come right away. I bought the tickets on Wednesday, flew on Thursday, and walked bleary-eyed into his apartment, aptly named "House of Picasso," three hours after getting off a Swissair flight Friday morning. He encouraged me to extend my stay to meet his friends Frank Tenot, the late French publishing mogul and longtime publisher of *Jazz* magazine, whom he had known since 1952, and Jacques Muyal of Geneva, an electrical engineer who had worked with Granz in later years to produce his films and videos for release.

The door opened again in October 2003, when Grete Granz invited me back to Geneva to look over the remainder of Granz's papers and effects and, more important, to penetrate the iron curtain around his private life. Grete's openness and the effort she made to pull things together and share her insights and memories countered a widespread impression of an emotional austerity and harshness in Granz's life at odds with the joys of the music he promoted. Even the remnants of Granz's papers and memorabilia add key insights into his personal and professional life: financial ledgers of the 1949 and 1952 seasons that detail the economics of his touring jazz concerts; over thirty pages of autobiographical writings; a handwritten tour highlighting museums and restaurants across the south of France; personal correspondence; photographs; and official documents, such as passports and military records. Granz had even preserved a March 1982 letter I had written him requesting his participation in my effort to chronicle his life.

Even though the depth of my research and my orientation intrigued Granz, my years of tracking his story did not result in a significant bond between us that might have produced a more in-depth personal portrait. Granz wrote some noteworthy and intimate reminiscences of his early days, which are quoted in this book. I wish there had been more. The chapter on his art collecting and his friendship with Picasso contains one of the richest lodes of personal material in this work. Those memories surfaced in a series of taped conversations with Grete that were made at his instigation in 2000 to detail some of his non-jazz activities and that he hoped would be published posthumously in a separate volume. Some friends, like Benny Green, had died by the time I began researching this book. Others, such as Oscar Peterson, opened up only upon his blessing, shared only what long-standing loyalty and discretion permitted, and clammed up when Granz occasionally let it be known that he was holding me at arm's length. And Granz himself, like Ella Fitzgerald and Duke Ellington, left little behind to reveal much beyond what he shared publicly.

That said, any biographer, especially when dealing with a living subject or one within living memory, encounters sensitive matters and wrestles (or not) with whether to publish all that is known about both the subject and others integral or peripheral to the story. I have withheld some personal details where the omission does not distort the story, and I resisted speculation when there was no corroboration to justify includ-ing it in this book. *Norman Granz* primarily recounts a professional life writ large upon jazz performance and recording, the life of a man with a gift for turning both into gold and a will to lock horns with anyone that got in his way, especially where racial justice and "his" musicians were involved. The intellectual and artistic currents that coursed through his life made Norman Granz not just an instrumental figure in jazz history but also a person who engaged the great social issues and high culture of his times. His effort to present and record jazz's reigning talents on a global scale remains one of the best breaks jazz ever had, and his commitment to the cause of civil rights ultimately takes his story to a higher plane.

Granz justified his monumental project to record Art Tatum in his last years on the belief that jazz "owed" Tatum. For all the luster Tatum had added to the music, there were perilously few recordings in the Tatum catalog to convey his massive stature. Granz vowed to remedy that himself. That notion animates this work on Norman Granz: con-sidering all that this gifted, heroic, difficult, and enigmatic man brought to jazz beginning almost seventy years ago, now is finally the time to reestablish his place in jazz history and among other notable social activists of the twentieth century.

But Granz's elusiveness did not foreordain a bad "final act," any more than Duke Ellington's did; the difference is that Ellington cared about posterity whereas Granz only flirted with it on occasion. Neither need have worried. Ellington's music *does* speak for him. Granz's irreplaceable catalog of recordings, dearly held memories among those who packed his concerts, and the sense of racial justice that infused his life's work *do* speak for him. His attitude about how his memory would be interpreted reflected his view of the public's reception to JATP or his recordings: if you like them, fine; if not, that's okay too. He insulated himself against the frustration of history's neglect with the conviction that his contributions were long term. For someone who preferred the limelight to shine on others, it's finally time to acknowledge the obvious by borrowing an introduction he bestowed countless times on those he presented: "Ladies and gentlemen, I'm pleased to introduce one of the real giants of jazz: Norman Granz."

1

"All I Wanted Was My Freedom"

"I guessed from the odd spelling of my name, with a 'z' on the end, that at Ellis Island, when they passed through immigration, maybe the name was Granzinski, or something like that, [and] that my father had, I suppose, at some point chopped off the 'inski,' and left it with 'Granz,'" Norman Granz said, speculating on a common assimilation strategy his father might have employed when transitioning to a new life. He admitted that he had given little thought to his origins and cared about as much.[1] Granz, however, was the family name that Morris Granz, then a resident of San Bernardino, California, had used when he declared his intent to become a citizen in November 1907 at the age of twenty-two. In April 1910 he took his oath of citizenship in Los Angeles, renouncing his allegiance to Czar Nicholas II, emperor of "all the Russias." According to the 1910 Census, taken within days of his becoming a citizen, Morris Granz described himself as an English-speaking single boarder who could read and write and had been employed in the garment industry continuously over the previous year.

The exodus that brought Morris Granz and eventually three of his brothers to the United States resulted from the failed 1905 Russian Revolution that forced revolutionaries and hundreds of thousands of Russian and Eastern European Jews to flee for their lives and liberty in the early twentieth century up until the outbreak of the First World War. Morris left from the German port city of Bremen for the trip to Ellis Island in May 1904; Ida Clara Melnick, Norman's mother, and her parents landed in New York the same year. Granz recalls that she had done some sweatshop labor when she first arrived in the city and that his parents met and married in St. Louis on the way to their ultimate destination, Los Angeles.[2] Morris and possibly one of his brothers, both listed as salesmen and residing at the same address, first appeared in the Los Angeles city directory of 1911. By 1915 there were three Granz brothers under one roof, and by the following year yet another. In 1917 Morris peeled away from the family support network, although it was not until the following year, that of Norman's birth, that Ida Clara was identified as his wife in the city directory entry.

Morris was thirty-two and Ida Clara twenty on the morning of Norman's birth on August 6, 1918. The family resided at 1103 Twenty-third Street, bounded by Vernon Avenue and Central Avenue, an integrated area of Los Angeles where Norman Granz would return as a UCLA student to haunt jazz clubs in the early 1940s. "It is interesting that my parents settled in the Central Avenue area, which is like settling in Harlem," he said. He described an austere life growing up in a household shared from time to time by his parents and maternal grandparents. His grandparents never learned English, while his parents struggled with the language to get work and navigate daily life. Yiddish was Norman's first language. He went to Hebrew school as a youth at the same time that he attended junior high school in Long Beach. He spoke Yiddish to his grandparents but easily picked up English at school.[3]

Granz may have been raised in a conservative Jewish household, but it does not appear that the family regularly attended services or had a home synagogue. Ida Clara Granz maintained a kosher kitchen and lit candles every Friday night, as was the family custom in Russia. Her son got up at six every morning for prayers, and for the rest of his life he would be an early riser, though without the religious ritual. The cornerstones of Granz's early family life were religion and, more important, basic survival. "You have to survive. If I were to ask them [his parents], I don't think they had ever heard of Franklin Roosevelt."[4]

By 1920 garment manufacturing, along with clerical and blue-collar work in the emerging film industry, employed approximately two-thirds of the fifty thousand to one hundred thousand Jews in Los Angeles.[5] The senior Granz's work existed on the periphery of the men's garment trade—described as "gents' furnishings" on Norman's birth certificate and including fabrics, used shoes, remaindered clothing, dry goods, and factory rejects—but it never amounted to what could be considered a trade. By 1920 Morris Granz had ventured from Los Angeles to Riverside and Colton, both approximately sixty miles east of the city. Two years later, the family settled in Long Beach, where he managed the Golden Rule Department Store until the early 1930's, when the Great Depression closed its doors. Many accounts of Granz's life have mistakenly asserted that his father owned the store. "I wish it were true," he said. "My father never was successful."[6]

Granz's family life was squeezed both emotionally and financially, ever more so when his younger brother, Irving, was born eight years after Norman. The strain of their modest circumstances was more than sufficient motivation for people of his temperament to chart a course for moving on from, if not entirely forgetting, their origins. Adding to the tension at home was the Granzes' frequent bickering over "the precariousness, the insecurity" of their situation, aggravated by the greater success of their extended families. "My father had a very bad relationship with his brothers and nephews because they prospered," Granz said. "I guess they stopped helping one another."[7]

It is a measure of Granz's self-education that none of the building blocks of his later life—music, art, and ideas—were formed at home. "I don't think any ethnic group cared about anything, if they were immigrants, except making money," Granz said. "There weren't, for instance, any paintings on the wall. They couldn't afford it. And they were not inclined or maybe not cultured enough for it, or curious enough, to buy for ninety-nine cents just a poster or something and put it on the wall."[8] The same held true for music. Although his mother encouraged him to play piano when he was around seven, he soon quit. There was never any recorded music until Granz earned his own spending money.

A tattered hand-tinted studio portrait of the Granzes, taken when Norman was around six or seven and darkened to a bronze tone over the course of more than eighty-five years, reveals something of the social expectations imprinted on such formal occasions as a family sitting. The photograph shows up the poignant gap between this occasion and the grimmer reality the family faced upon leaving the photographer's studio. In the only surviving photograph of the family together, Morris stands protectively at the summit of the family tree, with Ida Clara seated in front of him and Norman on her lap, resting his head on her collarbone. Morris's suit, with a pin in the lapel suggesting some sort of affiliation, could easily be that of any small-town businessman or Rotarian. A faint, inexpressive smile on his wide mouth is accented by his unrevealing gaze and complements his receding hairline and close-cropped graying hair. His warmth toward his wife is conveyed by the sparest of gestures. He rests only his thumb on Ida Clara's fleshy shoulder, casting a trace of a shadow. Ida Clara, dressed in a sleeveless print dress and a pearl necklace, wears her dark hair in the short, bobbed style prevalent in the early 1920s. Her dark eyes and her slightly bowed mouth are mirrored in her son's features. With her left hand she clasps Norman's elbow as with her right she holds his right shoulder. Granz's small, solemn face is crowned with a shock of hair as golden as the buttons of his Cracker Jack sailor suit. His eyes capture the viewer's attention, as does a faintly arched eyebrow; in years to come, his bushy eyebrows would become a prominent and potent feature used to unsettling dramatic effect.

Norman began first grade and stayed until he graduated from junior high in 1932. There were few other Jews in Long Beach or among Norman's classmates—not that he particularly cared to seek them out. Long Beach, according to Granz, was "predominantly a midwestern community in its thinking. . . . I think I remember the Ku Klux Klan used to parade there in their nightshirts. But I don't think it had any influence on me at the time. I suppose that the reason I can mix so easily with minority members arose from my playing with kids on Central Avenue when it was a heterogeneous district with all minorities represented."[9]

The Granzes returned to Los Angeles around the time Norman finished junior high school to settle in the ethnically and racially mixed Boyle Heights neighborhood, which Granz described as "a Jewish ghetto." Shortly after the 1932 Olympics hosted in Los Angeles, Norman—sandy-haired, athletic, and, at over six feet, already taller than his parents—enrolled in Theodore Roosevelt High School. Like the neighborhood, Roosevelt teemed with recently arrived and unassimilated immigrants and minorities, including Mexicans, Japanese, Russians, Jews, and African Americans. The sons and daughters of white Protestants were so few in the school population as to be almost curiosities in this polyglot setting.

Granz's appetite for knowledge, energy, self-possession, and entrepreneurial instincts were obvious by the time he started classes at Roosevelt High. By Granz's own admission, "The best thing that ever happened to me in high school" was that he befriended fellow student and intellectual voyager Aaron Greenstein, who as Archie Green would over the next eight decades become a central figure among folklorists and labor, cultural, and social activists and would spearhead the legislation creating the American Folklife Center at the Library of Congress in 1976.[10] Born in 1917 in Winnipeg, Green came from a politically aware household—his father fled Russia after the 1905 Revolution, ultimately settling in Boyle Heights—and his influence was incalculable in Granz's early stirrings of intellectual passion in high school and the first couple of years at UCLA.

Granz, according to Green, made an impression on his classmates with his natural abilities as a student and as an athlete nicknamed "Speedy" for his prowess in basketball and tennis, a sport he continued to play for decades. "Norman was funny, he was intelligent," Green said almost seven decades after their meeting. "How could anyone miss the fact that he would succeed? He was an individual, and that rubbed a lot of people the wrong way. He wasn't the glad-hander, although he was nothing like a hermit either. Some people felt that he would come to no good. But I didn't."[11]

Granz was equally taken with his new friend. "It was Archie who introduced me to the wonders of reading political magazines," he wrote late in life. "We became friends, even though he was nonathletic and I was athletic, and I hung out with different people, different boys that lived in my neighborhood."[12] Granz began spending long evenings in the public library doing schoolwork and reading periodicals such as the *New Republic,* the *Nation, Harper's,* and *Atlantic Monthly,* as well as books that nourished his interests in literature, politics, and economics. These habits continued throughout his life; he maintained a sumptuous and ever-growing library in his London apartment until the late 1990s.

Equally significant were the excursions into what Green described as "New Deal culture"—dramatic, musical, and oratorical programs characterized by an internationalist, pluralistic outlook—experienced at a time when the two young men were awakening to culture as an idea but before, as Granz put it, "Archie went hillbilly and I went jazz." Among the productions Green remembered attending with Granz were the WPA Theater's production of *The Hot Mikado* and *The Swing Mikado;* the African American Hall Johnson Choir doing gospel, blues, and jazz; operas; Sinclair Lewis's play *It Can't Happen Here;* and Duke Ellington's short-lived, socially barbed musical revue, the 1941 *Jump for Joy.* Green added that music was not yet a central interest for either of them and that at the dawn of their lengthy friendship jazz had yet to seriously engage Granz.[13]

Granz and Green supplemented their interest in leftist writings and cultural activities with what they picked up in their classes and in lectures by radical thinkers. Almost sixty-five years later, Granz still recalled his excitement in the late 1930s at hearing two lectures given at UCLA by Harold J. Laski, the brilliant socialist theorist, economist, author, and lecturer from the London School of Economics, then at the height of his Marxist phase. Granz's brush with Laski left him thinking about becoming an economist and studying at the famed London institution. "I was enthralled. I had never heard words used in that fashion," Granz recalled.[14]

While still in high school, Granz took possibly his first-ever job on Saturdays at a men's haberdashery in downtown Los Angeles, which provided early training in gauging and influencing customers' tastes in addition to covering his school expenses. "My job was to act as a shill whenever anyone would stop and look at the shirts, etc., in the window. I would go into a spiel about what beautiful things we had inside and how inexpensive our products were," said Granz. He unfurled an even more imaginative example of his salesmanship on New Year's Day in the mid-1930s. He rented a truck, filled its bed with used wooden boxes for fruits and vegetables, and hawked his wares at fifty cents to a dollar to people hoping to catch a better view of the annual Rose Parade. This, arguably, was Granz's first brush with show business, and it was successful. He confidently predicted that he would be a millionaire by the time he was forty, a goal he would reach at least five years earlier. Even his signature in Archie Green's senior yearbook provides an ambiguous clue that he was looking ahead. "Norman Bradford Granz," he wrote near his portrait, which showed him wearing his mortarboard and gazing confidently into the future. Granz in fact had no middle name, and if he had, it would not be one sounding as if it came from an F. Scott Fitzgerald novel. Green saw in this signature Granz's sardonic, subtle wit rather than any WASPish pretensions on his friend's part.

My asking Green about his longtime friend tapped the great teacher in him. Green eloquently recounted the historical, social, and religious particulars of the Russian Jewish experience in Los Angeles from which Granz had emerged. He could talk with equal authority about his own and Granz's parents and about the mixture of rebellion and adaptation by which the sons of Morris Granz and Samuel Greenstein had distinguished themselves as they pursued the archetypal dreams of first-generation Americans striving for success. Within their respective realms of jazz and vernacular music, they were equally committed to transmitting cultural and political messages that were infused with New Deal values and the émigré politics of the First Russian Revolution.

In the shakeout, Granz found himself a secular humanist with self-confessed communist leanings that the leftist Green, for all his radicalism, never shared. Granz did not consider religion anything near a guiding force in his life. Green believes that Granz's parents, despite the quickly widening divergence between their beliefs and those of their son, made their own peace with his direction in life. "Norman's success was more important than his parents' adherence to Orthodoxy and superstition." In 1987, Granz rejected the idea that his Jewish upbringing had explicitly influenced his later life. "I don't think anything that I did or that I do, or whatever, could be ascribed to Jewishness or anything of that sort," Granz explained. "I'm not sure that I even understand that kind of generalization. As far as I'm concerned, being poor didn't fill me with any determination other than that it's better to have money than not to have money."[15]

Granz had considered studying international relations at Princeton University around the time he was getting ready to graduate from Roosevelt in 1935. He had the enterprise and intensity to gain entry into Princeton, had not the cost and possible religious discrimination been prohibitive. Granz approached a local stockbroker, head of the Los Angeles chapter of the Princeton alumni association, about getting into the school on scholarship, but the man offered Granz little encouragement.

Granz left home briefly after graduating high school but found the going a little too rough. "All I wanted was my freedom, because I had very difficult work, very difficult jobs. I tried to make it work, even coming back and living at home. But it was just too difficult. Getting up at four in the morning and then traveling to the job, and then studying until midnight. I had no privacy."[16] He appears to be referring to his $60-a-month job as a board marker in the Pasadena office of the Los Angeles Stock Exchange that he obtained soon after leaving home. The job required him to wear earphones and mark the chalkboard with the latest stock quotations from companies listed on the New York Stock Exchange. The Exchange started transacting business at 9:00 a.m., so given the three-hour time difference between New York and Los Angeles, the local exchange opened at six. Granz had to get up at four and walk several blocks in the dark to catch the streetcar to make connections to Pasadena, arriving an hour before the local exchange opened and working until it closed at noon. The work exposed him to the nitty-gritty of the business world and brought out the drive that distinguished him in later years. He memorized over fifteen hundred symbols of companies represented on the stock exchange. Granz became so proficient that he was soon teaching the tricks of the trade to aspiring board markers and was bumped up a notch to announcer, which required him to sit where the tapes came in and speak into the microphone.

Granz had to prolong his education at UCLA, taking time off from his studies to work for his tuition and other expenses. He waited until the fall of 1936, over a year after high school graduation, to enter UCLA as a student in the College of Arts and Sciences. School records show that Granz stayed until April 1938 the first time around, then reenrolled from September 1940 through June 1941, when he volunteered for the Army Air Corps. While in school Granz earned extra cash by printing and selling his class notes for a dollar each to incoming students. He also raked in about $50 a month working as a reader for professors he said were "too tired or too bored to read some of the papers that were turned in."[17] He was briefly a member of the freshman UCLA basketball team, but he dropped out because he missed too many practices. Home offered no refuge for studying. A friendly night watchman at the stock exchange let him into an office to study until midnight when he took a streetcar back to Boyle Heights.

Granz persuaded a UCLA dean to permit him to become one of the first multidisciplinary students in the school's history, which possibly explains why his student records state that he had "no declared major." Too impatient to suffer through survey classes of three hundred to four hundred students, where conversation with a professor was virtually impossible, he devised his own plan for combining the study of philosophy, political science, and economics. "In short, I tried to put together a learning apparatus," Granz recalled. "Rather than saying, 'I'm going to take economics and then next year I'll take political science,' take them together." Once the deal was finalized, he bent the rules further by sitting in on graduate-level economics classes. Still hoping to attend Princeton at some point, Granz took Latin, which he thought would give him a leg up. "It did one good thing for me. It gave me a great vocabulary."[18]

Not satisfied with the victory he had already gained in designing his own curriculum, Granz pushed academic tolerance almost to the breaking point when he decided to skip his final exam in a philosophy class. The incident is all the more interesting given that Granz's liberal views were compatible with his professor's. "It was a very beautiful day, and I just thought after they passed out the test: 'This is a waste of time.' So I simply wrote down in my blue book, 'Whether I know or don't know philosophy is not going to be judged by a grade.' And I turned my book in ten minutes after they were passed out, and every student thought I was out of my mind." The teacher called Granz into his office.

"This is ridiculous. I have to fail you."

"Well, I don't care. I've learned what I've learned from you and from what I've read."

"I'm going to pass you just to get rid of you."[19]

In the meantime, Granz had begun taking some classes available through the L.A. Stock Exchange. But his dismissal from a job at the Dean Witter office in Los Angeles, his second as a board marker, underscored a major obstacle to his success in the financial sphere: anti-Semitism. Shortly after he heard Harold Laski speak and turned his thoughts to the London School of Economics, Granz approached Phelps Witter, the managing partner at the local office, to ask if he would send a letter of recommendation to the English firm with which they did business, should he be accepted at the school. Witter instead tried to divert Granz with the offer of a promotion to a low-level broker position. "Well, that's very nice of you, but I'd rather finish my schooling, and if you could help me with just the letter I would appreciate it," Granz said.

"No, but I'll tell you something. Now I know I have a Jew boy working for me, you're not going to be around much longer," the man told the startled Granz.

Approximately one week later, Witter made good on his threat and fired him. Fighting mad and out on the street, Granz sought revenge by informing some of the brokerage's Jewish clients of what had happened, hoping they would cancel their business with the firm. "They looked at me like I was crazy. I learned a lesson then, too, which I've never forgotten. Anybody who thinks a rich ethnic member, whether it's a Jew or black or Japanese or whatever, is going to feel that it behooves them to help another member of the same group—forget it."[20]

Archie Green believed that whatever wounds Granz may have suffered from prejudice when he was growing up were cloaked by his poised and guarded demeanor. The scars he chose not to reveal nonetheless were never forgotten as he distanced himself from a past he largely shielded from all but his intimates. He had developed an enlightened, humanistic attitude growing up in racially and ethnically diverse circumstances, and the lash of anti-Semitism steeled him to confront discrimination and gave him insight into the African American experience. But he did not escape his early life without prejudices of his own. While Green could laugh at the fact that most of the class officers at Roosevelt High came from the tiny minority of white Anglo-Saxon Protestants, Granz permanently crossed WASPs off his list. An intense and deep-seated anger at the prejudice and ignorance he had seen and felt in his youth accompanied his rise to the top.

Granz's practical education soon encompassed the finer things of life, including a style of dress suitable for his planned future success, a taste for fine dining, and especially jazz. Granz's appreciation of culture was recalled by another friend from his Roosevelt High and UCLA days, the late Sandy Elster, a retired executive for a successful family refrigeration company that grew rich from military contracts during World War II. Elster met Granz shortly after he started at Roosevelt High School. They initially shared an interest in classical music, and Granz used to come by the store where Elster worked, which carried records, to listen and discuss what they heard. "Norman would go down to Brooks Brothers and buy clothes," Elster said. "That may have been a little later on. I remember one time he appeared with a real beautiful sweater and it cost about $35, which was a fortune of money at that time. . . . Another thing that Norman liked was, he loved to go to Musso and Frank's," Elster said of one the tonier Hollywood restaurants. "Here we were from Boyle Heights and going to Hollywood and eating dinner. It was inexpensive for the time, but it was not inexpensive for us. There, we could run into different Hollywood stars all the time. Norman liked that."[21]

Assessing his early life, Granz later wrote that everything he had experienced in his first twenty-one years was little more than a "preamble to the most important thing in my life: I met Coleman Hawkins! Or more accurately, I heard 'Body and Soul'! That introduced me to real jazz." Hawkins's treatment of the song was one that produced a rare confluence of critical raves and popular acclaim. "It kind of grabbed hold of me," Granz said on another occasion. "I think, too, that the more I listened, the more I found, which is really I think the mark of good jazz: that you keep finding things."[22]

2

"A Marvelous Crucible"

Norman Granz arrived on the jazz scene in Los Angeles just as the city was becoming a "giant boomtown" in the lead-up to World War II. During the war, as the city became embroiled in racial and ethnic conflict, Granz would make racial justice his signal cause. His first Jazz at the Philharmonic concert in July 1944 was a fund-raiser to overturn the verdicts in the notorious Sleepy Lagoon murder case. The repercussions of that trial, which began in 1942 when twenty-two defendants from a Hispanic gang were charged with the death of a rival gang member, partly contributed to the weeklong Zoot Suit Riots in June 1943. Such flashpoints for the city's ethnic tensions must have underscored for Granz the risks encountered by the "hipsters" who wore zoot suits and the musicians who played jazz. He was entrepreneurial enough to see audiences for his shows in the thousands of young people as restless as he, many of whom had come to Los Angeles to work in defense industries. His awareness of racial discrimination deepened as he saw it occur to his black musician friends, and he decided to become their champion by making jazz his business.

The most important musical figure to emerge in the late 1930s and early 1940s, who would for a while became Granz's closest friend and artistic confederate, was Nat Cole. The Chicago-born pianist, whose vocal talent eventually eclipsed his stellar keyboard artistry, came to Los Angeles as part of the 1937 revival of *Shuffle Along*, the 1920s hit revue by Noble Sissle and Eubie Blake. The national tour put together by the dancer Flournoy Miller ran out of money in Los Angeles in May. Cole's first important break came with an extended engagement at the Swanee Inn with his history-making trio consisting of Oscar Moore on guitar and Wesley Prince (and later Johnny Miller) on bass.

The nightlife of Los Angeles reflected the nation's quick mobilization in the early 1940s. Nightclubs suffered from periodic blackouts, particularly when fears of Japanese attacks unsettled the West Coast in the days after Pearl Harbor. By January 1942 the Coconut Grove was operating only on Friday and Saturday nights. Ciro's on Sunset Boulevard was the first major club to fold as a result of the shortened hours.[1] In one dramatic opening night at the Palladium in February, Claude Thornhill and his orchestra spent the night with several hundred patrons and employees during a blackout when the city's air raid sirens provided the only music for dancing until the "all clear" was sounded around seven the next morning.[2] But business quickly bounced back as fears of domestic attacks subsided. Exhausted musicians found additional opportunities to play as the twenty-four-hour schedules at area defense plants created the 4:00 p.m. to midnight "swing shift." By the middle of 1942, swing-shift dances usually went from two until five or six, ending in time to give musicians a break until eight, when the night-shift dances commenced.

Two districts—Central Avenue and the cluster of nightspots along the Sunset Strip and in Hollywood—gave Los Angeles a distinguished but underrated jazz scene during World War II. They existed side by side in the city that bassist Red Callender, a self-described "hip New Yorker among all the squares," called a "big, rambling country town."[3] For purposes of rough definition, Central Avenue in its heyday in the 1930s and 1940s was populated by nightclubs, music halls, and theaters located on thirteen blocks between Nineteenth and Forty-first Streets and was sometimes referred to as the "Black Broadway." Central represented that portion of underground Los Angeles where, as in the lyric of "Basin Street Blues," "dark and light always meet." It offered a freedom attractive to a handful of white rebels, pleasure seekers, and dilettantes who crossed a sharply defined color line in pursuit of nocturnal adventure or an escape from their everyday segregated existence. To say Central Avenue was black dominated is not to make any claim that it was black controlled economically. The area was already integrated by the late 1930s. Whites owned the businesses but hired few black clerks until widespread nonviolent picketing forced a change.[4]

Central Avenue began evolving into an entertainment district in the 1920s with the founding of the two-thousand-seat Lincoln Theater and the Florence Mills Theater. Another important event was the establishment, in 1928, of the Hotel Somerville, the first hotel offering first-class accommodations for blacks in the city. The hotel went under after the stock market crash the following year and reemerged in its more influential incarnation as the Dunbar Hotel. The Central District really began to take off after the repeal of Prohibition in 1933, when beer gardens, nightclubs, and after-hours clubs could operate under conditions far more conducive to the music scene. The election of reform mayor Fletcher Bowron in 1938 put pressure on the city's unrestrained nightlife and more overt illegal gambling activities, but even electorally imposed "virtue" could not long dampen Central Avenue's vitality.

Red Callender recalled Central Avenue as a twenty-four-hour-a-day "carnival of life, music and action. Every kind of cafe, restaurant, tailor shop, real estate, insurance broker, dance hall, social hall, beauty shop, music store—every kind of business numbering into the dozens was there."[5] At Twelfth Street, the famed and enterprising Benjamin Franklin "Reb" Spikes and his brother John ran a record store that served as the meeting grounds for the musical community of Central Avenue. Across the street, the Hummingbird Cafe and Adams Street Shop were favored perches to observe the panorama on the pavement. "It was common to meet celebrities like Jack Johnson, or view parades marching past by the Elks, Foresters, or Masons," Callender said.[6] The Dunbar Hotel, located next door to the Club Alabam at Forty-first, was the home away from home for the royalty of the black entertainment world. Duke Ellington, Count Basie, Jimmie Lunceford, Don Redman, and Billie Holiday all stayed there or made the scene at the hotel's renowned bar. The Clark Hotel at Central and Washington and the Torrence at Fifty-first also attracted traveling black musicians who played dances at such ballrooms as the Parish Hall and the Egyptian Hall.[7] The singer Ivie Anderson, who had retired in Los Angeles after ten years with Ellington, opened Ivie's Chicken Shack on Vernon just off Central in 1941 and added soul food artistry to her already celebrated reputation. Anderson did not present music, but the piano in the dining room attracted Art Tatum, Nat Cole, and the seminal and short-lived Ellington bassist Jimmy Blanton, who used to jam there.[8] Another Ellington singer, Herb Jeffries, worked as a host at the Club Alabam and elsewhere and found some success operating the Black Flamingo, a name evoking his greatest hit with Ellington. Hollywood celebrities figured prominently among those "slumming" on Central Avenue for the jazz and after-hours clubs in the early 1940s, according to Callender: "You'd see Mercedes-Benzes,

Cadillacs, Bentleys; people like Mae West, Barrymore, John Steinbeck. Stepin Fetchit was big then, he'd drive up and down Central Avenue in his chauffeur-driven Rolls Royce with a washtub of champagne on ice. He liked living it up. Bill 'Bojangles' Robinson, who worked in pictures with Shirley Temple, was on the scene. All the stars, both black and white, came to Central Avenue."[9]

The other main scene where jazz thrived—both small groups of players and many illustrious big bands drawn west by the allure of lucrative film work—was the cluster of showrooms along the Sunset Strip and in Hollywood. Unlike the clubs on Central Avenue, with their easy acceptance of outsiders, upscale white clubs in Hollywood feared the racial mixing that Norman Granz would later actively promote through his concerts; they typically either refused to hire black bands or, though hiring them, insisted on keeping the audiences all white. And their black musicians, generals in the development of jazz, earned buck privates' pay, approximately one-fifth that paid to white musicians.[10]

The Hollywood Canteen, which earned the reputation as the nation's "largest nightclub" for hosting some twenty-five thousand GIs weekly, was a glaring exception to the generally segregated Hollywood scene. Organized by approximately forty unions, including those of white and black musicians, and run by seven thousand volunteers, it regularly featured the music of such leading bands as Ellington, Basie, Carter, the Dorseys, Cugat, Crosby, and Spike Jones. In April 1943 some local women protested when volunteer dance hostesses at the club broke racial customs to entertain black servicemen, but the protesters were overpowered by such formidable celebrity hostesses as Bette Davis, Lana Turner, and Betty Grable.[11] According to the president of the all-black Local #767 of the American Federation of Musicians, some clubs that tried integration met with opposition from the Hollywood Chamber of Commerce, which in 1945 sought to get their licenses yanked (the chamber denied the charge).[12]

The racial tensions that separated bands from their fans separated black and white musicians as well. The black Local #767 of the American Federation of Musicians had sought parity with the all-white Local #47 ever since the entertainment business first gained a foothold in Los Angeles in the 1920s. It then turned its efforts toward seeking a merger, but the two unions would not be amalgamated until 1953, following three difficult years of negotiations.

Just as Norman Granz was born near Central Avenue when it was starting to become the entertainment district of black Los Angeles, he was reborn there by his exposure to the street's high-spirited music making and cutting sessions among jazz musicians. Early on he recognized that their music was profoundly democratic in its openness to anyone who could prove his talent, an attitude he would take into organizing jam sessions beginning in 1942 and integrate into his social thinking.

The time between 1940 and mid-1942 was a transitional period in Granz's life. He had resumed his studies at the University of California in Los Angeles, and part of the price he was still willing to pay was staying at his parents' home at 2747 Malabar Street in the Malabar section of Los Angeles until he left UCLA for good to enlist the Army Air Corps in June 1941, never to earn a degree. During these years he would become a more and more knowledgeable jazz listener, but the next decisive turn in his life would come when he undertook an active role in jazz.

Beginning sometime between the fall of 1940 and spring of 1941, Granz acted on his growing interest in motion pictures by obtaining a job as an apprentice editor, one route to becoming a director. He started out at National Films working on film trailers before moving on to General Studios, where he worked again as an apprentice editor on independent films. His experiences at the smaller studios landed him a job as an assistant editor in MGM's Foreign Department, where he helped clean up films that had been dubbed into English. The union job at MGM was an "accident," according to Granz, who said his friendship with the secretary of Walt Disney's brother, Roy, had gotten him a membership into the Film Editors Guild, a requirement for working at the major studios. Granz spent his workday using small brushes to dab spots of heavy India ink over pockmarks in the soundtrack to erase surface noises.[13]

Jazz soon eclipsed Granz's aspirations in film; throughout his UCLA years he spent many long nights and early mornings under its spell. In addition to frequenting clubs and the city's larger theaters, he listened to live remote broadcasts of big bands from as far away as the College Inn in Chicago.[14] "Los Angeles was a stop that all the big bands made, . . . playing at a theater called the Orpheum where they would play for maybe four to six weeks and do a half a dozen shows a day," Granz said. "So if you got there early enough you could sit through two or three shows. There would be good dance teams, good singers, and of course the band. Plus, there was a ballroom called the Trianon that played the big bands, and the big black bands, or 'colored' bands, as they were called then, who couldn't play in Hollywood at a place like the Palladium. As a result there was ample opportunity to hear live music in Los Angeles."[15] During this time, Granz first heard Duke Ellington and Ella Fitzgerald when she was in town with the Ink Spots, although he was not particularly impressed at the time.

The first issue of *Down Beat* for 1941 carried an item that might as well have been a late Christmas present for Norman Granz. "Lester Young, Count Basie Part Company," trumpeted a headline announcing that the tenor saxophonist, who had come to glory during his five years with the Basie band, had now called it quits. Why was a mystery that remains unresolved; the story ridiculously claimed that the break had occurred when Young refused to attend a Friday the thirteenth recording session.[16] But in any event, Lester Young, "the Prez," was coming to Los Angeles. Granz had befriended Lee Young, who had lived in Los Angeles since 1929, even before his brother Lester arrived, so now he got to know Lester as well. Granz's budding friendships with the Youngs, like his friendship with Cole, took him behind the curtain of black life largely closed to white outsiders.

Lester and Lee Young, born five years apart, were veritable strangers and near-total opposites temperamentally at the point when Lester arrived in Los Angeles. Lee had not seen him since childhood, apart from a ten-day stopover in Kansas City to visit their ailing father during Lester's years with Basie. Lester was the ultimate "shy" person (a term his family prefers over "introvert"), whose private, supremely hip jargon magnified his legend across the jazz world in the late 1930s. Young's nonengagement with the practical side of the jazz business, or life for that matter, made it all but impossible for him to lead his own groups for more than short periods. His sextet with the trumpeter Shad Collins washed out shortly after its three-week engagement at Kelly's Stables in early 1941. Young was already a heavy drinker and on the way to becoming a lost soul.

"Lester didn't know how to do anything but play saxophone," Lee once observed.[17] Compared to Lester, Lee was health-conscious from the beginning and kept his drinking to the soft variety. He still played golf until shortly before his death in 2008 at age ninety-four.

Lee persuaded nightclub owner Billy Berg to hire his group, including Lester, for a six-month engagement at Berg's first nightclub, the Capri, where Granz was gravitating almost nightly to a scene already among the hottest in town. Berg, a former vaudevillian, played an important role in the city's jazz life, operating a handful of Los Angeles's more notable clubs in the early to mid-1940s. Located near the intersection of Pico and La Cienega, the Capri was a spacious but plain room with small tables and a long bar. A tribute to Lee's stature on the local scene was the fact that the group was referred to as the Lee and Lester Young Band because of Lee's already established local reputation. Lester's second billing mirrored the diminished national coverage he received after he left Basie. Rounding out the group were Angelinos, saxophonist Hubert "Bumps" Myers, trumpeter Red Mack, bassist Red Callender, guitarist Louis Gonzales, and pianist Arthur Twine. Twine's untimely death in 1942 opened the way for the induction of the Spokane, Washington, native Jimmy Rowles into the ensemble. The sextet's sound benefited mightily from the work of skilled arrangers, among them Dudley Brooks and Billy Strayhorn, in town for work on *Jump for Joy,* and trumpeter Gerald Wilson. Rowles recounted a lively show that made him eager to come to work every night for the better part of a year. "On the same bill were Leo Watson, Teddy Bunn and the Spirits of Rhythm. Joe Turner sang the blues and Marie Bryant danced. She was tough." One night a white-haired older man, obscured in the haze of the club, caught Rowles's eye. On closer look, he made out the figure of conductor Leopold Stokowski. "Yeah, figure that one out."[18]

Granz's repeated visits to the Capri and other local nightspots caught the attention of musicians unaccustomed to seeing many white faces at their gigs. Their early descriptions were quite consistent. "He was there every night. That's before he became *the* Norman Granz. If he was flush, he didn't show it—tennis shoes and a pair of old dungarees or something like that," said Rowles, who, along with the Oklahoma-born guitarist and Charlie Christian acolyte Barney Kessel, was one of the rare white musicians accepted in the black L.A. jazz scene.[19] Lee Young remembered Granz "as a real Joe College type, with brown-and-white shoes, the open collar, the sweater and the general Sloppy Joe style. At first we wondered what he did for a living. He was a lone wolf. And before long I'd be going over to his side of town, and he'd be visiting mine, and we'd play tennis."[20] During Granz's UCLA years Young used to meet him at a court on La Cienega just off Wilshire, where many neighborhood tennis aces, among them future tennis great Poncho Gonzales, played and placed friendly wagers on their games.

Granz was amused at the three-times-nightly charade that the Lee and Lester Young Band had devised to introduce Lester, who was prevented by musicians' union rules from playing regular jobs until six months after relocating to Los Angeles. The rule effectively prevented national musicians from displacing local ones on their home turf until a formal transfer was approved. Accordingly, Lester, typically attired in finely tailored double-breasted pinstriped suits, tab collars, small trouser cuffs, and pointed shoes with Cuban heels in addition to his trademark porkpie hat, was considered an "act" who was randomly introduced. "You could only take occasional jobs, like recording or one-nighters," Granz said. "He'd sit in a chair in front of the band and play, as if he were not part of the band. It was a silly kind of subterfuge, but that's how it was."[21]

Granz discussed his friendship with Nat Cole in greater detail in unpublished autobiographical writings from the 1990s: "In the beginning of my jazz career, the man most responsible for my success was, without question, Nat Cole," he wrote. "Not only was he inextricably tied in my professional mode, but he became my best friend and mentor into the black musician's way of life: its vicissitudes, its dangers and its victories. In short, we hung out."[22] The two frequently got together to play records, have dinner, and discuss music, life, and race relations. Granz loved Cole's piano playing so much that he missed the import of and did not care for his transition into one of the leading pop singers of his time.

Granz's connections were beginning to pay off as he began keeping later and later hours watching the music take shape at rehearsals, jam sessions, after-hours clubs, house parties, and other places further off the beaten path where jazzmen gathered. Virtuosity was at a premium in this environment, where musicians played for their own enjoyment and to refine their skills in the competitive and intense arena Ellington once compared to "jousting" among knights. "I got to be accepted and treated the same way that other musicians might have been treated," Granz said. "So it gave me access, it was fun, and it was a chance to hear good music. But it also determined my attitude for the rest of my life about music and particularly about musicians. I began hearing jazz, if you like, being created. . . . You really had to be competitive, because you had to prove that you could play better than the other person. It was a marvelous crucible for young musicians to work in. So if they came up in it, they became better and stronger. A young musician might come in, and he didn't deserve to be there, he might not be good enough. It's just that simple. Charlie Parker had trouble with that in the early days, getting up on stage, because you had to be able to cut it. It's healthy if you can make it, if you can survive."[23]

One memorable example occurred early one morning when Granz ended up at a house party attended by one promising pianist, two luminaries, and another in reserve. "There was a wonderful lady and her husband from the May Company Music Department that was a friend of the musicians and would throw parties with a couple of bottles of scotch. It was Jimmy Rowles, Nat Cole, Count Basie, and Art Tatum," Granz began. "And the guitar player was Dave Barbour, who was married to Peggy Lee. I was in the kitchen with Basie. Jimmy played, Nat played, and Art played. I said to Basie, 'Aren't you going to go out and play?'"

"After Nat Cole and especially Art Tatum? You're asking *me* to play?" Basie asked. "I would die first."[24]

Granz had begun to ponder his future in his junior year at UCLA as war in Europe loomed. Germany had already occupied much of Western Europe by the spring of 1940, and the Battle of Britain was raging. Notices posted on the UCLA campus claimed that those who volunteered for military service could choose the branch they wanted and become officers, whereas those who waited would almost certainly be drafted into the army. Granz would end up both volunteering and, later, being drafted. He enlisted in the Army Air Corps in June 1941, six months before Pearl Harbor, and reported for training at Tulare near Los Angeles. He appreciated the irony of being expected to help marshal the nation's air forces when he couldn't even drive a car.[25] Indeed, he soon concluded that, having no appreciable mechanical aptitude, he would probably never become a pilot. Shortly after Pearl Harbor, he and his fellow soldiers went on patrol with wooden rifles to conduct nighttime guard duty. "I said to my commanding officer, 'These are wooden guns. What are we going to do? Club them?'"[26]

On July 10, 1941, Duke Ellington introduced *Jump for Joy,* a saucy paean to racial pride and exuberant music making, at the Mayan Theater in Los Angeles, in a hastily conceived but brilliantly executed production that its backers hoped would be the prelude to a Broadway smash.[27] Most who saw it, including Granz, who made the trip several times from Tulare, knew they had had a rare musical experience. Called by one writer "Duke's 'forgotten' L.A. musical," the production was a disappointment only in the respect that it never reached New York.[28] It played to sold-out houses at the Mayan Theater for twelve weeks before closing in September.

Granz recalled the ever-changing nature of the production over its brief life. "If you were a devotee, like most of us were then that went to see the show often, it was like going to the Orpheum to hear the band play," he said. "It didn't do very well at the beginning and so they brought Joe Turner in. So before Joe Turner, it was one *Jump for Joy,* and after it was another *Jump for Joy.* And I don't know that Joe made all that much difference to the public, because inevitably the show did not work economically."[29]

In the late 1960s, when *Jump for Joy* had become a dim memory, Ellington, challenged by black activists to speak out on civil rights, responded that he had done so in 1941 and would stand by that. Granz sympathized to an extent with Ellington's critics about his generally avoiding the topic head on, although Granz's views softened in later years. More significantly, Granz expressed ambivalence about the show's ultimate impact in spreading its message on race: "I mean, people say this in retrospect. . . . I would not have thought immediately that *Jump for Joy* made a social contribution. If you ask me about it now, I would say that it did. But I'm not so sure that it did have the impact that they had hoped that it might have initially, because the people that went to see the show already felt that way."[30]

One tragic sidelight was that the show marked the last appearances with the band of the trailblazing bassist Jimmy Blanton, who in his brief ascendancy had shown every sign of becoming a major force in modern jazz. In two years he had become one of the most influential and beloved Ellingtonians. Blanton left the band in December 1941 in hopes of recovering from the tuberculosis that was to kill him on July 30, 1942, at a Los Angeles–area sanitarium, where his room was adorned only with a photograph of Ben Webster on his dresser. Granz, who in 1973 would record a tribute to Blanton with Ellington and bassist Ray Brown, had become friendly with him. Blanton sometimes joined Granz, Nat Cole, and Lee Young on their rounds when Ellington was in town. Granz was one of his well-wishers when he was ill. "Jimmy was a friend of mine," Granz recalled. "He was a teenager then. And, in fact, when he was sick—he died in California—I sent him records and things."[31]

Of special note among the assemblage of *Jump for Joy* was the Mississippi-born dancer, choreographer, and singer Marie Bryant, who by all accounts became Granz's first girlfriend. The statuesque and elegant Bryant, admired for her talent, professionalism, and vivacious temperament, was at the time of *Jump for Joy* drawn to the Ellington trumpeter, violinist, and vocalist Ray Nance and the actor John Garfield, whose portraits hung on her walls. Bryant had first appeared with the band in 1939 at the Cotton Club, and her name appeared under Duke's on the marquee at the Apollo shortly thereafter. Bryant was the first to crash the color barrier as an assistant dance director at MGM, Columbia, 20th Century Fox, Paramount, and RKO beginning in the late 1940s, where she worked with the likes of Gene Kelly, Billy Daniels, Cyd Charisse, and Nick Castle.[32] Archie Green, Granz's friend from Roosevelt High, believed Granz had been slow to start dating because his parents had not had a warm marriage. "As I understand, and Norman didn't boast about it, it was as near as I could tell his first girlfriend, his first sexual experience," he said. "I think it's admirable that he was mature enough to date a black gal and someone in show business."[33]

Granz got acquainted with Billie Holiday when she made her first trip to Los Angeles, with Jimmy Monroe, her husband of five weeks, in October 1941 to open Cafe Society, the short-lived and unauthorized "western edition" of the two New York clubs by that name. Granz recalled that it took him a while to develop his ear to appreciate Billie's singing. "The way she sang represented jazz to me," Granz said in 2001. "Though I must say when I first heard Billie on the Teddy Wilson records I used to skip Billie so I could hear Teddy play, because he never had any records of his own. But then I finally began listening to her."[34]

Granz recalled an incident when he, Holiday, Roy Eldridge, and Marie Bryant were in a car heading to Holiday's gig in a nightclub in the Valley. "Roy drove and Billie sat next to him; Marie and I sat in back. During the trip, Billie—or was it Roy?—took out a reefer, took a deep breath, gave it to Roy and then Marie, who took their puffs, and then it was passed to me. Now I had seen musicians light up, but since I had never smoked anything in my life, I had no desire to smoke pot. On the other hand, I could hardly refuse the company I was in, especially Lady. So it came to me and I inhaled the same way as the others, but I made the mistake of saying, 'I don't feel anything.' Whereupon, Lady furiously shouted, 'Give me the goddamned roach. All you're doing is wasting it.'"[35]

Granz's days in the Army Air Corps, the first of two brief stints in the military, ended shortly after Pearl Harbor. Any hopes of receiving an interesting assignment pretty much evaporated when he failed his flight test. "On the final test, which was to fly solo, I flunked out. They gave me the opportunity to stay in the Air Corps as a navigator. I said no, that I would take my chances with the draft. I took the freedom."[36] Granz was mustered out from the Army Air Corps in Los

Angeles sometime in January 1942. Fearing that the draft might soon sweep him up, he bought a bus ticket to New York and promptly set out to immerse himself in the jazz scene on Fifty-second Street and Harlem as he had done earlier along Central Avenue. "I took a bus, the cheapest line I could. It was at that time that I saw snow for the first time in my life," Granz recalled. "I mean, I saw it and felt it, because the bus stopped everywhere. I was dressed as a typical Californian: T-shirt, sweater, cotton pants, no overcoat, no jacket, nothing. When we got to New York, I had never been so cold."[37]

Granz took a dollar-a-day room with a toilet down the hall at 116th Street and Riverside Drive, in a brownstone subdivided into a "rabbit warren" of cheap apartments on the edge of Harlem. There he would stay until sometime in April 1942. He quickly found employment on Wall Street as a board marker for the same $15 a week he had earned in Los Angeles. "I was really broke when I was in New York," Granz said. He managed to get by on his meager wages and to get around the city to accomplish what had originally brought him there. "The subway was a nickel. I would save that by walking to work. And when I finished work, which would have been three o'clock New York time, I would walk back to my apartment, and would stop at Billie Holiday's mother's restaurant, and she would feed me . . . Also Uptown, 126th Street was the Braddock Hotel. I remember running into Ben Webster there and Ray Nance. There was also, of course, the Hotel Theresa that was more famous and bigger. They had a long bar, but I couldn't afford going into a bar too many times."[38] He occasionally cobbled together the money for fifty-cent standing-room-only tickets to see Broadway shows.

Roy Eldridge was among the first musicians Granz called upon once he got to New York. He had met the trumpeter in California when he had played as a guest soloist with Gene Krupa's orchestra, and he already considered Eldridge one of his closest friends. Until his death in 1989, Eldridge epitomized Granz's idealized jazzman for his fiery, competitive spirit and unquenchable love of playing. "Roy invited me up to his home, and gave me a meal," Granz said. "He had at that time recently recorded some sides for, I think, Commodore. Especially duets with Chu Berry, the saxophone player. I remember he gave me some acetates." He recalled that Eldridge had once taken Marie Bryant and him to hear Billie Holiday and that Eldridge had got him into after-hours jam sessions with some of New York's finest. Granz also made friends and broke bread with a dance team featuring the three Step Brothers.[39]

Other prominent musicians, including Johnny Hodges, squired Granz around Harlem to the places where modern jazz was then taking shape. "In Harlem, I went out with a little drummer named Kansas Fields, and we ran into Sidney Bechet. Kansas knew him, and he introduced me. I asked him where he was playing. He said, 'I can't get a job. I'm a tailor.' I got to see these people as human beings, not as jazz personalities," said Granz. "I went to Minton's with some friends, including Kansas. At that time, Minton's was unique, whereas Fifty-second Street had 90 percent of all the jazz musicians of that era. So I spent most of my time there. The only time I would go to another area would be if I were asked. I saw Eddie 'Lockjaw' Davis at Minton's. But that's the only name I could recall."[40]

Granz enjoyed a brief romantic relationship with an African American woman who worked for the post office and whom he met at one of the left-wing political meetings he attended while in New York. "No show business here," Granz wrote in unpublished memoirs. "We were instantly, mutually attracted to one another. During that period there were blackouts in New York [because of the war] and I would stay with her. Our relationship was not only sexual but, inevitably, we talked about race." After some weeks, she felt comfortable enough with Granz to take him to a small party thrown by a friend and let it be known in advance that guests could feel comfortable with her lover. "This was a tremendous learning step for me."[41]

Another high point of Granz's stay in the East came in late February, when he went to Boston to see the smaller-scale, abridged performance of *Jump for Joy* at Symphony Hall and enjoy some time with Marie Bryant. "To see her, I had to go backstage," Granz recalled. "And it was funny. Barney Bigard came to me first and said, 'I hear you're going out with Marie. Now tell me about yourself.' I mean, it was like he was vetting me." He had the chance to meet and share some relaxed conversation with Duke Ellington. "Duke saw me hanging around, obviously . . . And that's how it started. It was a good way to meet Duke, because I didn't want anything. I didn't want an autograph. I didn't want anything. In fact, if I didn't meet him, it wouldn't have meant that much to me. I was more interested in the sidemen in the band."[42]

Little could Ellington, Lester Young, or Holiday have foreseen that with Granz, then still a college student, they had formed relationships that would endure until the end of their lives. Granz would draw on all the connections he had made in the jazz world when he began organizing his own jam sessions in mid-1942. He started out like a humble tramp steamer, not unlike the *African Queen,* making random stops from port to port. His cargo consisted of jazz musicians on temporary loan from Duke Ellington or other bandleaders who stayed around long enough for their musicians to have at least one night off. But he dreamed of the time when he would command an ocean liner, and he would not have to wait long.

3

Cole Train

His adventure in New York coming to an end, Norman Granz left for Los Angeles shortly after Easter 1942, riding the bus to the end of the line of his savings and hitchhiking the rest of the way back home. En route he was buoyed by the memory of a recent experience that had touched him for the kindness shown him during a time he was barely scraping by. Granz had befriended a woman who, along with her husband, ran an eatery opposite the stage door to the Apollo Theater, on 126th Street. Lulubelle Padron could see the deliberateness, born of hunger and not much money, with which Granz eyed the menu. Soon she let him eat there for free on his way home from work. Granz was thrilled when she proffered "the invitation of a lifetime" to join her family in their box for Jimmie Lunceford and his orchestra's annual Easter concert and dance, where dancers sported their finest, on Sunday, April 5, at the Renaissance Ballroom at 138th Street and Seventh Avenue in Harlem. "I was very, very honored and fortunate that they would take this total stranger and treat me that well."[1]

If anything, the demand for entertainment in Los Angeles had intensified during the time Granz was away. Following America's entry into the war, the need for armaments and manpower and the West Coast's role as a staging ground for the Pacific Theater combined to create an economic boom that made a lively music scene livelier still. Norman Granz's summer of '42 saw him organizing jam sessions with some of the finest musicians in jazz and producing his first recording session, now considered a classic. In the process, he revealed characteristics that, powered by his energy, intellect, and fearlessness, shaped the man, his career, and jazz in the decades to come. He developed these qualities as he reconceived a role that on the surface seemed wholly implausible in its chances for international success, that of jazz impresario. Events propelled him to come to terms with racism in practice as opposed to more abstract ideas he may have held as a UCLA student. His response pointed him toward an activism of the type practiced by civil rights organizations and even the trade union movement. Granz projected a self-assuredness verging on arrogance that helped him defy his skeptics as he set out on his controversial and productive journey.

"One day I came to work, and there was a jukebox in the middle of the floor," said pianist Jimmy Rowles. Club owner Billy Berg had abruptly lost his entertainment license to operate the Capri in April 1942 when a woman attending a film at a nearby movie house complained to the mayor's office about finding a musician in the backseat of her car with another woman. In late February Rowles had left Slim Gaillard and bassist Slam Stewart to play at the Capri in the Lee and Lester Young Band, where his race qualified him as an "unusual feature" since the band was otherwise black. Rowles got a call from Berg about a week later asking him to come to work at his new Trouville Club near the corner of Beverly and Fairfax. Whereas the Capri was plain, its successor was anything but. Patrons entered the club through two large doors framed by long drapes. Once they were inside, they were confronted with the flamboyant black-and-white zebra-patterned décor. Hollywood fixtures such as George Raft, Betty Grable, Jack Benny and his wife, Robert Taylor, and Barbara Stanwyck frequently showed up, and John Carradine, playing in a production around the corner, stopped by regularly in his cape to down a couple of nightcaps. The music at the club was stellar, and there was so much of it. Marie Bryant, back from her latest tour with Duke Ellington, was in her usual fine form, as was Joe Turner, who had remained in Los Angeles after leaving New York to appear in *Jump for Joy*. "Now that Joe Turner has his slightly used Packard car, he sings out the blues with more gusto," reported the black Los Angeles newspaper, the *California Eagle*.[2] The Spirits of Rhythm also made the move to the Trouville.

Lester Young, fortified by half-pints of Old Schenley bourbon provided by the case by Billy Berg especially for Young's copious consumption, remained the focal point of a scene that made history simply because he was there. Not only was Young playing well, he attracted and consistently outplayed the best local and nationally known tenor saxophonists intent on trumping him in the club's jam sessions. Billie Holiday came to the club on her second engagement in Los Angeles beginning in late May and revived the legendary partnership with the man she called "Prez." Nut-brown and beautiful, Holiday added spice to an already unforgettable scene by sometimes running around backstage holding a drink and dressed in little more than high heels.

Granz's early friendship with Holiday led to a conversation that, as he neared his twenty-fourth birthday, helped to crystallize his thinking on race by forcing him to see, as if for the first time, the partitioning of the races in jazz as in the rest of society. Though Granz had begun by seeing race relations in purely personal terms, in the early 1940s his understanding soon grew to encompass its economic and political aspects, and he began plotting a strategy to make a difference.

"Billie Holiday was really the one that provoked my first nightclub session," Granz recalled.[3] Up to that time, Berg had permitted a limited number of blacks, mostly performers, to watch shows at the Capri from a small alcove overlooking the stage, but he had provided no such accommodations at the Trouville. Granz got an earful from Holiday when they met to have a drink and talk at a Chinese restaurant across the street from the club, as they regularly did in between sets. This particular night, Holiday was in tears. "Billie came to me and said, 'I had some friends who came over from the South Side, and wanted to hear me, and they turned them away. That's what I've been facing, and I hate that.' She put it more strongly than that in her own colorful language. She was really destroyed by that, because at least on New York's 52nd Street, there was a mixed audience."[4]

Discrimination came home again with Granz's decision to date Marie Bryant. Their affair had gone well enough for Granz to want Bryant to marry him (though her mother did not quite approve of him and wondered why Marie would date a white man who did not have any money). Granz soon discovered that he could not enjoy so simple a pleasure as taking her to dinner without risking a humiliating episode. He had to do advance work of sorts just to find a place where he and Bryant would be seated, and he was irritated that by doing so he was conceding in advance the reality that they might not be welcome. "Marie told me the facts of Negro life. In short, my education in race relations had begun. I became more militant. There was no question about being embarrassed. The question was to effect the change," he later observed. "At the time I was just getting started. Later on I would make up for that."

"Later on" turned out not to be that much later after all. The opportunity presented itself when the locals of the American Federation of Musicians finally won their lengthy campaign to force club owners to close one night a week, guaranteeing musicians a night off. Most establishments chose Sunday. The new arrangement did not preclude Granz from coming in as an independent contractor and providing music. Suddenly, he could draw on a pool of musicians for jam sessions that would blend local talent and star soloists from national touring bands. Engagements of three and four weeks for major bands were not uncommon in the largest cities, such as Los Angeles, leaving time on musicians' hands for extracurricular opportunities to play. Granz set out on the first major initiative of his career with no name or money but with a workable and just idea with drawing power. "It was really kind of silly," he later said. "I really didn't have a penny."

The proposal Granz sprang on Billy Berg in June 1942 to begin Sunday afternoon jam sessions at the Trouville had all the hallmarks of his personal and professional ethic. He easily wielded a sledgehammer, take-it-or-leave it style, incorporating his background in philosophy and economics, to prove the radical proposition that integration was good business. Charles Emge, the Los Angeles correspondent for *Down Beat*, suggested in an article a decade later a measure of what Berg faced. "I remember Norman walking into our office, and that he endeavored to arouse my interest in some strong conviction he had on some subject or another," wrote Emge, who met the budding impresario around 1940. "The look of calm superiority he gave me when I failed to show proper enthusiasm has stayed with me through the years. . . . I enjoy seeing him turning it on others. I know how effective it is."[5] Nat Cole put it this way in 1957: "Even in those days Norman wouldn't knuckle down to anybody. A lot of people disliked him, but I understood his attitude. He knew just what he wanted and exactly how he was going to get it."[6]

Granz never wavered in his assertion that his primary reason for starting his jam sessions was "sociological." The plan he proposed to Berg was threefold. First, Berg would have to advertise the three-hour jam sessions in advance, and musicians, who regularly hunted down after-hours opportunities to satisfy their love of playing, were to be paid at least union scale, then around nine dollars for three hours. They would not be expected to just casually show up and play for free. Berg could keep the one-dollar admission and sell drinks. "I'll hire, and you'll pay because it's your gig, and everyone has to be paid," Granz informed Berg. Under Granz's proposal, only he did not benefit monetarily from the sessions. Deriving income from his work was to be another "later on" he factored into his agenda. Second, Granz insisted that tables be placed on the dance floor. In a format built around virtuoso jazz soloists, he was not interested in catering to dancers. This was music to listen to.

"Finally, you have to have to admit everybody, black or white, or whatever," Granz said. "They sit wherever they want to sit, and if it works, then you have to admit them the whole week. It's got to be that way. If you do that, then you'll have no problem. If I'm wrong, then okay, then I'm wrong, and we'll forget the whole thing."[7] At first, the club owner balked, and Granz said to forget it. Berg said he personally had nothing against blacks coming into the club, but he would lose too many white patrons. Granz scorned this excuse as "the lowest kind of cop-out." Berg acceded reluctantly to his terms despite his reservations.

Then there was the matter of getting the blessing of both the black and white local unions. Putting together legitimate jam sessions meant Granz had to wend his way through the labyrinth of rules designed to maintain local members' livelihood and support the unions' activities. The fact that his dates, minor events in the larger scheme, were paid engagements cleared one of the primary hurdles in dealing with unions that regularly dispatched stewards to look for and fine members playing for free in after-hours sessions. Some after-hours spots like Brothers were considered off limits. Threats of fines ranging from $100 to $200 could not be easily dismissed. The black AFM Local #767 routinely scuffled for the work not taken by members of the white Local #47, which considered first calls for lucrative studio jobs a virtual birthright. Strictly prohibited in both unions was the setup Granz had in mind: engaging traveling musicians in jam sessions in local clubs. His hopes of selecting the best soloists in their ranks was jeopardized until he agreed to pay an equal number of so-called standby local musicians who showed up and did nothing so that he could present the players he wanted. This was a variation on the rule protecting local musicians' incomes that had relegated Lester Young to the sidelines when he first arrived in Los Angeles.

That first Sunday show, held in middle to late June, marked the first occasion when Granz presented jam sessions before paying customers in a setting without racial discrimination, requiring arrangements that would compensate musicians fairly and treat them respectfully as artists. The sessions at the Trouville, which ran between four and seven, were the first such all-star events in the city's history. They were an immediate and resounding success in replicating the excitement and competition where musicians played for their own satisfaction and that of their peers. Billy Berg made more money than he ever had during the first Sunday he opened his club under the Granz regime with a lineup of the Lee and Lester Young Band, the Nat Cole Trio featuring Oscar Moore and Wesley Prince, Red Mack and Taft Jordan on trumpets, Eddie Barefield on clarinet, and Joe Ewing on trombone. Granz was perhaps the greatest fan of his own handiwork. "I used to listen to all my jam sessions. I was crazy about them."[8]

Berg was ecstatic and integrated the club seven nights a week to keep the shows after Granz reminded him of his promise. A few other club owners jumped on the bandwagon under way with the Trouville. In the coming weeks, the club's stage was graced with heady company. Jo Jones sat in for Lee Young when Basie was in Los Angeles, as did Jimmy Crawford, the Lunceford drummer who eventually went to work full time in an area defense plant. Another session featured a saxophone summit in which Ben Webster, Lester Young, and Lunceford tenor man Joe Thomas kept the audience on the edge of their seats. Another week, Don Byas went head to head with Young. Trombonist Trummy Young was another Lunceford section man that Granz inducted into his enterprise. Around this time Billie Holiday and Trummy Young went into Capitol studios and recorded his tune "Travelin' Light" with a Paul Whiteman–led ensemble. Basie's trumpeters Buck Clayton and Harry "Sweets" Edison and trombonist Dicky Wells could also be counted on to bring their horns to the musical melees. Alto saxophonist Willie Smith of the Lunceford organization became a lifelong Granz favorite starting in the Trouville days. There was also plenty of work for the best local musicians, such as bassist Red Callender and Dexter Gordon in the days when the tenor saxophonist was playing with Lionel Hampton's band.

Jimmy Rowles described one typical Sunday event where the ambience was more like the O.K. Corral's than a music venue's and the strong, silent hero wore a black porkpie hat. "We had what we called the Big Sunday Afternoon Jam Session—Norman's shows," he said. "Whenever there would be bands in town—Lunceford, Basie or Ellington—it was a roaring joint. It was ferocious. Here we were at the Trouville with Lester Young, and a lot of guys didn't care too much for him because he didn't play from the Coleman Hawkins school. They'd come to the club with blood in their eyes to wipe Lester out. Anytime anybody used to come out and try, he'd end up wiping them out. He was always ten miles ahead of Don Byas and all those guys. He used to blow out Joe Thomas, Illinois Jacquet, Johnny Hodges, and Ben Webster. Lester would sit over there in the corner and drink his straight whiskey, and wait his turn. I saw it happen more than once.

"I remember one time sitting at a table with Billie Holiday and my wife, Dorothy. That was the first time I had brought my old lady out. Anyway, they were playing 'Bugle Call Rag.' Nat was at the piano. Buck Clayton was playing and Billie was screaming at him, 'Go on play it, you blue-eyed sonuvabitch, you motherfucker, let 'em have it!' Dorothy's hanging on to me and saying, 'What's happening?' There was a big break before you played your solo, and everybody played some crazy, freaky thing. Lester sat up there on the riser listening, saying to himself, 'That's nice, that's nice.' He'd see some chick in the corner, and he'd say, 'Damn, I like that.' When it was his turn, Prez emptied his glass, got up there, and all of a sudden started playing 'Bye-Bye Blackbird' as a break with that fake fingering of his. He then got into 'Bugle Call Rag.' There was nothing left when he got through."[9]

Cole served as the "house pianist" for the weekly events at the Trouville as he would do for the early Jazz at the Philharmonic concerts two years later. Oscar Peterson, a devoted Canadian admirer of Cole then coming up through the Johnny Holmes Orchestra, assumed that role in the JATP juggernaut after Cole concentrated on his skyrocketing singing career and edged away from pure jazz. Granz credited Cole with being the foundation of the success of the jam sessions, even more than the reeds and brass that aroused the crowd. He was a sparkling and distinctive piano stylist and could set the pace for a rhythm section that supported the musically robust programs. "Nat Cole was closer to all of the people he accompanied," Granz said, "whereas the tenor saxophones only did their solos."

The content of the shows, in addition to their equal-opportunity access, became the buzz of local black newspapers and the jazz press. "Nice thing about the Trouville, you and I are welcome there," wrote a columnist for the *California Eagle*. "The cats are groovy . . . and it's Sunday afternoon. Highballs and colas were jumping like mad ants. There's Ben Webster coming up to the bandstand. Oh look, there's Trummy Young, Willie Smith, Joe Thomas, King Cole, etc. What a deal, kids, it's a royal flush, doubles. . . . The whole thing is solid kicks and knocking us to our knees."[10] These words were published July 2, 1942, two years—to the day—before Granz presented the first Jazz at the Philharmonic, a concert that would be based on the same musical and social precepts being established then.

Granz's first recording, on July 15, 1942, brought together his two best musical friends, Lester Young and Nat Cole, to record what he envisioned as a purely private memento but is now viewed as an important record of both artists. The session required no more forethought than sitting down for instant portraits in a photo booth, Granz recalled. The four sides were recorded in about an hour on glass discs because of wartime shortages of shellac. The recording was made at Music City, a record store at Sunset and Vine owned by Glenn Wallichs, who at the same site a few months before had founded Capitol Records along with movie producer Buddy DeSylva and songwriter Johnny Mercer. Granz and the musicians had waited in vain for hours for guitarist Oscar Moore to show and ultimately recorded the date as a trio when bassist Red Callender joined Young and Cole in the studio. The four standards they recorded that day—"Indiana," "I Can't Get Started," "Tea for Two," and "Body and Soul"—stood out for several reasons. They marked the first time Young had recorded in a trio and were the only sides he ever made without drums. The recordings evince a more melancholy sensibility on his part than during the early Basie years. They are considered among the finest examples of Cole's jazz playing, a "quintessential jazz statement," according to Cole's biographer Daniel Mark Epstein.[11] They demonstrate Granz's willingness to go outside the standard instrumentation and his instinct for producing high-quality music. Another aspect of Granz's style became apparent after the recordings were commercially issued on a patchwork of different labels. "For years, Norman made sure we got royalties from that date," Callender wrote over four decades later. "He was always fair with musicians."[12]

Granz's maiden voyage was cut short when the draft notice he had anticipated since he left the Army Air Corps finally arrived, ordering him to report for duty at Fort MacArthur in San Pedro, California, on August 4, 1942. The scene at the Trouville had begun began to dissipate as Lee and Lester and their group went east in late August to play at Cafe Society Downtown in New York. Rowles went on to a short-lived residency with Benny Goodman, and the Youngs hired pianist Clyde Hart. Granz's induction put the music on hold with just about everything else in his life for the better part of the next year. The *Los Angeles Sentinel,* another black journal of the day, reported his departure and hailed him as "the extremely likeable ofay" who "could sponsor a jam session better than anyone else, and has made a place in our hearts because he has a thorough understanding of racial problems and not just in theory. His has been an almost one-man campaign in the

Hollywood spots to practice democracy, and stop preaching it. So the next time you walk into the Trouville, and you are immediately seated and served at the best available table in the house, drink an audible toast to Norman Grant [sic] of the United States Army, a friend we can ill-afford to lose."[13]

An interesting sidelight to this early phase of Granz's career is that Lee Young later stated that *he* had been the one to first develop the concept of the all-star sessions and that he had handed them off to Granz. Young made the assertion in a 1977 interview and again in the 1998 book *Central Avenue Sounds,* a collection of oral histories with key figures in the black Los Angeles jazz scene. "It's a funny thing how a guy will have an idea," Young said. "You have a million dollars in your pocket, and you just don't realize it. I used to call all the musicians to get to these things, and I started giving Norman names of the guys to call, and he took it a step further. And I'm certain this is how he came up with Jazz at the Philharmonic."[14] Granz, after reading *Central Avenue Sounds,* vehemently denied Young's account and at one point stopped just short of publicly challenging his remarks.

Wren T. Brown, a Los Angeles–based actor who was Lee Young's grandson and was very close to him, has found a middle ground that holds both of their accounts to be true. Young was an influential and well-liked musician around town whose ties to the union put him in touch with a lot of musicians looking for gigs large and small. By Granz's own recollections, jam sessions were under way by the time he began making the scene with Young and Cole. What may have been splendid occasions for companionship, music making, and a few extra dollars in Young's hands were for Granz part of a larger vision that he kept expanding as he made his way to the top of the jazz business.

Granz's second tour of duty took him from Fort MacArthur to Fort Sam Houston in San Antonio, Texas, between August 1942 through the late spring or early summer of 1943. He was itching to apply the lessons of his "sociological" experiments at Los Angeles nightclubs in a new setting. Granz could not resist the opportunity to poke the U.S. Army in the eye over the issue of equal treatment for black soldiers.

Granz surely caught the attention of his superiors when he showed off his civilian connections by presenting concerts by the Nat Cole Trio and the Count Basie Orchestra at Fort MacArthur. He had hoped that the shows might demonstrate his fitness for Special Services, but that would not happen. He was eventually assigned to a regular infantry unit in Texas in the spring of 1943. One Granz sighting occurred on his way to San Antonio. The late Phil Elwood, a longtime Bay Area jazz writer for the now-defunct *San Francisco Examiner* as well as a broadcaster, educator, and historian, recalled meeting the "tall, intense Army Pfc" in April amid the bins at the Record Exchange store on Eddy Street in San Francisco. "If you find any Vocalion or Brunswick-label sides by Billie Holiday or Lester Young, let me know," Granz asked. Elwood politely told him that he was scouting similar material but suggested that they might pool their resources. They exchanged addresses, and Granz asked his new acquaintance to put together a wish list he could hunt down in Texas. Elwood's mother later told him that Granz had knocked on their door in Berkeley later that day to look through duplicate records and make a few purchases. True to his word, Granz shipped two boxes of 78s to Elwood from Texas a few weeks later, including recordings by Ida Cox, Bessie Smith, and Louis Armstrong.[15] Ellwood later recalled his chagrin in learning that his mother had had to pay $50 for the C.O.D. package.

The timing of Elwood's meeting with Granz in April indicates that his military career lasted about two months after he got to Texas, given that he was discharged and back in Los Angeles by early summer. One of the first things Granz noticed was that black soldiers were barred from the base dayroom where soldiers went to smoke, read the newspaper, or buy a Coke. The same held true for the post exchange. Accommodations for black soldiers were no better than wooden shacks. At best, Granz observed, their treatment was on a par with, or worse than, that accorded prisoners of war. Once while he was out on a day pass, Granz went into San Antonio and returned with a stack of jazz records. The mostly southern recruits were amazed when he brought the records back to their rec area and invited them to listen. "I became friendly with them, and they would listen to the records until my commanding officer told me to stop," Granz recalled.

The same commanding officer recommended Granz for officer training in Washington, with the expectation that he might qualify for a position in intelligence. Granz's superior, a draftee more relaxed and down to earth than most career military officers, informed him that his appointment appeared doubtful. About a month later, he confirmed to Granz that he had indeed been turned down for officers' training for political reasons, namely, fraternizing with black soldiers at Fort Sam Houston.

"Great," Granz responded.

"I'm so irritated," his commander continued. "I checked your file. Did you know that you have an I.Q. of 146? That's higher than mine."

"Well, what are you going to do about it?"

"There's nothing to do. If they don't want to take you, they don't."[16]

Granz kept up his relationships with black soldiers, serving as their company clerk, and, on his own, mailed their letters and performed other favors. His desire to get back to Los Angeles fueled his determination to figure out a way to ensure that the time came sooner rather than later. His tenacity paid off when he read the entire Uniform Code of Military Justice and discovered a provision that said a person who had been turned down for officers' school for no stated reason could petition to leave the service.

"Goddamn, I never knew that was there."

"I can tell you everything about it."

Granz used the obscure policy to receive a medical discharge on May 7, 1943, whereupon he hitchhiked from Texas back to California.

Upon Granz's return, the *Los Angeles Sentinel* published a passionate account of his reaction to the official discrimination he had encountered in the service.

COMES THE REVOLUTION

The Army, we imagine, was pretty glad to get rid of Norman. He was stationed at Fort Sam Houston, deep in the bowels of Texas (we refuse to subscribe to the libel that Texas has a heart). . . . He was continually in the Southerners' hair as regards the race question.

There are thousands of Negro soldiers, and theirs is a pretty miserable lot, Norman said. Until his efforts, they had almost no share in the recreation planned for the white soldiers. What he was able to do, he insists, was not too much—a chance to swim in one of the pools a few days a week; seats, though segregated, in the post theatre; participation in post sports— but more than they had.

It is interesting to note the change in the white boy. Before he went in the Army, he was fairly militant on the race question.

. . . But now, there is no Negro soldier returning from training in Texas or Mississippi, whose resentment against American fascism is deeper dyed than Norman's. He is bitter. He doesn't feel sufficient kinship with the Southern whites who embrace racial hate and the Northern whites who tolerate it to feel shame for them. . . . They really must have an anti-lynch law in the South as regards whites, because we don't see how Norman escaped being lynched otherwise.[17]

The column is invaluable in pinpointing the timing and depth of Granz's growing militancy regarding civil rights. One can almost hear him speaking those passages. Also of interest is the respect accorded to the nondiscriminatory practices that Granz adopted from the beginning of his career, his insightful analysis of the racial situation, and his penchant for direct action. Granz had cultivated the friendship of the *Sentinel*'s editor, Almena Davis (later Lomax), and the columnist Alyce Key, and that friendship had deepened as the three talked at length of their mutual aims. "It was for those days a very aggressive paper," Granz recalled admiringly. "I used to come downtown during the daytime, and I'd go to the paper. Almena Davis was a forerunner of really aggressive black women's rights with her little newspaper."[18]

The intersection of Granz's activism and the black press during the war years, when the newspapers were cornerstones of their communities and had an estimated four million readers, was important for both.[19] Granz soon built on these relationships to include the black press as part of the publicity machine for his endeavors that addressed other issues of mutual concern.

With this powerful segment of black opinion makers in his corner, Norman Granz set to work rebuilding a circuit of clubs interested in presenting his jam sessions immediately upon his return in June 1943, the month the Zoot Suit Riots engulfed Los Angeles. He endeavored to employ as many local musicians as possible along the lines he had introduced at the Trouville. Some club owners aware of his success sought him out. He made the rounds to others with the standard provisions that musicians would be paid scale and that admission would be open on a full-time basis. The 331 Club, still the home of Nat Cole's trio, was the first to open its doors, on Monday nights; its owner, Herb Rose, was delighted with the response. The opening show at the 331 featured a group drawn mostly from the Count Basie band. Cole was back in the cockpit of the rhythm section for the first program, joining drummer Jo Jones, bassist Red Callender, trumpeters Harry Edison or Snooky Young, and tenor saxophonist Buddy Tate. As with his sessions the year before, the capacity audience was filled with Hollywood celebrities and other figures from the world of show business. The *California Eagle*, in a reference to the recent Zoot Suit Riots, praised the "sepia and ofay lineup that spelled Democracy peculiar after the riots in L.A."[20] Billy Berg, now operating the Swing Club, invited Granz to book Tuesday nights.

Other club owners rejected Granz's offer out of hand. At least one found democracy just a little too unnerving, even though his cash register told a different story. "He was so much of a racist that he would rather give up the money than allow me to prove my point, because in each place I insisted that the rest of the week had to be open," Granz said.[21]

Granz presented a rotating group of artists in his shows in the coming weeks and continued to draw on the ranks of big band stars playing extended engagements at the Trianon or Orpheum theaters as well as local talent. As a rule, Granz said, members of the Basie band were eager to participate. With the exception of Ben Webster, the Ellingtonians were more "team members" than soloists outside the band.[22] Duke never came down to see his shows, while Basie always came to cheer his men on when they were on the bandstand. "I was too dumb to use Basie because I had Nat Cole all the time," Granz said. "Basie used to come out because he liked to party and hang out."[23] Billie Holiday returned to the Granz fold when she was in Los Angeles. Wynonie Harris was regularly on the bill singing the blues. Another favorite was the Texas-born singer and guitarist T-Bone Walker. Granz frequently paired him at the 331 Club with Cole, whose guitarist Oscar Moore regularly bypassed the minor extracurricular club dates. A Los Angeles resident since 1935, Walker came to prominence with the Les Hite band. His work on the electric guitar and as a singer was influential in the development of rhythm and blues, but he had a special knack for playing jazz. His inclusion pointed to Granz's affinity for the guitar and his view that blues was a primary building block of jazz. Granz, as taken as he was with Cole's instrumental mastery, never asked him to sing. More surprisingly, Granz never asked Ella Fitzgerald to sing on those occasions she was in Los Angeles. "In those days, I never dug Ella."[24]

By the end of 1943, Granz had begun implementing his radical vision to use jazz as a vehicle to pursue a social agenda in a hostile real-world setting and had seen that there were profits and plenty of good music to be made along the way. He denied in later years that the step up from nightclubs to the concert stage in 1944 was part of any fixed plan; rather, he had simply moved forward as new opportunities presented themselves. It might be hard for him to argue otherwise. The array of factors that precipitated the successful debut of Jazz at the Philharmonic in 1944 came together from too many directions for him to have controlled them all. He could only instinctively absorb and react to such circumstances, beginning with the opportunities he had exploited to get started. Within jazz, bebop, with the degree of listening and virtuosity it required, marked an important turning point in the culture of the music. By challenging the status quo in ways that swing had not, bebop engendered a lively internecine battle between the advocates of

Dixieland and swing and the infidels of modern jazz regarding the role of the jazz musician as an artist and in society and the meaning of the music. Granz showed his own allegiance by attaching his first concert to the cause of the defendants in the Sleepy Lagoon case and consequently began to stir a new mass audience for jazz. The opposition Granz stirred up when he began retooling the jazz concert from occasional events or limited series into major tours was not limited to those who saw august auditoriums as the preserve of rarified culture. He had plenty of critics from within jazz who for different reasons chafed at the idea of jazz traveling so far from home. Granz was already showing himself adept at putting the pieces of the puzzle together in ways more conventional thinkers could not begin to imagine and thereby recasting the fate of jazz, its musicians, and himself.

The lessons he absorbed at the beginning of his career took on far greater significance in the early 1950s, when Jazz at the Philharmonic had become a serious economic force and enabled Granz to effectively agitate on a larger scale. "I used jazz because I loved jazz," he told the Scottish record producer Elliot Meadow in 1987. "Primarily, the players were black, so it was insane to have black musicians primarily working for white audiences. I looked at it as an aberration. And the fact that I could do it with good music at the same time is really how my jam sessions developed. I stopped doing what I thought I might be doing as a film editor, and began doing sessions. That became my life."[25]

4

"The Opener"

The story of Jazz at the Philharmonic, the longest-running and most influential series of jazz concerts in the music's history, beginning in 1944, can be traced in part to the decisive role that the Second World War played as a social and cultural icebreaker. High-paying jobs in the defense industries stimulated growth in the affected cities and changed the expectations of the new residents. World War II and its hardships on the home front provided another set of opportunities for Norman Granz's ideas about the jazz concert to take off. Tight rationing of gasoline and rubber restricted normal travel and left the millions of civilian war workers effectively stranded in the cities where they lived and worked. They were flush with cash for entertainment that might divert their concerns, however briefly, from the unrelenting war effort. Concert hall owners and promoters quickly seized the idea that popular musical performances presented a potentially lucrative way to fill vacancies in their schedules. Furthermore, the ambience and acoustics of concert halls translated into higher ticket prices. For performers, one show in a concert hall paid, with far less stress, as much as or more than they could earn playing several shows a day in smaller theaters or clubs.[1]

The musical environment, of course, also contributed to the rise of JATP. By 1944 jazz had been shown to have the staying power to at last merit a definition in *Webster's New International Dictionary* as "a type of American music, especially for dances, developed from ragtime by the introduction of eccentric noises and Negro melodies, and now characterized by melodious themes and varied orchestral colorings."[2] The first great jazz concert of the year was presented, not in Los Angeles, but in New York at the Metropolitan Opera House on January 18 with *Esquire* magazine's premiere All-American Jazz Band, an event paired with War Bond sales. Selected by jazz critics and experts, the meteoric cast included Louis Armstrong, Roy Eldridge, Coleman Hawkins, Art Tatum, Benny Goodman, Billie Holiday, Mildred Bailey, Red Norvo, Lionel Hampton, Teddy Wilson, Jack Teagarden, Barney Bigard, Al Casey, Sid Catlett, and Oscar Pettiford. The concert, and the recording that preserved it, represented one of the classic Swing Era events even as bebop knocked at the door. In September Granz's alma mater UCLA sponsored a conference entitled "Music in Contemporary Life" that included a forum chaired by Artie Shaw, conferring the blessing from other branches of music that jazz was a distinct art form.

Granz was ready to accommodate the public's shifting taste in entertainment. After all, he had studied, encouraged, and channeled those impulses, on a modest, yet tantalizing scale, for the past two years. Archie Green, his friend from Roosevelt High School, attended several concerts with Granz in the late 1930s. He suspected even then that Granz was evaluating the concert as a social experience first and a musical experience second. "I had a funny feeling when I went to concerts with Norman," Green said. "He didn't look at it as a musicologist or a fan looks at it. A concert was a happening, a fusion of people, rather than a series of notes."[3]

The economic viability of the jazz concert had pretty well been established almost a decade before Jazz at the Philharmonic. Jazz historian Scott DeVeaux points to a December 1935 appearance by Glen Gray's Casa Loma Orchestra at New York's Paramount Theater as a breakthrough event. The drawing power of jazz concerts was no longer a serious debate by March 1937, when Benny Goodman's Orchestra, also at the Paramount, tore the place up. At first concerts by jazz bands were sandwiched into entertainment packages that might have also included comedy, dance, and specialty acts by vaudeville performers. It was not unusual in the early days to see jazz musicians or singers supplementing their performances with jokes and other nonmusical entertainment. For example, Ellington's trumpeter, violist, and vocalist Ray Nance occasionally performed a little soft shoe. The attire and spit-and-polish precision movements of the Jimmie Lunceford Orchestra suggested the showmanship required above and beyond the music. Instrumentalists selected from within groups also presented onstage jam sessions. *Variety* noted this trend in 1938 as "the new phenomenon of a transplanted 52nd Street jam session into a more or less decorous auditorium."[4] Jazz concerts in theaters, dating from the 1930s, instructed audiences on how to comport themselves on such occasions, not that the audiences always followed instructions. Widespread revelry in the aisles had already begun to chip away at the traditional decorum surrounding classical concerts.

Just when and under what circumstances Granz stopped holding his nightclub jam sessions, which peaked with around the half dozen or so clubs he was booking by late 1943 or early 1944, is not clear from contemporary press accounts. By early 1944, when he briefly worked on a labor gang for a dollar an hour at Warner Bros., he was turning his thoughts to larger things. "A good concert is better for music making than a nightclub full of patrons more interested in drinking than listening," said Granz of the evolution in his thinking. "A good acoustically alive theater or hall is the best place to hear jazz. A dark, smoky cellar may look romantic in the small hours, but late night sessions produce more bad music than people are capable of realizing at the time."[5]

Granz settled on Music Town, a small hall capable of seating between 150 to 200 people, located near Jefferson and Normandie in the heart of the West Side's African American neighborhoods, to begin his move away from nightclubs. What the *California Eagle* called one of the city's "emerging art centers" resembled a school lunchroom and had no liquor license. Music Town, its small stage jutting out at one end of the hall, was adequate for hosting parties, church affairs, and community concerts and dance programs. Some of the Sunday afternoon concerts, beginning February 6, 1944, were co-produced with the actress and Los Angeles social activist Frances Williams. She recalled that the shows drew fans and curiosity seekers from the nearby University of Southern California. "People had never seen such fully integrated audiences out here and the USC art students would come over and sketch them."[6]

The shows at Music Town can be seen as early rehearsals for the first Jazz at the Philharmonic concert, barely five months away. In 1954, Los Angeles *Down Beat* writer Charles Emge nostalgically remembered the hall's homely charms. "Music Town was a shabby, run-down hall rather than an 'auditorium,'" he wrote. "The acoustics were terrible. This was the point at which jazz emerged from the smoky, smelly hotspots, reeking of stale perfume, alcohol, and other drugs. The atmosphere at Music Town was clean; listeners and performers were relaxed. Never again would I be able to enjoy jazz as much as I did at the Music Town concerts. I think Norman Granz feels the same way."[7]

Musicians were paid from gate receipts divided up at the conclusion of the three-hour shows after such expenses as the rental of the hall and folding chairs were paid. Even in 1944, the war had not completely disrupted the touring of the most sought-after national bands. Granz regularly drew from the Basie, Ellington, and Cab Calloway bands, mixing and matching the players with local talent in what turned out to be a short-lived series. Among those musicians making the scene were some of the future stars of JATP, among them Illinois Jacquet and the drummer J. C. Heard. Listed as appearing in the first program were Shad Collins on trumpet and Gene Englund on bass, both of them then with the Stan Kenton Orchestra. (Granz had recorded a session with Cole, Heard, Collins, Englund, and Jacquet in February 1944 that was later issued on Disc Records.) Guitarist and Charlie Christian devotee Barney Kessel began his long association with Granz at Music Town. In Kessel's words, Granz hired him "instead of at least five other better-known, more experienced guitarists." A transplanted Oklahoman, Kessel moved to Los Angeles in 1942 as part of a band fronted by the comedian Chico Marx (including the teen-aged Mel Tormé as well) but actually under the baton of the veteran California bandleader Ben Pollock. "There was a shared feeling not only of acceptance, but where you really felt they looked at you as an equal and that you had something to say," Kessel recalled.[8]

The concerts, unlike the nightclub jam sessions, never sold out, and Granz discontinued the Music Town concerts a few weeks later. (The last reference to Music Town in *Down Beat* was on April 1.) "I kept it up until finally it began to fall of its own weight," Granz said. "Nat Cole, I think, got a little tired of being the house pianist. He suggested to me that it might be a good idea if I kind of laid off for a while. I could see that it was a no-growth proposition."[9] Years later, when Granz was touring saxophonist Sonny Rollins and trumpeter Don Cherry in Europe, Cherry recalled that his father had taken him to Music Town, in part because there was no alcohol served and they could focus on the music. "You are one of the few who remember," Granz said.[10]

In 1942 and 1943, at the time Granz was beginning to produce his jam sessions, several events were stirring up racial and ethnic tensions in Los Angeles. One of these, the notorious Sleepy Lagoon case, would intersect with Granz's career in an explosive musical moment on July 2, 1944, when Granz, then twenty-five, presented his first Jazz at the Philharmonic concert.

Conservatives often portrayed zoot-suit culture and bebop as explicitly political acts of rebellion. But although both ultimately came to challenge the political status quo, as Granz conceived his jam sessions and later Jazz at the Philharmonic specifically to do, it is problematic to characterize the emergence of zoot-suit culture or bebop at this time as political. Rather, both may be seen as aspects of a youth hipster culture that had been developing since before the beginning of the war. Zoot-suiters and jazz musicians defined their distinctiveness by contrasting themselves with what had come before, as in every generational succession. Jazz had already changed directions several times since its establishment as an identifiable musical form around the turn of the century, and bebop was its latest turn. Zoot-suiters, as African Americans in the East and Hispanics in the Southwest were known, sought out the comforts of unity within their subcultures and proclaimed their separateness from the larger society by their garb when such visible signs of difference during wartime were especially risky.

On a purely functional level, loose-fitting zoot suits, or "drapes," allowed dancers a freedom of movement to respond to the beboppers and launch themselves effortlessly into a lindy hop or applejack that would have been impossible in the formal attire of a Fred Astaire. The garb finds its counterpart today in baggy hip-hop clothing, which sends a similar message. Though modern jazz would later advertise itself as a listening experience rather than a medium primarily for dancing, it was only just then being worked out by Charlie Parker, Dizzy Gillespie, Thelonious Monk, and the drummer Kenny Clarke in establishments such as Minton's Playhouse and Monroe's Uptown House where the bebop movement was germinating. Zoot-suiters also wore gaudy accessories such as elongated gold watch chains and low-crowned "pancake" hats—many with a long feather shooting out backwards at a defiant angle. The term *zoot suit* probably appeared first in a sketch entitled "Made to Order" in Duke Ellington's *Jump for Joy,* performed by the comedy-and-song team Pot, Pan and Skillet.[11]

By World War II, zoot suits, as a style of black and Hispanic hipsters, carried many negative connotations of purported antisocial behavior, criminality, drug use, sexual freedom, antagonism toward the work ethic, and draft evasion. The War Production Board's decision in 1942 to cut back the production of wool suits effectively banned the manufacture of zoot suits and inspired a busy underground network of tailors in New York and Los Angeles.[12] The result was "victory suits" sans lapels or cuffs.

The legal nightmare for the seventeen defendants convicted in the Sleepy Lagoon case began on the afternoon of August 1, 1942. A sensation-seeking reporter had given the case its name, which might have been lifted from the title of a current hit song by Harry James.[13] Henry Leyvas, a member of the Thirty-eighth Street gang, had taken a girlfriend to a pond near a gravel pit in East Los Angeles that doubled as a makeshift swimming pool when they were roughed up by members of a rival gang called the Downey Boys. Later Leyvas and some of his neighborhood allies returned to the gravel pit to look for the assailants. When the search proved unsuccessful, they stumbled into a party at a nearby residence but were soon run off after scuffling ensued. In the early morning hours of August 2, a teenager by the name of Jose Diaz was found lying wounded and unconscious on a dirt road near the house where the party had been held and was taken to a local hospital, where he died. The cause of death was inconclusive, according to the coroner, who could not even ascertain that a murder had occurred, and police could not produce a weapon. Two friends who had left the party with Diaz were not even called to testify.[14]

Police rounded up twenty-four alleged Thirty-eighth Street gang members and charged them with first-degree murder (charges were dropped against two insisting upon separate trials). Seventeen of the men were convicted of second-degree murder and lesser offenses on January 13, 1943, in the largest multiple-defendant murder trial in the county's history. The Axis powers were quick to capitalize upon the verdicts by publicizing them in a Spanish-language broadcast to Latin America that ruffled diplomatic feathers from Mexico City to Washington. "The 360,000 Mexicans of Los Angeles are reported up in arms over this Yankee persecution," the broadcast stated. "The concentration camps of Los Angeles are said to be overflowing with members of this persecuted minority. This is justice for you, as practiced by the 'Good Neighbor,' Uncle Sam, a justice that demands seventeen victims for one crime."[15]

Ironically, the incident that sparked the Zoot Suit Riots on June 3, 1943, followed a meeting at a police substation between Los Angeles police and a group of Hispanic youth seeking to reduce gang violence. Almost immediately after police drove them back to the neighborhood, the youths were beaten by a group of vigilante policemen out to avenge a group of sailors who had been assaulted earlier that night by Mexican gang members near one of the city's worst slums. Beginning the night of June 4, violence erupted when about two hundred sailors and Marines stationed at the Naval Armory near Chinatown cruised the city's Mexican East Side in twenty taxi cabs. They halted their procession four times, leaving the street littered with severely beaten zoot-suiters. Nine sailors were arrested at one point, although charges were never pressed. Likewise, police made no attempt to interfere on June 5 when servicemen marched through the streets to warn zoot-suiters to hang up their drapes by the following night or else. Up to this point, there had been no reports of reprisals from the Mexican community.[16] On June 6, the second full night of rioting, police again followed sailors and ended up arresting forty-four severely beaten boys and men.

One particularly telling signal of the city's defensiveness about the civic brawl occurred June 17 when the *Los Angeles Times* reported comments by Eleanor Roosevelt. "For a long time I've worried about the attitude toward Mexicans in California and along the border," she told a press conference, adding that the riots "have roots in things which happened long before" and "elements which have little to do with youth."[17] The following day, the *Times* printed a rebuttal by Preston Hotchkis, president of the California Chamber of Commerce, who wrote in part, "These so-called 'zoot-suit' riots have never been, and are not now, in the nature of race riots. The trouble commenced several months ago as sporadic clashes between juvenile gangs . . . without regard to race or color."[18] An editorial further expressed the Los Angeles establishment's fury over the First Lady's comments by comparing them to the Communist Party line and adding, "It seems incredible that the wife of the President of the United States in wartime would deliberately seek to create a vicious international racial antagonism without a foundation in fact."[19]

In Mexico, official opinion in the government-controlled press gave priority to maintaining good U.S.-Mexican relations. But it also criticized an internal Los Angeles Police Department report on the riots for having "entered the regions of Nazi biology" by asserting that Mexicans had inborn criminal tendencies—an allegation that had "an extremely undemocratic, anti-American, anti-Roosevelt flavor."[20] Chester Himes, who reported on the riots for *The Crisis,* was equally blunt: "The outcome is simply that the South has won Los Angeles."[21]

The riots in Los Angeles ignited zoot-suit-related disturbances in San Diego, Philadelphia, and Evansville, Indiana, in the days immediately following; other large-scale race riots occurred between June 16 and August 1 in Beaumont, Texas, Detroit, and Harlem.[22] One incident suggests the collateral damage visited upon jazz musicians, zoot-suiters, and other cultural rebels during World War II. On June 10, clarinetist Buddy DeFranco and pianist Dodo Marmarosa, then members of the Gene Krupa Band, were assaulted by two sailors as they waited on a Philadelphia subway platform. Apparently, the sailors mistook the musicians' band uniforms for zoot suits.[23] According to DeFranco, Marmarosa never fully recovered from head injuries sustained in the beating.

The Zoot Suit Riots and the Sleepy Lagoon case revealed the struggles around race, ethnicity, class, and culture in America's rapidly diversifying cities and the willingness of the authorities to countenance a brutal suppression of challenges to the established order. Norman Granz would draw on the cultural changes represented by modern jazz and the zoot suit to challenge the status quo as he took jazz on the road and into history.

One can only guess how the fates confer their blessing on those situations where the right people, time, and place come together. But that was exactly the outcome when, on July 2, 1944, the music—high-spirited and compelling—soared from the stage of Philharmonic Auditorium in Los Angeles. Granz had spent the previous two years sifting what he had learned from his first forays presenting jazz. But there was another drama playing itself out that afternoon. By offering to stage a benefit on behalf of the Sleepy Lagoon defendants, Granz had forever tied his beginnings as an impresario to one of the defining moments in the history of Hispanics in Los Angeles. He admitted at the time that he was only partially aware of the details when he offered his services to the Sleepy Lagoon Defense Committee. "There were so many kids accused that it smacked of a prejudice case," Granz said. "I didn't even know where Sleepy Lagoon was, and I didn't know what the hell was going on with the case. This was a chance to try out one of my ideas, which was to put on a jazz concert at Philharmonic Auditorium."[24]

The Sleepy Lagoon verdict might have gone unchallenged were it not for its power to attract the attention of high-profile activists and Hollywood celebrities to a homegrown international cause celebre. The Mexican-born actor Anthony Quinn, Henry Fonda, Rita Hayworth (whose ancestors came from Spain), and her husband at the time, Orson Welles, all lent their prestige to the Sleepy Lagoon Defense Committee, which was chaired by the writer and activist Carey McWilliams. Granz and the defense committee split the work to advance both of their causes: Granz hired the musicians and attended to all production details, while the committee dealt with publicity and ticket sales. Granz had posters printed to display in the windows of black barbershops and record stores and rewarded each store owner with two tickets for helping get the word out. He nailed other posters on telephone poles. The posters themselves have entered Jazz at the Philharmonic lore, for the printer took it upon himself to edit the original copy from "A Jazz Concert at the Philharmonic Auditorium" to "Jazz at the Philharmonic" to fit on the posters and handbills advertising the event. Jazz journalists and fans communicating in a kind of shorthand extending over the next forty years soon abbreviated the name to "JATP." "I really can't claim credit for the title," Granz said in 1972. "It was such a good name for the public to hold onto, that wherever we played after that, even at Carnegie Hall, we said, 'Jazz at the Philharmonic is coming to your town.'"[25]

Not everyone was enthusiastic. The *Los Angeles Times* music critic Isabella Morse Jones turned down Granz's offer of tickets: it was simply "beneath her dignity" to attend a jazz concert.[26] Granz's audacious plan raised eyebrows even among his friends. Nesuhi Ertegun, who with his brother, Ahmet, founded Atlantic Records in 1948, was then owner of a Los Angeles jazz record store. He recalled his first reaction: "Philharmonic Auditorium was where the symphony played. I didn't think there had been pop concerts there before. It was a place for quote 'serious' music, like this music wasn't?"[27] News of the concert must have been startling to Jones and those of like mind. To them, the Baptist-owned auditorium was the city's most prominent musical venue, one that demonstrated L.A.'s arrival on the national cultural scene. Founders of the Los Angeles Philharmonic had set out with just this goal in mind when they chartered the symphony in 1919 and leased the former Clune Auditorium at Fifth and Olive near Pershing Square as its home the following year. The symphony itself had established something of a populist tradition by attempting to bring larger audiences to classical music. Shortly after its founding, the Philharmonic scheduled concerts with ticket prices as low as twenty-five cents and sponsored other events at area high schools, in addition to holding concerts at outdoor venues such as the Hollywood Bowl. But as far as the Philharmonic was concerned, "populism" assumed a whole different meaning after July 2, 1944.

The complexion of the estimated crowd of over two thousand people who attended the concert was as much a revolution in the history of Philharmonic Auditorium as the music was. The racially and ethnically mixed audience of mostly young blacks, Hispanics, Jews, and "ofays" like Granz who followed jazz where it led them were a different clientele than the hall had ever assembled. Granz had encouraged the musicians to take their time and stretch out the music for its maximum emotion-grabbing effect, and fans responded to the crackling excitement of the jam session concert with an equally wild enthusiasm that provided the model for future JATP hell-raisers. The whistling and stamping might at times drown out the music and distract the performers, but it also ratcheted up their intensity. Granz's knack for expanding his audience permitted him to contemplate presenting a wider cross section of jazz musicians and achieving the profits necessary to take his ambitions to the next level.

Other cornerstones of the JATP format were in place from the start. The opening jam session by a small ensemble of seven or eight, composed of edgy brass and saxophones pushed to their limits by a crack rhythm section, left little to the imagination as to where the evening was headed. The musical fare was a mixture of jazz standards, ballads, and improvised blues riffs that incorporated emerging rhythm and blues trends and gave maximum leeway for soloists to display their highly individualistic styles with abandon. The swing-based format stressed virtuosity in extended improvisation that easily integrated the bebop revolution after Charlie Parker and Dizzy Gillespie played a legendary West Coast debut at Billy Berg's in late 1945 and found time to play JATP concerts as well.

For Les Paul, the morning of Granz's concert was interrupted by an urgent phone call from Nat Cole to step in for Oscar Moore at that afternoon's 2:30 concert. Paul, long before he was known for multi-track recordings and his inventive genius in electric guitar design, had led a well-regarded jazz trio in Los Angeles. "Oscar's been shacking up in a room with a chick for three days, and we can't get him out," Cole said. "We're shoving pizzas under the door. So come and play." Paul was then serving in uniform as part of the Armed Forces Radio Service and was prohibited from playing civilian gigs. Paul observed the regulation to the extent that he stripped himself of all his military identification before stepping into the breach, using the alias of "Paul Leslie."[28]

The curtains opened up on a group made up mostly of familiar faces from Granz's jam sessions playing the Ellington standard "C-Jam Blues." The group included the trumpeter Shorty Sherock, then with Horace Heidt's band, Bumps Myers and Joe Thomas on saxophones, Buddy Cole (no relation to Nat) on piano, bassist Red Callender, and drummer Joe Marshall, who like Thomas was a member of the Jimmie Lunceford band. They also accompanied the long-forgotten singer Carolyn Richards on "The Man I Love."

The music continued with a moderately upbeat "Lester Leaps In," featuring a sextet of the trombonist J.J. Johnson, tenor saxophonists Illinois Jacquet and Jack McVea, and a rhythm section of Nat Cole, Les Paul, bassist Johnny Miller, and drummer Lee Young. The lusty roar of Johnson's trombone brought the crowd's mounting excitement to an even higher pitch. Cole's restraint, by contrast, entreated his listeners to pay close attention to absorb his piano artistry, whether in his fluid melody lines or in the block chords he chose for his solo on the languid early choruses of "Body and Soul." If anyone could be said to be emblematic of Jazz at the Philharmonic, especially in the early days, it was Jacquet. His and Granz's feelings about engaging audiences at a primal level were perfectly in sync. The scrappy saxophonist, who rose through the ranks of hopping Southeast Texas blues and jazz bands, came to JATP already the master of a rough-cut smattering of wails and squeals barely contained in irrepressible surges of playing that proved to be as much instant crowd-pleasers as they were fodder for critics.

After "Tea for Two," the ensemble went into a blues number. It was one of those moments when, like tumblers in a lock, all the elements fell into place that would make JATP the attraction it remained for years to come. Jacquet's tour de force solo on "Blues No. 2" made the record a hit when it was issued; decades later he would copyright it. But Granz shared the view of Les Paul that the interplay between the guitarist and Cole offered the purest moments of improvisational magic. "Nat played something, and I decided I was going to play cat and mouse with him," Paul said of the runs the men swapped back and forth. A former piano player, Paul injected runs he hoped Cole might have the hardest time responding to. He said of one in particular, "When I threw that one at him, he just slapped his hands down on the piano, took his hat off, and threw it out in the audience. The audience threw their hats all up on the stage, and the place went crazy."[29] "Everybody gets keyed up about the Jacquet solo with all the screaming and everything," Granz said. "The exchange between Nat and Les Paul was more interesting in that the give and take of what a jam session could accomplish was there in its purity."[30]

Chicago jazz received its due in a set with Joe Sullivan on piano, Barney Bigard on clarinet, Charlie Peppie on trumpet, Randall Miller on trombone, and Bud Hatch on bass. Sullivan played piano solo. Pianist Meade "Lux" Lewis, whose career had been resuscitated by the boogie-woogie revival of the late 1930s and early 1940s, performed a short set of four tunes that concluded with his 1927 composition "Honky Tonk Train Blues." Vocal kudos went to Nat Cole, who performed one of the greatest hits of his career. "Sweet Lorraine," first recorded by Cole in 1939, gave full expression to the mature crooning style that launched him toward almost unimaginable acclaim. Granz's paramour Marie Bryant also sang.[31]

The concert concluded with "Bugle Call Rag," a song played by a combination of musicians that ensured the program's conclusion on a high, if frenetic, note. A backstage photograph taken shortly after the concert shows Granz and Cole with, among others, Shorty Sherock and his wife at the time, Jean Bach, who would direct the 1994 Oscar-nominated jazz film *A Great Day in Harlem*. In the picture, a proud, erect, and stylish Granz folds his hands neatly together, his blazing eyes and tight-lipped smile betraying a heady satisfaction with what he had just accomplished. "That concert made Norman Granz," said Les Paul. Granz was a month short of his twenty-sixth birthday.

Bach, who had met Granz the previous year, has strong memories of the afternoon. "It was a success, a milestone in jazz history. But the thing that really got me was Illinois Jacquet, well, he shrieked a lot. I think he's wonderful. But, boy, the thing that got through to the crowd was the shrieking. And I developed this terrible headache, and it became my 'Jazz at the Philharmonic headache.' It's all psychosomatic."[32] The typically immodest Jacquet described his JATP pyrotechnics differently: "My high notes are inspired by the Lord."

The concert's impact was magnified by hundreds of thousands of listeners when Granz allowed the program-hungry Armed Forces Radio Service to record the show for later broadcast to the troops in return for the master recordings free and clear. Coincidentally, the engineer was Jimmy Lyons, the future founder of the Monterey Jazz Festival. The records inspired Granz to regularly record his concerts and shortly thereafter to release the first-ever commercially issued "live" recordings. Granz instantly understood that they documented valid and exciting musical experiences that potentially had a wide market.[33] (In April 2011, the recordings were inducted into the Library of Congress National Recording Registry, to be made available into perpetuity, as were selected programs of legendary Voice of America broadcaster Willis Conover.)

Down Beat applauded JATP for hitting a home run in "what was once the sacrosanct last stand of the staid symphonists," although the reviewer wondered whether the result was more like nightclub entertainment than "serious jazz." "The kids went wild over the screaming harmonics produced by Illinois Jacquet from his tenor sax," wrote Charles Emge. "They screamed with glee as guitarist Les Paul produced novelty sound effects on his electric guitar. . . . . Nat (King) Cole did everything but card tricks on the piano." Emge acknowledged the obvious when he wrote, "Notwithstanding this spotty performance at this first event, impresario Granz (who reports have it was strictly a Sinatra fan only two short years ago) had rung up an achievement, both for the music and the racial unity so important right now in this city. . . . Los Angeles newspapers missed the boat completely. Not one carried a line about the concert, either as a significant news event, which it certainly was, or as a musical affair."[34]

"The concert was a tremendous success in every way. It was one of the highlights of the whole campaign," recalled Alice McGrath, who began her decades-long career as a social activist at the age of twenty-four as executive secretary of the Sleepy Lagoon Defense Committee. The concert yielded almost $1,000 for the organization as part of an effort that eventually raised around $100,000. Even more surprising than the success of Jazz at the Philharmonic was the legal victory: a landmark ruling by unanimous decision in *People v. Zammora* on October 4, 1944, by California's Second District Court of Appeals, junking the verdict for lack of evidence and egregious violations of the Bill of Rights.[35] The court roundly criticized prejudicial remarks by the original trial judge, who, in addition, had refused to permit defendants even to sit or adequately communicate with their legal counsel. Defendants had not been allowed to shower or put on fresh clothes, further prejudicing the jury, which had convicted them even though the evidence placed none of the men at the scene of the alleged crime. By the time the charges were formally dropped later that month, nine defendants had been imprisoned at San Quentin for almost two years. The same press that had inflamed the passions surrounding zoot-suiters and the trumped-up murder trial begrudgingly printed the trial's outcome. But even then, the newspapers were all but silent in reporting the substance of the judges' ruling that had reversed the charges.

Granz had not even left the theater before the opportunity arose for him to segue to a second triumph of his young career that summer. Among his well-wishers backstage at Philharmonic Auditorium was a renowned *Life* magazine photographer whose work Granz already admired. The Albanian-born Gjon Mili had come to the United States in the early 1920s to study engineering at MIT. He was taking pictures long before the introduction of photo flashbulbs in 1931 prompted him to master artificial light in order to freeze motion in extremely sharp, dramatically lit images. Later he worked with a team from MIT experimenting with ultra-high-speed electronic flash. He used a prototype of the flash unit to become one of the most stylistically advanced innovators in photo-journalism of his day, one whose love of jazz was already well documented. A layout of photographs from jam sessions he had produced in his Manhattan loft with such musicians as Duke Ellington, Count Basie, Lester Young, Billie Holiday, Dizzy Gillespie, James P. Johnson, and Mary Lou Williams was published in *Life* in October 1943.

Mili was in Los Angeles at the invitation of Warner Bros., who had asked him to produce a short film on a subject of his choosing to see whether he was director material, when a friend suggested that they take in the concert. "He could have made a film on flowers if he wanted, but he wanted to do a jazz film," Granz said. "He was so impressed by the Jazz at the Philharmonic concert that he suggested we could work together and make a jazz film."[36] Mili outlined his plan for a jazz short to Gordon Hollingshead, head of short films at the studio, during an August 1 meeting. Hollingshead fired off a note to Jack Warner, stating in part, "He seemed to be a very talented man and might make a good director. It is his idea to get some of the greatest jive musicians, both colored and white, in the country and put them in this short."[37]

They had a couple more discussions before Warner Bros. signed off on the picture. In actuality, Mili performed more as a photographer than as a director, in part because the union, which was nearly impossible to get into without strong studio backing, would not admit him so that he might direct more openly. Under the arrangement Mili shot the film while Granz contracted the musicians, singers, and dancers. Hollingshead was formally listed as producer of *Jammin' the Blues,* as he was with all of the projects passing through his department. Granz was designated technical director in the film's credits.

The concept was to re-create the atmosphere of the nightclubs and after-hours spots where Granz had developed his ear to create a film conveying the essence of the jam session experience. *Jammin' the Blues* would not be an ordinary "soundie," a brief filmed performance on a special coin-operated viewer or brief footage of big-name bands that was often inserted into feature films. Granz and Mili created a work of art in which the music and the spirit of creation were foregrounded along with the musician creators. Mili set out to produce "an abstract motion picture treatment of pure jazz."[38] The cast of musicians was a compromise with Warner Bros., although Granz did the lion's share of the hiring. The Count Basie Orchestra was in Los Angeles for an engagement at the beginning of August, permitting Granz to select from among players whose friendship and musicianship had influenced him so profoundly. First among these was Lester Young, who had rejoined the band since leaving Los Angeles, along with drummer Jo Jones, trumpeter Harry Edison, and trombonist Dicky Wells, who dropped out after the first night and did not appear in the film. Warner Bros. had angled for Louis Armstrong to star in *Jammin' the Blues*. This gave Armstrong's manager Joe Glaser some leverage to include drummer Sid Catlett, who had played with the trumpeter between 1938 and 1942 and was leading his own groups in Hollywood. However, the arrangement to include Armstrong in the proceedings did not pan out.

Pianist Marlowe Morris, who worked with Catlett, was a good fit in a rhythm section rounded out alternately by Jones and Catlett, with Red Callender or John Simmons on bass. Completing the roster were Illinois Jacquet and Barney Kessel. Garland Finney, a pianist who played some early JATP concerts and later with the Los Angeles tenor saxophonist Maxwell Davis, appeared on "Sweet Georgia Brown," a segment that was excised from the final product. Granz contemplated asking Leo Watson, the drummer and singer with the Spirits of Rhythm, but was overruled. On the second day of filming, Granz was abruptly told to include a singer who could also dance. He was still seeing Marie Bryant, so he invited her to appear in the film. Granz asked Archie Savage, the lead dancer with Katherine Dunham's dance company who later appeared in such films as *South Pacific* and *La Dolce Vita,* to do the lindy sequence with Bryant. "I never wanted it in the film, but the studio did. I was even then a purist," Granz said.[39]

The ten-minute film devolved into a series of headaches in a brief but tense shooting schedule played out over four days, up from two, and the postproduction work in August and September required to get it to the big screen within weeks. Granz did not let his ambition to rise from his job on a Warner Bros. labor crew prevent him from becoming a thorn in the studio's side. "The film almost didn't take place," Granz recalled.[40] Warner Bros. was nervous about producing a jazz picture, even if it were just a short packaged along with a major film for national distribution. The studio's concerns were heightened when Granz invited Barney Kessel to join the otherwise all-black cast of musicians. Breaking the color line in this way raised fears among executives that southern theater owners might reject the short and hurt the feature film with which it was paired, in this case *Passage to Marseille,* starring Humphrey Bogart.[41]

Granz and the studio initially butted heads over the issue of simultaneous live recording versus prerecording of the soundtrack. Granz had argued that jazz was created on the spur of the moment and thus that it was especially difficult for musicians to go back and recreate their physical motions in sync with a recording, as was the standard practice in moviemaking up to that time. In the end they compromised. Because some of the passages were so intricate, especially drum solos, the sound and images for the majority of the film were recorded on the set. Prerecording for the film had been completed by mid-August and filming got under way on September 13.

When the studio intruded further by inviting an unwanted studio audience for the first session, which kicked off around midnight, Granz was put off even more. "It was almost as if we were monkeys in a cage. I had a foreboding that it was going to be a disaster," he said. "By the time the filming started, some of the musicians were drunk. The whole thing wasn't going to work."[42] The evening was a complete washout.

On the second day, Granz led the musicians on strike after learning that Warner's was paying Bryant and Savage each $50 for the day while paying musicians a lower union-scale rate of $30. Granz insisted to Gordon Hollingshead's assistant that the musicians be paid the same as the singer and dancer. Warner's objected. "Well, you don't have a contract with the musicians. Your contract is with me to provide the musicians," Granz said. "So, if you won't give them the $50, I'm calling them off the set." At that point, he recalls, "pandemonium broke out, and they called Hollingshead, who came downstairs furious. 'How dare you do this? You'll never work in Hollywood again.' A lot of typical threats and stupid things. One of his associates kept saying, 'Remember your ulcer.' It was kind of bizarrely funny."

Filming hadn't even begun when Granz called for the bus he had put in the contract to transport the musicians back to the hotel. Mili, distraught, called Granz to arrange a meeting. Granz told Mili that the previous day's recordings were unusable, given all the distractions, food, and drink that had been laid out for the cast, crew, and hangers-on. Mili called back to say that Hollingshead had agreed to equal pay for the musicians. "So, in effect, I won the strike," Granz said. The bus made the return trip to the studio the following day, although with some substitutions in the ensemble.[43]

There was more anxiety in store for Hollingshead and company before the shoot was over. They had yet to decide how to finesse Barney Kessel's appearance as the film's only white player in *Jammin' the*

Blues. It would have been less controversial if the cast had been strictly an all-black project rather than depicting any form of equality or amity between the races. Again, Granz did not budge. This time the studio didn't either, mostly. Kessel stayed in the film, but in various ways his race was obscured. "They went into having me in the shadows," Kessel said in 1985. "We finally thought that the big, big compromise, which today would be out of the question, was that they stained my hands with berry juice."[44] This was all the more unfortunate given Warner's reputation as one of the more politically liberal of the major studios. It had already broken the color barrier with the Benny Goodman Quartet in the 1937 film *Hollywood Hotel*, although the scene was edited out for distribution in southern states.

That the filming was completed in the midst of such conflict was a miracle. Out of the chaos, Norman Granz, Gjon Mili, and the musicians salvaged a sliver of high art, all the more provocative given the period in which it was made. On September 14, the day after filming began, Hollingshead commended Mili's work and convinced Warner to see rushes because the images were so startling and unconventional.[45]

Mili's roots as a still photographer are visible in his style of building scenes around stark, striking compositions and special effects sculpted by sinews of light in sync with the pace of the performances. His trademarks asserted themselves in a series of dreamlike episodes populated by arresting images that transport the audience beneath the surface of the creative experience of the jam session. The uncluttered set provides a blank canvas alternating from black to white throughout to reveal nuances of feeling and intimate, intense expression. Mili introduced the players through direct- and backlit portraiture and medium-range and wide-angle shots that establish relationships among the musicians at any given moment. This technique extended to clearing the set of all but the soloist to emphasize without ambiguity the musician's individuality. In addition to capturing faces, Mili uses closeups to depict the nuances of music making: fingers plucking bass strings or depressing valves, brushes lightly caressing the drum's surface, Lester Young's hands squeezing the keys as smoke wafts upwards from his cigarette.

Jammin' the Blues opens with a device that immediately draws the viewer into the subliminal world at the film's core. Chiaroscuro lighting rims only the crown and brim of Lester Young's porkpie hat with a trail of smoke curling up the right side of the frame. The image morphs into the man himself as the saxophonist lifts his head in a slow diagonal movement, pulls the mouthpiece toward his lips and begins to play the slow blues "Midnight Symphony" as the scene pans out to show Young perched on a stool on an empty set. Only as Harry Edison begins his solo does the scene show Young as part of a group of musicians who up to this point have just been heard accompanying him. They are casually dressed in fashionable high-drape pants, some with suspenders, long-sleeved shirts, and hats, with the exception of Young and Jacquet, who wear tailored pinstriped suits. Their street attire, which reinforces the "inside" feel of after-hours sessions, furthers the dramatic break with the more typical, idealized view of jazz on film, which featured exquisitely dressed musicians on spacious extravagant sets that reinforced the separation between audience and artist.

Mili's eye creates fluid transitions between the three songs in the film that contribute to the unity of the entire production. For example, as Edison is winding up his solo, Marie Bryant appears from nowhere to sashay like an apparition through the musicians, waving to Catlett, who smiles and tilts his head back in acknowledgment as she passes by. As Bryant begins singing "On the Sunny Side of the Street," the camera pans to the underside of the piano lid, where her distorted, wavy figure cuts into the frame at a right angle before dissolving into a tight shot of her face against a white background.

The up-tempo "Jammin' the Blues," the film's final number, begins with a showy changing of the guard from Sid Catlett to Jo Jones in the song's percussive introduction. Catlett does not skip a beat as he tosses a drumstick to Jones, who crashes a cymbal as Catlett rises from his seat, hands Jones the other stick, slightly bows, and exits. Jacquet and then Edison cascade across the screen in a stream of multiple images before Bryant and Savage enter the set for their lindy dancing against a dark backdrop as Young solos behind their routine. Only in this final number does Kessel at last appear onscreen. When one knows the real reason behind the guitarist's near-disappearing act, it is almost comical to see how the camera concentrates on his dizzying flights up and down the frets and intense strumming, never showing his face beyond a dimly lighted, double-rendered profile. Kessel is decamped to the extreme right edge of the frame, making it almost impossible to definitively apprehend his features. The film concludes with an explosive burst from Jo Jones's drums and Jones's transfixing, radiant smile, maintaining the audience-grabbing intensity until the final bar.

Jammin' the Blues opened in December 1944 to unexpectedly wide notice beyond the jazz press. Reviews appearing in *Time,* the *Nation,*

Ebony, Esquire, Theater Arts, and *Life,* which devoted a layout to its staff photographer's handiwork, attest to the interest aroused by the film. The *Chicago Defender* reviewer saw cause for optimism that Hollywood might be looking at subjects involving blacks with "new eyes."[46] *Time* magazine reported that the buzz on the Warner's back lot was that the picture might single-handedly rescue the genre of the short film. The writer praised the experimentation in cinematography, so lacking in mainstream Hollywood, which enabled *Jammin' the Blues* to present "the most honest down-to-earth popular music yet recorded for the screen."[47] But James Agee, best known as the author of the Depression-era classic *Let Us Now Praise Famous Men* with photographs by Walker Evans, dismissed the film in a rather disjointed review as being "too full of the hot, moist, boozy breath of the unqualified jazz addict" and as resorting to overly dramatic pretentious lighting techniques. He finished with a swipe at "middlebrow highbrows" whose tastes were inimical to the creation of substantive works of art.[48]

Commentary on the film continues in the works of contemporary scholars. Arthur Knight, writing in 1995, called the movie "a consummate 'crossover' product," made by outsiders, that "combined small group hot jazz and art photography, inserted them into the mechanisms and forms of Hollywood, and distributed the results to theaters everywhere." Knight insightfully assessed the relationship between Jazz at the Philharmonic and *Jammin' the Blues* as "a complex market-driven and market-responsive answer to a racist situation" that sought to "change the rules of assimilation, to alter what assimilation would look like, and to shift the ground for the meaning of that term." The film, Knight wrote, functioned as "the first national advertisement for the JATP ideology."[49]

The "ayes" within the film community had it when *Jammin' the Blues* was nominated for an Academy Award for Best Short Subject in a year remembered for such classics as *Going My Way, Double Indemnity, Gaslight, Laura,* and *Meet Me in St. Louis.* The film eventually lost out to Paramount's entry, *Who's Who in Animal Land.*

Granz believed that *Jammin' the Blues*'s chances to win probably suffered from the studio's ambivalence about pushing the film in the Oscar race, partly because of the disputes surrounding its production (when the filming was completed, Warner Bros. paid Granz the $240 due him and promptly banned him from the lot for life). Shortly after the film's release, Gjon Mili sent a telegram thanking Charles Einfeld, his editor at Warner's, and adding, "Would like to do another [short film] next summer. Suggest get Granz for preparatory work. Granz good smart boy. Mili."[50] The suggestion would be resolutely ignored.

Meanwhile, Granz lost no time in following up on the success of the July 2 concert and booked Philharmonic Auditorium for the last Sunday of the month. Unlike the first concert, the July 30 show would be strictly commercial. He noted, "The response to the show meant to me immediately that a lot more people wanted to see jazz than went to nightclubs to drink and be out on the town."[51] The lineup underwent last-minute changes when the management of the Orpheum, where the Basie band was due to open August 1, threatened to sue if Granz followed through on his plan to build the show around Lester Young, Jo Jones, and Harry Edison. (Edison appeared after all, as did the other Basie tenor saxophonist, Buddy Tate, and the vocalist Jimmy Rushing.)[52] Nat Cole headlined with bassist Johnny Miller to perform duets when Oscar Moore again failed to show. Other performers included bassist Charles Mingus, J. J. Johnson, tenor saxophonist Georgie Auld, pianists Joe Sullivan and Buddy Cole, Les Paul, trumpeter Corky Corcoran of Harry James's band, Red Callender, Lee Young, Jack McVea, Barney Kessel, Illinois Jacquet, Jacquet's brother trumpeter Russell Jacquet, vocalists Marie Bryant and Carolyn Richards, and drummers Buddy Rich and Sid Catlett.[53] Some 1,200 people attended the second show, confirming that what had begun earlier in July was no fluke, but the results were hardly conclusive.

The third concert, on a rainy November 13, drew enough fans to finally pack the 2,670-seat hall at between one and two dollars a person, and that was on a Monday, a night when Lionel Hampton's band was playing at the Orpheum. The occasion was no doubt primed by plugs from one of the city's foremost broadcasters, Al Jarvis, who had founded the original *Make Believe Ballroom* radio program on Warner Bros.' KFWB station and who served as master of ceremonies for the occasion. The Granz/Jarvis partnership ended that very night when the two men argued backstage and Jarvis succeeded in pushing a last-minute appearance by singer Frankie Laine to do a blues number against Granz's wishes.[54] The evening was more noteworthy for the addition to the lineup of two musicians who became mainstays of Jazz at the Philharmonic, trumpeter Roy Eldridge and tenor saxophonist Joseph "Flip" Phillips. Eldridge was then touring with Artie Shaw, while Phillips's star was rising with the Woody Herman Orchestra. Among others joining

them were the Jacquet brothers, Barney Kessel, Buddy Rich, Slim Gaillard, pianist Duke Brooks, tenor saxophonist Maxwell Gordon, and
bassists Callender and Chubby Jackson, who played with Herman.

Granz adopted the entire Woody Herman rhythm section for the last
concert of 1944, on December 18, with drummer Davey Tough, pianist
and arranger Ralph Burns, guitarist Billy Bauer, and Jackson. Featured
soloists included Willie Smith, Corky Corcoran, Phillips, and T-Bone
Walker singing the blues. Sid Catlett also appeared before the estimated
crowd of 2,200. Granz tried to get the army to furlough Lester Young
from Fort McClellan, Alabama, to play the show but did not succeed.[55]

December was also notable for the release of *Jammin' the Blues* and
the naming of Lester Young as best tenor player in the annual *Down
Beat* poll. In that same month Private Lester Young reported for duty as
an infantryman at Fort McClellan.[56] Young, who had famously coined
the phrase "feeling a draft" for times he sensed racist vibes in the air,
had felt the real thing. In September, shortly after the completion of
filming of *Jammin' the Blues,* an FBI agent whom Young had avoided
for the better part of the month when the band had been in Los Angeles
served him and Jo Jones their induction notices on the bandstand. The
draft board, in upholding his draft status, disregarded Young's medical conditions: syphilis, contracted in the late thirties, that appeared to
be worsening, as well as periodic epileptic seizures. In addition, Young
acknowledged in a questionnaire that he smoked marijuana and on
another occasion reported drunk for a spinal tap and was confined to a
padded cell for over a day. But he was inducted into the army on September 30, and the legendarily traumatic fourteen months that followed
would forever change him and his playing.[57]

Among those applying outside pressure on the draft board were
Granz and Milt Ebbins, Count Basie's personal manager. "I tried to get
people to help keep him out. If anyone was ever less suited to the discipline the army required, it was Lester," said Granz in 1980. "He didn't
want to go. No blacks wanted to go. It may have been a popular war
in white America, but not among a disenfranchised group of blacks.
I'll grant that he could have played in an army band. But Lester never
had the basic toughness that many had. He was always one who would
rather walk away from a bad scene. He was an original. Originals have
to be treated differently. There aren't that many of them."[58]

Many of the outstanding performances that unfolded in the summer
of 1944 were turned in by Norman Granz. His unflinching tenacity in
his disputes with the powerful—whether the bosses at Warner Bros. or

the scions of Philharmonic Auditorium—offered a preview of his way of doing business long before his future and that of his enterprises were assured. Granz himself was an improviser, still eager in his idealism to battle on behalf of his causes and to accumulate the wealth, respect, and power to eventually lead the charge for those causes most dear to him: jazz and justice.

5

Let Freedom Swing

In 1945 and 1946 Jazz at the Philharmonic rose to greater prominence as suddenly as it had when it changed venue from the Trouville
to the Philharmonic Auditorium. Norman Granz maintained his pace
of monthly bookings at the local symphony hall but soon turned his
attention to developing regional and then national concert tours, once
and shortly thereafter twice a year. "I proved what *could* be done, so I
took it on tour in '45," Granz said of early JATP road tests.[1] After that,
he used the West Coast only as the jump-off point for a monthlong
national tour that concluded with a successful series of concerts at New
York's Carnegie Hall in May and June 1946, only to be followed with
a second sweep east in October.

Thus was born the idea of seasonal concert presentations of jazz. Bop
hit Los Angeles in December 1945 when the two most important exponents of the new music, Charlie Parker and Dizzy Gillespie, opened for
their legendary appearance at Billy Berg's. The next month they were
in the JATP lineup. Granz furthered his recording aspirations in a big
way when he linked up with the record producer Moe Asch, who, like
Granz, appreciated the unvarnished JATP performance recordings.

Granz's conviction that jazz deserved a platform equal to that
afforded "serious" music predictably rankled many inside and outside
of jazz. The management of the Philharmonic Auditorium, unsettled by
the concerts and the audiences they had drawn since their inception and
rebuffed in its attempts to make Granz enforce decorum, asked him to

move on in early 1946. Within the jazz world, some criticized Granz regarding the content of his shows and the conduct of his audiences, while others attacked his move to give jazz more formal recognition as a misguided attempt to raise its stature as an art form. The only voices that mattered to Granz, however, were the cheers that greeted his concerts (and the cash registers they filled) and the satisfaction of the musicians he employed. That support was all he needed to take his ventures to a level of success few could imagine then or dispute later.

All the basic elements on which Granz built his career fell into place in 1945 and 1946, when he maximized jazz's commercial potential by presenting it in new ways. He set out to carve a niche on a national level by engaging musicians of established reputation to attract attention to his shows and recordings. And in 1946 he began inserting nondiscrimination clauses in his touring contracts.

The forebears of Jazz at the Philharmonic had gone back at least a generation. In the early decades of the century, black bandleaders and composers such as James Reese Europe, Will Marion Cook, and W. C. Handy, as well as Paul Whiteman, presented concert programs that showcased a spectrum of African American music from spirituals to ragtime, blues, concert music, and, sometimes, jazz or jazzlike music. But concerts devoted entirely to jazz did not begin to emerge until the mid-1930s, and when they did, as DeVeaux points out, they came "'from below' as the outgrowth of the ordinary situations in which jazz was performed."[2] Specifically, he argues that "the imaginative arrangements and brilliantly improvised solos" of swing as it transitioned from black dance band styles were the necessary precondition for the music to be considered as a listening experience supposedly divorced from dancing and other sources of the music's creation.[3]

The writer and jazz historian Albert Murray celebrated the roots of jazz in the dance hall and deplored the automatic canonization of the concert hall by some jazz writers too eager to accept the notion that the best thing for blues and jazz was to leave dance halls behind. For him the jazz concert, like the phonograph record or live music delivered via radio, exerted pressures on musicians to deliver near-perfect performances and thus in some ways inhibited the music's continuing evolution. But he saw both types of venues as offering benefits for jazz's expression. "[The concert hall] provides a showcase for the new and serves as a permanent gallery, so to speak, for the enduring . . . Thus the concert hall recital at its best is in a very real way also an indispensable extension of the dance hall . . . Inasmuch as all occasions and circumstances seem to generate musical responses sooner or later, there is nothing intrinsically inauthentic about blues music composed for concert recital."[4] Duke Ellington voiced a similar attitude when someone asked him, during a Tuskegee, Alabama, nightclub engagement, whether he continued to play dance music to gain a larger audience for his concert works. "Don't pay any attention to those guys, sweetie," Ellington said. "When you get so goddamn important that you can't play places like this anymore, you might as well give it up, because you're finished. We try to play everything."[5]

Benny Goodman looms large in the history of jazz in concert. One witness to Goodman's historic 1935 engagement at the Palomar Ballroom in Los Angeles said he was not sure whether he was "attending a dance in a ballroom or some new and weird type of orchestral recital in a music hall."[6] However, ebullient crowds of jitterbuggers testified that although jazz was moving in the direction of art music, it would not abandon its dance hall past. Goodman's January 1938 concert at Carnegie Hall, seasoned by Count Basie and five members of his band including Lester Young, proved to be the most influential marker in the history of the jazz concert up to then. On August 2, Goodman appeared at Ravinia Park, the summer home of the Chicago Symphony near Chicago, the first presentation of jazz at that site. In that same year the producer John Hammond, Goodman's brother-in-law, held the first of two Spirituals to Swing concerts, employing a completely black roster; the second, in 1939, concluded with a mixed Goodman Sextet. (It should be noted as well that Goodman figured in the history of integration within jazz for bringing Teddy Wilson and Lionel Hampton into his small groups in the mid-1930s.)

Jazz concerts proceeded along two main lines during World War II. A series of annual Carnegie Hall concerts begun by Ellington in January 1943 regularly concentrated on multimovement suites, such as *Black, Brown, and Beige, The Perfume Suite,* and *The Liberian Suite,* all composed for the occasion. The move to the concert hall showed once again that the great innovator could enlarge his appeal in new settings without forsaking what he considered to be music's roots. That first Carnegie concert in 1943 led to a flurry of similar appearances that year and a return engagement in December when Ellington premiered *New World A-Coming.* The luster of these shows led to his being honored by special recitals at Harvard and other Boston area universities alongside Bela Bartok and Igor Stravinsky. (Stravinsky showed that the jazz-classical influence went both ways when he composed *The Ebony*

Concerto for the Woody Herman Orchestra and conducted its inaugural performance in 1946.)[7]

Jam session–style concerts were the second major way live jazz entered the concert arena during the war years. The *Esquire* All-American Jazz Band in January 1944 opened the Metropolitan Opera House in New York to jazz. The event was broadcast live and recorded on V-disc for distribution to the military and remains in print today. *Esquire* magazine's second annual swing concert edged its way in as the first major jazz concert of 1945. The concert was notable as much for the talent as for the imaginative live coast-to-coast radio broadcast emanating from the Philharmonic Auditorium in Los Angeles, the Blue Radio Network studio in New York, and Municipal Auditorium in New Orleans.[8] Anchored by Duke Ellington and his orchestra in Los Angeles, the broadcast concluded with a "three-way jam session" with Ellington taking the lead on "Things Ain't What They Used to Be," Benny Goodman following in New York, and Louis Armstrong wrapping it up from New Orleans.

Jam sessions instigated by guitarist Eddie Condon that continued through the war years at Manhattan's Town Hall and later Carnegie Hall were the clearest precursors of Jazz at the Philharmonic in terms of a jazz concert *series*. Both Condon and Granz realized the changing economics of the music business that were upending the big bands during and after the war, in part because of the large payrolls they required.[9] Musically, the two shows could not have been more different. Condon's affairs, aided by friendly newspaper and magazine coverage, reflected his Dixieland/Chicago roots and boosted the careers of the musicians he featured, such as the clarinetist Pee Wee Russell and the trumpeter Muggsy Spanier. Granz and his shows rode a more contemporary wave of some of the best known and emerging artists of the day.

The February 12, 1946, concert marked the introduction into the JATP fold of the man most responsible for bringing Granz to jazz, Coleman Hawkins. Hawk's return to play Billy Berg's on February 1 marked the first time he had been in Los Angeles since he came through with Mamie Smith in 1923. He brought with him a quintet made up of Sir Charles Thompson on piano, Denzil Best on drums, Oscar Pettiford on bass, and trumpeter Howard McGhee, who had joined Hawkins only two months before. Thelonious Monk, Hawkins's regular pianist at the time, was not keen on playing outside New York.[10] Granz was not alone in wondering what to expect of Hawkins given his long absence from Los Angeles and his status as one of the leading swing figures to follow the trail blazed by Charlie Parker and his associates. Hawkins is credited with making the first bop recording, in 1944, with a group that included Dizzy Gillespie. "When they came, they said, 'Oh, man, what a band! We haven't heard music like that, ever,'" Howard McGhee said. "So I guess Coleman was the one who opened the West Coast as far as modern sounds in jazz." Some who heard the show, like Kid Ory, wished Hawkins would revert to his earlier style.

Slim Gaillard brought Granz and Hawkins together after Granz saw the saxophonist during an engagement date at Billy Berg's. "I remember getting a lot of coins together and going to a pay phone," Granz said. Gaillard made the call to New York, introduced Granz, and handed him the phone. "If you're coming out here, I'd be pleased to put together a Jazz at the Philharmonic, and have you on it," Granz said. "What's it pay?" Hawkins asked. ("One thing I liked about Hawk was that he was up front.") Hawkins wanted $100 for his services. "I was lucky to pay musicians $20, $25. But I said, 'No, I'll do it.'"[11]

Hawkins headlined a JATP lineup that included Charles Mingus on bass, Dave Barbour on guitar, Corky Corcoran, Neal Hefti, and Shorty Sherock on trumpets, Milt Raskin on piano, and Dave Coleman on drums. Billie Holiday, apparently still in town from the *Esquire* concert in Los Angeles the previous month, was on the bill along with Howard McGhee, alto saxophonist Willie Smith, and tenor saxophonists Wardell Gray, Illinois Jacquet, and Charlie Ventura. In addition, there was a group led by Gene Krupa and a performance of the comical *Opera in Vout (Groove Juice Symphony)* by Gaillard and the bassist Tiny "Bam" Brown, the second of Gaillard's partners after Slam Stewart.

Granz was suitably impressed, and cowed, when he came face to face with Hawkins's haughtiness. "Coleman's attitude was undistilled arrogance," Granz recalled. "I mean, he could have been royalty, for me." At the point when musicians from the previous sets assembled for the finale, Hawkins was packing up. In deference to Jacquet, they had selected "Flying Home," his monster hit with Lionel Hampton, to bring the evening to a close.

"Listen, don't put your horn away. You're in the finale," Granz said.

"I don't play numbers like that. Now would you pay me?" Hawkins answered.

"But you're supposed to do it. (Here I was, naive.) You're supposed to play the whole concert."

"I'm not going to play that number, and I want you to pay me."

Granz stumbled through an "Okay, yes sir, of course" as he peeled off $100. Hawkins's visit, however, returned immediate dividends after he began praising Granz among musicians. "Coleman passed the word that I was honest, which was unusual," Granz said.[12]

Granz planned a busy spring, with two concerts in March and five between April and May, including Jazz at the Philharmonic's initial ventures up and down the West Coast. It was somewhat risky for Granz to bring Duke Ellington back to Philharmonic Auditorium on March 5, slightly less than two months since the orchestra had played the *Esquire* concert. However, he was vindicated by a full and enthusiastic audience, though one more subdued than the JATP norm. Hawkins was on the first out-of-town JATP trips to what were off nights at the Curran Theater in San Francisco on April 16 and the Russ Theater in San Diego the following night. Also on the bill were the Nat Cole Trio, Willie Smith, Slim Gaillard, and Tiny Brown, plus local musicians. Granz explored the possibility of booking the Shrine Auditorium for a concert scheduled to include Art Tatum in late May, but he pulled back when low ticket sales forecast a bust. At around $5,000, projected expenses for the 6,600-seat Shrine concert would have more than tripled the $1,500 he had shelled out to rent the Philharmonic Auditorium and pay his musicians from $40 on up.[13]

Granz held no illusions that the success of his concerts was winning the hearts and minds of those running large venues in Los Angeles. Reactions did not vary much from those of club owners he had approached three years before, except that the higher visibility made them more cautious about being associated with his events. If anything, the halls were becoming more protective of their role in allocating critical cultural exposure and the legitimacy it might have conferred. In June the Hollywood Bowl rejected Granz's offer to produce a Jazz at the Philharmonic concert as part of its Festivals of Popular Music, a four-concert series from June to September that included Frank Sinatra, Dinah Shore, and Carmen Miranda. It fell to Dr. Karl Wecker, managing director of the Bowl, to give Granz the brush-off. The Bowl, Wecker said, objected to the jam session format of JATP and did not want the word *jazz* used in connection with any event there. Wecker said that he approved of popular music concerts, as long as the music was "the best of its kind."[14]

Granz returned to New York in August for the first time since 1942 to catch up on the music scene and scout talent for the first national tour of Jazz at the Philharmonic, which was scheduled to leave Los Angeles in November and wrap up in New York a month later. He ended up knocking the beboppers and some old friends alike. "Jazz in New York stinks," Granz said. "Even the drummers on 52nd Street sound like Dizzy Gillespie. . . . I can't tell you how disappointed I am in the quality of the music here. We keep hearing out west about 52nd Street, but I'd like to know where it is."[15] He said of the moderns, "Maybe Gillespie was great, but the 'advanced' group that Charlie Parker is fronting at the Three Deuces didn't knock me out. It's too rigid and repetitive." He then unloaded on Ben Webster ("wasn't playing anything when I heard him") and Billie Holiday ("I'm sorry"), adding that the bright spots for him had been trumpeter Hot Lips Page, the Woody Herman Orchestra, pianist Erroll Garner, and guitarist Bill De Arango. "Otherwise, the West Coast may not be the happy hunting ground of modern jazz, but, brother, neither is 52nd Street these days," Granz concluded. His comments are interesting from two standpoints. First, they confirm the obvious: his musical sensibilities were rooted in swing. Second, his statements indicate that when he asked Gillespie and Parker to play JATP in January 1946 during their engagement at Billy Berg's either his tastes were quickly changing or he was willing to take a chance that Los Angeles audiences would like modern jazz.

Another aim of Granz's trip to New York was to find a label to release his recordings, and he found it when he met Moe Asch. The partnership that resulted briefly paired two of the more distinctive record producers in the annals of twentieth-century recording. Granz's view of his live concert recordings as documentaries meshed perfectly with Asch's expansive, esoteric tastes. His various labels, which were eventually consolidated into Folkways Records, boasted one of the largest, most diverse, and most eclectic catalogs in the world at around two thousand entries. Field recordings of native music of the Zulus and Eskimos and ballads from Britain and Siberia were listed alongside recordings of Huddy Ledbetter (Leadbelly), Pete Seeger, Woody Guthrie, and Cisco Houston, in addition to those of jazz artists Mary Lou Williams, Erroll Garner, Joe Sullivan, Sidney Bechet, and Baby Dodds and blues singer Lonnie Johnson. No record was ever deleted from his catalog.

Shortly after Granz heard the acetates from the July 2, 1944, concert, he conceived of issuing his live recordings with no editing or other manipulation required or desired. Mainstream record companies, however, were locked into the notion that recording required the controlled environment of the studio. Granz was turned down in a face-to-face meeting with one of the most important recording executives in the business at the time, Mannie Sachs, president of RCA Records. Sachs was put off by mistakes, crowd noises, and the freewheeling ways of JATP.

"That's exactly the reason you should put it out," Granz told Sachs. "You don't want a retouched photograph if it's a documentary."[16]

Granz received a warmer reception from Asch when he brought two sets of acetates to the offices of Asch Records at 117 West Forty-sixth Street after looking him up in the phone book. Asch received Granz's first call because he topped the alphabetical listings. Granz's first order of business was on behalf of a friend, the Scottish singer and B movie actress Ella Logan—the aunt of jazz singer and actress Annie Ross—whose career would crest with her leading role in the 1947 Broadway musical *Finian's Rainbow*. Asch turned down the Logan discs but perked up when Granz got around to the JATP records. He played a version of "How High the Moon," JATP's anthem in the early years, that had been recorded at the February 12 concert. Asch immediately concluded that the potential here easily outstripped that of his normal fare, and he made Granz a generous offer on the spot: $2,000 for costs and a royalty of fifteen cents per record. Returning to the Belmont Plaza Hotel where he was staying on Lexington at Forty-ninth, Granz wrote Asch authorizing him to subtract $150 off the total for his own commission and promising to get the masters, artwork, and liner notes to him by the following week. He asked that a contract containing a clause that protected his royalty rate should the masters change hands be sent airmail to California for his signature. That provision would become an issue later when Granz joined forces with Mercury Records in 1947.[17]

Also in August, Granz worked out other practical details involved with launching the next JATP tour from Los Angeles on November 26 and scheduling multiple dates across the three thousand miles to New York. Up to now, JATP had pretty much been a local affair, with little thought given to transportation, accommodations, and other logistical headaches, which in this case were exacerbated by booking a national tour of an integrated production. Granz signed with Chicago band manager Berle Adams, although that deal fell through before the tour began. It is testimony to the novelty of Granz's creation that it was neither well understood nor taken seriously. *Billboard* said the tour was "similar to one-nighter bookings of name bands under usual flat figure and percentage."[18] As the date got closer for the tour to begin, Granz signed with Joe Glaser and MCA to promote an itinerary that started in Los Angeles and continued to San Diego, San Francisco, and Victoria,

British Columbia. The eastern swing of the tour was scheduled to pick up seamlessly in Denver or Minneapolis.[19]

Granz was back in the recording studio in the fall of 1945, producing records for the Philo label in Los Angeles under the ownership of brothers Eddie and Leo Mesner. The pair later changed the name of the company to Aladdin Records following pressure from the neighboring Philharmonic Auditorium, which thought the company name implied an affiliation between the two. In early September, Granz produced a session led by trumpeter Howard McGhee and featuring tenor saxophonist Teddy Edwards, followed up by an October date with a quintet headed by another trumpeter, Harry Edison, with alto saxophonist Willie Smith. Like many other recordings from this period, these were also released on the Los Angeles label Black and White, with which Granz had recently signed a deal obligating him to produce twelve sessions.

Meanwhile, Moe Asch released *Jazz at the Philharmonic, Volume 1*, on Asch Records in late October. Three twelve-inch records contained "How High the Moon" and "Lady Be Good" from the February 12 concert. At nearly twelve and fourteen minutes respectively, each song was spread across three discs, with fadeouts from disc to disc suturing the music together. "The audience is very much a part of the recordings. . . . People pay the admission not only to hear jazz as presented by the best exponents of this art, but to participate," a press release written at the time asserts. "During these concerts, the audience sometimes does everything but play the instruments, and like the bleachers in a baseball game, excite the musicians' creative powers."[20] *Metronome,* reviewing the album in its December issue, explicitly noted the album's place in jazz history. "To the best of our knowledge, this is the first time an actual jam session has been recorded and marketed on a commercial label," the review said, noting the clarity of sound that preserved the music and the spontaneity of the occasion.[21]

The significance of *Jazz at the Philharmonic, Volume 1*, cannot be overstated. The recordings introduced a fundamentally new technical direction in recorded music. The enthusiasm they engendered among the record-buying public mirrored that expressed toward the concerts themselves. Sales of around 150,000 copies demonstrated beyond a doubt the viability of recording live music.[22] But it was the album's positioning within Granz's manifold endeavors that multiplied its impact. As the records mesmerized thousands more new listeners on the radio and jukeboxes, they became calling cards that publicized the concerts and the artists, thereby building up a demand for additional concert records that further swelled the audiences of JATP. They soon became integral to Granz's marketing strategy.

A measure of the records' impact is provided by the recollection of the late St. Louis veteran broadcaster and critic Charlie Menees some thirty-five years after the thunderous reception that greeted *Jazz at the Philharmonic, Volume 4,* from the July 2, 1944, concert. "Of all the years I've been on the radio since 1944, I've locally premiered four or five recordings that brought immediate and dynamic reaction from my listening public," Menees said in 1981. "And that record ["Blues, Parts 1 and 2"] with Nat Cole, Illinois Jacquet, Les Paul, and others was my unforgettable first. St. Louis went berserk. I was ecstatic." His advice to local record dealers: "Get as many copies of that record as you possibly can!"[23]

No feature of Granz's albums over the next decade, other than the music itself, came to signify his recordings more than the drawings of David Stone Martin, beginning with *Jazz at the Philharmonic, Volume 1.* A trumpet player drawn from a downward right angle on the album cover became JATP's trademark image that would still be appearing on record labels, concert programs, advertising, and reissues over five decades later. Martin's style, with his immediately recognizable signature, was as distinctive in its lines as the sounds of Parker or Young. His drawings resonated in communicating the spirit of jazz with weblike tangles of lines that turned twelve-inch album jackets into works of art. Martin began his work as a jazz album illustrator for Moe Asch by creating a 1944 cover for his lover, the pianist, composer, and arranger Mary Lou Williams. After that, Asch appointed him art director of his labels, Asch, Disc, and Stinson.

Born in 1913 in Chicago, Martin was a graduate of the Art Institute of Chicago whose primary early influence was Ben Shahn. He credited his work as art director for the Tennessee Valley Authority in the 1930s with raising his social consciousness that would permeate his later work. His professional life would intersect decisively with Granz's in 1948, when Granz lured him away from Asch to oversee art for his labels. The two men's collaboration over the next seven years would result in around 250 covers by the mid-1950s. The late Manek Daver, a Hong Kong–based businessman and Martin enthusiast who compiled two books featuring his jazz drawings, noted the convergence of Martin's images and Granz's flair for promoting his product in the concert hall and on vinyl. "Hundreds of record companies started up and faded quickly," he wrote. "The demands of packaging and marketing defeated them. One rare independent who went on to join the majors was Norman Granz. . . . Granz gave packaging considerable attention."[24] Granz gave Martin a free hand.

JATP got out of town in October 1945 for a sellout date in Portland and a less-than-successful appearance in Seattle, where a newspaper strike prevented Granz from adequately publicizing a program that included Hawkins, Eldridge, pianist Meade "Lux" Lewis, and former Count Basie vocalist Helen Humes. Further, Granz had difficulty locating a good hall and settled for a venue that he said more properly "should have housed alfalfa," disappointing musicians and audience alike.[25] The lesson was not lost on Granz, who shortly afterward found himself spending as much time on the road doing advance work for the shows as he did on the actual tours themselves.

Granz's problems with the management of Philharmonic Auditorium, which had endured crowds that shook the rafters and rattled their nerves for fifteen months, came to a head as he prepared for the November 26 concert. Their fundamentally opposing views can be found in Granz's aims for JATP published in the concert program. "It's gotten to the point where jazz is being called an Art (and see that you spell that with a capital 'A,' Jack)," Granz wrote. "The critical boys have picked it up, applied nice big descriptive words about it, and before you know it, a jam session becomes a jazz concert. Or as they sometimes like to put it, jazz is a folk music with its 'roots sunk deep in the people.' Actually, though, jazz is the one kind of a thing more than anything else that brings people together as spectators and participants with a complete disregard for race, color or creed. And that, Jack, is more important than anything else that may be said of it as an 'Art.'"[26]

In 1945 the Philharmonic Auditorium's general manager, C. H. Brainard, informed Granz that he had to find a new name for his shows that did not include the word "Philharmonic" if he wanted to continue presenting concerts there. Further, Brainard sought a pledge that Granz would keep the number of black musicians from exceeding 50 percent, limit print advertising to metropolitan dailies (thereby excluding the black press), and curtail promotion over the radio. Granz, for the time being, conceded on the show's name, changing it to "The Norman Granz Concert."[27] "That confirms what I thought," Granz said some five decades later, alluding to the racist motive of Brainard's proposed restrictions on advertising. "Of course, Brainard couldn't say that he was against mixed audiences. I don't think he was in a position to do that."[28]

The fall 1945 concerts that got under way in Los Angeles under the sponsorship of Philo Records, according to Granz, were a "rather strange, hybrid" group of East Coast musicians accompanying Coleman Hawkins. The rhythm section was Hawkins's own, consisting of Thelonious Monk in his one and only Jazz at the Philharmonic tour, Al McKibbon on bass, and Denzil Best on drums, and, for at least two appearances before he quit, saxophonist Lucky Thompson. Granz recalled, "At that point, Monk had not even begun to make any kind of noise or be acknowledged. I don't think people even knew his name."[29] Meade "Lux" Lewis played intermission solo piano. Helen Humes became JATP's first regular vocalist. Willie Smith filled in on a couple of dates until Granz could replace Thompson with a Chicago tenor man by the name of Tom Archey, and Roy Eldridge played some of the concerts as well.

The tour crawled out of town in an ancient bus for the first dates outside Los Angeles: San Diego, Portland, and Victoria, British Columbia. Granz realized as the troupe began its way up the coast that it was unlikely they would find integrated hotels or restaurants that would serve them. As a result, he sought assistance from African American ministers along the way who were willing to house the musicians for the night in their homes or elsewhere. The excursion was not any easier for the fact that Jazz at the Philharmonic was hardly known outside Los Angeles. An advertisement announcing the JATP's appearance at Portland's Mayfair Theater on December 4 sent mixed signals, sowing confusion about what kind of music an audience would hear. According to the ad, "Norman Granz' 'Jazz Symphony'" promised "an all-star aggregation of America's most versatile musicians playing everything from Brahms to jazz!" One Portland newspaper reporter pronounced himself a "cynic," so dashed were his expectations. "To call two tenor saxes, a bull fiddle, trumpet, piano, and drums a 'symphony' is to make a louse of *Webster's*," he wrote. "Maybe we were disappointed at not hearing an honest effort to bring Brahms and boogie woogie together. But when we read Mr. Granz's fine words at the top of the program, we realized that we were there as a member of the joy-through-jive movement."[30]

The end of the road for the first "national" tour came prematurely in Victoria when turnout no longer justified pressing on. Granz promptly canceled the second portion of the dates back east. "The tour was a disaster economically," Granz recalled. "Nobody knew the show, nobody knew what it was about. I was my own advance man. I went up and tried to get some publicity, but nobody knew what the hell Jazz at the Philharmonic meant. And the first records hadn't come out."[31] He called the musicians together and broke the bad news, lightened only to the extent that he would provide them with first-class train tickets to the destinations of their choice. He was not the first rookie promoter to go bust on the road, but his response, like his stance on racial discrimination, revealed another facet of working with Granz: he did not let musicians down in the clutch. He hocked almost all of his belongings to pay for the tickets. "The musicians, though they lost the gig, discerned the way I was," he said, "and I got a reputation immediately, because the guys in New York told me that I was honest, that no matter what, I wasn't going to strand them." Joe Glaser gave Granz the chance to keep the show on the road by doing some engagements in Texas, but he was not ready to confront the segregationist ways of the South just yet. *Billboard* must have thought it was publishing JATP's obituary instead of a temporary setback for a very determined and resourceful man. It derisively reported personnel problems as the cause of the tour's premature end before declaring, "Gag drew okay while it lasted."[32]

Though the concerts tanked, December 1945 was still an exciting month for Granz. Lester Young flew back to Los Angeles with a ticket Granz had provided the day he left the army on December 1. Granz did not want Young to suffer Jim Crow train service in the South following the ordeal he had already been through. His return was a year to the day of his induction and ten months after court-martial proceedings landed him in the stockade and confirmed Granz's and others' worst fears about the effect military life might have on Young. On the tenth of the month, Charlie Parker and Dizzy Gillespie opened at Billy Berg's and exposed a gap between the city's musicians, many of whom were captivated by the new music, and its audiences, who for the most part did not comprehend what they had heard. These two episodes loom large among the legends of the musicians and can be found in greater detail in numerous treatments of their lives. Accordingly, they are mentioned here only in relation to the opportunity they afforded Granz to present and record Young, Parker, and Gillespie in what would be the beginning of long ongoing relationships.

During Young's time in the army, Granz mostly kept up with him by reading the letters he sent to his wife, Mary, who lived in Los Angeles. Young was released from detention two months early, and Granz was eager to manage him as he got his music career back on track in the studio and with personal appearances. He was equally concerned to cheer Young up. He took him to local record shops to hear the latest jazz recordings, noting Young's interest in the recordings of Don Byas. On another occasion, he attempted to distract Young by taking him to the ballet. "I was a ballet freak," Granz recalled in 2001. "I remember that Jerome Robbins, the great choreographer, was one of the dancers. At intermission, he said, 'Well, I've had enough.' And that was the end of Lester's connection, if you like, with the ballet."[33]

At Granz's prompting, Young signed with Aladdin Records, and before December was out he had recorded some classic tracks produced by Granz. Appearing on the date that produced "D.B. [detention barrack] Blues," "Lester Blows Again," "These Foolish Things," and "Jumpin' at Mesners" were his former colleagues with Basie, the trombonist Vic Dickenson, as well as Dodo Marmarosa on piano, Henry Tucker on drums, and Red Callender on bass.[34] Granz and Young were back in the studio on December 22 to record Helen Humes with an octet. Granz assisted Young in getting lucrative bookings without a contract and on the road when he became a major attraction at black dances at clubs such as the Pershing in Chicago and other clubs capable of holding hundreds or thousands of patrons. "Lester had reached the stage shortly after he got out of the Army where he became suddenly enormously popular playing for black dances," Granz recalled. "They were very special kinds of gigs in America. It was better for him to be touring on his own than with JATP."[35]

Granz had known of Charlie Parker since the alto saxophonist's days with the pianist and bandleader Jay McShann in the early 1940s. Merle Anderson, a Kansas City tenor saxophonist in Los Angeles looking for work, had presented him with acetates Parker had recorded with the band. "I don't think Charlie had recorded commercially up to then," Granz said. "I must say, I didn't understand what I was listening to. It was not until later that I got to know Charlie."[36] He was not alone, as shown by the sharply divided reaction that greeted the group when they brought the music west to Billy Berg's. The trumpeter and bandleader Gerald Wilson, in Los Angeles since leaving Jimmie Lunceford in the spring of 1942, had known Gillespie since 1938 and been aware of Parker since the early 1940s. He spoke for many musicians when he said that "these great geniuses" were "the future of jazz." Wilson recalls being at Berg's with Granz on opening night, although not his reaction.[37]

After a year and a half producing jazz concerts, Granz was invited to serve as a judge for *Esquire*'s 1946 All-American Band contest. His comments are as revealing in what they say about the jazz scene the year the war ended as they are about Granz's tastes and his status as a promoter. His main criteria came down to ability as an individual and as a part of a musical unit of any size. He selected Harry Edison over Roy Eldridge, with Joe Guy and Howard McGhee as up-and-coming trumpeters to watch; trombonist Lawrence Brown of the Ellington Orchestra over a second-place Bill Harris, who would become a JATP star in later years; alto saxophonist Willie Smith over Benny Carter (Charlie Parker rated a "very strong" honorable mention); tenor saxophonists Illinois Jacquet and Don Byas; clarinetists Rudy Rutherford, then with Count Basie, and Ellingtonian Jimmy Hamilton; pianists Nat Cole and Erroll Garner; drummer Gene Krupa and Cab Calloway drummer J.C. Heard; bassists Billy Hadnott and Chubby Jackson of the Woody Herman Band; and guitarists Oscar Moore and Barney Kessel. He cited Eckstine and Woody Herman as his top two male singers, and Billie Holiday ("the greatest vocalist in jazz") and Jo Stafford as his two top female singers. Rounding out his choices were Ellington's baritone saxophonist Harry Carney, vibraphonist Lionel Hampton, Ellington and Billy Strayhorn as the best arrangers, and Ellington and Herman as the top bandleaders.[38]

Jazz at the Philharmonic stepped out front before Granz's peers in a big way when Granz accepted an invitation to program a concert in conjunction with the *Down Beat* Awards ceremony honoring West Coast recipients at Philharmonic Auditorium on January 28, 1946. Two thousand disappointed fans were turned away at the door. Granz gathered some of his usual players and others new to the mix, such as Howard McGhee and Al Killian on trumpets; Nat Cole, winner of three awards, and Arnold Ross, then with Harry James, on piano; Billy Hadnott on bass; Lee Young; and the Gene Krupa Trio with Charlie Ventura on tenor saxophone and Teddy Napoleon on piano. Mel Powell, in town with the Benny Goodman Orchestra, was honored along with Goodman, as was vocalist Helen Humes.[39] Making the evening an historic fulfillment of Granz's labors, however, were the initial JATP appearances by Lester Young and the celebrated visitors Charlie Parker and Dizzy Gillespie. Given the low attendance at Billy Berg's, most of the audience was hearing Parker and Gillespie in person for the first time. They were scheduled to play during the first half of the show so that they could make their way back to Billy Berg's.

Parker's JATP debut was a cliffhanger that almost didn't happen. He failed to show at first because he was out securing a heroin connection to carry him through a full evening of playing. When he finally returned, the ensemble had struck up "Sweet Georgia Brown" to conclude the set. Gillespie opened playing the melody, followed by a solo by Mel Powell when Bird walked onstage unannounced during his first chorus. An unidentified musician is heard on the recording saying "Hey" as Parker moves into the lineup. Further evidence of the commotion attending Parker's late entrance can be heard by the applause halfway through Powell's second chorus and another musician asking, "Say, man, where have you been?" Gillespie concluded "Sweet Georgia Brown" with phrases from "52nd Street Theme," used to finish sets back east, possibly to avoid calls for encores featuring Parker that would have put him late to work at Billy Berg's. Accordingly, there is only one recording of the two together from the concert. Parker stayed for four numbers into the second set, beginning with an improvised blues, "Blues for Norman," and "I Can't Get Started," which were issued on disc as *Jazz at the Philharmonic, Volume 2.* But the tension was far from over, as pianist Ross, who replaced Powell, told jazz historian Phil Schaap. "On this one tune, I remember Bird stepped forward and he didn't play for a whole chorus. He just stood there with the horn in his mouth," said Ross, who slipped from comping to taking a solo himself to fill the gap.[40]

The next three tunes—"I Can't Get Started," "Lady Be Good," and "After You've Gone"—likely represented the first significant joint appearance of Young and Parker. The latter had clearly absorbed much from his illustrious predecessor. Of the three tunes, Parker's stunning bluesy solo on two choruses of "Lady Be Good" proved to be of enduring interest. Parker's colleagues onstage immediately realized its import and hesitated to step forward to follow him. This explains why Hadnott filled in with what turned out to be JATP's first recorded bass solo until Killian, McGhee, and Willie Smith nudged Lester Young from the wings. The musicians were acknowledging memories of Young's classic version of "Lady Be Good" in his 1936 debut recording with a Count Basie small group. An incident forty-four years later illustrates the impact of Parker's solo on musicians at the time. Ray Brown was deep in conversation with Hank Jones, tenor saxophonist Jimmy Heath, and the late pianist James Williams during a February 1990 rehearsal for an all-star tribute to Ella Fitzgerald at Lincoln Center. Williams asked Brown how he knew whether a musician was hip during the time he was coming of age. "They could sing Bird's solo on 'Lady Be Good' note for note," the bassist answered before breaking into an impromptu unabridged performance.

The *Down Beat* show brought the house down in more ways than one. It marked the final occasion that JATP actually played at the "P" forever embedded in its name. Philharmonic Auditorium managers refused to hold any more Granz concerts, citing disturbances in and around the auditorium as the final straw. The magazine reported complaints that some patrons unable to obtain tickets had tried to break into the hall, infractions of the theater's alcohol and smoking bans, and trouble with ushers. Hall manager C.H. Brainard said he had no quarrel with Jazz at the Philharmonic musically or Granz personally but that Philharmonic Auditorium was not going to host events where the peace had to be maintained by the police. Granz fired back that the contretemps represented "reactionary views" against the mixed crowds and the interracial couples regularly in attendance. Reports of any disturbances, he said, were overstated as a cover for the Philharmonic Auditorium to do what it had threatened for a long time. The decision, however, carried few consequences for Granz's plans. Los Angeles had served its purpose as the launching pad for JATP. Henceforth, the city became one among scores of destinations on Granz's annual itinerary and remained the hub of his business and recording activities for decades.

Granz worked nonstop in the months leading up to a projected twenty-one-city tour in the third week of April 1946. In January he recorded for Aladdin a Lester Young small group including Willie Smith, Howard McGhee, and Vic Dickenson; then, in March or April, he recorded a trio with Young, Nat Cole, and Buddy Rich, which he would hold for release until he began working with Mercury Records in 1947. Recordings released on Black and White as part of a "Norman Granz Specialty Series" included sessions by pianist Arnold Ross and trumpeter Gerald Wilson, as well as the Ella Logan records that Moe Asch had rejected.

The second Jazz at the Philharmonic tour, unlike the ill-fated one four months earlier, made the distance. MCA's Los Angeles office handled the bookings as far as Denver, while the Moe Gale Agency of New York booked the remainder of the dates as the shows moved east.[41] The tour, which opened at the Embassy Theater in Los Angeles on April 22, was billed as the "Battle of the Saxes," an only slightly hyperbolic title for an event featuring Young, Hawkins, and Parker. The alto saxophonist had not returned to New York with Gillespie and the others as planned in February. Parker had been gigging around town, getting more strung out on the way to a full-blown nervous breakdown and hospitalization at Camarillo State Hospital in July, and had begun his seminal recordings for Ross Russell at Dial Records. Trumpeter and Basie star Buck Clayton, an old friend from the Capri and Trouville days, had not been out of the army a week when he got the call from Granz to play the tour. Fattening up the bill at the Embassy Theater were Willie Smith, Kenny Kersey on piano, Irving Ashby on guitar, Slim and Bam, Joe Guy on trumpet, Red Callender, Buddy Rich, Meade "Lux" Lewis, and Billie Holiday.

On the opening evening, one particularly striking passage in "I've Got Rhythm" provided a shorthand reading of the changes occurring in jazz at that moment and the genius of the JATP format in presenting them as irresistible entertainment. Following the opening measures by Kersey, Willie Smith sailed through a buoyant solo, followed by Buck Clayton, whose attack had grown brassier after three years playing in army bands compared with his sound during the Basie years, when the Count had encouraged his use of mutes. "The louder, the better as far as Norman was concerned," Clayton recalled in the 1970s. Clayton laid the bridge to a succession of solos by Hawkins, Parker, and Young. Each of the saxophonists had his partisans. "I would have to give the decision to Hawkins—just listen to how he throws the rhythm into overdrive," wrote jazz critic Bob Blumenthal in a 1977 reissue.[42] Hawkins's biographer John Chilton favored Young, on different grounds: "It is Lester Young, whose solo is full of understated, lithe phrases, who creates the most effective work."[43] Finally, the jazz historian and noted Parker authority Phil Schaap insisted that Parker, whose style had absorbed the harmonic sophistication of Hawkins and the rhythmic and lyrical sensibilities of Prez, gave the exchange its lasting meaning: "This [solo], while marred by a squeak, is brilliant in a Swing Era portion, and while playing with Swing masters, we can hear just how much Bird had changed jazz."[44]

Four days later, JATP, with Parker playing intermittently, began its trek east by plane, playing Oakland, San Francisco, Seattle, Portland, and Victoria through the end of April and picking up again in Denver, Kansas City, Pittsburgh, Chicago, and Minneapolis before performing multiple dates in New York City as part of the Carnegie Hall Pops Series beginning on May 27.[45] Ads in the local press show the concerts cropping up under varying names—"Norman Granz All-Star Jazz Concert," and simply "Jazz Concert"—until mid-May, when the name "Jazz at the Philharmonic" stuck once and for all.

The concert at Oakland's Shrine Auditorium on April 26, 1946, had a lifelong impact on one sixteen-year-old jazz fan. Clint Eastwood had grown up hearing jazz and rhythm and blues in this very African American city, but Jazz at the Philharmonic presented an aesthetic turning point for him. The wonder began with a lineup of Coleman Hawkins, Flip Phillips and Lester Young ("the cat's ass, you know, for tenor saxophone"). But Charlie Parker, also on the bill that evening, provided the moment of rapture, the fundamental insight, that helped shape Eastwood's acting career and general artistic vision. Parker was "a whole shock to the system. It was just amazing to see somebody do anything with that kind of confidence. He wasn't arrogant or anything, he was just a guy standing there in a pinstripe suit, and when he started playing, it was like some kind of free painter, who'd just jump right on in there and start slapping paint up there, a totally unplanned deal. . . . There was no show business to it in those days. This guy just stood and played, and I thought, God, what an amazing expressive thing." He came away contemplating what it might be like to apply that same confidence to any endeavor he might strike out upon.[46] Eastwood's love of Parker's music and inspiration was fully returned to the source when he directed the Parker biopic *Bird* forty-two years later and became an influential champion of jazz in his films and as a jazz pianist.

The concerts' ambitious schedule and star power began to draw attention in the trade press, as well as in local newspapers reacting to the hubbub the concerts were creating in their towns. One thing obvious from the trades was how assiduously Granz fed them his glowing box office figures. Around 4,600 people packed Detroit's Masonic Temple, a number swelled by a standing-room-only crowd of 200. What space onstage at the Moore Theater in Seattle was not occupied by the musicians accommodated another overflow audience, and according to the *Seattle Times,* "Every nook and cranny of the theater held a happy jazz addict."[47] The *Denver Post* noted the lack of printed programs and the music's abrupt improvisatory nature, observing that "the evening was a successful experiment in Denver, showing that jazz can be treated like music, like a true art form in its own right."[48]

The May 13 concert at the Carnegie Music Hall in Pittsburgh demonstrated Granz's desire to strengthen his ties to black communities in the cities JATP visited, in more ways than just integrating concert halls and other public accommodations. For example, he invited the *Pittsburgh Courier's* theatrical writer George Brown to serve as the emcee, giving him the chance to share the stage with the likes of Young and Hawkins. He also contracted Lee Matthews, one of the city's best-known black promoters and head of the Pyramid Club. In an issue of the *Courier* that contained two stories promoting the concert, Granz took out a quarter-page ad with photographs of the stars prominently displayed.[49]

The promised land of the second national tour was the Carnegie Hall Pop Series. Carnegie Hall's commitment to popular music and light classics presented an alternative view from that held by the more conservative Philharmonic Auditorium and Hollywood Bowl. In New York, the idea of presenting concerts of popular music and jazz in elegant and prestigious surroundings was welcome programming that helped to enlarge the hall's constituency. Ready to convert to a "proletarian palace" where sandwiches, pretzels, and beer were sold in the boxes before the show and during intermission, Carnegie Hall scheduled seven weeks of programs between May 4 and June 22. Tickets sold for one to three dollars. The series was notable as well for the support of the influential Detroit chemical executive and arts philanthropist Henry Reichhold, who personally called upon Granz to provide some needed additional programming. The week of June 2 provides an example of the varied schedule, which included "Viennese Night" with the seventy-member New York Philharmonic, JATP, "An Evening of American Folk Music," a tribute to George Gershwin and Jerome Kern, and two more concerts by the New York Philharmonic.

Four JATP concerts on consecutive Monday nights, including a June 3 broadcast by the city-owned radio station WNYC, gave Granz the chance to pull out all the stops as he presented JATP in the city's most revered concert hall in the country's jazz capital. Being in New York permitted him to replenish his lineup with some of the best jazz talent in town. Sarah Vaughan, already the leading vocalist to have emerged from bop, guest-starred on the opening show on May 27. Billie Holiday met up with her friend Granz for the June 3 show. Illinois Jacquet rejoined the lineup for the first time since the California concerts. Other guests included Dizzy Gillespie, trombonist J. J. Johnson, Ray Brown, Gene Krupa, and the bands of J. C. Heard, Edmund Hall, and Mary Lou Williams. Of the first three Carnegie concerts, Leonard Feather observed that Granz was doing "a good thing for jazz by presenting, for the most part, modern music and progressive musicians; he is using almost all Negro talent; and he is featuring saxophones (all tenors) very extensively." He did complain that JATP suffered from "nothing but solos and uncoordinated ensembles" and gave too little time to Coleman Hawkins.[50]

Halfway through the New York shows, Granz and the Gale Agency took out two full pages in *Variety* dominated by a large photograph of a packed hall to ensure that the entertainment industry would understand that JATP, with its "jazz in concert style," represented "a new kind of showbu$íne$$."[51] The ad, which referred to Granz's work on *Jammin' the Blues*, quoted box office figures and reviews from the tour, including one in the *Chicago Tribune* that hailed JATP as a "financial wow" and one in the *Chicago Herald-American* that stated, under the headline "Jazz Biz a Whiz," "A milling crowd [of around 2,500], policemen, and attendants shouting, 'Sold Out' one half-hour after the start of a concert is a strange sight at any musical event in Chicago."

The figures speak for themselves in revealing the economics of the jazz concert business Granz was bringing to fruition. The top-earning hall in 1946 for JATP had been the Civic Opera House with a gross of $12,000 per night, followed closely by Detroit with $11,500. Figures from the other cities included Los Angeles, $6,500; San Francisco, $5,200; Seattle, $4,800; Dayton, $3,600; Minneapolis, $5,000; Denver, $4,600; and Carnegie Hall, $4,200 per night for the first three concerts in the Carnegie Hall Pops series and $4,400 for the last concert. This last concert, held on June 17, yielded a profit of only $500 after expenses and commissions were paid, including $1,700 paid out in musicians' salaries.

JATP played a second date in Chicago for good measure to wrap up a successful tour. Looking back fifty-four years later, Granz said of the first Chicago show, "Chicago was the most important because it was the breakthrough concert. It was because I had Lester and Hawk together, the idea of having the leading exponents of the two schools of the tenor. That was the dream team. It was like having Duke play Basie at the Savoy. Until Chicago, we never made it really big because I think the cities we went to were not too heavy. When we got to Chicago, it was insane. The tickets sold out the same day. Even I was surprised. The musicians and I talked about it. They couldn't figure it out. Then I learned. It was Lester and Coleman. That why the show had a gross which for that period was unbelievable."[52]

While still in New York, Granz announced his intent to sue the Stinson Trading Company to get an accounting of royalties from *Jazz at the Philharmonic, Volume 1*. He added that he planned to maintain his ties with Asch, who had helped finance the concerts.[53] Also in June, he appeared to be negotiating again with the Hollywood Bowl to present the Duke Ellington and Woody Herman orchestras, although the Orpheum Theater, which had originally booked Ellington in Los Angeles, ultimately barred his participation.[54] Britain's *Melody Maker* reported in July that Granz was even then looking to book a series of JATP concerts in Europe, beginning with Paris shows on September 1.

However, it would be another six years before his hope of building a concert circuit on the Continent came to pass.[55]

The *Pittsburgh Courier* applauded another "significantly important precedent" established by Jazz at the Philharmonic: the nondiscrimination clause Granz had inserted in his contracts. The provision giving the contract its economic teeth stated, "It is the essence of this agreement that there is to be no discrimination whatsoever in the sale of tickets, and that there is to be no segregation of whites from Negroes. In the event of any violation of either of these provisions by you, the management of the hall, or anyone else, Mr. Granz has the privilege of refusing to give you the concert, in which case you will forfeit one-half of the contract price to him."[56] Granz told the *Courier* that he had already sacrificed bookings, especially in the South, but that other southern promoters had been willing to accept the shows under those conditions. "This merely proves that the enlightenment is gradually spreading all over the nation," Granz remarked at the time. "I realize that in those places where there are state statutes on the books it will be impossible to insist on adherence to such a clause. However, it will probably insure the arranging of equal accommodations for all patrons." The *Courier* reported that Granz was seeking the cooperation of leading black bandleaders to insert nondiscrimination clauses in their touring contracts because, "after all, it is they who can really strike most effectively at this insidious thing if they have but the courage of their convictions and a deep interest in their self respect." The paper added that booking agencies handling black bands were watching Granz's experiment with great interest before following suit.

According to a *Detroit Tribune* article from around the same time, Granz also fought discrimination on his tours in another way.[57] He would book confirmed reservations for first-class hotel accommodations for the musicians and himself and wire the funds in advance. Then when he showed up with his racially mixed group he would quell any resistance he encountered by producing a contract and insisting on bypassing the quaking clerk to personally threaten the hotel manager with a lawsuit if the contract was not honored. These episodes were forerunners of the increasingly public campaign against the racial status quo that Granz would wage the following year.

Granz spent the remainder of the summer and part of the fall preparing for the tour to get under way with concerts in San Francisco and Los Angeles on October 6 and 7. He tried to patch things up with the Philharmonic Auditorium in late August but was coolly and completely dispatched. The hall refused his offers to share a percentage of the proceeds, allow preapproval of advertising, post a bond of $10,000 to cover any possible damage, or book two nights instead of one. "The board's position is that a jazz crew attracts an undesirable element," *Variety* said, referring to the fracas in January 1946.[58]

He must have been amused to read the headline of an article announcing the appearance of the JATP's Third National Tour at a half-full Shrine Auditorium: "First L.A. Bash of Season Too Heavy on Talent." The lineup in San Francisco the previous night—Roy Eldridge, Buck Clayton, Coleman Hawkins, Illinois Jacquet, trombonist Trummy Young, pianist Kenny Kersey, trumpeter Rex Stewart, and Helen Humes—became a virtual armada when joined in Los Angeles by Billie Holiday, Erroll Garner, Barney Kessel, Howard McGhee, Willie Smith, trumpeter Sonny Berman, Bill Harris on trombone, and drummer Jackie Mills. Making his second JATP appearance that night was tenor saxophonist Flip Phillips. Some new and lucrative stops further off the main route now supported the tour on its way east: in addition to Chicago and Detroit, Cleveland and the Brooklyn Academy of Music.

The concerts drew mixed critical reviews. One in particular, D. Leon Wolff's *Down Beat* review of the October 24 concert at the Civic Opera House, has been widely quoted over the years and elicited a caustic but carefully reasoned response from Granz. The review, entitled "Granz Bash a Caricature on Jazz; Everything Bad in Jazz Found Here," contains all the most common criticisms of JATP's commercialism, the bluster of its musical presentation, and the deportment of its fans.[59] "Of all the wretched music ever inflicted upon the earnest devotee of *le jazz hot,* nothing, I regret to say, has yet to equal Norman Granz's Jazz at the Philharmonic," it begins.

To Wolff, Illinois Jacquet was "the loudest tenor in the country making more than $60 a week," and Rex Stewart "should have been yanked off the stage during the second number, the most sickening and obscene demonstration ever perpetrated before a mixed audience." Even the venerable Hawkins "sounded like a sewing machine" compared to his work on records. Helen Humes's suggestive phrasing turned her material into "worthless blues" with "no emotional validity, no musical attraction, no justification whatsoever, except for the adolescent or mentally retarded drips, who knock themselves out over suggestive lyrics." Along the way, Wolff denigrated artists performing what he considered were tired hits from the 1930s: hyped-up, flag-waving tunes interspersed with sleepy ballads.

Granz responded with a letter as long as the original article. "We'll try to keep personalities out of this, including even such a strong personality as D. Leon Wolff," Granz wrote, but he would immediately break that promise in a full-scale counterattack that bashed Wolff point for point while unapologetically setting forth Granz's own philosophy for synthesizing art and commerce.[60]

Though Granz's irascible response showed that he wasn't exactly impervious toward his critics, what they said didn't matter in the sense that it didn't alter his course in any way. If anything, such broadsides presented welcome opportunities to publicly defend his musicians and audiences. He relegated critics to the wilderness as long as he had the public in his corner and the cause of racial justice to advance. While his critics were not as unitary in their condemnation as one might believe listening to Granz, he had a point. "I came across the article by Leon Wolff in some papers I had," Granz said in 2000. "It didn't mean a thing, it never bothered me. I learned from the first JATP concert and then onward that there was nothing that the critics could do either affirmatively or negatively . . . I don't know who Wolff was or what his credentials were, but I could have eaten him alive."[61] Granz never gave any hint that he had erred by refusing to take his critics seriously. His ascent over the next few years was testimony to the belief that the only instincts he could count on were his own.

6

Norman Granz versus . . .

"Victory abroad," the first plank of African Americans' "Double-V" campaign, was fulfilled with the Japanese surrender on August 14, 1945, ending a war in which an estimated one million African American men and women had served. The bill for the second half of the charge—"victory over racism at home"—came due immediately thereafter. The agenda of the civil rights movement in the 1940s reflected vigorous thinking and activity that eventually led to the undoing of many of the more egregious manifestations of segregation in the law, politics, education, voting and housing rights, public accommodations, and to a lesser degree economics over the succeeding decades. Though Norman Granz, in his two brief stints of military service, never saw a battle, he would head to the home front time and again to fight against racial discrimination. The period was equally distinguished by other symbolic events, primarily in the areas of sports and the arts, which inescapably hastened a turning point in the wider struggle for equality. Undoubtedly, the most dramatic of these happened on April 15, 1947. The same week that JATP played Detroit's Music Hall, Jackie Robinson, an illustrious example of a different kind of swing, suited up for his first day as second baseman for the Brooklyn Dodgers, and hit the issue of integration from home plate of the nation's pastime into the upper decks of its consciousness.

By 1947, smartly packaged and aggressively marketed semiannual tours and recordings had moved JATP to the forefront nationally in transmitting both jazz and Granz's social agenda. Granz used the sky-rocketing appeal of Jazz at the Philharmonic tours to piece together a national network of concert halls and theaters, lodging and transportation, and friendly newspapermen, broadcasters, promoters, and record distributors. He continued to consolidate his gains in the concert field while also branching out further into recording with the founding of his first label, Clef Records. (Granz was so plugged into the music scene that he managed to join the Los Angeles Musicians Union in the late 1940s by claiming to play the triangle.) He kept his focus on both the substance of the shows and the deeper meaning he hoped to communicate in keeping the spotlight on civil rights through jazz. "As in genuine democracy, only performance counts," Granz told *The Crisis,* the magazine of the National Association for the Advancement of Colored People (NAACP), in May 1947. "Jazz is truly the music of democratic America."[1]

Granz's own civil rights activities directly absorbed the unfolding agenda, means of communication, and strategies of the 1940s civil rights struggle. The Double-V campaign during World War II employed two broad sets of strategies that would also characterize the civil rights movement in the latter half of the twentieth century: peaceful but aggressive direct-action protests and a coordinated national legal assault. Its achievements, hard won during dangerous days by a pantheon of heroes, among them A. Philip Randolph, Thurgood Marshall, Bayard Rustin, James Farmer, Walter White, Roy Wilkins, and Paul Robeson, have been obscured to some degree by the more recent fame accorded the movement successes of the 1950s and 1960s. But those successes, which would seal the reputations of towering figures like Martin Luther King and Malcolm X, could not have been achieved without the groundwork arduously performed by the previous generation of civil rights warriors.

The Congress of Racial Equality (CORE), founded in Chicago in 1942, was the most influential example of the pressure that nonviolence was capable of exerting. CORE's protests were distinct from those in the 1930s in their long-range, sustained efforts and their reliance on interracial groups of volunteers that were usually more white than black. The organization adopted more confrontational tactics of picket lines and sit-ins at restaurants, theaters, barbershops, and recreational facilities, such as amusement parks, bowling alleys, skating rinks, and swimming pools, in the border states of the old North/South divide.[2] On another front, in early 1947 an interracial committee in the Washington, D.C., and Baltimore chapters of the National Association for the Advancement of Colored People began a lengthy desegregation campaign by Actors' Equity against the sister National and Ford theaters, a development that Granz watched closely.

Under Thurgood Marshall, general counsel for the NAACP, the civil rights organization shifted its legal strategy in the mid-1940s from pressing southern states to abolish their separate-but-equal laws to more directly assaulting segregation. Beginning in 1946, Marshall, who went on to win twenty-nine cases before the Supreme Court before becoming the Court's first African American justice in 1967, won major victories in the areas of public accommodations, access to graduate and professional schools, and restrictive property covenants; most famously, he headed the legal team that in 1954 secured the historic—and unanimous—*Brown v. Board of Education* decision outlawing segregation of public schools.

President Harry Truman, not known for publicly promoting the cause of racial justice, nonetheless lent the prestige of his office to help advance civil rights during this period. In June 1947 he became the first president to address the NAACP when he spoke to the thirty-eighth annual convention in Washington. Four months later, the final report of the president's Commission on Civil Rights, *To Secure These Rights,* articulated four basic freedoms: safety and security, citizenship and its privileges, freedom of conscience, and equality of opportunity. "It contained more than I'd dreamed possible. . . . All the developments [made] 1947 an exhilarating year for the NAACP," Roy Wilkins wrote.[3]

Harry Truman was not the first chief executive to have to contend with A. Philip Randolph, president of the all-black Brotherhood of Sleeping Car Porters and the most powerful African American union leader of the twentieth century. In 1941 Randolph had threatened his predecessor with an African American march on Washington to protest the lack of access to well-paying jobs in defense plants, and Roosevelt had responded with an executive order establishing the Fair Employment Practices Commission. In the years after the war, Randolph loudly protested segregation in the military and advocated that blacks avoid conscription. On July 26, 1948, Truman avoided a collision with Randolph when he issued Executive Order 9981, officially desegregating the military. When Truman was asked days later at a press conference if the order's intent was to totally end segregation, he answered with a terse "Yes."

Esquire magazine's *1947 Jazz Book* caused an uproar in the music world, one in which Granz himself would take a part. The annual series of special issues was designed originally to chronicle trends in jazz across the board over the preceding year, and previous issues had ranged across the jazz traditions from New Orleans to the modernists redefining jazz in the mid-1940s. But with the latest edition, under the direction of Ernest Anderson, Eddie Condon's manager and promoter of his Town Hall concert series, the publication, according to the critic Leonard Feather, "was quite unsubtly transformed into a virtual publicity outlet for Condon and his associates." The usual profiles of poll winners and judges' comments were cut out so that twenty photos of the (all-white) Condon group could be included, along with articles by Condon's booking agent and friends. Though Sarah Vaughan won the award for best female vocalist, the publication merely listed her name, devoting instead a full-page story to a non-award-winning female singer who had appeared with Condon's group. The ensuing controversy ended the series. Granz resigned from *Esquire*'s board of judges, foreshadowing a mass exodus of eighteen remaining judges over the next two weeks that left only four of the original twenty-five-member board in place. He also returned the check for his services, calling the book a "disservice to jazz." A similar blast came weeks later in a letter signed by thirty-four poll winners—Louis Armstrong, Duke Ellington, Billie Holiday, Nat Cole, Ella Fitzgerald, Coleman Hawkins, Roy Eldridge, Miles Davis, Tadd Dameron, and Sarah Vaughan among them—who decried the work "as an insult to the musical profession and to the jazz musicians who have helped *Esquire* by taking part in its jazz activities. As long as the present unfair set-up continues, we do not wish to vote in any future polls, and we will refuse to accept any future awards."[4] Granz was far from alone in his rebuke, but the episode showed that he was not aiming to get too tied up with the jazz establishment, such as that represented by *Esquire* magazine.

The spring 1947 Jazz at the Philharmonic tour was set to open February 6 with a concert at the Brooklyn Academy of Music featuring a lineup of Coleman Hawkins, Willie Smith, Roy Eldridge, Buck Clayton, Trummy Young, Buddy Rich, Kenny Kersey, and Helen Humes. Flip Philips began an unbroken string of seasons with JATP continuing through the last domestic tour in 1957, a record matched only by bassist Ray Brown. Banner national advertising, such as that published in *Variety* in late January, was just one indicator of the activity that made Jazz at the Philharmonic a top-grossing musical phenomenon by its fourth year.

The semiannual tours soon stretched over three months and required an approximately equal amount of time in advance work for the next tour. The Granz approach to concert promotion was as well oiled as the shows themselves. Upon arrival in a new town, he bought papers at the airport so that he could visit the midnight disc jockeys, most of whom had not heard of Jazz at the Philharmonic, and try to get some plugs for the shows. By six o'clock he did the same with those hosting the morning shows. His next stop was the hall so that he could scale the seating and order tickets; then he visited the newspaper offices and found hotels that could accommodate the group. "Then I would go on to the next city and it would repeat itself," Granz said. "I was literally on the road 50 weeks out of the year."[5]

Around the time of the April concert in Detroit, Granz hired Martha Glaser to assist him on the road. Glaser, best known as Erroll Garner's longtime manager, described the promotion she had done for the Detroit date, which filled the two-thousand-seat hall and netted around $3,800. She had booked radio interviews for Granz and some of the musicians, singly and in groups, on four local stations after delivering copies of Jazz at the Philharmonic records in advance, methods that *Down Beat* termed "unorthodox."[6] She had also met editors and spread advertising dollars among a dozen community newspapers, including the local African American and Jewish press. Furthermore, she had held a press conference that featured a showing of *Jammin' the Blues* to familiarize local writers with the JATP concept and better prepare them for what they were about to see. Promotional tie-ins with local record stores demonstrated how the concerts and the recordings were logical extensions of one another. Glaser scheduled four autograph sessions with musicians at local record outlets, and met with some fifty record dealers, whose posters promoting the concerts made up for any lack of other outdoor advertising. Granz met with distributors of the major record dealers and department stores to discuss jazz and the opportunities for sales presented by JATP concerts in their city. Such thorough preparation went a long way toward holding successful events that accommodated the needs of the public, the musicians, and the local promoters and businessmen.

The Bay Area critic Ralph Gleason wrote of a similar blitz in Oakland and San Francisco in November 1948, in which advance work for JATP succeeded to the point that concerts at the Oakland Auditorium and the San Francisco Opera House outdrew competing events by Nat Cole, Duke Ellington, and Stan Kenton. As Granz had commented, fans "won't come to hear individuals, but will line up at the box office because they know JATP means fine music."[7] Gleason praised Tony

Valerio, Granz's local representative in the five-week lead-up to the concerts, for his work in JATP's good showing. Valerio saw to it that a dozen stations saturated the airwaves with JATP recordings; he also held disc jockey promotions and pushed for stories in the local press. The result was that the concerts grossed around $11,000, and hundreds of fans were unable to get tickets. "They were not only the best promoted concerts ever held in this area, but despite the usual mic and spotlight horrors, they were most successful from the audience standpoint," Gleason wrote.[8] As Oscar Peterson later observed about the confluence of tours and recordings, "Jazz at the Philharmonic was like having your record collection come to town."

Granz not only ensured that his JATP musicians got major public buildup before the tours but also rewarded them with top pay and first-class travel, accommodations, and attire. "I was the first one to have jazz musicians come out in tuxedoes, in dinner clothes. The essence of Jazz at the Philharmonic was that I wanted to get respect from everybody in the house. I wanted to get the best dressing rooms, I wanted the best pianos. They had to treat my musicians like they treated classical players. I wanted to make sure they enjoyed the cities that they had to spend time in, instead of trying to find a place to eat. Finally, I think, too, that the public sensed that they should react to the artists in a different fashion from the way they might have done in some nightclub. So, in a sense, we established a precedent for these people."[9]

Clearly the JATP musicians returned the appreciation. Helen Humes, a hardworking and sweet-natured professional, fondly recalled life on the road during her two years as the featured singer. "When we'd get on the train, we just played cards all over the United States . . . Norman used to take us to places and go into hotels where they didn't have colored. He said, 'They're going to stay here,' and we stayed. Of course, every once in a while one of the boys would try and show off. But they were sweet to me, and I had all kinds of service."[10] Trummy Young was equally positive about his time with Jazz at the Philharmonic in the late 1940s. "Norman was first class," he said. "He was one of the first guys I knew that really started paying the musicians some money when he made it, some fairly decent money, you know . . . He fought that thing [segregation], I know he took us once to, I think it was Lexington, Kentucky. And he told them if they didn't mix up the audience, he wasn't going to play. Now this is true. I saw him do it."[11]

With the opening of the spring tour, Granz expanded his activity against segregation in the presentation of live music. Specifically, he tried to persuade major bandleaders to adopt clauses in their contracts similar to his that would stipulate against playing before segregated or all-white audiences. Granz contacted bandleaders by telegram and publicized the initiative in trade publications, black newspapers, and any mainstream press that might be sympathetic. The telegram that he sent to approximately thirty top bandleaders stated, in part: "Thirty-six of the leading playwrights in the country, and leading producers, directors, and members of Actors' Equity either pledged or promised to investigate the possibility of pledging themselves to a clause whereby they never would be forced to play a segregated theater. The obvious corollary to this is that those of us in music either should do something similar or at least find some comparable method whereby we can add our voice against discrimination. . . . I am suggesting that bandleaders find some way to fight this disgraceful situation."[12]

Among the bandleaders Granz contacted were Gene Krupa, Cab Calloway, Woody Herman, Artie Shaw, Bob Crosby, Lionel Hampton, Ray McKinley, Billy Eckstine, Sammy Kaye, Louis Prima, Harry James, Jimmy Dorsey, Count Basie, Charlie Barnet, Tommy Dorsey, Stan Kenton, Benny Goodman, Duke Ellington, Erskine Hawkins, and Nat Cole. Cole, a draw significant enough to demand such terms, stood by his longtime friend by telling his manager to include a nonsegregation clause in his contracts. Others signaling their approval were Shaw, Tommy Dorsey, Barnet, Buddy Rich, and Coleman Hawkins. Hawkins spoke for many in a telegram to Granz that was reprinted in the *New York Amsterdam News*: "Am firmly convinced that one of the key ways for ending undemocratic practice of Jim Crow is through the entertainment media, particularly the jazz field which has wide interdenominational, interracial participation and following. Will work with you to line up the band industry behind non-discriminatory pledge."[13]

Granz told the New York daily *PM,* "Except in a few Southern states which have statutory regulations against mixed audiences, there is no reason why a band can't enforce such a clause. . . . So far as the Southern states are concerned, big bands at least can stay out of them until the statutory regulations are changed."[14] He talked about using his mailing list of around ten thousand young people to form clubs around the country to promote jazz and race relations, an idea he later said never came to fruition. The paper states that Jazz at the Philharmonic had played occasional fund-raisers on behalf of the passage of federal antilynching legislation and the interracial Sydenham Hospital in New York. In the same article Granz took the opportunity to hit his critics within jazz "who have a hard time agreeing among themselves on what constitutes good jazz," asserting, "I would rather sell mediocre jazz to 9,000 people, and sell my pitch on race relations along with it than operate in a vacuum. Whatever bandleaders and musicians can do will be a step forward, and when their effort is combined with those of Actors' Equity and other branches of the entertainment field, we will be a long way toward eliminating Jim Crow practices in this country."[15]

A report in the *Washington Afro-American* coincided with a week-long series of concerts by Jazz at the Philharmonic at the Howard Theater in February. Granz talked of the obvious difficulty in building a unified front to defy segregation during remarks to the Capital Press Club in which he explained his nondiscriminatory contracts. "Granz admitted that as liberal as many of the musicians might be, there is a reluctance on their part to adopt the clause because many of the bands . . . have to make trips into the South to survive," the paper said.[16]

Documents in the NAACP archives at the Library of Congress show that Granz communicated about his antidiscrimination activities with NAACP's national offices in New York through his assistant Martha Glaser. An incomplete set of letters between Glaser and the NAACP Legal Department in early 1947 shows one of Granz's strongest intuitive traits: consulting and then following expert advice for whatever he wanted to know. Granz was working in support of a Democracy through Music fund-raiser. This exchange of letters establishes at least an informal relationship between Granz and the NAACP that gives credence to his statements at the time and later that he checked out in advance the status of antidiscrimination practices by cities on his touring schedule.[17]

Granz's campaign stirred a lot of headlines and even more passions but did not get near to accomplishing the sweeping changes he sought. After all, it was 1947. Despite Granz's contention, it was not only second-tier bands that had to play the South—or, for that matter, other regions throughout the country where discrimination also prevailed—to earn a living. Keeping solvent was problematic enough for many bands that they could not make the life-or-death decisions that carrying through on the contract entailed. Losing $100,000 in bookings for JATP, as Granz claimed to have done in 1947, was a loss he was willing to absorb to make a point, but Count Basie and Duke Ellington did not have that luxury. They supported Granz but did not change their contracts. Granz felt that Duke's legendary aversion to controversy or confrontation, as well as the high cost of maintaining the band, was at the root of his reluctance to act. Other bandleaders, such as the Dorseys, either did not play the South or had all-white bands that barely intersected, if at all, with black audiences. Granz acknowledged forty years later that expecting bands to adopt antisegregation clauses might have been more than black bands could have been expected to do. "[Many of] the bands literally had to stay in the South, and for them, it was just survival," he said. "So it was wrong for me to say, 'Hey you have to include that clause when you play Mississippi. They would say, 'We can't get the gig, so I might as well break my band up.' . . . And they had to play one-nighters with jumps that would insure that they could survive. And, of course, once you get past Chicago, you don't play 100 miles later on. You have to go 500 miles, so you take whatever gig you can, and the whole Midwest was prejudiced. Indiana was like playing Birmingham, Alabama."[18] Though the issue would remain unresolved for many years in the future, Granz took any opportunity to publicize the examples of Jazz at the Philharmonic and Actors' Equity. He was still speaking out on behalf of nondiscrimination clauses as late as 1961, but it was not until the 1964 Civil Rights Act was signed on July 2, the twentieth anniversary of the first JATP concert, that the matter was finally settled.

Granz spread what he had learned from the NAACP and elsewhere as he crossed the country. In late 1947, when he met with fifty-eight student newspaper editors in Philadelphia, they peppered him with questions: "What would you do if a Negro could not get in a hotel? Do our city and state have civil rights laws to cover things like that? What can schools do to better race relations?" The black students were mightily impressed and asked Granz if he would "tell our whole student body the same things." As school appearances required a faculty invitation, Granz met the students on the lawn the next day and was invited by the principal to return whenever he was in town.[19]

The fourth national tour took twelve weeks to complete its coast-to-coast schedule. JATP hovered along the East Coast in the first two weeks of February 1947, playing dates in New York, Washington, Philadelphia, New York again, and Boston. In March the show left from Montreal for performances in the Midwest, Vancouver, and Shrine Auditorium in Los Angeles. In April JATP made dates at Carnegie Hall, Vancouver, and Detroit before returning to New York in May to perform three concerts during the Carnegie Hall Pop Series. The low point of the spring tour, and certainly the most embarrassing from a personal point of view, came in Granz's hometown in the third week of March. JATP "laid an ostrich-sized egg," or an "omelet" as another publication more diplomatically called a last-minute date at the Shrine Auditorium.[20] The hall's management, like Philharmonic Auditorium before it, had considered giving JATP the boot but was giving the show another chance. It didn't help things that the concert started an hour late as the local promoter haggled with the musicians' union before he agreed to cover the guarantee for standby musicians retained for the concert. Attendance was low, perhaps because Granz had not significantly revised his show and because many of his black patrons were among the hardest hit in a soft postwar economy. The event grossed a mere $1,000, the "slimmest take any jam session ever copped here, and definitely the worst gross of the entire tour." Granz put the blame on MCA, which was then still booking JATP, and on the local promoter, who took a major loss on the concert. He attributed low turnout to a lack of print and radio advertising, including the failure to notify the local black press of the event.[21] "I'm through with Los Angeles forever," he sniffed. "I'll never play here again even if they beg me."[22]

If Los Angeles was the nadir of the spring season, Billie Holiday's impromptu appearance at the May 24 Carnegie Hall Pop Series show would take the prize for high drama. The performance came eight days after federal narcotics agents finally lowered the boom on Holiday, who was in Philadelphia to play an engagement at the Earle Theater opposite Louis Armstrong. The agents moved in on May 16 after finding heroin in her room at the Attucks Hotel. This precipitated Holiday and her driver's famous getaway when he hit a parked car and eluded police bullets (although this detail of the legend remains disputed) on a furious trip back to New York. She opened at Club 18 on Fifty-second Street, formerly the Onyx, the following night. Holiday was driven to Carnegie Hall during an intermission at the club and gave an enchanting ten-minute recital backed solely by her pianist Bobby Tucker. The program, consisting of "You Better Go Now," "You're Driving Me Crazy," "There Is No Greater Love," and "I Cover the Waterfront," gave no hint of the turmoil the singer faced as she went from Carnegie Hall to trial, sentencing, and a federal penitentiary in Alderson, West Virginia, in four dizzying days.

In June 1947 Granz added another layer to his enterprises with the founding of his first label, Clef Records, as a series on Mercury Records. No matter how instrumental Moe Asch had been in getting his records before the public, Granz was too independent to have viewed the relationship as anything but a temporary arrangement that would end when he devised new arrangements more rewarding to his artists and himself. Accordingly, he had more to worry about than preparing to release recordings and establishing a distribution network. He had to disengage from his increasingly unworkable relationship with Asch, who unlike Granz was never known for keeping his business affairs in order or on the level.

Negotiating the rapids of the record business was a formidable proposition. But the incentives of the postwar years were great. The number of records sold annually had jumped nearly fourfold from 1940 to 1946, from 75 million to 287 million.[23] An estimated five million record players, a half a million of them jukeboxes, were thought to be in American households and commercial establishments. In another sign of the times, manufacturers' orders for "radio-phonographs" outpaced those for radios, changing a long-standing trend in home entertainment. A surge in advertising by record companies, especially major labels, encouraged magazines to devote more space to reviews of recordings.

In 1947, four major labels—RCA Victor, Decca, Columbia, and Capitol—dominated a national market swelled by another 250 to 300 small independent labels. That spring, Congress was investigating monopoly practices among the large firms. Independent record companies faced major obstacles in the marketplace. "Investigation of the disc industry [demonstrates] that the giants are getting more gigantic, and the little fellows are wishing that they had invested their gold in those nice little chicken farms," one writer noted. The majors, despite an economic recession, saw their profits rise an average of two and eight times between 1945 and the following year.[24]

Independents, to succeed, first had to solve fundamental promotion, marketing, and distribution problems. However, independents offered certain advantages to their artists. Smaller labels did not normally have surplus recordings sitting in the can; they released what they had almost immediately. They took chances in developing new artists, while facing the constant risk of watching their top talent wooed away by the majors. Their operations could be swamped if they had an unexpected major hit on their hands and had difficulty locating adequate and timely pressing facilities.

Independents made available music typically neglected by major labels, such as folk and international music, more obscure classical recordings, and children's records. The independent labels scuffling around jazz in the late 1940s made this one of the most important periods for recorded jazz. Among the leading indie labels were three with which Norman Granz already had a relationship—Black and White, Aladdin, and Disc. Apollo, Blue Note, Keynote, and Musicraft also made a mark in jazz recording.

Granz's separation from Asch might have been an insignificant event given that their original contract expired on March 31, 1947.[25] However, it turned out to be the beginning of a dispute that would involve years of litigation. Granz said at the time that the split had been "amicable." Asch implied it was he who had decided not to renew his option, but that is debatable, for Jazz at the Philharmonic records had speedily risen to join politicized folk songs and traditional jazz as the mainstays of the Disc catalog. On the other hand, Asch may have found the handling of JATP recordings too distracting, given his responsibilities to maintain the rest of his massive catalog.

Despite Granz's public statement about an "amicable" split, the tug-of-war with Asch had been escalating. In April Granz began seeking return of the original JATP masters. Asch had sealed the recordings and placed them in the vault of another partner, who retained many of Asch's masters as collateral against the cost of pressing future recordings.[26] Thus began more than five years of litigation in state and federal courts that left several early JATP masters out of Granz's reach. By 1948 Asch would be bankrupt and the masters would be scattered among several of Asch's partners and ex-partners. Granz, who argued his own case in some of the proceedings, finally secured satisfaction from the U.S. Court of Appeals in New York in August 1952. Yet despite his victory, he never regained total control over *Jazz at the Philharmonic, Volume 1,* and a few other early sessions. Recalling the imbroglio from a vantage point of three decades, Granz said, "That's the only thing I ever lost."[27]

Granz's high school friend the folk and labor historian Archie Green knew both men, given his widening contacts in folk music circles. He recalled the personal and professional contempt Granz expressed for Asch after their falling out. "It was a contradiction that Moe Asch was an unscrupulous businessman, but also idealistic," Green said. "Records were more than a business to Norm. He would have paid Moe anything to get his masters back. Norman didn't like Warner Bros. or nightclub owners, but they were just businessmen. But with Moe Asch, he had a special animosity."[28]

In the hectic month of June 1947 Granz began producing new recordings under the name Clef Records by releasing a new version of "How

High the Moon," recorded in March 1947 in Pittsburgh, in hopes of recapturing some of the glow and financial remuneration from the immensely popular *Jazz at the Philharmonic, Volume 1*. The ensemble included Buck Clayton, trumpet; Trummy Young, trombone; Willie Smith, alto saxophone; Coleman Hawkins and Flip Phillips, tenor saxophone; Kenny Kersey, piano; Benny Fonville, bass; and Buddy Rich, drums. Also around this time he severed his relationship with MCA, which until then had promoted a portion of his concert dates. In addition, Granz was among those to be honored at a June 16 Negro Freedom Rally at Madison Square Garden. The event, featuring music by JATP, was scheduled toward the conclusion of the tour's second annual weekly Carnegie Hall Pops Concerts. However, Granz backed out after the June 7 concert, citing fatigue and a desire to return to California. The pianist Hazel Scott, co-chair of the event and then wife of the Harlem congressman Adam Clayton Powell, announced the decision to honor Granz and JATP. She mentioned Granz's work among bandleaders to fight discrimination and his willingness to sacrifice bookings when venues refused to allow integrated audiences. Scott had planned to join the JATP troupe in the first such affair to be held at Madison Square Garden.

The fifth national tour was the most ambitious yet. On the bill for the 1947 fall schedule of more than fifty cities were Coleman Hawkins and Flip Phillips, trombonist Bill Harris, trumpeter Howard McGhee, pianist Hank Jones, Jackie Mills on drums, Ray Brown in his JATP debut on bass, and Helen Humes. The tour would open on September 24 at the Brooklyn Academy of Music and would be followed, over the next four days, by concerts at the Baltimore Coliseum, the Philadelphia Academy of Music, the Newark Mosque, and Carnegie Hall. It yielded fresh examples of how Granz maintained the pressure of his civil rights agenda. One episode occurred in September at a Dayton, Ohio, department store that carried Clef Records. The musicians were staying at one of Cincinnati's best hotels after Granz again had strong-armed his way to secure the rooms for which he had contracted. He had released Charlie Parker's 1946 "Lady Be Good," and he asked some of the musicians, among them Ray Brown, if they wanted to go to the record store and hear the recording, since customers were allowed to play recordings in listening booths before making a purchase. The store had the recording but told Granz that blacks weren't allowed to listen to music in the booths, although he suspected that blacks would have been permitted to buy the records outright.

"Call in your manager," Granz instructed the salesman. When the manager appeared, Granz asked him, "You're distributing my records?"

"Yes," the manager replied.

"Well, I'm pulling the whole line, so you can forget selling my records."

Granz ordered his Cincinnati distributor to clear out the remaining stock and to make no further sales there. "I think he was more surprised than anything," Granz told Nat Hentoff in 1994, "because it's rare that you go to someone and say, 'I don't want you to sell my records.'"[29]

By default, the November 29 concert at Carnegie Hall turned into the fund-raiser for the NAACP Legal Defense and Education Fund that had been discussed the previous spring. The original plan had called for the evening proceeds of over $4,000 to go to Billie Holiday, then entering her third month at Alderson. Granz's assistant Martha Glaser had told a *New York Daily News* columnist that Holiday was broke and that she had been writing friends for records, chewing gum, and other comforts during her imprisonment. But as it turned out, Holiday's manager, Joe Glaser (no relation to Martha), had announced around the same time that the tribute/fund-raiser was unauthorized and that he had a letter from Holiday stating she neither needed nor wanted the tribute. The concert was then turned into an NAACP fund-raiser, but partly because of the lack of coordination Carnegie Hall was only about two-thirds full. The episode caused temporary bad feeling between the two men. Granz said he felt that Glaser had made things unnecessarily difficult but conceded that he should have notified Glaser before scheduling the event to aid his client. For his part, Glaser put out a vague threat that he had pressed "various legal agencies to investigate Granz's activities." "Well, you gotta learn it doesn't pay to do anyone a favor," was Granz's parting shot.[30]

Also in November Granz met with members of the Progressive Citizens of America chapter in St. Louis on the afternoon JATP played Kiel Opera House. A PCA member himself, Granz sought the organization's support in pressuring bandleaders not to play segregated venues. He urged the group to better understand discriminatory practices in their city as a way to fight them, whether these were social custom or law. He described to the PCA how his NAACP-aided research into the status of civil rights laws and ordinances in the locales where JATP played had enabled him to strategize an informed plan of attack. "Know your civil rights laws," Granz exhorted. "Make them work. Prejudice is an economic matter. Make it unprofitable." The *Pittsburgh Courier*, which related Granz's account of the event, added, "Granz wants people to demand the highest standards from the bandleaders, Negro and white—not only good music, but militancy in fighting all forms of discrimination."[31] Granz claimed around this time that he had sacrificed over $100,000 in lost bookings for the year to date.[32]

The Baltimore concert on September 25, held in a boxing ring, proved that even in a format that thrived on spontaneity there could be such a thing as too much spontaneity. The din of popcorn, peanut, and hot dog vendors that continued through the show had already prompted Granz to cut the evening short before the final insult. A local electronic mandolin ace by the name of Flash Mallory did not let the fact that he had not been invited stop him from plugging into the sound system backstage in the midst of the finale, "Flying Home." Howard McGhee played his solo following Hank Jones's introduction and was handing it back to the rhythm section, which that night included Kenny Clarke on drums, when the mystery guest suddenly began to play. Flash was quickly silenced after police found him plucking away backstage during his brief turn in the limelight. Pandemonium reigned as Granz came out and stopped the concert. Marvin Wildstein, a retired New York art gallery owner, recalled him bellowing into the microphone: "Even if Benny Goodman were to show up, he would not be allowed to sit in! Now you can play the whole night, we're leaving."[33]

Then someone in the audience shouted up from the darkness, "We want our money back!"

"I'm not going to give you your money back. You heard the concert. That's all we play," he said on the way to the getaway, or so he thought. "We couldn't get cabs and couldn't get a bus. We had to walk all the way to the railroad, with the equipment and musical instruments and all these people screaming. All that was needed was for one person to punch somebody. You can't begin to tell people what it was like."[34]

The tour also had its lighter moments. During the weeklong engagement at the Howard in Washington in February, Roy Eldridge mischievously alluded to critics' dismissal of JATP as a lot of grandstanding musical exhibitionism. With the aid of a saxophone borrowed from Coleman Hawkins, the trumpeter said, "I could play the tenor sax a bit in B flat. When it came to my turn to go onstage, I went out with Hawk's sax and started blowing this low-note phrase over and over again. It broke the audience up. People were screaming and hollering. I handed the sax back to Hawk, and that was that. But when we went back to Washington all sorts of people came around and asked, 'Are you going to play the tenor sax?'"[35]

During 1947, in the contexts of civil rights and jazz, it was striking to see the discipline—practical, intellectual, and creative—that helped make Granz a force to be reckoned with. He took on all comers: theater, hotel, and restaurant owners, record retailers, *Esquire* magazine, Moe Asch, the critics (always the critics), and the uncertainties of the road and the marketplace in a year marked by a national recession that reverberated through the entertainment industry. In just over three years, he had redefined how jazz was presented. The jazz concert had arrived as an economically viable way of drawing nondancing audiences. Granz was poised to use the economic position of Jazz at the Philharmonic to underwrite his burgeoning ambitions as a record producer, and even then he was aspiring to extend his ventures abroad. In the following year, he launched his spring tour with a purely bebop show, signed Charlie Parker to his new Clef label, and promoted a string of non-JATP jazz events. Through a chance encounter with Ella Fitzgerald on the road he foresaw the luster she could bring to his enterprise and the historic partnership that lay ahead of them.

1. Norman Granz and his parents, Morris and Ida Clara, gather for a rare family portrait, taken at a Los Angeles photo studio, ca. 1924. Grete Granz's private collection.

2. Granz was well respected by peers for his brain power and athleticism, as his 1935 Roosevelt High School yearbook shows.

3. Granz beams after the first Jazz at the Philharmonic concert, held July 2, 1944, at Los Angeles Philharmonic Auditorium. Joining him backstage are, from left to right, Jean Bach, Nat Cole, Arlene Thompson, and Shorty Sherock, then Bach's husband. Courtesy of Jean Bach.

4. A dramatic portrait of the budding impresario in 1945 shows Granz holding a copy of *Jazz at the Philharmonic, Vol. 1*, which sold around 150,000 copies and was one of the first "live" concert recordings commercially released. The drawing of the trumpeter by David Stone Martin soon became the trademark image of Granz's productions. Photograph by Gjon Mili/Getty Images.

5. The Oscar-nominated Warner Bros. short film *Jammin' the Blues* (1944) was directed by *Life* magazine photographer Gjon Mili with a cast of musicians who were regulars in Norman Granz's jam sessions. From left to right are Red Callender, Marlowe Morris, Jo Jones, Lester Young, Illinois Jacquet, Harry "Sweets" Edison, and Barney Kessel. Photograph by Gjon Mili/Getty Images.

6. The spring 1947 Jazz at the Philharmonic tour, which kicked off in February, passed through Buffalo, New York, on one of its notoriously snowy days. Hot swingers braving the chill are, from left to right, Coleman Hawkins, Buck Clayton, Hank Jones, Benny Fonville, Flip Phillips, Granz, Willie Smith, Helen Humes, and Trummy Young. Collection/Courtesy Hank O'Neal.

◄ 7. In September 1950, Granz and Gjon Mili joined forces again to shoot a short film, tentatively called *Sitting In,* in the tradition of *Jammin' the Blues.* Granz converses with Lester Young in this triple-exposure photo taken in Mili's studio at Sixth Avenue and Twenty-third Street in New York. Photograph by Paul Nodler. Paul Nodler Estate/Institute of Jazz Studies, Rutgers University.

◄ 8. Granz said at one point that he "felt most at home in the studio," in contrast to his peripatetic life shepherding Jazz at the Philharmonic. In this June 1952 session he marshaled the talents of Charlie Parker, left, and Johnny Hodges. Completing a trio of supreme alto saxophonists for the first in a series of studio jam sessions was Benny Carter. Photograph by Esther Bubley/Courtesy of Jean Bubley.

9. In December 1952 Fred Astaire went into the studio to be recorded with jazz musicians performing some of the standards he had introduced in his films. The result was *The Astaire Story,* one of the more stunning tributes to an artist recorded and packaged up until that time. Photograph by Gjon Mili/ Getty Images.

10. Oscar Peterson beams as he looks out the window of an old Buick "woodie," as cars with artificial wood paneling were known (photo ca. mid-1950s). Early Jazz at the Philharmonic tours were often caravans of cars or bus rides, but later Granz provided nothing but the best in travel and accommodations for musicians in his employ. Flip Phillips Collection/Courtesy of Hank O'Neal.

WHOEVER TAKEN MY WHISKEY —

I'M HIS MOTHER'S VERY BEST MAN.

11–12. The tenor saxophonist Flip Phillips, one of the more steady musicians on the JATP roster through the years, chronicled the life and times of his fellow musicians in photographs. Here he shows a photo of Lester Young on the road (top) and appends to it a caption (bottom) quoting a threat of Young's. Flip Phillips Collection/Courtesy of Hank O'Neal.

13. A visibly angry Ella Fitzgerald is comforted by her assistant and cousin Georgiana Henry as they, along with Illinois Jacquet and Dizzy Gillespie, cool their heels following a bust for a dice game backstage at a Jazz at the Philharmonic concert in Houston, Texas, on October 7, 1955. Houston Metropolitan Research Center, Houston Public Library.

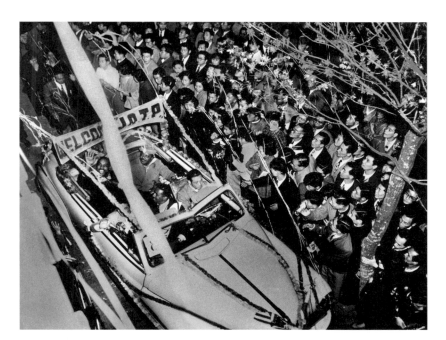

14. When Jazz at the Philharmonic arrived in Tokyo in November 1953, a boisterous crowd greeted them, and the musicians were paraded through the streets of the city in open cars—surely the most exuberant welcome in the history of JATP. Seen acknowledging their Japanese fans are Benny Carter and Charlie Shavers, with Ray Brown visible in the front seat. Institute of Jazz Studies, Rutgers University.

15. Granz noodles around on Ray Brown's bass as he talks with Buddy Rich on the set of filming in Gjon Mili's studio in September 1950. Photo by Paul Nodler. Estate of Paul Nodler/Institute of Jazz Studies, Rutgers University.

16. A moody and intense Norman Granz was featured on the December 15, 1954, cover of *Down Beat* when he was fully on top of his game as a jazz impresario and record producer. Courtesy of *Down Beat* magazine.

17. Granz, tennis racket in hand, and Ella Fitzgerald share a moment at the 1957 Newport Jazz Festival, when their historic partnership was beginning to crest. Photograph by Ted Williams/CTS Images.

18. Granz and Oscar Peterson were both amateur shutterbugs who occasionally recorded their experiences in the studio and on tour. Peterson captured one such moment of Granz made while they were recording sometime in the late 1950s. Courtesy of Kelly Peterson.

19. Pablo Picasso and Granz prepare to bat a ping-pong ball around the artist's home in the south of France, probably sometime in the late 1960s. Grete Granz's private collection.

▶ 20. Granz posed for Picasso several times. After one sitting he showed Granz half a dozen or so pictures prefaced by a comment as elliptical as his art: "I can't understand it. I want the color blue, but the color red comes up." The color of this portrait from April 9, 1969, drawn with a felt-tip pen, was indeed crimson. Grete Granz's private collection/© Estate of Pablo Picasso/Artists Rights Society (ARS), New York, 2011.

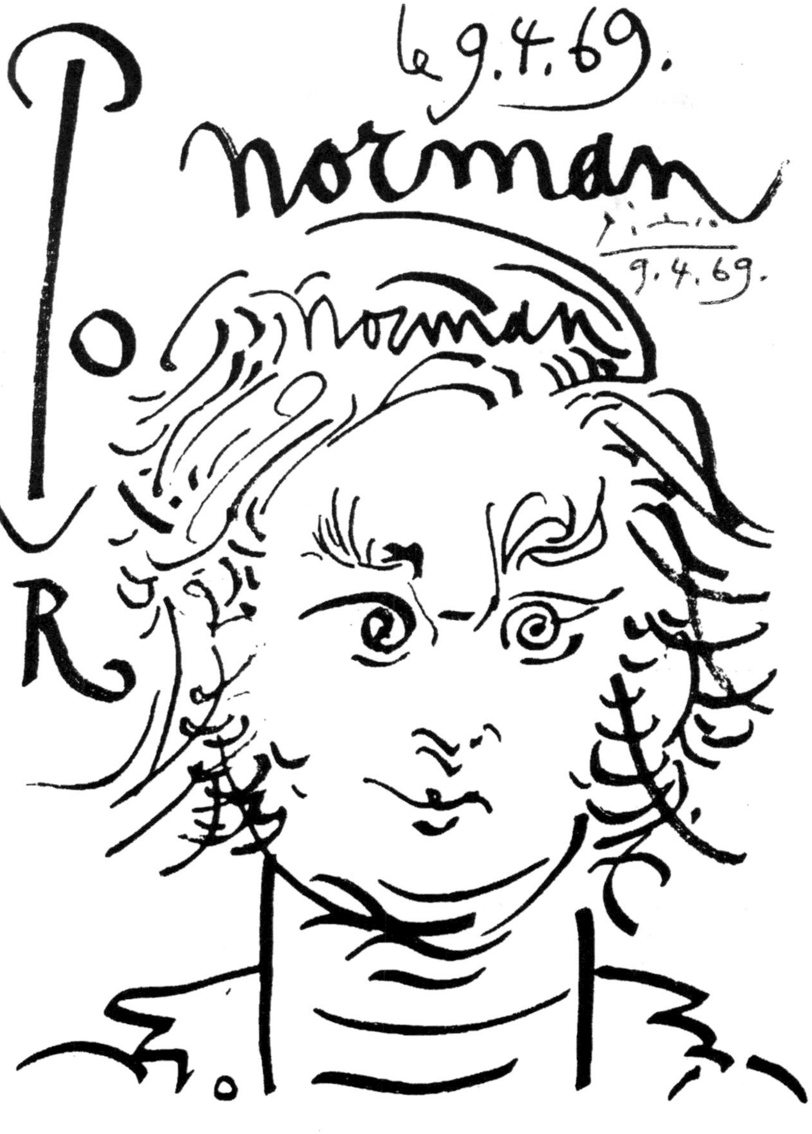

21. Count Basie and Ella Fitzgerald, seen here during a concert in San Antonio in December 1979, made regular appearances together during the Pablo Records years. Aside from a session for Verve in the early '60s, their work on Pablo represents most of their recorded work together. Photograph by Tad Hershorn.

22. Norman Granz, seen in his office in Beverly Hills in 1987, poses before an enlarged sketch of Ella Fitzgerald by Picasso in 1970. He reportedly hardly knew what Fitzgerald looked like, but that did not stop him from penning a striking impression, done mostly with a single line. Photograph by Tad Hershorn. Sketch © Estate of Pablo Picasso/Artists Rights Society (ARS), New York.

23. Though Norman Granz remained on the go even after his retirement around 1987, he and his wife Grete were constant companions in his last years. Grete Granz's private collection.

24. Granz writes on the balcony of his sixth-floor apartment about four months before his death of cancer on November 22, 2001. Grete Granz's private collection.

7

Mambo Jambo

By the end of 1947, the entertainment industry was celebrating the drawing power of jazz concerts, a far cry from the attitude it had displayed when dismissing JATP concerts as a "gag" a couple of years earlier. In the parlance of the time, *Variety* announced in a banner headline in October that such events were "Wham Coin for Jazz 'Longhairs.'" That, translated into more conventional journalistic language, is "The jazz concert field is rapidly becoming one of the most profitable outlets in live entertainment" and "The intangible element of prestige attaches itself to playing in major halls. Billing 'direct from Carnegie' or Town Hall is an important factor to many and invariably pays off."[1] The singer and guitarist Josh White had "nabbed" $3,500 during a recent concert at New York's Town Hall. The much-ballyhooed September 29 concert at Carnegie Hall starring Dizzy Gillespie, Ella Fitzgerald, and Charlie Parker pulled in $5,700, some $3,600 less than the $9,300 garnered by Jazz at the Philharmonic's Carnegie Hall concert two days before.

The appeal of the concert hall prompted Duke Ellington to perform some one hundred such events in 1947, and Count Basie anticipated revving up for a series of similar dates. Furthermore, Nat Cole had capped a successful string of concert one-nighters with his own Carnegie Hall date on October 18. The bandleader Phil Spitalny, who had become popular because of his all-girl bands, walked away with $18,000 from one Cleveland event. Spike Jones and his band netted some $94,000 from nine shows during a Midwest tour, while the harmonica player Larry Adler earned around $25,000 during a week of Christmas concerts at Town Hall. Hall managers across the country might have become more enthusiastic about jazz concerts because of lower-than-expected box office receipts from their classical programming, but even owners of sports arenas showed interest in hosting jazz events. The increasingly lucrative returns from jazz concerts also had the benefit of providing musicians a respite from their punishing and far less financially remunerative nightclub appearances.

Enthusiasm for concerts within the jazz world was mixed. Even some of those who disapproved conceded that the concerts might yield some benefits to the music and to diehard fans. *Down Beat* took a critical position on jazz concerts, among them those produced by Granz. One of its articles, by the critic Paul Eduard Miller, attacked the proposition that concerts represented a qualitative advance for jazz but was short on identifying specific offenders. Miller believed that a decade of jazz concerts had not given jazz any more prestige than that "accorded third-rate concerts in the classical field" and asserted that "mediocre" concerts had earned the respect of neither musicians nor fans. Disparaging one of Granz's cornerstone musical values, the article criticized concerts for "taking too many chances," thus totally missing the point of JATP.[2]

An editorial in the magazine took on Granz for promoting contemporary jazz, Rudi Blesh for promoting New Orleans vintage jazz, and Eddie Condon for promoting the Chicago school, using as its pretext an attack on Blesh by the eminent New Orleans clarinetist Albert Nicholas, published in the same issue. It is a feast of supercilious criticism of the type that Granz summarily dismissed. "Granz at least makes no pretensions to musical authority, and in his own screwball fashion is concerned with doing something good in the world. . . . None of them overpays his musicians, with the possible exception of Granz, who was so overwhelmed with accusations of connivery when he started that he has made a point of paying well ever since. . . . When they start telling musicians how to play, what to do, and just what art is, this is time to call 'halt,' as the musicians are already doing. It's only unfortunate that in this sense, a vast fraud has been perpetrated upon the public, which will take a long time to expose."[3]

Granz took "violent issue" with the conclusions. He responded in part, "I simply have presented jazz to the public as a promoter primarily, and secondarily as a producer. I have been concerned with selecting men who were musically important and commercially able to sustain the cost. . . . Since the responsibility for the show falls on the producer,

I reserve the right to put on the type of shows that maintain what I feel are good standards at the same time pleasing the most people. JATP seems to do this."[4] He emphatically denied the editorial's insinuations regarding his business dealings.

Jazz at the Philharmonic was also repeatedly attacked for the kinds of crowds it drew. Granz had democratized access to the concert hall and the prestige it afforded, with implications for jazz as a listening experience. JATP triumphed as entertainment in part because it encouraged the lively bond between artist and audience that was central to the creation of the music. But for those who saw musical culture as the preserve of an elite, that very liveliness was threatening: the large crowds, mixing and fusing races, ethnic groups, and classes in one shared, vivid experience, might become dangerously excited, with unpredictable results.

A brief historical comparison reveals that issues raised about the alleged excesses of JATP's audiences were hardly novel. Either of the following passages could have been written about any random stop on the JATP circuit, but these criticisms are separated by just over a century. The first describes a singer being met by "screams, whistles, clapping of hands, hisses, trampling of feet, roaring, menacing outcries, and gesticulations of every kind, [as if] the inmates of some half a hundred mad houses had broken loose."[5] The second describes "present-day audiences" as being "of a different and more warlike tribe. They rarely move from their seats, yet they manage to give off through a series of screams—the word 'go' repeated like the successive slams of the cars on a fast freight—bloodstopping whistles, and stamping feet creating a mass intensity."[6]

The first piece recounts the reception greeting tenor Sesto Benedetti's performance during the opera *Norma* in New York's Astor Place Opera House in December 1848. The second (which concludes with "that would have made Benny Goodman pale") is from a famously critical piece on JATP written in 1954 by the critic Whitney Balliett, entitled "Pandemonium Pays Off." (His revision of the piece for a book of essays published in 1959 interpolates that the mass intensity "would have soothed Hitler.") Though Balliett looked back nostalgically to the relative gentility of Swing Era crowds (apart from those of Goodman and Sinatra), he had to block out the memory of such episodes as the "jitterbug riot" at a Jimmie Lunceford concert at the Shrine Auditorium in Los Angeles in March 1940. At that event a crowd of around six thousand, fueled by free liquor, suddenly exploded, "smashing windows, flashing razors, and swinging fists." Lunceford sought to calm the crowd but had to struggle to be heard above the melee and eventually escaped from the hall with his orchestra. The ensuing brawl left seven injured, in addition to a policeman who suffered knife wounds. It took about twenty-five officers to eject troublemakers into the street, where fighting resumed when it was announced no refunds from the concert were forthcoming. Officials of Shrine Auditorium decided then to ban future such events.[7]

The cultural historian Lawrence Levine has shown that until late in the nineteenth century large audiences for public concerts and opera behaved much as popular music audiences do today, with "spontaneous expressions of pleasure and disapproval in the form of cheers, yells, gesticulations, hisses, boos, stamping of feet, whistling, crying for encores, and applause," and that audiences had to be "tamed" to new norms of silence and passivity.[8] It was these norms that Granz helped to destabilize with his concerts. Levine's own enthusiasm for jazz extended back to his teenage years in New York in the late 1940s, when he heard the music in the heyday of Fifty-second Street and attended Jazz at the Philharmonic concerts at Carnegie Hall. Levine recalled that attending JATP at Carnegie Hall was akin to a nineteenth-century concert hall experience. "I sat in the balcony and there was just an incredible spurt of energy. They were wonderful things . . . The audience participated by clapping, stomping, and dancing in the aisles. For the most part, there was a tremendous amount of interaction. There was a sense of familiarity; people understood the music. It was an integrated audience, and they understood what was happening. What Granz did in places like Carnegie Hall was have jazz jamming, and it was not highfalutin' at all. Although it was hard in that huge place, they interacted . . . The jazz musicians that Granz was introducing all over the country were signs of urban American culture. That's why the audience responded as it did. Granz treated jazz as a living music," Levine said.[9]

Granz had no incentive to totally suppress audiences' conduct to placate his critics. Why risk squelching the excitement that made JATP so appealing? On the other hand, Granz did rein in crowds when they crossed the line by distracting performers and disrupting the listening of other paying customers. The boorish behavior of a few audience members could also lead concert halls to ban further jazz concerts, as in the case of the Philharmonic Auditorium in January 1946, which arguably seized on this excuse to do something it had wanted to do for a long time. For theaters that did not publicly admit to racial or ethnic discrimination, disruptive episodes presented convenient rationales for banning JATP. The mainstay populations of his audience, according to Granz, were large numbers of Italian Americans, blacks, and Jews, mostly in their teens and twenties. "I mean, these were people who got very emotional about their music and the musicians I had," Granz said.[10]

"I insisted that audiences respect the musicians, because in the early days some of the houses we played were not to be believed," Granz said in 1972. "If anyone made noise, I stopped the show. I even passed out little handbills ('How to Act at a Jazz Concert'). Now it didn't make me well liked by the public, but I think the public that did want to hear the artist, and didn't want to hear noisy exhibitionists, liked it too."[11] Granz rebutted critics who wrote that the musicians pandered to the crowds' base instincts. "I think it's presumptuous to say that the artist solicited, by their performances, noise and raucousness from the crowd," he said, somewhat disingenuously. He did not have to ask certain artists to showboat. "I don't think they did. The point is they played the way they played wherever they were. I would have never asked any of my people to change what they were doing. I used to have some problems with Ella when she'd get into a ballad and somebody would yell, 'Work it, girl,' or something like that. And she would promptly get terrified and go into 'How High the Moon.' I felt there were some exhibitionists in the audience. It only takes three or four people out of 3,000 people making noise. There were a lot of them who quieted those who did make the noise. But at least the jazz concerts, for whatever they were worth, were happy concerts."[12]

The criticism directed at JATP audiences suggests, as Lawrence Levine would argue, an anxiety regarding a new, highly charged relationship between artists and audience that defied established norms. Though Jazz at the Philharmonic transposed the context of jazz performance from clubs and dance halls to concert halls, no one could argue that it failed to connect with its audience. Albert Murray, in his 1976 book *Stomping the Blues,* expressed his unwavering belief that dance halls remained a critical source of inspiration for jazz and blues musicians, yet he also insisted that a concert hall setting could still nourish a lively artist-audience relationship. And he noted special benefits to the music of this new venue: "It provides a showcase for the new, and serves as a permanent gallery, so to speak, for the enduring. Moreover, as in the case of the great masterpieces of European church music, it affords opportunities for the music to be heard on its own apart from its role as an element in a ritual, in other words, as a work of art *per se.* Thus the concert hall recital at its best is in a very real sense also an indispensable extension of the dance hall."[13]

Murray added that phonograph records served a similar role of "a concert hall without walls" and that the radio energized and prepared listeners for what they would hear in concerts in terms of a recognizable repertoire and style. "Even as Chick Webb kept them stomping at the Savoy Ballroom on Lenox Avenue in Harlem, and Earl Hines kept them shuffling at the Grand Terrace on the South Side in Chicago, their orchestras were also playing what to all intents and purposes was a finger-snapping, foot-tapping concert for listeners huddled around radios all over the nation."[14] His comments might help to explain an insight that Norman Granz and Moe Asch shared: that record buyers were ahead of mainstream record companies in their appreciation of "live" recordings that simulated what they had become accustomed to on the airwaves.

The success of Jazz at the Philharmonic can be partly attributed to the growing confidence in American cultural identity after the war and its relation to jazz and the African American experience. The change in attitudes can be discerned over the course of the few short years that separated John Hammond's Spirituals to Swing concerts in the late 1930s from the successes Granz scored with JATP in the following decade. The folk revival of the 1930s might be typified by Alan Lomax's condescending presentation of the blues singer and former prisoner Leadbelly in concert in prison stripes and performing atop hokey bales of hay. This overly serious search for authenticity figured into the aim of the Spirituals to Swing concerts to explore the entire history of African American music that culminated in jazz. Lomax and Hammond, along with such figures as Leadbelly and Woody Guthrie, were all part of that period's movement to identify American "roots" music.

The commercially powered Jazz at the Philharmonic came out of a viewpoint that was virtually opposite to that of the "roots" movement. Granz recognized what Hammond and Lomax failed to fully grasp: jazz represented the melding of many regional cultures on a national scale that resulted from the widespread migrations of African Americans taking place during the Depression and World War II.

A picture layout of a JATP concert at the Chicago Civic Opera House in the September 1946 *Ebony* magazine conveys the splendor of the event and the racial pride felt by the audience. The photos show an interracial crowd, estimated to be half white and half black, milling around in conversation between sets in their finest suits and evening gowns, framed by the colonnaded foyer of the opera house. Some five hundred frustrated fans cooled their heels on the pavement that night, unable to get tickets; other patrons slipped in under the wire to occupy the aisles. In the meantime, Buck Clayton, Lester Young, and Kenny Kersey counted off the time to curtain. Shadow Wilson warmed up on drums borrowed from the house after his were misdirected in transit. Meade "Lux" Lewis adjusted the Chicago telephone directory in his chair to get into position to play. Lester Young signed autographs for admirers gathered around him on the way into the hall. Granz appeared tense as he peered from behind the curtains to survey the house just before he came on to introduce the musicians. "The triumph of jazz concerts climaxes an uneven, not-too-aggressive, 50-year battle by jazz for true recognition," *Ebony* concluded.[15]

Lee Rowe, a retired registrar from the University of Michigan living in Washington State, recalls how at age fifteen in the late 1940s she cultivated her appreciation of jazz by standing outside the "black and tan" clubs in Detroit to listen to the music. Once she was escorted back to a white neighborhood by a concerned policeman. Later she attended a string of Jazz at the Philharmonic concerts at Detroit's Masonic Temple from 1949 through 1953. Rowe was swept off her feet not only by the music but by the elegance of the crowd. "People dressed like they were going to the opera," she said. White patrons generally wore coats and ties; blacks, she added, came out in the height of fashion. "There were top hats, gold-headed canes, and capes. Capes! This was the height of the music. Jazz was as much a deserving music for that kind of place as classical music."[16]

Granz kicked off 1948 with the announcement in New York in January that Jazz at the Philharmonic would build on its dominance of the U.S. jazz concert market by accepting an invitation to play at the International Jazz Festival on the French Riviera and other European destinations between February 16 and 25. The festival, instigated by Hugues Panassié and the Hot Club of France, was the first of its kind in the history of the music and an opportunity to fulfill his ambition of exporting Jazz at the Philharmonic. Scheduled to make the European trip were Coleman Hawkins, Flip Phillips, Howard McGhee, Ray Brown, J. C. Heard, and Helen Humes; a pianist, an alto saxophonist, and another tenor saxophonist were still to be determined.[17] The announcement marked the second time Granz had floated the idea of a European tour, the first being in July 1946, when he was reportedly finalizing details for a tour kicking off in Paris in the fall.[18] Granz was proceeding with his goal of extending American musicians' influence and earning power in

Europe, since he believed that Europeans had an awareness of modern American music matching that of Americans.

Granz had agreed to six continent-wide broadcasts after the opening concert in Nice, including broadcasts planned during concerts in Paris, Geneva, and Copenhagen. Granz was to host two broadcasts in French, but financial reasons forced him again to cancel his plans. Granz had much to learn about the intricacies of the international jazz business before he finally began staging concerts overseas: he had to build a network of local promoters and learn about the currency, exchange, taxes, laws, and union politics in different countries. Such a jump surely required more financial and organizational clout than Granz could muster at the time. In the grand scheme of things, JATP's advance into Europe came soon enough, in 1952. Granz said toward the end of his life that his hopes in the early years had been little more than pipe dreams. He could direct only limited resources and experience toward building an international circuit while still consolidating JATP's domestic operations.

Granz's plans upon returning from Europe appeared to be somewhat unsettled. The abrupt cancellation of the European tour, possibly at a late date when it might be hard to contract a package of headliners and complete the arrangements for a full season in the United States, could help to explain a fragmented series of concerts with varying personnel that carried the Jazz at the Philharmonic banner beginning in late March. Mercury Records, which had been distributing Granz's records since 1947, put him in charge of scheduling a "caravan" of eleven concerts, beginning in Indianapolis, that would feature Frankie Laine, Helen Humes, and Carl Fischer's orchestra with Flip Phillips and Buddy Morrow. The most intriguing package was one that paired Sarah Vaughan with Charlie Parker for dates in at least seventeen midwestern and East Coast cities over four weeks beginning April 18. Rounding out Parker's ensemble were Phillips and Dexter Gordon on tenor saxophone, guitarist Barney Kessel, and trumpeter Red Rodney, while pianist Jimmy Jones accompanied Vaughan.

During the fall tour, on October 2, 1947, Norman Granz met Loretta Sullivan, the first of three women who would become his wife. Seeing the Monroesque blonde beauty from Saginaw, Michigan, distributing fliers for the JATP concert outside the city's Municipal Auditorium, he immediately fell in love. As their affair got under way, it hardly mattered—to either of them—that Loretta was not only married but the mother of a daughter, Sheridan. Although they did not marry until the day after

Christmas in 1950, in Las Vegas, Granz settled in Detroit in 1948 and 1949 until he could figure out what was next for his family and career.

The late veteran Detroit advertising man Arthur Schurgin published JATP concert programs and allowed Granz to use a desk and phone over the next three or four years on his whirlwind trips through town. "Loretta lived here and was pregnant at the time. She was really a very voluptuous woman," he recalled in 2002. "And for him to be in one place for two days, well . . . Norman was always on the go. He really had a lot of energy. I might see him in the airport, and he's on his way to Europe. I'd see him at the airport again and he's just back from Europe. He did much of his business here by phone. He was a great phone man. Norman knew the people."[19]

On October 9, 1949, Loretta bore the couple a daughter, Stormont. Arthur Schurgin was on hand at the hospital, since Granz was presenting JATP in Buffalo. Thus it was on the road that Granz first received news that his infant daughter was developmentally disabled, apparently because of being deprived of necessary oxygen during birth. "The child's problems became apparent very early," Schurgin said. Loretta's life became ever more complicated: with a largely absentee spouse, she had to look after her daughter Sheridan while managing the care of a newborn seriously ill from the beginning. Sheridan remembers that her stepsister underwent a series of medical tests but that nothing surfaced that could alleviate her condition.

New York was the next stop for the Granz family. Sheridan remembers living at the Algonquin Hotel and attending a bustling public school in the city, one of ten schools she attended in the period her mother was married to Granz. "I can remember walking along the New York streets trying to keep up with Norman's long determined strides. I was sort of swept off my feet as I flew along beside him," she said. Then, around 1950, the family moved back to Norman's home base in Los Angeles. (Loretta had taught Norman how to drive, and he drove them all out west in a new Cadillac.) When Granz was in town, there was plenty of time for days at the beach, shopping at the farmers' market, and dinner with his parents on Friday nights. "This was great fun because the food was so good, and it was like a real family," Sheridan said. "Ida did all the cooking and I would drink Manischewitz wine and watch Friday night boxing with Norman and everybody. Morris, his dad, was there, and other members of the family lived upstairs and across the street."

As Granz's music business grew increasingly prosperous, he moved his family into a series of increasingly more expensive houses, ending up on Rodeo Drive in Beverly Hills in a mansion with a swimming pool and tennis court. Granz's unshakable devotion to work would have taxed the strongest marriage, and the Granzes' marriage was pretty well over by the time they moved to California, although it had already begun to fray after Stormont's birth. "I believe Norman's absence and Loretta's love of going out spelled disaster for the marriage," Sheridan stated. Loretta filed for divorce against her husband on grounds of cruelty in January 1953, with a final decree coming down in January 1955. Word of the Granzes' divorce trial hit Los Angeles tabloids in one of the rare examples of his personal life playing out in the press, with the titillating detail that Granz had tossed his wife's fur coat in the kitchen sink in a fit of rage. For her part, Loretta drolly told Leonard Feather in 1956 that the couple had split after "I was ill-advised enough to tell him I disliked some of his records."[20]

On March 5, 1953, Granz bought his now ex-wife a home where she would live for the rest of her life. He was a frequent visitor and, according to Sheridan, loved the role of being a dad. "He bought us a collie, which he named JATiP. He had a line of wonderful cars and always took us out to dinner and to amusement parks. He taught me how to use my eating utensils in the European way when I was really young."[21] One telltale sign of Granz's undiminished affection for his former stepdaughter was that he sent her postcards from all over Europe during JATP's spring tour there. He also underwrote the cost of her junior year abroad in Europe.

Granz struggled, however, to come to terms with the tragedy of his stricken daughter Stormont. He established a trust fund for her to ensure lifelong care, which remains in effect as of this writing, but apparently stopped seeing the child when she was around nine years old. He spoke virtually nothing of her outside his most intimate circle of friends, such as Benny Green, who also had a developmentally disabled child. But for the remainder of Granz's life he always displayed photographs of her in his home and office.

Even at this point in JATP's history, the owners of venues that contracted with Granz were not always sure what they were getting. Such was the case when Humes, Phillips, Eldridge, Davey Tough on drums, Mickey Crane on piano, and Al McKibbon on bass showed up for a two-week engagement beginning May 21 at the College Inn of the Sherman Hotel in Chicago, famous for its remote broadcasts. It was the first time that Jazz at the Philharmonic had played in a nightclub. "Everyone wanted to play there because they had broadcasts," Granz said. "It was great publicity for an orchestra."[22]

In his initial meeting with Ernest Beifeld, owner of the Sherman Hotel, Granz persuaded him to provide musicians with free rooms in the hotel. He was less successful in getting him to completely abandon his whites-only seating policy; the best he could get was integrated seating on the two weekends. "That's important, because the college kids would come in with their girlfriends," he said. "But it turned out that I don't think he knew what Jazz at the Philharmonic was all about. Beifeld had a reputation that when a new group came in, he would have the best table in the house for the first show. At the end of the show—he didn't even sit through the show—I got a call from his secretary. 'Mr. Beifeld would like to see you immediately.'

"So I went up there, and he said, 'What is that noise? I thought you were a symphony group.'

"You mean Jazz at the Philharmonic?"

"Yeah. That's a lot of noise to me."

"Look, if you don't want us, pay us for the two weeks, and we'll go tomorrow morning."

"No, but I'm not going to come hear you anymore."

"That's up to you."

"We did work it out," Granz recalled, "but it was not heaven."[23]

Granz flexed his muscles as a promoter in the fall of 1948 with a triple header. He and Mercury Records promoted a JATP tour of twenty-eight concerts, headlined by Charlie Parker, Coleman Hawkins, Howard McGhee, Flip Phillips, Al Haig, bassist Tommy Potter, trombonist Tommy Turk, alto saxophonist Sonny Criss, and singer Kenny "Pancho" Hagood. The show kicked off the season at Carnegie Hall on November 6. In addition, he booked a national tour of around thirty dates by Sarah Vaughan and Illinois Jacquet and another forty-five for a tour by the Stan Kenton Orchestra. Other than booking the bandleader, Granz apparently had little use for the Kenton sound, as he made clear in 1950. "It hasn't got a heart. It's not jazz," he said. "There's so much over-arranging, and so many of his effects are there just for effect's sake."[24] He also disdained Kenton's seemingly endless takes in the studio, which he believed squeezed the life out of the music.

One of the more unusual stops in the fall JATP itinerary, which, like the spring tour had a decidedly bebop flavor, was Salt Lake City, Utah, on November 15. The concert, however, drew a packed, mixed crowd the night Charlie Parker played South High School Auditorium.

(Even Norman Granz did not even try to book the city's best room, the Mormon Temple.) The review in the Mormon-owned *Deseret News* failed to mention a single musician by name. "Different is the only word to describe Norman Granz's Jazz at the Philharmonic (which drew a crowd only of teenagers) last night," wrote one Harold H. Jensen. "This writer has reviewed every kind of concert from a 500-piece symphony in the Kaiser's box in Berlin to the first colored band after World War I, in London, billed as 'American Indians,' but never has he heard music like that which came out of seven artists in their own right. . . . By the time of the grand finale, everyone including the artists and audience had worn themselves out, but there was no denying it was different."[25] Different? It is hard to conceive a stranger cultural landing spot than Salt Lake City. A critic for the *Salt Lake City Tribune* wrote more appreciatively though hardly more perceptively about the first major jazz concert presented in the city. "The troupe must be complimented, in addition to its virtuosity, upon its honesty," the reviewer wrote. "These men believe in jazz. They play like it, which is more than can be said for a lot of pseudo-legitimate concert artists who try to be both longhair and popular, and turn out to be neither grist nor chaff."[26]

But all was apparently not all right with Charlie Parker, whose performance at a November 22 concert at the Shrine Auditorium was criticized by the local *California Eagle* as leaving his fans dissatisfied. *Down Beat* was more specific. "The complete disappointment of the evening was the performance—or nonperformance—of Charlie Parker, who came on late to the session to a screaming, stomping ovation, and then blew nothing but clinkers and meaningless, disconnected passages that sounded as though they tumbled from a dream—almost completely alien to the architectural structure of the composition attempted," the magazine stated. "In contrast, Coleman Hawkins was brilliant. . . . In like manner Flip Phillips showed that background and musical experience ring the bell more often than wild unschooled ideas."[27]

Parker's weak showing in Los Angeles was symptomatic of the frustrations Granz occasionally endured taking jazz musicians on tour. To the extent that he could, he attempted to shield Parker from the drug pushers so that the alto saxophonist could fulfill his obligations on stage. Mostly, "Charlie was fine on the whole tour," Granz said later. "He might have had some 'connections' in certain cities, but he made time, and he made the gig." But in Los Angeles the pushers were all over Parker and Granz needed to stash him somewhere out of harm's way until at least after the performance. The pressure was on with a sellout crowd at the Shrine (most likely the November 22 concert, based on the details of Granz's recollections). Granz thought he had found an answer when he called a friend of his, a black detective at the Los Angeles Police Department, to recommend someone from within his ranks who could act as Parker's chauffeur while at the same time keeping watch over Parker and making sure that he made it to his engagements on time. Granz booked Parker into a motel on the outskirts of the city and pumped his ego by saying he was worthy of having his own car and driver. "Apparently, Charlie said he was going to go to sleep, and I think the young detective thought he could sack out, too," Granz said. "When he woke up, Charlie had taken the keys to the car and gone."

Granz had arrived at the Shrine a couple of hours before showtime to get the sequencing of the program down when the detective showed up with the bad news that Parker had given him the slip. Granz told the detective that the alternative to finding Parker was announcing that the audience could stay and hear the concert for free and suffering a total loss for the evening. "You'd better be sure that he's either going to be here at some time before eleven o'clock, so that I can effectively say I put him on," Granz said. "If that's impossible, then I've gotta make my announcement at eight o'clock." The detective was flummoxed until Los Angeles tenor saxophonist Teddy Edwards volunteered to search for the wayward Parker in haunts unfamiliar to the lawman. "He found Charlie, and he was virtually unconscious. He was really out of it," Granz continued. "There was no way for Charlie to go on effectively. Coleman Hawkins was playing, and I kept signaling when Coleman would finish a number that finished his set, to play. I'd say, 'One more.' Poor Hawk was out there interminably, it seemed." At that point, Granz had Parker under a running faucet to bring him around. "Charlie, I'm gonna kill you if you don't get yourself together. (I mean, I was that tight with Charlie. I could say anything I wanted. He knew that)," Granz said. "He got himself together, and went onstage. I think he played one or two numbers, and I brought the curtain down. They had seen Charlie Parker, so technically I was okay. I didn't blame him for that. If you're taking someone out on tour, you know whom you are taking. I mean, there were a lot of musicians I knew who were not straight. As long as they did their show, it wasn't up to me to tell them what to do and what not to do offstage."[28]

Granz was in the audience on September 29, 1947, for a date significant beyond the debut of both Dizzy Gillespie and Ella Fitzgerald at Carnegie

Hall as part of a show touring since the previous November. The concert, which featured a last-minute appearance by Parker, was important for mixing two streams of modern jazz: bop and Afro-Cuban jazz. The result, known as "Cubop," had come into being earlier that year when the legendary and short-lived conga player Chano Pozo joined Gillespie's big band. The performance proved to be a breakthrough for Afro-Cuban music, which had flourished in New York beginning in the late 1930s and edged toward full expression a decade later.

The recordings of the concert show that Gillespie and Parker had a spirited reunion. The artistic highlight of the night was the introduction by Gillespie's big band of George Russell's two-movement "Afro-Cuban Drum Suite," a vehicle for Chano Pozo's stunning chanting and playing that was recorded commercially three months later as "Cubana Be" and "Cubana Bop." A "shadowy figure" who became "more legend than human" after being shot to death in a Harlem bar in December 1948 in an argument over drugs, Pozo would eventually be described as "more responsible than any other musician for establishing the playing field for Afro-Cuban jazz," according to a 2002 review of a major reissue of his recordings. His stagecraft, which involved an initial ritual of taking off his shirt and oiling his chest and arms, was as dramatic as his playing.[29] As a composer, he shared credit with Gillespie for "Manteca" and "Tin Tin Deo."

Though possibly overshadowed by the musical pyrotechnics of the Gillespie band, Ella Fitzgerald showed how far she had traveled stylistically during her ten months touring with what many still consider to be Gillespie's greatest orchestra. Her treatments of "Lady Be Good" and "How High the Moon," two bop-era flag wavers from this period, never left her repertoire. Her popularity contributed to making the tour a success.

One can almost hear the gears whirring in Granz's head at the Gillespie/Parker/Fitzgerald show, as they had years before when he first heard musicians jamming in Los Angeles nightclubs. The difference by the fall of 1947 was that he had the mechanisms in place to translate his enthusiasm for Afro-Cuban jazz into a handful of recordings that would prove influential, especially among musicians. Between 1948 and the mid-1950s, he produced recordings that captured the integrity, excitement, and contributions of the music and gained it wider exposure. He signed Charlie Parker onto his Clef series on Mercury Records in November 1948 and was soon free to include him on recordings he produced with the Cuban master Machito and his later sessions with one of the foremost composers and arrangers in Cubop, Arturo "Chico" O'Farrill.

According to Machito in a 1980 interview, O'Farrill was the one to introduce Granz to Latin American jazz by taking him to Birdland one night to hear Machito's band. This incident probably occurred in November or December 1948, when JATP was in the area. "Norman Granz was connected with Chico O'Farrill, because Chico already had a name as an arranger," Machito said. "That particular week, Norman came to New York, hit Birdland, and he flipped!"[30] Shortly thereafter, Granz took Parker to hear the band rehearse at the Palladium, which had become the premier showcase for Afro-Cuban jazz in midtown. At the rehearsal Parker and the Afro-Cubans, along with Flip Phillips, started out with "Mango Mangue," an instrumental with no solos but a spot for a vocal group where Parker would come in. After two run-downs, Parker assembled his horn and "played all through the arrangement, like he had known that number for 20 years," Machito recalled. "That fellow had a photograph, a machine in his brain. Anything that he heard he kept like a sponge. It was no problem because he was so far advanced, so well equipped in the analysis of chords."[31] In addition to "Mango Mangue," Parker, Phillips, and the Afro-Cubans would record "No Noise, Parts I and II."

Surprisingly, Parker's recordings with Machito and later O'Farrill succeeded despite his disinclination to adapt his phrasing to their style. The late historian John Storm Roberts observed, "The frame of the full band [was] strong enough to contain him."[32] Despite Parker's reputation for unpredictability, Machito said that he was always prompt to the sessions and that playing with Parker was the highlight of his career. In January 1949 Granz reconvened Parker and Machito to record "Okiedokie," the latter co-written by Machito and Rene Hernandez, the Afro-Cubans' pianist but named by Parker himself after a favored expression of his. On the heels of the Afro-Cubans' recordings with the alto saxophonist, Granz invited the band to play as part of the JATP spring tour kickoff at Carnegie Hall on February 11, 1949. A partial release of the concert by Pablo Records in 2002 did not include Machito's portion of the concert.

Granz's next outing with Parker and Machito, which took place on December 21, 1950, is best remembered for a masterpiece written and arranged by O'Farrill, the eight-part *Afro-Cuban Jazz Suite*. Machito's band, including Mario Bauza, was supplemented by such jazz players as Phillips, trumpeter Harry Edison, and drummer Buddy Rich. O'Farrill said in 1998 that Granz was generous in giving him an opportunity to record the *Suite* but that he had minimized the costs of recording a big band by cutting out rehearsal time. "He would tell me, 'Chico, let's do a jazz date or a mambo date,' but he would point out to me what he was hoping for. I have never worked for a producer who was more amenable, who let you do whatever you wanted. You know what Norman used to say? 'You do what you want. You fall on your ass, I'll pay.' He loved music, yes. Basically, he was a very good businessman. I don't think he made any kind of big money with these recordings. He did it because he was a gambler. When he had Jazz at the Philharmonic, he made a lot of money, so he gambled with [my music]." *Gambler* was something of a misnomer where Granz was concerned. He never had to place anywhere near all of his chips on the table. Huge profits from Jazz at the Philharmonic concerts where he indulged the famous and familiar continually replenished Granz's coffers and granted him wide latitude to subsidize the more esoteric in jazz.[33]

The relationship between Granz and O'Farrill on the Clef and later on the Norgran label extended over five recording dates in New York and a final one in Los Angeles in April 1954. According to the writer Oscar Huelos, author of *The Latin Kings,* the recordings, which included the two Afro-Cuban suites and other notable selections such as "JATP Mambo," "The Peanut Vendor," and "Cuban Blues," showed that O'Farrill had progressed "from some kind of apprenticeship to a master's glory."[34] O'Farrill later confessed his disappointment that he had not recorded more extended suites during this period. "I guess Norman was looking for commercial successes," he said. "What I should have done, but didn't, was start at a point and build up over a period of time to something specifically recognizable, something commercial. Instead I had a ball."[35]

His time with Granz ended unhappily in 1955 when Granz refused to release O'Farrill from his contract, rendering O'Farrill unable to accept an offer from Capitol Records. Capitol aimed to develop him as a rival to Perez Prado, who recorded for RCA around that time. O'Farrill considered Capitol's offer the opportunity of a lifetime and was disappointed and confused by Granz's position. He continued to work such usual haunts as Birdland, the Blue Note, and the Apollo, but jobs for the band were not easy to come by. He was so discouraged he turned down an offer from Granz he later regretted: to record a band stocked with star trumpeters, such as Gillespie, Maynard Ferguson, and Thad Jones. "Let's do the most way-out trumpet battle with a 40-piece orchestra. Do anything you want!" Granz said. "If somebody told me something like this today, I'd say, 'When do we start?'" O'Farrill commented in a later interview. "But at the time, I told Norman, 'I can't do anything anymore.'"[36] He promptly returned to Havana and in 1957 went on to Mexico City, where for eight years he prospered, leading his own bands and doing studio and television·work. Then, coming back to the United States in 1965, he continued his career for the next three decades, writing for leading musicians and bands, including, on one occasion in 1975, Gillespie and Machito, who played together again in a session produced by Granz for Pablo Records.[37]

O'Farrill said that his recordings with Granz, such as the Machito/ Parker records, were widely noted among musicians and aficionados of the New York Afro-Cuban jazz scene, but he acknowledged their limited impact on the listening public. Parker was impressed with the music, though he hardly brought Afro-Cuban jazz into his repertoire much beyond these recordings. Dizzy Gillespie, however, remained a major force in the music for the rest of his life. Nearly forty years after the first of his Afro-Cuban recordings were made, Granz said that Gillespie's involvement in the music should force a reevaluation of the trumpeter's role in jazz history. "I'm not sure that Dizzy has ever been given his proper niche in jazz," he said. "I don't think people really understand the contributions he's made. I mean, yes, Dizzy and Bird were in at the beginning of bebop, but look where Dizzy went beyond that. He was the first one that introduced the Cuban rhythm section. I'm not sure that Dizzy isn't more important than Bird. That discussion seems to go on. I think Bird was an incredible soloist, but so was Dizzy. Bird had a big impact, but so did Dizzy."[38]

By 1948 Granz, in four and a half years, had obtained exclusive access to some of the music's most enduring talents early in their careers and had put together a machine that, fueled by publicity, promoted mutually supportive recordings and concerts. The combination of strategies made JATP the leader of the jazz concert field. Granz cultivated the loyalty of a mass audience by producing highly charged concerts that maintained the emotional connection between audiences to jazz and that expected the artists to stand and deliver in a competitive format. The previous year had been distinguished by Granz's emphasis on experimentation with the content of the concerts. Beginning in the spring, he had focused on bebop's contributions to jazz with the Sarah Vaughan/Charlie Parker concerts around the time when bebop reached its zenith. Again that fall JATP went on the road with Parker in what was most likely the widest live exposure bop had received beyond the coasts up to that time. As pianist Oscar Peterson once said, Parker's tours with Jazz at the Philharmonic transported him beyond the mists of East Coast jazz mythology.

No factor was more critical for the long-term health of JATP and Granz's recording endeavors than the arrival of two key figures in 1949. Ella Fitzgerald began her association with Jazz at the Philharmonic in February. Seven months later Granz presented the twenty-four-year-old Oscar Peterson to an unsuspecting audience at Carnegie Hall for the JATP fall season opener. In Fitzgerald he secured the services and drawing power of a leading singer of striking musicality and charisma who soared with bebop, had a facility with pop music, and could muster up a physical stamina matching that of any instrumentalist. Granz would guide her to unimaginable heights of achievement over the next four-plus decades. As a soloist, trio leader, and hub of JATP's rhythm section, Oscar Peterson recaptured what Granz felt had been lost with the prodigal Nat Cole. Peterson was the most prominent example of Granz's transforming a largely unknown talent into a world-class artist. Fitzgerald's and Peterson's careers soared under Granz's management, and in turn Granz's prospects as an impresario rose immeasurably because of their popularity and prodigious output. Both artists became among the most recorded artists in the history of jazz (some have said overrecorded, although Granz argued just the opposite).

The links between the concerts and recordings forged by Granz produced dramatic results in a few short years. By 1949, Granz had signed Charlie Parker, Bud Powell, Coleman Hawkins, and Flip Phillips and had produced around eight recording sessions for Clef. Five years later, he created a second label, Norgran, to ease distribution bottlenecks at Clef and supervised nearly sixty sessions with a vastly enlarged roster of jazz greats. But although the addition of Peterson should not be underestimated, only with the acquisition of Fitzgerald did JATP become "an important package." The success that the mature Jazz at the Philharmonic achieved from 1949 to 1957, when Granz discontinued domestic touring, allowed him to take his crusades on behalf of jazz and racial equality to new heights.

8

Enter Ella and Oscar

Given the influence Norman Granz was accumulating, his statements at the time about jazz and its marketing offer clues to his success. Granz elaborated on the seat-of-the-pants marketing he employed to keep JATP fans coming back for more year after year. "I consistently check the song popularity polls and radio disc jockey surveys to get new ideas," Granz said in a March 1949 interview. "We have found this system helpful in forming well-balanced programs, from bebop to blues and boogie woogie that will appeal to teenagers as well as jazz savants. Too many 'progressive orchestras' make the mistake of playing numbers which are sometimes too advanced or technical for the lay public."[1]

It is all the more surprising, then, that Granz took exactly the opposite direction when he produced one of his greatest recordings, *The Jazz Scene,* a compendium presenting the full spectrum of contemporary jazz. Here commercial potential was clearly secondary to the elegant presentation, and the remarkable recordings delved into the avant-garde in ways Granz would not have attempted with Jazz at the Philharmonic, which was predicated on mass popular appeal. The album is on a par with his other key professional achievements of the 1940s—the nightclub jam sessions, JATP, and *Jammin' the Blues*—in confirming his focus, energy, and growing financial resources, not to mention his originality and taste. All of these had a part in making *The Jazz Scene* a genuine happening in jazz recording that showed just how diverse his ambitions were.

Granz said in his original liner notes that *The Jazz Scene* was not intended merely to chronicle jazz's past or predict its future. He revisited the rationale behind the project in 1989, when he said *The Jazz Scene* had been inspired by Gjon Mili. "After seeing what Mili had done on *Jammin' the Blues,* photographically, I thought it would be a good idea to put out an album that would try in some way . . . to give you the image and the record," he said. "I wanted to get as representational a kind of an album as I could in terms of what was happening in jazz then." Granz's hopes for the participation of some artists were dashed by recording contracts that prohibited them from taking part. "I was much too small then to convince any major to do a side using their artists."[2]

To achieve the "distillate" of the musicians' artistry he sought, Granz offered unlimited freedom. The artists could select any composition, arrangement, and instrumentation for their performance and could take the necessary studio time within reason to produce a result that met their standards. The album's release in December 1949 was the culmination of three years of recording on both coasts and an investment of between $12,000 and $30,000.[3] Signed and numbered in a limited edition of five thousand, *The Jazz Scene* sold for an unheard-of $25, possibly the highest price for a set of records up to that point. The price and its limited circulation further militated against the project's commercial success. As the British jazz historian Brian Priestley points out in his notes for the 1994 reissue of *The Jazz Scene,* Granz's expansive concept enabled him to underwrite the creation of important works that have withstood the test of time. The finished product combined the work of Duke Ellington, Coleman Hawkins, Lester Young, Flip Phillips, Willie Smith, and Ellington's baritone saxophonist Harry Carney (featured in a rare starring vehicle) with a newer era represented by Charlie Parker, Bud Powell, and the Machito Orchestra. The project was equally driven by the contributions of six leading arrangers: Ellington, Billy Strayhorn, Ralph Burns, Neal Hefti, Mario Bauza, and the obscure but memorable George Handy, whose meteoric talents flourished and then all but disappeared in the postwar years.

Granz returned to his roots in jazz to again pair Lester Young and Nat Cole with Buddy Rich in the first session on the set, recorded in April 1946 in Hollywood. Their rousing "I Want to Be Happy" recalled the casual brilliance that had distinguished Granz's recording debut in 1942. Ralph Burns, who was among the first to hear of the project, recorded his composition, "Introspection," the following October, also in Los Angeles. "We were on some kind of vacation, and I remember

Norman was some place else and offered to sublet his apartment," Burns said later.[4] "Introspection" emanated from that period when Burns, a onetime student at the New England Conservatory of Music, was making his name writing, arranging, and playing piano for the orchestras of Charlie Barnet, Red Norvo, and Woody Herman. The recording for Granz came about a year after Burns had left Herman's band in 1945 to devote more time to writing and arranging. As such, Burns's piece for a big band of fourteen featured many musicians who had been in Herman's band at the same time as Burns, including the trombonist Bill Harris, who began his periodic involvements with JATP in 1947. Burns's band doubled in size that October day to spend no less than five hours recording George Handy's "The Bloos."

Handy was already nearing the end of his brief period of fame as one of the top jazz arrangers. His work had reached its peak of both quality and quantity in his collaborations with Boyd Raeburn and Dizzy Gillespie, as well as his arrangements of his own compositions and some vocal pieces. Handy supplemented standard big band instrumentation for "The Bloos" with a French horn, oboe, bassoons, a violin, and cello. *Down Beat*'s suggestion that "The Bloos," with its jagged modern classical ambience, amounted to a send-up of "what George Handy thinks of the gentry who keep on leaning on the blues for musical assistance in composition," may help explain his comment, in a cryptic biographical sketch he provided to Granz, that aside from his wife and son, "the rest stinks, including the music biz and all connected."[5]

Duke Ellington's unique identity as a bandleader and composer was acknowledged in *The Jazz Scene* by recordings of two rarely recorded compositions, "Sono" and "Frustration," featuring baritone saxophonist Harry Carney with fellow Ellingtonians Billy Strayhorn on piano, guitarist Fred Guy, bassist Oscar Pettiford, and Sonny Greer on drums, supplemented by three violins, a viola, and cello. The results so pleased Granz that he issued both. "Duke came down and sat in the booth, and actually supervised the session," he said. "We worked in kind of tandem, because I didn't do anything musically. Duke did it, I think. He was intrigued with the idea since he didn't work with strings often, or maybe at all."[6] Granz was pleased to offer the spotlight to Carney, whose identity was so tightly bound with Ellington's sax section. Ellington may have been motivated by these recordings to more fully indulge his appetite for strings in the late 1940s and 1950s. Willie Smith's selection for the album was "Sophisticated Lady," recorded in Hollywood in November with a group that included pianist Dodo Marmarosa, guitarist Barney Kessel, bassist Red Callender, and drummer Jo Jones. It was a tasteful if conventional treatment compared to an otherwise daring group of selections.

The December 1947 Charlie Parker date is justly celebrated as much for an encounter that fell through as for an unexpected and fortuitous collaboration that came together on the spot. Granz had booked Carnegie Hall for a recording double-header when studios all over New York were jammed in anticipation of the second recording ban in a decade that had been ordered by the American Federation of Musicians to begin on January 1, 1948. To produce two recordings simultaneously, Granz reserved the recital hall for a Parker quartet. Downstairs on the main stage, an orchestra called together by Neal Hefti was preparing to record two of his pieces, "Rhumbacito" and "Repetition." Parker and company dashed off a composition of his, "The Bird," in what turned out to be his longest-ever solo on a studio recording. When Parker dropped in on the Hefti session, Hefti hastily switched gears to include him on "Repetition." By so doing, they created one of the best-remembered recordings of Parker's career. "Norman asked me about two days before if I could come up with two other sides [in addition to "Rhumbacito] for a ten-inch single," Hefti told jazz historian Phil Schaap. The recording got under way about eleven o'clock or midnight, in part so that Granz might snare musicians making their way from other last-minute record dates. "We had about 15 minutes left to do the other side of the proposed single, and that was 'Repetition,' which was just the way it was before the Charlie Parker solo. . . . We ran it down a couple of times, and Norman came over and said, 'Charlie Parker is here. Can you use him?' I said I hadn't really hadn't planned it for any kind of soloist, but if he wants to just jam over the last chorus when we reprise the melody, there's no problem."[7]

Gene Orloff, concertmaster for the date, recalled what happened next. "It was the most phenomenal thing I've ever seen," he said. "The lead sheet for him or whatever he had to blow changes on was spread out, a sheet of about ten pages, and he had it strewn out over the piano. He was like bending down, then lifting his head up as the music passed by, reading it once or twice until he memorized those changes, then proceeded to become godly."[8]

The original plan had called for Parker to record duets with Art Tatum. The pianist was playing at Kelly's Stables when he got the call from Granz. "I had rented Carnegie Hall for an afternoon to record just the two of them in this enormous place. I thought it would be great to get that big sound," he recalled. Both Parker and Tatum agreed to do the session, but Tatum was nowhere to be found at the appointed time. "Bird came in early, ready," Granz said. "Art didn't show. He didn't even call. He did nothing."[9]

Tatum's change of heart left Granz scrambling to find musicians to accompany Parker. "In those days in New York, you could get on the phone and get fantastic musicians on short notice, and Hank Jones came down," Granz said. Ray Brown also got the call, and Granz begged, borrowed, or stole Shelly Manne from Hefti long enough to record "The Bird." Afterwards, the group, minus Manne, made a few attempts at a drummerless trio but gave up when Bird's tempos defied winging it without a driving percussive underpinning to sustain them. The missed Tatum/Parker date provided Granz with one of the few regrets of his career, but he bore no Tatum ill will. "I accepted that [his decision to skip the date] because I respect genius. And if he did things which were maybe out of the norm, it was a price I was glad to pay. I never even asked him about it."

The next recording for *The Jazz Scene* was the unreleased remake of Mario Bauza's "Tanga" with Machito's Afro-Cubans from December 20, 1948, in which Flip Phillips, who had soloed on "No Noise, Part I," had the lead role.

In the midst of a project that gave prominence to composers and arrangers, Coleman Hawkins's unaccompanied solo "Picasso" roared like a lion in its solitary majesty in a piece notable for its lack of easily discernible harmonic, rhythmic, or tonal themes. John Chilton, the saxophonist's biographer, hailed Hawkins's conception of "Picasso" as "revolutionary," and the results as "positively *avant garde*."[10] According to Gunther Schuller, Hawkins influenced a new generation of saxophonists, notably Sonny Rollins, with his triumph as "a solitary soloist sans accompaniment of any kind, on a single-note instrument. . . . 'Picasso' is one of his most visionary and personal, though also thorny, expressions."[11] Hawkins tried to diminish the effort it took to record this difficult number by saying afterward that he had come up with the idea for "Picasso" that morning. Granz said Hawkins had painstakingly worked out the construction of the piece on a piano for about two hours and then spent another two trying unsuccessfully to record a satisfactory take. They reconvened in the studio about a month later, and Hawkins went through another four-hour lead-up to the recording of a masterpiece.

The final number recorded for *The Jazz Scene*, a sparkling version of "Cherokee" by a Bud Powell trio with Ray Brown and Max Roach, dates from January or February 1949. The perfection of the recording was like a brief glimmer of light breaking between two dark clouds. Powell had been hospitalized for mental problems for about a year beginning in November 1947 and was readmitted in early 1949 for two to three months shortly after these recordings were made. Later still he would record for two years for Granz and Blue Note.

What *Down Beat* writer Mike Levin heralded as Granz's "slightly delayed love child" was issued as twelve selections on twelve-inch 78s in packaging befitting classical recordings.[12] The albums prefigured deluxe box sets of today in that the packaging itself was a work of art. The records came in sleeves enclosed in a black cloth notebook with the title displayed in simple gold-leaf lettering at the center and with Granz's name in the lower right corner. The package also featured a panoramic drawing by David Stone Martin of a lone trumpeter practicing in his room lit by a naked bulb and strewn with empty chairs, instruments, and cases, with a sultry ingenue sprawled out on the bed. Accompanying Gjon Mili photographs showed musicians who were represented in the recordings and others who were not but whom Granz still considered to be leading figures. The portfolio, entitled "And This, Too, Is the Jazz Scene," displayed photographs of Louis Armstrong and Roy Eldridge, Dicky Wells, Ella Fitzgerald, Gene Krupa, Teddy Wilson and Benny Goodman, Harry Edison and Illinois Jacquet, Stan Kenton, Mary Lou Williams, Count Basie, Art Tatum, Sarah Vaughan, Dizzy Gillespie, John Simmons, and Billie Holiday. Granz saw *The Jazz Scene* as the prototype for an annual review of jazz. Rather than meeting that lofty goal, the album is striking as a showcase for Granz's visual and musical aesthetics of production and as a work of art commensurate with the music making. Numerous projects to come would be similarly ambitious.

No night since the one when Ella Fitzgerald had made her way to the stage during an amateur night contest at the Apollo Theater in 1934, not knowing until shortly beforehand whether she would sing or dance, was more significant for her career than one in Akron, Ohio, some fourteen years later. She was attending a Jazz at the Philharmonic concert to see bassist Ray Brown, whom she had met in September 1947 on tour the previous year when he was with Dizzy Gillespie's big band and whom she had married two months later. The crowd quickly recognized her, and the resulting applause and commotion prompted Granz to invite her onstage. Helen Humes, completing her time as JATP's featured vocalist, could only watch as Fitzgerald's performance of "How

High the Moon," in which she traded fours with the ensemble, brought the house down. Her performance inspired Granz to ask Fitzgerald to join JATP.[13]

Fitzgerald began her JATP career on February 11, 1949, in the series' spring opener at Carnegie Hall. Her auspicious beginning coincided with a show packed with leading bop players, including Charlie Parker, Bud Powell, trumpeter Fats Navarro, Hank Jones, and Ray Brown, as well as Coleman Hawkins, Flip Phillips, Sonny Criss, Shelly Manne, and trombonist Tommy Turk. Machito's Afro-Cubans appeared on the concert on the heels of their recordings with Parker, although neither toured with JATP that spring. A portion of the concert that featured Parker taking part in one of the jam sessions was bottled up for fifty-three years before its release on Pablo Records in 2002. Navarro was twenty-six and still in good form, as these long-awaited performances attest, when he made his only tour with JATP. The concert illustrates one of the perplexing challenges Parker encountered as a revered figure who exerted a vast influence. One wonders what his reaction was as Criss, one of many who had absorbed his style, channeled his musical mentor, who was standing only a few feet away. Jimmy Rowles, who toured with Parker up the West Coast into Canada in 1952, once speculated that Parker may have been driven to the edge in part because it was not easy for him to hear new ideas: too many people were playing him.

Fitzgerald's reputation had the immediate desired effect of bolstering the attention JATP received during a tour that concluded on March 30 with a concert at the Brooklyn Academy of Music. In the Carnegie Hall set she was backed by Jones, Brown, and Manne in performing "Robin's Nest," "I Got a Guy," "Old Mother Hubbard," "Lover Man," and "Royal Roost Bop Boogie" (or "Ool-Ya-Koo").[14] The San Francisco critic Ralph J. Gleason reported that in advance of JATP dates in San Francisco and Oakland, "the magic name of Ella Fitzgerald had every platter spinner in the Bay Area mad with joy." That draw, combined with Granz's crack publicity effort, led him to predict that the impresario would gross "a fat, five-figure sum for the two dates."[15] From the beginning, Fitzgerald joined the finale that pushed her into competition with the JATP lineup, with crowd-pleasing results.

By tour's end, Granz found himself in something of a double quandary where Fitzgerald was concerned. First, her contract with Decca prevented him from issuing concert recordings of her. He reportedly considered making an end run around Decca on the grounds that her contract pertained exclusively to her studio recordings, but he backed off when the company rightfully took exception to his specious interpretation.[16] The tour had convinced him that Fitzgerald had a bright future away from the nightclub circuit in both concert halls and other prestigious venues where she had failed so far to gain entry. Granz may have already been the foremost factor in her personal appearances between 1949 and 1954, but he merely presented her as part of a lineup of other musicians in Jazz at the Phil. Accordingly, he held back from offering too many suggestions about her material in case he might offend the singer or her longtime manager, Moe Gale. Fitzgerald had been successful during the years Gale oversaw her career, but he simply had no plans to take her career beyond jazz clubs. His background was the Savoy Ballroom and patterns of managing African American talent stemming from that. He neither had the imagination nor the connections to do what Granz was prepared to do for her career.

Granz was typically occupied on a number of other fronts. Mercury Records, one of the earliest labels to move in the direction of long-playing records, would soon begin issuing Jazz at the Philharmonic records in the new format. Granz also planned to step up the release of two sets of JATP records annually to coincide with the semiannual tours, a practice that ended with the 1949 fall season, after which the concerts toured domestically only in the fall.

In April 1950 Granz announced plans to travel to Europe early that summer, but these hopes, like past attempts to take his shows abroad, ended in frustration: still consolidating JATP in the United States, he had not yet learned the ropes of foreign tours or acquired the financial means to take the risk. But his interest was reciprocated, for European jazz fans were as excited about the prospect of seeing his shows as their American counterparts had been. The French jazz writer Charles Delaunay had expressed interest in bringing Jazz at the Philharmonic to France.[17] In March 1949 the French record producer Nicole Barclay—who along with her husband, the bandleader and pianist Eddie, had formed Blue Star Records in Paris in 1946—caught up with Granz at a JATP concert in Pittsburgh. Granz, a leading A&R man for Mercury Records at the time, signed off on a preliminary deal with the label to manufacture and distribute JATP singles and albums on Mercury in France, Switzerland, Italy, and Belgium. By 1953 the Barclays were running a $5-million-a-year business serving diverse listeners, including a label dedicated to instrumental dance music, which was hugely popular in Europe.[18] Granz had planned to visit with record companies in countries outside Blue Star's network to discuss recording and touring prospects, but he had to postpone the trip.[19]

Canadian-born Oscar Peterson's determination to succeed was a signature characteristic that drove his decades-long career. The young prodigy had catapulted to fame in his teens when an amateur contest earned him a weekly fifteen-minute radio broadcast in Montreal, a chair in the Johnny Holmes Orchestra, a popular touring dance band, and a contract with RCA Canada. Training in both classical and popular music pushed him toward a florid keyboard technique that incorporated the traditions of jazz piano while maintaining his strong individuality. "I decided if the only way I was going to make it was to frighten the hell out of everybody pianistically, that's the way I was going to make it," Peterson recalled in the 1980s.[20]

When Norman Granz first became aware of the pianist is not clear, but, as Granz later admitted, he missed the import of and did not like Peterson's early boogie-woogie-influenced recordings made for Canadian RCA. According to Granz, his relative obscurity in the United States until he took the stage at Carnegie Hall was partly due to the long-standing insular attitude of the United States toward its Canadian neighbor. Peterson was largely unknown to American jazz fans, though not to musicians, who came away amazed at the youthful piano phenomenon. His name first appeared in *Down Beat* in 1944, when Count Basie praised his work and at one point asked him to consider sharing piano duties. Jimmie Lunceford also eyed the young pianist for his orchestra.[21]

Coleman Hawkins began talking Peterson up around 1945. Among others to take an interest in him were Ella Fitzgerald, Duke Ellington, Billy Strayhorn, and Flip Phillips. Dizzy Gillespie went head over heels for Peterson after the audience prevailed upon Gillespie to call Peterson up to sit in during an appearance with his big band at Montreal's Chez Maurice Danceland in late 1948. The son of one of Peterson's teachers witnessed the event and later told the Montreal jazz historian John Gilmore that Gillespie had pulled the band's most difficult piano chart to stump Peterson. "It was of those things where the band wails, and then stops dead, and the piano is supposed to play. The whole brass section stood up . . . [and] Diz just stared at him for a minute, and started shouting, "Blow! Blow! Go ahead and blow, man!" After the engagement the two repaired to an after-hours club and, according to Peterson, stayed up playing until six the following morning.[22]

"I had heard about Oscar from various people I respected," Granz said. "The first one to tell me about Oscar was Coleman. Hawk was very enigmatic in the way he said, 'You know, Norm, I don't want to tell you how to run your business, but you better hear a young piano player up in Montreal, Oscar Peterson.' Duke Ellington told me about him, and Billy Strayhorn, especially, told me about him. So I was quite keen to hear this new piano player."[23]

Peterson had had one disconcerting experience with Granz in 1948 when he was performing with his trio at Montreal's Alberta Lounge and thus was unable to get away for Granz's JATP concert. He later caught up with a delegation of JATP musicians at the Saint Michel. Granz had come to join them but was refused entry into the packed club by a doorman unaware of his identity. Peterson tried unsuccessfully to mediate the face-off, but Granz turned on his heel and left.

The meeting that changed both of their lives occurred in the late summer of 1949, when Granz was in Montreal finalizing details for Jazz at the Philharmonic's September 28 appearance at Verdun Auditorium. As Peterson and Granz have told it, Granz was in a cab heading toward the airport when he heard what he assumed was recorded music on the radio. On learning that the music he was hearing was actually a live broadcast, he ordered the cabbie to take him to the club.[24]

Peterson picks the story up here.[25] "The first thing I saw was the buckskin shoes with the sort of tan stripe across them," he said. "That was one of his trademarks. I still remember as my eyes started following up the legs, seeing the tweed outfit he had on—he was very English at that time. The next trademark was the eyebrows, the huge eyebrows. It was Norman."

At set's end Granz invited Peterson back to his hotel for a talk. Of the pianist's Canadian RCA recordings, Granz asked, "Why do you make those terrible boogie-woogie records? That's not you. You don't play like that."

"Well, that's what they've asked me to do," Peterson answered.

Granz wasted no time in getting to the point. "I'd like you to take a shot at the American jazz market," he began. "I think you could bring something to it. I think it would be a tremendous innovation. First of all, the playing. Secondly, the fact that you're not an American. I think it would be great." He offered Peterson a slot on the tour he was then organizing, but Peterson demurred. He was not ready to take such a leap so quickly. He acquiesced to Granz's request to make a guest appearance with Jazz at the Philharmonic to get a reading on American audiences' response to his playing.

"When I finally agreed to do it, he decided it should be at Carnegie Hall," Peterson continued. "I was thinking a smaller city. He decided the proper place would be Carnegie Hall."

"Take your best shot, and you'll know immediately. You won't have to dilly-dally. If you make it, you'll know it. If you don't make it, you'll know that, too."

Granz adopted the ploy of inviting Peterson up from the audience as a "surprise" guest whom he had seen out in the audience and invited to perform on the spur of the moment. The ruse allowed Granz to sidestep immigration and labor issues that would have complicated his plans for even such a brief appearance. Peterson got to Carnegie Hall that Saturday, September 17, with time to spare and took a seat near the stage to contemplate the memorable evening ahead. True to form, Roy Eldridge came early to warm up. The competitiveness and feisty exuberance that fired the trumpeter's playing and pushed him to be in fighting trim for every concert were traits that especially endeared him to Granz. He reassured Peterson, who confessed his excitement in seeing a show featuring a lineup of Ella Fitzgerald, Coleman Hawkins, and Lester Young, who was returning to JATP for his first tour since 1946. Charlie Parker made a special appearance but was not scheduled the remainder of the tour.

The night got under way with the JATP jam session consisting of Flip Phillips ("the exciting one," according to Granz's intro), Charlie Parker ("the cool one"), Young, Tommy Turk, and a rhythm section of Hank Jones, Ray Brown, and Buddy Rich, who also backed Fitzgerald. Between two extended bluesy riff-based bookends, "The Opener" and "The Closer," and the sounds of a Parker fan blowing a high-pitched birdcall from the audience were "Lester Leaps In" and "Embraceable You." By her second season with JATP, Fitzgerald ("the greatest thing in jazz today") was *the* headliner, a position accorded her alone among the musicians. She cruised through her first set beginning with "Robin's Nest" and cleared the decks a half a dozen songs later with "Flying Home."

Peterson, meanwhile, was preparing to take his bow at the beginning of the second set. He had planned on playing as a trio. Granz originally wanted him to play solo but had arranged with Buddy Rich and Ray Brown to accompany the newcomer. Rich begged off after a draining first set. Brown had heard Peterson in Montreal and was enthusiastic about joining him when Granz made his way to the microphone.

"Now for the second set, we have a surprise for everybody, something we couldn't advertise, because we ourselves didn't know it was going to happen," Granz began. "Up in Canada, there's been a very wonderful piano player. All the bands that have traveled through Canada have heard about him and raved about him. Today, he flew to New York to hear our concert. I saw him in the audience and prevailed upon him to join our group. I think he's very wonderful and something you ought to hear, because we think he's going to be one of the coming giants of jazz. From Canada, for his first appearance in the United States, Oscar Peterson."[26]

Peterson's initial nervousness is audible on the recording, which captures the uncertain moments leading up to his brisk "Fine and Dandy": a cough and then three notes of a false start virtually sucked back into the air, such was his speed. He left his boogie-woogie licks at the border and displayed a maturing style that would soon thrust him into the international limelight when he began recording for Granz the following spring and joined Jazz at the Philharmonic in the fall of 1950. Applause and whistles thundered down on Peterson in the best JATP tradition as he brought his set to a close with "I Only Have Eyes for You" and his own "Carnegie Blues," which he had just sketched out that day. Peterson demonstrated the presence of mind necessary to pass this most important audition and the ability to make the most of the many opportunities Granz would soon give him.

It would have been understandable for Peterson to think he was playing in a dream sequence, for he was followed by Coleman Hawkins, who led off a twenty-five-minute segment with "Body and Soul" before Fitzgerald returned for her second set. An evening that featured Fitzgerald, Parker, Hawkins, Eldridge, and Young and the introduction of Peterson was historic for the music itself. But that early Sunday morning one transcendent moment seemed especially to foretell the future of JATP and Granz all at once. Fitzgerald took her cue from Granz, who wanted the musicians to spike the pace on "How High the Moon." "Up, up. Up, he wants it. He wants it up," she shouted above the din as Hank Jones picked up the pace. "He wants it up!" By late 1949, the question for JATP was not whether this moon-orbiting jazz would rise to meet Norman Granz's expectations but rather how high it would rise. "Up" he wanted it, and up it would be.

9

The Continental

Norman Granz's fortunes zoomed ahead in the three years beginning in 1950 when Ella Fitzgerald and Oscar Peterson became JATP's mainstays. Jazz at the Philharmonic had come a long way from its beginnings as a dynamic experiment in Los Angeles that went on to tour the West Coast. After six years, JATP had become an eagerly anticipated annual highlight for tens of thousands of jazz fans across the country, and by 1952 it had refashioned the music industry to make concerts the dominant vehicle for reaching jazz audiences.

Much later, John McDonough, looking back at Granz's business practices during this time, proclaimed in the *Wall Street Journal* that Granz's accomplishment was comparable to that of Charlie Parker, the great genius of modern jazz. "Two mavericks changed the face of jazz in the 1940s. Parker changed the way it was played. Norman Granz changed the way it was sold. . . . Jazz at the Philharmonic jump-started a selling reciprocity between box-office and record sales no one had imagined possible. The albums leveraged the concerts. The concerts generated more live records. . . . Some called him a monopolist. He probably was. By controlling his product from raw material to distribution, he built the closest thing America has seen to a vertically integrated jazz conglomerate."[1]

Furthermore, Granz finally pulled the sword from the stone as far as touring Europe, with resounding success that almost immediately made him the most important jazz impresario from across the Atlantic.

Granz easily moved into a new phase as a record producer. He continued to profit handsomely on the margins of the record business with his live recordings. However, he vastly enlarged that base with an outpouring of studio recordings featuring the likes of Count Basie, Benny Carter, Billie Holiday, Stan Getz, Johnny Hodges, Ben Webster, Anita O'Day, Charlie Barnet, and Teddy Wilson. He also regularly produced studio recordings of artists associated with his concerts, such as Charlie Parker, Lester Young, Oscar Peterson, Barney Kessel, Illinois Jacquet, Roy Eldridge, Bill Harris, Flip Phillips, and Gene Krupa.

Even Granz's time and seemingly limitless energy could be stretched only so far. He reserved his comprehensive approach to artist management for an elite few. Granz moved in on Peterson in the aftermath of the pianist's triumphant 1949 debut but was forced into a holding pattern with Fitzgerald. In the case of both artists, Granz appreciated their strengths, challenged them to move outside their artistic comfort zones in ways that respected their talents, earned their allegiance, and guaranteed their futures.

Peterson had swiftly ascended to stardom in his storybook New York recital. The reaction to his playing rippled among musicians stunned at the clarity of his ideas and execution. In his famous *Down Beat* review, Mike Levin wrote that the Canadian had "stopped the concert cold dead in its tracks" with his "flashy right hand, a load of bop and Shearing-styled ideas, as well as a good sense of harmonic development. . . . He scared some of the local minions by playing bop ideas single finger on his *left* hand, which is definitely not the common practice."[2]

Peterson returned to Montreal to absorb the implications of his initial triumph. He wanted to take care of outstanding obligations and generally take stock of his life. He returned south of the border in the interim between his debut and his first gig with JATP for a week at Bop City in the spring of 1950. He began working closely with Granz to plan the next phase of his professional life every bit as carefully as an actor or classical musician would.[3]

Peterson's popularity in Canada and the headlines from New York gave him the leverage to disregard money as a primary consideration for joining up with Granz for recordings and touring. He reportedly earned $1,000 a week during his Bop City engagement, so he might well have commanded a roughly equivalent sum in the short run if he had chosen to strike out on a solo career independent of Granz.[4] Over the long haul, however, the association with Granz was incalculably beneficial for both. Granz recalled in 2001 that Peterson had reached his decision on the basis of his desire to play among illustrious company. "I became Oscar Peterson's best friend after one night," Granz said. "People had been asking him for years whether he would like to come to America, and he refused them. I do not know whether he didn't want to travel or whether he wanted to stay in Canada."[5]

The pianist characterized the immediate post-Carnegie period as one of "confusion," although his bond with Granz was solid from the start. "We had an immediate connection. The first thing I admired about Norman was something that I think a lot of people who don't care for him too much saw in him. He is a very honest man who spoke his mind. Sometimes he did not care if it bruised a couple of people . . . Norman came out and said what he was thinking and what he wanted to do."[6]

In addition, Peterson appreciated the absence of pressure to draw up a management agreement on the spot. "If you want me to manage you, I will try and do my best," he remembers Granz saying. In answer to Peterson's question about when a contract would be forthcoming, Granz said a handshake would suffice. That remained all the contract they ever had over the decades he managed Peterson's appearances and recordings. There were early practicalities to be resolved, such as securing a visa for Peterson so that he might legally travel and work in the United States.[7] Musically, Granz advised Peterson on his artistic development and future club work. The trick, he said, would be for Peterson to respond to his growing popularity without risking early overexposure or situations that might inhibit the artistry he was striving to attain. Peterson characterized Granz's attitude as "Let's just cool it and see what the reaction *really* is, and then plan it from there. I don't want you coming in and being just another saloon pianist."[8] In retrospect, Granz's measured and deliberate approach matched Peterson's own. Peterson had long felt that his wait until 1950 to join JATP, rather than his spectacular 1949 introduction, led to his enduring success because it gave him the requisite mental preparation.

Plotting Peterson's debut was nowhere near as complex as the daunting set of calculations involved in steering a veteran of Ella Fitzgerald's singular talents into the Granz orbit. Relationships with her longtime manager, Moe Gale, head of the Gale Agency, and Decca Records set the boundaries that left Granz dreaming and scheming about the day he might coordinate these arrangements under one roof—his. Gale, who was then co-owner of the Savoy and also operated as Consolidated Radio Artists, had raised the prominence and earning power of the Chick Webb Orchestra after taking over the band's management in late 1929. Gale had also delivered the band to Decca as one of the new label's earliest attractions and had pressed Webb to bring a female vocalist into the band, so he had known Fitzgerald from her earliest days as a professional singer.[9] Gale felt proprietary enough about his client's welfare in 1942 to help secure an annulment of her brief first marriage to a small-time hustler with a criminal record named Benny Kornegay. The marriage confirmed his fears that she had gotten involved with a man who saw her as a meal ticket and who Gale knew skimmed gate receipts on road trips.[10]

Granz concluded in the midst of Fitzgerald's first year with JATP that her talent was being seriously underutilized and that at best she was randomly managed and supplied with a diet rich in musical junk food. This view, only partially true, downplays the fact that Fitzgerald recorded many satisfying and important dates on Decca, especially in her later years there, and that she was capable of choosing questionable material on her own. For example, Fitzgerald carried the day in 1951 when she recorded a cover of Rosemary Clooney's "Come On a-My House," a hit Clooney herself detested. Milt Gabler, who produced Fitzgerald's recordings from 1943 until 1955 and whose jazz credentials were beyond question, was straightforward in justifying Decca's approach of balancing her recordings between the strictly commercial and jazz to take advantage of her undisputed crossover appeal. Gabler guided her through an enviable array of popular hits and jazz classics to earn a respectable reputation, and their successful working relationship was strengthened by the ease and affection they felt toward one another. Any rap against her Decca recordings, which is far from justified, has lingered mainly because the contrast with the Granz era would have been profound under almost any circumstances. Fitzgerald was intrigued by Granz's offer to improve her recording opportunities in much the same way that he was upgrading her personal appearances.

Granz first attempted to take Fitzgerald from Decca by going directly to Gabler to plead his case for buying out the remainder of her contract in 1951. Gabler has since stated that Fitzgerald waged a sub rosa campaign, abetted by Granz, to extricate herself from her Decca contract when it expired. "She had about a year, maybe a year and a half [on her contract]," Gabler recalled. "So I said, 'Norman, I love Ella just as much as you do, and I wouldn't sell her contract for any money in the world. I'm not even going to tell the president of our company, Milt Rackmil, that you offered $25,000. If you want her, you'll have to call him yourself. He's liable to take it because there's only 12 months or so left.'"[11]

It seems likely that Granz and Fitzgerald were working in tandem to enlist Moe Gale to allow Granz to record her. That they had to maneuver in this manner is testimony to the fact that the authority with which she approached her art did not extend to a similar boldness in managing her affairs. Besides, Gale was still exercising the power of attorney she had granted him to make such decisions. That she participated at all in disparaging Decca ran counter to her reputation as a self-effacing artist heretofore unwilling to air her complaints publicly. One example was a column by George Hoefer in early 1950 that reported her growing dissatisfaction with her recordings. "Strange as it may seem to jazz fans, her favorite songs are of the ballad type, rather than the blues, scat or bebop vocalisms," he wrote. "As for some of the pop tunes she had recorded, her talent has a tendency to make mediocre material appealing, yet she agrees that Decca has made some poor choices of tunes for her to wax."[12] (In retrospect, her comments were ironic, for she made some beautiful sides with Louis Jordan and Louis Armstrong later that year; she also recorded duets with pianist Ellis Larkins on *Ella Sings Gershwin,* an album considered by some Fitzgerald fans to be her finest recorded work, as well as a precursor of the songbook series with Granz.) Gale had rejected a pitch similar to Granz's from John Hammond for Keynote Records, which subsequently went bankrupt. He did not take Granz's bait because of his feeling that Clef was not in a league with Decca in providing the necessary backing or stability for such a proven lucrative talent.[13]

Gale likely operated from at least two considerations in sizing up Granz. He clearly did not appreciate the potential effect on her career of Granz's proven one-two punch of national exposure via JATP and wide distribution for his discs through Mercury Records. He may well have also been attempting to erect a firewall against Granz to protect his own interests in Fitzgerald, who was already receiving a high percentage of her work and career direction from Granz. Gale surely understood that the stakes were high and that the indefatigable Granz would not be content to settle for a partial share where Fitzgerald was concerned. Using his power of attorney, he abruptly closed the door on Granz's offer in October 1951 by extending Fitzgerald's contract with Decca for five more years.[14] But Gale was not around to make that decision when the question of her Decca contract came up again. Norman Granz would be.

Within weeks of releasing *The Jazz Scene,* his monument to modernism, Granz was at Hambone Kelly's in the East Bay of San Francisco recording Dixieland revivalist trumpeter Lu Watters and his Yerba Buena Jazz

Band. Watters was one of the main forces behind the revival of traditional jazz in San Francisco. On January 15, 1950, Granz conducted the first of two recording sessions that he presided over that month at Watters's nightclub in El Cerrito. According to clarinetist Bob Helm, Granz told Watters that his interest in traditional Dixieland jazz was strictly pragmatic, to fill a void in his catalog. Granz then purchased Watters's Down Home label, a vehicle the trumpeter had created in 1949 for his own recordings. Between the time Granz began producing or leasing new recordings for the Down Home series on Mercury and the time he sold Verve in 1961, he offered a small stream of recordings by such New Orleans and San Francisco stalwarts as trumpeter Bob Scobey, pianists Joe Sullivan and Ralph Sutton, trombonists Santo Pecora and Turk Murphy, and clarinetist George Lewis. However, his only producer credit appeared on a June 1956 session by Roy Eldridge and his Central Plaza Dixielanders.

In March 1950 Mercury executives formally asked Granz to oversee the company's jazz, race, and folk divisions in recognition of the focus he had brought to developing the company's jazz catalog beginning with the JATP records. He was one of five appointments made in the wake of the departure of Mitch Miller for Columbia. Under this arrangement, Granz and four other executives reported to Art Talmadge, the Chicago-based vice president in charge of public relations and advertising.

Irwin Steinberg began his thirty-seven-year association with Mercury Records as its comptroller fresh out of the University of Chicago shortly after the company was formed in 1946 and rose to become president of the label. He recalled the mutual attraction that had led Granz to affiliate with Mercury after his break with Moe Asch. One of the preconditions Granz insisted upon was that Mercury would not own the rights to his masters and that he would take them with him when he struck out on his own as an independent producer. "In the jazz area, we made our first moves through Norman, primarily through the Jazz at the Philharmonic series," Steinberg recalled. "I respected him very much. All his thinking went into his love for jazz and the artists who represented what he thought were the best in the field. He was simply who he was. He would dress down. To this day, I can see Norman in tennis shoes at the finest of halls."[15]

Steinberg added that partly because of Granz's marketing savvy Mercury began coordinating new releases with live appearances and radio as well as relying on sophisticated market and demographic research, a practice rare at the time for an emerging independent label. "Norman gave us the impetus to recognize that that was an area of business that could be interesting and profitable to us," he said. "Obviously the selection of the talent, without question, was as good as it could be, as was the coordination with radio. He was also a catalyst in moving us in that direction. I think he chose us because we were the new kid on the block, and we were very effective."

About the time Mercury promoted Granz, he got back together with Oscar Peterson in New York to produce his first records for Clef, while simultaneously pressing Canadian RCA to release Peterson from a contract with options that he had signed in the spring of 1949. In any event, his last dates for RCA were recorded the following November. In March 1950 Granz recorded several sessions that included Peterson as well as quartets led by Flip Phillips, Lester Young, and Charlie Parker using a common rhythm section of Hank Jones, Ray Brown, and Buddy Rich. Granz paired Peterson with Brown, whom the pianist found simpatico musically and personally, in a partnership that lasted in one form or another until the mid-1960s. Peterson returned to the studio in May with bassist Major Holley and again in August with Brown to build anticipation for his appearances with the fall JATP tour.[16]

Granz next went to London, Paris, Stockholm, and Rome in mid-March on what was becoming an annual nonevent: the announcement of a spring European tour, followed by a last-minute cancellation. This year was different in that he had discontinued semiannual national JATP tours in the spring, underscoring his expectations that spring tours of Europe were in the offing. Henceforth Granz would launch his domestic tour from Hartford, Connecticut, in September. He told the British music publication *Melody Maker* of his plan to bring Jazz at the Philharmonic for concerts in London and other continental European cities as soon as May. Granz conceded that he needed to reach an accord with the British Musicians' Union if he had any hope of doing business there.[17] The union staunchly maintained a protectionist line excluding American artists from playing within their jurisdiction without reciprocal arrangements on behalf of British musicians. Granz approached the union with an offer for JATP to hold a benefit concert for its Musicians' Benevolent Fund or to a charity of its choice. But his plans sank once again.

He ventured to Europe for the second time in 1950, in June, to try to put together six weeks of concerts that would begin the following March. He met with the board of the British Musicians' Union and again offered to stage a fund-raiser as a way out of the impasse. Granz assumed that the publicity JATP would reap would be worth anything he would sacrifice in ticket sales. The union board concluded the meeting by asking him to submit his request in writing.[18] "In any European country, an American group can get an audience simply out of curiosity," Granz said at the time. "They've heard our cool cats and our smart cats. They've never heard my in-between type."[19]

Granz gave country-by-country impressions of the jazz that he had encountered during his trip. Sweden was the most advanced in its appreciation for modern jazz. "Sweden is completely on a bop kick," he said. "Since there are no nightclubs there, jazz musicians do most of their work in concerts, on the radio, and on records. And disc jockeys in Sweden don't talk. They just pick the records and play them." Sidney Bechet was influential in steering England in the direction of earlier jazz traditions. France teetered in between bop and New Orleans advocates, again influenced by Bechet, who relocated permanently to Paris in 1951. Italy, according to Granz, was largely indifferent. He came away with some recordings from Italian jazz musicians, only to find that Italian boppers did what many musicians all over the jazz world did: follow the Bird.[20]

Granz spent twelve hectic days in Europe in January and February 1951 nailing down three weeks of concerts scheduled to get under way in Copenhagen on March 18 and to conclude with six nights in Paris starting April 9. Many reasons were cited for the complications in late February that again scuttled the tour. Ella Fitzgerald and Ray Brown reportedly reconsidered because of salary differences with Granz. Buddy Rich and Harry Edison were the next to announce they would not make the trip, since Rich did not want to dissolve the big band he was leading at the time. Finally, the British Musicians' Union held the line against admitting JATP. (Granz had approved a live broadcast from Paris to the British Isles in order to effectually bypass the union and take his music directly to the public.)[21]

Granz told the critic Ralph Gleason early in 1950 that he and Gjon Mili were concluding two years of discussions to film a sequel to *Jammin' the Blues.* The project came to fruition in September 1950 around the time of the JATP fall tour. Most significantly, *Sitting In,* as it was tentatively known, contains only the second film clip of Charlie Parker known to exist. Granz originally hoped to market the short for viewing in movie theaters or on television, provided he reached an accord with the American Federation of Musicians.[22] Filming got under way at Mili's New York loft studio at the corner of Sixth Avenue and

Twenty-third Street in New York, where he had photographed jazz musicians since the late 1930s.

The production was hampered by a shortage of funds that precluded the multiple cameras necessary to properly film and record the event simultaneously. For all his complaining about prerecording parts of the soundtrack for *Jammin' the Blues,* Granz felt he had little choice because Mili's studio was not soundproof. "By that time, shorts were not really making it, so I could not have gone back to Warner Bros. and asked them to do another one," Granz said in 1987. "We prerecorded, and then we tried to match it later on by shooting to it. But it really didn't work."[23] In particular, Rich and Fitzgerald's performances eluded the filmmakers' attempt to synchronize image and sound. This footage, whose fate was a source of intense speculation for decades, was finally released in 1996 under the title *Improvisation,* a compilation of performances from the 1950s through the 1970s.

The film opens with Parker and Coleman Hawkins performing a duet on "Ballade," an improvisation on "As Long as I Live," backed by Hank Jones, Ray Brown, and Buddy Rich. Hawkins takes the first solo as Parker, in one continuous, playful movement, catches the eye of someone off set as he reaches in his jacket for a cigarette, arches an eyebrow, and nods approvingly in Hawkins's direction. In the up-tempo "Celebrity," Parker anchors the scene with the intensity of his playing and stage presence. Members of the 1950 Jazz at the Phil unit, with the exception of Oscar Peterson, are featured in the film, which begins with a trio and builds up to the larger ensemble of Lester Young and Harry Edison, both veterans of *Jammin' the Blues,* along with Fitzgerald and Flip Phillips. This later effort does not quite clear the bar Mili and Granz set with the singular *Jammin' the Blues.* That said, the footage has undeniable documentary value, for like *Jammin' the Blues* it is one the few examples of moving images to convey a sense of Jazz at the Philharmonic concerts.

The 1950 JATP tour, which got under way at Carnegie Hall on September 16, featured the leanest frontline ever fielded by Granz, with Harry Edison, Bill Harris, Flip Phillips, and Lester Young assuming the leading roles and Jones, Brown, and Rich providing backup. Until the arrival of Fitzgerald and Peterson, Phillips was the undisputed star of JATP, although his role hardly diminished with their addition. Edison had ended his thirteen-year association with Count Basie the previous February when the bandleader dissolved his big band and temporarily led a septet until he re-formed a big band in 1952. Edison replaced Roy

Eldridge in his first appearance on the tour despite his long association with Granz. The replacement of Tommy Turk by the lanky Bill Harris returned to JATP one of its most distinctive, idiosyncratic, and hard-swinging trombone stylists. Harris and Phillips had known each other since their time in the Woody Herman band from 1944 through 1946 and had been occasional centerpieces of a quintet that worked when the two players were not otherwise engaged. Charlie Parker and strings were accompanied by pianist Al Haig, bassist Tommy Potter, and drummer Roy Haynes. The group was assembled especially for the Carnegie Hall show and played the following night at the National Guard Armory in Washington but did not make the remainder of the tour.

The tenth national tour leaving from New York and arriving in Los Angeles around the middle of November was scheduled to play forty-one cities in the United States and Canada, in addition to staging concerts at universities in Iowa, Michigan, and Missouri.[24] Jazz at the Philharmonic continued to pack halls in virtually every stop along the way. Ten of eleven dates leading up to the October 15 concert at the Civic Opera House were sold out. Some 4,200 fans at the Opera House filled every seat, occupied the pit, and crowded the stage with folding chairs.

But Peterson was the main story. In Chicago he had to beg off after half a dozen numbers to maintain the pace of the program "as he's been doing in every other town."[25] The grooming to prepare Peterson for his entry into the big leagues had begun immediately after Granz brought him to New York. Phillips fondly recalled helping Peterson learn the ways of the road, literally and figuratively. "Norman told him, 'You ride with Flip. He'll take care of you,'" said Phillips, who frequently had Granz as a passenger. Phillips taught him how to drive as well as rules of the road for a successful career. "He learned very well. I told him to stay away from the drugs and the drinking part. A couple of the guys used to get high, and there was a lot of drinking going on. Oscar stayed away from it."[26]

Peterson estimated his income for the year at around $60,000.[27] His first season with Jazz at the Philharmonic had been exhilarating but also intimidating. "That first tour with JATP was a strange thing," he recalled in 1952. "I was a rookie, a kid of twenty-five. I was like Mickey Mantle starting with the Yankees. I had heard about these big names, and now I was playing with them . . . To tell you the truth, I wasn't relaxed. I couldn't be sure of myself, of how the musicians and the public would accept my work. That tour was pretty rough for me just for that reason."[28]

"My real kick was being able to sit backstage and listen to Prez and Hawk and Roy Eldridge, and people like that," he said. "When I was playing the jam session, their needs took precedence over everything else. I wasn't looking to be a star . . . Most of the work with those various soloists was as an accompanist. Interspersed between it, I inevitably got a chance to play solo. I had to step very carefully, musically speaking."[29] With Lester Young, Peterson adjusted to the saxophonist's lyricism and provided the "harmonic carpet" that gave him the comfort margin for his solos. ("To me, Prez did a song from its title on.") Playing for Hawkins required him to adapt to a style based as much on his sound as on his harmonic complexities. ("We would lay some harmonic changes that he would run through as if he had planned them.") And then there were Eldridge's "strollers" that punctuated his irrepressibly fiery playing. ("That would be for me and the drummer to lay out. And it would just be the bass. Then he liked to have the rhythm section to come to full tilt behind him, and that's when he would explode on it.") "I learned a lot from the horns," he said.[30]

In 1952, Peterson and Granz decided the time had come for the pianist to move from duos into trios. They followed the model of piano, guitar, and bass introduced over a decade before by Nat Cole, an idol of Peterson's. The first to hold down the guitar chair, Irving Ashby, was famed for his association with Cole, which dated from when he had replaced Oscar Moore in October 1947. Ashby linked up with Peterson in March, just in time for Jazz at the Philharmonic's first European tour. His residency could be counted in months as Ashby gave way to Barney Kessel and shortly thereafter to Herb Ellis.[31]

Granz added to the string of luminaries on Clef with the signing of alto saxophonist Johnny Hodges, who made his first recordings for the label in January 1951 and then left the Ellington Orchestra within weeks. The date of Hodges's sudden departure from the band remains as unclear as the precise role Norman Granz may have had in encouraging the alto saxophonist to leave. Adding to the impact of the news was the simultaneous defection of trombonist Lawrence Brown and drummer Sonny Greer to join Hodges. Brown, a prominent member of the band since 1932, had never been particularly fond of Ellington and had been making noises for some time that he might leave over pay and other disputes. Greer's departure represented the end of an era for Ellington. The drummer was the last remaining member of his original band, the Washingtonians; however, his drinking and attendant unreliability had forced Ellington in 1950 to employ Butch Ballard as a backup drummer.[32] As with Brown, money issues figured to some extent in Hodges's decision, even though he was reportedly the highest paid member of the band. Hodges was also known to resent Ellington for cashing in on hit songs derived from his solos or catchy phrases. Many of the longer works increasingly featured by Ellington reduced opportunities for him to shine as a soloist. Also, Hodges, who had often recorded with small groups from within the band in the past, wanted a format that put his talent front and center. For his group, Hodges supplemented Brown and Greer with former Ellington tenor saxophonist Al Sears and ex-Basie trumpeter Emmett Berry, then filled out the rhythm section with Joe Benjamin on bass and Leroy Lovett on piano.

Granz's strongest statements about his role in instigating Hodges's departure from the Ellington Orchestra can be found in Derek Jewel's 1977 Ellington biography. Jewell described Granz's role as "crucial" in what writer Jack Chambers, writing from an extreme position of Ellington partisanship in 2001, called a calculated attempt by Granz to "ruin Ellington."[33] "Sure, I pulled Johnny and the others out of the band," Granz told Jewell. He and Hodges had known each other from the time *Jump for Joy* played Los Angeles and Granz was staging his first jam sessions, some of which featured Hodges. And when he presented Ellington in concert after the war he came to the conclusion that Hodges's talents were being underutilized. "I wanted to record him outside the Ellington context, and that's why he and the others came out," Granz said. "Harry Carney almost came too, but he was afraid to quit, and, anyway, we didn't need him." Further comments by Granz suggest that there might indeed have been a trace of malice in his action. "Duke liked things to go smoothly. If anything disturbed his equanimity, then it was a great drag to him. He was incredibly *égoiste* in the French sense."[34] Granz later offered a more nuanced (or revisionist?) account, saying that he did not exactly recall whether the move was his or Hodges's idea.[35]

What Ellington really felt about the sudden, wrenching loss of his favorite soloist remained his secret. He did not speak to Granz for a year, and there is little doubt that the episode affected the relationship between the two imperious men for years to come, though their paths crossed regularly for the remainder of Ellington's career. Within three weeks, Ellington was already rebounding after conducting a raid on Harry James's band in what came to be known as the "Great James Robbery." It netted him the services of alto saxophonist Willie

Smith (later replaced by Hilton Jefferson) and drummer Louie Bellson. Another bonus was the return of the valued trombonist Juan Tizol. Tizol, composer of such Ellington classics as "Caravan" and "Perdido," had been with the band since 1929 before linking up with James in 1944 and returned to him in 1953. Bellson won over his colleagues with his upbeat temperament and with playing that worked up the band "into more enthusiasm than they have known in years."[36] Ellington surely must have felt Granz was gunning for him when, shortly after Bellson joined the orchestra, the impresario dropped by a Detroit theater where the band was playing. "Bellson was my boy," Granz said. "As soon as Duke saw me, he said, 'Oh my God, you want Bellson,' and the bags under his eyes flopped to the floor. I told him, 'Man, I need a drummer,' and almost apologized for saying it, the way he looked."[37] Bellson actually stayed with Ellington until early 1953, when he got involved with his future wife, Pearl Bailey, and began to work for her. But he eventually played for a season with JATP in 1954 and thereafter frequently recorded for Granz.

Hodges returned in October 1955 to what Granz termed the "protective womb" of the Ellington Orchestra with a newfound appreciation for the sheer grit required to lead a musical organization. "Too many headaches," Hodges himself said succinctly of the experiences that led him to return to Ellington, armed with a well-paying contract renewal from Granz that allowed him to lead small groups in the studio when he wished, thus escaping other burdens of keeping a group together.[38]

If Granz had rocked Ellington's boat in 1951, he provided a safe harbor for two old friends, Count Basie and Billie Holiday, early the following year. Basie used a two-year hiatus after disbanding in 1950 to front a septet including Clark Terry, Wardell Gray, and Buddy DeFranco. With the encouragement of Billy Eckstine, Basie reconstituted a band with a musical identity and sound based on arrangements and ensemble playing that maintained the Basie tradition of swing and an unshakable bond with the blues. The so-called New Testament band propelled him into a new era of popularity that ended only with Basie's death in 1984. The sound that burst on the scene at Birdland and on Clef Records, though linked to the past through Basie and rhythm guitarist Freddie Green, departed from the rough-riding improvisation and celebrated individualism of former days that had been central to the band's style and presentation. Granz signed the band for a series of recordings that figured largely in Basie's resurgence. "I have to say that all those records that Norman began bringing out on Mercury and then

Clef and then Verve labels were very, very important," Basie remembered in his autobiography. "That was the main way the new band got nationwide exposure. Those first records were not big hits or anything like that, but there were disc jockeys playing them, and they were on the jukeboxes; and when we went out on those early tours, everywhere we went there were almost always some people waiting for us, mainly because they were aware of how the new band sounded."[39] For Granz's efforts, Albert Murray, who had assisted Basie in telling his life story, told Granz that he was nothing less than "the man who engraved the first tablets of the New Testament band."[40]

The band hit its stride when singer Joe Williams joined in 1954 and scored big with the hit vocal "Ev'ry Day (I Have the Blues)" and the instrumental "April in Paris." In announcing the signing, Granz aimed to continue producing a stream of big band recordings as well as featuring Basie's spare pianism in small-group settings. He did so in December 1952 by recording him with trumpeter Joe Newman, tenor saxophonist Paul Quinichette, Freddie Green, bassist Gene Ramey, and Buddy Rich. The following August, he used Basie for the second in a series of studio jam sessions. Basie was amenable to mixing it up in different musical settings in ways Granz believed other bandleaders were not. "You could do that with Basie," he said. "He really dug it, because Basie was the most 'down' of all the bunch of them."[41] Basie shared his enthusiasm for his new band toward the end of a series of concerts that Granz promoted featuring the band, Billy Eckstine, and George Shearing in the fall of 1952. "I'm crazy about this big band, Norman Granz, and Mercury," Basie said. "I've had better men, but none so enthusiastic and energetic. I'd like to keep the group together forever."[42] Granz's idea of recording him apart from the band, however, did not reach its full fruition until twenty years later with the founding of Pablo Records in 1973, resulting in some of Basie's most distinguished award-winning recordings.

Billie Holiday desperately needed the knowledgeable and compassionate guidance Granz provided to make a series of recordings that acquit themselves well alongside masterpieces she recorded for Columbia between 1933 and 1944 and her solid but more commercial recordings for Decca from 1944 to 1950, largely under the direction of Milt Gabler. By the early 1950s her scrapes with the law, continuing drug addiction and alcoholism, and unreliability had reduced avenues of work for her and undermined her chances of making quality recordings.

One episode during a 1952 Jazz at the Philharmonic concert showed what Granz faced during the next five years when he recorded Holiday.

Granz had hoped the evening would be an important one in reviving her faltering career, although it could not compensate for her loss, after a 1947 felony drug conviction, of the New York City cabaret card that had permitted her to work in the city's nightclubs. Oscar Peterson, with whose trio she made her first studio recordings for Granz, recalled that Holiday got off to a good start. "Norman thought it would be a great idea to have her as a surprise guest, even though he already had Ella. Ella thought it was a great idea, too. The first show was magnificent, and Billie's set was a thing of beauty."[43] The response to Holiday's set got a bit out of hand when whistles and catcalls marred the ambience as she sang "Lover Man." "Hold it," Granz instructed the pianist as he played the introduction to the next tune. "Ladies and gentlemen, I'm getting a little sick and tired of you few idiots who are spoiling the show for everybody. If it's going to continue, we're going to stop the concert until those people are thrown out. Now will you please shut up and let Billie Holiday sing!"[44]

In between shows, however, Holiday surrendered to her heroin addiction and was barely coherent when it came time for her second set. Peterson saw the worried look on Granz's face when it was time to bring Holiday back on. "She was like a sphinx, a graven image." Three attempts that he made to guide her into "I Only Have Eyes for You" went right past her. The whispers buzzing through the hall made the moment all the more grueling. "It was horrible," Peterson said.[45] No attempt by Peterson to jump-start her into the song broke through her stupor, and Granz finally came and led Holiday offstage, where she cursed the pianist and blamed him for the disaster.

Peterson later reflected on how the evening had affected Granz. "I knew what must have been going through his mind and his heart," he said. "I know that represented a huge failure for him, because he wanted this to be her really triumphant return to the New York scene."[46] Granz for his part was philosophical. "It was an unfortunate incident that Billie, physically, was unable to complete two shows," he said. "But it was one of those things. I don't think I ever held it against Billie."[47]

The eleventh national tour headlined by Fitzgerald and Peterson in 1951 saw the return of Roy Eldridge after a year's layoff and Illinois Jacquet playing his first full JATP season in five years. They joined a lineup that included Flip Phillips, Lester Young, Ray Brown, and Hank Jones. In addition, Granz took the opportunity of the breakup of Gene Krupa's second big band following the drummer's emergency appendectomy to entice him into the fold for what turned out to be three seasons ending in 1953. The talent alone cost Granz $12,000 a week.[48] The trademark hectic atmosphere of the concerts was counterbalanced by the addition in 1951 of a tasteful new feature. The ballad medley, knitted together by Oscar Peterson, gave players a chance to select songs they liked that often differed from night to night. Reviews of the midnight concert at Carnegie Hall blasted the audience and gave the music ratings from mixed to excellent. The *Down Beat* critic made some straightforward, if condescending, admissions about the gap between critics' and audiences' judgments of JATP: "Let's face it, JATP is not designed to please critics. The mere fact of our understanding music, and writing about it for a living, disqualified us from judging it from the viewpoint of the people for whom it was presented. . . . The fact is, too, that the worse the guys blow, the better the audiences will like it, and the musicians are cynically aware of this; as a result, to quote Bill Harris, 'You can't tell what a guy can blow from concerts.' To Norman's credit, though, something should be pointed out that his detractors overlook. He is bringing to crowds all over the country several great artists that no audience can spoil."[49] One has to wonder whether even this relatively balanced review of JATP might reflect how little effort Granz expended to court the jazz press or how much writers feared his merciless responses, often all-out personal attacks, to even the most glancing criticism.

Toward the end of his life Granz summarized his attitude toward most critics in remarks expressing a defiant pride in his ability to make shows happen and deliver work to musicians. "Leonard Feather or the *Metronome* duo of George T. Simon and Barry Ulanov or Nat Hentoff—or, above all, Whitney Balliett—none of them, they never left New York. I went places they never heard of so I could break even and keep the tour alive. Plus all the other aspects: hotels, food, being able to go to a restaurant, whether the bus would break down. They didn't even understand it. My position has been with the critics, quite simply, well, fuck 'em."[50]

Two dispatches from the road in 1951 confirm the impact that JATP and other jazz concert tours were having on the entertainment industry. The opening of the film *An American in Paris* in Houston was postponed to avoid going head to head to with a Duke Ellington/Nat Cole/Sarah Vaughan package called The Big Show *and* Jazz at the Philharmonic, both of which would be playing there on October 30. Granz had originally rescheduled from the thirty-first to the thirtieth to bypass the traffic and congestion of the Shrine Circus's performance in an adjoining venue that evening. He felt he would still come out ahead even after he became aware of the competing jazz triple-header. He was right. JATP, making its third annual stopover in the Bayou City, attracted some four thousand fans, while the Ellington/Cole/Vaughan show drew only half as many.[51] For three concerts in the Bay Area and Sacramento in mid-November, JATP produced one of the oddest footnotes in its history by outcompeting, not The Big Show, but the Biggest Show on Earth and grossing $37,000 in the process. The San Francisco Fire Department blocked the doors of the Civic Auditorium after four hundred extra chairs pushed attendance at JATP to just over eight thousand; another six thousand people saw the Oakland show. In contrast, the weekend engagement of the Ringling Brothers Circus at the Cow Palace in San Francisco the previous June had drawn only six thousand people.[52]

The popularity of jazz concerts was beyond dispute in the fall of 1951 when four major shows—JATP, Ellington/Cole/Vaughan, Stan Kenton, and Billy Eckstine and George Shearing—were on the road simultaneously, though some feared the music might be reaching a saturation point, particularly for the African American audiences at whom the shows were directed. But something else was afoot that indicated how completely Granz had succeeded in transforming how jazz reached its audiences. In December he pointed to evidence that the main impact of the proliferation of concerts was a decline in the business of ballrooms. Concertgoers were stretching their entertainment dollars by selecting events that offered several big names rather than those built around single artists. Success could be attributed as well to what he believed was actual growth in the number of fans. In some cases, he filled houses with two shows a night in cities where JATP had formerly played one; in others, venues that historically had been partially full were delivering standing-room-only business.[53]

Within months, Granz made the long-awaited announcement that JATP would be traveling abroad, where questions of a glut of touring jazz shows were nonexistent. "It's finally going to happen," he announced in March 1952 from his new headquarters at 451 North Canon Road in Beverly Hills on the eve of the tour's twelve-city sweep.[54] Making the tour were Ella Fitzgerald, the Oscar Peterson Trio with Ray Brown and Irving Ashby, Flip Phillips, Lester Young, Hank Jones, and Max Roach. The company left for Stockholm on March 26 in time to get acclimated for a continental swing that began there four nights later.

The scene that greeted their arrival on the tarmac was underwhelming, even though the audiences had snapped up all available tickets in six hours for two packed shows at the 2,100-seat Stockholm Concert Hall. "I've read that certain jazz groups were met by crowds ranging from 5,000 to 50,000 in size, and I looked forward to such a greeting," Granz wrote later. "Unfortunately, there were but two small boys who met us. One thought Oscar Peterson was Joe Louis, and the other was there to meet his mother. We rapidly surrounded them and made them take our autographs."[55] As expected, Fitzgerald and Peterson were the biggest hits, but each musician had fans who were thrilled to hear them in person. Photographs in a local newspaper depict a surreal postconcert reception that threw together members of JATP with the cast of a Stockholm production of *Porgy and Bess* still in blackface makeup.

The musicians traveled to do two shows each in Gothenberg and Malmö, with four concerts before a combined sixteen thousand people in Copenhagen squeezed in between. They landed in Paris for a midnight concert on April 6, closing out the second Paris Jazz Fair at the Salle Pleyel concert hall, where those without tickets shelled out between ten and twenty times the face value of tickets to get in the door.[56] It adds a symbolic touch of the meeting of future and past that Sidney Bechet was seen pushing his way through the crowd in the foyer of the Salle Pleyel to get to the JATP concert that followed his own.[57] The concert got under way only after the assertive Paris audience got a taste of its own medicine from the man who was on the verge of becoming the most important source in bringing American jazz musicians to Europe for the next twenty years.

Charles Delaunay, the director of the festival, had warned Granz that French fans boo and shout and whistle, but Granz countered that he would not allow the concert to begin until the hall had settled down. He simply stood silently at the microphone until he got the desired result. "I introduced the musicians on the jam session—Lester Young and Roy Eldridge receiving the biggest applause—and the concert started," he recalled.[58] As Flip Phillips went into "How High the Moon," the most boisterous of those who took seats on the stage ended up sitting on the floor at the feet of the musicians and were eventually cleared by gendarmes. "I don't think that Flip knew it, but the bedlam that broke loose didn't come from his playing but from the French police versus the French jazz fan. But finally everything quieted down, and from then on the concert was a beaut."

The musicians enjoyed three days off in Paris before picking up again with a concert in Brussels. Meanwhile, Granz, Peterson, and Phillips slipped into London on April 8, the same day the British Musicians'

Union notified Granz by letter that it had rejected his final offer to perform a charity concert. Granz met with Jack Chilkes of Melodisc about distributing his recordings in the British Isles before taking the musicians to a Savile Row tailor and a store specializing in fine Sheffield cutlery. Photographs in *Melody Maker* show the trio at Westminster Abbey and posing in the sports car of the magazine's columnist Max Jones.[59] Two days later, JATP performed in Brussels under the auspices of the Hot Club of Belgium. Granz put Belgian jazz fans on a par with the Swedes for being the most discerning. The Dutch press boycotted the concerts in Amsterdam after Granz begged off staging an airport news conference, although advance publicity had drummed up capacity crowds for the four shows in Amsterdam and The Hague on April 11 and 12. The tour continued with concerts in Geneva and Zurich on April 16 and 17 before closing out with two concerts in Frankfurt two days later. Granz chartered a bus in Geneva to show the musicians the splendor of the country that would become one of his homes beginning in 1959. In Bern, they lunched on escargot, a meal that went well enough until Phillips playfully informed Fitzgerald that the snail he had seen crawling up the wall minutes before had made its way to her plate. "That ended the snail proclivities for Ella," Granz said.[60] The two Frankfurt shows played before audiences composed predominantly of American soldiers; the musicians also performed a benefit concert at a local hospital.

Concertgoers and writers alike reacted to Lester Young's playing, ever more reflective of the alcoholism at the root of his physical and mental deterioration, with sadness and bewilderment. Reviews indicated that Phillips's playing had exceeded expectations, partly because of the contrast with Young's. Indeed, Phillips had been coupled with Young to compensate for the latter's weak physical condition and apparent indifference. "Lester's playing on record in the past few years has caused me much disappointment," wrote the British writer Mike Nevard of the Paris concert. "His solos at the Salle Pleyel dropped him even further in my estimation. In the second number, 'Undecided,' his playing was saturated with tricks. . . . Phillips's stage manner is more vaudevillian than Lester's, but his playing is more legitimate."[61] Of the Brussels concert, Nevard's colleague at *Melody Maker,* Steve Race, wrote, "Maybe I was too disappointed with Lester's playing to think of anything but how disappointed I was with it. If that is cool jazz, I'll take chili."[62] According to the late French publishing and broadcasting magnate Frank Tenot, who would later work for Granz as the label manager of Verve Records in France and promote his Paris shows in the 1960s, Granz had said it was not unusual for Young to play at full strength for only the ten minutes or so it took him to complete his featured numbers. The situation went even further downhill in subsequent tours. "In 1953 and '54, you see, Lester came to Paris with JATP, and he'd play quite nothing," Tenot said in 2001. "With JATP, you had Roy Eldridge, Charlie Shavers and all of these people, and they'd play solo after solo after solo, and Lester would only play 'I Cover the Waterfront' and then he'd go to a club and play all night."[63]

Granz was clearly elated that European audiences had embraced Jazz at the Philharmonic after so many thwarted attempts to export his concerts. He was impressed by fans' respect for the musicians and by well-informed daily and music papers that provided ample coverage. Support for jazz existed even though jazz programming on the radio was practically nonexistent. The biggest conduit for the music in postwar Europe was the American Forces Network and, beginning in 1956, Willis Conover's seminal jazz broadcasts for Voice of America. European fans were generally older than JATP audiences in the United States and as a result were equally appreciative but more restrained than in America. "They listen to you, applaud, and stamp their feet," Granz wrote. "But there is no shouting or whistling during a solo, or any of the outcries that mar a pretty tune."[64] He did not, however, adopt the commonly expressed view that fans' appreciation for jazz was *greater* in Europe than in the music's homeland; it was just different. The older cultures of Europe accounted for audiences that were more steeped in all the arts and were prepared to accept jazz as part of a bigger tapestry.

Another refreshing aspect of the European tour was the virtual absence of racism. Granz noted only two "drag incidents," both involving Americans, "who evidently haven't yet learned the meaning of the word 'democracy.'" In the first, two soldiers so obviously avoided Ella Fitzgerald and her cousin seated at the bar of the Victoria Hotel in Amsterdam that the other patrons left their tables and filled the remaining barstools in a show of support. In the second, Roy Eldridge was refused service by an American headwaiter in a German club where he had gone with friends. However, Granz was troubled by the attitude of some European jazz fans, especially the French, who he thought practiced a form of reverse racism by presuming black musicians to be more authentic jazz artists than white players simply on the basis of skin color. He hoped, prematurely as it turned out, that the positive reaction to Flip Phillips in Paris signaled a move away from the reverse discrimination of "Crow Jim." "This is just as wrong as the bias in the U.S. that's directed the other way," he wrote. "As a leader of a show which has both Negro and white musicians, I certainly intend to make the European tour a yearly one, since I like them to live as, and be treated like, normal human beings."[65]

Roaring drum battles between Gene Krupa and Buddy Rich set the pace for the twelfth national JATP sixty-one-city tour in 1952, which musically ran "the gamut from hot to frenzied."[66] For the Carnegie Hall concert, alto saxophonist Benny Carter made one of his rare trips east to join a bill starring Ella Fitzgerald; the Oscar Peterson Trio with Barney Kessel; a Krupa trio with Hank Jones and Willie Smith; a Rich quartet filled out with the Peterson Trio; Flip Phillips; Lester Young; Roy Eldridge; and trumpeter Charlie Shavers, fresh from one of his many stints with the Tommy Dorsey Orchestra. It was also the night of Billie Holiday's abbreviated drug-addled recital.

In October, in the midst of the JATP tour, Granz appears to have made a trip to Havana to add a little-noticed footnote to his already illustrious career by recording the first *descargo,* or jam session, in Cuba. The thirty-four-year-old pianist Bébo Valdes, pianist and arranger for Armando Romeu's Tropicana Hotel Orchestra, was approached by an American owner of a local record store who conveyed a message from Granz stating his doubts about Cubans' ability to play jazz. This challenge resulted in four sides being cut at the Havana Panart Studios by "Andre's All-Stars," named for the record store.[67]

Thus only ten years after Granz had begun his floating jam sessions in Los Angeles nightclubs, he was poised to become a jazz figure of global scope. This end was all but guaranteed after he was finally able to take advantage of the European concert market, with plans to more than double the schedule of concerts there the following year, including shows in London. Granz's visibility escalated in 1953 with a tour of Japan that, as in Europe, was endorsed by sold-out crowds every bit as enthusiastic as those in New York, Chicago, or Saginaw. He also found the time to produce some seventy-five sessions between 1950 and 1952 by using the profits the concerts yielded to become the most prolific independent jazz producer of the decade.

10

"I Feel Most at Home in the Studio"

A photograph of Frank Sinatra in March 1949 showed the singer admiring what he could not then have known would be the salvation of his career after his fabled postwar professional drought. Sinatra held a copy of his Columbia 78 rpm album, *The Voice of Frank Sinatra.* Edward Wallerstein, president of Columbia, and Mannie Sachs, one of the record executives who had dismissed Norman Granz's pitch on behalf of concert records four years before, likewise beamed as they displayed the company's revolutionary 33 1/3 rpm long-playing album of the same title.[1] Though Sinatra's comeback had begun with his 1953 Academy Award for *From Here to Eternity,* it was primarily due to his epic thematic and richly orchestrated "concept" albums for Capitol Records in 1955. LPs would preserve his most distinguished musical legacy. Such was also the case for his only rival in the arena of classic American popular song in the coming decade, Ella Fitzgerald.

Exploitation of new technology came naturally to Granz, who used the increased time available on LPs in two ways. He could finally reproduce the extended improvisations of JATP in studio recordings. Time was no longer the issue it had been when music had to be recorded on a 78 rpm record, which at best could capture a single solo or a portion of a symphonic movement. Granz's *The Jazz Scene* had revealed him to be a record producer who was thinking ahead of his time. The album was a precursor to such projects as *The Astaire Story,* the Art Tatum solo and group sessions, and ultimately the Ella Fitzgerald songbook series, in addition to encyclopedic recordings by Charlie Parker, Billie Holiday, Lester Young, Dizzy Gillespie, and the Oscar Peterson Trio, among others.

"As the originator of the recorded concert in jazz, with all the crowd noises, applause, and so forth, I have a special affection for the innovation of the long-playing record," Granz wrote in September 1953. "Apart from the classics, which normally are long works that are written out by the original composers, I know of no other musical form that has benefited as much as jazz has, and will, from the long-playing record."[2] The excitement that an artist strove for, Granz said, "was a cumulative one, and the jazz man must have the time to pace himself and build." The LP, along with the introduction around this time of magnetic tape, put an end to his practice of stretching improvisations over three and sometimes four sides. It permitted artists to record music at the length they might perform in personal appearances. Granz pressed the argument, maybe to the breaking point, that in jazz recording quantity equaled quality. "I think that this makes sense, because isn't it better to get a tremendous instrumental by a band on one number instead of four average performances?"

Whatever the medium, Granz's style of recording took on an assembly-line quality closely linked to JATP. A closer look at recording dates shows that he increasingly congregated multiple sessions around the start or conclusion of tours to take advantage of times when his artists were in one place at the same time long enough to produce a lot of records. The long-playing record came at a time when Granz was flush with cash to record the stars of JATP, sign other top jazz talent, and spend as much time in the studio as he could. "I feel most at home in the studio," Granz said around this time.

A typical spate of recording in Los Angeles between July 31 and September 7, 1955 (picking up briefly in New York), shows Granz's hectic schedule. Such periods of activity were common through the Clef and Norgran years and would continue to be when he founded Verve in 1956. On the last day of July Lionel Hampton recorded an album featuring Teddy Wilson and Gene Krupa. On August 1 Hampton was on deck for a recording with Stan Getz and a trio date with Art Tatum and Buddy Rich. On August 2 the vibraphonist returned to the studio for a big band recording and the next day as part of a sextet, for a total of five albums in four days. Granz recorded Getz, in town for the production of the film *The Benny Goodman Story*, for an album entitled *West Coast Jazz* on August 9 and completed the record six days later before recording him again on August 19 in a quartet with pianist Lou Levy, bassist Leroy Vinnegar, and drummer Shelly Manne (all of whom had participated in the *West Coast Jazz* sessions). On August 10 and 11, the vocalist and guitarist Stan Wilson recorded an album. Also on the eleventh, Anita O'Day recorded four titles with Jimmy Rowles, guitarist Tal Farlow, Vinnegar, and Larry Bunker on drums, while Farlow came in the next day for a date with clarinetist Buddy DeFranco. On August 23 and again two days later, Billie Holiday recorded with Benny Carter, Harry Edison, Barney Kessel, John Simmons, Bunker, and Rowles, all of whom played under Buddy Rich's leadership on August 26. De Franco completed his album the same day; three days later, Granz recorded Joe Sullivan playing solo piano. Hampton closed out the Los Angeles summer dates with a sextet on September 6 and with Tatum, Edison, Kessel, Red Callender, and Rich on September 7. In New York, Granz recorded Johnny Hodges with a small group, Ben Webster and strings, Dizzy Gillespie with a big band, and a Lawrence Brown group between September 8 and 14 before JATP started at Carnegie Hall on September 17.

Granz centered his labels Clef and Norgran on mainstream jazz, the blend of swing and bop era styles long associated with Jazz at the Philharmonic. The volume of recordings grew so swiftly that he had to parcel out his artists between Clef and the newer label and channel them through different distributors. At that point, Clef, which became independent in 1953 and included his entire Mercury catalog, became home to such artists as Charlie Parker, Art Tatum, Count Basie, Gene Krupa, Oscar Peterson, Illinois Jacquet, Teddy Wilson, Benny Carter, Roy Eldridge, Flip Phillips, Billie Holiday, the studio jam sessions, and Jazz at the Philharmonic. Norgran hosted the talents of Dizzy Gillespie, Stan Getz, Johnny Hodges, Buddy DeFranco, Ben Webster, Lester Young, Charlie Ventura, Buddy Rich, Louie Bellson, Bill Harris, and Chico O'Farrill.[3] Granz's choices as to which artist went with which label often appear to be arbitrary ones to solve his problem of getting his records before the public.

Despite the losses incurred by many of his recording enterprises, Granz was able to use both concert revenue and the tax code to keep the records coming and make his company larger than other independent labels. "The records were, as far as I am concerned, a labor of love," Granz said in 2000. "I recorded people who would never recoup. Never. I did it because I liked what I was doing, and I could afford it.

It was tax money. I mean, if the concerts made $1,000, $500 went for taxes. So if I lost $500 on a recording, the government paid half."[4] Not all observers of the jazz scene made the connection. Bill Coss of *Metronome* wondered "where the money-making side of Granz fits into the record company," as "so much of what he has recorded . . . is really out of the commercial jazz class that dominates the releases of most major labels—and Clef and Norgran are major labels, make no mistake about that."[5] Coss was prescient, however, in identifying Granz's contribution: though Granz might be "too closely eying the past, . . . in so doing he has made sure that we will have much to listen to in the future" in ways that made him "more of a benefactor than a impresario."[6]

The upswing in Granz's recording schedule becomes visible during the last three years he produced jazz on Mercury. Between 1950 and 1952, he produced 20, 19, and 60 sessions, respectively, followed by 44, 75, and 59 studio dates in the years 1953, 1954, and 1955 for a total of around 357 recording sessions between New York and Los Angeles over the six-year period.[7]

If Granz was opinionated about the artists he recorded, he held equally strong views about recording jazz. "He would say, 'I've got the best musicians in the world. One take, that's it,'" Ray Brown recalled. "Nobody said, 'Aw, we want more than one take.' It gets you off your ass."[8] Granz believed, quoting Ellington, that the "virgin take" caught the truest rendering of the jazz musicians' art. "That really was the purest and the best," he said. "I don't hold with people that review that in the eighty-third bar the third trumpet player made a mistake. I don't accept that. That's ridiculous! You can keep recording forever until you get a perfectly sterile record. I wasn't selling perfection."[9] Likewise, Granz was not enamored of all the possibilities available with magnetic tape. The development of stereo and later multitrack recording transformed what went on in the studio into what he called an "engineer's domain." This extended to determining the sound mix and the ability to splice tape to create "perfect" takes. On Granz's wall at his Beverly Hills office in the 1950s was a David Stone Martin cartoon, presented to him by Fred Astaire, of a man hanging from a tree by his toes with a caption reading "He suggested intercutting at a Granz date."[10]

That Granz wanted to record what he ideally hoped to be the first and best impression did not mean he conducted recording sessions with one eye fixed on the clock. The photographer Herman Leonard recalled that the freedom Granz encouraged in the photographing of the sessions was the same he extended to musicians to produce work that satisfied their standards. "He never told me what he wanted specifically. He said, 'Go ahead and shoot,'" Leonard said. "I approached it from a *reportage* angle."[11] Leonard said that among Granz's skills none were more important on occasion than those of a "strong diplomat." "He handled artists' idiosyncrasies with great skill, but was firm about what he wanted," Leonard continued. "But he was also very encouraging of the musicians in allowing them to do what they could do without trying to filter it, alter it, or direct it in any manner. He had no qualms about going into overtime. He just spent money like there was no tomorrow as long as he got the results . . . I worked with a lot of other record companies and other A&R men. They were more invasive in the product—Norman was freer, less critical. I think the guys had more fun with Norman. See, he was independent. They other guys were not independent. He couldn't lose his job."

"If you listen to Duke in the early days, he recorded on one mic, period," Granz said in a 2001 interview.[12] Soloists like Johnny Hodges worked the mic by edging closer or further away and hearing all the other music going on around them. "What came out were the dynamics of the musicians hearing themselves play and recording the way they wanted it to sound." Later, when musicians regularly wore headphones and were sometimes partitioned off from one another, Granz could hear hairline fractures in timing when players were prevented from hearing each other's sound directly, creating recordings he found artificial and in need of an engineer's work to revive as best they could a natural sound.

Granz had a similar philosophy about his concert recordings in that he favored minimal amplification and saw concerts as events for the audience first and recording opportunities second. "When I did a concert, it was a pure concert. The recording was in a sense a happenstance," Granz said. "I wouldn't even allow photographers to come to my concerts on the theory that, if you paid five dollars, why should you look at the rear end of a photographer? I'm not stupid of course. If the *New York Times* or someone sends a photographer, I want publicity. But at what price?"[13]

The Astaire Story was a four-LP set of Fred Astaire singing, with jazz backup, the Great American Songbook standards that he more than any other jazz or pop artist had been responsible for introducing on stage and in his films between 1926 and 1944. Begun in late February 1952 and released in 1953, the project shows Granz's dual role as an A&R man and as an ardent and original chronicler of American music. The collaboration with Astaire at Radio Recorders Studio in Los Angeles added another distinguished volume to Granz's recorded works. His love of Astaire dated back to Roosevelt High School when, by his own count, he had seen *Top Hat* at least twenty times. Granz had memorized the lyrics and dance steps in the hopes that he might get a role in the chorus at one of the studios and maybe appear in an Astaire movie. He secretly enrolled in a night dance class in the Wilshire District and made the trip by streetcar from Boyle Heights two to three nights a week. "I bought a pair of Capezio tap shoes, put them in a plain brown bag, and happily made the trips. Of course, I had no place to practice," Granz wrote in an unpublished memoir. Despite that, he did fairly well and retained the basic elements of tap dancing. "It all came to nothing as far as becoming a professional, but most importantly, it brought me closer to my idol Fred Astaire." He credited to Astaire his lifelong love of composers like George and Ira Gershwin, Cole Porter, Irving Berlin, Dorothy Fields, Johnny Mercer, and Jerome Kern.[14]

Granz originally conceived of *The Astaire Story* as a personal project to be presented exclusively to friends "for kicks." He got Astaire's number through a mutual acquaintance and called to query him about his idea. "He'd never heard of me, said he wasn't interested. He was curious as to why I wanted to do it. Astaire was going out of town for the weekend, and asked that I call him [the following week]. I knew I was dead and nothing would come of it. For starters, Astaire was no fan of his own singing, and could not understand why anyone else wanted to record him."[15]

That same day Granz decided at the last minute to attend an Ellington concert at the Shrine Auditorium. "During intermission, I looked around and right behind me, out of all those thousands of people, were Astaire and his son," he recalled. Fred Jr. had all the Jazz at the Philharmonic albums and Astaire heard the music at home. Astaire signed off on the project when Granz showed him *The Jazz Scene*. "As he explained his purpose and how it would be done, I began to see it," Astaire said. "The idea was attractive to me because of his attitude and approach to the concept."[16]

Granz "practically lived with Astaire for weeks," poring over every song in his repertoire, closely questioning Astaire about the music, and including many verses largely unknown outside their original settings in plays or films.[17] The two men eventually selected a program of thirty-four tunes representing a roll call of composers who had written especially for Astaire, in addition to four improvisations, three of which Astaire danced to. Granz set aside his original idea of big band arrangements and brought in Oscar Peterson to meet Astaire and work through further preparations before five other musicians convened. "I was struck by the meticulous preparation and research Norman had done. He'd chosen the musicians for versatility, studio know-how and breadth of idiomatic grasp," Peterson later recalled. Barney Kessel, Ray Brown, Flip Phillips, Charlie Shavers, the drummer Alvin Stoller, and Peterson made up the group, and the project expanded into fifteen sessions in December 1952. Gjon Mili's pictures show Astaire not in his customary finery (except for an ascot) but casually dressed like the musicians in a fedora or straw hat and deeply engrossed. During one rehearsal, Astaire, a closet drummer with a trap set in his living room, temporarily assumed Stoller's place, leading Peterson to observe, "What a riot! To hear his time with Ray's vast sound was quite an event, and the look of rapt intent on Fred's face was a joy to behold."[18]

The marathon sessions produced results of an understated conversational beauty. Restrained, expressive, silken solos revealed and complemented the intimacy of Astaire's performances and confirmed the depth of Granz's conviction regarding his affinity for jazz singing. The signed and numbered limited-edition set, with a sale price of $50 (like *The Jazz Scene,* a benchmark in the price of a recording), carried the imprimatur of a Granz production, complete with a portfolio of David Stone Martin drawings on cotton rag paper, photographs by Mili and his assistant Paul Nodler, and pressings on high-grade virgin vinyl imported from India. The session had obviously meant a great deal to Astaire, who presented each musician with a gold identification bracelet bearing the legend "With thanks, Fred A."

Astaire was so impressed with Granz that shortly after the project was complete he offered to enlist as a partner in Granz's record companies—no small offer from a man whose films with Ginger Rogers had saved United Artists Studio during the Depression. Granz demurred. "I'm flattered, Fred," he said. "I think it is very generous of you, and I am totally sure you would lose your investment. My company is run on a strange personal basis, as I have no intention of making money, but rather making unique and special recordings. My concerts support the record company, the company is not successfully self-supporting."[19]

Around the same time as the Astaire project, Granz also brought together three of the greatest alto saxophone players in jazz history, Charlie Parker, Benny Carter, and Johnny Hodges, in their one and only jam session, and indeed the only time they would ever play together. Granz saw his opportunity to fulfill a long-standing dream when the three saxophonists had simultaneous engagements in Los Angeles in June 1952, and he immediately corralled them into the studios of Radio Recorders. Filling out the roster was a rhythm section composed of Oscar Peterson, Ray Brown, Barney Kessel, and drummer J. C. Heard, tenor saxophonists Ben Webster and Flip Phillips, and Charlie Shavers. The resulting recordings, commonly known as "The Funky Blues" session, would later be reissued as *The Charlie Parker Jam Session,* although actually Carter was the group's leader, in his recording debut for Granz.

Scattered photographs from the session that also produced "Jam Blues," "What Is This Thing Called Love," and a ballad medley have been published almost since the date of recording, including a famous image of a forlorn-looking Parker in a rumpled white suit sitting on an empty horn case. In the mid-1990s, Hank O'Neal, the photographer, photo historian, and president of the jazz label Chiaroscuro Records, saw the Parker image in a Sotheby's auction catalog and tracked it to its source. He was astonished when he met New York magazine photographer Esther Bubley, who had taken over three hundred photographs at the session. After David Stone Martin had met her in the lobby of their Los Angeles hotel, he had spontaneously invited her to join him in watching the musicians at work. She worked so inconspicuously that almost no one recalled her ever being present. Bubley supplied Martin with prints that he eventually used to sketch the album cover. In 1996 Bubley and O'Neal published a book of photographs from the session that was artistically satisfying in and of itself as well as being an invaluable document in the history of jazz and of Norman Granz.

The pictures are striking given Bubley's unfamiliarity with jazz and the artists she encountered. She never heard the recordings, even after O'Neal gave her a reissue on a compact disc over forty years later. (She did not own a CD player.) Bubley's freshness permitted her to improvise on her own skills as a photographer to convey the individuality of the musicians and the essence of the proceedings. Her pictures focus on the humanity of her subjects: sharing a joke or road story; lighting a cigarette; Hodges at the keyboard explaining an idea to Peterson; Parker and Granz gesturing through the glass of the control booth; instrument cases and horns at rest amid studio risers; Kessel meditatively listening to a playback; Shavers in mid-solo; and Parker, Kessel, and Peterson sequestered in a corner of the studio as the clock inched toward seven in the evening.

In Bubley's photographs, Granz, dressed at his most casual, appears only periodically and mostly on the fringes: sitting with head bowed and face cupped in his hands as the musicians deliberate; ensconced in the control booth; passing the time with Shavers in between takes. His willingness to stay at the sidelines subtly suggests his surefootedness in directing a congregation of independent-minded jazz giants with strong personalities. As O'Neal pointed out, Granz's philosophical embrace of the primacy of improvisation limited his capacity to control the session even if he were so inclined. He could not foresee the results, only that he expected to record enough music for one longplaying record. As it turned out, there was enough for two, *Norman Granz Jam Session #1* and *#2*.

Around this time, Granz took it upon himself to repay what he saw as a debt jazz owed Art Tatum by single-handedly producing a library of the pianist's work. It remains one of his most audacious recording projects and one he considered a high point of his career. Aside from a record Tatum made for Capitol Records with bassist Slam Stewart and guitarist Everett Barksdale in 1952, he had not recorded between late 1949 and December 1953, when Granz began a series of solo and small group recordings. Granz even thought about creating a special label named for the pianist to release the recordings. The first session, held on December 28 and 29, 1953, was scheduled to get under way around nine o'clock. Granz supplied a case of beer and Tatum came equipped with a portable radio to hear intermittent snatches of a UCLA basketball game. After listening to the game and sipping his brew for around half an hour, Tatum said, "Let's go."[20]

Tatum told Voice of America broadcaster Willis Conover in a rare interview that they cut around one hundred tunes over the next four hours, although it hardly matters that the actual number was only an astonishing sixty-nine. Furthermore, with Tatum, no playback was required to slow them down. "Every master you go straight down," Tatum said. "There are no retakes. You can do that when you're playing piano solo, and you don't have to worry about anybody else."[21] Granz recalled that a tape ran out as Tatum was playing the final number of the evening, "Mighty Lak a Rose." "Art being almost blind, we couldn't send him a signal, so we let him play on two minutes until the end of the number," Granz said. Afterwards Tatum, rather than taking it from the top, asked to hear only the last eight bars. He would pick it up from there and complete the take. "In that two minutes, Art wasn't one second out of his timing," Granz continued. "His time on the second take was the same as we'd timed on the first."[22]

In additional sessions in April 1954 and January 1955, Tatum recorded a total of 120 solos issued on Clef as fourteen single albums or three boxed sets called *The Genius of Art Tatum* and later reissued on Pablo as *The Art Tatum Solo Masterpieces* and inducted into the Grammy Hall of Fame in 1975. Tatum's biographer James Lester stated the obvious when he called the project "unprecedented in the recording industry."[23] Granz's offer to Tatum placed no restrictions on material or time. It was Tatum's call to focus on long-established interpretations of standards and other tunes from his repertoire, ranging on average from three to six minutes long.

Beginning in June 1954 and continuing until within weeks of his death in November 1955, Granz recorded Tatum in what he later called the group masterpieces. The series includes sides with Benny Carter, Roy Eldridge, Lionel Hampton, Ben Webster, Buddy DeFranco, Harry Edison, Barney Kessel, drummers Louie Bellson, Buddy Rich, Jo Jones, and Alvin Stoller, and bassists Red Callender, Bill Douglass, and John Simmons. Although all of the group recordings are excellent, those with Hampton and Webster have been deemed most successful, probably because Tatum's collaborators here were comfortable enough not to attempt to compete with Tatum on his terrain. In turn, Tatum held in check as best he could his busy accompaniment that sometimes distracted soloists when they realized he was, in effect, soloing simultaneously behind them. Red Callender, Tatum's regular bassist in Los Angeles who was on the Webster date, recalled, "They were old buddies. It was beautiful because Ben was playing Ben and Tatum was playing Tatum. That was the idea of the thing. But most people who played with Art usually got all shook up."[24]

DeFranco recalled his date with Tatum in February 1956 as an "intimidating" experience, compounded by a bad case of flu. He let Tatum call the tunes, while Granz may have also weighed in on a few. "I deferred to Art because of his stature," he said. "I never wanted to impose on a genius. He called most of the shots and the keys. It was okay with me because he was the top man. He was very encouraging, a delightful guy."[25]

Louie Bellson, who played on the Tatum/Benny Carter session, said that at one point Carter had called a tune the pianist, famous for his scope of knowledge of tunes and their verses, did not know. "He told Benny just to play the melody on the saxophone, which Benny did, you know, no chords or anything. And when he played it, Benny Carter looked at me and he said, 'Do you realize this man didn't know the chords and he played all the right chords and went way beyond that!'"[26] Tatum later told Callender that the Carter session had been a little too tedious for his taste. "It was a kick when Art told me about the date because Benny is a very dominating character," Callender wrote. "Art says, 'That cat was really screwing around with his horn. We cut something, and he wanted to do it over again, his solo wasn't right, he tells me. Finally I had to tell him, Man, I wish you'd get yourself together because I can't hang around here all day.'"[27]

It is hard to imagine that such a uniquely comprehensive, overdue, and timely undertaking drew any critical reproach. But the solo masterpieces, in particular, gathered their share of fire. The most severe came from French critic André Hodeir, who thought Tatum should have stretched beyond his normal repertoire of what he termed "popular hits." In his controversial 1955 review of the first five-album boxed set, Hodeir conceded that Tatum was at the top of the heap among jazz pianists but nonetheless concluded, "He shows no evident desire to depart from the main theme. It is all played according to the rules. One need hardly say that Tatum does this better than anyone else, equipped as he is with greater technical means and a better imagination than one finds in any other pianist."[28] In fact, Hodeir's remarks are consistent with the oft-repeated observation that Tatum's best performances were in after-hours settings where he felt less inhibited about opening the spigot on his seemingly limitless abilities and where he was known to play more pure blues and even sing than in his public repertoire of mainly standards.

But Gunther Schuller spoke for many in challenging Hodeir. He claimed that "the uniqueness and solitary nature of [Tatum's] art" defied stylistic changes in jazz and criticized jazz observers "who require everything in jazz to fit neatly into definable classifications."[29] Schuller praised the pianist's astonishing technique, which he felt was continuing to advance even at the time of the Granz recordings. "Certainly this heroic effort does not deserve the petulant, caviling, unreasonable, and often incoherent criticism unleashed upon it by André Hodeir."[30]

Granz's extensive recordings of Billie Holiday required another type of commitment. "Norman will keep the studio open as long as I think I can make it. He'll cut anything. That's why I like working for the cat," Holiday confessed to her longtime friend, the pianist Jimmy Rowles, in August 1955 as they prepared to go into the studio for Granz the next day.[31] At the time hardly any other record producer would have even thought of employing her, much less signing for an extended series of dates, and her problems required all of Granz's skills to address. For many years Holiday had primarily performed relatively slow- and medium-tempo songs and used them as standbys in her concert and club appearances. "It hurt her in some of the gigs, because the critics would jump on her and say, "She's doing the same 'Miss Brown to You' and 'What a Little Moonlight Can Do,' you know, her repertoire," Granz said.[32] So Granz began enlarging her offerings to include standards by top composers that she had long overlooked. He also worked hard to create a comfort level for Holiday by surrounding her with veterans from her 1930s and 1940s recordings. The result was that he produced the best work of her remaining years. "Everyone wanted to work with Billie," said Granz, who let Holiday make the final choice. "There was never a scintilla of doubt that I couldn't come up with the best accompaniment. My relationship with Billie was like with any other recording artist. There was nothing unique or difficult about it."[33] However, her physical and emotional state was such that he did not dare interrupt a take to ask her to pick up the tempo or offer suggestions, as he might have with other artists. "I knew her too well, and it would just cause her to get worse."

Rowles accompanied her on all of her recording sessions in Los Angeles in what were easily some of her best with Clef and Verve, featuring Harry Edison, Barney Kessel, Benny Carter, and Ben Webster. "The Verve sessions usually started around 2:30. There was always enough to drink, and Norman sent out for sandwiches if anyone was hungry. Billie and I would be working out keys and a basic set of chords so we would have an idea of what was going on. The key we recorded in depended by and large on what she had been doing the night before. If she had been celebrating, her voice might be a little rougher than normal. We got into some pretty weird keys trying to smooth over the ups and downs of her voice. The sessions were totally relaxed. They were really like jam sessions. Norman's head is one big jam session." Engineer Bones Howe recalled one day when Holiday came to the studio. "There was no greater legend than Billie Holiday," Howe said. "She came in one day, spent about a half an hour coughing and spitting, and recorded 'Sophisticated Lady.'"[34]

Herman Leonard, who first photographed Holiday in 1949, remembers being shocked at her appearance, obviously worn down and drunk, when he attended a June 1956 date in New York for the *Lady Sings the Blues* album. She was in such obvious distress that Leonard has never displayed or published all the photographs. "I was afraid to even take the pictures," Leonard said. At one point, he retreated into the booth with Granz as Holiday studied arrangements with the musicians.

"You can't use these pictures on your album covers, she looks awful," Herman said.

"Get your ass out there and shoot because it may be your last time," Granz replied.

It was.[35]

Among Granz's recordings, none remain as controversial as those with Charlie Parker. Parker was one of the seminal figures in jazz, who before the Granz period had completed his most prolific period of recording at his creative peak. Parker's output between 1947 and 1949 was approximately eight times that between 1944 and 1946.[36] The volume of previous recordings alone intensified the historical scrutiny on Granz when he obtained exclusive rights to record Parker in 1948, rights he would keep for the remainder of Parker's life, and made these recordings more widely available through a distribution network superior to those of Dial and Savoy. The Granz era took off when the saxophonist's popularity was on the rise, as registered by his hit recording of "Just Friends" and the naming of the nightclub Birdland.[37] As with Billie Holiday, chronic drug and alcohol abuse blunted his creative impulses and made him more unpredictable than ever. Where once he had practiced exhaustively from dawn to well past dusk perfecting his technique, now his habit and extracurricular activities eviscerated his practice routine and made it virtually impossible to maintain regular accompanists. Granz often resorted to the tactic of making up for a musician's loss of direction and vision concerning his career by placing him or her in different, often one-of-a-kind settings. His ability to ante up substantial financial resources certainly redirected Parker's recording career.

Many critics have discussed the "what-might-have-beens" of Parker's potential. Most cited are comments from the late 1940s onward about his love of classical composers, from Debussy and Beethoven to such leading modernist figures as Hindemith, Schoenberg, and Stravinsky. But Parker, unlike John Coltrane, was unable to return to his earlier revolutionary "woodshedding" period to find a new musical direction for himself at a time when his life on the whole was disintegrating.

Norman Granz's plans for recording Charlie Parker began in earnest in 1949 with a series of recordings ending in 1954. The ever-changing conditions under which Granz recorded Parker, especially during the 1950s, opened him up to criticism about whether his Parker recordings lacked coherence. The Parker case energized and may best illustrate issues raised by critics about aspects of Granz's recording philosophy in general and whether he adulterated the music of jazz artists to popularize them. Yet the output of sessions was more likely to reflect the musician's wishes and other exigencies of the moment, such as the availability of musicians on a specific date and an artist's choice of material, than any design by Granz. The strongest argument on Granz's behalf is that he had the sharpest instincts in jazz for reaching a mass audience but hated the idea of diluting the spirit of the music. His growing financial success meant he was able to take chances on projects that other small independent labels might have considered too expensive, of insufficient interest, or involving material that would challenge an artist's identity based on previous work.

Granz recorded Parker six times during 1949. In January, Parker and Machito's Afro-Cubans joined forces to record "Okiedokie," co-written by Machito and the band's pianist Rene Hernandez. Then came the February 11 JATP Carnegie Hall concert recordings released in 2002. Parker went into the studio, probably in March, with his regular working group—trumpeter Kenny Dorham, pianist Al Haig, bassist Tommy Potter, and drummer Max Roach—plus trombonist Tommy Turk and Carlos Vidal on congas, a mainstay of the post–Chano Pozo Afro-Cuban jazz scene, to record two Parker compositions, "Cardboard" and "Visa." On May 5, Granz hastily assembled just Parker and his working group (no extra players) for the only time in a studio setting. The jazz historian and broadcaster Phil Schaap, who assembled *Bird: The Complete Charlie Parker on Verve,* attributed this circumstance to Parker's imminent departure for the Paris International Festival of Jazz and Granz's desire to have some material on reserve with the group Parker used at the event. "There was a code: get to your best shit fast," Roach told Schaap. "Don't fool around, get to your climax now . . . And I know we did this in about three hours. I know that was it."[38] Granz recorded Parker as part of the group that opened the fall JATP tour at Carnegie Hall on September 17.

The final and best-known collaboration of the year, *Charlie Parker with Strings,* was the most acclaimed by the public but also the most attacked by critics. Granz turned to Mitch Miller, who was then head of A&R at Mercury and later would hold the same position at Columbia, to serve as the contractor for the date. Miller, who played oboe, in turn hired his lifelong friend Jimmy Carroll to prepare and conduct arrangements of standards for Parker with three violins, cello, viola, harp, and a rhythm section consisting of the studio pianist Stan Freeman, plus Ray Brown and Buddy Rich. Parker would be paid $4,100 for the sessions.

One telltale sign of the confusion surrounding the recording of *Charlie Parker with Strings* is the uncertainty regarding actual dates for the six tunes issued as an album the following spring. It has never been established whether November 30, the date given for the recordings, represents the opening session when Parker recorded only one number or the occasion when the remaining five numbers were completed. In any event, Granz recalled that Parker had come to the studio so disoriented he could barely play but had managed to polish off a complete take on "Just Friends," the undisputed masterpiece of the series.

"We started and Charlie was physically out of it," Granz said. "We did 'Just Friends,' and everything went magnificently. After that, everything went downhill. I remember one of the violin players said, 'Look, we know what a drag it is. You don't have to pay us.'" Freeman said that there were no formal rehearsals and that the arrangements were worked out at the sessions. Three or four other sessions were scheduled and then canceled because of Parker's addled condition, which made him unable to focus on the task at hand. At one point, Granz told an irritated Mitch Miller that Parker was too overcome by the beauty of the music to play and denied that Parker had been sidetracked by drugs.[39] "I was living in New York then, so I could adjust the program to suit the musician," Granz recalled. "Charlie came back, and we finished the album. Everybody raves about 'Just Friends.' It was nothing that I did."[40]

The single of "Just Friends" was the best-selling record of Parker's career. It was the sole recording he felt was good enough to play as an example of his work for the physician who attended him in the days leading up to his death in 1955. Likewise, the record-buying public warmed to the album rounded out by "Everything Happens to Me," "April in Paris," "Summertime," "I Didn't Know What Time It Was," and "If I Should Lose You"—all solid songs worthy of Parker's efforts.

Metronome and *Down Beat* squared off on the issue of the album's merits. *Metronome* noted that its review of *Charlie Parker with Strings* was late because of a feud with Granz that had kept the magazine from getting an advance copy. "We're here to state that with the exception of 'Just Friends,' we're *not* for it. . . . Bird with strings may have seemed like a good idea, and 'Just Friends' proves it could have been."[41] The review in *Down Beat,* by comparison, was high praise: "These are the much-heralded Parker sides with a kicking jazz rhythm section, and Parker playing. Listen to the man run on in 'Just Friends,' 'tis enough said. . . . The boys who feel that boppists play no melody whatsoever are in for trouble with this Norman Granz date."[42]

Opinion long after the fact remains mixed. The critic Martin Williams, writing in 1970, dismissed the recordings as he did most of Parker's work for Granz: "It was perhaps in some search for form beyond the soloist's form, and for refuge from the awful dependency on the inspiration and intuition of the moment (as well as a half-willing search for popular success) that he took on the mere *format* of strings, the *doo-wah* vocal groups, the Latin percussive gimmicks." Over twenty-five years later, Carl Woideck conceded the brilliance of "Just Friends" but pronounced the concept second rate. The playing, he said, was pumped up with "common Hollywood arrangements" that added nothing substantial to Parker's discography.[43] Schaap believes that such "purist" criticism found its mark, "influenc[ing] a generation of record buyers to such an extent that these wonderful recordings have been passed over for too many years."[44]

It has been long suggested that recording Parker with strings was an idea foisted on him by Granz, but in fact it was an opportunity the saxophonist had long coveted.[45] Parker himself said, "I was looking for new ways of saying things musically. New sound combinations. . . . Why, I asked for strings as far back as 1941, and then, years later, when I went with Norman, he okayed it."[46] But comments Granz made in London in April 1950 raise questions about the provenance of the project and the initial appeal to Parker. "Well, he was pretty skeptical when I first suggested the idea to him," he said. "I finally talked him into coming along, however, and when he met the fellows accompanying him he began to show interest. In fact, Charlie thinks now that the results are some of the best he has made, and really treasures them."[47]

Granz remained forever galled by what he considered unfair and ill-informed criticism of the records and by accusations that Bird had somehow compromised himself. "To say Charlie Parker played differently means that he was really dampened by strings, but that's untrue," he said in 1972. "That's the whole point. Because he was so strong, which is why he was great, he could supersede any kind of a background." On another occasion, he said, "They bitch about *Charlie Parker with Strings,* and that always seems to be a pet peeve of everyone, well, without that, there would have been an important part of Bird's life out the window."[48]

Yet another Granz project was the June 6, 1950, session reuniting Parker and Dizzy Gillespie for their last studio recording together, one of five Parker sessions recorded for Granz that year. The date is also

noteworthy for the appearance of Thelonious Monk in his first recording since July 1948, possibly to give him exposure after a dearth of
recent recordings. Bassist Curly Russell resumed his place in the quintet
that made history at the Three Deuces in 1945. Feathers were ruffled,
however, by the inclusion of Buddy Rich rather than Roy Haynes, who
was in Parker's working group at the time. Ross Russell, the owner
of Dial Records, sarcastically called the substitution one of Granz's
"brainstorms,"[49] and Haynes himself complained that Granz had denied
Parker's request to include him. "Before a session, Bird would show
Norman the list of musicians he'd like to use," Haynes said. "Everything would be all right until he got to my name."[50] Granz, however,
batted back this allegation in a 1987 interview. "Maybe Charlie Parker
wanted Buddy," he said. "That's obviously what happened. I'm too old
to be amazed or astonished by people. I've never used an artist that I
would impose on by saying, 'You've got to use this other musician, or
not. . . . If I want to get the best out of Lester Young or Artie Shaw, or
whomever, the first thing I would say is, 'Who do you want?'"[51]

The May 1953 choral recordings resulted from ideas Parker had
been discussing with the arranger Gil Evans since 1947. Evans was
then in his second stint with bandleader Claude Thornhill, who favored
unusual instrumentation and choral backup. "One of Evans' greatest
triumphs was grafting Parker's innovations onto the Thornhill sound
without spoiling either," wrote Phil Schaap.[52] Again, the concept of
working with a chorus had been brewing in Parker's mind, as evidenced
in an interview with Nat Hentoff around that time. Parker had in mind
something closer to Hindemith's *Kleine Kammermusik* than to popular
standards. Evans had already begun translating the general idea into
arrangements and had tapped Dave Lambert and his singers (including Annie Ross, his future partner in Lambert, Hendricks, and Ross).
Max Roach recalled that Granz had rebuffed Parker's more adventurous "Third Stream" suggestions for the date, which fell into disarray
so quickly Granz halted the session after three songs. "He [Parker]
mapped out things . . . , and Norman Granz would holler, 'What's
this? You can't make money with this crazy combination. You can't sell
this stuff!'"[53] Parker, Evans, and Lambert were more optimistic about
the results after hearing a test pressing disc (two songs were eventually
released on a single), but Granz refused to schedule another session
even after the three went to see him and offered to work for free to
record enough tunes for a full album.

There is no question that Parker and Granz did not always see eye to eye musically, leading to occasional arguments over Parker's recorded repertoire. One particularly harsh comment Parker made to a friend shows his ambivalence toward Granz and raises questions about just how fully Granz understood the musicians he championed and how far he would go in subsidizing risky projects if they required elaborate production. "He's made one million dollars, and he's on the way to making two, yet he's the most frightened man in the world," Parker reportedly said. "He takes jazz musicians, and he removes them from others. He puts them in a box."[54] It is difficult to assess Parker's remark within the context of his and Granz's lengthy relationship. On the one hand, Parker, a musician profligate with his talent, passions, and self-destructiveness, might well come into conflict with a jazz advocate who was at the same time a strong-willed, calculating businessman with a guiding sense of what the public would buy. On the other hand, Parker's observation echoes the views of some other jazz musicians who felt that Granz and the format and creed of Jazz at the Philharmonic unduly subjugated musicians' instincts to the goal of popularizing the music.

In 1965 Granz reflected that although he was glad he had recorded Parker, "in some ways, other companies did it better than I. They got Charlie when he was fresh. I think there are certain times in an artist's development when, even if he is more polished and more mature later on, the rough, first cut, if you like, is a wonderful thing. Those companies that had Charlie, Billie Holiday, or Lester Young did things I never could have done. What I did was, in a sense, after the fact."[55]

Parker's wife, Doris, had her own take on the dynamics between Parker and Granz, which she recalled in 1991. "Norman was very supportive of Bird, and Bird was glad to have him. Norman subsidized him $50 a week, and, yeah, I think he was the best thing that had come along for Bird up to that point. I don't know how Norman profited from that, but for Bird, he had somebody that was behind him, and Norman was recording him like mad," she said.[56]

The debate remains lively as to whether Granz functioned equally well as a producer of concepts and as an A&R man bringing together small groups of like-minded musicians or combining them with others from different schools with unexpectedly satisfying results. The Clef and Norgran years are distinct because of the flood of studio recordings made "Under the Personal Supervision of Norman Granz." Granz's success as an A&R man is in some ways comparable to that of a short-order cook in a well-stocked kitchen.

Who else but Granz would envision the compatibility of the cool-schooled Stan Getz and the fire-breathing Lionel Hampton? The two were in Los Angeles in August 1955 to record the soundtrack for Decca of the film *The Benny Goodman Story.* Hampton and Getz had both emerged from the big band era with an interest in newer forms of jazz, so it was not surprising that the vibraphonist vindicated himself just fine in the heavily bop-influenced session. Of the meeting of Getz and Dizzy Gillespie in April 1953, more logical on its face than that of Getz with the much older vibraphonist, Granz said, "Here we have two different types of musicians, each a star soloist in his own right, and a key representative of a particular style. Playing together they illustrate that skilled jazzmen, combining their individual efforts, can summon up fresh and lasting ideas beyond their own special contributions." The session between the two exhibits one of the aces Granz brought to impromptu recordings: the accessibility of a wonderfully tasteful house rhythm section of Oscar Peterson, Ray Brown, and Herb Ellis, with the addition here of drummer Max Roach.[57]

Meticulously crafted works such as *The Jazz Scene, The Astaire Story,* and, later, the Fitzgerald songbooks showed that Granz was capable of being a thoughtful, even brilliant, producer. Even before recording Fitzgerald in those breakthrough albums, he induced Oscar Peterson to do a songwriters series devoted to the works of Gershwin, Porter, Berlin, Ellington, Kern, Rodgers, Youmans, Warren, Arlen, and McHugh beginning in 1952. Granz hoped that the relatively short selections of standards timed for radio play and the pianist's dazzling talent could improve Peterson's crossover appeal.

Ben Young learned the Granz catalog thoroughly during his years producing reissues for Verve in the 1990s. He believes on the whole that Granz's overriding "concept" as a studio producer up until 1955 was "X Meets Y."[58] "He put jazz masters in the same room who more or less spoke the same language," Young observed. Granz was not a "hands-on producer," a trait that showed up positively and negatively all the way through to final release. For example, his occasionally "slapdash" approach was evident when Young studied master tapes and saw that, in many instances, little afterthought was given to sequencing the songs to sharpen the logic of an album. Producer Michael Cuscuna agrees that Granz was not "an in-studio" producer. One trademark of Granz's recordings was that in small informal sessions "he let the musicians do what they wanted, and turned that into an LP. But is that really what makes a record as special as it can be? I believe overall the quality holds up, but the output had a sense of hit-and-miss that goes back to the lack of preparation and involvement."[59]

The longtime Columbia Records producer George Avakian has spoken admiringly of Granz's ability to pull together recording sessions from a deep bench of talent. "I envied him many, many times, because I would have loved to have done nothing but jazz recordings," Avakian said. "I would have had a big stable like he did, except that he had most of the people that I didn't have . . . I think Norman was vastly important in the expansion of different kinds of jazz recordings, especially small groups. His philosophy was to catch the guys while they were hot, and not just live, but in studio packages. And he worked very fast, which was good in that he could put out a lot of product. And sometimes not so good, because frankly some of it, and I guess he would have to admit it himself, wasn't quite up to standard. But it kept the hula-hoop going, you might say. So there was a lot of activity that was great for his label, but also good for the business. I cannot stress enough that Norman was a very potent force in the popularization of jazz quite apart from what you might say was the pure jazz public."[60]

Granz was a man of great style in an art form defined by rapid change. He made more than enough to enjoy the good things life had to offer, but for him part of living well was taking money he earned from live jazz and putting it back into recording the music. The scale on which he did so in the 1950s allowed Granz to be described as a patron of the arts while being in the thick of commerce. Few others have managed that balancing act, and none with better and more bountiful and enduring results.

11

Starry Nights

Norman Granz had been news for a long time in the music press, but by the early 1950s, as he entered his second decade in the music business, he attained visibility and acclaim in the nontrade press as well. To a degree, this measured his increasing influence in the entertainment industry as a leading independent record producer and concert impresario, not only in the United States but in Europe and the Far East. It also showed the respectability—deserved or not—that can attach itself to those enjoying financial success. Many outside observers saw Granz primarily as a business story and marveled at how he put the numbers together from jazz. *Time* magazine ran a story in March 1953 on JATP's second annual tour of Europe, which began in Stockholm and had been extended from the past year's three weeks to five.[1] Sold-out Swedish audiences cheered wildly as if they were at a sporting match rather than a concert and required forty-five minutes to exit the packed theater in Stockholm afterwards. "If I didn't make $100,000 take-home pay a year, I'd quit," Granz informed the magazine, which went on to report that he had grossed an amount ten times that of the preceding year. "Jazz in Clover" ($4 million annually in 1954 dollars) was how *Newsweek* characterized the Granz saga. Both articles noted Granz's success in recording and his reputation for paying musicians handsomely; neither mentioned his efforts on behalf of civil rights.

A more rounded picture of Granz appeared in a September 1953 profile for the *New York Times* during an interview the day following a double-header at Carnegie Hall launching the thirteenth national tour.[2] Granz said his involvement in JATP had gone from reluctantly serving as emcee to regularly doing grassroots give and take with fans. "I do like to talk about jazz, and I always make it a point to go down in the audience during the intermission and argue. It's good first-name stuff. I don't pretend to be taking a Gallup Poll, but if some kid says, 'I don't like your trumpet player,' it's a good thing for me to do some listening."

Granz's business success was also highlighted in a 1954 article by Whitney Balliett, the future *New Yorker* critic, entitled "Pandemonium Pays Off." Granz, said Balliett, was pulling in some five hundred thousand people annually for his shows and putting out approximately half the jazz records in the United States. The unruly world of jazz had "finally run into its potential master," who "sends out single-handedly over a good part of the Western world a yearly series of jazz concerts . . . , owns a record company that has mushroomed so violently in its first year that it has to be split in two to accommodate overworked distribution facilities, and, as a canny, granitic businessman . . . is generally regarded as the first person who has been able to successfully mass produce jazz."[3] Balliett credited Granz for his stance on race and for improving working conditions for musicians but criticized JATP concerts for their use of banal materials and their restrictive concentration on solo as opposed to collective improvisation, which according to Balliett had impeded the growth of many of his players. He also described the audiences of JATP concerts as screaming, whistling, and stamping their feet with a "warlike . . . mass intensity." His conclusion, that in the next year, "to at least half a million customers around the world, Granz will be doing for jazz what another prestidigitator, P. T. Barnum, did for midgets," earned Balliett Granz's lasting animosity and probably an entry in the notebook that according to his publicist Virginia Wicks he kept to remember those who had crossed him. Granz told me in a 2001 interview that he had invited Balliett up to his New York office and threatened to sue him for libel over statements he construed as implying he had embraced civil rights as "a good business tactic." A later version of the article, published in an early anthology of his work in 1959, shows that Balliett did indeed make the changes specified by Granz.[4] Balliett denied in 2001 ever having met Granz but admitted he'd never particularly warmed to his enterprises.

The JATP players themselves viewed the tour's effects on their musicianship far more positively than Balliett did. Asked about how leading the rhythm section for Jazz at the Phil had influenced his skills as an emerging player, Oscar Peterson said that playing behind some of jazz's most individualistic soloists kept him on his toes and tutored him in a multiplicity of rhythmic, harmonic, and stylistic variations and musical philosophies. He recalled, for example, how Lester Young might enter the ballad medley part of the program by telling him, "I'll take a little bit of 'Tea for a Deuce.'" "Meanwhile—this is while we're playing—I'd say, 'What key?' And Prez would say, 'Well, you know, the right key,' and walk to the mic. So right away the computer inside of me was like, 'What keys are within his range, and this and that and the other.' I'd have to yell to Ray Brown and Herbie Ellis what we were doing. So that was where the spontaneity of Jazz at the Phil was. It was not tailored to the nth degree as some people like to suggest." On one occasion at the Forum in Montreal, it was Peterson, sitting behind a twelve-foot concert grand with its top removed, who threw Young a curveball, according to Bobby Scott, an eighteen-year-old pianist whom Young had taken under his wing on the tour. "All great comedic talent—and Lester was—had timing, and Prez could take a ribbing," Scott said. Young had selected "I Didn't Know What Time It Was" for the ballad medley and Peterson went through the normal introduction. "Then he started going through manifold different changes, moving here, there and everywhere. That's how he put the needle into Prez. You could see Prez's eyes. He liked simple chords back then. He started moving backwards over towards the piano, took the horn out of his mouth, unaware that there was a microphone near Oscar, and asked: 'Lady Pete, where are you motherfuckers at?' The whole place came apart. There must have been thousands. The laughter came down like a waterfall. It was the ballad medley so it was out there in the clear."[5]

Peterson's comments address a persistent criticism of Jazz at the Philharmonic as a caricature of the jam session, reduced to a formula in order to appeal to a wider audience. Critics were not the only faction Granz contended with in this regard. Some musicians who returned season after season, drawn by the promise of wide exposure, good pay, opportunities to record, and the other perks of working for Granz, also harbored mixed feelings about the shows. A nuanced answer to the criticism involves assessing Granz's role in the creation of the shows. He obviously set the basic parameters of what type of show he offered the public. But his time-tested format incorporated compatible combinations of musicians and room for play and experimentation, thereby keeping both himself and his audiences entertained. If he argued with success, he did so quietly and incrementally.

Though Granz could be manipulative, he clearly felt a bond with his musicians as their friend, patron, and boss all at the same time. Stories are legion about Granz the businessman calling a deal with a musician on his own terms, but so are reports of quiet moments where he unselfishly helped to guide musicians' careers or offered encouragement and assistance in surviving the chaotic world of the traveling jazz artist.

Pete Cavello was in his early thirties and already weary of working one-nighters as a road manager for bandleader Ralph Flanagan when he met up with his friend the trumpeter Charlie Shavers at a Manhattan tavern in early 1953. The gangly, laconic Brooklyn native had learned the music business in the postwar years by first driving a truck carrying instruments and equipment for local bands, then graduating to serving as a "roadie" for Tommy Dorsey.

"There's a guy looking for you," Shavers informed Cavello. "I want you to go see him. He's got a job for you. A guy named Norman Granz."

"Never heard of him. But what have I got to lose?" responded Cavello.

Shavers's tip resulted in thousands more one-nighters for Pete Cavello. Proving himself indispensable, he spent the next thirty-seven years, first for JATP and then for Ella Fitzgerald, until he collapsed in the set of a Grammy Awards rehearsal and died two days later in 1990. As road manager, especially from 1958 on, when he accompanied Fitzgerald exclusively, Cavello saw to it that everyone made it to the venue and back to a hotel or airport to make the next date. He collected money, dealt with promoters on the ground, kept in touch with Granz or the office in Beverly Hills, dealt with medical and other emergencies, knew a city well enough over time to know whom to call if an instrument turned up missing or damaged, and located food and drink after hours. Cavello, who married in 1953, said in later years that he was "married to two women"—his wife and Ella. His catch-all responsibilities kept him hard at work, and continual life on the road could be lonely sometimes.

His first meeting with Granz was at a small suite at 522 Fifth Avenue in Manhattan. Granz's secretary Alice de Pamphillis, once described as the "eye" of the Granz hurricane, ushered him into the impresario's office. "He had two phones—one in each hand," Cavello recalled almost thirty years later.[6]

"I'm in a great deal of a hurry," Granz stated. "Can you be fast?"

"Yeh, Charlie Shavers told me to come, that you may have work for me," Cavello said.

"I've heard about you, but we don't go on tour until September," Granz responded.

Cavello told Granz that September was too long to delay his search for work, especially since he was on the verge of getting married, so Granz put Cavello on the payroll doing office work and running errands starting the following Monday. Thus Cavello was available for Jazz at the Philharmonic's second European tour beginning in February and was brought in early to prepare for five weeks of shows. "We had a get-together about a week before we went to Europe. It wasn't really a meeting, just a talkover. I hardly knew too many people on Jazz at the Phil," he said. "I knew Shavers, of course, and I knew both Krupa and Flip Phillips. I met Ella and Lester Young for the first time."[7] Surveying the room, he saw Oscar Peterson, Barney Kessel (in the final months of his tenure with Peterson before being replaced in July by Herb Ellis), Ray Brown, J.C. Heard (a late replacement for Buddy Rich), and Willie Smith. The group discussed the itinerary and travel arrangements, followed by a breakdown of the show: the jam session, segments by the Peterson Trio and Ella Fitzgerald and her trio, and a return of the horns for the finale with the singer.

Others confirm the essentials of Cavello's description of JATP's pretour planning and expand on Granz's role in structuring the program and, from the sidelines, its content. From the time he joined JATP in the fall of 1950, Peterson gained Granz's respect both personally and musically to perform as a kind of first among equals. This extended to working with musicians on their parts of the program and settling details concerning the entire production. This authority came both from his role leading the rhythm section for the ensemble parts of the show and also as a rising star in his own right. Drummer Louie Bellson approvingly called the pianist Granz's "straw boss," capable of intervening in musical matters where the impresario was not keen on rushing in.

"Norman liked to be very loose," said Bellson, a member of the 1954 tour. "The meeting was us getting to know one another, and saying, 'Well, what would you like to play on the program? What key would you like to it?' Then we'd work out an outline for a program. Norman was never one to get into a rehearsal. There was nothing to read. Everything was ad lib. He wanted it to be pure jazz, swing, you know. Those meetings were wonderful because Oscar was more or less in charge. He was easy to work with, as he understood every performer and had that great ability to communicate. Oscar would say, 'Well, okay, during the ballad medley, what do you want to play, Roy [Eldridge]?' We'd work this out. I know that a lot of Norman's success was the fact he had a giant like Oscar Peterson handling the programming. It's like he wasn't the leader, but he was. Then Buddy Rich and I would talk about what kind of tune we wanted to play, what tempo. Once that was outlined, we were ready to go on the bandstand and play."[8]

Herb Ellis, another fan of the Granz approach, said that Granz "played a bigger role than you might think," and that his influence stemmed from his deep appreciation for jazz and the essence of what made the music swing. "He would put groups together, like he'd have another piano player other than Oscar," Ellis said in 1996. "Oscar would just play when he played with his trio, or sometimes he would come out and play a couple of numbers with Ella. Anyway, Norman would put these things together. He'd have Roy Eldridge and Coleman Hawkins. Their styles blended, so he'd put them together. Then he'd have Stan Getz with Dizzy Gillespie. Thank God, he knew about music. He knew the main thing was the groove."[9]

Peterson said Granz would occasionally call just before the tour with proposed additions to the lineup and would ask about how a given musician might interact with those already on the bill. "He would say at different times, 'What do you think about so and so? I'd like to have this person on the tour,' and it might be someone you would have never thought of right away as being a viable member of the JATP crew. He not only wanted that person but could imagine the setting in which he would present them."[10] However, Granz's unabashed advocacy of JATP as a vehicle for "excitement" (or incitement to frenzy) collided with what many musicians viewed as their prerogative to entice audiences into their creative world on their own terms. The format, which opened with an up-tempo and medium-paced ensemble blues, sections set aside for all-star small groups, and sets by the Peterson Trio and Fitzgerald, capped by such flag wavers as "How High the Moon" or "Perdido," can hardly escape a charge of being called formulaic. But it would be simplistic to conclude that all the musicians felt constrained by it.

For example, clarinetist Buddy DeFranco turned aside Granz's initial invitation to join JATP when they met by chance at a recording studio in New York sometime in 1953. "I was rehearsing one day, and Norman was working with some group in another part of the studio and he said, 'I'd like to have you come with Jazz at the Phil.' I didn't particularly like JATP at the time. I kind of considered it a circus or something. I think I was pretty nasty at the time, and I refused Norman.

I just wanted to play my kind of music, and all that nonsense. Every young musician goes through that if they have any talent at all. Each of us think we're doing our own thing, to quote a cliché, when, in fact, nobody's doing their own thing. Norman was kind of disappointed." DeFranco changed his tune when they encountered each other again and Granz, showing no sign of the earlier rebuff, pulled out his checkbook and asked, "Here, would this help you come with JATP?"[11]

"I said, 'Yes, it certainly would.'" DeFranco inquired about his part in the show and was delighted when Granz allotted him twenty minutes backed by the Peterson Trio and Rich. "Of course, when I heard that, I said, 'Holy smoke, this is fantastic. This is some backup group.'" DeFranco also spoke admiringly of the freedom JATP gave him. "Norman gave you a latitude, free rein, gave you the choice of playing what you wanted the way you felt it."[12] Musically, it turned out to be an enriching experience, and Granz "made sure everyone was treated equally, that everybody got the best treatment, the best hotels, the best services, and the best transportation."[13] DeFranco was one of the few interviewed for this book to provide specifics on the financial advantages of working with JATP. Normally, the clarinetist's agent booked a single concert date for his group for $1,500. DeFranco would give $225 off the top to his agent, and after paying for the group plus transportation, he might wind up with $600 or $700 for the night's work. Granz paid him around $1,200 per night and picked up all expenses for his accommodations and transportation.

During his seven years with JATP, Hank Jones alternated between criticizing what he viewed as Granz's approach of calculatedly provoking crowd response and acknowledging the good that Granz and JATP did for the music. "Jazz at the Philharmonic was more oriented toward the visual, as far as appealing to the crowds," Jones said. "Norman was more interested in exhibiting showmanship. That's why I eventually left. My idea is to explore the musical possibility of the tunes played without regard to audiences. Audiences are not trained. It's up to the performer to set the tone." The pianist went on. "He never told us what to play. In a rough sense, Jazz at the Philharmonic gave some idea about how jazz was balanced, but jam sessions at Minton's, for example, were not held to impress other people or other musicians. They were learning experiences. JATP reversed that impression. I don't think impressing people should be the aim of jazz musicians."[14]

Jones may not have liked the means, but he appreciated the end. "Jazz at the Philharmonic changed a lot of things. The name was very significant. Presenting the shows in symphony halls gave people the chance to listen to jazz in concert. This gave the music prominence and circulation on a large scale. It made jazz an attraction. We were appreciated as performers. It increased my exposure, made more people aware of me, and gave me the chance to sell more records. I still get a lot of questions about Jazz at the Philharmonic."

Dizzy Gillespie similarly had many reasons to be thankful to Granz over their nearly five-decade association, but he criticized the musical values of JATP in his autobiography. "Norman Granz always tried to get the top soloists together in a package for a Jazz at the Philharmonic tour by calling up who he thought were the top instrumentalists on their respective instruments and offering them a lot of money," Gillespie wrote. "JATP wasn't much musically because Norman got his nuts off by sending two or three trumpet players out there to battle one another's brains out on the stage. And he'd just sit back and laugh. . . . It was funny, battling all the time. Norman had a weird sense of competition. . . . The importance of Jazz at the Philharmonic is that it was the original 'first class' treatment for jazz musicians. You traveled first class, stayed in first class hotels, and he demanded no segregation in seating." On another occasion, Gillespie called Granz "at the forefront of the best in jazz."[15]

Lester Young, too, recoiled at the demands of the format: his JATP performances in the 1950s were mostly lackluster in comparison to his earlier appearances, even though the tours provided substantial income. John Hammond, who had a large stake in Young's early years, wrote, "'Prez' was always too much of an artist to pander to the JATP crowds, and it wasn't much fun for him to play second to Flip Phillips and Illinois Jacquet in the various tours. He made innumerable recordings for Norman's Clef and Verve labels, but the zest and invention of the old days were pretty well dissipated."[16]

Other stories further reveal Young's dwindling interest in performing with JATP. The French jazz writer Charles Delaunay told Nat Hentoff, "The first time he came over with JATP [in 1952,] his short, mediocre stage appearance disappointed nearly every one of his fans. But pianist Henri Renaud and a few other musicians managed after the concert to take him to the Tabou, where he sat in with the local band and really *blew*. There we discovered that Lester could still blow when he wanted to, when he was in the right environment or mood."[17] During the troupe's 1953 European tour, Young confessed, "I'm tired of all this noise. I like to play cool."[18] On still another occasion, he referred to Jazz at the Philharmonic as "a flying plantation."[19] The suggestion of exploitation would be difficult to dismiss if Young had not benefited from Granz's friendship and patronage for the past eleven years.

In the summer of 1953, a quarrel between Buddy Rich and Norman Granz brought this debate into the pages of *Down Beat,* with Flip Phillips serving as the arbiter between the two men. The magazine reported that Rich had signed with Harry James for an annual salary of $35,000 and quoted Rich as saying, "I don't want any part of Granz or his Jazz at the Philharmonic. You can make that plain. In the first place, it's not jazz. It's just honking and noise. He may be trying to prove something, but it has nothing to do with jazz as I know it. This guy Granz talks about doing so much for jazz. What has he done? He takes top jazz stars—Flip and Bird and everybody—and makes them play loud stuff that he calls jazz. A lot of noise, not jazz."[20] A spokesman for Granz, then traveling in Europe, dismissed Rich's statement as personal, not musical, "a clash of personalities."[21]

Phillips countered that working with Jazz at the Philharmonic did not betray his own sense of himself as an artist. "Look, I'm playing what the people want," he said. "Is that bad? In my basement, I'm the coolest. But when I play for people who spend money to hear me, I play what they want to hear. After all, look at the business JATP has been doing."[22] He went on to note that club dates during the JATP off-season gave him the chance to explore different sides of his playing. He argued as well that musicians could do worse for their careers than satisfying their listeners.

For his part, Granz said that he had heard no complaints from Rich over the four tours since he had started playing JATP in 1945 or during an estimated one hundred sides he had cut for Granz over the years. "Never at any time have I told him or anyone else that Buddy has recorded with or concertized with how to play," wrote Granz, adding that critics had often cited Rich as the noisiest of the troupe and then dismissing him as a "boor" and a "liar."[23] "I'm sure those of you who have heard JATP through the years will agree that apart from occasional changes in personnel and presentation, there has been little change in JATP's sound or format, and this is the way I would have it, because this is the type of jazz I like." The skirmish spilled more ink than blood, for whatever their real differences might have been, Rich was back on tour the following year.

Trombonist J. J. Johnson took much the same pragmatic approach to assessing JATP as he did to his career as a professional musician when he balanced the demands of his artistry with those of entertainment and commerce. "Let's face it, jazz is a part of show biz," he said. "Some of us don't like to recognize that, but it really is. We're in the business of entertaining people. A guy pays ten or twelve bucks to come into a club, he wants to be entertained, maybe on a different level than a guy who comes into a club and wants to see tap dancers or snake charmers. But it's all entertainment. It's all business, in the sense that it *is* the entertainment business."[24]

With musicians especially Granz's kinder side came through time and again. Oscar Peterson has written that life on the tour bus was a world unto itself governed by rules that helped preserve breathing space, respect, and sanity in tight quarters over three-month tours. "Being a heavy player in the concert halls and arenas bought you no favors in this college-on-wheels: living on a bus had its own specific rules, and you either lived by these or became a non-entity."[25] The seat on the bus that a musician took was his for the remainder of the tour. Any conversations were to be moved to the rear of the bus if nearby musicians were sleeping. Personal property was sacrosanct. Peterson recalled one night after playing a university date in Kansas where Granz had hot food not only waiting but ordered according to the musicians' preferences. "He would go to great lengths to customize our meals to our individual tastes," Peterson said. "I recall Coleman Hawkins being handed the very special kind of brandy that he had been unable to pick up for the last few days."[26]

Sharing stories about musicians and making music were normal ways of killing time on the road, according to Peterson. "I remember Ella asking Roy Eldridge if he recalled the way that Billie Holiday used to do this tune or that tune, then Lady Fitz would launch into a 'Lady Day' version of 'What a Little Moonlight Can Do.'" She would motion to Herb Ellis to get his guitar, and before too long she would be joined by Eldridge on muted trumpet, Lester Young on sax, and Ray Brown balancing his bass in the aisle. "Try to picture the scene as I saw and heard it, and try to envision what a cameo it was, both visually and musically. Here was this great big Greyhound bus rolling down the Kansas highway on a picture-perfect evening; inside some of the greatest jazz people that could possibly ever be mustered at any one time and place."[27]

Granz, who was typically tense backstage and confessed to screaming every five minutes at stagehands or anyone else in the way, was a different man once he joined the musicians on the bus and laid down his burden for the night. "The Norman Granz that people saw walk out on the stage to introduce the players was not the Norman Granz that got on the bus," Peterson said.[28] "He became a member of JATP in the full sense of the word. He laughed with them, he cried with them. Very seldom did he ever have to revert to being Norman Granz the impresario."

There were, of course, occasions when unfinished business from a performance caused Granz to arrive back at the bus steaming. One evening overly long battles between Illinois Jacquet and Flip Phillips and, later, Roy Eldridge and Charlie Shavers prevented a timely transition between shows and left the theater manager threatening to shut off the lights during the second. Peterson recognized all the signs of Granz's anger as he got on the bus and, with his top coat's collar turned up, almost covering his face, and his hands jammed in his pockets, made his way toward the rear. At this point, according to Peterson, Lester Young intervened to defuse the situation by beginning a comic monologue in the voice of his alter ego "Dr. Willis." "'Does Lester feel a draft?' He paused measuredly. 'Say what? Say what?!! The Midgets fucked up? What?! And Lady Granz is about to kick their asses?' Snickers now from various seats. He senses a gathering momentum and pushes on. 'What's that, Dr. Willis? You say Lady Flip and Lady Jacquet are 'bout to get their buns kicked too? My, my; and Lady Granz got her feelings all hurt and everything. Ugh!' By this time, Ella is in convulsions. Norman's hat is bobbing up and down with laughter, along with everyone else, and Prez had accomplished what he set out to do."[29]

Herb Ellis gratefully recalled that Granz and Peterson had extended every understanding to him when his alcoholism got the better of him in 1954 as JATP prepared for its third annual trip to Europe. On the morning he was to leave, Ellis was too drunk to catch the flight from New York's Idlewild Airport and ended up in a hospital. Ellis disappeared into a second alcoholic fog for about a month in New York the following year. But following a meeting with Peterson, Ellis firmed up his commitment to Alcoholics Anonymous and swore off drinking.[30]

"Oscar and Norman were both great," Ellis said. "If they had not wanted me to come back, I don't know what would have happened to me. Norman would do great things, but he was embarrassed sometimes. When I came back on the tour, in order to show his appreciation, we were going somewhere on the train, and he gave me a little package. It was a Patek Philippe watch. That's one of the best watches in the world. That was his way of saying, 'Everything's okay, that you're still one of us, and we don't hold any ill feelings.'"[31]

Stan Getz was more problematic. A violent alcoholic and drug addict, Getz was arrested for heroin use at his home in the Laurel Canyon section of Los Angeles in December 1953. His wife, Beverly, who was seriously addicted herself, flushed his stash down the toilet when she heard the commotion with the police at the front door. Getz pled guilty in January, with the judge turning aside the saxophonist's request for a postponement in serving his sentence so that he could make the upcoming 1954 European JATP tour. He was ordered to return for sentencing in February but had time for an eight-day West Coast tour for the promoter Gene Norman. When he decided to lessen his desire for heroin by taking barbiturates, he became so desperate by the fifth day of the tour that he attempted an early morning holdup of a Seattle drugstore across from the group's hotel by pretending to have a gun in his pocket. For the second time in a month newspapers across the nation publicized his arrest for drug violations. He nearly died in the Seattle jail after he swallowed the remainder of his barbiturate capsules and was eventually charged with being "a habitual user of narcotics." Three days into his four-month incarceration, his wife gave birth to a baby girl. Soon she was reduced to selling furniture to buy food and drugs. A friend later said, "Norman Granz really came through." He provided Getz's wife with a weekly allowance during the time the tenor saxophonist served behind bars.[32]

Other band members would also look back later on what Granz had done for them. An ailing Barney Kessel, writing to Granz in 1996 after his stroke, recalled, "You were the first one to take me to Europe, where I learned to feel right at home. I remember how you took the country boy I was and tried to add a bit of sophistication. You told me to stay at the Algonquin in New York, you took me to a French restaurant and showed me what to order, you told me the best wristwatch to buy. You were always good to me and taught me so much."[33] Roy Eldridge, in an oft-quoted statement, said, "What impresses me about Norman is that everything he's achieved, he's gotten by himself. Like most of us musicians, he had to start from scratch to get things going. But he broke through. . . . He made sure the cats got a decent living. He was the first to break down all that prejudice. He put the music up where it belongs. They should make a statue to that cat, and there's no one else in the business end of the music business I would say that about."[34]

Granz was capable of administering tough love when he felt the occasion demanded it. Again, it is Oscar Peterson who, as is so often the case, reveals the more private side of Granz. Granz's fifty-two-year relationship with Peterson was that of friend and mentor, and Peterson was one of the few artists Granz actually managed. Peterson's time to be called on the carpet came a few years into their association. The pianist had been regularly failing to repay Granz for annual loans to deal with hefty Canadian taxes as well as falling behind on commissions but still continuing to live beyond his means. Granz called Peterson into his office to tell him he felt he was being taken advantage of. Trying to be Peterson's best friend was becoming more of a hindrance than a blessing. "The thing that was hurting him most of all was that I was not making any financial progress at all, and in fact was digging a deeper hole for myself year by year. He then said he wanted his money and he wanted his commissions paid, and that he didn't care what I did with the rest of the money from there on. . . . I told him that I would put things right regardless of time and cost. That might have been one of the hardest days in Norman's life; from the end result, now that my operational status is the way it is, it turned out to be one of the happiest. He had done something that only a true friend could have done."[35]

Granz could be generous, not only in response to disasters, but also on a whim. Peterson recalled that once during a stopover in Stuttgart Granz took Fitzgerald and himself over to a Mercedes showroom to look at one of their deluxe models. "He decided to give it to her. And she was all ecstatic about it, of course. Then afterwards, he said to me, 'Which car do you like?'

"Oh, come on. Are you kidding? There's only one car here that I'd . . . and that's the 300 SL."

"Fine, I'm going to get that one for you."

"No, you're not."

"Yes, I am."

There was an Adriatic Blue 300 SL sitting out in a row of cars. Peterson recounts, "And I said, 'If I had to pick a car, that would be the car, but you're not buying it for me so forget it.'"

Norman said, "I'll tell you what. I'll give you a choice. You let me buy you that one, if you like that color, or, if you won't let me buy it, I'm going to buy you a red one. I know you hate red." ("Which is true. So he bought it.")[36] In 1974, the JATP troupe collectively repaid Granz on the event of his marrying his third wife, Grete, by chipping in to buy the couple a Mercedes 450 SL that he had been admiring for some time.

In February 1953 the North Sea floods hit the eastern coastal areas of England, killing hundreds, leaving tens of thousands homeless, and drowning hundreds of square miles of agricultural land. Jazz at the

Philharmonic was solicited to play London, with the Ministry of Labor relaxing its ban on U.S. orchestras for the first time in eighteen years on the condition that the proceeds be directed to the Lord Mayor's emergency fund to help flood victims. The British promoter Harold Fielding and *Melody Maker*'s Mike Nevard were in negotiation over relief concerts when Granz called from Stockholm to say that he would pay the musicians' travel expenses from Paris for afternoon and evening shows on Sunday, March 9, and would donate all proceeds toward their effort. Fielding rented the Gaumont State Theatre in London. Since the ban against U.S. orchestras remained in principle, no work permits were issued; rather, Granz and company came into the country with a special entry note from the British Home Office. The lineup consisted of the Oscar Peterson Trio with Ray Brown and Barney Kessel, Ella Fitzgerald, Lester Young, Flip Phillips, Willie Smith, Charlie Shavers, Hank Jones, J.C. Heard, and Gene Krupa, in addition to four British bands, including one led by the tenor saxophonist and later London club owner Ronnie Scott.

In anticipation, Granz uncharacteristically gushed to *Melody Maker,* "I've been running my unit for 12 years. To play London will be the biggest thrill of my life. I'll give you the biggest and best show we've ever staged."[37] The musicians even planned to rehearse for the London date, which Granz said was virtually unprecedented. "They're so scared, I fear they'll have a fit of nerves on Sunday," he said, no doubt with some tongue in cheek.[38] On a whirlwind visit to London in early March he assured his hosts that although JATP had already played some twenty-six concerts in the preceding two weeks his musicians were "strong as horses." Within a few days approximately 8,239 tickets for the two shows had been sold by mail order and at the box office.

Ecstatic reports on JATP's arrival and the concerts themselves read in places more like accounts of liberation than reviews of a jazz band. *Melody Maker* reported ecstatically before the show that "the fog that shrouded London for a week lifted on Sunday morning, and Jazz at the Philharmonic flew into town in brilliant sunshine. Twenty-one hours later, as the fog was closing in on London Airport, the unit flew out again to the Continent. . . . The miracle had happened."[39] Left out of this account was the unfriendly reception of the musicians by British customs officials, who rifled their baggage for any evidence of drugs. When they wanted to body-search Fitzgerald as well as her cousin and attendant, Georgiana Henry, Granz had had enough and yelled, "Cancel the concerts! If this is what we have to be subjected to in order to do these benefit concerts, forget it! We'll just go back to the Continent and continue our tour."[40] Customs immediately backed off.

In a review for *Melody Maker,* Tony Brown noted that the confident playing and complex chord changes marked the most obvious differences between American and British jazz. "What was striking," wrote Brown, "was the sheer physical power of the horn men and the tremendous rhythmic urge behind the playing of every musician in the unit. The vast majority of the excited crowd felt it and responded to it. The exhibitionistic spell-binding was all part of the circus, but it certainly was not overdone. . . . We just don't swing like Americans do. Too many of our musicians are worrying about the notes played when the essence is *how* they are played."[41] The results were certainly satisfactory for the cause: the concerts delivered some £4,000, or $11,000, into the treasury for flood relief.

One footnote to the 1953 tour was Granz's encounter in Paris (the tour's penultimate stop) with Django Reinhardt, whom Granz had first heard during his New York performances at Cafe Society Uptown in December 1946 following the guitarist's appearances with the Duke Ellington Orchestra. Granz hoped to record Reinhardt with Oscar Peterson and Ray Brown after finishing the tour's last stop, but Peterson, exhausted by the end of the tour, begged off.[42] And the opportunity was lost, for Reinhardt died weeks later on May 16, 1953, at the age of forty-three.

The European tour ended in late March with gross receipts of over $100,000. Granz told *Billboard* that the trip had enabled him as well to finalize agreements to further distribute his recordings. Blue Star would be the distributor in France and Belgium, the Music Record Company in Italy, and Karrusel Records in Scandinavia. As for Great Britain, Granz was thinking of starting his own label there in light of his failure to conclude a distribution deal during the tour.[43] As far back as 1951, Granz had concluded that his only option there was an independent operation. But he dropped the idea after running it past the British Board of Trade, which told Granz he would not be granted a license to operate unless he guaranteed a minimum export. Two years later he was able to meet the minimum in addition to pressing discs in England. He returned to Britain in late June to establish his own network to distribute Mercury masters that would be pressed by British Decca. Earlier attempts had reportedly foundered when the percentage of the profits that Granz sought was too high to generate any offers. During this trip, he also proposed that the Ted Heath Orchestra perform at Carnegie Hall, if the American Federation of Musicians would permit it. He hoped this suggestion might capitalize on the momentum of JATP's London shows and eventually lead to ongoing reciprocal arrangements.[44] However, the AFM was as leery as the British Musicians Union to grant access to foreign musicians, and the plan was dropped.

Granz returned home on April 1 to help manage what would become one of the most bizarre and widely publicized fiascoes in jazz history: a tour pairing Benny Goodman and Louis Armstrong that began two weeks later. Granz and Goodman's relationship had begun badly when John Hammond approached Granz about touring his brother-in-law during the time (the late 1940s) that the two men worked for Mercury and shared an office in New York. Goodman's fortunes were ebbing, and Hammond thought some exposure with JATP would help boost his career. "The idea of bringing Benny back after so many years was John's," Granz recalled. "He came to me and said, 'How would you like to tour Benny Goodman?' And I said, 'Well, if the conditions are right.' I should have known what was going to happen."[45]

Hammond arranged for Granz and Goodman to meet at Manhattan's Colony restaurant. Granz arrived in tennis-shoes casual. "I got there at the time we were supposed to meet, like two o'clock," Granz said. The headwaiter greeted him and went off with the message to Goodman, who asked that Granz wait until he was finished eating to consider their business. "I thought, 'This is weird. You'd think he'd say, 'Come and have coffee, or come and have a glass of water.' I sat there like a damn fool, and he didn't invite me."

When they did finally sit down together, Goodman started out by asking, "Now what is it that you're trying to interest me in?"

"I'm not trying to interest you in anything," Granz said. "If you want to work with me, we can look at what I have to offer, and then you tell me what you have to offer." Granz then showed Goodman the latest JATP program. "Why don't you look at this? These are the people you'll be playing with. You tell me who you want. I'd give you Teddy Wilson, Gene Krupa, Lionel Hampton, or the Benny Goodman Sextet. Just tell me what you want."

Goodman looked at Granz and said, "You expect me to play with this circus?"

"So I said, 'Benny, Lester Young plays better saxophone than you play clarinet, Coleman Hawkins would blow you out of the room, and

Ella sings better than anything you can play. In short, there isn't a musician in that group that you could even touch, so go fuck yourself and forget the tour.'"

Despite this unpromising meeting, Hammond persisted in trying to bring the two men together again, and shortly afterward Granz suggested building a tour around Goodman and Armstrong, thus bypassing the notion of trying to accommodate the clarinetist within the framework of JATP.[46]

Goodman put together a mix of veterans from his big bands as well as non-alums. Signing up for the tour were Teddy Wilson, Gene Krupa, and Ziggy Elman, the trumpeter whose star rose with Goodman between 1936 and 1940, and Helen Ward, the band's first vocalist. Also returning to the Goodman fold were Georgie Auld and Clint Neagley on tenor saxophone, and trombonist Rex Peer. Filling out the rhythm section was bassist Israel Crosby. Guitarist Steve Jordan, formerly with Ray McKinley, was recruited, as were Sol Schlinger on tenor saxophone plus trumpeters Al Stewart and Charlie Shavers. The Armstrong ensemble featured Joe Bushkin on piano, Cozy Cole on drums, bassist Arvell Shaw, Barney Bigard on clarinet, trombonist Trummy Young, and Velma Middleton sharing vocals with Armstrong.

A taskmaster who had always provided ample time for rehearsals, Goodman played dates in Manchester, New Hampshire, and Portland, Maine, on April 10 and 11 so that the band could get up to speed with the arrangements before linking up with Armstrong for the beginning of the tour in New Haven on the fifteenth. The first encounter between the show's principals foreshadowed problems that inadvertently broke up the tour. Two days before the concerts began, the Goodman band was practicing in a Manhattan rehearsal hall. With no notice, Louis Armstrong, his band members, their wives, and assorted friends suddenly swept in, with Armstrong at the helm playing "When the Saints Go Marching In." Virginia Wicks, the publicist for the tour, said that what had been intended as a goodwill gesture backfired.

"Louis was, of course, a gregarious man, so everybody greeted him and there was bedlam for about 20 minutes," Hammond wrote. "Benny took it as long as he could, then asked Louis if he would mind sending his entourage out so the rehearsal could continue. Louis took offense. He considered himself a co-star, although actually Goodman was the boss."[47] The next day tensions mounted when Armstrong and the musicians unit failed to show for a scheduled rehearsal. Then Armstrong unilaterally decided to increase his time on the program to that of the

Goodman band—an hour and twenty minutes rather than the original forty. Finally, he left Goodman in the lurch when he did not return for a planned duet concluding the show.

Goodman invited Armstrong to come early to the next show at the Newark Mosque concert hall to try to patch things up. Again, Armstrong failed to appear as showtime grew perilously near.

Norman Granz picked up the story at this point. "Benny was backstage fuming," he said.

"What's going on?" the clarinetist asked.

"Listen, I don't know what happened to Louis, but you're going to have to go on," said Granz.

"I'm not going to open the show," Goodman told Granz, who had agreed that in a concert with a big band and a small group that the big band should be the second act.

"There is no show," Granz said. "You're going to have to go out there."[48]

According to both Granz and Hammond, Goodman in his fury threw a bottle of scotch into a full-length dressing mirror, shattering it. Hammond's question to Goodman, "Who do you think you are, the Jewish Marlon Brando?" drew one of the few laughs of the night.

Afterwards, Granz discovered that Armstrong and his group had been outside hiding in a car the whole time, waiting for the show to get under way before they entered the hall, so that Goodman would be forced to go on first and Armstrong would be able to close. "Louis said, 'Is he on?'"

"Yeh," Granz assured him.

"Louis came on and he closed the show," he continued. "Flip Phillips came with me just to hear the band. Benny was so angry, he lost himself. He was taking all the choruses, calling numbers wrong. Everything was a disaster. He motioned tenorist Georgie Auld to take a solo. He had a wonderful sense of humor. So he played eight bars, and in the mic said, 'That's all he wants me to play. Bye-bye.' The whole thing was complete chaos."

The two Carnegie Hall concerts scheduled for April 17 had been an early point of contention between Granz and Goodman over the pricing of the tickets. Normally, they would have sold for around two dollars; Granz marked the price up to five dollars. He was in Europe when he got a call from Hammond, who said Goodman believed he was trying to kill his career with such a steep price. "I'm paying Benny," Granz said. "I've got a contract. Your man's going to get paid and Louis is going to get paid. So just relax, because I can tell you now, it's going to be a sellout."[49] Indeed, both shows sold out within hours and, according to Hammond, racked up the largest grosses of any jazz concert playing the hall up to that time. According to one Broadway columnist, the Goodman-Armstrong fight continued backstage when Goodman asked that Armstrong delete Velma Middleton's "comedy" split dancing, to which he instructed her, "You go ahead and do it, honey."[50] "In both [concerts]," Hammond wrote, "Benny played atrociously. . . . According to the Saturday papers it appeared that Goodman had returned in all his glory. Those of us in the audience who knew better . . . recognized that his performance was less than glorious."[51]

Goodman and the band's subsequent performances the next day in Providence were much improved over the Carnegie date; however, that day was to be the last in a concert series that still had a week to go. On his way to Boston for the next day's concert, Hammond learned that Goodman was incommunicado after a sudden bout of bad health. At first he heard that Goodman might have suffered a heart attack; then Virginia Wicks said he had genuine breathing problems. Other speculation centered on nervous exhaustion, and Goodman's doctor was unable to determine a cause. Gene Krupa took over the leadership of the band, and Armstrong graciously emceed the show, as well as playing.

Over the next few days, everyone wondered whether Goodman would return to finish the tour. Granz, like Hammond, believed Goodman had manufactured his health problems to scuttle what had turned out to be an ill-conceived venture and to keep Armstrong from performing. The upshot left few of the principals untouched or unruffled. Goodman fired Hammond as his personal manager even though Hammond, after overcoming his initial resistance to getting professionally involved with his notoriously finicky brother-in-law, had worked diligently to help make Goodman's portion of the program a success. The consensus was that Goodman had been well enough to rejoin the tour but had instead chosen to cause havoc by not doing so. Reportedly he had even tried to go through the American Federation of Musicians to keep the band from fulfilling its obligations without him. Granz "expressed several opinions about Benny's actions, none of them printable," Down Beat noted.[52]

On the eve of the 1953 fall tour, the marriage of Ella Fitzgerald and Ray Brown ended in a quickie divorce in Juarez on August 28, with Fitzgerald getting custody of their son, Ray Jr., who was actually the son of Ella's sister. They had patched things up after a trial separation in the summer of 1951, but they could no longer simultaneously maintain dual careers and a semblance of family life. Furthermore, Fitzgerald was overweight and sorely conscious of it, which made her all the more emotionally needy, while Brown was a more dashing figure who was a magnet for female admirers. By all accounts, they soldiered on gracefully in close proximity through what must have been a difficult period. "They were professionals," Granz said of the breakup.[53] Virginia Wicks recalled the aftermath as an agonizing moment in the singer's life. "In the dressing room, she would put her head down in front of the mirror. She shed real tears," recalled the publicist. "Then she'd wipe under her eyes where the mascara had dripped and put on new mascara and say brave words, like 'I can't let this win' or 'I can't let this stop me.' She just kept saying, 'I'm so hurt' but provided no specifics about what had occurred between them."[54]

Oscar Peterson felt trapped in the middle in that Fitzgerald was his friend and Brown an inseparable member of his trio. "I was busy tiptoeing through the tulips. She still had feelings for him after the divorce." He recalled one night on tour in Britain when Brown was signing autographs and chatting with some English lovelies. "She walked past him and got on the bus. For some reason, she hit me. I mean, I saw stars for a couple of seconds, you know," Peterson said. "She said, 'I know what you're up to, Oscar.' I realized she wasn't, in essence, talking to me. She was talking to Ray."[55]

Saxophonists Benny Carter and Ben Webster were the notable newcomers to the forty-two-stop thirteenth national tour, which was Carter's only domestic tour and Webster's first. "This year's JATP has been strengthened by the addition of Webster and Carter," wrote Nat Hentoff of two September 19 concerts at Carnegie Hall.[56] "Carter, in a sense, was the dominant instrumental figure in this brace of concerts. His skilled musicianship and wondrous ease, swing and imagination seemed to serve as criteria during the full-group numbers." Rejoining the contingent was the ever-welcome Bill Harris, rounding out a program featuring Fitzgerald, the Peterson Trio with Herb Ellis (who "meets the difficult challenge of replacing Barney Kessel"), Willie Smith, Gene Krupa, Flip Phillips, Roy Eldridge, and Charlie Shavers. Lester Young had played a section of the concert on some of the East Coast dates. "In any case," he said, "this is a stimulating JATP that manages to bridge the difficult problem of satisfying a hyperthyroid audience in need of intense emotional purgation while retaining long sections of first-rate improvised jazz."

The biggest moment of the fall campaign, however, was half a world away when JATP swept into Japan for three weeks of concerts in fourteen cities during November. In Tokyo JATP played at the Nichigeki Theatre, where Granz estimated around sixty thousand people would attend the concerts. He also scheduled shows for GIs at the Ernie Pyle Theatre in Nagoya, named for the popular American newspaperman killed covering the war in Japan. Gene Krupa, following a successful May 1952 trio concert in Tokyo at the end of a Pacific tour, told Granz about his reception and the hearty welcome he could anticipate in Japan. The formal invitation came from Taihei Records, distributor of some forty 78-rpm sides of Granz's Mercury/Clef records in the three months leading up to the tour. The concerts occurred as some of the more stringent restrictions of the postwar occupation were being eased and as American culture, including jazz, was being devoured by a populace that followed Armed Forces Network broadcasts. The jazz musicians were not the only Americans in Tokyo around this time: Xavier Cugat and his band were making their second tour of Japan, and the New York Giants baseball team was in the midst of a series of exhibition games.

Nothing in the history of Jazz at the Philharmonic could have prepared the musicians for the welcome they received when the Pan American flight carrying them from Honolulu landed at Haneda Airport in the early afternoon of November 2. "I remember I was sitting with Ray Brown, and when we landed there were thousands of people waiting at the airport," Herb Ellis remembered. "'Who are all these people here for? I wonder who's on the plane. Is it for us?' Ray replied, 'Oh no, it must be the vice president or somebody big.' It turned out they were there to see us, Jazz at the Philharmonic."[57] The airport welcome was the prelude to a ticker tape parade in which the musicians and Granz were feted through the cobblestone streets of Tokyo on the way to a reception with the president of the record company and other dignitaries.

Ellis recalled a round of practical jokes that did not stop until the beginning of the following year. The first was a trick played by Granz and Peterson on Ray Brown. The trio was waiting to go on with Fitzgerald when Peterson loosened Brown's G-string so that it had no tension whatsoever. "When she walks out, she wants to start immediately," Ellis said. "Ray started to play and it was clank, clank, clank. It sounded terrible, and Ella was not too pleased with that."[58] "Okay, all right," Brown responded when he saw Peterson and Granz laughing at the prank. Between shows, the bassist went out and played a few rounds of pachinko, a game where the winner receives small steel balls that are turned back in for prizes. Then, just as Peterson was playing the introduction for trombonist Bill Harris on "But Beautiful," he leaned over the piano and dropped the pachinko balls on the strings, causing a jangling clatter when Peterson hit the keyboard. "Bill Harris tried to play through this, and the audience didn't know what was going on," Ellis continued. "But Bill was the butt of the joke, and he had nothing to do with any of this. When he came off, he didn't look at any of us. He just walked by Oscar, Ray, and myself, and just said, 'Don't worry. You'll get yours.'"

And they did, in Rome in 1954 after Granz had persuaded a reluctant Peterson to sing a number on the program. (Normally Peterson refused partly because his singing voice so closely resembled that of Nat Cole.) He chose "Tenderly." As he completed the opening line, "The evening breeze caressed the trees . . . ," Harris positioned himself next to a waiter's cart stacked high with plates and glasses that had been placed at the edge of a flight of stairs leading to a basement. When Peterson hit the word *tenderly,* Harris nudged the cart, sending it crashing down the stairs and bringing the performance to a halt. Granz was so angry that Harris didn't confess what he had done until a year later.

The next mishap was not the result of a practical joke, but it none-theless stunned the audience and the musicians. Peterson had bought a suit he hid away especially for the Tokyo concerts. "I put it on that day and came out to the gig," Peterson said.[59] "That's when the piano stool broke. All I knew was I fell. When I opened my eyes, I was look-ing up at the sandbags and wires along the ceiling of the theater. I just started talking quietly to myself on the floor, lying there saying, 'Oscar Peterson, this can't be you, in your new suit, on this stage in Tokyo.' Meanwhile, Norman was ranting and raving backstage. 'Get him a piano bench! Get him a piano bench or I'll stop this concert!' So I got up and picked up the pieces and walked off. Not a person laughed, not one person in the audience. They got another bench. I came out with it and they applauded. We got into the next tune, we were playing along, then I heard this crack. I grabbed the front of this grand piano to pull my weight off the seat. All I could think of was that spoke in the middle of the seat. I started yelling, 'Ray, Ray!' He didn't know what had hap-pened. He decided I was trying to put him on or something. He was saying, 'Stop it, Peterson, and play the piano,' or something like that. I said, 'Ray, the bench, the bench.' When he realized what it was, then he came apart. Then the whole group came apart, and then the audience."

The Tokyo newspaper *Yomiuro Shinbun* explained the incident by saying that Peterson "played so hot that he fell down with his chair."[60]

The November 18 concert that was broadcast live on a Tokyo radio station made its way to a bootleg edition, which some twenty years later Peterson picked up during a Japanese tour. He forwarded a copy along to Granz, who issued it for the first time on Pablo Records.[61] One fascinating item from Granz's personal papers is two sheets of yellow legal-sized paper containing his handwritten introductions in phonetic Japanese, a revealing gesture directed toward cultivating his shows' new fans.

The trip to Japan proved to be as much of an education for Americans as it was for audiences hearing Jazz at the Philharmonic for the first time. Herb Ellis was impressed at the methodical, studious way the Japanese took to jazz, an affection that led to many return visits by Fitzgerald and Peterson over the decades. "When they come to hear a jazz show, they not only know who's playing—who the players are—but they know their records, or if they've had a particular solo on a particular record that was kind of popular. And they're autograph crazy, but they're very polite about it," Ellis said.[62]

Road manager Pete Cavello recalled some of the practical aspects of the tour. The trains the musicians rode to make a series of one-nighters ran with maximum efficiency. "The train only stopped in each station for barely a minute, necessitating that musicians line up near the windows with instruments and baggage. "Four or five of us ran off the train so that the guys by the windows could throw the bags to us to get them off the fastest way possible because the trains don't wait. We would have our bags lined up, and the next thing you know the train's not there. Whatever you left in the train, forget it."[63]

One incident involving a trio of drunken soldiers turned nasty. They made the mistake of heckling Fitzgerald with catcalls of "Fuck you, Ella" and other obscenities from the balcony of the Nichigeki as she was singing "Body and Soul." The yelling, as Granz told it, distracted and frightened Fitzgerald. After the finale, he turned to Benny Carter, who was known for rolling up his sleeves now and then when insulted. "Follow me." Oscar Peterson joined them as they made their up two flights of stairs to where the offenders were seated. "'Are you the man who's been shouting while Ella was singing?' Granz asked. "He said, 'Yes, fuck you' or that kind of thing. Another soldier broke a bottle, and Carter said, 'Don't you get into it. You stay out of it.'" Peterson and Carter stood in between Granz, the soldier, and his friends to keep the fight even. Granz twice sent one offender flying into curtains behind him. Carter punched out another who was ready to lunge at Granz. Their chivalry on Fitzgerald's behalf earned them the applause of some audience members who had suffered through the soldiers' behavior.[64] It also prompted one letter to the editor of Tokyo's *Asahi Shinbun*. An office worker who had witnessed the incident wrote to say, "It was as if I were being shown the American type of justice in this brave action."[65]

Granz expected to have a lock on the Japanese jazz market into the foreseeable future, if only because the high cost of transportation and accommodations virtually prohibited competition. He predicted similarly large audiences if he carried through with a tour late the following fall. However, he never found it practical or profitable enough to make Japan a regular stop. The only other time JATP returned to Japan as a touring unit, for two shows in Tokyo in 1983, was to mark a thirty-year anniversary of the original, and represented the last JATP concerts ever. Granz was enthusiastic about one Japanese jazz musician discovered by Oscar Peterson playing in a nightclub in the Ginza district. He recorded Toshiko Akiyoshi, who had been classically trained but turned to jazz in 1947, with a rhythm section of Ellis, Brown, and Heard before JATP returned to America. The pianist/bandleader was acknowledged as Japan's leading pianist before immigrating to the United States in January 1956 on a scholarship to study at Berklee College of Music in Boston and embarking on a career that has spanned seven decades.

Granz estimated that JATP had rung up a $600,000 gross from its three tours in 1953.[66] The twenty-two Japanese concerts contributed around $50,000 to the total, and the European tour of fifty concerts in thirty cities grossed around $200,000. The domestic tour took in $350,000, a 20 percent decline over the previous year. Granz attributed the fall-off in attendance to presentation of "the same old names" year in and year out. The uncertainty about JATP's future in the United States was only one indicator of major changes in American life since the late 1940s that were beginning to affect Granz's fortunes and to alter entertainment in general. Four factors explain the changing environment in which Granz was operating by the mid-1950s. First, the suburbanization of America in the years after World War II dispersed audiences from the core of the older cities and left established entertainment venues to fend for themselves. Second, Granz's audiences were ten years older than they had been when JATP was a part of the emerging youth culture, and the young were increasingly turning toward folk music or rock and roll. Third, television, by offering new stay-at-home entertainment, drew consumers away from live entertainment. In the four years between 1950 and 1953, the number of homes with televisions grew twenty-fold, from around one million to twenty million. Finally, changing tastes within jazz also affected how Granz programmed Jazz at the Phil in the next few years.

A November 1954 *Time* magazine cover story on Dave Brubeck surveyed the state of jazz in the wake of the pianist's emergence and popularity especially on college campuses for his more cerebral and cool approach.[67] This music, according to the magazine, was spearheading "a new type of jazz . . . that is causing a tremendous boom in all jazz—the birth of a new kind of jazz age in the U.S.," one that "evokes neither swinging hips nor hip flasks. It goes to the head and the heart more than to the feet." Thus it is ironic that a comment by Granz in the Brubeck story became its headline. "Says Jazz Promoter Norman Granz, who does not always understand Brubeck's 'far-out music': 'He's way out on Cloud 7.'" (JATP was listed first among the pianist's "competition" with respect to jazz events in 1954.) That did not prevent Granz from fielding a package called the "Modern Jazz Concert" with Duke Ellington and his orchestra, Brubeck, Gerry Mulligan, and Stan Getz, in October 1954, but later he declared it a failure. "Jazz has always been, to me, fundamentally the blues and all of the happy and sad emotions it arouses. I dig the blues as a basic human emotion, and my concerts are primarily emotional," Granz said. "I could never put on a cerebral concert; I'd rather go the emotional route. The biggest flop I've ever had was the tour I put on with some of the cerebral musicians like Brubeck and Gerry Mulligan. A critic told me that Bud Powell's a better pianist than Oscar Peterson, but I could put Powell on the stage and he'd die like a dog."[68]

Also on the horizon was the Newport Jazz Festival, initiated in July 1954, which began to take over from Jazz at the Philharmonic as a mass jazz event. It was emblematic of a new approach, devised by George Wein, that has now been working for nearly six decades. Instead of taking a particular set of jazz stalwarts on a season-long tour of audiences' hometowns, it involved staging single events, sometimes spread over days, in one location, with the aim of exposing audiences to a broader range of what was happening in jazz and poplar music from year to year, a trend that Miles Davis early on dismissed as "jazz supermarkets."[69] Davis's comment resembled criticisms leveled at Granz as he endeavored to take jazz to the world's finest concert halls and encouraged a fresh evaluation of jazz as an art *and* as commercially successful music.

The next few years presented other cultural and musical challenges to jazz and resulted in Granz's decision in 1957 to stop touring Jazz at the Philharmonic domestically. In the meantime he was fast acquiring the international connections that would allow him to move much of his business to Europe. By 1955 Granz had acquired the rights to be Ella Fitzgerald's personal manager and record producer. The founding of Verve Records the following year would take them both to new levels of fame, fortune, and critical acclaim.

12

"That Tall Old Man Standing Next to Ella Fitzgerald"

The Japanese tour of 1953 was still in progress when Granz acquired the Hope Diamond of his career. On the flight between Tokyo and Osaka, he talked with Ella Fitzgerald about taking over her personal management when her contract with Moe Gale at Associated Booking Corporation would expire that December. Gale, one of the owners of the Savoy Ballroom, had been involved with Fitzgerald since the beginning of her career as part of his managing the Chick Webb Orchestra from late 1929. Gale had also delivered the band to Decca Records as one of the new label's earliest attractions and had pressed Webb to bring a female vocalist into the band.[1]

"I'd been thinking for years about taking over Ella's personal management. . . . Ella was afraid. She thought I was too much of a blow-top," Granz reflected.[2] "So I told her it was a matter of pride with me, that she still hadn't been recognized—economically, at least—as the greatest singer of our time. I asked her to give me a year's trial, no commission, but she wound up insisting on paying the commission. We had no contract—mutual love and respect was all the contract we needed." In 2001, he added, "I didn't claim to be the *only* manager. I never had a contract with Ella or Oscar or Basie or Duke. I told Ella, If you want the luxury of saying, 'Norman, I quit,' you're off. Go for yourself, but I want the luxury of quitting you, too. So we had a nice relationship. Ella lasted for maybe forty or forty-five years, Oscar well over fifty."[3] After she agreed to go with Granz, he satisfied an IRS debt that Gale had allowed to pile up and that the government was pressing to settle.

Together, they worked to polish her talent and enhance her reputation. Granz had plans to widen her scope musically and upgrade the venues in which she appeared, as well as to get her higher pay that would leave what Granz called "Fifty-second Street money" in the dust.

Signs were abundant that Fitzgerald was ready to enjoy a deeper appreciation of her talent. In May 1954, on her opening night at New York's Basin Street East club, the entertainment elite gathered to celebrate her nineteen years in the business. She received eighteen awards, ranging from those given by the trade press to those given by international jazz federations from France, Italy, Spain, Iceland, India, and Australia. Decca Records presented the singer with a plaque citing her sales of over twenty-two million records since the Chick Webb days. Among those paying tribute to Fitzgerald during the program emceed by Steve Allen were Pearl Bailey, Dizzy Gillespie, Harry Belafonte, and Eartha Kitt. A flurry of telegrams from Louis Armstrong, Lionel Hampton, Lena Horne, Billy Eckstine, Rosemary Clooney, Benny Goodman, and the Mills Brothers among others added to the festiveness of the occasion. Asked to sing, she humbly told the crowd, "I guess what everyone wants more that anything else is to be loved. And to know that you love me for my singing is too much for me. Forgive me if I don't have all the words. Maybe I can sing and you'll understand." *Newsweek*'s coverage of the evening captured the essence of what Granz would capitalize on in the years ahead when he coordinated her personal management and recording activities. "Other popular singers tend to become identified with a particular musical groove," the magazine reported. "Ella Fitzgerald plays the field, exerting a talent which, in addition to an unmatched pliability, has demonstrated an uncommon staying power."[4]

Granz used that acclaim to book the singer into more prestigious clubs and hotel showrooms that had previously been closed both to black artists and to jazz in general. "I can get her into the right clubs with just a few phone calls," he said.[5] Fitzgerald expressed similar aspirations to her onetime press agent Jules Fox as they passed Sunset Strip on their way to the Tiffany Club in the Wilshire district. "I know I make a lot of money at the jazz clubs I play," she said, "but I sure wish I could play at one of those fancy places."[6]

Granz and Fitzgerald were not alone in thinking that her talent deserved a higher profile. In early 1955, Marilyn Monroe lent her prestige to help broker Fitzgerald's first appearance at the Mocambo on Los

Angeles's Sunset Strip. Monroe, a committed Fitzgerald fan, had heard of her desire to play more upscale clubs.

The actress took up her case directly with Mocambo's owner, Charlie Morrison, and called Granz urging him to follow suit. When Morrison repeatedly failed to return Granz's calls, Monroe again spoke to the club owner and pledged to occupy a front table every night of Fitzgerald's run at the Mocambo if he booked her. Morrison relented in the face of that appeal. Monroe recruited Judy Garland and Frank Sinatra to attend the opening night of Fitzgerald's two-week engagement in March 1956. The run was extended to three weeks after sold-out crowds brought Morrison completely around and led him shortly thereafter to book Nat Cole and Eartha Kitt. Fitzgerald returned to the Mocambo twice more in the next year and a half, generating the club's largest business after release of the Cole Porter songbook in 1956. The success of Fitzgerald's appearance also helped usher in the opening of integrated nightclubs in Hollywood, among them Pandora's Box, the Purple Onion, the Crescendo, and the Renaissance.[7]

Word of Fitzgerald's drawing power at the Mocambo spread across the industry, and within a month Granz had booked her for three weeks at the Venetian Room of the Fairmont Hotel in San Francisco, marking the first time the room had ever booked a jazz act. In November 1955 she returned to Las Vegas after a five-year absence for a date at the Flamingo Hotel. Another show of support for Fitzgerald came when Marlene Dietrich came into the whites-only casino arm in arm with Pearl Bailey and Lena Horne.[8] Fitzgerald was feted during a star-packed after-hours concert at the Flamingo, beginning with a sextet led by Jack Teagarden, and was greeted by an emotional ovation lasting five minutes when she hit the stage and swung into a fifty-minute set with her trio.

Granz's campaign for Fitzgerald's recording contract became more aggressive as the deadline to re-sign with Decca Records approached and her apparent frustrations with her longtime label surfaced. Nat Hentoff prefaced a particularly revealing interview published in February 1955 by noting, "Very little is known about what Ella really thinks on subjects closest to her career and emotions. . . . But she is conscious of the scope of her vocal skill and warmth, a potential that has never been realized as fully as it deserves—for reasons that have nothing to do with her undeniable talent."[9]

One can almost hear Granz's prompting behind her unusually frank and public airing of what she considered missed opportunities with Decca. For example, she had incorporated into her act an arrangement of "Teach Me Tonight," a best-selling pop hit of the day, but had not had the chance to record the tune. This, she said, was one example of how Decca rerouted "hot" pop material to other singers. "It's been so long since I've gotten a show tune to do," she said. "Or a chance to do a tune like 'The Man That Got Away.' Frank Sinatra came into Basin Street East often when he was working at the Copa, and he asked for that song every time. And he also asked, 'How come, Ella, you don't have a number like *that* to record?'"

Fitzgerald also complained that Decca had failed to adequately promote her recordings, noting that she had personally purchased copies of her album *Ella*, a rematch with pianist Ellis Larkins, for West Coast broadcasters in order to gain airplay. "Now I don't like to say anything against anybody, but maybe the recording company is more interested in pictures [Decca began acquiring substantial holdings in Universal-International Pictures in 1951 and full control a year later] now that they don't give as much attention to the records. But I sure would like to be with a label that would give me something to record."

Granz finally had the opportunity to pry Fitzgerald away from Decca ten months later and swooped in like a hawk. In June 1955 Universal had begun prerecording the soundtrack of *The Benny Goodman Story,* starring Steve Allen as Goodman. The cast featured not only a handful of contemporary musicians but many of the musicians from the clarinetist's former bands playing themselves. But up until late in the game Decca did not know, or did not think it mattered, that Gene Krupa, Teddy Wilson, and Stan Getz were all under exclusive contract to Granz (Lionel Hampton also recorded extensively for Granz but was not similarly bound contractually). "It's astonishing how major studios can make mistakes. But then you think, it's people. People make mistakes," Granz said. "It never occurred to them to check with me whether they had the right to use them. They finished the picture and the music was recorded. Then they discovered that I had the artists under contract and might have to throw out the album because Gene Krupa was on everything. Gene came to me and said, 'I think you better get together because they're going crazy now. They're afraid to put it out. I wish as a favor you would let it come out.'

I said, 'Don't worry about it. I'll do it. Just don't say anything.' I mean, how could they have a *Benny Goodman Story* without an album? It would be crazy."[10]

When Decca finally came to Granz seeking a release for the musicians, he expressed his willingness to negotiate. "I then proposed that if they wanted the soundtrack badly enough, in return I wanted a release of Ella from her Decca contract. It was that simple."

Decca had despaired of ever releasing what it knew would be a lucrative soundtrack album. Granz, ever the wily bargainer, knew he held all the cards. The label finally ceded Fitzgerald in the first week of January 1956, barely a month before the film's release on February 2.

Granz, anticipating Ella Fitzgerald's arrival, announced the formation of Verve Records almost as soon as she departed Decca. Thus began the second and greatest of the three major phases of her recording career, the last being the Pablo years in the 1970s and 1980s. Granz insisted that her leaving Decca and the establishment of Verve were unrelated. His plan, he said, had been to merge Clef, Norgran, and Down Home into a broader-based entity that would include popular music as well as jazz. Rather than being created merely as a vehicle for Fitzgerald, Verve was his solution to another long-standing problem: the hemorrhaging of money from his jazz labels, whose finances had up until then depended exclusively on the tours. Granz said the wider focus of Verve allowed him to design a more effective network of disc jockey promotion and other activities more associated with pop music.[11] Among the first artists making the move to Verve were Anita O'Day, Buddy Rich, Oscar Peterson, Joe Williams, Count Basie, and a newly formed big band led by Gene Krupa. Granz stated that the first Verve recordings— six LPs, six extended-play seven-inch discs, and four singles—would come out in February.

Granz also reached an agreement with the American Record Society to form a mail-order jazz record club and selected releases from new recordings or previously unreleased masters, none of which carried Granz or JATP trademarks. The recordings were promoted as an adjunct of ARS, and Granz agreed to develop a jazz education component as part of the program.

"Granz will have no connection with Verve except for owning it," Down Beat reported. "All central operations will be handled by 24-year-old arranger-conductor Buddy Bregman."[12] The two had met in November 1955 on the tennis courts at Rosemary Clooney and Jose Ferrer's home in Los Angeles. Bregman had recently had hits with an R&B-flavored Leiber and Stoller tune, "Bazoom (I Need Your Loving)," for a group called the Cheers and Bobby Short's "Let There Be Love." Bregman had been a fan of Granz and JATP since seeing the concerts at the Civic Opera House in the late 1940s. When they were introduced, Granz said, "I just heard a record by Buddy Bregman. Was that you?"[13] He was referring to "Bernie's Tune," the B side of the Cheers' single. According to Bregman, Granz told him of his plans to begin a new label and asked if he would consider going to work for him. Bregman's early successes with popular music and his enthusiasm gained Granz's confidence. Granz may have also felt that Bregman's youth would make him more affordable, more controllable, and better attuned to the contemporary pop markets than an established arranger. He reported for work at the Granz offices at 451 North Canon Drive in Beverly Hills as head of pop A&R at a weekly salary of $500, plus scale for all orchestrations and sessions. "I started on a Monday, we did not have a name on Tuesday, and by Wednesday, Norman had come up with Verve," Bregman recalled.[14]

A native of Chicago, Bregman was the son of a wealthy steel executive and the nephew of the composer Jule Styne, his mother's brother. The self-taught arranger, whose tastes were formed in the Swing Era, came up through a high school music program playing clarinet and took early opportunities to produce arrangements for UCLA drama students before getting his first professional jobs. When Granz gave him a list of artists to choose from on Clef and Norgran for his first projects, Bregman elected to produce an album with Anita O'Day, whose sales with Clef had previously been between three and four thousand albums. According to Bregman, the result, *Anita*, sold in the vicinity of 185,000 albums and was deemed a critical success for O'Day. "That made me a star in that area," he recalled.[15] In January 1956 he followed up with an album of Buddy Rich singing songs by Johnny Mercer and four singles by Fitzgerald that marked her recording debut for Verve and Granz (not counting all the live JATP recordings that Granz had been previously barred from issuing because of her Decca deal).

Granz had wanted Fitzgerald to do a Cole Porter album for many years and had unsuccessfully appealed to Decca to undertake such a work. "They rejected it on the grounds that Ella wasn't that kind of singer," Granz said in 1990. "I could understand it from their point of view, because they had one thing in mind and that was finding hit singles. I was interested in how I could enhance Ella's position, to make her a singer with more than just a cult following amongst jazz fans. . . . So I proposed to Ella that the first Verve album would not be a jazz project, but rather a songbook of the works of Cole Porter. I envisaged her doing a lot of composers. The trick was to change the backing enough so that, here and there, there would be signs of jazz."[16]

Granz's ideas about what would be best for Fitzgerald's recording career were evolving over time, as seen in an exchange of letters with Milt Gabler, Fitzgerald's former producer at Decca. "I have the utmost respect for your knowledge of your end of the business and feel at this point that you should inject yourself personally into Ella's recording," Gabler wrote Granz in December 1954. "If you have any suggestions, I am willing to listen. If you would like to help produce a date at our studio, I am sure we can work it out. The most important thing we both want to achieve is a hit for Ella." Granz waited until the following July, when he was within months of gaining her recording contract himself, before responding. "I certainly wish something could be done to get Ella some material of a pop nature, instead of just the standards alone," he said. "My suggestion that Ella do standards was primarily directed to the package trade, but at the same time I certainly feel that she should be given as much pop material as possible. . . . The standards that she has done ought to be released in an album."[17]

Granz prepared for the Porter songbook with the same methodical zeal that he had shown in producing *The Jazz Scene* and *The Astaire Story*. He instructed his main assistant, Mary Jane Outwater—*secretary* would be too narrow a term to describe the role Granz entrusted her with—to track down two copies of every Cole Porter song in publication and then winnow them down to about fifty songs for Fitzgerald to consider. His first choice to arrange the thirty-two-song, two-LP set was Nelson Riddle, the former Tommy Dorsey trombonist and arranger who had made his mark in the early 1950s when Nat Cole selected him to oversee his Capitol vocal sessions. Frank Sinatra credited Riddle for virtually reviving his career on the same label. However, Riddle's boss at Capitol, Carlos Gastel, was not keen on loaning him out. Finally Granz chose to "take a chance on Bregman. He knew all of the songs and had an affinity for the material."[18]

Bregman has long asserted that he influenced Granz on key decisions concerning Fitzgerald, including signing her with Verve. He says he was the one who informed Granz that Decca was recording his artists for *The Benny Goodman Story* and that the infraction might provide the leverage to get Fitzgerald's contract. Granz, according to Bregman, initially dismissed his idea, saying, among other things, that she couldn't sell many records—a remark that strains credulity. Likewise, Bregman claims he preceded Granz in conceiving the songbook concept, beginning with Porter and followed by Lorenz Hart and Richard Rodgers.

Bregman seemingly overstates his case. It stretches the imagination to believe that Granz, then nearing fifteen years in the business and having already toured Fitzgerald for seven years, needed direction concerning Fitzgerald from Bregman, who was then still at the beginning of his career. Bregman may have thought of gaining Fitzgerald's recording contract or redirecting the repertoire that relaunched her career at the same time that Granz did, but it is more probable that he simply helped to carry out plans Granz had hatched long before.

That said, Fitzgerald, Bregman, and Granz had a successful collaboration. Granz provided the backing and was responsible, along with Fitzgerald, for settling on the material and providing the instrumentation. Bregman's varied arrangements played by top-drawer Los Angeles jazz and studio musicians gave a pop feeling to the songs while retaining room for jazz feeling and some improvisation as well as accommodating Fitzgerald's jazz instincts. Granz also pushed Fitzgerald to sing all the verses to the songs to feature the full scope of the lyricists' art and make the albums that much more distinctive and authoritative. "Most singers, maybe excluding Frank Sinatra, rarely sang a verse and the composers used to go crazy," Granz said. "They never got a verse, and some of them were beautiful. Ella would get uptight and say, 'Why do I have to do this [learn the verses]?' Translation: She had to spend time doing it and she didn't want to. . . . The verses were a problem because it meant working hard on them. For the most part they were written for shows. On a three-minute single no singer could give up a chorus for a verse, but this was an LP, so I didn't care about time."[19]

With recording set to begin on February 7, 1956, at the Capitol Records studio, Bregman and Fitzgerald had begun rehearsing for the Porter songbook about three weeks before at Zardi's Jazzland, the club where she was then appearing. "I doubt the bartender realized he was witnessing history," recalled Bregman in 2002.[20] Granz was back in New York during part of this time recording Lester Young and Teddy Wilson; then he returned to Los Angeles to record sessions with Buddy DeFranco and Art Tatum.

The songbooks required a different approach from what Fitzgerald had been used to when she went into a studio with a trio and reeled off tunes in two to three takes before quickly moving on. Granz noted, "When I recorded Ella, I always put her out front, not a blend," he said. "The reason was that I frankly didn't care about what happened to the music. It was there to support her. I've had conductors tell me that in bar

23 the trumpet player hit a wrong note. Well, I don't care. I wasn't making perfect records. If they came out perfectly, fine. But I wanted to make records in which Ella sounded best. I wasn't interested in doing six takes to come back to where we started. My position has always been that what you do before you go into the studio really defines you as a producer. Choosing the musicians, the songs, the arrangers, all of that nails down the effect I have on the session. . . . All my decisions as producer really have been made by the time I walk into the studio. The die has been cast. I have very little to do other than to say one take is better than another."[21] Pianist Paul Smith, who came in with Bregman and accompanied Fitzgerald intermittently over the next thirty-five years, played on all of the songbooks. He remembered, "There were hardly any second takes. The Cole Porter and some of the others were sort of *ground* out. That's the only way I can describe them. We'd run down the verse, just to make sure she knew it and bang, we'd record it."[22]

One of Bregman's memories from the Porter recording dates, specifically the wrap-up to a rehearsal on "Just One of Those Things," typifies Granz's recording studio practice and philosophy. Unbeknownst to Bregman, Granz had arrived at the studio in time to hear the run-through of the song. "That was a take," Granz's voice crackled unexpectedly over the studio loudspeaker.

"What do you mean that was 'a take?'" Bregman asked. "I want to try it one more time."

"It was fine," Granz responded. "Let's get on with it."[23]

Though Granz and Cole Porter had been friends through Fred Astaire since around the time of *The Astaire Story* in 1952, and though Porter was notoriously picky about how singers recorded his work, Granz chose not to involve him in the process. Instead, once the recordings were done, he took a stack of the acetates with him to New York to play for Porter. "He loved them," Granz said after two hours with the composer at his Waldorf-Astoria apartment.[24] Porter was delighted by Fitzgerald's treatment of his work, including her diction. And if Porter was happy, the listening public was ecstatic to hear the old and familiar "Day and Night," "In the Still of the Night," "Begin the Beguine," and "I Love Paris" side by side with less well-known songs such as "All Through the Night," "Ev'ry Time We Say Goodbye," or "I Am in Love." The collection revealed the depth and craftsmanship of Porter's art by demonstrating in retrospect how time and again Porter had adapted his music and lyrics to fit the narrative of stage and film productions, some of which had sunk without a trace apart from his music.

Down Beat's five-star review fully recognized the significance of *Ella Fitzgerald Sings the Cole Porter Song Book*, which it described as "a delightful 32-course feast of much of the best of this stimulating sensual and intelligent diarist of our overcivilization. . . . This set also, however, indicates a wider adaptability to shades of considerably varying moods than Ella has generally had a chance to display before. . . . The recording, as has been the case on Verve, is superior to the average of Norman Granz's other labels."[25]

The songbooks did have a few critics. One was Bill Coss of *Metronome,* who wrote, "There was no attempt to make a jazz album here, although Buddy Bregman's sometimes heavy scores skirt that issue and there are pleasant moments by Oscar Peterson and Herb Ellis [actually Paul Smith and Barney Kessel]. But Ella with Cole Porter music and lyrics should have been the album to end all albums, jazz or not. *Should have been,* I say, because it isn't. There's an unreal quality about much of this, which isn't altogether explainable at first." Coss then unfavorably compared Fitzgerald's reading of "I Get a Kick Out of You" with those by Frank Sinatra and Billie Holiday, concluding that maybe the lyrics were too far from her experience to be credible. "The fact remains that however pleasant the album is, it is not good Ella or good Cole Porter."[26]

The Porter songbook took off beyond Granz and Fitzgerald's wildest expectations both commercially and artistically, becoming one of the top-selling jazz records of all time. Sales boosted the fortunes of the young Verve and laid the groundwork for the remainder of its signature series in the years to come. When sales hit one hundred thousand in the first month, the album went to no. 15 on the *Billboard* charts, and two weeks after its release it was ranked second in a *Down Beat* poll of best-selling jazz albums. "It was the eleventh biggest LP of the year. That was insane for me. Verve put me in the commercial market for the first time," Granz said of the best-selling album of his career.[27] Around the same time, Granz booked Fitzgerald into the Starlight Room of the Waldorf-Astoria with the Count Basie Orchestra in what for her was a significant move upward. The warmth between the singer and bandleader extended as well to her relations with the band—who called her "Sis"—and to the emotional depth of the performances.

On August 15, 1956, a spectacular concert at the Hollywood Bowl featured Louis Armstrong and the All-Stars and Art Tatum alongside Fitzgerald, the Oscar Peterson Trio, and a JATP ensemble filled out by Roy Eldridge, Harry Edison, Flip Phillips, Illinois Jacquet, and Buddy

Rich. The album, *Jazz at the Hollywood Bowl*, became effectively the 1956 volume of the JATP recordings. Granz later received a letter from the Hollywood Bowl telling him that the concert had been the best-attended jazz event in the history of the outdoor facility—ironic given that eleven years earlier the Bowl's management had told Granz that they did not want to host any event with the word *jazz* in its title.

Fitzgerald and Armstrong went into the studio with the Oscar Peterson Trio and Buddy Rich the day after the Bowl concert to record the first of three albums that not only sold well but are thought to be among the finest of Granz's career. Armstrong was unusually hard to corral given his seemingly nonstop touring schedule, and often his trumpet playing was barely up to par when Granz had the chance to record him, so that he was often forced to compensate by singing more. His manager Joe Glaser didn't make it any easier by approving dates for Armstrong at the last minute, leaving Granz with only a day or two at most to prepare, as was the case with all three of the Ella and Louis records from 1956 and 1957. Granz later said that Armstrong, unlike Fitzgerald, with her perfect diction and loyalty to the music as written, "never deferred to the material. He did what he did, and that was the thing I was trying to capture. You could hear his breathing or sighing or, instead of the word, he'd come out with a sound. But to me, that's its quality."[28] The contrast between their styles was pure magic. Fitzgerald deferred to Armstrong to make the final choices on the songs and keys. Photographs taken during the sessions show Armstrong and Fitzgerald, dressed in casual summer clothes, thoroughly enjoying one another.

Shortly afterwards, on August 21, 1956, Granz, Bregman, and Fitzgerald returned to Capitol Studios to get started on the Rodgers and Hart songbook and thereby capitalize on the momentum provided by the Porter release. Granz was a little the worse for wear, sporting twelve stitches in his chin and a broken cheekbone from a car accident ten days before in Benedict Canyon that had resulted in his Mercedes Benz being totaled after careening into a cliff.[29] Granz had decided to spotlight the music Richard Rodgers had written with Lorenz Hart because he felt Hart's words had inspired Rodgers to write with a leanness and edge, whereas Rodgers's work with Oscar Hammerstein was more schmaltzy. "I talked to Cole Porter about this once," said Granz, "and he thought that Rodgers should have teamed with Johnny Mercer after Hart's death. Mercer would have been perfect. His work would have had Hart's thinking and that edge."[30]

The Rodgers and Hart songbook followed the pattern set by the Porter, featuring big band, band with strings, and small-group arrangements. Though the content of the songbooks was pretty much set by Granz in consultation with Fitzgerald, there was still give-and-take in the studio when the singer occasionally resisted her manager's wishes. For example, during the recording of Rodgers and Hart, she refused to sing "Miss" as in "Have You Met Miss Jones?" Granz recalled, "It was not a woman's lyric. So she changed it to 'Have you met *Sir* Jones?' I was very unhappy about that, but we were in the midst of recording and Ella was very firm. I had to think of the whole project, and I didn't think it warranted a stand on principle. I could have eliminated the song, and I considered that. But since it was such a good song and Buddy's arrangement was good, I gave in."[31]

A dispute in which Fitzgerald ended up acquiescing to Granz's wishes was captured on tape from a rehearsal on Porter's "Let's Do It," reproduced as part of *The Complete Ella Fitzgerald Song Books on Verve.* "This is so *long!*" an exasperated Fitzgerald exclaimed.

"Whose idea was it to do it all?" the engineer Val Valentin inquired.

"It's Norman's," Bregman said.

"He wants it," Fitzgerald said.

"If it's Norman's idea, we better give it to him and let him pick [a longer or shorter version]," replied Valentin.

"Let's do it!" Fitzgerald said, laughing at the play on words of the song's title.

Bregman's younger brother Bobby, who had met Granz at the Beverly Hills Tennis Club, worked for Verve for two years beginning in mid-1956 and was in the studio for some of the Rodgers and Hart sessions. "What always sticks in my mind was 'Manhattan' and that she did it in one take," the junior Bregman said. "It was so great, and Norman was such a perfectionist. It was a wonderful thing to be there. I was a big jazz fan, and to be around these people—working and getting a paycheck . . ."[32]

Fitzgerald had a busy and lucrative fall and winter of 1956 and 1957, according to an itinerary that also shows her fees, quoted here to indicate her rising economic status. The day after she recorded *Ella and Louis* on August 16, she performed at the San Diego Palladium Ballroom ($1,500 guarantee, plus 50 percent of gross over $3,500).[33] Fitzgerald had almost a month off before picking up with the Jazz at the Philharmonic tour between September 15 and October 15 at $6,500 per week. On October 16 she began a two-week engagement, her third, at the Mocambo in Los Angeles ($2,500 weekly) before heading off for three weeks at the New Frontier Hotel in Las Vegas, where, as with JATP, she received $6,500 per week. Afterwards she spent one week at the Chi Chi in Palm Springs (November 19–25, $2,500, plus a three-bedroom suite), three weeks at the Fairmont in San Francisco ($2,000 a week, plus suite), three weeks at Zardi's back in Los Angeles (December 18 to January 7, $4,000 per week), and just over a week at the Versailles in Miami Beach (January 11–19, 1957, $6,500 plus accommodations).

The benefits of Granz's management, which like Fitzgerald's singing found distinctive ways of melding jazz and pop, can be seen in an infatuated review in the *Hollywood Reporter* of her October 1956 Mocambo appearance backed by pianist Jimmy Rowles, guitarist Barney Kessel, Max Bennett on bass, and Larry Bunker on drums. "'Ridin' High,' Ella Fitzgerald's opening number, set the theme and ignited the enthusiasm of the usually blasé first-nighters at the Mo. The contagion grew to such proportions that they wouldn't let the gal go after 13 songs and 50 minutes. It was a beg-off. . . . Miss Fitzgerald, spurred on by such idolatrous acclaim (heralded, of course by her smash LP album of Cole Porter songs), has never been in finer form. . . . Not to be minimized—and these are very important angles in summing up the current Fitzgerald craze—are her bright and flashy arrangements and conducting, all by Buddy Bregman. Seldom has such fine music come from such a small group as the combo that backs Miss Fitzgerald."[34]

"Ella was easy," Granz said late in life. "All Ella needed was a good manager, which I was for her compared to what she'd had—and the record company, that was total. Decca did good things for her and Milt Gabler was a good producer, but she was one of many artists at Decca. When I formed Verve, she became *the* artist and she had the advantage not only of someone to manage her, but also presenting her concerts. I was unique among managers, in that I owned the record company and I was also an impresario."[35]

The exact nature of their relationship has long been a subject of fascination, with some believing that Granz exercised a disproportionate and overbearing influence over the singer's affairs. But Fitzgerald told her old friend Leonard Feather that she and Granz had had many confrontations over the years and that she had never been just putty in his hands. Rather, the two of them combined formidable qualities in making their partnership successful. "Granz has an irascible side;

Ella says she has learned to live with it," Feather said. As Fitzgerald explained, "The idea was, get him to do the talking for me and I'd do the singing. I needed that. Sometimes we'd argue and wouldn't speak for weeks on end, and he'd give me messages through a third party, but now I accept him as he is, or I may just speak my mind. We're all like a big family now."[36]

Granz's focus on Fitzgerald's career demonstrated the attention to detail he had so fully mastered over the years. Pianist Paul Smith said Granz selected about 99 percent of the music Fitzgerald sang and recorded in the ensuing decades. He also handled the messy duty of hiring and firing musicians, always acting in concert with Fitzgerald's wishes. Granz noted, "There were times I let musicians go that, personally, I would have preferred keeping. But Ella, for whatever reasons she might have had, thought maybe that they didn't try enough or didn't play well enough when she was onstage."[37]

"At the very beginning, I turned Ella's career around by merely dictating different approaches—work at the Fairmont Hotel, not the 331 Club. But that was an economic decision," he said. "When I first broke the Fairmont in San Francisco with Ella, she asked me what she was getting. I told her and she said, 'But that's not right. We're getting less than in a club.' I said, 'Yes, but you're building a reputation for playing the Fairmont Hotel. Next time around, you'll get ten times more.'"

Fitzgerald was a reserved person who often preferred solitude and opened up to only a few close friends. She was insecure despite her renown and needed some coaxing to come out of her shell to help Granz promote her career. For example, Virginia Wicks, both a personal friend and her publicist during this period, said Fitzgerald feared interviews partly because of her general shyness around other people. "She knew there were many intelligent people coming to interview her," Wicks said. "She didn't think she had the vocabulary or knowledge to deal with them. That is one reason she was reluctant to have interviews with *Time* and other major publications. You almost had to trick her into an interview. It was very important to Norman. Yet Ella would really sulk. She would be sitting in a corner of the room. The interviewer came in and she would be uncommunicative until either the interviewer or I said something that brought her out of it. But she didn't do a lot of talking. She kept a lot inside her head."[38]

Some have charged Granz with overworking Fitzgerald in the giddy years when she began to roam the upper echelons of the entertainment world. But those who knew Fitzgerald better describe someone for whom work—and lots of it—was her life. Her pianist Paul Smith did his first extended tour with Fitzgerald in South America and Europe lasting six months in 1960 and another forty-six weeks in 1962. "She was fun. How could you not have fun playing with her?" he said. "As far as the amount of work, Norman was kind of trapped in between. Ella would complain that she was working too hard and he would not book her for about two weeks, then she would say, after about the first week, 'Why aren't I working? Don't people want to see me?' Norman was damned if he did and damned if he didn't. Ella really didn't have much of a home life. Her home was the stage. When she was onstage, she was loving it."[39]

Smith acknowledged that sometimes Fitzgerald got extra nervous when she knew Granz was coming in to hear a show and that sometimes Granz imposed his views on her repertoire in ways she didn't like. For instance, Granz "disliked anything Stephen Sondheim ever wrote" and made sure Fitzgerald didn't perform it. "Benny Carter wrote a beautiful arrangement of 'Send in the Clowns,'" Smith said. "Norman came in and said, 'What are you playing this for?' He made such an issue of it we took it out of the book."

Granz was also irritated, according to Smith, by the idea of Fitzgerald recording with Mel Tormé, who was Fitzgerald's friend and was, like her, a master of scat singing as well as a gifted songwriter, arranger, and all-around musician who had signed with Verve in 1958. The mentions of Granz in Tormé's later memoirs are not entirely complimentary. After a concert tour with Fitzgerald to Australia, which Granz oversaw, Tormé came to the conclusion that "Norman was not one of nature's noblemen."[40] Later he wrote, "What Ella needed was direction. She was in danger of falling into the 'cult singer' trap, an abyss wherein only jazz fans and musicians appreciated her. This was not the way to gold, and, even though she was solidly committed to singing in her jazz-oriented, jazz-influenced manner, she wanted more out of life than smoky joints and out-of-the-way venues in which to ply her trade. . . . Her help came in the form of Norman Granz. This Svengali-like handling of Ella has produced astounding results. . . . He had her embark on a series of 'songbooks' that elevated her into a new category, a 'pop-jazz' singer. These songbooks were landmark recordings and led to Ella becoming persona grata in every part of the civilized world. Her fame spread to the four corners of the earth, and in this country, she played where she wanted to."[41] Granz, however, disputed the "Svengali" image and the idea that he had begun to totally run the singer's life from top to bottom. "None of that bothered me. I had a job to do and I did it."[42]

Granz explained his relationship to Fitzgerald and how he saw his role in a 1987 interview with the record producer and broadcaster Elliot Meadow. "If I'm standing next to Ella Fitzgerald, and people want her autograph, and someone in the line says, 'I don't know who that tall old man is standing next to Ella, but I think I'll get his autograph, too. Who knows who he is?' That's all right," Granz said. "My ego's just as large as any performer's, because I know my function. . . . Don't worry. I know what my contribution was just as much as I know Ella's contribution."[43]

Granz's interest in seeing that Fitzgerald's artistry and dignity were protected did cross over into her personal life. When Fitzgerald moved to Los Angeles to be closer to the center of action with Granz, she bought a home on Hepburn Avenue on the predominantly black West Side. But as Granz later recalled, "Finally when she really made big money, I suggested she move to Beverly Hills. The people who wanted to sell the house wanted the money, and they happened, by coincidence, to be Ella fans. They were delighted to be able to sell the house and say, 'This is Ella's house.' I talked to the real estate agent, bought the house in my name and gave it to Ella in her name. That way, we circumvented the racism that existed. Ella was always shielded from economic choices, but she was always made aware of them."[44] Fitzgerald was put on an allowance, though certainly a comfortable one, to help maintain the budget that Granz allocated for her expenses, upkeep, and securing of her long-term economic well-being.

"There was a kind of naiveté about her," Paul Smith said. "She was like a little girl. If she was unhappy she'd pout like an eight-year-old, which in a way she was. I always thought of her as a lady who never quite grew up. She always had that little girl quality about her. Her feelings could be hurt very easily. Ella was a very tender lady. She loved kids. She was kind of like a kid herself, inside. She never had a romantic life. Ella was a lonely lady and every once in a while one of those guys would come by and they'd have a live-in relationship for a short while. . . . Ella's naiveté permeated her relations with men."[45]

One of her romances that ended up causing friction with Granz involved a Norwegian man whom she had met while touring Scandinavia with JATP and whom she had begun a long-distance affair with in the late 1950s. In July 1957, Reuters reported that she had married

Thor Einar Larsen and was staying for the time being in a suburb of Oslo, a rumor she soon denied, although she indicated she might like to see it happen. She maintained an apartment in Copenhagen for four years. Granz, at her request, was working to help Larsen gain a visa to come to the United States. "Ella had called me from Europe, which she didn't very often do, and said, 'I'm in love.' I think there came a point where Norman was losing patience with the man," recalled Virginia Wicks, who was present backstage one night when the subject turned to Larsen. "There were words between Norman and Ella. I think that Norman realized before Ella did that Larsen was taking advantage of her. Norman tried to explain what was going on, and she was angry with him, saying, 'You don't run my life. You don't run my personal life. You don't know what goes on.'"[46] As it turned out, Larsen had been convicted of defrauding a previous fiancée and had received five months' hard labor in Sweden for his offense, so he was not even eligible to enter the United States for another five and a half years.

Phoebe Jacobs met Fitzgerald during the singer's Decca period in the early 1950s and got to know her better over the next three decades at her uncle Ralph Watkins's Basin Street East club in New York. Jacobs first dealt with Granz when she working for the publisher Simon and Schuster. The company was on the verge of issuing a series on American popular music, and Jacobs called Granz to see if he might be interested in doing a tie-in with Doubleday and the Liberty Music Shop on the recently released Rodgers and Hart songbook. He was. "I took him back to the office," she said. "He was a stunning man. He had an exquisite manner. Norman was a hunk, but he was unassuming about himself."[47]

Granz was determined to prepare Fitzgerald for superstardom, Jacobs continued. "He ruled her life. I remember his buying her a sable coat, and Ella saying, 'He bought it for me because he thought I should have one.' Ella could have cared less whether or not she had a Rolls Royce. Norman saw to it she had one. He wanted her to have the best. She was his star."

Jacobs, now president of the Louis Armstrong Educational Foundation, concluded that Fitzgerald and Armstrong were similar in many ways. "They were very much of the same mentality toward work and they trusted their managers. They were dedicated to music and the artistry of performing. They were both childlike in their imagination, in their ability to play with things, whether it was melody or with people. That's where you get improvisation, like a kid making up a story . . . I don't know whether Norman and Ella were a good pairing. It was truly a professional relationship. They didn't socialize. Norman was never a great extrovert. Music was the common denominator. He treated her like she was a queen. He was dedicated to presenting her in the atmosphere she should enjoy befitting her talent. He was a very savvy guy and Ella respected and trusted him implicitly." That trust and love would be the basis of a shared enterprise that would fill record bins and concert halls and create a legend.

Fitzgerald said as much in a brief, undated telegram that caught up with Granz in Paris: "Even half asleep, I love and appreciate you. Thanks very much. Ella."

13

The Jazz Hurricane

"The chief of our Norman Granz department collapsed in front of the public library just before press time," *Metronome* reported in June 1954 in a tongue-in-cheek but accurate allusion to the futility of keeping up with the peripatetic impresario. "Fortunately, however, the guy has a telephone, and a daily call will keep you posted on what part of the world Norman was in as of that hour." In short succession, the magazine learned Granz was in London "battering" the Musicians Union, flying Buddy Rich, Lionel Hampton, Buddy DeFranco, and Oscar Peterson into New York "from the four corners of the United States" to record with Ray Brown, and pushing forward with his efforts to promote Ella Fitzgerald. "As we said, it's hard to keep up with the guy. Lots of us have been following him for years and have never been able to see him."[1]

Publicist Virginia Wicks remembers all too well the torrent of words that regularly poured forth from the receiver when the "Jazz Hurricane" phoned in from the road with rushed reports and concise instructions. "When he called, it was a roar, and you had to get down every single word," Wicks recalled affectionately. "He would call from anyplace, overseas, wherever it was, and he had his notes in front of him in a phone booth or a hotel room. He wouldn't say, 'Are you busy? Are you talking to someone else? Do you have an appointment you have to go to?' He never asked a question. He would start just talking. Boy, the people who were in the office with me knew when it was a Norman Granz call. I didn't have to say a thing because I probably turned white.

"I grabbed a pencil and the nearest piece of paper, and I would start scribbling," Wicks continued. "He was telling me positive things, like how much money for this and how much money for that, and what date was this, and this man's name and that man's name, 'Don't even speak to so and so,' and on and on. He would say all these things in a period of a few sentences, but I had reams of papers and notes to go over and decipher and figure out exactly what he had said, and act on some of it immediately. It would always scare me to death. I said to him once that I didn't take shorthand, but he just went on. I don't remember once not knowing the amount of money or how to scale the seats in the theater—rows one to six, rows eight to whatever they were—'but leave room for,' and he'd tell me how many seats to reserve for some of the people that he had dealt with. But all of this was positive stuff. 'All right, goodbye.' Then he'd be off. When I look back, I don't know how I did it."[2]

According to Bobby Bregman, who did postproduction work for Verve and was the younger brother of the arranger Buddy Bregman, all the mercurial Granz had to do to shake up the office was to walk in the door after weeks on tour. "He was there about half the time. He would be out with JATP or whoever. Mary Jane Outwater would say, 'Oh my God, Norman's coming tomorrow.' When he got back, all hell broke loose for a day or two, a lot of top-of-lungs yelling. And then he'd kind of mellow. There were days when he'd say, 'Hey, Bobby, come on in and listen to this. I just recorded Ella and Louis.' When we went to play tennis, everything was fine."

Many years later, Bregman recalled being dazzled by Granz's expertise in the minutiae of European travel and food and his gusto for imparting that knowledge. "One of the things Norman absolutely loved was planning people's European trips, because he knew all of the out-of-the-way places. He lived at least half his life in Europe. When I married my present wife thirty years ago he planned our extended honeymoon trip. Norman gave us the most wonderful places we didn't know about. One day when we sat at the tennis club for maybe two and a half or three hours, 'Do this, go see this, stay here.' He'd send a letter or make a phone call, make a reservation at this place. He was dead on. If Norman told you to go to an out-of-the-way place—great food, great atmosphere—he was 100 percent right."[3]

In one of the most perceptive pieces ever written on Granz, Leonard Feather told of spending the day with him in January 1956, beginning with Granz's arrival at his Beverly Hills office one morning after a painful session at the dentist. He came in "with an expression of aloof disdain even more pronounced than usual."

"Boy! What a session that was," he told Outwater.

"Well, he's a good dentist," she responded.

"Good dentist my foot," said Granz. "He butchered me. Let me have an Anacin."

On the wall of his small office were a Picasso print, a framed photograph of Fred Astaire, and another of his daughter, Stormont, and Loretta Granz's daughter from a previous marriage, Sheridan Sullivan. The first order of business was a call to the Hollywood Bowl, which had contacted him about putting together its annual jazz concert. He offered to either oversee a show of the Bowl's choice for $5,000 or to program a show using his artists for free. "They took the free deal," he told Feather. He called Chicago about a recording session he had produced there two days before with the Basie Band. "Basie shouldn't have recorded that way, all that flute stuff and the same tunes Jo Stafford has recorded," he said. "Basie's is a blues band. But he wants to do it, so let him do it." Next, Granz tangled with someone from the American Record Society, with whom he was negotiating to provide material from Verve Records. "Your so-called expert's views and mine are antithetical," he said. "If you want it that way, maybe you should take my name off the whole thing." Turning to Feather, he said, "People don't know how to delegate. I always feel that if you trust someone, you have to let them go for themselves. I don't know who my distributor is in Minneapolis. I don't know what tunes Buddy Bregman is making with Ella today. If Buddy's a good musical director, it will come out all right; if not I can always bounce him." He then called out, "Mary Jane, show me the Stevenson contracts. Set up the studio for the Tatum session. And get me John Hammond in New York."

Following two hours of calls and brief meetings with Outwater and Verve's distribution manager Bernie Silverman, Granz and Feather drove over to Romanoff's for lunch with Spike Jones, the musical satirist and bandleader who was about to make his debut with Verve. Granz ruminated a bit about some of his recent activities outside of music. He was arranging a benefit concert for the Thalians, an advocacy group for developmentally disabled children like his daughter. He also discussed shipping a Cadillac chassis to an automobile designer friend of his in Turin to adapt a body based on specifications Granz himself had drawn up, at a total cost of $15,000. Next, the trio headed for the

Radio Recorders studio to hear some of Jones's test pressings. Granz took away one of the discs, saying, "My kid will like this."

Granz then walked the short distance, where Fitzgerald and Bregman were laying down the first session she recorded for Verve. Observing from the booth, Granz stated, "Now that she's on my own label, she'll make more records during her first year than she's made in the whole 19 years she was with Decca. What's more, she'll have the complete freedom to record anything she likes. Eventually, I want Ella to make enough bread so she can afford to take a couple of months off every year; if she can make 200 grand a year, why should she knock her brains out? That's what I'm looking for—that and her dignity, which I don't think has been respected enough."

After the session ended around 6:00 p.m., Granz and Feather stopped off at the home of his former wife, Loretta, for him to play with his daughter, as he did daily when he was in town. They arrived in time for an eight o'clock reservation at Chasen's, where Granz gave Feather an account of his relationship to food. "I began to become conscious of the art of cooking around the time we began visiting Europe. I'm a firm believer in eating whatever is indigenous to the country you're visiting. It's like anything else. When I become interested in something, I like to know it thoroughly. I bought a whole bunch of cookbooks. Every once in a while I like to cook dinner specials at home. One evening, I had Oscar Peterson's trio and we went the whole route, with caviar and vodka along the way." Granz usually was in bed by 9:30 to be up in time for a 6:30 a.m. tennis match. "He has a chronic distaste for the kind of life led by New Yorkers and by the majority of jazz musicians forced by the virtue of their work to stay up until 4 in the morning," Feather observed. This early-to-bed policy was coupled with a disinclination to attend many musical events other than his own, one exception being Duke Ellington.

The evening ended at Granz's Benedict Canyon apartment, where piles of classical records far outnumbering those of jazz, a television Granz "hardly ever turned on," and shelves loaded with books filled the living room. Granz was in a contemplative mood. "I don't want to be king of the mountain in America," he began. "I don't dig ostentation. What does one live for? I want to be casual, I don't want any big rush, and I'd like to be in a place where competitors think in the same way. That's why I dig Italy. I'm going to spend six months a year there from now on. I'm not as eager as some of our friends along Broadway. I want a peaceful existence."

Feather identified a global convergence of attention on jazz in 1955 and early 1956 that he felt could be traced back to Granz's activities. Ten thousand people had greeted Louis Armstrong in the West African country of the Gold Coast when he arrived to present the first jazz concert ever performed there. North Texas State Teachers College in Denton was the first to incorporate jazz into its curriculum as a legitimate course of study. Venues such as the Music Barn in Lenox, Massachusetts, Lewisohn Stadium in Manhattan, and the Stratford Shakespeare Festival in Ontario all opened their doors to jazz musicians during the period. It was at the Stratford event in 1956 that the Oscar Peterson Trio was captured at its peak. Furthermore, Dizzy Gillespie's interracial band, during a concert in Yugoslavia as part of its Near East tour under the auspices of the State Department in 1956, motivated the American ambassador to wire back to his superiors, "Gillespie's band just made my job much easier."

Feather jumped from there to a sweeping endorsement. "That jazz, which a decade ago was hardly ever heard in a concert hall, far less recognized by the U.S. Government, could have reached this summit of prestige and propaganda value was astonishing to some, incomprehensible to others," he said. "To many observers, it may have seemed like nothing more than the logical outgrowth of the efforts on the part of one man to launch jazz as an international commodity. The man in question is Norman Granz, an irascible, slangy, expensively-casually-dressed, impulsive, epicurean, much-hated and much-loved man who, at 38, is not only the world's foremost jazz impresario, but also can claim to have made more money exclusively out of jazz than anyone else in its short and turbulent history."[4]

Granz's fortunes were at a crossroads between 1954 and 1956, just as they had been when he had made the leap of turning Jazz at the Philharmonic into a national touring enterprise ten years before. JATP, now hailed as an institution, was graying at the temples as the tours charged into their last four years in the United States. Reports surfaced as well that the concerts were being accorded some of the most respectful receptions in their tumultuous history. "For the first time, the emphasis was beginning to shift away from the jam session as the cornerstone of JATP," wrote jazz historian Bob Porter of the 1954 concerts. "Despite the crackling success of 'The Challenges' [the opening ensemble jam number], it would be the last year for that section. JATP was coming of age."[5]

Granz had been diverted from his plans to raid drummer Louie Bellson from Duke Ellington in 1952 when he hired Gene Krupa, but he doubled back to secure Bellson for one year only, 1954. In the year and a half leading up to Bellson's joining the tour, he gave the drummer the red carpet treatment in the recording studio, beginning with a big band date in July 1953, followed by five additional orchestra and quintet dates between September 1953 and August 1954, in addition to opportunities to serve as a sideman on recordings with Benny Carter, Art Tatum, Meade "Lux" Lewis, and the Johnny Hodges Orchestra. "I understood that Norman wanted somebody that could really play time and swing, and yet be a soloist," Bellson said in 1999. "He liked the idea of the drum battle, which was very exciting. Norman knew that I had already made a mark playing 'Skin Deep' with Duke Ellington, which was quite a hit as far as jazz records were concerned in those days. I seemed to fill the bill, according to Norman." Bellson recalled his first drum battle with Rich. Afterward, Rich said, "'Boy, you play long drum solos, don't you?' I said, 'Well, you tell me. Was it too long? I'll shorten it because, I don't know, it is my first year.' So the next night, Buddy played his ten times longer and I cut mine short. Norman came to me and said, 'Ah, 'The Monster' got to you, huh?' I said, 'What do you want me to do?' He said, 'I'm the one who signs the checks, so you go out there and play, hear?' We never had any problems after that."[6]

In 1953 Granz first included Dizzy Gillespie a in the Jazz at the Philharmonic tour, replacing Charlie Shavers. In doing so he provided a lifeline to an important musician whose career was drifting as he struggled to redefine his role in jazz. Granz's intervention immediately opened the way to the next phase of the trumpeter's career through his appearances with JATP and in a flood of new recordings. Granz began by throwing him into the mix of his studio jam sessions: alongside Roy Eldridge, Johnny Hodges, Illinois Jacquet, Ben Webster, Lionel Hampton, Oscar Peterson, Ray Brown, and Buddy Rich in early September in New York and as part of a sextet with Stan Getz, the Peterson Trio, and Max Roach in December. He recorded Gillespie on ten occasions in 1954, including two big band sessions; two small-group recordings with the tenor saxophonist Hank Mobley; a small Latin band; a date with Eldridge and the Peterson Trio with Bellson; a Benny Carter date with Bill Harris, the Peterson Trio, and Rich; and the 1954 fall JATP tour.

Granz organized two concert packages that autumn. In addition to JATP, he booked a series of concerts featuring the Duke Ellington Orchestra, Gerry Mulligan, Dave Brubeck, and Stan Getz. The fifteenth national tour by Jazz at the Philharmonic got under way at Bushnell Auditorium in Hartford on September 17. Buddy DeFranco, Gillespie, Bellson, and a returning Buddy Rich were added to the old standbys: Fitzgerald, the Peterson Trio, Roy Eldridge, Ben Webster, Bill Harris, and Flip Phillips. Lionel Hampton made a surprise guest appearance with DeFranco, Rich, and the Peterson Trio, breaking it up with his theme song, "Flying Home," and a fiercely competitive drum battle with Rich.

Two seminal civil rights victories of the mid-1950s—the Supreme Court's May 1954 decision to desegregate the public schools in *Brown vs. Board of Education* and the Montgomery bus boycott beginning the following year—created a backlash and a particularly volatile racial situation in the southern states where Jazz at the Philharmonic was touring. One incident, which occurred at a benefit concert on September 27, 1954, in Charleston, North Carolina, nearly turned into a full-scale brawl. For this leg of the tour, Granz had flown the musicians around in a DC-3. The first sign of trouble, according to the road manager Pete Cavello, occurred as they arrived at Charleston County Hall to find blacks conspicuously relegated to the balcony of the arena-like venue. "Norman went over to the people who brought us there, and he said, 'No, I don't operate that way.' He wanted them integrated, but they wouldn't do it," Cavello said. "Norman said, 'Well, I'm not going to give you a show.' Back and forth. The man who brought us there figured he better go and move some people up and see what happened because he had too much at stake to blow the show then. They moved a couple hundred black people toward the middle of the theater, and the show went on."

About half an hour before the end of the show, Granz and Cavello noticed a crowd of local toughs gathering in the area outside the stage door aiming to harass them as they left the theater. The pilot, copilot, and stewardess were in the audience seeing the show, while the limousines and drivers waited outside. The crowd building outside grew from around a dozen to more than twenty and then more. Cavello said, "The stage manager told me, 'There's going to be trouble tonight. They're waiting out there.'" He passed the word to the drivers, who waited in a small gated area next to the building out of direct view of the crowd to be ready to move out in a hurry. The musicians started preparing to exit while onstage Fitzgerald was doing a number with the rhythm section and Louie Bellson. "I put the spotlight down to Ella only," Cavello said. "The rhythm section started getting their gear and heading for the back door. We were passing the stuff into the limos quietly on the side where nobody saw us. As Louie was doing his thing, I was taking his drums apart. All he had left up there was a snare drum, because we had to get out of there fast. The eventual losses for the evening were one sweater that Cavello took off as he was setting up, a shaving kit and drum accessories belonging to Bellson, and one of Fitzgerald's shoes.

"We loaded up the cars in the matter of a few minutes. We told the drivers, 'Get us to the airport as fast as you can.' These four limos went out like hell, man. It took them about five or ten minutes before they found out we were gone. Norman had sent the crew out 15 minutes before. They had one propeller going on the DC-3 as we ran on that plane. You never saw us load up a plane so fast in your life. As we get on the runway, we saw dozens of cars coming up this little road to the airport after us. We were up in the air looking down at the headlights, and I said, 'Oh, boy, that was one we got out of.'"[7]

Two months later Granz filed a federal discrimination suit in New York against Pan Am World Airways for a more routine but equally pernicious form of racial prejudice. In July, Fitzgerald, her cousin and assistant, Georgiana Henry, the pianist John Lewis, and Granz were bumped from a flight that was supposed to take them to a series of concerts in Australia and the Antipodes. The flight from San Francisco to Sydney, for which the musicians had first-class tickets, was interrupted during a refueling stop in Honolulu. The airline's actions to accommodate some white travelers forced a three-day delay in leaving Honolulu and the cancellation of concerts in Sydney. The airline furthermore denied Granz and Fitzgerald the opportunity to retrieve their luggage and other personal effects before the plane left. The suit alleged that Pan Am's behavior had violated the federal civil aeronautics act prohibiting racial discrimination. Granz sought approximately $270,000 in actual and punitive damages against the airline when the case was heard in U.S. District Court, but the court dismissed the case without trial in July 1955. A three-judge federal appellate court returned a favorable ruling in January of the following year. The airline settled the case out of court in early 1957 for a reported $7,500.

As a coda to the 1954 season, Nat Hentoff spoke for many about what he considered to be Granz's major unheralded contribution over the previous ten years as jazz's leading impresario. "Granz, more than any other single force in jazz since the war, has consistently supported those artists that form the mainstream of the jazz tradition, those artists whose roots are life-deep in jazz and without whom there could have been no modern jazz, cool or turbulent," he said, referring to Granz's patronage not only of mainstream musicians but also of more modern ones such as Parker, Gillespie, and Bud Powell. "Granz has also issued recordings of such artists as Eldridge, Carter, Hodges and Webster not solely with an eye to the sales charts, but because he feels that these men still have a lot to say and that it would be musically criminal to leave them relatively unrecorded or badly recorded by someone who is exclusively interested in the quick buck."[8]

The 1954 European tour, which got under way in Brussels in early February, showed that the Europeans' relationship to Granz's productions still had its problems. Hopes that Jazz at the Phil could return to Great Britain were dashed when the Musicians' Union refused to grant the necessary permission Granz hoped would follow the 1953 concerts. On another score, he was perplexed by what he considered overly harsh reviews of the tour by local jazz writers. To get their attention, he choked off their supply of free tickets until he had a chance to meet them face to face. "In Sweden, in Europe, the critics have a more serious approach," he said. "That doesn't mean they're more knowledgeable. In Sweden, where we had enormous success, we were also terribly criticized . . . I said to my local promoter, 'I want you to invite every critic who might want to see the concert, and at that juncture, I'll decide who gets tickets.'" He tersely brushed aside the promoter's concerns as he summoned and prepared to lambaste a half a dozen or so writers. "I see you're a jazz critic," Granz said, calling one after another forward like a drill sergeant.

"Yes."

"Prove it to me," Granz said. "What do you know about jazz? Are you a musician? Are you a composer? Where are you coming from that says you're a critic?"

"And, of course, it broke up in a terrible scene," Granz recounted later. "But I stood my ground, and the next time we came around, we may have had only one critic, because they thought, 'Well, we can boycott this.' Boycott! What difference does it make?"[9]

In late January 1955, Granz announced the itinerary of Jazz at the Philharmonic's fourth annual European tour. It began with a two-week series of concerts beginning in Stockholm on February 7 and 8, followed by engagements in Copenhagen, West Berlin, Frankfurt, Munich, Stuttgart, Zurich, Basel, Geneva, and Lyon, and concluded with concerts in Paris on the nineteenth and twentieth at Le Théâtre des Champs Élysées. Stockholm sold out two weeks in advance and treated the musicians as celebrities. Young women selling Swedish glass and pottery in the city's largest department store recognized them from the newspapers and competed to take voluminous orders for shipment back to the United States. Granz presented a streamlined program with relatively restrained playing featuring a constant rhythm section of the Peterson Trio with Louie Bellson and soloists Bill Harris, Roy Eldridge, Dizzy Gillespie, and Flip Phillips, the sole saxophonist. Another sign that JATP was moving toward a more diverse program, less flamboyant and more quietly musical, was a duet between Eldridge and Ray Brown, along with the ballad medley.

Granz displayed a rare light touch when he permitted reporters and photographers to observe backstage preconcert activity. "Granz was in a particularly good mood, and even the Swedish photographers, flashing off bulbs within six inches of his eyes for close-ups, failed to draw more than a good-natured response from him," said a detailed account in *Melody Maker*. "Dizzy and Roy were blowing high notes at each other from opposite sides of the room; Bill Harris, a laconic humorist with a pungently dry sense of fun, was playing an outrageous burlesque of Tommy Dorsey's 'Getting Sentimental Over You'; Flip was playing arpeggios at the wall; the others were talking and laughing. But when Granz called, 'Hey, fellers! Dig this!' the resulting silence was immediate and complete. 'Let's get this thing routined. Take the opener—'The Blues'—Bill, you open it. Diz, Herb, you follow on. Then Flip. And 'Jazz' [Eldridge], you lock it up.'" Afterward, Granz was ready with "wads" of one-hundred-crown notes for musicians who were ready to hit the town or otherwise needed an advance. He also made sure Gillespie had a chess partner to engage him constantly in one of his most beloved backstage pastimes.[10]

In Paris, Granz performed the near impossible at Le Théâtre des Champs Élysées when he cowed a rowdy Paris audience determined to send Buddy DeFranco packing. He believed the incident stemmed from reverse racism that devalued white jazz musicians and a dislike of the clarinet in jazz among some Parisians. Granz and DeFranco have slightly differing recollections of what started the chorus of boos, catcalls, and shower of coins that forced DeFranco to leave the stage angry and near tears. Granz said it was a "musical problem" when the clarinetist went into a seemingly unending number of choruses of "Just One of Those Things." "It's got, not a trick ending, but it's got an ending that you've got to know where you're going," Granz said. "They got to the second or third chorus, and instead of going out, Buddy did another chorus. Oscar looked at me. As it turned out, Buddy couldn't get out of it." DeFranco said, "It was a terrible welcome. I don't know why I thought I could ingratiate myself with Parisians by playing 'April in

Paris,' but I did. But I'd just begun playing, and all of a sudden this hooting and hollering went up. It was so bad I just quit playing and walked off the stage."[11]

Granz brought the concert to a halt by walking onstage with a stopwatch and a chair and sat down. "I got real chauvinistic. I told them I wouldn't speak French to them, and that they were either going to listen to two hours of music or two hours of yelling and booing. They kept on screaming, but finally shushed each other into silence. I never got so many congratulations backstage. People were telling me: 'Well, someone finally defeated a French audience.'"[12] DeFranco adds, "I didn't realize until many years later through some very close friends of mine in Paris that a group of jazz players who not only did not like white jazz players but especially didn't like any clarinetist had assembled a group there that began this booing. So it was a kind of conspiracy. I went back to Paris several times after that and never had any trouble."[13]

In Hamburg, West Germany, Granz pulled no punches when most of the musicians on the tour, other than Fitzgerald, were accommodated at a premium hotel only after he threatened to cancel the concert in the city. "They suddenly found rooms like magic," said Granz, who was shortly thereafter contacted by the concierge with a request from a large radio station for an interview. "I said okay."

"Well, Mr. Granz, you're back in Hamburg, and I guess you like it here," asked the interviewer. "What is it that you find attractive?"

"You people lost the war and you were Nazis. Now I find out that you won't admit a black musician into a hotel because of racism. That's my reaction to your country and specifically to Hamburg," Granz said. The interview abruptly ended. "That afternoon I received a call from the manager of the hotel, saying, 'I am so sorry. It was some stupid room clerk who was new here, and we are delighted to have you and Miss Fitzgerald and your great show.'"[14]

Following the 1955 continental swing, Peterson and Fitzgerald and her pianist Don Abney peeled off from the group to play a handful of dates in Great Britain. Peterson's Canadian citizenship and Ella's being a vocalist rather than an instrumentalist allowed them to bypass the Musicians' Union strictures restricting performances by American musicians. Work permits for Brown and Ellis were applied for but were rejected, necessitating that Peterson work with local musicians.

The late Frank Tenot, a longtime Granz associate, said that one of the first impressions he had of Granz dating back to the early 1950s was his insistence that every comfort and courtesy be extended to "his" musicians. "It was not a reputation. It was a reality," Tenot recalled nearly a half century later. Granz was exacting in securing comfortable transportation, decent hotel rooms, adequate backstage accommodations, good food, and, of course, the money. "For musicians, he did everything," Tenot said.

Once, he recounted, Jazz at the Phil had been booked at Paris's Olympia Theater playing concerts at six o'clock and midnight opposite Edith Piaf, France's most beloved entertainer at the time. Olympia's manager Bernard Coquetrix found himself in the unenviable position of telling Granz (and giving Tenot heartburn in the process) that he did not have a dressing room for Fitzgerald, except for a small room off the bar. "Norman said, 'No,'" Tenot said. "'Ella must have the same dressing room as Edith Piaf. If she doesn't have the same dressing room as Edith Piaf, no show.'" An English magician on the show who had overheard the exchange approached Tenot with an idea and gave up his dressing room to Fitzgerald. Coquetrix took the sign bearing Piaf's name from the door of the dressing room and put it on the one intended for Fitzgerald. Tenot added, "Norman doesn't believe this, but it was a good approach, and it saved the show."[15]

Melody Maker made a couple of stabs at explaining the complexities of Granz to its readers. Under the headline "Keeper of Giants," the music paper reported in 1955, "He is a big man. And his physical dynamism matches well his conversational punch. . . . He works hard and is usually at his Hollywood office an hour or more before his staff arrives. By 10 o'clock he has sewn up several business deals and has played a sharp game of tennis. He reads his mail thoroughly. He will quote, word for word, a tucked-away viewpoint in a *Melody Maker* six months old, and argue his counterpoint furiously."[16] The following year another *Melody Maker* writer, Mike Nevard, offered a keen analysis of how Granz had negotiated the jazz wars of the mid-1940s and later up to that time when "Granz's idols were buried in the debris. The great Hawkins, Roy, Lester, Krupa were condemned to obscurity in the polls. Creation of Jazz at the Philharmonic was his way of digging them out. . . . Thousands endorsed his policy. . . . He doesn't talk about his war against segregation. There is no self-aggrandizement in his attitude toward the Negro. . . . Yet success didn't iron out his craggy personality. . . . His dogged determination to win on every count has been the prime feature of how he bulldozed his way to the top. Meet Granz once, and you realize that he is the most immovable, irresistible figure in the jazz world today."[17] As if to underscore the story's emphasis on Granz's aggressiveness, the photo depicted a dour, fedora-wearing Granz wolfing down a meal, impaling his food on a fork in one hand and gripping a mug of ale in the other as if to suggest his muscular way with his detractors.

In a cable from Paris in March 1955 updating the success of the tour, Granz was ecstatic, reporting sold-out concert halls in Stockholm, Copenhagen, Berlin, Frankfurt, Munich, Zurich, Geneva, Basel, and Paris.[18] He clearly appreciated the critical and economic climate for his tours that followed the building of a loyal fan base across Europe just as he appreciated audiences who embraced jazz as part of the panoply of the fine arts. He felt that the praise given the artists and the music extended as well to his role, which had been given an enhanced status in Europe.

Shortly after Granz returned from Europe, Charlie Parker died, on March 12, 1955, at the age of thirty-four. Granz lamented, "I think it is a shame that finally, when jazz has reached its peak in public acceptance, the man who should be given the most credit for innovating and originating the ideas that are currently popular (ideas for which other musicians are being credited) should be completely forgotten."[19] Dizzy Gillespie met with a committee of Parker's friends chaired by an attorney to consider funeral arrangements and what to do about Parker's compositions. Complicating matters, Doris Parker and Chan Parker, his third and fourth wives, fought over possession of the body. "They had a big mix-up about the body and were getting ready to bury him in New York, but there was some discussion about sending it to Kansas City," Gillespie said. "They didn't have any money to send it to Kansas City, and at this meeting in the lawyer's office they asked me, 'What should we do?'" Gillespie called Granz to explain the lack of money to bury Parker as well as the question of where Parker would be buried. Granz said that after a decision was made he would pay the bill if the body was to be flown to Kansas City, which was indeed the final decision.[20]

In addition, Granz offered to lend his services to record an all-star fund-raiser for Parker's two sons that took place in late April at Carnegie Hall. Among those appearing on the midnight program that finally ended at 3:40 a.m. were Billie Holiday, Lester Young, Dinah Washington, Herb Jeffries, Hazel Scott, Pearl Bailey, Stan Getz, Mary Lou Williams, Kenny Clarke, Oscar Pettiford, and a jam session that included Red Allen, Buster Bailey, Thelonious Monk, Gerry Mulligan, and Gillespie, who had rushed in from a Philadelphia show to pay homage to Parker.[21] Granz's hope to issue the disc of the concert on one of his labels or on another label, depending on possible contractual conflicts of some of the artists, was dashed when Lennie Tristano, a member of the committee that planned the concert, complained to the union about his participation. The resulting decision was that no recording would be permitted.

Addie Parker, the saxophonist's mother, held a soft spot in her heart for Granz for the opportunities he had given her son, aside from his role in getting Parker's body returned for burial. Shortly after his death Mrs. Parker had Granz to dinner during a stopover in Kansas City and presented him with one of the late saxophonist's *Down Beat* awards.

Granz led the seven-week sixteenth national tour out from Hartford, Connecticut, on September 16, 1955, with Lester Young and Illinois Jacquet returning to the fold along with Gillespie for his second tour and Ella Fitzgerald, Roy Eldridge, Buddy Rich, Flip Phillips, the Oscar Peterson Trio, and a Gene Krupa quartet. Young was a last-minute replacement for Stan Getz, who canceled because of scheduling conflicts. Granz had originally wanted to showcase Getz and Gillespie, as their 1953 recording had proven to be extremely popular. The change of plans prompted Granz to change the structure of the concert from the previous year. He deleted "The Challenges," which pitted all the horn players against one another, in favor of the "Swing Set" and the "Modern Set" and added an opening blues that featured the lineup as a whole. The "Modern Set" included the only example of Gillespie and Young fronting a small group together, while Phillips, Jacquet, and Eldridge held similar roles in the "Swing Set."[22]

Two sold-out houses at Carnegie Hall the following night yielded a $24,000 gross, up 30 percent from 1954, foretelling another season of box office success for Granz and company, especially given that there were no other major jazz tours to compete with during the forty-seven-city fall tour whose weekly payroll was around $20,000. The early take on the program was that Granz had turned down the volume somewhat to focus on less histrionic music making, with the glaring exception of the red-meat Rich-Krupa drum battle. Similar results were reported from the early East Coast swing taking in Boston and Brooklyn. In its first full week, JATP grossed around $76,000, with stops along the way in Montreal, Toronto, Pittsburgh, Philadelphia, and Newark. That figure takes into account the $6,000 in ticket receipts Granz had forsaken when he canceled a September 22 date less than an hour before curtain time at a movie theater in Buffalo, whose narrow stage, Granz thought, was too dangerous to safely accommodate the concert. This followed the closure to JATP in 1953 of the city's premier theater, Kleinhans Music

Hall, because of the management's unhappiness about the hyperactive crowds it drew. The hall rejected Granz's offer to post a $10,000 bond to cover any potential damages. "It's incredible that a city like Buffalo, which boasts of possibly the finest auditorium in America, doesn't see fit to hold jazz concerts there," Granz said. He added that the audiences, whose age at that point averaged between thirty and forty, "are not swept off their feet emotionally, even by music they like."[23]

As in 1954, JATP's 1955 tour included a racial incident in a southern city that was provoked by Granz's integrationist policy: in this case, a trumped-up gambling arrest backstage at Houston's Music Hall during an October 7, 1955, double-header that made headlines internationally. Granz later said he wanted to challenge segregation in the South even more than he wanted to deliver good music, and Houston's wealth and power made it an especially tempting target. "Usually a city that's very rich is difficult to break and change tradition. The people who run things, the rich whites, could come on as strong as they wanted, and the police department would of course agree with that. Their point is, 'Don't come here.' But I wanted to play one southern city where, being a rich city, we had a chance to sell out."

Granz met with the ticket taker and worked out what would be printed on the tickets. He advised the man that there was to be no discrimination in the sale of tickets, that Jazz at the Philharmonic was an integrated show. "I'm not sure that it registered with him because he kept mouthing, 'Yes, yes, of course.' It was only after the tickets were being put on sale that he called me. He said, 'You realize that you can't have integration here.' I said, 'Yes, I can. I checked. There's no law that says I have to segregate, just custom, so you just sell the tickets the way they are.' And he said okay." The day of the concert, Granz told the theater manager that he wanted to make a few changes for the evening and personally removed signs designating "white" and "Negro" bathrooms from the doors.

"The concerts were an enormous success," Granz said. "A lot of people had never seen Ella, or they may have seen Ella but not a lot of the musicians. I got to the concert hall early, and somebody came up and wanted to change tickets because they were sitting next to a black. And I said, 'No, you can have your money back, but we're not going to change your seat.' (The customer took the money.) We did everything we could, and of course I had a strong show. People wanted to see my show. If people wanna see your show, you can lay some conditions down."[24]

Gene Krupa and his group were onstage when Granz noticed three or four men milling around backstage who identified themselves as Houston police detectives and Krupa fans when he queried them. He had already taken the precaution of hiring some off-duty policemen to help maintain security during the show. Granz warily relaxed his normal policy of not permitting outsiders backstage during performances. As the first concert neared its conclusion, the detectives suddenly burst through Fitzgerald's dressing room door, guns drawn. The singer was enjoying a piece of pie with her cousin and attendant, Georgiana Henry, as musicians including Illinois Jacquet and Dizzy Gillespie shot small-stakes dice to while away the time between appearances.

"Suddenly, these plainclothes guys broke in," said Granz. "I mean, they could have turned the handle and gone in easier. But they broke in and said, 'You're under arrest for gambling' and that kind of thing. I rushed over and asked what was going on. They said, 'You're under arrest too because you're managing the gambling.'" Granz moved in to block the path of a detective heading toward Fitzgerald's toilet on the assumption that he might attempt to plant drugs to seriously inflate the charges. "He said 'What are you doing?' I said, 'I'm just watching you to see whether you try to plant any shit.' He got furious and said, 'I ought to shoot you.' He put the gun in my stomach. I knew if he shot me all the police would say that I was resisting arrest. You don't have a chance when a policeman has got other colleagues there. The witnesses of Dizzy and Jacquet I don't think would have counted for much, since they were also 'gambling.' And I said, 'Well, if you're gonna shoot me, I mean, shoot me.' The whole thing was just jive. The thing was that in the South they don't like the idea that we'd 'mix' everything because that sets a precedent. That's the thing they were bugged about, 'cause if you could prove that black and white could sit next to each other, you could break up a lot of shit down there."[25]

The police, who had confiscated about $185 from the floor, informed Granz they were going to arrest and book him, Fitzgerald, Henry, Gillespie, and Jacquet immediately. Granz summoned the Music Hall manager and said, "Look, you'd better tell this guy you've got three thousand people sitting in the hall and you've got three thousand people coming in for the second show. You're gonna have the biggest uprising you ever had, because I'm going to go out onstage and tell 'em the concert is canceled, and I'm going to tell them why it's canceled. So you'd better talk to these guys." The police agreed to book the five in between shows and get them back in time for the second show. The crush of reporters and photographers at the Houston police station confirmed what Granz had suspected: that their arrests were a setup. The *Houston Post* carried a photograph of a forlorn Fitzgerald sitting on a bench in a blue taffeta dress and mink stole, while another showed her directing a chilly glance at one of the officers. "One of them had the nerve to ask for an autograph," Fitzgerald sniped afterward. The paper went on to add, with more than a dollop of condescension, that the singer was "one of the most handsomely dressed women ever to visit the Houston Police Station."[26] Gillespie later wrote, "They asked everybody their names, and I told them my name was 'Louis Armstrong.' I acted pretty smart."[27]

Granz paid the $50 bail and a trial date was set. "I got pissed off about that, and I hired a lawyer. I'm sure they were confident that nobody would fly all the way back to defend $10," said Granz, who was particularly upset at the treatment accorded Fitzgerald. Granz retained the services of Abe Herman, attorney for the prominent Fort Worth newspaper publisher Amon Carter. Herman successfully fought the charges against what one headline writer called Granz's "'Guys and Dolls' Dice Bit."[28] When the affair was over, Granz had spent approximately $2,000 to get the charges quashed. The local press that had first splashed the story then turned on the officers. One newspaper recommended that a special patch depicting a chicken on a field of yellow be presented to the detectives participating in the raid, a detail Granz still relished even after the Music Hall was demolished in 1999.

Don Freeman, a San Diego newspaper reporter who wrote many of Verve's liner notes, caught up with a reflective Granz on the last stop of the 1955 tour, the city's Russ Auditorium. "Isn't that great? Not a peep out of them. They're *listening*. Three years ago, this would have been just about impossible—20 minutes of nothing but pretty ballads and no one out there yelling 'work man' or 'go, go, go.'" The nearly three-hour program had dropped many long-standing hits and featured little scat singing by Fitzgerald, who instead emphasized standards and popular songs. "Up in San Francisco, some of the kids—not just one either—came up to me and said, 'You didn't have to yell at us this year, Norman.' It was that way all over, everywhere we went. More mature audiences are one reason. Another may be that we've priced ourselves into dignity." With top ticket prices of $4.75 and low seats selling for $2.75, the just-completed season was the most financially successful in JATP's history, with six cities yielding grosses of $25,000. "I've guess we've become institutionalized. There's no pattern. We'll draw in places like New York and Chicago, where there's a lot of jazz all year, or we'll make it big in Portland, where they don't see Diz or Oscar or Ella very often. The audience really doesn't come to see any one or even two special artists. They come to see Jazz at the Philharmonic."[29]

The changes in programming on the 1955 tour, most notably the addition of the Modern Jazz Quartet, were well received during the following year's fall tour, the penultimate outing for Jazz at the Phil in the United States. The concert opened with a thirty-minute jam session set up by the Peterson Trio with Jo Jones on drums accompanying a lineup of Eldridge, Phillips, and Jacquet and brought the temperature down with a subsequent fifteen-minute set by the MJQ. The quartet's rhythm section of John Lewis, Connie Kay, and Percy Heath then fell in behind Gillespie and two newcomers to JATP, saxophonists Stan Getz and Sonny Stitt. A quartet led by Gene Krupa opened the second half of the show, followed by the Peterson Trio and Fitzgerald. One of the more interesting commentators on the new JATP sound was the Newport Jazz Festival co-founder George Wein, then reviewing jazz for the *Boston Herald*. "I don't know whether it was the quiet dignity of the Modern Jazz Quartet, the resplendent tuxedos in which all the musicians were attired, or the spectacles worn by Stan Getz," Wein wrote, "but this writer felt a sense of maturation to the jazz concert. This desire to mature has been evident in the last two or three Norman Granz efforts. However, in my opinion, it is not until this year that Jazz at the Philharmonic has completely come of age as a totally sincere jazz concert. While the moments of inspired music were few, the high level of performance by the musicians made for one of the most enjoyable evenings I have ever spent at a Symphony Hall jazz concert."[30] Granz implicitly acknowledged his own long-standing preference for jazz laced with high-octane emotion at the opening of the sixteenth national tour at Carnegie Hall when he introduced the Modern Jazz Quartet as a group "foreign to our background."

Granz had another project close to his heart—to launch a solo concert tour of Art Tatum in the fall of 1956. Over a year earlier, in June 1955, word had begun circulating of Granz's intention of touring Tatum in Europe. It was slated to be a solo tour, beginning October 15 in Paris, of both classical music and jazz. The British Musicians' Union announced that it would oppose any attempt to reclassify Tatum as a "concert pianist," given the fact that he had gained fame as a jazz musician. It did not matter to the union that pianists Teddy Wilson, Mary Lou Williams, and Lil Armstrong had been admitted into England for appearances or that Tatum himself had performed in London night-clubs in 1938. Plans were firming up a year later for a series of concerts in which he would simply be billed as "Tatum." He had even bought the white tie and tails in preparation for his concert hall appearances. However, the pianist's final concert was the August 15, 1956, Granz extravaganza at the Hollywood Bowl. With an audience of nineteen thousand, the concert marked the largest crowd Tatum had ever played. However, his years of hard living and heavy drinking, resulting in an increasingly debilitating case of uremia, had taken their toll. In September he made his final recording, the Granz-produced date with Ben Webster, bassist Red Callender, and drummer Bill Douglass, and in the following month he performed dates in Washington and New Jersey. He abruptly canceled the remaining engagements and returned home to his wife in Los Angeles. It was obvious that Tatum was sinking fast, and many of his oldest friends in town made the pilgrimage to his home. One of his last requests was that Oscar Peterson come down from San Francisco, where he was playing a nightclub engagement. Trumpeter Harry Edison made the call imploring Peterson to make the trip, but the club owner held Peterson to his contract, forcing him to make a late-night flight. The man who had once anointed Peterson his musical heir ("You're next after me") died November 5, hours before Peterson reached Los Angeles.[31]

In 1956 Norman Granz's connections to the Communist Party ten years earlier were dredged up briefly, though to no marked effect since he was by then the reigning capitalist of the jazz world. McCarthyism, which had peaked in the early 1950s, had not fully run its course when the House Un-American Activities Committee (HUAC) scheduled hearings in Los Angeles to investigate communist activity in the music industry. The committee summoned thirty-five musicians to appear during a week of hearings beginning April 16. Granz had been tipped off in advance that he was to be subpoenaed to appear before the committee, where he would need to either answer questions publicly or refuse to answer. He took the threat seriously enough to avoid being served a subpoena by going abroad. An April 5 memorandum found in Granz's FBI file said HUAC had reported to the Bureau that Granz was on the list of those wanted for questioning before the committee but that the FBI did not believe he would appear. The memo reported that, as of March 15, Granz was living in the Lancaster Hotel in Paris. Granz said in 1998 that he also hid out in Mexico for several weeks to avoid the committee.

The FBI papers included a quote from the *Hollywood Reporter* that Granz was "en route to the Soviet Union."[32]

In later years, Granz kept two special types of clippings from his career—those he thought were so offbase they were funny and those that he felt could harm him. In the latter category was a piece by the right-wing columnist Westbrook Pegler that pilloried him as a communist. Granz received an overseas call from Mary Jane Outwater telling him about it. "I was in Rome on a tour with Ella," Granz recalled. "Mary Jane called and said one of the newspapers came out with a front-page story that I was a communist and had fled to Russia. I said, 'When am I supposed to flee to Russia? I've got a concert tonight—in Rome.'"[33]

Granz was not alone in resisting HUAC's questions. Only six of the thirty-five musicians who had been summoned were considered to be "friendly" witnesses; others largely asserted their First Amendment right of freedom of speech and their Fifth Amendment right prohibiting self-incrimination. Those refusing to testify could have been subjected to further congressional scrutiny. On the fifth day of the hearings, which were repeatedly interrupted by protests in the Federal Building, Granz was publicly identified as having been a member of the musicians' branch of the Los Angeles County Communist Party. His accuser and that of thirty-three others was Donald Christlieb, age forty-four, a veteran bassoonist in Hollywood studio orchestras and a party member between 1941 and 1946.

FBI inquiries into Granz had gotten under way in late February, about two months before HUAC convened in Los Angeles, and throughout the spring and summer had bounced back and forth between Washington and Los Angeles, as well the State Department and embassies in London, Paris, Rome, and Bonn. In an April 13 letter from J. Edgar Hoover to the State Department's Office of Security, the FBI director said that there was no need for the State Department or the Central Intelligence Agency (which received a copy of the letter) to investigate Granz any further. He stated that the matter had been referred to the legal attaché in Paris. But Hoover did express interest in what the State Department might do about Granz's passport.[34] A May 14 report from the FBI's Los Angeles office concluded that Granz's links to the Communist Party were more than a decade in the past and that as a result no inclusion in the Security Index was warranted.[35] In July the State Department instructed all consular and diplomatic posts that if the opportunity presented itself Granz should be asked to submit an affidavit concerning his past Communist Party affiliation. The legal attaché in Paris wrote Hoover in October that since Granz's passport was due to expire soon he would be on the lookout for Granz to sign a loyalty oath if he sought a new passport in the French capital.

Although Granz, unlike film, radio, and television people blacklisted in the 1950s, was self-employed, he was not willing to risk the bad publicity. To conclude the matter, he set up an appointment to be interviewed by two FBI agents in Los Angeles on October 18. "It was wonderful, the way they were dressed—the black ties, the white shirts, the dark blue suits, and the hats. It was almost like a Woody Allen film, except that they were serious," Granz recalled of the men who paid a midmorning call to his office.[36] They went off to a nearby coffee shop for the interview. Granz told the agents how his interest in fighting racial discrimination had led him to accept an invitation to join the musicians' branch of the Communist Party, and he recalled attending meetings in private homes that had drawn as many as sixty people. He stated he had taken a film-cutting course from Edward Dmytryk, one of the Hollywood Ten, at the so-called People's Education Center in 1944 and 1945 but that he had not known that Dmytryk was a party member or that the organization had been designated as a Communist Party front by the attorney general of the United States.[37] He said his travels with Jazz at the Philharmonic beginning in 1945 had necessarily cut into his participation and that he had finally drifted away in 1946.

"They asked all kinds of silly questions," Granz recalled. He had little difficulty in convincing the agents that he had no desire to overthrow the United States by violent means. "I wouldn't give any names, except Gus Hall, but he had run for president several times. Finally, they gave up, and left. I was fortunate that I was an independent operator. I wasn't hurt in the way that a lot of screen people were, and the television people especially."[38] The agents who interviewed Granz in Los Angeles concluded by saying he had answered all their questions, had volunteered information about his activities, and had been cordial throughout the interview. They agreed with earlier assessments that he presented no threat to the republic.

The matter was not as dead as Granz might have been led to expect, given the government's interest in having him sign a loyalty oath the next time he applied for a new passport. In February 1957 Granz received the questionnaire containing the oath when he applied for a passport extension in Zurich. He could not simply deny his past membership in the party, as that would have constituted perjury. "I was afraid of losing my passport, so I decided that I would go to Zurich on the theory that, if they took my passport away, I would simply be a political refugee, and the best place would be Switzerland. They were neutral and it wasn't against the law to be a Communist," he said.

He went to the consulate in the morning. The secretary at the desk looked over his passport and said that, given he was an American citizen, it would be no problem for her superior to stamp it that afternoon to extend it for an additional three years. She then asked Granz to fill out the questionnaire. "She was going down very fast with her pencil, and when she came to the X [indicating his membership in the Communist Party] her eyes popped."

"Are you sure you're putting this down right?" she asked.

"Yeah, I'm telling the truth," Granz answered.

The secretary backed off her earlier promise that the matter could be completed that day. Fine, he would be around for a few days.

"I went back on the day they rang me, and they said that the State Department had canceled my passport," Granz continued. "I said, 'In that case, I will seek political refugeeship in Switzerland. As you know, I'm on a concert tour, and there's going to be a lot of publicity. Are you sure that you want that?' They said, 'Well, let us think about it.'"

The consulate ended up clipping the corners of Granz's passport that allowed him to finish the tour, but the passport was to be picked up as he prepared to board a return flight back to the United States. "I was living in New York then," he said. "I got a lawyer, a very good lawyer who was general counsel for CBS. We went to Washington. We sued for the passport, which you could do only on a very narrow basis. I had to go in and write so many events that correlated with what they thought I had done. Two months went by. They had to think about it. Then they gave me my passport and, surprisingly, sent me my old one with the clipped pages."[39]

Granz never forgot about these incidents and never forgave those whose testimony against former party members often destroyed their professional lives. For example, Granz and John McDonough disagreed about whether the film director Elia Kazan could ever be forgiven for his infamous congressional testimony in 1952 during which he had volunteered the names of former communists among his colleagues. The issue arose when Kazan was to be honored with a special Academy Award for Lifetime Achievement in 1999, over the protests of many in the film industry. Granz thought Kazan should not be given the award. "His work was not an issue," he said. "He gave names, the names of friends of his. The party used people like me and other idealists. Fortunately, the party didn't trust me too much."[40]

Almost twenty years later, Granz took a moment to stick it to his onetime accuser, Donald Christlieb. His son, the tenor saxophonist Pete Christlieb, was part of a big band led by Louie Bellson being recorded in the mid-1970s for Pablo Records. Granz inquired about the status of the elder Christlieb.

"He's retired," Christlieb replied.

"Please tell him Norman Granz said hello," Granz said.

"I never heard back on that," he recalled.

14

"The Lost Generation"

Oscar Peterson and Ella Fitzgerald turned in their usual polished sets on Saturday, July 17, 1954.[1] But on that particular night, they made history not for Norman Granz but for George Wein, who broke new ground by presenting the first U.S. jazz festival. It was held outdoors on the grass tennis court of the Newport Casino in Rhode Island. Jazz and high society had become somewhat surprising bedfellows.

The Newport Jazz Festival in Newport, Rhode Island, for seventy-five years the home of the international tennis and social set and site of a bustling navy base, was the brainchild of Wein, the Boston pianist, nightclub owner, columnist, and sometime lecturer, and local socialites Louis and Elaine Lorillard. With a second-night audience of six thousand, bringing the total number of spectators to thirteen thousand from an estimated thirty states, Wein and the Lorillards had every reason to think that Newport would become a perennial on the jazz scene.[2] It did, but it also marked the beginning of a new way of presenting jazz. Though the idea of a festival dedicated solely to jazz had begun in Nice, France, in 1948, it was Wein's vision and energy that eventually supplanted Jazz at the Philharmonic. The festival committee presented an ambitious agenda to honor jazz in performance, education, and learned discussions that overlapped with aims Granz had long articulated. It issued a statement that laid out a basic goal of the festival as establishing "jazz as an art form in the eyes of the American public. Europeans consider jazz our most important cultural contribution to the world. We must give jazz this same position in the minds of our people."[3]

Newport received major national and international coverage that included the *New York Times* and the *Herald-Tribune, Life, Look,* the *New Yorker, Newsweek, Esquire, Seventeen,* and newspapers from as far away as Mexico City and Paris. ABC Radio broadcast forty minutes live from the Saturday night show. The buzz was heightened, no doubt, by the festival's elegant surroundings, seen in abundance in the film of the 1958 festival, *Jazz on a Summer's Day.* The event generated mixed responses among the local gentry: some objected to the introduction of jazz to the community, especially on such a scale, while others enthusiastically attended the concerts. (The festival's success prompted the board of the Newport Casino to demand that it find a new location. The festival obliged, moving to Freebody Park in 1955.) *Down Beat* captured Newport's significance in the lead sentence of its review: "America's first major jazz festival—the largest held anywhere in the world so far—has opened a new era in jazz presentation. . . . Never before were so many of the major names in jazz gathered together for one brace of programs and never before was so comprehensive an attempt made to present jazz artists in the framework of a living history of jazz. . . . Though there were a few of the 'Go! Go! Go!' adolescents, the consensus among musicians and long-time jazz observers is that this was the most mature and intelligently attentive audience ever attracted to a major jazz presentation."[4] The seeming swipe at JATP was at best an afterthought to a story that also quoted Miles Davis's characterization of Newport and the festivals that followed as "jazz supermarkets." Festivals concentrated audiences for single events that diminished the demand for the one-night concerts in a location that Granz had pioneered.

After Wein and the Lorillards went their separate ways in the late 1950s, Wein succeeded in remaining the sole longtime producer by his ability to forge partnerships and sponsorships to underwrite his concert packages. Here he differed strikingly from Granz, who personally bankrolled the vast majority of his events. The two maintained a professional respect and occasionally collaborated, as when Granz recorded most of the 1957 festival and served on the Newport advisory board, but they were never close.

George Frazier, writing in *Esquire* the following year, extolled the virtues of the Newport Jazz Festival and Wein, then went on to draw critical comparisons with JATP and Granz. He described Granz as overbearing and suggested that Granz had promoted JATP to serve his own ends rather than that of the music. He also charged that Granz's musicians played "wearing unpolished shoes and suits that look as if they had been purchased at a maternity shop" and dismissed the majority of his recording efforts as "pretty awful."[5]

The article provoked a spirited defense of Granz by Leonard Feather and, predictably, from the man himself a few months later in a letter that ran over four columns. Granz contrasted the highbrow pretensions of the Newport organizers with his own projects and motives for bringing people together to enjoy the complete social and musical experience offered by jazz. "I think putting on the festival was a good idea, in that it afforded employment for musicians and allowed fans to hear some jazz," Granz wrote, "but that it provided the chance for the social Newporters to go slumming musically and meet all 'those jazz musicians' is at best a rather depressing idea, and even in some ways a little disgusting."[6] Ironically, Granz's sentiments resembled those of earlier critics who had dissed JATP for taking jazz to concert halls.

The differences between Jazz at the Philharmonic and the Newport Jazz Festival were as much about cultural and political trends in the decade between 1944 and 1954 as they were about changes in jazz. JATP originated during wartime, when the expansion of industrial production, which benefited some groups more than others, exacerbated social tensions and prompted struggles over employment that would open up further struggles for equality in the years ahead. Through JATP, Granz set himself up as a provocateur on behalf of democracy, especially where racial issues were concerned. The allure and success of Newport can no more be separated from the prosperity of its time than the excitement and challenge of JATP can be separated from the conflicts of its time.

Looking over the bulging list of Verve titles in between 1956 and 1960, even Norman Granz might think he was perusing someone else's catalog. In addition to Buddy Bregman, Barney Kessel had a hand in producing popular music for the label. A group under Kessel's direction in March 1957 resulted in the first four recordings of a teen idol then making his breakthrough on television, Ricky Nelson. Granz found out that Nelson's father, Ozzie, a former bandleader, was, in contrast to his warm, fuzzy image on *Ozzie and Harriet,* a tough and unpleasant negotiator. But the contract drawn up was rendered moot by a judge's decision that it was unenforceable given Nelson's status as a minor at the time.

Granz allowed Buddy Bregman wide leeway, though not complete freedom, in bringing talent to the label. "It was Norman's authority:

'Sign anyone you think will do well for us, but check with me first,'"
Bregman recalled.[7] Among the artists Bregman brought in during his
two years with Verve were actress and singer Jane Powell; composer and
arranger Conrad Salinger, orchestrator for *Singing in the Rain*; Count
Basie with Joe Williams; Oscar Peterson and the Bregman Orchestra;
vocalist Joan O'Brien, who had made her name on the Bob Crosby
radio show; and the vocal group the Skylarks. Bregman also produced
the musical *Ruggles of Red Gap* by Bregman's uncle Jule Styne and Leo
Robbins (featuring Jane Powell, Michael Redgrave, Peter Lawford, and
Imogene Coca) and one of Bing Crosby's most notable jazz records, *Bing
Crosby Sings Whilst Buddy Bregman Swings*. Then there was an album
of Fred Astaire singing his own songs; Granz thought it fairly mediocre
but furthered his relationship with Astaire by issuing the soundtrack of
the 1957 film *Funny Face*, which costarred Audrey Hepburn.

During this time Granz extended his range as an innovator by producing the earliest live comedy albums. Granz, a fan of stand-up, invited
comedian and political satirist Mort Sahl to begin the series for Verve.
Beginning with a show at the hungry i club in Los Angeles, Sahl made
five albums for Granz. Sahl was followed by Shelley Berman, who was
the opening act for Rose Murphy (the "chi-chi" girl), another Verve
artist, and then Jonathan Winters and Jackie Mason. Berman was unexpectedly Verve's single most lucrative star. "Shelley Berman, if you like,
helped subsidize Ben Webster," Granz said. "Then I got Jonathan Winters. Jonathan I was really crazy about. He was really great."[8]

Granz got close to signing Lenny Bruce. However, the brilliant but
drug-crazed comedian who made headlines with biting social commentary laced with obscenities that landed him in and out of jail in the 1950s
and 1960s was one headache he could live without. "I heard Lenny, and
of course, he was wonderful to listen to if you liked that kind of stand-up
comedy," Granz said. "I asked him if he wanted to record, and he said
yes. So I told him I'd be in touch, and I guess I didn't call him back the
next day or the day after that because I was recording Ella.

"Suddenly he burst into the studio and said to me in Yiddish, 'You're
working with the schvartzes [black people] more than with me.'

"I said, 'You come in and you break up a session and you want me
to record you?'

"Bruce then said, 'I already know the album cover. And I want
to sing.'

"'No, I'm not going to let you sing on an album. You want to do
your routine, fine.' So we broke it off and I never bothered."[9]

Even more unusual than the comedy records was a series of spoken-word recordings that appeared on Verve in the late 1950s, featuring, among others, Linus Pauling, Jack Kerouac, Evelyn Waugh, the Italian novelist and playwright Alberto Moravia, Angus Wilson, Dorothy Parker, Alice B. Toklas, Joseph Cotten, and Elsa Lancaster. Granz believed that for Verve to live up to his expectations as a quality label he had to release prestige projects that he believed in, even if sales from them were low.[10]

By mid-1957, Granz and Fitzgerald were at work on the third album in the songbook series, one devoted to the music of Duke Ellington. Obtaining the right to record the Ellington Orchestra required a little horse trading. Duke had signed a contract with Columbia in 1956 and had become an especially "hot" item again following his legendary performance at the Newport Jazz Festival in July of that year when tenor saxophonist Paul Gonsalves rocked the festival with his twenty-seven choruses on "Diminuendo and Crescendo in Blue." The ensuing publicity for the Ellington Orchestra was beyond anything associated with JATP and had George Wein in a panic. *Time* magazine even put out a cover story on Ellington in August 1956.[11] With Duke's blessing Granz approached Columbia and negotiated with the veteran producer George Avakian for permission to use the Ellington Orchestra on the Fitzgerald recordings, using alto saxophonist Johnny Hodges, who had been in and out of Ellington's band before going back permanently in 1955, as his bargaining chip. Granz relaxed his exclusive contract with Hodges for Avakian and in return received the release.

Granz understood that Ellington and his musical alter ego Billy Strayhorn would write arrangements for the occasion, but their lack of preparation, which led to the controlled chaos under which they thrived, was not quite what Granz or Fitzgerald had expected. Ellington and Strayhorn came to the studio on the first day of recording with only the band's existing arrangements, some selected because Ellington thought they accommodated Fitzgerald's range.

The session with the orchestra then had to be supplemented to fill out the two-album set. First were small-group sessions with Ben Webster, the idiosyncratic violin virtuoso Stuff Smith, and a rhythm section led by Paul Smith with Barney Kessel, Joe Mondragon on bass, and Alvin Stoller on drums. Webster also fronted a quartet of Oscar Peterson, Herb Ellis, Ray Brown, and Stoller while the Peterson Trio backed Fitzgerald on "Mood Indigo." The orchestra recorded a sixteen-minute *Portrait of Ella* containing four movements, "Royal Ancestry,"

"All Heart," "Beyond Category," and "Total Jazz," that interpreted different aspects of her musical personality. Just as Fitzgerald had honored his work, Ellington repaid in kind with spoken testimonials to the singer separating the movements of *Portrait of Ella*.

Critic Irving Kolodin, writing in the *Saturday Review,* supported Granz's highest hopes concerning the songbooks' likely effects on Fitzgerald's reputation. "If there is any doubt, after her volumes devoted to the songs of George Gershwin [the Decca recordings], Rodgers and Hart, and Cole Porter, whether Ella Fitzgerald is the greatest jazz vocalist of the day, her mammoth collaboration with Duke Ellington and the band should resolve the question," he stated. "She has rarely been engaged with the kind of material invented by Ellington and such able associates as Billy Strayhorn, Barney Bigard, Juan Tizol, Toby Hardwicke, etc., or by the small ensembles. . . . One of the special pleasures of this project is the opportunity to review the spectacular collection of fine tunes Ellington has piled up in the last three decades, as well as the others in which he was a collaborator or generative force."[12]

The sixth spring European tour, slated to begin in February 1957 in Scandinavia and then to continue through Italy, Germany, Switzerland, Spain, France, and Holland, was postponed until April and extended through June after Ella Fitzgerald suffered a stomach abscess that required immediate surgery. She had fallen ill during what had been a highly successful week at the Paramount Theater in Manhattan with Nat "King" Cole and the Count Basie Orchestra and was unable to complete the date despite her desire to do so.[13] Making the 1957 tour were Dizzy Gillespie, Roy Eldridge, Coleman Hawkins, Stan Getz, Sonny Stitt, the Oscar Peterson Trio with drummers Jo Jones and Gus Johnson, and Fitzgerald, who was back in top form by May.

Granz continued to fill his calendar with commitments aside from concert and record productions. He agreed to take part in the first sessions of the School of Jazz to begin in August 1957 at the Music Inn in Lenox, Massachusetts. Headed by John Lewis, the school ran for three weeks, during which forty musicians worked with twenty nonpaying students. The curriculum included composition, arrangement, the history of jazz, and two hours a week of individual instruction. Many on the faculty had close associations with Granz: they included the Peterson Trio, Dizzy Gillespie, vibes player Milt Jackson, drummer Max Roach, saxophonist Jimmy Giuffre, and Stan Kenton's arranger Bill Russo. Duke Ellington, pianist Lennie Tristano, trombonist Wilbur DeParis, historian Joachim

Berendt, poet and writer Langston Hughes, and composers George Russell and Gunther Schuller were also involved.[14] Granz continued toying with the idea of capturing jazz on film. Even though the sequel to *Jammin' the Blues* that he and Gjon Mili had filmed in 1950 was never completed, Granz announced plans in Milan in June 1957 to film Fitzgerald, the Basie Orchestra, and the JATP unit at a studio in Rome sometime in November. He added that he had already written a script and planned to direct the project. This film, too, apparently came to naught.

The 1957 Newport Jazz Festival ran from July 4 through 7 and drew a record fifty thousand fans before it was all over. The event showed a rare intersection of the careers of George Wein and Norman Granz: Wein staged the festival, while Granz provided a fair amount of the talent and issued twelve albums from the festival on Verve featuring some of his regular artists as well as others not in his orbit. Many of the recordings were held up for decades before they were released on Pablo Records long after Granz had sold the company. Granz also participated in an onstage panel discussion alongside George Avakian, Nat Hentoff, George Shearing, John Levy, Bert Block, and Gerry Mulligan.

Chuck Suber, then publisher of *Down Beat,* recalled being with Granz during the festival at an excruciating moment for both of them when Billie Holiday came onstage for her set. Holiday, visibly distressed, struggled through a short and tired set of familiar material, near breathless and with an unbearably cracked delivery. They heard the set from the rear of the pavilion. "As soon as she started to sing, Norman began shaking his head slightly," Suber recalled. "It was obvious that it was agonizing, particularly the reaction of the audience. They gave very nice, polite applause, but it was like, 'Please, Billie, don't come back for an encore.'" At one point, Suber looked over and saw tears in Granz's eyes as he sadly remarked, "This is the end." The recital was to be her last recording for Verve.[15]

Granz didn't hesitate to embarrass the Newport management, whom he had previously dismissed as the "Madison Avenue–Ivy League social crowd," over what he saw as the cheapness of their hospitality toward the musicians, especially when compounded by racial discrimination that made it difficult for some to secure local hotel rooms. On the Friday night of the festival, musicians were invited to a party that the Lorillards gave "for their Eastern friends," as Granz put it. "It's typical of the rich. They're going to have a buffet. They have a buffet of hard-boiled eggs or something. This one was organized by John Hammond. I got so teed off by how chintzy they were that I took over the hotel restaurant where the musicians were staying—some of them—and invited all the musicians who participated in Newport to come, but I wouldn't let the Lorillards in. I had a fantastic spread for everybody, and that evening, Coleman Hawkins jammed, which was unusual for him. Why? Because I made things the way they should have been."[16] As George Wein later said of the incident in his autobiography, "Norman liked to do things like that; upstaging the Lorillards helped reinforce his feeling that the jazz world revolved around him, like planets around the sun."[17]

Though not caring for Granz personally, Wein approached him about possibly becoming partners in owning and managing the Newport Jazz Festival. "He wanted to take me in as a partner because he didn't have enough money," Granz said. "The Lorillards that put the money up got bored . . . and threatened to kill it. George came to me and said, 'If you can give me $10,000, I can give it to them, and they'll give us Newport. Then you and I could do it together.'" "I did not want it," Granz said, declaring that he had preferred to continue producing shows as he had done in the past. "And that was it."[18] Wein, for his part, did not recall talking to Granz about taking over Newport, but he did not dismiss the possibility that the conversation had occurred.[19]

Louis Armstrong and Ella Fitzgerald were back in the studio for Verve during July and August of 1957 to record their second album of standards, *Ella and Louis Again*. Less than a week later they recorded *Porgy and Bess* with arrangements by Russ Garcia. The timing was fortuitous, as interest in the Gershwin opera was on the rise. From the studio, Granz would drive over to Ira Gershwin's Beverly Hills home and the two would sit up late listening to acetates from the session. Gershwin took the initiative in getting to know Granz. "I received a call one day from a gentleman who asked for me. 'This is Norman Granz. Who are you?'"

"This is Ira Gershwin."

"I almost fainted," Granz recalled. "I thought, my God, this great man is calling me. What's it about?"

Gershwin explained that Granz's recordings of instrumental versions of George and Ira Gershwin songs, such as Oscar Peterson's songbook, made no mention in the liner notes of his own contributions as the lyricist. Granz accepted Ira and Lee Gershwin's invitation to take this up at dinner—"an early six o'clock"—at their Beverly Hills home the following day. He was impressed by the kindly man he met who had achieved so much after his brother's tragic early death two decades before, not to mention the iconic work they had created together.

"There was a strange chemistry that was formed almost immediately," he said. "I became kind of adopted by the Gershwins. . . . The more I visited, the more I saw what a sweet little man Ira was. I don't think he ever possessed a negative thought. He looked with a poet's eye on what he was, one of the greatest lyricists in the history of America."[20]

The Armstrong/Fitzgerald rendition of "Summertime" made Gershwin weep. "Ira was overwhelmed by the poignancy of Louis's voice, and said he wished that George were alive to hear the records." In gratitude, Ira presented Granz with an early lead sheet for "It Ain't Necessarily So" in George's hand. The Catfish Row saga opens with a nearly eleven-minute overture before the voices of the bell-like Fitzgerald and gravelly Armstrong are heard. Armstrong's chops were not in the best of shape, which led him to do more singing. "We spaced it out and gave him some breaks in between and then had him sing some solos that we might have done instrumentally," Granz recalled. "And Ella was so proper that she had wanted to sing 'It isn't necessarily so,'" a memory that made him laugh twenty years later.[21] Granz and Gershwin's late-night conclaves continued when Fitzgerald recorded the epic George and Ira Gershwin songbook in 1959.

Jazz at the Philharmonic came to prominence at the tail end of the Swing Era, well before the luster of its star players had begun to fade. The disbanding of many major bands around the time JATP was becoming a national touring act greatly enhanced the players available and the prestige they in turn gave JATP during its early formative years. However, in the late 1950s, some longtime observers of jazz as well as musicians had begun to bemoan and resist trends in jazz that were beginning to seriously affect Jazz at the Philharmonic's future viability. These trends, along with other factors that converged around the same time, caused Norman Granz to make the eighteenth national tour the last. Billy Taylor, writing in *Esquire* in 1958, called the warhorses of the Swing Era, then only in their early to mid-forties, the "lost generation." Among them were many of Granz's musicians: Coleman Hawkins, Roy Eldridge, Benny Carter, Jo Jones, Lester Young, Harry Edison, and Stuff Smith. Taylor argued for a broader view that would embrace a greater range of jazz styles. "In today's world of jazz everything happens 'right here' and 'right now.' . . . The tragedy is that the creative part of a musician soon becomes outdated at a time when his 'interpretative half' has reached a plateau of excellence." For Taylor, the broadcast of *The Sound of Jazz*, presented as part of CBS's Seven Lively Arts series in

December 1957, and stocked with still more of Granz's stars such as Count Basie, Billie Holiday, Ben Webster, Jimmy Giuffre, and Gerry Mulligan, was the most obvious sign of veteran musicians' continuing relevance. "Yet today too many of these men must scrounge around for weekend dates and hope for occasional recording dates with Norman Granz or some independent recording company which still appreciates what they are playing," Taylor said. "And they *can* play, right now, with all the power and authority of great musicians, if anyone will bother to listen."[22]

Nat Hentoff had made a similar argument a couple of years earlier: "The melancholy fact concerning jazz adherents is that only a relatively small segment of the jazz audience and of the younger musicians does have enough feeling for jazz roots to be aware of the continuing richness and resourcefulness of the *whole* of the language's tradition. . . . Were it not for Norman Granz's determination to continue to utilize older jazzmen of continuing creativity on his Jazz at the Philharmonic tours and on his recordings, it is doubtful whether even so maturely masterful a jazz improviser as Roy Eldridge would still be playing to large audiences in large halls at least part of each year."[23]

The stellar lineup for the fall 1957 JATP tour demonstrated Granz's gift for adapting his show to changes in the jazz world. It was Coleman Hawkins's first tour in ten years, and there were two musicians on the bill who had appeared at JATP's first concert on July 2, 1944, Illinois Jacquet and J. J. Johnson. The combination of Stan Getz's muscular plaintiveness with the driving passion of Johnson proved brilliant. Hawkins and Roy Eldridge were paired with the rhythm section of the Modern Jazz Quartet, John Lewis, Connie Kay, and Percy Heath. Fitzgerald had the backing of the Peterson Trio with Jo Jones. The show made critics sit up and take notice from its opening in New York on September 14. After all, the Modern Jazz Quartet was a far cry from Jacquet and others who had first lit JATP's fuse. Lester Young, who did not get a set to himself, nonetheless received some of the highest praise in his many years with JATP.

Russ Wilson, jazz critic for the *Oakland Tribune*, could not have been more complimentary about the October 5 concert, which as it turned out would be one of the last reviews of a domestic Jazz at the Philharmonic tour. "Miss Fitzgerald proved anew that she has a sweet, clear voice for ballads, can run the changes with any of the competition, and retains her impeccable phrasing and sense of rhythm. . . . The

Peterson trio has developed an even greater cohesiveness, if that is possible. . . . The Modern Jazz Quartet, which for several years has topped
the jazz polls in the combo division, played mostly the blues, and excel-
lently. . . . Coleman Hawkins, the 'inventor' of the tenor saxophone,
was teamed with trumpeter Roy Eldridge and the MJQ rhythm section
in a set which unequivocally proved that both soloists still are among
the important jazz figures and have not let the years pass them by. . . .
Trombonist J. J. Johnson has a golden tone, a beautifully precise attack,
and fine ideas, while Getz has added warmth to his tone that, to these
ears at least, increases his appeal. Their counterpoint was delightful and
their individual ballads were thrilling."[24]

Music from the 1957 fall tour appeared on four Verve albums. The
concerts were recorded on two occasions: the Civic Opera House on
September 29 and Philharmonic Auditorium in Los Angeles on October
7. The Chicago date was recorded in stereo; the concert in Los Angeles
was in monaural. The series " . . . at the Opera House" included discs
by Fitzgerald; the Peterson Trio and the Modern Jazz Quartet; Johnson
and Getz; Hawkins and Eldridge; Young, Jacquet, Phillips, Stitt, and
the Peterson Trio with Jo Jones in a jam session; and Getz, Johnson,
Eldridge, Hawkins, and a rhythm section of Lewis, Kay, and Heath in
a second jam session.[25]

Granz concluded that Jazz at the Philharmonic had finally run its
course as a touring vehicle for jazz, at least in the United States. He was
no sentimentalist when it came to investing energy in a project with
diminishing returns, especially given how long JATP had been successful.
Audience numbers had been down all over the country since the opening
of the show's twenty-one-city tour in New York in September, despite
its blockbuster lineup. For example, JATP attracted only 3,500 people
to the San Francisco concert and a scant 2,500 in Oakland.[26] At Boston's
Symphony Hall, where JATP had normally filled two houses a night,
only enough tickets were sold for one performance, and not even that
was sold out. In addition, Granz said that after 1957 he could not afford
to pay Fitzgerald as much as she commanded in her jobs away from
JATP. "She was better off not touring with Jazz at the Philharmonic and
going on her own, even though I was her manager," Granz said.[27]

The maturation of the audiences at Jazz at the Philharmonic and
the evolution of their musical tastes, along with Granz's appreciation
for styles of jazz just then coming into their own, could be seen in the
programming in 1955 and 1956. Thus in 1957 Granz was willing to
withdraw his long-running show in order to concentrate on managing

Ella Fitzgerald and Oscar Peterson, as well as running Verve Records and building upon his considerable and expanding business in Europe as he prepared to move there two years later.

Nat Cole and Granz's paths crossed in the twilight of Jazz at the Philharmonic just as they had at its beginning. On November 15, 1957, many of the musicians from the tour were featured on Cole's NBC show, *The Nat King Cole Show,* from Los Angeles in JATP's only televised appearance in the United States. The show opened with an introduction from Granz and Cole. "In 1944, it was my privilege to found Jazz at the Philharmonic," Granz began. "No one would have guessed at that time, least of all myself, the extent to which these concerts would grow. It's been a fabulous experience. It's been my life."

Like JATP, Cole's show was not long for this world. The program, the first ever starring an African American, had proved to be one of the most highly rated on television during its yearlong run, although it failed to attract a single sponsor. Many top-flight entertainers appeared on the show for union-scale pay to raise its chances for survival, but to no avail. NBC dropped it two months later.

The recording activities in Granz's studio were most fast-paced and economically rewarding in 1957, when Verve Records realized some $10 million in sales, what with the Ellington songbook, another volume of Ella and Louis, the Newport recordings, and a flood of others; *Down Beat* reviewed around fifty Verve releases in that year alone.[28] In some ways, the most surprising news was that Count Basie was leaving Verve for Roulette Records, especially given Granz's patronage in helping him achieve a midlife musical revival five years before. It is generally conceded that Granz wanted to push Basie in the direction of more frequently featuring his piano playing but that Basie could or would not go against the bandleader's all-for-one-and-one-for-all ethic that had been his code. As was the case when Basie signed with Granz in 1952, Willard Alexander, the bandleader's aggressive manager who almost scuttled the deal with excessive demands, tried to up the ante five years later with a push from Morris Levy, the Birdland owner who went on to found Roulette. "I think that Willard just felt he wanted to get the best deal he could," Granz told Albert Murray, who at the time was working with Basie on his autobiography. "Levy was always trying to get Basie, and so Basie went with Roulette. I think that was the only time Basie and I came close to having any differences."[29] The recording relationship was renewed in the early 1970s with the formation of Pablo Records, after which Count Basie as pianist was frequently brought to the fore.

Among the independent jazz labels, Verve was the commercial leader in a field also populated by such companies as Blue Note, Roulette, Prestige, Riverside, Epic, Coral, ABC-Paramount, Atlantic, Bethlehem, Dot, Fantasy, Debut, and World Pacific. In the majors, Capitol was focusing on the bands of Stan Kenton and Les Brown as well as producing such jazz-oriented singers as Frank Sinatra, Nat Cole, Peggy Lee, and June Christy. Columbia, under the guidance of George Avakian and Teo Macero, stayed with jazz and jazz-influenced popular music, producing the likes of Miles Davis, Duke Ellington, Louis Armstrong, Dave Brubeck, and Erroll Garner. Decca came too late to the ball to employ a significant amount of unsigned talent.

The shelving of JATP turned out to be the earliest stage of Granz's withdrawal from America; it was followed by the January 1961 sale of Verve to MGM with its noncompete clause that mostly kept him out of the recording studios for seven years. He had already moved to Lugano, Switzerland, in 1959, and had begun to undertake a slightly different and expanded role in the music business. He continued to present JATP in Europe but also acted as a promoter, underwriting the costs of bringing American talent to the fields of popular, gospel, and rock and roll and using the contacts built up over years. Granz later considered this aspect of his career to be of little consequence beyond making money. At the close of 1960, his vast influence had reached its apogee. He followed some of his heroes into the sunset in the 1960s before starting a new jazz label in the 1970s. But never again would Norman Granz—or jazz—take center stage to the extent that they had during the first two decades of his career.

15

Duke, Prez, and Billie

The relationship between Norman Granz and Duke Ellington, to appropriate the words of Winston Churchill, was "a riddle wrapped in a mystery inside an enigma," as subtle as an Ellington/Strayhorn arrangement. Two proud men with healthy egos to match, they became more intertwined professionally than ever over the eight years beginning in 1958, when the bandleader accepted Granz's offer to help manage the band for no fees or percentages. Granz saw his managerial assistance as a service he could perform on behalf of jazz based on his paramount regard for his music, if not always the man himself, and Ellington was equally ambivalent toward Granz. At this time Ellington may well have needed Granz more than the other way around.

Granz spoke admiring of Ellington's élan as a showman, his sense of drama, and attention to the details of his appearance and presentation that made him a musical and cultural icon without compromising his musicianship. "His whole attitude [made Ellington distinctive], that whole seignorial attitude of his," Granz said. "He was a very imposing man—very tall and quite graceful. Duke always did a little dance step when he was moving around, almost like a little shuffle. Duke prided himself on his small feet, almost 'petite,' as he put it, and he did a little dance all the time . . . And Duke's band . . . stomped more than swung. Duke almost hammered you, because that was the way he wrote. I think he liked the idea of being an entertainer. . . . He let you know when he did his so-called jungle music that he knew where it was and he knew what the roots were and that is probably what kept him alive in terms of his own people. In effect, he said, 'I didn't sell out,' and the public sensed this."[1]

Granz said that he "kind of fell into" managing Ellington. He found dates to book the band with Ella Fitzgerald, but Granz did not feel that he could manage the band with its special needs, such as making a payroll. "I could only come up with a spot thing," he said. "And it was much easier when Duke didn't have to pay a commission."[2] Granz sent his proposals through the Associated Booking Agency, with whom Ellington was contracted during this period.

A bud from this new relationship bloomed on Easter Sunday 1958 at Carnegie Hall. Granz had organized the first joint appearance on a New York stage of Ellington and Fitzgerald to re-create some of the selections in the Ellington songbook. The late photographer Paul Hoeffler, then a student at the Rochester Institute of Technology, arriving early, ambled down to the apron of stage left and was startled to overhear Granz recounting a row he just had with Ellington over a matter of staging. "Duke wanted the band onstage as the curtain opened," Hoeffler said. "Norman wanted to introduce each player in the band as the artist each was, with individual respect. He was using language that I had heard from Norman at Newport, which I had covered for a couple of years."[3]

Granz went to work on Ellington's behalf organizing a thirty-city, six-week tour of Europe, beginning with three weeks in Great Britain on October 5.[4] The British concerts, on which Granz partnered with promoter Harold Davison, marked the first time since 1933 that the band as a whole had played in the United Kingdom because of the same restrictive British Musicians' Union rules that had long been the bane of Granz's existence. During Ellington's previous visit, in 1948, he had appeared as a soloist along with trumpeter Ray Nance and singer Kay Davis and had been classified as a cabaret act. Two years later, when Ellington toured Europe in 1950, the band again could not play on British soil. Part of Davison's strength as a promoter came from the fact that he was then negotiating band exchanges between the United States and England. Stan Kenton was the first major American band to perform in the British Isles under a new agreement that went into effect in March 1956. He was followed by tours of Louis Armstrong, Count Basie, Eddie Condon, Lionel Hampton, Bill Haley, Jack Teagarden and Earl Hines, the Modern Jazz Quartet, and groups led by Gerry Mulligan and Sidney Bechet. The Ellington band's appearances in Great

Britain in 1958 were made possible by a reciprocal tour in the United States by the Ted Heath Orchestra.[5]

Granz said Ellington's reception in Great Britain was as good as could be expected given the band's long absence. But he lamented what he saw as Ellington's failure to diversify the programming and his overloading of concerts with medleys of his popular hits. He attributed some of the fall-off in attendance during the second tour he organized for Ellington, in 1959, to Ellington's failure to present different music before audiences who expected more challenging material. "I told Duke, 'You have the most incredible library of any band in the world. It's all your material. I should think you'd want to hear something different or better. Why not rehearse and play something new that you've just done?'"[6] Moreover, Granz felt that Ellington underutilized his players, and he would have loved to move them out beyond the Ellington standards. "In a sense, maybe that was the weakness of Duke, because he was beyond having to milk his audience for the applause. . . . I think it was more contempt for the audience." At least one band member, trombonist Buster Cooper, asked Granz about after-hours jam sessions where he could go out and jam in the European cities they visited. "Man, we play the same stuff every night."[7]

Granz prodded Ellington to branch out when he requested that one of his own favorites, the vintage "Stompy Jones" from 1934, be inserted into the program. "Of course, it was an old number which he rarely did. I remember Duke making a thing about it. He always went through the introduction with a tinge of sarcasm as if to say, 'I'm only doing this because this cat has asked me to do it.'"[8] Sure enough, such a moment was recorded during the October 29 concert at the Alhambra Theater in Paris at the conclusion of "Stompy Jones." "That was in answer to a request by our impresario, Mr. Norman Granz . . . Mr. Granz?" Ellington said coyly.

Granz's criticism about "recycling" past hits—standards from his own pen—is almost comical given that he was criticizing Ellington for a supposed quality about which his own concerts had often been attacked. Granz, after all, had made his career on the fame of a supercharged version of the familiar, whether established talent or a formula for presenting jazz that relied on blues and a thousand versions of standards like "Perdido" and "How High the Moon?" Ellington addressed the question in a 1956 interview. "I know they say that I have 200 numbers in the book I never play. I'd like to hear them too. But you can't hear 200 different numbers in one night. And you can't go around the country and *not* play 'Mood Indigo' and 'Sophisticated Lady' and 'Solitude.' . . . Another thing is, I don't want to educate people. I'm as interested in modern music and jazz as anyone else. I love to do it and listen to it, and there are some people in it who knock me out. But I have to respect an audience, too."[9]

One source of amusement among the press was what journalists thought was Ellington's first trip by plane, although in fact he had flown once seventeen years earlier. His aversion to air travel, long the source of his preference for trains, cars, buses, and ships, was expressed in a clause of the contract that specifically stated that Ellington was not required to fly. The band had made the excursion to Europe on the *Ile de France,* landing at Plymouth, England, on October 3. The band received the full Granz treatment during the voyage. In an interview with Granz in 1989, jazz historian Patricia Willard recalled Ellington's ecstatic report of the trip over. "I remembered his telling me afterwards what a delight and joy it was to work for you, because he had never traveled so elegantly on a ship," she told Granz. "'When you work for Norman,' he said, 'he seats you on a lovely satin pillow and sees that you are waited on hand and foot, and you feel so elegant and so important that it spoils you to ever work for anyone else again.' As he told me this story, I got a mental picture of Duke sitting atop a huge ocean liner on a satin pillow."[10]

But if Ellington was to reach Berlin for a concert at the twelve-thousand-seat Deutschlandhalle without laboriously traveling through East Germany by bus, he would have to fly. Ellington agreed to make the short flight from Frankfurt. As Granz told the story, "Duke sat next to me by the window, and I sat on the aisle seat. It was so foggy you couldn't even see the wing, and Duke kept saying, 'You sure that this baby's going to take off?'"

"Yeah, don't worry about it," Granz replied.

"I can't even see the wing," said Ellington.

"Well, don't look," Granz answered.[11]

Trumpeter Clark Terry remembered the flight. "Duke was sitting on the plane with his prayer beads." Ellington again became concerned when he saw the captain pass through the cabin, only to be told by Granz that he had put the plane on automatic pilot. Amazingly, Ellington became an instant convert to air travel, according to Terry, who said he bubbled over with his newfound love. Ellington's debt to Granz went beyond overcoming his fear of flying. Its economic ramifications kept the band on the move with greater efficiency and economy and saved wear and tear on everybody. "Norman taught him how necessary it was to eliminate all that wasted time getting there and getting back when he could be making money," Terry said.[12]

Granz's connections extended Ellington's opportunities, most notably when film director Otto Preminger called on Granz in 1958 to help secure Ellington's services for scoring *Anatomy of a Murder,* the first of a run of such work for major motion pictures. Ellington went to Ishpeming, Michigan, where the film was shot, to appear in his on-camera role as a combo leader called "Pie Eye." The soundtrack for the film was recorded in Los Angeles between May 29 and June 2, 1959. Ellington, to his surprise and delight, received three Grammys for his work on *Anatomy of a Murder*—Best Musical Composition of the Year, Best Performance by a Dance Band, and Best Motion Picture Soundtrack of the Year—during the Recording Academy's televised awards ceremony in November 1959. It took Peggy Lee's lyrics to the main title music, renamed "Gonna Go Fishin'," to give the melody life beyond the film. Ellington followed up the success of *Anatomy of a Murder* by working on a second film score, *Paris Blues,* which began filming in France in the autumn of 1959, when he would be in the midst of his second European tour for Granz.

The 1959 Ellington tour, a monthlong concert series beginning with two days of concerts in the Netherlands on September 18 and ending October 18 in Vienna, was pared down from the year before because of a lack of shows in Great Britain. After two days at Salle Pleyel in Paris, the band headed for a week in Sweden and eleven dates in Germany and Switzerland.

Granz fully appreciated Ellington as a towering figure in jazz. This helps explain why, in the late 1950s or early 1960s, he met with Columbia Records president Goddard Lieberson, one major executive Granz respected, to broach an idea reminiscent of what he had done with Art Tatum, but on a much larger scale: to record everything that Ellington had ever written or wanted to record. "Goddard was unique in the recording industry in that he was the president of a major label, and he was still essentially an A&R man," Granz said. He suggested that, "since Ellington was the only *major* composer in jazz at the time," Columbia ought to record anything Ellington wanted to record, lest anything be lost. He called it "a cultural imperative." Granz estimated that if the band worked for scale it might cost Columbia $100,000 annually to undertake such a project and that any loss the company suffered could be partially written off. "The important thing," Granz said, "was to get all that stuff recorded and ready for the future, for

posterity . . . I tried to convince him that it had nothing to do with economics. This was subsidizing something that was very important, that
it was creative." Granz additionally argued that the project would pay
off over time ("Nobody ever lost money on Ellington"), but Lieberson
shut down the discussion by saying that his responsibility to Columbia's
shareholders nixed the proposal.[13]

The "some other spring" in the lives of Lester Young and Billie Holiday finally came due in the spring and summer of 1959, robbing the
jazz world of two brilliant and equally troubled leading lights from the
Swing Era and Granz of some of his earliest and most influential friends
in the music. Holiday's relationship with Verve had ended with her
pitiful 1957 Newport Jazz Festival appearance. Young had remained
more closely allied with Granz, both in his recordings and in his tours
with Jazz at the Philharmonic in 1955 and 1957. The paths of the two
men crossed frequently under varying circumstances as Young's health
deteriorated because of relentless alcoholism, illness, and depression.

During the 1955 JATP fall tour, Young's quirky valor that allowed
him to see it through until the end was described in a sympathetic 1983
essay by his pianist on that tour, Bobby Scott.[14] Young suffered a nervous breakdown upon his return to New York, and his wife had him
admitted into Bellevue Hospital, where psychiatric help and alcohol-
free nourishment put him back on his feet. It was about this time that
Young relinquished his last regular group. Granz paid his hospital bill
and helped provide for his family in the weeks before Young went home
around Christmas. He was so encouraged by Young's recuperation (and
playing) when he came from California to see him in January 1956 that
he quickly booked back-to-back dates with old friends of Young on the
twelfth and thirteenth at the Fine Sound Studio in New York to record
his last undisputed great studio sessions.[15]

In the first album, *The Jazz Giants '56*, Granz brought Young
together with Roy Eldridge and Vic Dickenson and a rhythm section
of Teddy Wilson, Freddie Green, Gene Ramey, and Jo Jones, much as
he had lovingly selected musicians that helped Billie Holiday make outstanding records during this period. "That January '56 session was very
good," Granz recalled. "Lester had just come out of the hospital. He
felt good. Roy remarked that it was the best he'd heard Lester play in
years." Young returned to the studio the next day with Wilson, Ramey,
and Jones, and the mood that had graced the January 12 proceedings
carried over to those made by the quartet. Then Young was not back in

the studio for Granz again until July 31, 1957, and February 7 and 8, 1958, backed by the Oscar Peterson Trio with Louie Bellson and Harry Edison. The weaknesses of the performances were especially apparent when Young played some of his rare recorded performances on a silver clarinet. "He wanted a silver one, so I went out and bought him one," Granz said. "Then he complained that he had to get it together and practice. It was always one thing or another. I could never get him to record with it. I think he liked the clarinet, but lacked the confidence to do it. By the time I did manage to do it, it was really too late."[16]

In the spring of 1958, Young's instability finally broke apart his family, at which point he moved into the rundown Alvin Hotel overlooking Birdland, where he would die the following year. That September, Young severed his ties with Verve in an effort to "start afresh" and signed with United Artists. He fulfilled engagements in New York and was supposed to be on the 1959 European JATP tour. In the end he decided to accept an offer to appear for eight weeks at Le Blue Note in Paris. Young had his last reunion with Billie Holiday during their stay, as she was singing at the Olympia Theater and the Mars Club through February 22. Occasionally, she even got onstage with Young at Le Blue Note and performed sets with him.[17]

In his dying days Young gave the most substantial and longest interview of his career to Paris journalist François Postif. In it he discussed his early life as well as his musical aspirations and plans for when he returned to New York. Monte Kay, founder of Jazz in Central Park in the 1950s and a producer at United Artists, wanted to record Young with strings and even gave him an advance. However, Young was still under contract with Granz, and Granz refused to let the project go forward. "I got a man in New York now, writing some music for me when I get back," Young said. "I got bass violin, two cellos, a viola and a French horn . . . It's my first time and I always wanted to do it. Norman Granz never did let me make a record with no strings, you know. Yardbird made millions of records with strings."[18]

Another critic of Young's Verve recordings was Granz's old friend and Young's younger brother, Lee. "I think the things that Norman was doing were really almost demeaning, because it did not show the scope of the man as a musician. Norman was into the blues, you know, so he wanted you to play some B-flat blues, because that was about what he could understand," he said in 1977. "But, to me, if you listen to any records where Lester played solos on ballads, he was a very melodic musician."[19]

The homesick and terminally ill Young, now in severe distress from his ulcers, cut his Paris stay short one week early, on March 13, and returned to the United States. Young was in such pain during the trans-atlantic flight that he bit through his lower lip, but he refused to be taken to the hospital when he landed. He instructed his female com-panion, Elaine Swaine, to take him to the Alvin Hotel, where he spent his last night watching the comings and goings at Birdland from his window and polishing off a bottle of vodka and most of a bottle of bourbon. He died in the early hours of March 15.

Granz was among the mourners who gathered to celebrate Young's life during the funeral four days later at Universal Chapel on the corner of Fifty-second Street and Lexington Avenue. Billie Holiday, who would die around four months later on July 17, had been asked not to sing at the service out of a fear that her declining abilities might cause embar-rassment. Granz took out a full page in the April 30 issue of *Down Beat* with a photograph of a baleful Lester Young playing bordered by black. The legend read, "We'll all miss you, Lester. Norman Granz."[20] The tribute to Young was the only time he had so honored a musician.

Granz was often asked why he had not reunited Holiday and Young, who had made what were some of jazz's finest records together in the 1930s but had become estranged over the years when he had them both under contract. His answer, that most of his recording activities were based in Los Angeles and that scheduling problems had interfered, sounds unconvincing or incomplete. The man who had moved moun-tains to accomplish his feats in jazz could certainly have reunited the two artists in a studio in New York. The question remains essentially unanswered.

The Fitzgerald-Granz partnership proved particularly rewarding in the three years leading up to when Granz left the record business. Fitzgerald recorded the Irving Berlin and George and Ira Gershwin songbooks in 1958 and the following year, the latter of these being the most lavish tribute in the series at five albums. Even when she did wrong, she did right. She flubbed the lyrics with "Mack the Knife," a recent smash hit for Bobby Darin and Louis Armstrong, during the February 20, 1960, *Ella in Berlin* concert and came out the other end with her best-selling record to date at over a half million copies and Grammys for best vocal and album. The song never left her repertoire.

In selecting Irving Berlin to be celebrated by a songbook, Granz took an especially convenient request from the composer himself. It seems his children had taken to singing Cole Porter and Rodgers and Hart songs around the house after falling in love with the Fitzgerald performances of their songbooks. Would Granz consider similarly honoring Berlin's work with a Fitzgerald set so he could save face within the family? "As a matter of fact, I'm researching you now," Granz assured Berlin, whose work had preceded the other composers and lyricists and had framed some of the earliest twentieth-century American popular songs, beginning with "Alexander's Ragtime Band" in 1911.

Arranger Paul Weston, a West Coast A&R man for Columbia and husband of singer Jo Stafford, finished his obligations for the label in time to accept Granz's invitation to work on the Berlin songbook, which was recorded between March 13 and 19, 1958, at Radio Recorders. Weston concurred with the decision to keep Berlin out of the studio, given his memories of working around Berlin during production of the 1941 film *Holiday Inn*. "He was a real stickler . . . very intense," said Weston, who recalled that Berlin had once sneaked into a secretly scheduled rehearsal (intended to keep him away) to hear how his music was being played. "Berlin would have been all over Norman with suggestions. . . . Norman and I put in a lot of time together—Ella may have been in on one of those meetings—and Berlin had a huge book. Some of the verses were very nice, and the music was really superb. I think I underestimated Berlin. Norman had a sense of how to balance a project like that with enough familiar stuff to get people to listen, but enough unusual stuff to make it interesting."[21]

Weston said it usually took him five to six hours to write an arrangement at around $200 apiece after the selections and scoring decisions were reached. "Sometimes I'd have an idea where I was going, but Norman never made the slightest interference as far as the arrangements were concerned. He never asked to change a note." Berlin was so thrilled with the results, especially since Fitzgerald and Granz had helped to revive some of the lesser-known works in his catalog, that he cut his mechanical royalties in half, from two cents per song to one.

Just as Norman Granz had crafted *The Astaire Story* by absorbing Fred Astaire films in his teens, he had an even more direct connection from his youth with George Gershwin, who, with his brother, Ira, was the subject of the next songbook. Granz, a UCLA student at the time, had been studying in the library on September 28, 1936, when it was announced that Gershwin would be presenting the school's new fight song in the gymnasium. Granz was in the audience when Gershwin performed a reworked previous hit as "Strike Up the Band for UCLA," a mere nine months before the composer died of a brain tumor.

Work on *Ella Fitzgerald Sings the George and Ira Gershwin Song Book,* given the scope of its ambition, began over a year before the first track was recorded. Nelson Riddle, always on Granz's shortest short list to do the arranging for the songbooks, was available. "All commercial good sense seemed to take leave of Granz in the grip of a project that he was convinced was to be a masterwork," John McDonough wrote in the liner notes for the complete reissue of the songbooks. "Granz was utterly fearless in going deluxe."[22]

Fitzgerald, Granz, Ira Gershwin, and Riddle managed to whittle down the Gershwin catalog to fifty-nine songs written by the two brothers between 1924 and George's untimely death in 1937 at age thirty-eight. Gershwin, the only one of the composers whom Granz permitted to collaborate on the album honoring his work, helped compile the music and occasionally revised a lyric. Granz made one memorable contribution to the album when he suggested that Fitzgerald sing "Lady Be Good" as a ballad rather than as the up-tempo scat showpiece she had made famous.

Hildegard Handel of Frankfurt, Germany, a recording engineer at Capitol Records in Los Angeles between 1958 and 1983, shared the controls with Val Valentine when the Gershwin songbook was recorded on monaural and three-track tape in Studio A in January, March, and July 1959. Granz was firmly in control of the sessions, although "he never pushed anything on anybody." With Fitzgerald, she observed him as warm, gentle, and solicitous. "She knew that Norman guided her through these trials and tribulations. Norman was very smooth, very quiet, very determined," she said. "Ella needed special care. When she was singing, she was absolutely in command of her voice, the phrasing and everything. When you hear them today, the records are masterpieces." One sharply etched memory was of Fitzgerald walking into the studio in a green dress with green silk high heels. "Ella couldn't stay in those pumps anymore, so she just took them off and stood barefoot in the studio."[23]

The series continued with Harold Arlen in 1960, although it was clear that the Gershwin production would be its apex as far as volume and the recordings' impact on Fitzgerald's career. The series would be resumed three years later with the final two songbooks, tributes to Jerome Kern and Johnny Mercer, both arranged by Nelson Riddle and completed in October 1964. Granz ended the songbook series because he thought he and Fitzgerald had fully covered the composer-lyricist teams worthy of such treatment. Kern had turned to many lyricists to produce his work, and the lyricist Mercer had searched out a variety of composers. "So the sense and impact of a single team's work was necessarily being diluted," Granz said.

Fitzgerald did not have to say much to acknowledge the fruits of her labor after hooking up with Granz. "[It] was the real turning point in my life," Fitzgerald said in 1983. "Norman felt I had more to offer than bop, so he started our songbooks."[24] On another occasion she said, "Norman thought I could do different kinds of songs, and how right he was. I will always be grateful for that."[25]

British jazz critic Benny Green, a close friend of Granz's from the late 1950s, agreed that Granz was prescient in realizing the works of the classic popular composers as "authentic works of art, miniatures that had never been treated as they deserved. . . . It has to be remembered that in 1956, when the grand strategy was first set in motion, most of the men whose work was to be featured in the series were still alive. . . . Granz was on terms with more than one of them. This was to prove a huge asset, which became apparent as the series began to unfold."[26]

These Fitzgerald/Granz masterworks not only raised critical consciousness about the canon of work that they celebrated but constructed the platform for the remainder of Fitzgerald's career. McDonough, writing upon her death in 1996, pointed to a sobering undercurrent of the tributes undetected as they were being created. "[The] barbarians were already at the gate," he wrote. "The Presley phenomenon and the rock 'n roll revolution that issued from it would signal the collapse of the composer's place in American popular music. That it should happen precisely at the moment Miss Fitzgerald offered a new perspective on its appreciation and demonstrated that their work could be treated in a definitive manner as a body of literary work seems an astonishing irony. The songbook project would become an unexpected and historic elegy to a vanishing age of literacy, intelligence and elitism in American music."[27]

A profile of the singer in *Ebony* in 1961 in the afterglow of her most defining success, one of the most revealing ever written about her personal life, showed Fitzgerald ensconced in the leafy, comfortable, and private retreat in Beverly Hills that her talents had secured for her but that she had little time to enjoy. Rather staged-looking photographs depict her coaching her son on his music lessons, sitting poolside with him in the backyard, serving drinks, and playing cards with her traveling companion, Georgiana Henry, and her aunt, Virginia Williams, who had helped raise Fitzgerald and did the same for Ray Brown Jr.

"I'm fortunate to have been on top for so long," Fitzgerald said. "When you've done so well so long and won so many honors, it gives you the feeling that the first time you do one little thing wrong, people are going to be down on you." She said she was especially sensitive about her weight. "I've found that one of my biggest problems was not being too happy as far as my love life was concerned, and I just didn't care about my weight. . . . With all the glamour, there's still nothing like it [romantic love]. You can have love of family, love of children and all that, but you've got to have your man. . . . When you're in the public eye, you don't want to do things that will make people feel that you're not right. But then when you're sitting at home, you ask, 'Who am I pleasing now?' . . . But for two years, I've sat right in this house with the TV and the ice box, and it's no good."[28]

16

Joie de Verve

The April 9, 1959, recording session for the album *Ben Webster and Associates* at Nola Studios in New York brought together musicians that Norman Granz loved to produce in a fashion he had long since mastered. "I was recording Ben Webster, and Coleman Hawkins came up just to watch the session," he said. "I was going to record Ben again the next day, and he said, 'Hawk, do you want to do it?' His fellow saxophonist said, 'Sure.' Ben was at the barber shop the next morning when he ran into Budd Johnson. So he invited him and Budd showed up with his tenor. In the meantime, I called Roy Eldridge and asked, 'Roy how would you like to come down and do an album with Coleman and Ben?' He said, 'I'd love that.' So the session came out as Budd, Hawk, Ben and Roy plus the rhythm section. With people like that I couldn't do anything wrong. I'm not saying everyone would like or have to like it, or feel it was great, but it was a fantastic thing for me to have the right to sit in and listen to these people play. I mean, that's what I wanted to do."[1]

A 1957 date with Lee Konitz in New York provides a good example of how Granz was increasingly extending the good offices of Verve to support a diversity of jazz voices. Granz was pretty much nonplussed by Konitz's music and was nowhere to be found at the studio. But he appreciated that Konitz—one of the few major alto saxophonists who grew up in the shadow of Charlie Parker but did not follow in stylistic lockstep—had a valid musical statement to make and fans who appreciated his work. "I was very friendly with Lee. I liked him," Granz recalled.[2] Konitz, for his part, said of Granz, "I liked what he did with the Jazz at the Philharmonic guys. I didn't care for the show-business part of it, but I know it's part of the game. In some ways Norman found a happy medium with the product he presented." Between 1958 and 1960, when Konitz started a family, Granz put him on salary at $100 a week and gave him the opportunity to record seven albums for Verve. "He was really great with me, and considering I wasn't one of his favorite players, I just assumed that, somehow, he regarded what I was doing enough to keep it going for some years. I was grateful for that. I don't know if I was ever able to express that to him."[3]

Other players, Dave Brubeck among them, were not satisfied with a hands-off producer, especially one not sympathetic to their music. Producer Bones Howe, who dated back with Granz to the Verve days, recalled with chagrined amusement a story Granz told about what he thought was a sweeping and generous offer to Brubeck, on the heels of his early huge success with Fantasy Records.

"Dave had just left Fantasy and was available to record for other labels," Howe said in 2003. "Norman had this conversation with him. 'You can come to my label, you can do anything you want to, we make the studio available to you, you can stay in there as long as you want, you can make any record you want to.'"

"And apparently Dave said, 'Will you be there at the sessions?'"

Norman said no, and Brubeck asked why not. "Because I don't like your music."

"Norman couldn't understand why he would turn down the opportunity to have that complete freedom to make any record he wanted to, and he turned it down because he couldn't stand being on a label with a guy who wasn't a big fan. So he went to Columbia and did *Take Five,*" Howe continued. "Norman was so honest with some things. Norman could have had him; he probably would have signed with him. But he didn't want to go to the sessions because he didn't like the way he played. He didn't like the quartet. It was so honest of him and that tells you a lot about him."[4] (Granz, on the other hand, did like Brubeck's alto saxophonist Paul Desmond and recorded him in an inspired and highly regarded encounter with baritone saxophonist Gerry Mulligan in 1957.)

Who could blame Brubeck? The red carpet treatment he received from Teo Macero at Columbia Records, who produced a series of hit albums that made him a solid international star, was as essential to Brubeck's future over the next half century as what Granz had accomplished on behalf of Ella Fitzgerald through the recordings they did together.

More significant was Granz's attempt to expand his musical boundaries by underwriting and promoting the short-lived, well-traveled, and much-loved Concert Jazz Band under the leadership of baritone saxophonist, arranger, and composer Gerry Mulligan from the spring of 1960 through December 1964. Mulligan stated that his aspirations for the band were to achieve "the same clarity of sound and interplay of lines that I had in smaller groups."[5] Doubling on piano, he brought out the talents of the thirteen-member all-star band with arrangements by himself, Bob Brookmeyer, Johnny Carisi, Bill Holman, Johnny Mandel, George Russell, and a twenty-seven-year-old Gary McFarland.

The Granz touch was visible in the extensive promotion for the Concert Jazz Band, which included a full-page ad in *Down Beat* in late October 1960 announcing the release of its first album, *Gerry Mulligan: The Concert Jazz Band,* and the beginning of a seventeen-city tour of the West and Midwest before three weeks of concerts in Western Europe.[6] The Mulligan outfit played to four standing-room engagements within six months at the Village Vanguard, where one of the band's recordings was made in December 1960. The band's renown brought in a host of honors in 1960 and 1961 from the public and critics alike, including *Down Beat*'s annual international critics' poll and *Billboard*'s annual jazz writers' poll.[7]

Granz absorbed similarly high costs for other instrumentalists and vocalists to utilize big bands for their recordings. Whereas the major record labels, broadcasters, and movie studios had staff musicians, Granz could quickly assemble equally impressive numbers of musicians and arrangers necessary for full-scale productions when necessary, including the continuing popularity of recording with strings. During this period, Louie Bellson made three big band records, followed by Gene Krupa, vibraphonist Terry Gibbs, and Dizzy Gillespie, who each recorded two such albums for Verve. Oscar Peterson made a record with the Russ Garcia Orchestra; Sonny Stitt recorded with another band led by Ralph Burns; and there was a similar work by pianist and vocalist Bobby Scott, who had emerged from the Gene Krupa Quartet.

Terry Gibbs approached Granz about recording the latest version of his big band for Verve. Granz was interested and Mercury released Gibbs from his contract, allowing him to record three albums for Granz in the next two years. He went into the studio in February 1960 on the day after his release from Mercury to record *Swing Is Here* with the band. The following month, Gibbs recorded a quintet on *Can Can,* one of his favorite albums of his career. The following January, Granz recorded the band live at the Summit Club in Los Angeles for an LP entitled *The Exciting Big Band of Terry Gibbs*. Gibbs was impressed with Granz's generosity. At that time, union scale called for $100 per tune for soloists and principal performers but only $33 for sidemen. Granz paid everyone $100 a song.

Ella Fitzgerald aside, Granz had a resplendent group of jazz and popular vocalists recording for him in the late 1950s. Anita O'Day, who recorded the label's first volume and whose contract extended through 1963 and ten albums, continued recording throughout and beyond Granz's ownership of Verve. Her 1980 autobiography presents a mixed and not always plausible picture of her experiences with the label and its owner. On the one hand, her gratitude for the high-quality material, musicians, and arrangers (Russ Garcia and Marty Paich were her favorites) is palpable. Her Verve recordings, beginning with *Anita* in 1956, resulted in more personal and broadcast appearances and a renewed respect for her reputation as one of the most influential of all jazz singers. Yet despite her success at Verve she had suspicions about where she fit into Granz's overall priorities. Thus she states, "It soon became obvious Ella was Norman's main girl. Ella wasn't going to get most of the good stuff—she was going to get it all. I was an afterthought, a tax write-off. Even second best wasn't bad." O'Day describes Granz as someone who "could be charming or heartless depending on which would get him farther." All likely enough, but her credibility suffers with the charge that Granz preyed on drug-addicted musicians to maintain an upper hand during negotiations. At the same time she somewhat paradoxically praises his honesty compared to other label owners or executives because while he charged for recording he underwrote advertising costs.[8]

Certainly Granz made no bones about his bias in favor of Fitzgerald, whose insecurities, real or imagined, made him think twice about getting involved with managing other major female singers. This was evident when Granz received a letter from Carmen McRae virtually begging him to manage her career. "Lord knows I need you," McRae wrote.[9] Though Granz refused to honor her request, he felt bad about it, especially since McRae was one of his favorite four jazz singers alongside Billie Holiday, Sarah Vaughan, and Fitzgerald.

This was also a time when Granz rewarded some of his devoted regulars, such as Ray Brown, Herb Ellis, and pianist Paul Smith, with the chance to have their own recording sessions. Granz continued to produce a number of recordings for Verve's Down Home series of traditional jazzmen. Between 1958 and 1960, he released half a dozen albums by the great clarinetist George Lewis as well as others by trombonists Turk Murphy and Kid Ory and trumpeter Henry "Red" Allen. He leased recordings by foreign jazz groups, including John Dankworth, the British saxophonist and bandleader and husband of singer Cleo Laine, as well as musicians from Argentina, Italy, Cuba, and Austria. There was also room for others that do not immediately leap to mind where Granz is concerned: the Ink Spots, Memphis Slim and Willie Dixon, Herbie Mann, Sammy Davis Jr., and Paul Robeson. Verve even released a record by the Hawaiian jazz accordion player Lyle Ritz, *Jazz from the 49th State.* Granz had little doubt that the company could adapt and survive handsomely in the changing musical climate of the late 1950s and early 1960s. But in late 1958 he had begun to put out feelers for someone to buy the company. Much later he told an interviewer, "I'm sure we would have gotten our share as a viable label with getting people to come to us. I may not have had anything to do with it. I'm sure I could have had an assistant to do pop or rock or whatever. I loved to go into the studio and produce albums, but I hated the business side of the record business."[10]

In 1958, when Granz detailed his plans to assert his claim on Europe as he had in the United States, *Melody Maker* declared him the "dictator of jazz," adding, "As from now, he is crashing the European market with the intention of becoming the biggest importer of American jazz. It sounded simple the way Norman Granz said it." "Broadly," Granz announced, "my plan for Europe is this. I shall supplant 50 promoters in 50 cities, or 25 promoters in 25 cities. Where a proper organization exists, I shall use it. Where it is missing, I shall supply it. I am ready to tour Europe in parallel. It is a two-pronged contribution. The local impresarios have certain advantages over me. They live in the country and they can promote more economically than I can, and they are better acquainted with the local pattern of promotion. As against that, I have the advantage of offering a standardized tour through the American agency. I don't doubt that it will go all right." Granz envisioned having as many as two shows crisscrossing Europe simultaneously, JATP being the old standby. He might offer an agency the chance to put together a tour made up of such artists as Count Basie, Billy Eckstine, Benny Goodman, Louis Armstrong, Duke Ellington, Stan Kenton, and George Shearing.[11] Thus he was preparing to act both as an impresario for new talent, as he had through the years with Jazz at the Philharmonic, and as a promoter of established acts in and out of jazz.

The 1958 edition of Jazz at the Philharmonic got under way on May 2 at the Gaumont State Theater, Kilburn, London, for its first regular tour of Great Britain with a troupe consisting of Dizzy Gillespie, Roy Eldridge, Coleman Hawkins, Stan Getz, Sonny Stitt, Gus Johnson, Max Bennett, Lou Levy, the Oscar Peterson Trio, and Ella Fitzgerald. The program maintained the structure Granz had devised in the last years of JATP's domestic touring, one that featured swing and modern sets and the ballad medley.

Traveling through the English countryside by bus, the musicians relieved their boredom by betting on whether Gillespie could beat Granz in a footrace. Oscar Peterson asked the laconic Coleman Hawkins if he were going to ante up, to which he replied, "No, I was thinking of running." The bus pulled into a small street in a village about ten miles from Manchester and the group entertained a gathering crowd not by playing music but by holding the race. Granz easily outran the trumpeter, who mugged to the crowd as he made an exaggerated display of warming up. Actually, it was Sonny Stitt who bested them both as he kept the pace all the way to the finish line to witness the outcome.[12]

The lawyer Roberto Capasso had begun promoting Granz's shows in Rome in 1954. Capasso booked the theater, rented the piano, provided sound and lighting, wrote contracts, and scheduled advertising. He attended to press relations, provided complimentary tickets, obtained police permits and performance rights, secured hotel reservations, and organized airport receptions. "Italian audiences—and Roman audiences in particular—were warm, although they were not huge," Capasso said. "Of course, performances of such stars as Armstrong, Ellington or Ella were usually sold out, as these artists could count on a wider non-jazz following. Not-so-famous musicians could only count on jazz devotees, who mostly preferred mainstream styles."[13]

Capasso was on the scene to witness, survive, and repair the damage from one of the most stupid and arrogant miscalculations of Granz's career. This occurred at Rome's Teatro Sistina on May 26, 1958. Granz had befriended a young Italian beauty named Maria Scicolone, the younger half-sister of Sophia Loren and later the wife of Romano Mussolini, a jazz pianist and son of the Italian dictator. The night of the concert, Granz and Scicolone were invited for dinner at her illustrious sibling's apartment. In Rome Granz's concerts typically ran from 5:00

to 7:00; second shows started around 9:00 or 9:30 or even 9:45, reflecting Granz's experience that they were usually late filling up.

As Granz told the story, the invitation to Loren's apartment was "the dream, I think, of every man. As it happened, Sophia was a big fan of Ella's, and they became friends when I brought Ella to Europe, and to Italy, specifically. The dinner she made was spaghetti." Granz ignored Scicolone's reminders that it was getting late and that he needed to get to the show because he thought the rest of the audience would be similarly tardy.[14] So he might have wished. However, the scene was already verging on chaos by the time he finally showed up about an hour after curtain time, knowing full well the musicians would not begin without him. Granz further delayed the proceedings to get dressed. The delay stretched to fifty-five minutes as the audience began protesting and calling out the musicians' names. By the time he finally walked onstage, he was greeted by a barrage of coins, screaming, and boos, at which point the concert was almost beyond saving. Stan Getz played, and then Dizzy Gillespie was ready to come on, but the public wanted an encore by the saxophonist.

"Then Granz took a chair and sat down on the stage, grinning," Capasso said. "Of course, the audience couldn't help reacting. Some rolled paper sheets into balls and as a couple of these were thrown at Granz, a loud chorus rose: 'Buffone! Buffone!' Granz, furious, ran offstage and ordered the curtain lowered. An unknown voice from the audience shouted that the show wasn't over—Dizzy Gillespie had not played yet—and tickets had to be reimbursed. Granz ordered Gillespie to go onstage and play one piece only." The show ended after barely fifty minutes. Granz had decided that Joe Turner and Pete Johnson would not perform.

The scene slid into anarchy as the enraged audience refused to leave the theater. Capasso viewed Granz's behavior as demonstrating utter contempt for Italy and Rome in particular. "What happened in the wings," he said, "defied description. Personal abuse of Italian journalists, critics, and musicians was but the beginning of a veritable tirade." The police derailed Granz's plans to meet the musicians for an after-show dinner when they cordoned him off in the dressing room to protect him from angry concertgoers until around 2:00 a.m. They took him back to the hotel, where he was similarly barred from leaving. One Rome newspaper the following day captured the general mood of the public after the fiasco at the Teatro Sistina when it called Granz "the Maria Callas of Jazz." A report on the episode by the American embassy quoted Granz as telling *Il Tiempo,* "The Roman public is stupid. There will be no more jazz concerts in Italy, because I *am* jazz."[15]

Eventually Granz did make his apologies, and a few years later Capasso promoted another Jazz at the Philharmonic concert in Rome. The emcee for the evening was the well-known Italian entertainer Walter Chiari, who asked the audience "to behave in such a way that no one could say, '*Hic sunt leones,*'" a Latin saying that means "Here is the land of lions" (that is, a land of savage people). The concert lasted almost three hours. "There were endless encores, endless applause. Finally, Granz asked me, 'Are you satisfied now?'"[16]

Granz occasionally imported European talent he heard during his extensive travels. He achieved what turned out to be a critical and commercial coup in September 1959 when he presented the French singer and film actor Yves Montand for the first time in the United States. If the American public knew him at all it would have been from the 1953 film *The Wages of Fear,* his interpretation of "Autumn Leaves," or his marriage to actress Simone Signoret, then basking in the success of the film *Room at the Top* with Laurence Harvey. Granz booked Henry Miller's Theater on West Forty-third Street for three weeks of concerts. American audiences were largely unfamiliar with Montand's repertoire, described as one that explored "the modest hopes, the silent joys and sufferings and loves" of common people, music that could form the basis for future folk music.[17] Granz first proposed the idea when Montand was in the midst of shows at the Étoile in Paris during December 1958. Montand and Signoret knew of Granz as a successful impresario and record company owner and as the manager of Ella Fitzgerald and Oscar Peterson. They were also devotees of *The Astaire Story,* which Signoret praised as "a splendid example of good taste, intelligence and affection. . . . That evening, in the dressing room, Norman Granz was, for us, the gentleman who had the idea for *The Astaire Story* we were so proud of owning. Norman Granz isn't always affable; often he is rather abrupt—and he's stubborn. But that evening, he was smiling, charming and direct."[18]

Granz envisioned presenting Montand in a small Broadway theater on the scale of the Étoile. He would take care of all of the arrangements, including obtaining the visas for Montand and Signoret for the shows beginning on September 22, 1959. A few days later Granz returned with the necessary official forms to get the couple into the country in time for the concerts, but the consul's office soon informed them that their visa requests had been refused. Apparently suspicions had been raised by Montand's and Signoret's well-known leftist sympathies. As Signoret tells the story, "Norman had decided that he would be the first to import Montand to New York, to open his 1959 autumn season. But at the moment we weren't *grata,* as they say when they allude to certain *personae.* We were soon to learn that Norman was made of stern stuff. He took this refusal as a personal insult. On top of all the other things I've said he is, Norman Granz is also touchy."[19] Granz "moved heaven and earth, agencies and consulates," according to Montand, to get visas approved by the end of January 1959 that allowed the pair one entry into the United States between July 15 through December 15.[20]

At the last minute, one of the musicians that Montand had counted on playing with, clarinetist Hubert Rostaing, was forbidden by the American Federation of Musicians to accompany him. Granz asked Jimmy Giuffre to assume the role in a group that already included Billy Byers on trombone, Jim Hall on guitar, Nick Perito on accordion, Al Hall on bass, and Charlie Persip on drums. Though the six American musicians Granz had hired were unfamiliar with Montand's style of storytelling through his songs, their jazz background enabled them to adapt quickly to what was expected of them.[21]

The show was a hit, and the Montands suddenly found themselves famous. Granz had booked a second three weeks at the Longacre Theater at the conclusion of the run at the Miller. *Time* praised Montand as "the most brilliant music-hall artist to have made his presence felt on stage since the Second World War," and many reviews commented on the simplicity of staging, the "common man" theme of the repertoire, and the polish of Montand's execution.[22]

The success of the show exceeded expectations. Montand and Signoret were wined and dined at the city's top night spots and became regulars at Sardi's during the remainder of their stay. "We were simply royalty," Signoret recalled.[23] One highlight of their visit was an invitation to dinner at the apartment of Arthur Miller and his wife, Marilyn Monroe, with whom Montand would later have a much-publicized affair when they were filming *Let's Make Love* in 1960. Montand was booked for shows in Montreal, Toronto, Los Angeles, San Francisco, and Japan, concerts Granz had scheduled in the event that Montand's New York shows failed to hit the mark. Once during the "royalty's" six weeks in New York, Montand apparently became imperious enough in his ongoing demands to nettle Granz, who had gone back to Europe after the show opened. Granz flew to New York in a rage specifically to berate him and then retreated just as quickly to Geneva.

Granz's next major outing was the 1959 spring European tour, which made headlines when the British Ministry of Labour barred Stan Getz from entering the country because of his drug use, although no official explanation was given. Granz used Sonny Stitt to make up a horn section consisting of Roy Eldridge on trumpet and Eddie Wasserman on tenor saxophone and clarinet. Joining them were the Gene Krupa Sextet and a quartet led by pianist Lou Levy, who also served as Ella Fitzgerald's accompanist. The European dates were the first extensive performances of the reconstituted Oscar Peterson Trio. Drummer Ed Thigpen had replaced Herb Ellis, who had served his notice the previous year, citing the exhausting travel schedule and his decision to settle with his family in California.

Peterson credits Granz with helping him decide on Ellis's replacement. "Norman was always at his best whenever an apparently insurmountable problem arose," Peterson said. "He exuded total control, and his voice would take on a quasi-casual, but highly determined candor; furthermore, he took clever care to ensure he was not interrupted. After asking about my future plans, he demolished my worries about finding another guitarist by issuing a completely new challenge. He informed me that a lot of people—players and listeners alike—were curious to see if I could retain my command of the piano and the group if Ray's immense sound were to be complemented by a drummer." Granz further pressed Peterson not to "coast," suggesting to the pianist that he might have already begun to do so.[24]

With Brown's encouragement, Peterson asked Thigpen, the son of Ben Thigpen, drummer for the Swing Era bandleader Andy Kirk, to round out his new trio. When he was first approached in the late summer of 1958 his salary request was too high for either Peterson or Granz. "I could have kicked myself," Thigpen said later of the self-inflicted threat to his longtime desire to play with the trio.[25] Peterson then asked drummer Gene Gammage, who had played occasional dates with the trio, to join instead. During Gammage's brief tenure, the trio recorded a jazz version of *My Fair Lady*. But Peterson soon reconsidered and again turned to Thigpen, who began his six years with the Peterson Trio on January 1, 1959. Thigpen stayed in the Granz fold for the better part of the next fourteen years, accompanying Ella Fitzgerald in 1966–67 and 1968–72.

The year 1960 presented Granz with the opportunity to demonstrate the seriousness of his plans to upgrade his European operations by holding four to six concert tours annually. He launched two consecutive

Jazz at the Philharmonic tours in Great Britain and on the Continent in early February. One of them, spearheaded by Ella Fitzgerald and the Paul Smith Quartet with Jim Hall, had an unusual West Coast jazz coloration. The Shelly Manne Quintet featured pianist Russ Freeman, trumpeter Joe Gordon, tenor saxophonist Richie Kamuca, and bassist Monte Budwig, while Jimmy Giuffre, who had topped *Melody Maker*'s clarinet poll that year, headed a unit with Hall and Budwig.

The second tour under the JATP banner—featuring the Oscar Peterson Trio, the Stan Getz Quartet, and the Miles Davis Quintet with John Coltrane, Wynton Kelly on piano, Paul Chambers on bass, and Jimmy Cobb on drums—played in twenty-two cities, beginning on March 21 in Paris's Olympia Theater. The Davis booking in particular heralded a new direction in that Granz was not as directly involved in devising groups of musicians of his choosing as he had been with JATP. Granz had to step in before the beginning of the tour when Coltrane almost backed out because he wanted more money. Granz offered to supplement what Davis paid him to increase his pay to a thousand a week. "In his autobiography that was ghosted, Miles talked about Coltrane not wanting to go on tour," Granz said. "He got a $1,000 a week from me. Now that's the story. Miles was getting enough to pay him, but he wouldn't pay him any more."[26] Granz bit his lip on another occasion when Davis decided at the last minute not to play on three half-hour shows that Granz had negotiated with German television.

Despite that, Granz and Davis had come to a meeting of the minds early on that allowed the two prickly characters to peacefully coexist. "Miles and I got to be very tight in the sense that we talked to each other, as much as you could talk to Miles," Granz said. "I told him, 'I want you to know, I know you don't like me, but I don't like you either. But let's respect each other. You give me the full amount of time I want for my concert and I will pay you the full amount of money that I promised to give you. Just don't be late or I will deduct it. Just be cool like that.' From then on it was fine."[27]

In May of 1960, Granz promoted a three-week tour for Nat Cole that played in England, Sweden, Denmark, Switzerland, and Germany. Granz invited Quincy Jones and his all-star band—which included trumpeters Clark Terry and Benny Bailey, saxophonists Phil Woods, Budd Johnson, and Jerome Richardson, and trombonists Jimmy Cleveland and Melba Liston, all of whom were all stranded in Europe—to accompany Cole.[28] Jones's band opened the show with a forty-minute set before Cole came on to perform. Like Granz, many of Cole's

European fans were at the very least perplexed that the singer had wandered far away from his jazz beginnings. Jones recalls a show in Zurich when the audience was giving Cole a hard time. "They were hardcore jazz people and they didn't want to know anything about pop music," Jones said. "Nat was singing things like 'Mona Lisa.' The audience wasn't receptive to it when he opened his show with the first tune. He felt it, and came back to me and asked, 'Why don't you let the band go back out there for a while?'" Jones suggested that a dose of "Sweet Lorraine" would probably do the trick. "He did it and tore it up. That's what they wanted to hear. They viewed him as a pianist first."[29]

Granz said little of the camaraderie between him and Cole had survived over the previous twenty years. But around the time of the 1960 tour, Granz appears to have resolved many of his feelings that Cole had somehow diminished himself artistically by concentrating on being one of the greatest pop singers. Getting ready for the tour, Granz, who paid Cole $3,000 a night, asked if he would play a couple of piano numbers, but Cole replied that he really did not care for playing much anymore. "He may have privately liked to hear jazz, but from what I knew of Nat, I think he just gave up the idea, and for him it was the right decision," Granz said. "I don't fault any artist who decides to change what he's doing. I think it's presumptuous as I read jazz writers or reported jazz writers who say he sold out or he's commercial or his record company twisted his arm. That's bullshit, flat out bullshit. With someone like Nat, the decision, by his standards, was a proper one."[30] Quincy Jones echoes the sentiment. "I'm not that dogmatic. I think a person has the right to express everything they want to. He was a piano player first and he was a singer. He was the greatest who ever lived along with Sinatra. So be it. I loved to hear Nat sing."[31]

Granz rebuked Cole in print following an interview that the singer gave to *Variety* in Frankfurt in which he, like many jazz artists of the time, predicted (or hoped) that rock and roll was on the way out. Cole pushed Granz's buttons when he downgraded the state of jazz. "Jazz in the U.S. is at the bottom of the commercial barrel," he began. "It doesn't draw enough business and that's why rock 'n roll came into being." The interviewer wrote that "while other American jazz artists have been interrupted in the German concerts by rioting fans brandishing chairs, attacking each other with water pistols and jamming in the aisles, Cole says, 'I don't sing that type of music. Through the years, I have maintained my own style of popular music and it's not primitive.'"[32]

"First of all, Cole, if he's quoted accurately, is talking through his hat by saying 'Jazz is at the bottom of the commercial barrel,'" Granz shot back. "Nat should know better, because jazz in every conceivable form is bigger than ever, being used not only in films, but on television and obviously on records. Let him check the sales of Brubeck and Garner on Columbia and Ella Fitzgerald on Verve. And he only need look at the jazz concert grosses to know how well they're doing." Granz was especially upset by Cole's statements about chaos interrupting German concerts by American jazz artists. "I'm sure Nat must have been misquoted," he wrote, "because he's never been to Germany before and so, obviously, he couldn't have commented about the state of jazz concerts in Germany. I have presented concerts in Germany for almost ten years, . . . and never has anything happened such as the brandishing of chairs or the water pistol bit. . . . By the way, if anyone is curious about my authority in writing this letter, I was the man who brought Nat Cole to Europe and paid the tab."[33]

In May 1960 Granz arranged for Marlene Dietrich to tour Germany as the kickoff of a tour that eventually came to New York. Granz either did not anticipate or would not surrender to the controversy he would be stirring up by bringing back one of Germany's most notorious expatriates. Dietrich was the biggest film icon Germany had ever produced when she left the country shortly after the Nazi regime came to power in 1933, and she found herself pilloried through the years of the Third Reich. "Germans in 1960 knew little more than what Nazi papers had written, and they had been too busy digging themselves out of their own rubble and building their economic miracle with the help of the Marshall Plan to admit curiosity about 'a traitor.' But they were curious," wrote her biographer Steven Bach. "She was German, the most famous German woman of the century, their one true world star, a culture symbol whether she wanted to be or not."[34]

Granz entertained the thought of touring Dietrich as he basked in the success Yves Montand had enjoyed in his American and Canadian appearances. "I thought doing a tour with her would have been as exciting an event and, if lucky, economically beneficial to her and me, but I didn't imagine the aggravation factor in dealing with dear Marlene," said Granz.[35] Unable to get Dietrich to answer his calls at the Raphael Hotel in Paris, Granz asked Simone Signoret to intercede with Dietrich on his behalf. Dietrich left Granz to cool his heels in the hotel lobby for a couple of hours, until he called her and suggested that they forget the whole deal, at which point she met him in the salon of the hotel rather than inviting him up to her suite. The key to Granz's proposal was that playing Germany, hopefully opening in Berlin, was nonnegotiable. "Absolutely not," she snapped. "I will not set foot in Germany."

Dietrich finally agreed, whereupon she asked Granz to seal the deal by paying her hotel bill in Paris. After he moved her to the Hotel Lancaster, Granz discovered that Dietrich had charged clothes, shoes, and other items to her hotel bill after they had talked. Granz put his foot down as far as paying any additional personal expenses. He agreed to her requests for Burt Bacharach to serve as her pianist and musical director, a group of female dancers (they settled on the Blue Bells out of London), and Aimill Barelli, who would put together and lead the orchestra.

Germans barraged the media and the Titania-Palast in Berlin, where she would play (and where in 1945 she appeared before American soldiers, earning the lasting enmity of many of her countrymen), with their thoughts about her homecoming, pro and con. One letter writer in the Rhineland presumed to speak "for all my German brothers and sisters" when she wrote, "Aren't you ashamed to set foot on German soil as a common, filthy traitor? You should be lynched as the most odious of war criminals."[36] In comments to columnist Art Buchwald, Dietrich put up a valiant front when she said she would make the trip no matter what. "Before the war, I was attacked by Göring for becoming an American citizen," Dietrich said. "After the war I was attacked by the German press because I wouldn't come to Germany, and now they're attacking me because I'm going. The logic . . . escapes me."[37]

The controversy surrounding Dietrich's return showed up at the box office as the seventeen-city tour sank to twelve cities and the five days originally planned for Berlin were reduced to three. Berlin mayor Willi Brandt met her plane and escorted her into the city after her arrival. The management of the Titania-Palast gave away hundreds of tickets to entice concertgoers, although not enough to fill the 1,800-seat house or dampen the sentiments behind "Marlene Go Home!" posters that smeared the building during her appearances there beginning May 3. In a dramatic program opening with "Falling in Love Again" in German and including "Lili Marlene," the haunting German wartime song banned in the waning days of the Nazi regime, Dietrich gracefully and courageously embraced the risks inherent in her situation. In Berlin, she returned for eighteen curtain calls. Her Munich show ended with thunderous applause as she performed encore after encore before returning for sixty-two curtain calls.[38]

A friend of Dietrich's thought one of the motivations behind her concerts in Germany was an attempt to see if passions toward her had cooled to the point where she could possibly return from exile. He witnessed the most brutal of Dietrich's public humiliations during the tour which occurred outside the Park Hotel in Düsseldorf. Some two thousand fans were jamming the street to try to get a glimpse of her when an eighteen-year-old woman edged toward Dietrich and tugged at the sleeve of her mink. As Dietrich turned to respond, she yelled, "Traitor!" and spat in her face. Dietrich's friend concluded, "That made it clear she could never go home again, because they didn't want her."[39]

"I thought they would love to have her back," Granz said later. "Well, I was not only wrong, but shocked as well at the reaction when the news broke about her return."[40] What is more shocking is that someone as politically astute as Granz could fail to foresee how inflammatory the Blue Angel's return to Germany would be at a time when its people had scarcely yet come to terms with their past during the Third Reich or with a famous figure who had chosen not to share their fate. That Granz may have seen in Dietrich's return a way to torment Germany, just as he had used JATP to shame a nation back home, cannot be ruled out as a motivation.

Granz fielded two European tours again in the fall as he had in the spring. Ella and Oscar were both absent in November 1960 from a lineup including Dizzy Gillespie, Coleman Hawkins, Benny Carter, J.J. Johnson, Roy Eldridge, Don Byas, Jo Jones, Candido, and the Cannonball Adderley Quintet with Adderley's brother Nat on trumpet, Victor Feldman on piano, Sam Jones on bass, and Louis Hayes on drums. Granz also booked some of the individual musicians and their groups, such as those led by Gillespie and Adderley, aside from their participation in Jazz at the Philharmonic. In October, Miles Davis was again on the road for Granz with a quintet in which Sonny Stitt took the place of John Coltrane and the rhythm section consisted of Kelly, Chambers, and Cobb.

Granz, at the age of forty-two, cited exhaustion and dislike of the record business as his main reasons for unloading Verve Records. Dissenting voices within Granz's camp included some of his attorneys, who advised him that if he held on for another five years he might sell Verve for a far higher price than the $2.8 million he eventually received at the end of 1960. (One longtime observer, Granz's mother, Ida Clara, had another take on her son's windfall from the sale of Verve. As Oscar Levant tells the story, "With great pride he showed the enormous check to his mother. 'I always knew you were lucky,' she announced.")[41] Granz had three suitors for Verve when he began looking for someone to buy the record company: the international European record conglomerate Poly-Gram, MGM Records, and Frank Sinatra. According to Granz, Poly-Gram wanted to buy Verve with the caveat that Granz would stay with the company as A&R director for all of Europe. The company flew in a handful of country managers from all over the world in an attempt to entice Granz, all to no avail given that he would have had to maintain a schedule similar to the one he wished to abandon.

Sinatra's initial moves to form his own label went back to 1956, when he founded the Bristol Corporation to handle his film work and Essex Productions to handle the recordings. Sinatra proceeded to tell the trade press that Essex was fully independent and that he was "only nominally a Capitol artist" in that his work was distributed by the label. But Capitol executive Alan Livingston later said that Essex was an entity established for tax purposes and that the company remained the sole owner of Sinatra's recordings. Sinatra's campaign in 1958 and 1959 to bring Capitol chairman Glenn Wallichs around to permitting him to recognize his vision of Essex as a genuine subsidiary was unsuccessful. The singer responded by dramatically slowing his recording schedule over the next few years.[42]

Sinatra may have gotten wind of Granz's plan to sell Verve because they shared the same attorney, Mickey Rudin. But Granz's animosity toward Sinatra was such that he would not have wanted to put his catalog in Sinatra's hands. This meant it was impossible for Verve to produce any Sinatra sessions or to pair Sinatra with Fitzgerald and Peterson. "We had a strange situation," Granz recalled. "Rudin represented me and Frank, which was 100 percent against the law, or whatever they call it."[43] Sinatra wanted Granz to continue running the company even if he lived in Europe. But the one thing Granz did not want to do was run a label and possibly take orders from Frank Sinatra. Sinatra reportedly made a $2 million offer to wrap up the deal.

Sinatra's biographer Will Friedwald relates two versions of why Granz ultimately sold to MGM. The first is that MGM sweetened its offer by an additional half-million dollars over Sinatra's bid on the ground that he take it immediately and not return for a possible counteroffer by Sinatra. The singer said later he would have met and even exceeded the MGM offer. The second story holds that someone in the Sinatra organization may have purposely undermined the deal by delaying signing the papers or by returning time and again to examine Verve's books. The latter story was supported by Sinatra's longtime pianist Bill Miller, who had heard that Sinatra's offer might have been sidetracked for as long as six months until Granz finally lost his patience. Sinatra went on to form Reprise Records. Although he did not purchase Verve, he raided some of the label's personnel, most notably Granz's chief financial man, Mo Ostin, who stayed with Reprise and successor Warner Bros. until 1994.

By the time the ink was dry on the contract in December 1960, MGM owned the masters of Mercury, Clef, Norgran, Down Home, and Verve. Granz took payment in deutsche marks because of the higher exchange rate. A noncompete provision of the contract put Granz unhappily on ice for seven years as far as going back to the recording studio. By then Granz had made his move to Lugano, Switzerland.

17

Across the Sea

"In America I was a manager, but here I am an impresario," Norman Granz said in May 1960, two years after he had revealed his intentions to carve out a still larger slice of the European concert business. In doing so, he was benefiting from his understanding at the time that American entertainment and culture on a broader scale were following jazz in search of markets abroad, in no small part because of his efforts. Jazz would always be at the heart of his passion, but that did not stop him from plugging other musical acts into the circuit he had developed to satisfy European promoters who wanted to present lucrative American pop and rock stars, although he largely kept these endeavors at arm's length. "Granz is another example of the internationalizing of American show biz," observed one European correspondent for *Variety*. "Film people have made the crossing for foreign stints long before him, but the growing popularity of U.S. jazz, which he pioneered with his JATP concerts, and the burgeoning give and take culturally between the States and Europe, now make it possible for American impresarios to headquarter here if they so desire."[1]

Granz so desired. Though he continued to manage Fitzgerald and Peterson and a 1967 JATP farewell tour, memories of him as a key player on the jazz scene dimmed in America. The 1960s saw the music take off in directions for which he had little affinity and in the process marginalized the music and players he loved, while rock virtually eclipsed jazz altogether. Although he always claimed not to care much for what the jazz world thought about him (or anyone else on anything for that matter), he was clearly testy in comments he made to Leonard Feather in early 1972 in one of many interviews tinged with the bitterness that had begun to crop up over the previous several years. "Whenever there's any writing on jazz nowadays," he said with undisguised frustration in his voice, "people dismiss me as though I were a retired man. Hell, right now, I'm promoting more jazz concerts than anyone else in the world, including George Wein."[2]

Semiretirement, if the term could even apply to Norman Granz, never suited him. But he was not so burdened with work that it could interfere with his enjoyment of the good life in an environment rather like that of Southern California, where others shared his zest for fine art, music, food, wine, clothes, and a bohemian pace of life. After the sale of Verve Records, he enjoyed an unprecedented degree of financial independence, and numerous European cities became personally familiar to him. He maintained tastefully appointed apartments in London, Paris, and Geneva, and he had places to stay at La Colombe d'Or in Saint Paul de Vence in the south of France, the Algonquin Hotel in New York, and the Beverly Hills Tennis Club when he was in town on business. The south of France, where some of the country's (and the world's) most renowned artists were living, was not far from Geneva, so he could regularly mix with them as well as with film stars, musicians, writers, and restaurateurs.

Just how completely Granz's delights and avocations became entwined during his years in Europe can be observed from a guided tour he once prepared of museums, galleries, and restaurants across the south of France with a stopover in San Remo across the Italian border. Granz's tip sheet, complete with estimated driving times, distilled his twenty-plus years of hitting the road in a succession of high-performance sports cars. He directed the reader to his menu choices as well. Hectic travel schedules had never interfered with his quest for good food. As Simone Signoret wrote about him in her autobiography, "Norman Granz had had his breakfast in Stockholm, his lunch in Rome, tea on a British Airways plane and a champagne cocktail on the Air France plane bringing him from London just in time to have dinner in Paris in a restaurant where he had reserved a good table for 11 42 days before from Lausanne."[3] In the next generation of flight, Granz and his wife, Grete, would occasionally take the supersonic Concorde from Paris to New York for dinner. French cuisine topped Granz's menu. Beginning in the 1950s, Granz came to know French food and wine through annual gastronomic tours to sample the best regional cooking and visits to every three-star restaurant in new editions of the *Michelin Guide.*

"He knew I loved food and that I loved women. He did too at the time," Quincy Jones recalled in 2003. "I could feel his enormous capacity for beauty and art—he knew art, he had taste. He was discriminating about everything in life. He was a serious gourmet. He laid out all these amazing restaurants: Le Pic, Oberseno, Moulin de la Mougins, Chez La Mis Louis, the cream of the crop. I still go to those places." Mike Zwerin, jazz critic for the *International Herald-Tribune,* similarly recalls that when he ran into Granz in San Tropez Granz gave him impromptu directions to out-of-the-way restaurants between there and his destination. Zwerin later marveled at the four-star restaurants hidden in tiny hamlets across the south of France that uniformly lived up to Granz's billing.[4]

One apocryphal story told by guitarist Barney Kessel recalls Granz letting a passenger off at the curb when he suggested where to find the best burger in Beverly Hills. Not all musicians had exotic palates matching Granz's and preferred to go American when overseas. Flip Manne, widow of drummer Shelly Manne, recalled one such incident involving her husband during the 1960 Jazz at the Phil tour in Europe. "Norman took all of us to some restaurant famous for their hors d'oeuvres someplace in France," he said. "So they [Shelly and his band] took off to find a hamburger, and I don't think Norman ever respected them again."[5]

For whatever reason, Granz indulged Oscar Levant—a seemingly unhinged and finicky pianist, composer, George Gershwin acolyte, and host of a local Los Angeles talk show at the time—and kept his temper as the two of them shared an agonized and fruitless search for a suitable place to have lunch. "My reaction to the [first] place was so violent that I could not stand to eat there," Levant wrote in the late 1960s. "We went to another; that looked worse. . . . By the time it was four-thirty, we had canvassed seven restaurants. I had found fault with them all. So Norman took me home. 'Say, Norman,' I said as he let me out of the car, 'how about dinner?'"[6]

Granz found novel ways to mix business with pleasure that played on his devotion to food. During the Pablo Records years he once added a clause into a contract with his Italian distributor that, while requiring low advances and royalties, directed the company to provide him with a kilo of rare white truffles for each of the three years covered by the agreement, a figure that added up to thousands. Bill Belmont, director of Fantasy Records' international sales, heard years later about the frantic response by the Italian company when Granz called them up demanding the truffles. "The Italians thought he was kidding. They didn't think it was a real deal," Belmont said. "He says, 'No, I'm not kidding.' Three kilos of truffles. They were hysterical. A lot of pigs worked very hard to find them truffles."[7]

Granz's appetite might have been Napoleonic, but he went Anglophile in his choice of his attire beginning in the early 1950s. He drew on Fred Astaire's fashion recommendations to integrate haute couture with the casually chic and understated insouciance that had been characteristic of him even a decade earlier, when his friends uniformly recalled his laid-back "Joe College" look. Photographs from around the time Jazz at the Philharmonic began show Granz in sport jackets and flamboyant ties and sporting porkpie hats most famously identified with Lester Young. That look changed when Astaire, who had inspired Granz to take tap dancing lessons, directed Granz to his Savile Row tailor shop, Anderson and Sheppard, in the wake of *The Astaire Story* in 1952. Granz was one of a score of illustrious customers Astaire had steered to the venerable firm. Norman Halsey, Granz's tailor for most of the fifty years he went there, said that his clothes and the way he carried himself made people look twice at him walking down the street. "He looked that good," Halsey said. "He was very laid back and had the money and could do what he liked. This meant top quality, top to bottom and not a bit ostentatious, nothing at all."[8]

Halsey confirms Granz's habit of ordering multiples of a favored style and fabric at a time. Once Granz went to the famous fabric shop Max's along the Champs-Élysées and selected material by the bolt for his suits to be shipped back to Anderson and Sheppard. After he had settled on forty to fifty fabrics, the order that arrived in London filled a delivery truck and lasted over decades. "He instinctively knew what was good for him; a wonderful thing when you have that," Halsey said. Granz frequently sent musicians and friends to stop by the tailor shop to be outfitted from his stock and on his tab. The crowd included Michel Leiris, the French author and anthropologist, whose wife was one of his Paris art dealers; Duke Ellington; Oscar Peterson ("He took a lot of cloth"); the guitarist Joe Pass (he didn't); and Pablo Picasso.

Halsey recalled Granz's occasional requests for special creations that the impresario had conceived for Picasso, orders more unusual than what the traditional clothing establishment would normally fill. "His requests always had intelligence. And, of course, you had two satisfied people. You had Norman happy about it and you had Picasso." One order called for a pair of trousers with one red leg and one blue leg, as if they had leapt out of a Picasso painting.

Granz's fancy for luxury sports cars went back to the early 1950s, most conspicuously when in 1954 he bought a custom-built car from the Pinin Farina factory in Turin, Italy, famed for its design of the Ferrari and other European roadsters. At a European automobile show in Geneva that he had attended with Oscar Peterson, he had met the company's president, Sergio Farina, when he stopped at the company's exhibition space to inquire about a Lancia that had caught his eye. Farina invited Granz to see the factory. This worked out well, as Turin was on the concert schedule. "If you like cars, it was unbelievable," Granz said. When Granz said he planned to buy a Lancia and ship it to California, Farina advised him against purchasing a car impossible to service at such a distance; instead, he suggested, Granz should purchase an American-engineered chassis and engine to facilitate easy maintenance, and they would do the rest. "We will make you a car that will be the only one of its kind in the whole world," Farina assured Granz.

The car, a Cadillac, was given a leather interior, and engineers cut the chassis in half and reduced its length by almost forty inches to make it a two-seater, closer to the scale of Italian sports cars. In an act of friendship, Pinin Farina charged Granz only for materials; however, Farina requested that he ship the car back to Turin annually so that the company could show off its handiwork at trade shows to its peers and potential customers. Granz lost the Pinin Farina Cadillac with the Verve Records sale in 1960, since he had listed the car as company property.

A 1996 article in the London *Daily Mail,* one of a series of stories recounting "first loves," describes Granz the lover around the time he met his third wife, Grete, with whom he stayed for the remaining thirty-three years of his life. The writer, Sue Arnold, recalled meeting Granz in 1968. "Norman was more than twice my age, witty, worldly, world-weary, and very, very wealthy. I had never met anyone like him," wrote Arnold, who had just relocated to the city for a summer job at the *Evening Telegraph,* which she promptly lost along with her apartment. She had stopped in front of Magli's to look at a pair of shoes for what would have cost her two weeks' wages. She fidgeted in her purse for a cigarette as she decided whether to take the plunge on the shoes. As Arnold put the cigarette up to her lips, "Snap, a gold Dunhill lighter appeared over my shoulder, and a deep American accent said, 'Allow me.'"[9]

Arnold went on to describe Granz as extravagant and imperious, "an archetypal male chauvinist" capable of dispatching her opinion, about a play, for example, with a curt "I'm not interested in your opinion. The play was lousy."

Their relationship ended as quickly as it had begun. Arnold had invited Granz to have dinner at her apartment in time for him to catch a late flight out. He called to say he had scheduled an earlier flight and wanted the dinner to be earlier. She could not accommodate him. "He arrived on the dot, grim, cold, implacable," she said. "He neither would be having dinner, he said, nor would he be seeing me again. No one told Norman Granz they weren't ready; no one told Norman Granz to wait." She speculated that an invitation to dinner at her home might have suggested to him a domesticity he wished to avoid. Ending on what he apparently considered a gracious note, he had his travel agent call Arnold the following day, saying Granz would gladly pay for a one-way first-class ticket to Timbuktu. "If this is a problem," he said, "his second choice was Tehran." He was serious—Arnold had a job prospect in Iran—so Arnold seriously took him up on the offer: the next week she went to work for the *Tehran Journal*.

Mrs. Benny Green spotted the article in the *Daily Mail* when it appeared in May 1996 and sent it Granz. "Norman could not even remember her. I believed him. You could see it in his face," said Granz's widow, Grete. "But what she said was absolutely true about Norman."

Grete Lyngbye, a striking twenty-seven-year-old with honey-blonde hair who was a graphic designer and classical music enthusiast, was steered by a friend in the fall of 1968 toward a job in the classical department of a newly opened record shop on one of Copenhagen's main streets. Granz, in town to present Ray Charles, was heading back for a meeting at the Palace Hotel when he spotted a pretty woman walking down the street and began following her. When he spotted Grete through the window, he turned and walked into the store. He engaged her in conversation and afterwards arranged for her to receive two tickets to the concert that night. "In the meantime, I found out who he was from some of the people in the shop," she recalled.[10] She told the girlfriend who had gone with her to the concert that she wanted to thank Granz for his hospitality and tell him what a wonderful time they had had, so they went back to the stage door and waited for him to come out. He walked quickly past them, accompanied by a Danish model, Lisa Boudin; they headed straight for a convertible and drove off. Grete feared that glimpse would be the last she would see of him, but Granz returned the next morning about an hour after the shop opened to invite her for dinner.

By the early 1960s, Granz had recast Jazz at the Philharmonic to draw European audiences wanting to hear more contemporary jazz and had toured some of the players as spin-offs on their own as well. Musicians such as Cannonball Adderley maneuvered easily between JATP jam sessions and sections of the program set aside for their groups. Adderley had gained a large following after he formed his first quintet with his brother Nat on cornet ("our brass section") in 1956; then he moved on to join Miles Davis's legendary sextet with John Coltrane and Bill Evans. By 1959, again with the quintet, he enlarged his repertoire of hard bop and began to turn toward the "soul jazz" that enlarged his fame outside normal jazz circles, though to the consternation of some critics at the time. It did not hurt that Adderley possessed a sunny disposition, wit, and intelligence; that in his brother he had one of the finest trumpet players in jazz; *and,* on top of all that, that Norman Granz always enjoyed his southern cooking.[11] The 1960 JATP tour was the only chance Adderley had to play with one of his most important influences, Benny Carter, who took part in both the modern set with the alto saxophonist, Dizzy Gillespie, J. J. Johnson, and Lalo Schifrin, and in the swing set with Eldridge, Hawkins, Don Byas, Jo Jones, and Schifrin.

By the early 1960s the European concert market had diminished to the point that Granz had to devise new strategies to keep the tours profitable and maintain the benefits he offered his artists. The 1962 spring European JATP tour was almost his last, for he came down with a near-fatal case of hepatitis in Reykjavik, Iceland, just after the unit left Italy. Granz looked in the mirror his first morning in the city and saw that he was extremely jaundiced. He spent three months in Reykjavik in between his hospitalization and convalescence at the Hotel Saga. "Gee, I wish I could have come by, but as you know, I was not allowed, so *please,* please take care and do as they say," wrote Ella Fitzgerald in a brief note on her way to New York. "I'll miss you very much, but will get things fixed and taken care of (the music). Well, you are a good man, Norman. I mean that from my heart, in spite of our quarrels. I guess we're too good and think about other people too much."[12]

The next major European JATP tour took place in late 1966 with Dizzy Gillespie; Clark Terry; a saxophone dream team of Coleman Hawkins, Zoot Sims, Benny Carter, and James Moody; and a rhythm section of Teddy Wilson, Bob Cranshaw, and Louie Bellson, with

T-Bone Walker to boot. Moody said the tour, resulting in a broadcast from Royal Festival Hall in London on BBC television on November 26, had been a good experience. He noted Granz's regard for the musicians, and his generosity in distributing among them gifts of watches or sweaters, but was primarily impressed by the caliber of the musicians he played with. "All the musicians were ones I had admired most of my life—my heroes—Coleman Hawkins and Benny Carter. And of course Diz," he said.[13]

The 1960s and 1970s provide many unusual examples of Granz using his base and knowledge of live music in Europe to satisfy audiences eager to hear American stars of rhythm and blues, rock, and popular music as well as jazz. He tended to downplay this facet of his career as little more than "a financial arrangement." But he toured, among others, Donny and Marie Osmond, Gilbert O'Sullivan, Leonard Cohen, the Supremes, and Frank Zappa, as well as Barbra Streisand in several of her early U.S. shows.

There were clashes in style as Granz occasionally found himself irrevocably on the other side of the generational divide. He admitted as much when he recounted the story of a weeklong tour around 1973 by Carlos Santana's group. Granz had not heard the show until he arrived on the last night in Vienna. The house was full and the band had not yet begun the show. "The musicians were backstage and they just didn't feel like playing yet," Granz said. "I think the public has the right to a concert starting when it's advertised. But they [the audience] were quiet, smoking pot, not complaining. Finally, Carlos came out dressed in white with incense burning all around him, and said, 'Let's meditate,' and the audience accepted it. Fantastic! I couldn't get over it."[14]

Granz had great success in touring Ray Charles in Europe for nine years beginning in the early 1960s; throughout, he maintained a high regard for the man and his music. Charles's program was unchanging and never had encores, and if Granz was time conscious Charles was even more so. He started his shows at eight o'clock sharp, whether all the people were seated or not. "I respected that kind of attitude, because it meant I didn't have to worry about making time," Granz said. "I just had to worry about bringing my public."[15] It took time for their relationship to warm up, for Charles had been burned by many promoters in the past. Their friendship was partly established through a shared enthusiasm for jazz. "I remember when I would go in a limousine with him—because he wanted a limousine from the hotel to the concert hall—he made me put on Lester Young cassettes or Charlie

Parker . . . After enough years, Ray said to me, 'We don't have to have a contract anymore. I trust you. You're the only cat I would ever do it with. You just tell me when and where and what I'm going to be paid, and that's fine with me.' And we kept that arrangement."[16]

Granz witnessed and sometimes cringed at the strict discipline that Charles inflicted on his musicians. One night the drummer showed up for a concert in Bologna wearing brown shoes, in violation of Charles's rule that the band wear black shoes only. Charles, who heard about the infraction from his road manager/snitch, would not consent to start the show even though the man's shoes were an hour away in Milan and couldn't be seen by the audience anyway. He just sat backstage and played chess with one of the musicians until the matter was resolved, a tactic he employed as well if the sound was below his standards. Another night, Granz offered the Raelettes the chance to sit down as they waited for the final number. He came to regret it when he saw Charles berate them for violating his order that they stand while waiting to come out. "Ray was impossible," he said.[17]

One measure of Granz's influence is that his management of his shows in Europe established a standard for the reception of other American popular and rock-and-roll musicians when they crossed the Atlantic in the 1960s. Though rock groups at the time were not considered ready for prime engagements at major concert halls in the United States outside college campuses, they had no problem getting such engagements overseas. Bill Belmont witnessed this as a tour manager for Country Joe and the Fish, who first went to Europe when they performed a New Year's Eve 1967 concert with the Rolling Stones in London and by the following year found themselves playing at such halls as the Concertgebouw in Amsterdam and the Konserthuset in Stockholm. Belmont came to understand that many of Granz's business practices had become the norm for those who had promoted his concerts in Europe over the years. "We were offered the same basic deal as they said that Norman Granz and George Wein offered the groups they traveled," Belmont said. "We asked a lot of questions, and agreed to the legitimization of this way of doing business [where] promoters pay all the travel, internal transportation, all the hotels, per diem. Longtime European promoters I have gotten to know over the years basically considered Norman the role model for how it was done."[18]

However, Granz's jaunts in the early 1960s after retiring from Verve took him further afield than Europe. He was a frequent visitor to Rio de

Janeiro in the early 1960s, just when the bossa nova was getting white-hot internationally, and in later years he jetted down for New Year's and Carnaval celebrations in January and February to quench his thirst for Brazilian music. His reputation preceding him, Granz met musicians, attended rehearsals, balls, and street parades, familiarized himself with Rio's record stores, and returned with stacks of recordings daily to stay one step ahead of the country's high inflation. He became fascinated not only with the bossa nova but with a wider range of Brazilian music: samba carioca from Bahia and the Northwest and particularly the substyle of samba called batucada, which emphasizes fast-paced percussion. He came to view Antonio Carlos Jobim as the world's most important composer of popular music by the 1960s because of what Granz saw as his faithfulness to Brazilian music. He was especially taken with vocalist Elis Regina and sought out the city's vaunted samba schools, especially the Salgueiro Samba School. "They let me come in and watch them rehearsing the music and the steps. And when Carnaval came, they gave me the best seat to watch from," he said. "Europeans and North Americans don't imagine how great the rhythm of the samba schools is. There are very successful Brazilian musicians here who are unknown abroad—not for lack of quality, but for lack of opportunity and poor record company promotion."[19]

It is notable that the bossa nova megahit "The Girl from Ipanema" by Stan Getz, João Gilberto, and Gilberto's then-wife, the singer Astrud Gilberto, became the top-selling album in the history of Verve but was produced only after Granz had sold the company. Though Granz had been to Brazil earlier in his career, he had heard mostly jazz and foreign music in nightclubs and on the radio during his stays, even though the country had a lively indigenous music scene. "In Argentina, tourists listen to tango even if they don't want to," he said by way of comparison.[20] Not until the Pablo years did Granz end up producing some of the music and musicians he encountered during trips to Brazil. Among those he befriended and recorded were percussionist Paulinho da Costa, whom Granz assisted in emigrating to the states; jazz drummer Dom um Romao; and the vocalist Jorge Ben, whom he had first heard sing in a Rio de Janeiro nightclub. Granz, in turn, recorded Fitzgerald, Sarah Vaughan, Joe Pass, Dizzy Gillespie, and Louie Bellson playing Brazilian music, sometimes in Brazil. Fitzgerald had long featured bossa novas as part of her normal repertoire. Their mutual regard for Jobim led to the last in the songbook series, *Ella Abra Jobim: Ella Fitzgerald Sings the Antonio Carlos Jobim Songbook,* on Pablo Records, in 1981.

The 1960s also inaugurated a short-lived phase of Granz's career when he invested in theater production. The opportunity came while he was staying at the Algonquin Hotel in New York, for he met producers there, including Gilbert Miller, whose Broadway theater he had booked for the Yves Montand concerts. Granz agreed to become the largest investor besides Miller himself for a production of *Witness for the Prosecution* on Broadway in 1957. As he recalled later, the play was critically acclaimed and moderately successful financially. And his initial investment paid off when Miller, after buying off the investor who had backed the play only, divided with Granz the $400,000 proceeds gained from the film rights. Granz's friendship with film producer Henry Ephron and his playwright wife, Phoebe (parents of Nora Ephron, the author and film screenwriter, producer, and director), resulted in his backing her play *Take Her, She's Mine,* which closed shortly after opening on Broadway. This time Granz did not try to recoup his investment as the play headed to Hollywood, though as it turned out James Stewart was cast in the lead of what became a successful motion picture. "One might think I was foolish to invest in such risky ventures, but I was confident that I might get lucky as I did with *Witness for the Prosecution,*" Granz said of the loss of his investment in the play. He had just declined to invest in the smash hit *Hello, Dolly!* in 1964, a musical based on the Thornton Wilder play *The Matchmaker,* feeling that he had a long way to go in understanding Broadway and its "special public."[21]

Granz helped to underwrite two theatrical productions in London in 1968. *Soldiers,* by the controversial West German playwright Rolf Hochhuth, created as much of a storm as anything Granz had ever been involved with. Hochhuth, who according to the *New York Times* critic Clive Barnes had "a genius for controversy and a nose for publicity," had proven as much with *The Deputy* (or *The Representative*), an earlier play that charged Pope Pius XII with criminal cowardice for failing to directly address the Holocaust.[22] Hochhuth's latest World War II drama scandalously asserted that the 1943 plane crash that had killed General Władysław Sikorski, leader of the Polish government in exile, had actually been ordered by Winston Churchill as a way of placating Stalin. Staging the play was at that time as provocative an act as Granz's insistence upon bringing Marlene Dietrich back to Germany had been eight years before.

Britain's National Theatre had agreed in January 1968 to stage the play sight unseen. The board of directors, including many friends of the former prime minister who had died three years earlier, balked at

Hochhuth's criticism of the carpet bombing of German cities and at the insinuations concerning Churchill. On April 24, it banned the play from its stage, pitting the board majority against members of the theater's professional staff. One Labour Party backbencher even threatened reprisals in the form of cuts to the National Theatre's budget for even considering *Soldiers*. Among the theater's indignant staffers was its literary manager, Kenneth Tynan, whose writing Granz admired and who was one of the country's reigning men of letters. Tynan and Laurence Olivier, a board member, met with Hochhuth before the vote to suggest alterations in the text, but the changes were not enough to reverse the board's decision. Olivier was pressured not to take a leading role. Richard Burton's early expression of interest also fizzled.

Granz agreed to become involved with the enterprise, under the name of Norcor, Ltd., when Tynan and the producer Michael White approached him because he thought the move would open the door for him to get more actively involved as a producer in London theater. *Soldiers* opened in Dublin (other theaters in Britain exercised self-censorship), Montreal, New York, and Berlin, where it was booed at points, before opening at the New Theatre in London's West End on December 12, 1968. There it received a standing ovation, directed especially toward John Calicos, who played Churchill. But the hopes raised by the first night's gate success were illusory. The play ran only around four months. "It was a disaster, of course," Granz recalled.

The experience quickly soured Granz and Tynan's friendship. First, despite a prior agreement with Tynan and White in which Granz had declared his intention to be a hands-on producer, he felt he was systematically edged out of key decisions. This came to a head when Tynan and White agreed to a rental fee at the New Theatre that Granz thought unjustifiable. Further, though Granz was initially the play's sole backer, Tynan and White went on to cut a deal with a second investor, David Irving, the author on whose work the play was predicated and who in later years would become known as an inveterate and high-profile Holocaust denier. Granz believed the arrangement offered Irving disproportionate financial rewards if the play succeeded. Granz filed suit and eventually settled with his former partners. Tynan and White held onto the play, while Granz wrote off his loss and took pleasure in the success of the libel suit brought against them by the Churchill family.

The second play with which Granz became involved was *Jacques Brel Is Alive and Well and Living in Paris*. He had been delighted with the revue of the French poet and composer's songs when he saw it near the beginning of its lengthy run at the Village Gate in New York in the mid-1960s. His close friend Nat Shapiro, a jazz historian and music publisher, had struck gold around that time with the publishing rights to the hit musical *Hair*. Shapiro encouraged Granz's interest in getting involved with *Jacques Brel* on the basis of the soundtrack's continuing solid sales on Columbia Records and the skillful and appealing adaptation of the original lyrics into English. Granz opened a production at London's Fortune Theatre, which he felt offered the intimacy that had worked so well at the Village Gate. *Jacques Brel* was alive and well but survived in London for only twelve weeks. According to Granz, Columbia Records had offered no discernible support that might have helped the semiunderground musical to find an audience. Granz had pared down some of the production expenses to minimize any losses, but, like *Soldiers, Jacques Brel* was a financial washout.

Granz had a better run in film than in the theater. He had his fifteen minutes of frame when his voice was channeled by Peter Sellers in the role of Clare Quilty in Stanley Kubrick's 1964 film *Lolita,* based on Vladimir Nabokov's novel of the middle-aged Humbert Humbert and the young girl with whom he is obsessed. The emotionally unstable but brilliant British comedian and mimic had heard Granz at one of his concerts and wanted to appropriate his speaking manner, with its precise diction and flat enunciation. Kubrick called Granz to ask if he would consent to recording a few pages of script. "Peter says you have the perfect American voice," Kubrick said. "Nobody knows where you come from." In exchange, Kubrick offered to post billboards advertising Jazz at the Philharmonic along the roads that Humbert and Lolita would be filmed in their cross-country trip to California. That would not be necessary, Granz told the director. He would be glad to do it. Sellers practiced from time to time by calling Granz and mimicking him. "I saw the film, of course," Granz said later, "and I heard my own voice. You couldn't say I was from Texas."[23] When Sellers was hospitalized after a heart attack in the 1970s, Granz sent him a telegram to wish him well, saying in part, "I lent you my voice, but I'm sorry I can't lend you my heart."[24]

18

"Musicians Don't Want to Jam"

Nat Hentoff's description of the "increasingly bleak" state of jazz in the summer of 1964 paralleled Norman Granz's disenchantment as far as live music was concerned. Hentoff blamed the fragmentation of jazz into schools, developing in the 1950s, that drew "transitory listeners who were more interested in being currently hip than in reacting to the music itself"; the overly intellectual influences of the West Coast and Brubeck; soul music; a dwindling nightclub scene; the success of FM radio; and a proliferation of albums that normally sold five thousand copies or less. "A jazz partisan, therefore, can spend a much cheaper evening at home, sure of the brand of the liquor, than at a club," Hentoff said. The avant-garde was in even worse shape, since its eclecticism alienated more conservative listeners disenchanted by the lack of conventional melodies, harmonies, and rhythms.[1]

The 1960s found Granz perpetually enveloped in what Leonard Feather described as a "pessimistically cynical shroud." In part, Granz had pretty much lost faith in the United States, most likely its failure to move ahead on civil rights. His friend Jean Bach, after a long discussion about the 1960 presidential campaign, challenged Granz to at least come back long enough to cast a vote for John F. Kennedy. He couldn't be bothered.[2] On the other hand, Ella Fitzgerald flew round trip from Australia to appear for five minutes at Kennedy's inaugural gala organized by Frank Sinatra.

The next time Granz was heard in the United States was when, on October 25, 1961, he held a press conference in New York to advocate for standard touring contracts that would prohibit segregated audiences, picking up a fight he had begun waging fourteen years before. Joining him were John Hammond and Nat Shapiro, both of Columbia Records, Nesuhi Ertegun of Atlantic Records, and Nat Hentoff. The committee spearheaded by Granz fought to bar segregation in all clubs, arenas, auditoriums, and ballrooms and on all college campuses, citing support from the Shaw Agency, the Willard Alexander Office, and Joe Glaser's Associated Booking Corporation, which had begun inserting such clauses in its contracts a couple of months before.[3] "Freedom riders fight segregation, but jazz, which suffers from segregation, does nothing," Granz said. The cooperation of major artists could help raise standards for lesser-known artists held "at the mercy of promoters." Another three years passed before segregation in public accommodations was outlawed by the Civil Rights Act of 1964—exactly twenty years after the first Jazz at the Philharmonic concert.

Granz vented his feelings in a steady stream of interviews in U.S. and foreign jazz media. He frankly acknowledged that he was out of tune with much of the jazz then being created and thus unable to serve (and largely uninterested in serving) a younger generation of musicians and styles. "Norman was never interested in keeping up with where the music was going, only the type of jazz that he liked," said the historian Dan Morgenstern. "That is not to say he didn't tour people like Miles Davis and John Coltrane."[4] And indeed Granz still appreciated the importance of the new music and profitably toured some of its major exponents. "I never went into the studio and recorded Trane," said Granz of the man he had taken on tour with Miles Davis, on his own, and with Dizzy Gillespie in Europe. "I confess that I wouldn't have known what to do with him, because I wasn't into that kind of music. It would have been silly of me to sit down with Trane, 'Okay, let's think about the tunes you want to do.' Because (a) he wrote most of the songs himself, and (b) the kind of playing he evolved into that gave him his impact and his rating were not things I was familiar with or comfortable with."[5]

Granz's despair was evident when he declared in *Variety* in January 1964 that jazz had peaked commercially between 1945 and 1951 and that there was now almost "nothing left" of it in the United States. This assertion seemingly contradicted his argument with Nat Cole in 1960 in the same periodical after the singer panned the economic viability of jazz. Granz denied that jazz had been commercially successful in the postwar years, despite his own obvious success, and claimed that the Swing Era had been its financial heyday. "I'm the only one who ever really made money in jazz, and when I had my last Jazz at the Philharmonic tour in the U.S. seven years ago, jazz was already finished." Jazz festivals had proved to be the death knell for JATP-style tours, Granz continued. Yet if he had not chosen a graceful exit for JATP the radically different musical environment of the 1960s would have forced his hand, even in the absence of jazz festivals. Granz incorrectly predicted the demise of festivals, which he thought had proven by then that they couldn't support themselves financially apart from subsidies and sponsorships. He thought jazz had dropped the ball by not renewing its fan base. When an interviewer asked whether musicians shared in the blame by permitting jazz to become too esoteric, he answered, "Subjectively, I think yes. The kind of music being passed off today as good jazz has not attracted as many people as it might have. Also, folk music has drained off a tremendous amount of the potential jazz audience."[6]

A few months later, Benny Goodman lambasted Granz in the same periodical for his pessimism about the contemporary jazz scene. The clarinetist pointed out a handful of contemporary jazzmen—Thelonious Monk, Miles Davis, Ornette Coleman, and John Coltrane—who had succeeded handsomely on their own terms. "Granz has always been considered the patron saint of jazz, but when the business gets a little rough, he runs," Goodman wrote, referring to Granz's decision to stop American JATP tours in 1957. "And I think things had opened up a little for jazz before he came along. All he did was take a lot of established people and make a circus out of it. . . . But certainly anybody who runs away from jazz like that has no right speaking about it."[7] Perhaps Goodman's own memory of the 1953 tour with Armstrong that had turned out to be a fiasco made him impatient with Granz's complaints.

Granz's reply detailed his activities in jazz over the previous seven years: an average of five concert tours a year in Europe, Australia, and South America, involving some three hundred individual concerts that featured Duke Ellington, Count Basie, Miles Davis, Nat Cole, Quincy Jones, Kid Ory, Dizzy Gillespie, and the Adderley brothers, in addition to annual tours of Ella Fitzgerald and Oscar Peterson. Granz estimated that he had spent over a million dollars in artist salaries, transportation, promotion, theater rentals, and publicity. He also factored in around $250,000 that he spent annually on talent to produce jazz on Verve between 1957 and 1960.

"Why then do I say jazz was never really big and in fact, why do I continue with it?" Granz asked. "Well, I love jazz and feel I should subsidize it as best I can, as I did for example on Verve: the sales of

Ella and Shelley Berman paid for the Tatums, the Websters et al. And three weeks ago on Easter Sunday, I presented Duke Ellington at no profit whatsoever, at Carnegie Hall, because I felt he should be heard by America whenever possible." He concluded that Goodman, while focusing on a handful of successful jazz musicians, was failing to address the lot of hundreds of musicians unable to find work. "Benny's point of view about other jazz musicians is 'I've made it, now let them get out and do it.'"[8]

Part of Granz's negativity about contemporary jazz stemmed from his inability to convince many of the newer leading figures to break up their groups to participate in his all-star jam sessions. Accordingly, he was effectively stymied from presenting JATP as he wished. "Musicians don't want to jam. I mean, it's impossible to get Dizzy Gillespie and Miles Davis on the stage together." The rigidity of musicians on this score, he suggested, impinged on what he thought were his prerogatives as an impresario. "This destroyed any contributions I can make as producer of the concerts—when you can build a show so that the whole makes sense to the audience by combining musicians who have an affinity for each another and with succeeding jam session groups which can build on one another for a final climax," he continued. "You can't do this if you have fixed groups who compartmentalize their ideas so that they care only about what happens in their individual sets with no relationship to the rest of the concert."[9] (This criticism is bizarre, for the older and newer jazz musicians' styles and aims diverged so radically that the kind of collaboration Granz sought would have been impossible—something he should have recognized given the breadth of his artistic worldview. It was as if Granz had suggested that a meaningful crossing of an artistic chasm could be achieved by a collaboration between Grant Wood and Picasso.) Granz related a conversation with Eric Dolphy, then on tour for him, when he heard the avant-garde saxophonist playing straight-ahead blues after hours at a nightclub with some of Gillespie's musicians. He asked Dolphy why he couldn't play like that on the tour. "No, people say I have a reputation for being modern, so I have to play modern."[10]

Granz further noted changes and a decline in audiences for his productions in Europe in a conversation with Leonard Feather in October 1965 when he swept into Feather's New York office with his second wife, Hannelore, a former airline stewardess from Germany, whom he had married in Las Vegas. (The highlight of their marriage appears to have been their tempestuous divorce three years later when she fought for a large financial settlement.) Granz lamented that, using the standard of employment, "jazz is through. Sure a few cats like Brubeck and Miles make a lot of bread. But how does that help the rest of Local 802? Or the cats in Dubuque?"[11] Europeans were not any more appreciative audiences than Americans, and they did not greet American musicians on the tarmac with ten thousand cheering fans. Most of the musicians he was touring were not drawing as well as they had in earlier years. In addition, other American concert promoters had begun bringing shows overseas, a trend that had helped to flood the market and had lessened the "curiosity value" of his type of concerts. Granz also had to compete with festivals and even nightclubs subsidized by European governments with an eye toward tourism. "I've always funded everything myself. And I think it gave me more latitude in the end to do anything that I wanted, even touring those artists who didn't make money," he said in 1989. "I could take a Joe Turner on tour because I like to hear Joe sing. I was fortunate that I could subsidize it with what I did with artists who were more popular."[12]

During the interview with Feather Granz touched on the subject of racial discrimination in jazz. "There is a tendency nowadays to judge the employment situation not in terms of how well an artist performs, or how much he, therefore, deserves to be employed, but by the incidence of prejudice," he said. "I don't really think Ornette Coleman or Archie Shepp experienced more prejudice than Coleman Hawkins did; they just talk about it more. Perhaps they don't realize that men like Hawk broke down a lot of barriers for them. In an art form that is so largely individual, you have to give more weight to the artistic judgment as well as to the performance value of a Duke Ellington than to some young cat who can't find a job and decides that he is being discriminated against."[13]

Another exchange showed Granz at his most withering, all the more surprising because the person he lambasted over what was virtually a throwaway line was his longtime supporter and friend Nat Hentoff. In an October 1966 *Down Beat* column, Hentoff wrote that jazz labels ignored important talent and offered few good opportunities for veteran musicians such as trumpeter Red Allen and clarinetist Pee Wee Russell whose music merited recording. He advocated that small independent labels, run by musicians to promote their work and that of their musical colleagues, might help to remedy the situation. He and Charles Mingus had done as much with Candid Records beginning in the summer of 1960, forming the jazz division of Archie Bleyer's Cadence Records for thirteen months. He also raised the question of whether mail-order record societies might take up more of the slack. Tucked into his bill of particulars against the record industry was the observation, "Singer Sheila Jordan is another example. One Blue Note L.P. still in the catalog. But the facile Ella Fitzgerald albums pour forth."[14]

Granz began with an oft-repeated litany of complaints about "jazz reporters," whose work he said he generally ignored (although he didn't seem to have missed Hentoff's piece). "I say 'reporters,' because with the exception of two or three writers of jazz who qualify as critics, most are engaged in a reportage of their emotions—political and racial more often than musical," Granz said. "Finally one gets fed up with some of the amateurish nonsense that's printed in *Down Beat*." Granz branded Hentoff a "pseudo-social scientist" whose forays into the studio were not successful "statistically" or artistically. "What did he ever contribute of lasting worth in recordings?" he continued. "And his jazz concert impresario activities sank without a trace. Why? Too successful?" He then attacked Hentoff for his criticism of Fitzgerald. "He used to vote for her as the best singer in jazz. Now does he really feel that she's dropped down that much that her records shouldn't be released any longer?"[15]

Hentoff, in a brief response, corrected Granz's assertion that his career in concert promotion had sunk without a trace; in fact, he had never attempted one in the first place. Hentoff added, "Norman Granz's accomplishments for jazz, which have been considerable, have seldom been accompanied by a capacity to respect opinions differing from his own. That self-righteous incapacity has apparently grown in direct ratio to his distance from the current jazz scene."[16] The point about Granz's absence from the American jazz scene hit home: up to the end of his life, newer players, commentators, and others in the jazz orbit would be mere names to him, not familiar faces. Granz's diatribe against Hentoff, who chuckled when reminded of the exchange forty years later, demonstrated how Granz had adopted the dismissive manner of the powerful who elect to abuse rather than debate their critics. Yet it was more than fools that Granz did not suffer gladly—he could be as icily dismissive of the well informed and well intentioned.

This side of Granz eroded the goodwill of many in and around the industry who admired his work, leading one to refer to him as a "sore winner." "I was hurt that he was so bitter about the business," said the recording engineer and producer Bones Howe, who had known Granz since the Verve days. He recalled encountering Granz on the street in Beverly Hills in the mid-1960s, only to endure an earful of his bitterness. "I told him, 'What a good time we had doing that, and I learned so much on those sessions.' . . . I was sorry that he felt that way because I thought he made such a huge contribution and that he couldn't revel in that in some way. Certainly, what he left as a legacy is gigantic."[17]

Granz made only periodic trips back to the United States in the next dozen years, mostly tending to the business of managing Ella Fitzgerald and Oscar Peterson, until he began active recording again with Pablo Records in 1973. In 1965, Granz sold his music publishing business, which numbered around a thousand songs, to Major Music Management, the firm headed by Irving Mills. The songs included original music by Lester Young, Johnny Hodges, Oscar Peterson, Bob Brookmeyer, John Lewis, Coleman Hawkins, and Roy Eldridge.

Duke Ellington spent the first two months of 1963 touring Europe for Granz, beginning with eleven concerts in Great Britain. Granz recalled the band's deeply ingrained idiosyncrasies, which could not have been created, managed, or tolerated by anyone other than Ellington. The band's personality showed up in a couple of different incidents dating from this period involving tenor saxophonist Paul Gonsalves, whose alcoholism intermittently jeopardized his playing. Tenor player Eddie "Lockjaw" Davis told Granz of his reception from the band when he was called to sit in for Gonsalves on the spur of the moment. "Jaws is an incredible tenor player. He said to me that he sat down in his chair, and turned to—I guess it was Johnny [Hodges] . . . and said, 'What's my note?' And Johnny replied, 'Whichever one you want to play.' Jaws only stayed one night with the band. He said it made a nervous wreck out of him, because the band wasn't particularly helpful to anybody. I mean, they didn't hang out together."[18]

Once at London's Royal Festival Hall, Gonsalves again failed to show up as curtain time neared. Granz and Ellington were both concerned about the gaping hole that would exist if there were no tenor saxophone in the band for an especially big concert. Standing backstage were two of the best-known British saxophonists, Ronnie Scott and Tubby Hayes. Scott was on his way to a job, so Hayes took Gonsalves's chair. "Duke hit whatever the first number was, and the first soloist he called on was Tubby," Granz said, chuckling. "I think Jimmy Hamilton nudged him and said, 'You're on, go on out there.' That's what Duke would do. Tubby had to figure out the changes and everything for himself. He did great."[19] Ellington was pleased with Hayes's performance, but Gonsalves immediately reclaimed his chair. After all, as Billy Strayhorn noted, Gonsalves had not "murdered anyone."

On October 29, 1965, Granz and Ellington signed a contract to film his life story. Granz, who envisioned a screenplay written by Dalton Trumbo, had gone so far as to contact Sidney Poitier's manager about the actor playing the lead (one studio suggested Gary Cooper!) and anticipated that Ellington's band would provide the score. But the project collapsed when Ellington refused to stay put for the two to three months Granz estimated it might take to produce a screenplay that could also serve as the basis of a major autobiographical work. "Duke wouldn't take three days to do that," he said. "It was ridiculous, because we'd gone to a lot of effort to do a picture that Duke would own half of." Granz attributed Ellington's recalcitrance to the bandleader's long-standing refusal to divulge much about himself; typically Ellington deflected curiosity seekers by suggesting that people listen to his music in order to know him. "It seems to me that if he were being cagey with all the people who interviewed him or wanted to write about him and all the rest, . . . well, he accomplished it. He's still cagey, but to his own loss," Granz said years after Ellington's death. "He was an entertainer, and he really missed his last act."[20]

Ella Fitzgerald and Duke Ellington enjoyed many joint projects together over the next five years. Even when Verve was under new ownership, Granz maintained creative control over her recording projects and in October 1965 oversaw production of *Ella at Duke's Place* with the full orchestra. Two days of recording were needed to put the album to bed, with Jimmy Jones filling Ellington's chair. In January and February 1966, they were recorded live at the Teatro Lirico in Milan and the Circus in Stockholm and again in Rotterdam in January 1967.[21] An album of the Stockholm concert of February 8, 1966, originally broadcast on Swedish television, was finally released on *Pablo Live* in 1984.

In early 1966, Ellington undertook recording a third film score, the Frank Sinatra adventure drama *Assault on a Queen,* a project that Granz had brokered on his behalf for $25,000 plus travel and living expenses.[22] The work was more difficult for Ellington than that required for *Anatomy of a Murder* and *Paris Blues* because the film was incomplete when he began working on the score and last-minute editing called for significant revisions of the music. Ellington was displeased as well by what he considered the studio's interference with the score. He could not have been pleased either that the contract covered only himself as composer and not his orchestra, taking him away from the band's intimate informality and driving productivity.

Major concert events in 1966 and 1967 put Fitzgerald and Ellington at the center of two especially high-profile projects undertaken by Granz. The first was his film documenting a joint appearance in late July 1966 at the Sixth Festival Mondial du Jazz Antibes Juan-les-Pins on the Côte d'Azur, which he hoped to turn into a ninety-minute black-and-white feature and recording. Second was a three-month Jazz at the Philharmonic "farewell tour" starring Fitzgerald, Ellington, and Peterson that Granz had booked to play in the United States, Canada, and Europe.

Granz had originally planned to make a full-color documentary of the Côte d'Azur concerts and some of the rehearsals by the Ellington Orchestra during the '66 tour, but technical problems arose that precluded the use of color. Eventually the production, underwritten by Frank Tenot, was carried out by the German television producer Alexander Arens and a three-camera team from Paris shooting 16 mm black-and-white film.[23] *Jazz on a Summer's Day,* photographer Burt Stern's film of the 1958 Newport Jazz Festival, had been successful in depicting the idyllic combination of the Rhode Island coastline and the sights and sounds of jazz. Similarly, the Côte d'Azur film intersperses the jazz sequences with glances at European culture. Ellington is seen at the casino at Monte Carlo and observing a game of *boules* in St. Tropez. Granz also shows Ellington, bassist John Lamb, and drummer Sam Woodyard at the Fondation Maeght, a museum situated atop a hill overlooking the bay of Cannes at St. Paul de Vence. The Spanish artist Joan Miró, then in residence at the museum, has a cameo in the film. Miró and Ellington stroll in animated conversation through the grounds of the museum, where a concert grand piano has been positioned in the museum's art-filled courtyard. Thus the film can be seen not only as a musical documentary but as something of a Norman Granz travelogue and a hint at the landscape he traversed as he built up a world-class art collection during this period.

During the filming of the Côte d'Azur concerts, a rift developed in the relationship between Ellington and Granz that never completely closed. The most vivid account of their clash, which includes extensive comments from Granz, is given by Ellington's biographer Derek Jewell. Granz had sunk a lot of money into producing Fitzgerald and Ellington at the July 27 and 28 concerts. But days before the event, Fitzgerald's sister, Frances, died suddenly, so that Fitzgerald was forced into canceling her July 25 appearance. She caught an overnight flight back to New York to attend the funeral. Bearing up through obvious strain, she returned on the twenty-seventh, the day of her only joint appearance with Ellington. She was not at her best vocally and even appeared to be crying at times.

Ellington sought to relieve her misery by bringing the first half of the concert to an early conclusion and, not expecting Fitzgerald to return for the second half, preparing to carry the load for the remainder of the evening. From there, a war of wills developed between Ellington and Granz, who was fuming backstage. Ellington played on, bringing the crowd to fever pitch while blithely rebuffing Granz's shouted requests to bring Fitzgerald back onstage. "Either Ellington didn't hear, or he chose not to hear," Jewell said.[24] As soon as the show ended, Granz laced into Ellington, who reportedly ran for his hotel to get away. Ellington's friend Renee Diamond recalled Ellington's black mood that night back in his hotel room. "I've never seen him so sad. Not angry, but sad," Diamond said.[25] "He spoke a little about Norman not having consideration for *anyone*—which coming from Edward was quite hilarious." At Ellington's request Diamond went over to try to smooth things out with Granz, who launched into a bitter tirade about the bandleader—"terrible things." When he had calmed down somewhat Granz explained that he had wanted to get Fitzgerald back on stage because he had intended for her to have top billing in the film. Diamond comprehended his disappointment but not why he blamed Ellington: "Ella wasn't in any shape to go back on." Fitzgerald later admitted as much. The quarrel was not mended, however. Ellington and Granz took the same plane back to the United States the following day, but they only waved when they saw each other at the Nice airport and did not speak at all during the flight.

Years later Granz seemed to be revising his memories of the incident at the Côte d'Azur, suggesting that as time went by that he might have wanted to forget the details of a situation that had gone so terribly wrong. In May 1997 he attacked Jewell's account, saying he did not recall any such episode. "When Duke and I split up, it was a very personal matter. It had nothing to do with a concert, for Christ's sake," he said.[26]

Two angry and sarcastic letters from Granz to Ellington, dating from April 10 and April 11, 1967, during a Chicago rest stop on the JATP tour, show the continuing repercussions of the Côte d'Azur incident. Both were initially sparked by unwelcome early-morning phone calls to the impresario. The first read in part:

Dear Duke Ellington,

ITEM: Last Tuesday at 2:30 a.m., you awakened me in Toronto to wire money for you. Obviously I was supposed to get dressed immediately, rush down—on foot if necessary—implore Western Union to open its doors and wire the money urgently, so Duke Ellington's needs could be satisfied. But upon a moment's reflection and consideration, Duke Ellington could have known not a damn thing could be done until the next day anyway, and why not wait? On the other hand, why wait. What the hell does Granz mean trying to get a little sleep?

ITEM: Wake up Granz at 4:30 in the morning to tell him a great idea about putting the Antibes film on TV. Granz should immediately telephone Sarnoff, Paley and all the other heads of TV to see if they will take the film. Of course, for Duke Ellington to telephone Granz this urgent idea during normal and effective business hours (not Granz's normal and effective business hours since he has none; the business hours of Sarnoff, Paley, etc.) meant that Duke Ellington would have to get up at a ridiculous hour for Duke Ellington—that is somewhere between 9 a.m. and 5 p.m. to do this, and one needs one's (Duke's, that is) sleep and one's (Duke's) health, and so on, ad nauseam.

ITEM: Any idea or request or order, repeat, any, can wait a few more hours. If you're afraid you'll forget it, then write it down.

CONCLUSION: Between 12 midnight and 9 a.m., there will be a permanent and irrevocable Do Not Disturb on the Granz line. My life, my friend, is short enough as it is without having you make it shorter.[27]

Remarkably, Ellington placed another postmidnight call to Granz on the day he had penned the first letter. Granz's exasperated, caustic response reveals the breach that had opened up between them. It reads in part:

Dear Duke,

By now I trust you have received my first letter, so this second letter shouldn't come as much of a surprise to you.

I'm really afraid that you're using me not as a manager, but as a servant—and worse than that you are so incredibly, foolishly selfish in the way you do it that I think not even a self-respecting servant would accept it. Once again you rang me after 1 o'clock in the morning about something I absolutely could do nothing about until the next day—and more than that, about something which directly concerns [assistant] Mary Jane [Outwater]. . . .

I'm afraid, Duke, that I've had it with you and I think you are better off getting another so-called manager.

I'll be glad to give you whatever advice I can on any major issues that come up in your artistic life, but as far as sending your laundry out or wiring money to your friends, I don't think I can do that again; in fact, why don't you get yourself a secretary to do it for you? If you need money in advance on the tour I'll be glad to send it to Ruth [Ellington Boatwright, Ellington's sister] and you can direct her to take care of your little problems, but don't you ever call me again late at night, especially about such trivia, because I'm entitled to some consideration too.[28]

According to Granz, however, the incident leading to their five-year estrangement actually took place about a year later. After many years, he had finally succeeded in booking Fitzgerald for concerts in Eastern Europe and had invited Ellington to join the tour. He had labored to put together a tour that could succeed commercially, rather than going in as part of a State Department–sponsored event. The tough bargainer did not exactly walk over the Eastern European apparatchiks in charge of cultural exchanges. "I'd flown to Budapest and had three days hard talking," he said. "They *sap* you, those people, because they work in committees, but they've got only you, and they're obdurate, and they don't really care." Matters were even more complicated because Granz had been negotiating arrangements not only for Fitzgerald and her trio but also for the twenty or so members of the Ellington party. "I was exhausted, but I was elated, too, and the logistics of the trip were terrible," Granz recalled. He called Ellington's sister Ruth with the news, only to learn that she had booked the orchestra for a high school date that Ellington would not cancel, even though the proposed tour marked the first time the orchestra would have played in some of those countries. "I blew my top, and she was defending him . . . I'm sorry, I guess, that we had this terrible row, but I just canceled out the entire schedule I had arranged for Duke and I took Basie instead," he said.[29] Thus, aside from the 1967 JATP tour, the blowup at the Côte d'Azur marked the end of the two men's association until Granz founded Pablo Records in 1973 for what turned out to be Ellington's final months.

"Can JATP turn back the clock?" inquired one Toronto newspaper headline at the prospect of a revival.[30] Whatever reservations Granz felt through the years about doing a last concert tour by Jazz at the Philharmonic— reservations he later deemed well founded—weakened just long enough for him to do so in the spring of 1967. He was motivated partly by a sense of responsibility to expose young listeners to his brand of jazz. "I know it may sound corny, but this is my main reason for this one last American tour—and I think this will be the last," he told the Toronto interviewer. "I simply want to give the kids a chance to hear some real jazz." Granz announced in late March that the new tour would be based on the same concept as the original JATP concerts, with the only major difference being the inclusion of a big band. He asked Ellington to write special material to feature the jam session soloists and some of his own men.

Though the tour was anchored by Duke Ellington, Ella Fitzgerald, and Oscar Peterson, Granz also summoned Benny Carter, Clark Terry, Zoot Sims, and guitarist and blues singer T-Bone Walker to appear on some of the dates. Ellingtonians Johnny Hodges and Paul Gonsalves would step out from their normal roles with the orchestra to be featured in small-group formats to enhance interest in the event. The tour was a last hurrah for Coleman Hawkins, whose alcoholism had destroyed his appetite and drained his energy. His haggard appearance, unkempt beard, and ill-fitting clothes marked a sad contrast to the natty Hawk of old whose elegance had mirrored his supreme talent. Concerts recorded at Carnegie Hall on March 26, at the Hollywood Bowl on June 30, and in Oakland on July 1 would finally be issued on Pablo Records in 1975 as *The Greatest Jazz Concert in the World.*

Reviews of the concerts were mixed. Jazz at the Philharmonic was seen by some as nostalgia by the time Granz got around to reviving the onetime surefire concert series after a decade. Yet even somewhat critical reviews, such as the review of the Academy of Music concert in the *Philadelphia Daily News,* applauded the liveliness of the music. "The jazz these men play is mainstream, but it is not an archeological interest that puts them onstage. Their music is bright as new and, even in the old favorites, the force of new ideas keeps the music alive."[31] *New Yorker* critic Whitney Balliett, who had dismissed JATP as "pandemonium" in 1954, called the fare "safe and mild as fudge. . . . Granz has persuaded Duke Ellington to bring his band along on the current tour, and the result is as if General Motors had called in Chagall to mix its colors. The band, equipped with several new numbers, sounded fresh and ebullient."[32]

Coleman Hawkins's decline, sometimes noted in press accounts, occupied the time and concern of his musical colleagues who helped him make it through the tour. Trumpeter Clark Terry recalled Hawkins as being ill during most of the tour and drinking much more than he was eating. On the night of the Oakland concert, Terry and Hawkins were up front playing when the saxophonist ventured too close to the edge of the stage and began wobbling. Terry and Oscar Peterson moved on Hawkins simultaneously and rushed him backstage, where a doctor declared his touring days over. Terry recalls that during the dates at the Carter Barron Amphitheater in Washington, D.C., he and Zoot Sims encouraged Hawkins to eat and tried to stay on top of the situation. One day when they were in Hawkins's room, they looked in a wastebasket to find what looked like several days' meals.[33] Benny Carter remembered a similar episode in which a dinner he had left in Hawkins's Toronto hotel room went virtually untouched.

The JATP farewell tour played two concerts at the Civic Opera House on April 14. Mohammed Ali, who lived in the city at the time, came backstage in between shows, to the delight of the jazz heavyweights passing through town. The stopover in Chicago brought to the surface differences between Granz and Ellington on the subject of civil rights. Unlike Ali, Ellington shied away from explicitly political action, words, or deeds on behalf of civil rights, a stance that deeply troubled Granz. From Ellington's perspective, one he had long repeated, he intended his body of music to be seen as a tribute to the strength and beauty of African Americans. Granz overheard some Ellington musicians discussing an impending march before the show was to play in Chicago. "At that time, they were having a lot of marches, particularly outside of Chicago in Cicero, which is one of the most vicious racist cities you can imagine, a mean town," Granz said. According to Granz, Ellington's son, Mercer, a trumpeter and the band's road manager, said he wished his father would take part in the march, and when Ellington came into the dressing room Mercer asked him to do so. "Why in the hell should I march?" Ellington demanded. "My music is fighting the cause much more effectively and much longer than any march would do."[34] Granz could see both sides of it. He felt that Ellington should take a stand politically, supporting African Americans in a way that "might be more important than the subtlety" of his music. But he also understood Ellington's position that a one-shot appearance was not going to have any immediate dramatic effects. "So in a way, I think you have to judge it by your standards and where you're coming from," Granz said in 1989.[35] But he left no doubt that he felt Ellington could have risked a measure of his prestige on behalf of a critical cause that was at long last on the national agenda. "There was no escape," Granz said. "The issue was there, you see."[36]

How far could Granz reasonably go in presuming to judge Ellington about what he saw as his failure to step into the fray at a volatile time in the country's history when Ellington was engaged in an ongoing struggle to keep the band together and working? After all, Granz had designed JATP to strike a blow for racial justice by outcompeting more discriminatory tours economically. Ellington remained first and foremost a bandleader and prodigious composer; his low profile in the political world reserved the sanctuary that he needed to create his music. Granz had chosen to cast his lot with African Americans, but for all his awareness of the black experience in America he did not see that because he had never had to suffer the restrictions or assume the risks of actually of being black he did not have the right to dictate their responses to circumstances.

Granz was telling the press by late June that the 1967 concerts were to be his last in the United States, aside from booking Fitzgerald and Peterson. That was technically true inasmuch as he considered the Pablo tours of the 1970s and 1980s to be no more than promotional tours in response to dealers who wanted live appearances to help sell records. The tour had been successful financially with approximate nightly grosses of $25,000. "There were plenty of kicks and it was a sop to my ego, but I wouldn't do it again," he said. On balance, however, he thought continuing to work the U.S. concert market was too much work for too little financial return or personal satisfaction.

In September 1971, Granz and Jazz at the Philharmonic were feted at the Monterey Jazz Festival. The tribute, for which Granz was coaxed out of "seclusion" to serve as host and honoree, was staged by the festival's founder, the same Jimmy Lyons who had recorded the first JATP for the Armed Forces Radio Service. In what *Down Beat* called a "Granz night for swinging," the opening jam session featured Roy Eldridge, Bill Harris, Eddie "Lockjaw" Davis, and Zoot Sims, backed by the Oscar Peterson Trio with Danish bassist Niels-Henning Ørsted Pedersen and drummer Louis Hayes. Benny Carter and Clark Terry led a second group with pianist John Lewis, guitarist Mundell Lowe, Ray Brown, and Louie Bellson and then joined with Eldridge, Sims, and Davis. "The 5,000 fingers of Oscar Peterson, Pedersen and Hayes were on," the reviewer noted. The JATP redux ended with a set by Sarah Vaughan, who was "in fine form, meaning she swung, she mesmerized and she sassed."[37] Leonard Feather wrote, "Nostalgia being in trend this season, an evening with the JATP sounds could well have bogged down into nothing more than a trip down memory lane. Fortunately, Granz and Lyons were able to assemble a personnel strong enough to insure that the music would stand—and move—entirely on its merits by any standard."[38]

The timing of the Monterey event came fourteen years after JATP had left the scene in the United States and on the verge of Granz's getting started in the record business again with Pablo Records. Critical response to the tribute concert showed once again the power of Granz's jam sessions to entertain audiences with vibrant music and first-rank performances. Granz said in later years that a renewed sense of mission overtook him to work on behalf of those musicians whose work had driven his own over the decades. "I got back into records because I like recording the things I like in jazz," Granz told John S. Wilson of the *New York Times* in 1975. "I feel like I have a certain responsibility to jazz and certain jazz musicians that have made me successful—some who have been passed by—such as Roy Eldridge, Basie, and the rest. From a recording standpoint, nothing much was being done for them."[39]

Granz sensed as well that interest in mainstream jazz was beginning to revive to some degree in the early 1970s. Within months of the Monterey tribute, Granz had repurchased the masters of the Art Tatum recordings from MGM, which had no plans to reissue the material but turned down his offer to buy Verve back. In 1972 he was also making plans to record Ella Fitzgerald doing a new album of Cole Porter songs with Nelson Riddle arrangements as a run-up to starting up a new label. Leonard Feather wrote that Granz's renewed interest in recording was "symptomatic" of a trend then seen among some of the major labels around this time. At Columbia, Miles Davis's albums had been successful throughout the decade; so had releases as diverse as those of Charlie Byrd, Chuck Wayne, Tiny Grimes, John McLaughlin and the Mahavishnu Orchestra, and a reissue of classic Count Basie recordings. Chuck Mangione, who was experimenting by playing with the Rochester Symphony, was selling a fair number of records for Mercury, while RCA was releasing some fresh material by Buddy Rich and reissues covering Roy Eldridge's days with Artie Shaw and another reissue dedicated to Bunny Berigan.

More and more, the signs heralding a revival in jazz recording were influencing Granz and reawakening his desire to present opportunities and work for artists whose work he loved. Granz would take the plunge in 1972 when he turned an appearance by Ella Fitzgerald and Count Basie into an ad hoc Jazz at the Philharmonic concert in Santa Monica. Interest in recordings from the concert would guide him back into the studio for his next and final round as one of jazz's great record producers.

19

Picasso on the Beach

"One of the most joyful periods of my life was when I was in Europe and spent time on many occasions with Pablo Picasso," Norman Granz recalled in 2000. "He would show me his new paintings and things that he was doing."[1] Granz entered Pablo Picasso's circle late in the artist's life, after being introduced to him by the uranium magnate and art patron Joseph Hirschorn in 1968, although Picasso had long been one of Granz's main artistic heroes. He was close enough to the then eighty-six-year-old artist to get an inside view of his life. Lunch was a leisurely one-to-three affair, followed by a three-hour nap. Granz was present on many occasions to share teatime with Picasso and his guests from six until eight. Afterwards they were expected to leave, since Picasso would customarily work from then until around three in the morning.

Granz's introduction to modernism began with his first hearing of Coleman Hawkins's "Body and Soul." "Listening to Hawkins's 'Body and Soul' has nothing to do with nostalgia. It simply stands as a great work of art whether done yesterday or 50 years ago," he once wrote. "You look similarly at a Cubist Picasso which is 80 to 90 years old. It does not give me a warm feeling of nostalgia for that period—no! It stands on its own *NOW!!*"[2]

Granz gained experience in the world of fine art through a wide circle of postwar modern art dealers and collectors, most significantly Heinz Berggruen of Paris, Ernst Beyeler of Basel, and Otto Kallir of New York, as well as other friends throughout the cultural establishment.

Granz approached collecting fine art with the acuity that characterized his involvement in jazz: he gravitated only toward what he loved. He did not mind making a profit on his dealings, but mostly sold if he felt he had had his time with a given work and wanted to move on to acquire others. "I learned one thing: not to buy a picture for business reasons," Granz said. "Buy it because you love it, and if you ever sell it, you will get your money back. But if you're buying it to beat a dealer or a collector, the dealers will kill you all the time. You might as well go into the stock market."[3]

His timing and instincts in collecting modern art were as sure—and as fortuitous—as they had been when he began Jazz at the Philharmonic. A wide selection of works from major artists' important periods and styles was then selling in the tens of thousands of dollars rather than in the millions after the art market soared in the 1980s. As Granz once remarked, he had made his first steps into the art market when "you could buy Picassos cheap enough that you didn't have to sell too many records."[4]

Granz provided the greatest detail about his activities as a connoisseur and collector of art and his friendship with Picasso in a series of taped conversations with his wife, Grete. He also spoke of his education in art, furthered especially by gallery owners, other collectors, and much time spent in museums. Along the way he made choices about those artists he wished to collect and how to approach the art of the art deal in ways that mirrored how he had taught himself about the music business. From the very beginning he gravitated toward museum-quality modern art, which he bought "in bulk" in the 1960s, according to Olivier Berggruen, a New York– and Paris-based art historian and freelance exhibit curator whose father, the legendary modern art dealer Heinz Berggruen (d. 2007), Granz had known for over forty years.[5] Granz collected the Cubist paintings of Georges Braque and Pablo Picasso as well as the works of Paul Klee, Fernand Léger, Juan Gris, Egon Schiele, Joan Miró, and Jean Dubuffet. Of those, Picasso, Klee, Léger, and Gris were his favorites. Later, after he developed a taste for sculpture, he acquired works by Picasso, Alberto Giacometti, Henry Moore, and Alexander Calder.

Granz's views about music and art were decidedly nonacademic. "I don't think you have to 'understand' a painting. I don't think you have to 'understand' a piece of music. I think you need to listen to it or look at it. You have to be exposed," Granz said in a 1978 television appearance. "You can read something about a picture—and I know

how convoluted an art critic can be—and you come away more confused than ever. Why read it? Why don't you go to the museum and use
your own eyes?"[6]

"Norman's choices have been validated over time," says Berggruen.
"He was able to anticipate tastes that have become the focus of interest in later years." For example, Berggruen points to Picasso's work
from the 1960s, which had moved in directions that not even longtime
Picasso admirers could account for, much less praise. Most famously,
the critic and collector Douglas Cooper called this period "the scrib-
blings of a senile old man." "You're talking about the Baroque imag-
ery—circuses, theater of the mind, or musketeers—that characterized
this period," Berggruen said. "It was almost as if he was playing out his
own fears of death. He had almost a childlike way in his approach to
color. The work was very powerful. Norman recognized this."[7]

Berggruen added that Granz's sense of privacy trumped any idea of
using his art collecting as a tool to advance himself socially. He did occasionally show pieces to his friends and associates. Granz recalled taking
Ella Fitzgerald and Duke Ellington to his Curzon Street apartment in
London for a quick dinner in between shows, hoping to get their reactions to the artworks displayed there. During the two-hour dinner, neither of them said a word until Granz finally moved the conversation in
that direction. "I didn't expect Ella to be interested, but Duke was a man
of the world, a sophisticate," he said. "After I brought it up, he said,
'Oh, they're very good.' He took one second to turn his head around,
and said, 'Yeah, they're very, very good.' I'm sure if had asked him ten
minutes later, he wouldn't have known what to say."[8] Such was not the
case later when trumpeter Clark Terry stopped by Tite Street (Granz's
final London home). "Norman thanked me for noticing all of his Picassos," Terry said. "'You're the only Tommy Tucker who ever sat in that
chair who knew what he was sitting in the middle of. Basie sat there,
Erroll Garner.' He started naming off people and made me feel very
special that I recognized Picasso."[9] Oscar Peterson also enjoyed Granz's
art, frequently joining him in visiting museums. Ray Brown said weeks
before his death in 2002 that Granz had once advised him to invest in
fine art, a recommendation Brown came to wish he had followed. "I
might not have to be working so hard today if I had done that."[10]

Granz's relationship with Pablo Picasso was the most rewarding consequence of his involvement in art. With Granz, Picasso quickly overcame any wariness he felt toward many well-heeled collectors, especially

Americans, who wanted to come to his studio in the south of France and chat up the great man. "People were always saying, 'Mr. Paley would like to see you, Mr. Whitney would like to see you, Mr. Mellon would like to see you,'" Picasso's biographer and friend John Richardson said. "And Picasso would say, 'No, I have my American collector.' These tycoons, these great names were not nearly as welcome as these collectors whom Picasso felt really had got it. It came from within them. It wasn't that they bought Picassos because the neighbors had Picassos, or that it was a fashionable thing to do. That's what Picasso liked in a collector. I think Norman Granz exemplified that. . . . Heinz Berggruen used to show me what Norman bought, and he did seem to have had an extraordinarily sharp eye for quality and also for offbeat things. He didn't go for the conventional Picassos. He was way ahead of his time liking late Picasso, and he kept up with Picasso's changes in style. I think that Norman, who wasn't a 'fashionable' collector, bought things that we would only realize were great Picassos twenty or thirty or forty years later. Also, I went pretty regularly to see Picasso, and Picasso came to see me, especially when there was a bullfight. Picasso told us that he liked Norman so much."[11] Other crucial elements of their friendship were Granz's ability to amuse Picasso and the lack of demands he placed on their relationship.

Richardson said that although Picasso was not musically oriented, he "liked jazz, or more accurately, he liked the idea of jazz." He believed Picasso must have appreciated Granz's style and the glamour of show business that attached to him. The latter appears not to have been the case, for Granz recalled that Picasso knew of his activities as a promoter only in the broad sense. "He knew who was a world championship boxer, and he kept up with everything, and watched television," he said, "but there were certain things he didn't care about."[12] (Someone who shared this indifference to celebrity was Ella Fitzgerald, who turned aside an invitation to meet him at teatime when she had a day off in Juan-les-Pins. "I'm busy. I'm darning my stockings, and I have some other things I'm sewing, so I can't go," she said. "That's great," Picasso said, roaring with laughter when Granz told him. "Now I really want to meet her!"[13]) Granz added that Picasso had never seen so much as a photograph of Fitzgerald when he did a well-known sketch of her on a blank page of an art catalog on March 28, 1970, which Granz soon gave her. "He had no idea of what she looked like," he said. "But in his own genius way, the picture was perfect."[14]

Granz regularly made the trek to Notre-Dame-de-Vie, Picasso's villa and studio in Mougins, and indeed was one of the few welcome to stop by without a prior appointment in those final years. Granz's access to Picasso indicates that he had won over Picasso's wife as well. Grete Granz still believes that Jacqueline was in fact quite smitten with her husband.

Granz marveled at the vitality of the old man, who lived as active a life as was prudent for a man of his years and was justly proud of his physique as he headed into his tenth decade as a still-smoldering artistic force. His routine "was not one of fragility," Granz noted. Normally commanding, Granz gladly submitted to fetching and carrying when Picasso got the urge to show his guest treasures from his own vast private stash of paintings. Judging from examples from the Granz collection, Richardson correctly concluded that Granz was one of the few to engage in the kind of dialogue with the artist that he himself had experienced many times when Picasso laid out a group of recent works, usually a series executed closely together, and asked for comment. "He always asked the same question, 'Which is 'the strongest'?' It wasn't which was the most beautiful. It was 'the strongest.'" Richardson's remarks square with Olivier Berggruen's observation that Granz's taste favored Picasso's tougher works (and that Picasso appreciated as much), "not some of the more pleasing works of the women in his life," including works from the war years, the period after *Guernica,* or a portrait of his mistress, *Dora Maar* (1938), which would later be owned by comedian, actor, and writer Steve Martin.[15]

Their friendship brought out a lighter—almost bubbly—side of Granz. For example, he had his tailor make the artist clothing resembling something that might have come from one of his paintings. Once, when Picasso complimented Granz on a new pair of corduroy trousers from his Savile Row tailor Anderson and Sheppard but declined Granz's offer of a pair, Granz prevailed upon Jacqueline to loan him an old pair of Picasso's pants to get an accurate measurement. "I had the bright idea—or at least I thought it was a bright idea—of having every color made," he recalled. When Granz delivered his present, Picasso asked if he would amend the order to include a pair with one blue leg and one red leg. An order book from Anderson and Sheppard from April 23, 1969, confirms that Granz quickly complied.[16] He also supplied Picasso with expensive handmade shirts from Turnbull and Asser of London, which Picasso wore backwards as painting smocks.

Granz recalled with particular fondness the early days of their friendship when Picasso occasionally ventured from his retreat in Mougins. Norman and Grete once spent three days with Picasso and Jacqueline, beginning with a day at Carlton Beach in Cannes near the hotel of the same name. Though according to Granz "the beach boys who brought mattresses and umbrellas immediately set out space for the group of us so that Pablo wouldn't be bothered," one woman asked for an autograph. "Pablo signed a piece of paper, and then he turned to me and said, 'I should have autographed her ass.'"[17] The second day, the quartet drove in Picasso's Hispano Suiza, one of the world's rarest automobiles, to a nearby village to see the grandchild of a friend get married.

Jealousy on Jacqueline's part eventually tinged Granz and Picasso's friendship as it had others whom she suspected tried to get too close to her husband. Some found that their letters never reached the old man or that they encountered other obstacles. In this case, Norman and Grete concluded it was not Norman's attention to Picasso but Picasso's attention to Grete that had irked her. Sometimes Jacqueline turned them away with announcements that Picasso was busy, but such maneuvers were not determined or consistent enough to significantly curtail Granz's access.

While Granz had the opportunity to see Picasso sketching, he was never invited to watch Picasso paint. This did not dampen his intense curiosity about Picasso's work or his attempts to analyze Picasso's materials, such as paints and papers, with a view to assessing the artworks' permanence.

Granz's friendship with Picasso as well as his primary dealers in the late 1960s—Louise Leiris and D.H. Kahnweiler, her brother-in-law—enhanced his authority and ability to accumulate many of his later works, or "wet Picassos" as Granz called them, so close was he to the time of their creation. This constant exposure prompted him later to rightly proclaim that he could appraise the works of Klee or late Picassos as well as any dealer. Zette, as Madame Leiris was known, had early on placed Granz near the top of potential buyers when new works by Picasso came up for sale.

Despite Picasso's penchant for sequestering his works, he allowed Granz to initial the frames of canvases he ultimately wished to acquire through Galerie Leiris. Picasso also handed over some of his works to Granz as gifts. Once Granz was present at Chateau de Vie when Siegfried Rosengart and his daughter, Angela, dealers from Lucerne, looked over some unreleased work. "Pablo was behind them as they got close to a small wooden painting that was on the wall," Granz recalled. "He took it and threw it to me and said, 'Catch,' which I think was the only English word he knew. I was startled and I grabbed it, and he said,

'Don't let them see it.' I said okay, so we hid the picture and then he gave it to me after they left."[18] Other discoveries were right underfoot, as when Granz turned up a loose board that twisted in place every time he stepped on it. He finally pulled the board out to find a painting of a nude woman in repose on its underside. Louise Leiris was in the studio that day and negotiated its sale on the spot.

Granz acquired one late masterpiece, *The Rape of the Sabine Women* (1962), painted when the artist was eighty-two. In it Picasso reconceives the mythic theme, already captured by Rubens (1635–40) and David (1799), of the kidnapping of the women of the ancient tribe in mountainous central Italy who had fought the Romans in the eighth century B.C. The powerful image of violence and despair was reportedly inspired by the Cuban missile crisis and is believed to be the artist's last major statement on the violence and terror of war. "I was fortunate to get a great painting that was in the same passion as *Guernica,* but it was thirty or forty years different," Granz said of the work, which he eventually sold to the Beyeler Collection in Basel, Switzerland.[19]

Over the years, Granz came into contact with notable American dealers and collectors, such as Eleanore Saidenberg of the Saidenberg Gallery in New York and E. V. Thaw, an art professor at Rutgers University, whom Granz came to realize lowered his prices as his annual vacation neared. He bought a de Kooning and a Klee from Thaw. Although Granz never maintained a high profile in New York at the height of his art acquisitions, he became friendly with Alexander Rosenberg, who sold him a Juan Gris and the works of other painters as well as giving him entrée to private collections.

One of the collectors who most influenced Granz, the imposing G. David Thompson of Pittsburgh, was rather like himself, a hardshelled steel executive with a probing eye. Granz was speechless when he followed up Thompson's invitation to visit his home and browse his collection of European modernists. "He had an enormous collection of Klee, but only the best quality, museum quality," Granz recalled. "Then I went into a room that had Picasso, and he had all the Picassos that I had dreamt about, that I had seen in books."[20] It was Thompson who later sold Granz one of six bronze casts of *Baboon and Young,* a sculpture that Granz directed to be sold after his death to help defray estate taxes.

Thompson, who like Granz amassed a valuable collection partially by buying in bulk, imparted advice that Granz followed for the rest of his active collecting life. One edict was to buy the remainder of an exhibit after dealers had made their final choices. "I always remember that the last picture left is the one to buy because that's the tough picture, that's the difficult picture," he said. Once Granz was in town for a concert in Pittsburgh and stopped by Thompson's home. He offered no more than $60,000 for a painting, falling $5,000 short of Thompson's asking price. Granz ran into the Thompsons at dinner before show time when he urged him to rethink his position. "Norman, don't miss out on a sale for $5,000," he said. "If you love the painting, it's cheap at the price. If you really don't think you could pay another $5,000, you really don't care for the picture." Granz picked up two paintings on his way out of the city and bought a second first-class seat for them on a flight to the tour's next stop in San Francisco.[21] "Everything I bought from Thompson I kept the longest," Granz said. "His taste was just unbelievable."

Around the time Granz met Picasso he unexpectedly sold off a significant part of his collection. The main event was a sale of epic, record-setting proportions held at Sotheby's in London on April 23, 1968. "I have a lot of paintings, and I decided to refine my collection and keep a few of my favorites. It has allowed me, among other things, to buy different paintings," Granz said in an interview earlier that day. "I think a collection has to be alive all the time. It should not become a museum that's fixed, permanent. It really stops being fun. If you had all the money in the world you could do that. Short of that, you have to change, make substitutions, and I think all of our tastes change in any case."[22] The Sotheby's sale, broadcast live and in color in prime time by the BBC, represented a watershed for Norman Granz. Never before had he been so publicly identified as one of the major players in the art field.

The story of the Sotheby's auction began in July 1967, when Granz approached Peter Wilson, the company's innovative chairman credited with introducing high-profile blockbuster auctions and velvet-gloved, hard-sell marketing strategies. Wilson, impressed with the volume and quality of Granz's offering, suggested nonetheless that he come forward with additional works to achieve the critical mass that Wilson envisioned would result in a lucrative sale. Granz turned to his friend Heinz Berggruen, who augmented Granz's works with some choice paintings from his own inventory. The auction catalog previewed a sale that included works by Georges Braque, Juan Gris, Fernand Léger, Egon Schiele, Paul Klee, Joan Miro, Jean Dubuffet, and twenty-four pictures and one ceramic by Picasso ranging in dates from 1912 to the fall of 1967.

Announcement of the sale had the desired effect, packing Sotheby and Company's Bond Street sale house with some of the world's top dealers, all thrilled to see so many treasures on the block at once. The broadcast, beginning at 8:00 p.m., focused on the Picasso portion of the sale. It required close coordination between Peter Wilson, who served as the auctioneer, and the director to *slow* the pace of bidding in order to stretch the program out to the full fifty-eight minutes allocated.

The market for modern art was such that prices were a fraction of what they would become over the next two decades. With respect to Picasso alone, buyers could still purchase significant works from across various periods of the artist's career at what would today seem like bargain-basement prices. The Granz auction and another in New York held that same month were significant because previously so little modern art had been sold at an adequate volume that prices for works by major artists were not really known. A *Times* of London art writer, as part of a survey of modern art prices conducted with Sotheby's, cited the two auctions in an article published just over a month later to support her contention, based on a comparison of seven artists, including Picasso, that prices were skyrocketing for twentieth-century paintings: increasing twenty-fold, on average, between 1950–52 and 1968 and for Picassos 38 percent between 1967 and 1968 alone.

The British press covered the story of the auction adjacent to reports on the attempt by Granz's second wife, Hannelore, to use the court system in the midst of her divorce to interfere with the sale of the artworks, the majority of which her husband had either owned before the couple married or newly acquired from trades made out of his existing collection. Mrs. Granz, a German citizen whom Granz had married in 1965, took issues arising from their divorce into an English court in hopes of obtaining £300,000 from Granz's part of the expected proceeds. (To protect his other holdings, Granz temporarily sold the remainder of his collection to his friend Frank Tenot for one franc.)

The case had been brewing before the High Court as early as February 1968, when Granz petitioned the legal system not to remove the paintings from Sotheby's before the sale. His estranged wife and her attorney sought to designate the paintings as community property. Despite fresh motions from the Granzes' Swiss attorneys on the day of the sale, the judge tossed out Mrs. Granz's petition on the grounds that Granz, although still an American citizen, was domiciled in Geneva, as was she. Thus she had no standing to file her case in Britain. Under Swiss law, husbands were designated the party responsible for property until a marriage was dissolved. In any case, Granz was not dependent on his art collection to satisfy any financial obligations arising from his divorce.

Around the time of Sotheby's auction, the *Times* of London printed a story on Granz that mentioned his role in combating segregation through jazz. "I would much rather talk to you about your country's color problem than about my pictures," Granz said. "A weak anti-racialist law can vitiate real progress. Absolute enforcement is essential."[23] In the article Granz also expressed support for Stokely Carmichael and the Black Power movement. His FBI file reveals that these comments found their way back to Washington and resulted in an inquiry to the bureau's Los Angeles office in June 1968. But as with the original investigation of Granz in 1956, the probe went nowhere after agents checked with informants who said they knew of no activity by Granz on behalf of the Black Power movement in Southern California.[24] In a comment to Nat Hentoff in 1994, Granz expressed disappointment that A. Philip Randolph's radical economic and political philosophy of black advancement had been forgotten with the rise of Martin Luther King and Malcolm X.[25] Curiously, Granz did not rank King as high as Randolph, even though King had espoused the integrationist values that for so long were central to Granz's racial vision (and that Carmichael decidedly did not endorse).

Granz's public passion for Picasso resurfaced in a full-page open letter directed at French president Georges Pompidou in the weekly *l'Express* dated October 17, 1969. Granz vigorously urged the government to take the lead in establishing a museum in Paris to honor "the greatest artist in the history of mankind—Pablo Picasso," adding, "and it is not only astonishing but unforgivable that France, historically the most important of all countries culturally, has done absolutely nothing to honor this most important resident." Picasso doubted Granz's plea would cause a ripple in the French establishment, telling Granz he thought he was foolishly throwing away the thirty thousand francs he had spent on the ad.[26]

Picasso maintained a bemused interest in whether Granz would hear anything from the president, given the breach in protocol represented by Granz's attempt to directly communicate with him. Nonetheless Pompidou did respond indirectly: some weeks after the publication of the letter, Granz received word through Galerie Leiris that a representative from the Ministry of Culture wanted to find out whether Picasso would agree in advance to donate his pictures to such a museum. Granz met with the government emissary, telling him that Picasso probably "would make no such guarantee" but expressing the belief that in the end the artist would make an important contribution. He emphasized that if the museum was to be a genuine homage to Picasso the government would have to make the first move. The matter was dropped after the meeting. Granz expressed mixed feelings when an institution was finally built honoring Picasso only after his death.

Granz thought it equally sad that he could not properly commemorate Picasso after his death on April 8, 1973, at the age of ninety-one. He was in London when he received word from his longtime British promoter Harold Davison that Picasso had died. Granz flew to Paris, where he expected a message from Jacqueline concerning Picasso's funeral. It never came, for Picasso's widow, in her grief and confusion, kept friends at bay as she proceeded with plans to bury him near Aix en Provence.

Shortly before Picasso's death, Granz paid tribute to him in the form of a privately published, untitled book and again, prominently, when he formed Pablo Records the year Picasso died. He reproduced twenty paintings and drawings Picasso had drawn and signed for him, including sketches of the impresario and often, in the inscriptions, the words "pour mon ami," referring to Granz. The book, drawn from works executed between May 7, 1969, and November 27, 1970, had a run of fifty-one copies, with Picasso receiving twenty-six and Granz giving the remaining copies to friends and family. According to Olivier Berggruen, art had supplanted jazz for Granz as an opportunity where he felt he could still make a difference, given his bitterness about the direction of jazz and the music business from which he had drifted. Berggruen was grateful for astute lessons Granz passed on. "Norman was a master negotiator from all those years working with contracts for records and concerts. He told me, 'Buy what you feel strongly about. To recognize quality takes lot of work and requires a huge amount of background.'"[27]

Granz paid further homage to his friend by designating his airy sixth-story apartment in Geneva the House of Picasso. Scattered photographs made only glancing reference to highlights of his life in music: Granz with Ella Fitzgerald in the thick of recording the Gershwin songbook, a striking black-and-white photograph of Duke Ellington taken by Granz, a signed Gjon Mili photograph of Billie Holiday, and Mili's classic portrait of the cocksure impresario as a young man, holding *Jazz at the Philharmonic, Volume 1,* with David Stone Martin's iconic drawing of the trumpeter on its cover. Further inspection of Granz's holdings reveals three self-portraits of George Gershwin presented to Granz by Ira Gershwin, the third showing the composer in obvious physical decline or distress only shortly before his early death, and two self-portraits of Ira Gershwin himself, the impeccable lyricist and indispensable partner. Granz's collection of his own recordings was select and filled only a few shelves in the living room with more in his bedroom—a sign of Granz's sensitivity not to overwhelm his wife's equally strong devotion to classical music.

Picasso's effect on Granz, in contrast, made its presence felt in not only the quality but the sheer number of the artist's works displayed on the premises—some thirty sketches and paintings. In one large photograph, the two men, Picasso virtually swamped by Granz's massive frame, are batting the air with ping-pong paddles.

Granz's final label, Pablo Records, bore both the Picasso name and an abstract drawing many incorrectly believe is the image of a dog drawn especially for his friend's new enterprise. However, the origins of the crimson logo date back a quarter century before the label's founding in 1973. The design dominated the cover of a book of Picasso lithographs published in conjunction with *Le chant des morts (Song of the Dead),* a collection of poems by Pierre Reverdy shown at the Louis Carré Gallery in Paris in 1948 and edited into book form by Tériade, a giant among art book publishers of the twentieth century. The Picasso design, which Granz also had cast as a bronze medallion, commemorates the roles jazz and art played in Granz's life, as it is displayed near the top of his tall marble tombstone, inlaid in gold.

While Granz was devoted to Picasso, Picasso's feelings about Granz in his own words are largely lost. However, the artist's impressions may be divined from a handful of drawings and paintings of the impresario. Granz had often watched Picasso sketch and posed for him several times. Once Picasso asked Granz to grow the only beard he had ever had for a portrait. Some time passed before he showed Granz half a dozen or so pictures prefaced by a comment as elliptical as his art. "They're not finished," he told Granz. "I can't understand it. I want the color blue, but the color red comes up."[28]

20

"One More Once"

The last thing Norman Granz *needed* to do in the early 1970s was to get back into the record business for what would turn out to be almost fifteen years. But that is exactly what he did. Memories of Granz provided by the late British author, critic, and musician Benny Green, whose liner notes were regular features on Pablo Records, reveal the richness of the life Granz was enjoying during his first retirement from the studio. Green, one of the few welcomed within Granz's inner circle, came to appreciate the array of interests beyond music that occupied him. "He knows as much about modern painting as he does about jazz. He's a great collector and is friends with lots of the world-famous painters," Green would say about Granz later on, in 1987. "He has an obsessional interest in literature, P. G. Wodehouse, for instance, and has a complete set of Wodehouse's books. Norman has a *real* student's interest in cooking and food. He will go thousands of miles to find out how to make a dish. So he does have these other interests, but I think he doesn't display them to the outside world. Norman Granz is the kind of man, I believe, who would have been outstanding whatever he'd chosen to do. There are a few people like that. If he'd gone into the stock exchange or politics or architecture—whatever it was—he would have been the one of his generation, the same as he was in jazz. He was just one of those guys."[1]

Granz's return to creating and managing a new label would seem incomplete without musical fireworks heralding its arrival. That event, on June 2, 1972, was held, not in New York or any of the choice

European jazz capitals, but close to the locale of the first concert that had launched his career nearly twenty-eight years before. Advertised as "The BIG Concert of the Year" and starring Ella Fitzgerald and Count Basie, it drew a capacity audience to the Santa Monica Civic Center. "Good evening, ladies and gentlemen," Norman Granz began typically without introducing *himself*. "Tonight, I am very happy to present a most unusual concert, because it's more than you bargained for, a lot more than you saw advertised, a lot more artists than the featured ones."[2]

In a surprise unknown even to the headliners, Granz had planned a full-scale jam session loaded with all-star guests from the golden days of JATP—Count Basie, Ed Thigpen, Ray Brown, Stan Getz, Eddie "Lockjaw" Davis, Harry "Sweets" Edison, trombonist Al Grey, and Roy Eldridge—and had arranged for it all to be recorded. The group roared through Sonny Stitt's blues "Loose Walk," romanced the crowd with a ballad medley, and then resumed the blues with Eldridge's "5400 North," named for the Chicago address on North St. Louis Avenue of the local Public Broadcasting System outlet WTTW. Granz's next surprise came when Basie, seeing Oscar Peterson, who had just arrived from Honolulu, taking in the proceedings from the wings, got up from his stool and good-naturedly dragged him onstage to finish the set's final number. As "a little aperitif" before the Basie band and Ella Fitzgerald, Granz brought out Peterson and Brown, whom he proudly recalled introducing at Carnegie Hall nearly twenty-three years before. For their reunion, the two performed "You Are My Sunshine," imbuing the song with a gutsy blues feel.

Fitzgerald and the Tommy Flanagan Trio swung through a list of numbers before the singer, backed by the Basie band, did "Shiny Stockings," a Cole Porter medley, and a version of "I Can't Stop Loving You" that left the audience roaring their applause. Even then, she had really just been warming up for the finale, "C Jam Blues," the highlight of the evening. Dueling with each musician, she introduced them in song and imitated their styles and sound as they traded fours. Whether her interplay was with Al Grey's rambunctious plunger mute, Stan Getz's piercingly florid attack, the twists and turns of Harry Edison, the gruffness of "Lockjaw" Davis, whose exchange with the singer most audibly brought down the house, or the fierce incandescence of Roy Eldridge, Fitzgerald inspired some of the evening's most memorable and humorous peaks.

Granz, then fifty-three, was justifiably thrilled with the music from the Santa Monica Civic Center. Though offering no innovations, the

June 1972 concert, like the recent Monterey Jazz Festival concert, reminded people of the appeal of Jazz at the Philharmonic. The quality may have been enhanced by the fact that some of the musicians had been away from the JATP tours for at least fifteen years and could approach the experience fresh. In the coming months, Granz tested the market by offering four records from Santa Monica for sale by mail order. Though he certainly did not expect sales to match those of Verve, he was surprised when he sold only about 150 copies, a mere 1 percent of the sales of 150,000 copies of *Jazz at the Philharmonic, Volume 1,* when it had hit the record stores in 1945. "I couldn't give them away," Granz said.[3]

However, in early 1973, one copy ended up on the turntable of an executive at PolyGram in Hamburg, who called Granz wanting to know whether he planned to produce any more records. Granz said he had been finished with the record business since 1960. Undeterred, PolyGram was prepared to back a new label and handle international distribution if he could be coaxed back into the studio. Granz flew to Hamburg a free man and returned a player in the record business once more. Entrée into the American market came in 1975 in an arrangement with the late Ken Glancy, then president of RCA Records, who had become a friend when both lived in London.

Granz saw Pablo Records as an opportunity to produce new concert recordings, mainly from European venues and festivals. Studio dates would be held primarily in Los Angeles and occasionally in New York. He could always delve deeply into his library of unreleased material, some of which dated from the 1940s and had not been included in the Verve sale in 1960. He also saw his new label as a means of providing better venues for the many fine jazz musicians who had been forced to record material hardly suiting them or who had few or no recording opportunities at all. "It's criminal that someone like Sarah Vaughan was allowed to go without making a record for five years," he said in 1971. "And it's an outrage that of the 27 albums I produced with Art Tatum, not a single one is available. . . . The record companies have changed. Executives today are only concerned with the fact that they can gross $9 million with the Rolling Stones. They forget that a profit is still a profit, and that you're still making money if you only net $9,000. I keep telling people that, and they think I'm crazy."[4] Granz was by this time a man of substantial wealth, with interests other than music, and more than comfortable with the life he shared with his wife, Grete. "Now it is a lot of fun to go into the studio and do things on a relaxed basis," Granz said in 1975.[5] He didn't have to do it. Thus the Pablo years offer perhaps the finest examples of Granz showing his mettle as an uninhibited entrepreneur, patron, and advocate of jazz.

He wanted the freedom, naturally, to bring together musicians to produce the down-and-dirty jam sessions that had always been his forte. He approached Count Basie, then nearing seventy, and Duke Ellington, seventy-three and ailing, and invited them to participate in small-group settings where they would take a leading role. Granz thought them both underrated pianists. He even hoped at one time to produce a European concert tour featuring the Basie and Ellington orchestras on two band-stands in a competition like the fabled "battles of the bands" at the Savoy Ballroom in the 1930s. Basie, however, pooh-poohed the idea of competing, preferring instead a forum where the contrasts between the bands could be expressed. It was a matter of emphasis: Basie was not insecure about his own band, but rather held Ellington in such esteem that he did not wish to "battle" with him for supremacy.

That Ella Fitzgerald and Oscar Peterson's recording careers seri-ously needed priming factored as well into Granz's decision to establish Pablo. Having Granz back in the business made it easier for the two artists to resume working together in order to build on their record-ings with purpose and direction, especially given Peterson's emergence as a major piano soloist. Granz largely kept the Pablo roster reserved for such longtime associates (though occasionally bringing in someone new as a favor), since it was going to be difficult enough to generate profits across the entire catalog. Sonny Criss once approached Granz about being recorded shortly after Pablo began, only to be informed that Granz was having a hard time moving even Fitzgerald's recordings.

That said, Granz well understood the commercial benefits of encour-aging his artists to make new recordings. Granz had started Verve to help define Ella Fitzgerald in a broader context of jazz and popular music, much as he had done by brokering her entrance into the top tier of performance venues after acquiring her management contract in 1954. Pablo Records allowed him to send out a steady stream of promotional copies to help keep artists' names before the public. In Fitzgerald's case, Granz's continuing attention produced a steady stream of releases, as opposed to periodic revivals by various labels that might have been too diffuse to have done her any good. It is hard to think of another pro-ducer who would have teamed her with the Los Angeles–based guitar virtuoso Joe Pass for a series of recordings that were among the best of her entire career. Likewise, a new wave of Peterson recordings helped keep him near the top of the heap of touring jazz artists.

At its core, Pablo was a showplace for those artists Granz managed nominally and without fees, Ellington and Basie, as well as those he represented exclusively: Pass, Peterson, and Fitzgerald. Pablo quickly became a magnet for expatriate musicians, both newcomers and long-time Granz associates, who coveted his solicitous oversight. The writer Christian Renninger caught the essence of this in a story on Joe Pass. "Seated on stage with only his guitar, Joe Pass seems a little distant and perhaps ill at ease. Part of the distance, it would seem, has intentionally been created by impresario Norman Granz," he said. "With careful packaging of his Pablo artists—those relatively serious, all-business black-and-white photographs that usually reflect a somber side to virtuosity, the long-winded, reflective liner notes of British critic Benny Green, the sense of belonging to a prolific recording *club* of carefully selected musicians which may be beyond the reach of mere mortals—Granz has produced an aura that surrounds his touring clientele."[6]

The success of Pablo also depended on artists' willingness to plug into new musical settings provided by Granz. No better example of this willingness could be found than Count Basie. Basie was more available for recordings and touring than Ellington because of the latter's touring schedule and failing health. Furthermore, Basie, unlike Ellington, was not tied to an array of his own compositions. At some point Granz had tired of the Basie band's repertoire and arrangements and felt that little new could be done in recording the band, although he continued to record in deference to Basie. "I finally got Basie to play some piano," Granz said. "Usually with his band he wouldn't play anything. And so I got him to do a lot of these small groups, you know, get people who I thought represented something that would never be done again."[7] For example, Granz had cajoled Basie through the years to do an organ album, only to be gently but consistently rebuffed. So when Basie was in the studio to do some of his duets with Oscar Peterson, Granz saw to it that an organ was placed there just in case. Basie would walk over to the organ and begin fooling around on the keyboard. Eventually he recorded a few numbers on the instrument taught him by Fats Waller in the 1930s. "Before you know it, I'd managed to eke out of Basie two or three organ numbers," Granz said. "But he was that easygoing. If I suggested doing an album with Dizzy, that he do a jam session with other people, he'd say, 'Fine, let's do it.'"[8]

In a 1975 interview by the writer and jazz historian John McDonough, Basie, asked about his Pablo recordings, replied, "I just do whatever Norman tells me to do."[9] For McDonough this meant, not that Basie was indifferent about his music or in any way bereft of ideas, but only that he trusted Granz's judgment implicitly. And his trust paid off: Basie recorded a small-group album with Zoot Sims around this time that earned him a Grammy for best jazz solo performance (*Basie and Zoot,* 1976), and his band would receive a Grammy for best jazz performance by a big band for the album *Prime Time,* which came out on Pablo in 1977.

McDonough and Granz favorably compared Basie's flexibility to the rigid predictability of Lionel Hampton, which was well known within the business. "With Hamp, it almost became a joke, and I mean this in a nice way. I wouldn't put Hamp down," Granz said. "I used to talk to some artists who would say, 'I got a rehearsal with Hamp. We rehearsed "Flying Home," and then we broke up.' The times I would see him in his later years, I could almost rattle off all the tunes he played before the concert began . . . The band would sometimes just go through the motions."[10] Hampton declined Granz's offer to join Pablo, citing a grudge he had nursed for twenty years over what he considered a slight concerning his billing on an album he had recorded with Teddy Wilson and Gene Krupa.

The duet recordings of Basie and Oscar Peterson—polar opposites in their approach to the keyboard, except for their affinity for the blues—especially exemplify the benefits of Basie's renewed alliance with Granz. The albums grew out of the pianists' mutual affection and regard. They watched each other's performances nightly when they were on tour. "Basie used to threaten me at certain times, you know," Peterson recalled in 2000 of their joking play. "He'd say, 'I ought to come up there and beat your head in for what you played out there last night.'" Through the good offices of Norman Granz, they soon had the forum to settle their musical differences. It was Basie who came up with the title of their first album, *Satch and Josh,* named for two stars of the Negro Baseball League, in which he compared himself to the catcher Josh Gibson, and Peterson to the pitcher Satchel Paige. "The truth of it is that in this album, Oscar not only achieves his strike outs but at the same time Basie hits his home run," Granz said.[11] Whatever their keyboard personas—the powerhouse versus the minimalist—it was a love feast rather than a war when the two played together in the studio or on the road.

If Norman Granz had any illusions that he was reentering the same business he left behind in the last days of 1960, he soon found out otherwise. The jazz and blues historian, broadcaster, and record producer Bob Porter believes Granz may have miscalculated how the record-buying public of the 1970s would react to his return. "The public has a very short attention span without the regular touring, without the record label and without the constant visibility in the press," Porter said. "I think when he came back with Pablo he thought he could take up the slack because nobody was recording his favorite musicians and do the same thing he had done earlier. But he was very wrong."[12]

Even before the Santa Monica concert, Granz was producing new recordings of European concerts with blues singer Joe Turner and Count Basie. He also made a recording of a Paris concert by Muddy Waters, though Pablo wouldn't release it until 1997. The remainder of the first year's efforts included two Count Basie jam sessions from December 1973. The first album featured Basie in a small group with Ray Brown, Irving Ashby, J.J. Johnson, "Lockjaw" Davis, and Zoot Sims; the second featured Joe Turner backed by the same group.

Time was swiftly running out for Granz to record Duke Ellington. The two crossed paths again at the Coconut Grove in Los Angeles in 1972 and made their peace over whatever differences had fractured their relationship. Ellington was known for being pragmatic in his forgiveness; Granz had always been one of his staunchest fans and felt he finally had the chance to add to Ellington's recorded canon. Granz's two Pablo studio recordings of Ellington, combined with live recordings from European concerts and some leased material, partially redressed his long-standing regret that he had never gotten Ellington under contract at an earlier date and had the chance to take a comprehensive approach to recording him. "For some strange reason, I could never get Duke in the studio to record for me," Granz said. "Generally, the problem was that he was under contract to someone, so there was a real reason why he couldn't record for me. But when he was between contracts, which he was in the later years—and I mean in the late years when he wasn't recording for anyone—I'd sit down with Duke and say, 'I have an idea to do an album with you.' Of course, he wanted to know how much he was going to get paid and all of that. He'd say okay, we'd get it all laid out, . . . and then I'd never hear from him. The next thing I know, Duke would be signed for CBS or signed somewhere. It was curious considering my relationship with him."[13]

Ella Fitzgerald and Duke Ellington worked together again in late October 1972 for the taping of the Timex All-Star Swing Festival at New York's Lincoln Center. The program, which also featured the Count Basie Orchestra with Joe Williams, the Dave Brubeck Quartet, and Benny Goodman's quintet (with Lionel Hampton, Teddy Wilson,

Gene Krupa, and bassist George Duvivier), aired November 29 on NBC. The following week, on December 5, Granz and Ray Brown traveled to Las Vegas, where the Ellington Orchestra was playing at the Casino Lounge at the Hilton for four weeks. Granz planned to re-create the immortal sessions Ellington had recorded with bassist Jimmy Blanton in 1940 and 1941. For Brown, whose original desire to play had been fired by Blanton's revolutionary transformation of the bass from its role as accompaniment to a solo instrument, it was a dream come true. For Granz, it paid tribute not only to the Ellington-Blanton collaboration but to his own cherished friendship with the bassist, who had met with an untimely death in Los Angeles over thirty years before.

Less than a month later, Ellington recorded a quartet album for Granz when the band was in Los Angeles for the taping of a televised tribute produced by Quincy Jones for CBS. Duke, after all, did not need to be present for the rehearsal of the orchestra. Granz convinced Ellington to use guitarist Joe Pass in his first recording for Pablo Records, along with Brown and Louie Bellson. A videotape of the session, issued on record as *Duke's Big Four,* shows an exhausted and drawn Ellington amid a crowd of people he had invited to what was to be his penultimate studio recording. On January 11, shortly after it was over, he checked into St. Vincent's Hospital in New York with a viral infection and fatigue and stayed there eight days before resuming his waning days on the road. Granz nurtured Ellington in his own way by sneaking into the hospital and serving him gourmet food in bed. He also gave Ellington a private preview showing of the unedited *Duke's Big Four,* which Ellington satirically referred to as his own "adult movie."[14]

Ellington made his last cross-country road trip in the first three months of 1974 and soon thereafter, in late March, was hospitalized for the last time in the Harkness Pavilion of the Columbia Presbyterian Hospital on 168th Street. He died of lung cancer two months later. Granz saw him anytime he was in New York and reportedly sent him caviar daily. "He was on his way out and I brought him a big kilo of caviar because he would pass it out to the nurses and the doctors," he said. "It made him feel good."

The men saw each other one last time a day or two before Ellington died on May 24, 1974, just before Granz was scheduled to return to California to record a Basie trio album. Ellington was seated on a couch when he arrived for their last meeting, although he was too weak to talk for any length of time. Granz carried him back to his bed as their visit ended. Granz received one of the first early-morning calls from his sister, Ruth, confirming that he had died. Granz accompanied Ella Fitzgerald to the funeral in Manhattan, where she sang "Solitude" and "Just a Closer Walk with Thee" as part of a program that also included Earl Hines, Mary Lou Williams, Ray Nance, Hank Jones, Billy Taylor, and Pearl Bailey with Louie Bellson.

But even Ellington's death did not sever Granz's relationship to his legacy. Mercer Ellington and Stanley Dance met with Granz around this time to suggest that he take over the band's management so that Mercer could keep his father's band together. Granz declined their offer, believing that an effective manager for the band could operate only out of the United States and that he was unavailable too much of the time given that he was living in Europe. All three men did agree on the desirability of allowing Granz to issue on Pablo what Ellington had called "the stockpile," a cache of previously unreleased studio as well as concert recordings, mainly from 1969 to 1972, that Ellington had produced himself and that had stayed in the possession of the Ellington family. This material could now be added to live European recordings of the 1950s and '60s from Granz's own stash. In some instances, the albums, whose covers displayed Granz's own excellent photographs of Ellington, were released twenty years after the recordings had been made. Of special interest among *The Ellington Suites* was *The Queen's Suite,* inspired by Ellington's 1958 tour of Great Britain, when Queen Elizabeth had greeted him at a reception at Leeds Civic Hall as part of a festival of the arts. Ellington composed the six-part suite, paid for its recording out of pocket in April 1959, and had a single copy pressed and delivered to Buckingham Palace. He had refused all requests to release the music in his lifetime.

Granz later proposed to the Ellington family an idea he had unsuccessfully floated to Columbia Records president Goddard Lieberson about comprehensively recording the band's vast library in pared-down as opposed to big band or orchestral arrangements, both for documentation and for preservation. *The Intimate Ellington* and *Up in the Duke's Workshop,* both released on Pablo Records, are good examples of what Granz wished Columbia had done with Ellington. "I felt that the library wasn't in good enough shape for future bands, for posterity," Granz said. He recommended that the blind New York pianist and Ellington devotee Brooks Kerr prepare smaller-scale arrangements of the music. The deal fell through when the family proposed a more elaborate venture. Granz thought their alternative would drag out costs and time and thus defeat the whole purpose of undertaking a timely and economical survey of Ellington's work. "It was crazy," he said. "So I abandoned the project, and maybe again I should have pursued it. In any case . . ."[15]

The best single source of Granz's recollections, observations, and judgments on Ellington remains an August 1989 interview conducted by jazz historian Patricia Willard for the Smithsonian Institution's Duke Ellington Oral History Project. Even after two days of interviews, the normally articulate and incisive Granz doubted he had adequately expressed himself. "What he did in instilling respect for music—and I'm not talking about sacred music by the way—I mean the way when he walked onstage with his band and they played music for you, . . . one hoped that you would get joy out of it. I think you had to have enormous respect for the band, and respect for the dignity of the band was typified by Ellington . . . I think my liking for Duke was as a fan probably more than as a human being. In retrospect, I think I was maybe closer to the music than I was to Duke Ellington as a man."[16]

To say he was a diehard fan of Ellington's music did not preclude him from expressing privately, and later more publicly, unusually harsh views of Ellington and his later music. Just as Granz had given the Ellington biographer Derek Jewell an unusually frank account of the travails of the 1966 Ellington/Fitzgerald Côte d'Azur concerts, so he gave Jewell an unvarnished assessment of Ellington's later career. "Towards the end he did nothing musically and he was aware of that," Granz said before launching into a familiar complaint about how Ellington had "recycled" his hits too often. "It was a combination of sheer fatigue and the age of his sidemen. . . . The give and take of the early days was incredible, but later it became usual." He also attacked what he saw as inflation of the Ellington legend, such as stories that he kept a band together constantly so that he could hear his latest compositions the next day. "That kind of propaganda was in a way a crutch for Duke," he said. "He clung to the band like a crutch, just as old people cling together in marriage because they can't think of anything else to do."[17]

Jewell's own reactions to what Granz told him were mixed: "Such statements indicate that, as inevitably happens even with geniuses, someone somewhere will start a backlash once they are gone and (to be fair to Granz) once enthusiasm for their work has on occasions gone over the top. Granz has a point, even a useful antidote for hyperbole about Ellington, but it is exaggerated in terms of taste and sometimes in terms of fact."[18] Granz's comments in Jewell's 1977 book came four years after the publication of Ellington's autobiography, which contained

only brief and ambiguous sentiments about the two men's lengthy relationship, so perhaps Granz was retaliating in his own way. Ellington
complimented Granz for "never [taking] a percentage or a fee" and
expressed gratitude to Granz for representing him beginning with the
European tours of 1958; he noted how Granz had gotten Ellington a
$15,000 increase over the original offer he had received for his work
on the Sinatra film *Assault on a Queen* and said that the 1966 concerts
with Ella Fitzgerald at the Côte d'Azur had been "one of the highest
honors paid me." But his statement "The representation he [Granz]
gave me was great," was followed up by "It makes a difference when
the man who is doing the talking for you is a millionaire"—a comment
that could easily be interpreted as a subtle slap at Granz's financial success in promoting jazz.[19] Given Granz's hypersensitivity about anything
having to do with the financial aspects of his work, this statement might
well have rankled him.

Some years following Ellington's death, Granz was approached by
the British saxophonist and bandleader John Dankworth for a financial
contribution toward the building of a statue in his honor in New York.
"I refused," Granz said, "and the reason I gave was, 'If Duke were alive
then I would have contributed because Duke would have liked that. But
what the hell good does it do if Duke is dead? Why have this statue?
What does it benefit?'"[20]

One of the little-known aspects of the 1972 Santa Monica Center concert was a backstage meeting that resulted in the addition of a significant new artist to Granz's management portfolio. As the excitement
from the night's concert charged the atmosphere, Granz was introduced
to a guitarist friend of Stan Getz's who had attended the concert to hear
the tenor saxophonist. Although Granz had heard of Joe Pass, a bop-
inspired guitarist who had settled in Los Angeles to work as a studio
musician, recording artist, and club performer, he would not have recognized him.[21] As it turned out, Pass, then forty-three, was in the midst
of an engagement with Herb Ellis at the jazz club Donte's in North Hollywood. Granz and Peterson went the night after the concert and were
equally awed by Pass's command of his instrument and the precision
with which, as a solo guitarist, he used single notes to convey chords,
bass, and melody in ways that emulated saxophone solo lines and piano
accompaniment. Asked what struck him about Pass, Peterson said, "His
invention, it's his invention. The way he sat up and improvised, and it
just rolled out of him. But lyrically, Joe had such a sense of invention

with the ballads. Norm knew without saying anything what Joe stood for and who Joe was."[22]

No artist coming into Pablo Records rose further and faster than Joe Pass as Granz began managing his career and mixing him in among the giants of jazz on records and in live performance, as he had done with Peterson a generation earlier to such consummate effect. Yet Pass, whom Wes Montgomery once described as his favorite guitarist, traveled a circuitous route into the international spotlight, unlike the fairytale ascent of Oscar Peterson. Joseph Anthony Jacobi Passalaqua, born January 15, 1929, in New Brunswick, New Jersey, grew up in a working-class Italian neighborhood in Johnstown, Pennsylvania, where his father worked in one of the town's steel mills. His musical aspirations were awakened by the singing cowboy Gene Autry in the 1940 film *Ride, Tenderfoot, Ride,* and when he was nine his father gave him his first guitar so that his son would not have to earn a living under such grueling conditions. Pass moved to New York, getting gigs with various bands, including a three-week stint with the Ray McKinley Orchestra in 1949. He studied his heroes close up at the Royal Roost and Fifty-second Street and further refined his playing in after-hours sessions with seasoned and budding musicians. But soon he became addicted to heroin and spent the next dozen or so years in search of jobs and his next fix, drifting in and out of jails and in general surviving in "the cracks of society." Drifting through New Orleans, he lived in a dive with tenor saxophonist Brew Moore and writer/poet William S. Burroughs and "played bebop for strippers" whose only concern was tempo. In 1954 he was arrested in Las Vegas on charges of marijuana possession and sentenced to five years at a U.S. Public Service Hospital in Fort Worth, Texas, commonly known as a "narcotics farm," that July. He was released after serving three and a half years and returned to Las Vegas, where he played in show bands and small groups. A week before Christmas in 1960, Pass finally decided to kick his drug habit. He made his way from San Diego to Santa Monica, probably a step ahead of the police, and checked himself into Synanon, a rehabilitation facility known in the Los Angeles jazz community for its record in turning addicted musicians' lives around. He stayed there for three years and joined the institution's band. When Richard Bock, the owner of Pacific Jazz Records and a sponsor of Synanon, was persuaded to cut a record of the patients' music, he heard Pass and realized his enormous talents. *Sounds of Synanon,* featuring other patients as well but especially showcasing Pass, was produced while he was still in treatment.

Later, his weekend engagements at Shelly's Manne Hole in Los Angeles and his performances with Gerald Wilson's big band and under his own name would all be recorded for Pacific Jazz.

Thus it was natural that in 1973 Granz would have big plans for Pass. Whereas at Verve Granz had featured several guitarists such as Herb Ellis, Tal Farlow, and Barney Kessel (before Kessel went on to Lester Koenig's Contemporary Records in the mid-1950s), he tapped Pass to be *the* guitarist on Pablo. His first recording for Pablo came when Granz brought him into the studio unannounced on January 3 for the *Duke's Big Four* session. In a 1978 interview, Pass recalled the events that had uplifted his career in the hands of Norman Granz in the months after Granz first heard him at Donte's.

"I vaguely remember Norman saying, 'I'm going to start a record company and I'll record you.' I really didn't give it a thought. I had a lot of cats who said, 'You want to do a record?'" he said. "Six months passed or something. I just completely forgot it, and then the phone rang one day, and it was Norman. He said to come down to MGM Studios. 'I'm going to do a recording, at seven o'clock at night.' Actually, I was going to San Francisco to do a gig. I had to come back because it was a recording with Duke Ellington! I couldn't believe that. Hey, Duke Ellington? I had never heard him play with an electric guitar player in my life."[23] He passed the test with flying colors, as evidenced by the time Ellington gave him to stretch out. In mid-May, Pass made his first recording in the studio with Oscar Peterson, which marked the beginning of an immensely rich and occasionally contentious relationship over the next decade and a half.

Pass recorded his seminal album, *Virtuoso,* over three days in November at MGM Studios, socking away enough material for subsequent releases in the process. The title contained no hype; it simply stated the truth of Pass's overarching talents in the realm of solo guitar, much as Granz's marathon Tatum recordings had documented the pianist's better-known dominion over his instrument. Pass had developed his hypnotic technique over years of woodshedding and had as yet only teased his audiences with a couple of tunes that up to then had constituted his experimentation as a soloist. Granz challenged Pass to make that technique of solo playing his calling card. "It was Norman's idea to have me go out and play solo jazz guitar," Pass recalled, noting his own skepticism.

"Piano players do it. Segovia does it," Granz prodded.

"Segovia's a classical player," Pass countered.

"Yeah, but he plays a guitar, doesn't he? You play guitar, don't you?" said Granz, never one to take no for an answer or cater to resistance, especially when his instinct, which might have outdistanced an artist's concept of his own talent, proved correct. Pass recounted that "it was really hard in the beginning, no rhythm section to think about what to do."[24] (It is indicative of his international standing that these remarks were made during an interview in Hong Kong.) But *Virtuoso* went on to become one of the label's all-time top sellers, pleasing both Pass and his patron. *Down Beat* called Pass's solo album his passage to becoming "a consummate musicians' musician. . . . If one definition of genius is that it can make the impossible look easy, Pass certainly qualifies on this count alone."[25]

Ella Fitzgerald, who had recorded successful duets with pianists Ellis Larkins and Paul Smith as well as guitarist Barney Kessel, needed Granz's encouragement before working with Joe Pass. In August 1973 they recorded their first album, *Take Love Easy,* one month after their public debut at Carnegie Hall during a Newport Jazz Festival concert honoring Fitzgerald's fortieth year in show business. Pass arrived at the studio to find the singer, Granz, and a healthy stack of lead sheets. Fitzgerald, by then peering through a pair of thick glasses, breezed through the music until she found a song she wanted to record and hummed the tune until they settled on a key. "We did a whole album like that!" Pass said, recalling his awe of her casual command. "Without any rehearsing, just sifting through tunes . . . I could change keys with her, anything I wanted to do, she's there, she hears it, no problem."[26] The album convinced Fitzgerald that Pass would become a major part of her late career and led to a series of further recordings and appearances with him over the next seventeen years. Their recordings sparkle, not least because the format made judicious and emotive use of her steadily diminishing vocal resources and at the same time showed a pleasing maturity. "This is a record to be savored late at night, at subdued volume, for its dominant mood is relaxed and muted, suggesting a kind of intimate conversation between Fitzgerald and Pass that we are fortunate to overhear," noted one review. "The few solos he does take are intricate, but not flashy. A thoroughly disciplined musician, he never tries to upstage her."[27]

Oscar Peterson's recording renaissance at Pablo dates from late December 1972. He was then forty-seven years old and at the midpoint of his sixty-year career. His first studio session for the new label took the form of a retrospective, *History of an Artist,* reuniting Peterson with key members of his twenty-year career with Granz. Ed Thigpen, who had relocated to Denmark in 1972, was the sole holdout among major Peterson alumni that included guitarists Irving Ashby, Barney Kessel, and Herb Ellis; bassists Ray Brown, Sam Jones, George Mraz, and Niels-Henning Ørsted Pedersen; and drummers Bobby Durham and Louis Hayes. A second session on Valentine's Day 1973 finished out the first volume of the set; another volume was recorded later that year and completed the following year. This "history" not only surveyed the past but hinted at the future—most notably the growing importance to Peterson of Pass and Pedersen over the next decade and a half as well as his solo playing. The next album, *The Trio,* showed how seamlessly Pass had combined his own playing with the highly competitive dialogue of Peterson and Pedersen. It garnered a Grammy Award.

The robustness of the music on the album *Oscar Peterson in Russia,* featuring Pedersen and drummer Jake Hanna and complemented by a joyful reception by a supposedly jazz-naive audience in Tallinn, Estonia, produced yet another great Peterson album in the Pablo catalog. The pianist's first trip to the Soviet Union should have been a glorious occasion, judging from the Tallinn recordings. Peterson was invited to be the third in a series of prominent jazz artists under official sponsorship to visit the country, following Benny Goodman's State Department–sponsored tour in 1962 and Duke Ellington's enormously successful concert tour in 1971, also for the State Department.

The visit had been coordinated over a year of discussions between Granz, the Canadian Department of External Affairs, and Gosconcert, the official Soviet booking agency, which also handled transportation and hotel accommodations. The talks got caught up in the snarl of Soviet bureaucracy, complicated cold war politics, and Gosconcert's unwillingness to match concert fees that artists received in the United States and Western Europe. After suffering through many schedule changes, Granz and the musicians did not receive an itinerary for the trip until after they arrived, and even then it was incomplete. Dark clouds might have been gathering over the tour for other reasons as well. Two classical singers from the Ukraine, who had visited Canada in October and November, had been picketed by a large Canadian-Ukrainian crowd protesting Soviet domination of their homeland.

The tour called for four concerts in Moscow, eight in Tbilisi (the capital of Georgia) and Yerevan (the capital of Soviet Armenia), and three in Tallinn. All were sold out. One disappointment for Granz was that no concerts were scheduled in Leningrad (now St. Petersburg), the artistic capital of the Soviet Union. He and Peterson nonetheless flew into the city a couple of days before they were due in Tallinn so that they might see the Hermitage's Picasso collection, with which Granz was familiar. (Most of the best ones, he later said, were not on display at the time of their visit.) Granz complained to the driver over what he described as a broken-down bus that met them at the airport. "I told the Russians that if Herbert von Karajan or Leonard Bernstein were arriving, you wouldn't meet them like this. There was no point in my asking if this were racism because they wouldn't answer."[28] The next surprise came when they were told that they had to take a twelve-hour overnight train ride to Tallinn rather than the one-hour flight that was supposed to have been arranged. Yet the three nights of concerts went well, as did after-hours jam sessions with Russian musicians.

When they arrived in Moscow, however, they were held up for two hours because no one from the Ministry of Culture or the Gosconcert met the party of six, which included Grete Granz and Peterson's wife, Sandy. A representative from the Canadian Embassy finally arrived and located space at the Ural Hotel, a second-rate venue by Peterson and Granz's standards, especially compared to the promised Russiya, and a violation of the contract Granz had agreed to. "It was very bad news," Peterson later said. "They told us the Russiya was full. Someone told me that the Ural was the hotel where the farmers stayed when they brought their produce to market."[29] Granz and Peterson took their complaint to a Canadian Embassy attaché, saying that if they were not all moved to the Russiya Hotel they would cancel the tour. They became even more angry when they found, after moving to the Russiya, that some of their belongings had been pilfered. Grete Granz lost cosmetics, sweaters, and stockings. They were never sure whether the thefts were by government agents or the hotel staff.

The last straw during their brief stay in Moscow came when they were turned away from the hotel restaurant one night. As Granz and Peterson dined at a nearby canteen, they decided between them to scrap the tour before the Moscow concerts began. They broke the news the following morning to Canadian ambassador Robert A. D. Ford, who sympathized with them and said that Canada's hockey team had recently been treated shabbily as well. Ford believed the tour had run into problems because of incompetence and disorganization, "plus a distinct vein of racism" that he had seen before in Soviet attitudes toward African foreign exchange students.[30] The head of Gosconcert and an assistant deputy minister of culture came to the embassy to see if Ford might approach Peterson and Granz about changing their minds and going on with the tour. They apologized for "misunderstandings" and said they would not let such things happen again. "I told them I could not accept this," Granz wrote in a lengthy unpublished letter to the Polish jazz magazine *Jazz Forum*. "I had expected Peterson to be treated in Russia in the same way that any important Russian artist would be treated in the West."[31] Peterson would later accuse a KGB agent of jostling him in the elevator when he returned to the hotel to pack up. After this incident Ford asked Russian officials if they were blocking the Peterson party from leaving. He then sent them a contingent of his personal cars to get them safely aboard a flight for Helsinki and on to Copenhagen that evening.

In a report on the aborted tour, the Moscow correspondent for *Jazz Forum* parroted the Russian view behind Peterson's cancellation. "It was apparently felt that the world famous impresario Norman Granz was the person behind all Peterson's moves, and he played an unsavory role in building up a destorted [sic] image of Peterson locally," he wrote. "It was probably Granz's built-in arrogance (which incidentally impressed nobody here) and a lack of tolerance which did not allow him . . . to solve an uncomplicated accommodation problem in Moscow. Or rather, to help in solving the problem instead of canceling the tour."[32]

Granz and Peterson were invited to Ottawa by the Department of External Affairs about a month later for a briefing, since the repercussions from the incident had reached the highest levels of the Canadian government. The concerts, it seemed, had been caught up in the crossfire between factions in the Soviet government on issues of artistic freedom. "We were told that the tour was deliberately sabotaged by those who were hard on the idea of cultural *détente*," Granz said. "It seems that the soft group was successful in getting Peterson invited, but the opposing set was against it (which was purely an internal Russian political matter), and did their best to incur cancellation by harassment." Canadian officials admitted changing their minds about the trip's abrupt conclusion. "In retrospect," Granz said, "they were now pleased, because they felt it was time that people began taking a firm position with the Soviet Union."[33]

In 1971 Ella Fitzgerald had to abbreviate her European tour after a performance at the Nice Jazz Festival on July 21 in order to undergo treatment of a cataract in her right eye and a partial hemorrhage in her left. Granz had her checked into a hospital in Paris before accompanying her to the Massachusetts Eye and Ear Infirmary in Boston for treatment. Trouble cropped up again in 1972 in Verona, again after the Nice festival, when she began suffering from a leaking blood vessel in one eye. She returned to the Boston clinic and had a cataract from her left eye removed with laser surgery. Fitzgerald was initially fitted with contact lenses but found them too uncomfortable. She overcame her vanity about being seen in glasses in public, especially in concert, and was wearing them full time by year's end.

The last major phase of Fitzgerald's career, singing with symphony orchestras, began in 1973 when she sang engagements in Boston, Pittsburgh, Newark, Cincinnati, St. Louis, and Oklahoma City. The concert with the Boston Pops under the direction of Arthur Fiedler was seen on the orchestra's public television series, as was another appearance in 1976. The symphony arrangements commissioned by Granz allowed her to sing some of the material with strings and horns that she did not perform in nightclubs. By 1975, she had sung with more than forty symphony orchestras across the country. Sarah Vaughan's Grammy Award–winning 1982 collaboration with Michael Tilson-Thomas and the Los Angeles Philharmonic performing the music of the Gershwins provides a glimpse of what is missing from Fitzgerald's discography, for Granz never recorded her with a symphony.

Fitzgerald's achievements were further recognized when, in 1974, the University of Maryland announced its intention to name the new 1,200-seat concert hall on its Princess Anne campus the Ella Fitzgerald Center for the Performing Arts. It was one of the first major cultural facilities to be named for an African American artist. The honors that began piling up during this period suggested that she was succeeding in one of her most fervent desires of her later years—to remain a vital and creative artist who would not rest on her laurels or be satisfied with being venerated as a museum piece simply because she was still standing. As many have commented, the Pablo years document a steady diminution of her vocal powers, yet they preserve the spirit, joy, and musicianship that historically animated her performances. Any deterioration of her singing was measurable only against the standard of her own lofty achievements; unlike Billie Holiday, whose waning voice tracked a rapidly unraveling existence, Fitzgerald never ceased to dazzle and uplift audiences with her unbounded joyous musicality.

Despite her continuing renown, Fitzgerald was a woman of simple tastes, perpetually and sadly withdrawn and isolated when not in the public eye and enjoying few close relationships outside the profession. Among those with whom she maintained ties were Armstrong's widow, Lucille, and the vocalists Sarah Vaughan, Peggy Lee, and Carmen McRae, along with players in the Ellington and Basie bands she had gotten to know. One Friday night shortly before Granz founded Pablo Records, Oscar Peterson remembers stopping by her home when he had a free night in Los Angeles and she was in town. Peterson was her confidant as he was Basie's, whom he said suffered from a similar loneliness being away from home so much of the time. Fitzgerald, who was alone that night, answered the door. She invited him into the kitchen to join her for takeout Chinese food she had had delivered. "What a lonely, lonely existence," Peterson said. "Here's a woman that perhaps has the greatest voice in jazz at that time in the world. And here she is sitting by herself on a Friday night in this huge house, in this big kitchen with nothing else but four little cartons of Chinese food. That's a picture I will never forget." Peterson related the story to Granz, who said, "Well, unfortunately, that's her life. She's been unlucky so far in love. That's the way it is."[34]

These observations help to explain an exchange between Granz and John McDonough in the early 1980s concerning the possibility of a Fitzgerald autobiography. Granz had been urging her to sit down with a writer and wondered whether McDonough might take on the job. "I thought it about for a minute and I was certainly favorably disposed," McDonough said, recounting the story to Oscar Peterson years later. "And I said, 'A good autobiography has to be a story and it has to be told with a certain degree of insight. What kind of insight does Ella have into herself, into the people she worked with, into the times in which she lived, into the music she sang?' Granz leaned back in his chair and about as close a thing to a smile as I've ever seen began to cross his face and he said, 'Absolutely none.'"[35] That lack of introspection, second-guessing, or intellectualizing allowed Fitzgerald to pour her emotions directly into her music without ever becoming a caricature of herself, but on a personal level it left her an enigma to the last bar.

On a lighter note, Frank Tenot offers another story from the 1970s showing the contrast between the international First Lady of Song and the woman content to retreat and watch soap operas, snack on Kentucky Fried Chicken and pizza, or shop in her off hours. He tells of a night in Paris when he, Fitzgerald, and Granz ducked into one of the impresario's favorite restaurants in the City of Lights. The owner recommended fresh fish followed by a course of duck, then asked what they would like to drink. Granz requested a bottle of that season's Beaujolais. "No, no. I'll just have a Coca-Cola," Fitzgerald interjected.

"Ah, I'm sorry," the restaurateur said. "Zees is a French place. We have all kinds of wine. We have cognac. But we have no Coca-Cola."

"Oh, no matter. Pepsi Cola," she said.[36]

21

Takin' It on Out—for Good

In 1978 Tom Snyder, host of NBC TV's *Tomorrow Show*, provided Norman Granz a rare national audience for his thoughts concerning the state of jazz. He was joined on the broadcast by Oscar Peterson, Leonard Feather, and guitarist George Benson, then at the height of his popularity. In Peterson, Granz had a philosophical ally on the sanctity of jazz as a pure art form. Benson had realized a smash crossover success on Warner Bros. Records with *Breezin'* in 1976. The sole vocal track, Leon Russell's "This Masquerade," shot to number 10 on the pop singles charts and pushed the album to number 1. Feather, then writing for the *Los Angeles Times,* found himself mediating the forum on the popularization of jazz outside of clubs and small labels.

All agreed that there was a blurring of who was then considered a jazz musician. Peterson cited musicians such as Dave Grusin, Quincy Jones, and Lalo Schifrin, who had earned their reputations in jazz before translating their skills into more financially rewarding work in television, film, and popular music but were still labeled jazz artists.

Granz argued that unvarnished jazz could find an audience. "Whatever the form of the media is, people are afraid, afraid to do things that are honest or pure. Immediately, they want to hang onto the name 'jazz,' but they don't have the courage or the respect for the public that they might like something that is pure . . . Even if you listen to jazz stations, they are so afraid if they play pure jazz, good jazz constantly, that they modify, they compromise."[1] Granz pulled out an advertisement for the Kool Jazz Festival with Mercer Ellington, the Ojays, Ashford and Simpson, Johnny Taylor, the Voltage Brothers, and Gladys Knight. "Now Gladys Knight's a marvelous singer," he continued, "but she doesn't need to be called a jazz singer. Frankly she isn't. But here they go. They use the hook about a jazz festival, and apart from Mercer, there's nothing on it that approaches jazz. Why not call it a music festival? At some point in art, I think if you keep compromising, even if certain economic gains are made by all the participants, I think you destroy it, and that's what's so sad."

Benson, recalling his and others' experience in the jazz mainstream, said that only a few were well rewarded economically and even then they still had to endure grueling travel schedules to maintain their careers. Snyder asked Granz how he had guided Fitzgerald, Peterson, and others toward stardom in jazz without compromising their talent. "I have confidence in the talents of the people and ultimately that the public will accept it. None of the artists I record remotely approach millions of sales; you talk about a few thousand sales. But I don't think that you need to quantitatively measure success. I think you can do it qualitatively, and both the record company and the performer can be pleased and happy with that, especially if they're doing what they want to do." Granz added his wish that major labels would do more to subsidize jazz. "You give artists a hearing, just as a gallery might hang an artist for whom there's no chance to sell a picture," he continued. "Even from a tax point of view, the government would be paying half of it. The executives in the record industry don't have the courage and they certainly don't have the integrity or the honesty to back jazz . . . They won't sponsor, they won't subsidize good music."

Finally, Benson said jazz artists would benefit greatly from having an inside advocate at major labels overlooking how they could best serve jazz without making the bookkeepers too nervous. "I try to make the person who believed in me look good," said Benson to a round of laughter. Granz had the last word of the evening. "I question whether they would keep you if you didn't sell records."

Many longtime Granz favorites did not live long enough to see their recording careers extended by the advent of Pablo Records. The label earned a niche because of Granz's ability not only to select new material conforming to his catholic tastes in jazz, but also to draw on his treasure trove of unreleased recordings of jazz greats over the decades, many of whom were still recording for him. The greatest example was the re-release of his entire library of Art Tatum. Before starting Pablo, Granz purchased the Tatum recordings back from MGM for a reported $5,000; then in 1975 he released a thirteen-disc set entitled *Art Tatum Solo Masterpieces*. Granz was not alone in wanting to see the Tatum records back in circulation. The release generated a flurry of praise possibly even more appreciative than what he had received when he had originally recorded Tatum twenty years before. "There is nothing else like it: no other jazz musician has left behind him so full and so compact a self-portrait," wrote one critic for *Stereo Review*. The set was later inducted into the Grammy Hall of Fame.

Granz retrieved other vintage JATP tapes from the vaults along the way. When Oscar Peterson came across a previously unknown bootleg recording of one of the Nichigeki Theater concerts from November 1953 in Tokyo, Granz tracked down the source and released a three-record set of the event in 1977. Also issued for the first time were four records boiled down from fifty-four reels of tape from the 1967 JATP farewell tour. And JATP fans were treated to excerpts from a particularly exciting performance from Stockholm in 1955.

Granz was busy in the studio in 1976, recording multiple releases of most of his major artists. Ed Berger, associate director of the Institute of Jazz Studies and biographer of Benny Carter, describes two consecutive sessions in New York in November that illustrated Granz's flexible producing style. First the drummer Jo Jones came to the studio with no preparation and did not even have a list of songs he wanted to record. Granz grabbed the reins of the session, assembled the tunes, and parceled out the solos as they went along. Then the typically businesslike Carter arrived with everything in order; Granz sat back and read the *Wall Street Journal* as the master saxophonist and company cut the record without incident. "Is it all right that I have arrangements, Norman?" said Carter, poking fun at Granz for his predilection for unrehearsed recordings.[2]

Granz gradually worked to get up to the level of releasing around twenty-five albums a year. Among the more novel recording projects was the pairing of Oscar Peterson with five trumpeters for a series of "jousts." The first pairing, with Dizzy Gillespie in London in late November 1974, yielded the album *Oscar Peterson and Dizzy Gillespie*, which netted Gillespie his first-ever Grammy for best jazz performance by a soloist and was named Record of the Year in *Down Beat*'s international critics' poll. The series continued with Roy Eldridge, Harry Edison, and Clark Terry and concluded the following June with Gillespie protégé Jon Faddis.

Claude Nobs, the Montreux Jazz Festival director, gave Granz three nights of programming to convert part of the ninth annual event in 1975 into a runway for Pablo musicians. The Montreux Casino was equipped with television capabilities, so the proceedings were video-taped.[3] One image captured during the festival demonstrates life on the road with Granz at its best. Rather than another of the standard team photos on the airport tarmac, this photograph shows the entire casually dressed lineup lounging in lawn chairs in the gardens at the Montreux Palace, looking like visiting royalty. Another detail from the festival comes from a two-paragraph courtside summons Granz sent out. "The Montreux Casino has agreed to a take-all challenge tennis match between John Birks 'Dizzy' Gillespie and Norman Granz at 17.00 hours at the Montreux Palace Hotel tennis court. The winner gets 100 Swiss francs plus 75 percent of worldwide television, cinema and radio income and 25 percent to the loser. It will be a one-set match because of the advanced age of both players, especially Gillespie, who has to blow at the Festival tonight and doesn't want to blow his gig on the court."

In September of 1975, Frank Sinatra, Ella Fitzgerald, and Count Basie played for two weeks at New York's Uris Theater, reuniting the dream bill they had introduced the year before at Caesar's Palace in Las Vegas. The show grossed over $1 million, a Broadway record, during its brief engagement. However, behind-the-scenes maneuvering by Sinatra led Granz to privately communicate a deep-seated animosity toward the singer that may explain why Sinatra had failed to purchase Verve fifteen years earlier. The *New York Times* critic John S. Wilson had just reviewed the show, deploring, in the last paragraph, how little the Basie band had played and saying that its brief part of the show—three numbers before becoming part of the background—"was no way to treat Mr. Basie and his fans" and "bordered on the criminal."[4] Granz responded in a remarkably acidic and candid letter to letter to Wilson, written on September 12, 1975, two days after the review:

Dear John,

Bravo for your comments on Basie at the Uris.

Let me tell you a little bit more about Sinatra's arrogance. Last year, the same show with Ella and Basie appeared at Caesar's Palace with Sinatra. Basie was given six minutes! On opening night Basie, in his anxiety not to run overtime, played one number. The audience then had the pleasure of a ten-minute comic, and a twenty-eight minute Ella, and a one-and-a-half-hour Sinatra doing his mélange of songs, local jokes and, to no one's surprise, racist jokes. I said to no one's surprise because, a year ago when he opened at the Sands, his opening line was, "I'm happy to be back in Las Vegas; the dressing room they gave me was Lena Horne's, who appeared here before me and, man, you couldn't get in for all the watermelon rinds."

This arrogance carries into his allotment of time to artists whose asses he couldn't wipe today. At the opening rehearsal, I asked Frank Sinatra how much time Ella would have, and he replied that Basie would get fourteen minutes, Ella forty-five minutes and himself forty-five minutes. I protested to Basie, because you know Basie doesn't make any waves with someone like Sinatra. You heard only three numbers because Basie was fearful of exceeding his time limit. Incidentally, here is an example of his contempt for an artist. He told Ella not to close with "'Tain't Nobody's Business" and instead had her do "Caravan." Unfortunately, this was the third night and I was in California, so I could do nothing about it. And Ella, like Basie, was afraid to argue the point. You see, originally Sinatra wanted "Caravan" as a closer, but I changed it to "'Tain't Nobody's Business"; then he reversed it.

I thought you might like some of the insights as to what really goes on backstage. I think it was a gross insult to Basie that he wasn't given a decent time in which to play.

Sincerely yours,
Norman Granz[5]

(This was not the only time that Sinatra's occasionally inexcusable racial remarks or attempts at humor obscured his justifiable reputation for using his muscle to open up Las Vegas for African American performers. James Gavin, in his excellent 2008 biography of Lena Horne, traces a long-standing animosity Sinatra felt toward her that stemmed from her friendship with Ava Gardner during the Sinatras' tempestuous marriage in the early 1950s.)[6]

Ultimately at stake was whether Fitzgerald and Sinatra would ever blend voices in a recording of popular music's two finest talents. Clips of television appearances with them plus some rare recordings of the two backed by Oscar Peterson show the pair's natural compatibility. However, there were hints as far back as the early 1960s that this would never happen if Granz had his way. The late Nelson Riddle biographer Peter Levinson tells how once, when he was in the studio during the recording of *Ella Swings Lightly with Nelson* in March 1962, Mo Ostin, Granz's former business manager at Verve who went on to become president of Sinatra's Reprise label, arrived and Granz greeted him by saying, "Ella's singing so badly tonight, she's about ready to record with Sinatra."[7] Levinson wrote that plans for recording the two had been in the works, apparently without Granz's knowledge, at Western Recorders in Los Angeles for November 1967. Fitzgerald, Sinatra, and Riddle had just wrapped up three days of rehearsals with great anticipation and the project seemed headed for a historic consummation when Granz returned to Los Angeles and shut it down.

Granz was vehement but elusive in denying published reports of stormy scenes with Sinatra. One had supposedly occurred during the taping of *The Frank Sinatra Show* in 1958 or, by another account, in the following year during the taping of *An Afternoon with Friends,* both guest-starring Ella Fitzgerald, after Granz started suggesting songs the two might sing together; it had culminated in Granz's being thrown out of the television studio. The story, printed in the British first edition of Stuart Nicholson's 1993 *Ella Fitzgerald,* had circulated via the late Lou Levy, Fitzgerald's pianist from 1957 until 1962. Levy recalled, "Frank and Norman didn't see eye to eye. Norman would always want to be on top, and no one is on top of Frank Sinatra. Oh yeah! That's Caesar, you don't mess with him!"[8] Granz said he had never had the type of blowout with Sinatra that Levy had described, calling the incident "an event that never happened."[9]

Simply put, Sinatra's fame trumped Granz's power in a contest of wills between these two titans. Granz kept foiling future opportunities for Fitzgerald and Sinatra to appear together by demanding excessive fees. Once Sinatra contacted her directly about performing at a benefit, telling her that Granz had asked $75,000 for her participation. This time, Fitzgerald overrode her manager and accepted the invitation. She and Granz reportedly did not speak for weeks after the incident.

Sarah Vaughan's first recording for Pablo, the 1978 *How Long Has This Been Going On,* is the textbook illustration of the power of Granz's label on an artist's career. For *Village Voice* critic Gary Giddins, the album teaming her with Oscar Peterson, Joe Pass, Ray Brown, and Louie Bellson merited full-column treatment. The recording was cause for celebration as one of her finest albums. It got her back into a more purely jazz groove, even though Giddins noted that a couple of the rougher performances could have been remedied if there had been more than a one-day production schedule. "It will be interesting to see if she continues to work for Norman Granz, because if he parades the entire Pablo stock company through her sessions (including, one hopes, a set of Benny Carter arrangements), he will be mining the most valuable lode since Ella Fitzgerald discovered song books."[10]

Of particular interest was Granz's suggestion that she do a duet with each of the quartet members: "More Than You Know" with Peterson, "My Old Flame" with Pass, "Body and Soul" with Brown, and "When Your Lover Has Gone" with Bellson. "Just the idea that Norman had on that date [Vaughan recording with individual soloists], I use as a teaching tool in seminars," Peterson has said. "Now, who would think of recording Sarah Vaughan singing with just drums?"[11] Granz remembered Vaughan, an accomplished pianist herself, irritating Peterson when she went so far as to suggest the chords she wanted played behind her. Granz remembered, "Oscar said to me, 'If she touches that keyboard again, I'm walking out.'"[12]

Though he generally ignored the younger generation, Granz occasionally relented. Such was the case when he hastily put together a session for trumpeter Freddie Hubbard, whose playing he respected and to whom he offered a chance to repair his reputation after a series of poorly conceived jazz-pop recordings from the 1970s. Hubbard and Granz encountered each other at a festival in England when Hubbard said how much he had always wanted to record with Oscar Peterson "to get back to playing some real jazz and not this shit I'm into now."[13] Granz was quick to act when the opportunity presented itself a year or so later, in March 1980. Clark Terry was in town for a recording for Granz, while Peterson was there on personal business. Ray Brown, Joe Pass, and Hubbard all lived in Los Angeles and responded quickly to Granz's call. He turned up the heat on Hubbard when he prevailed upon a reluctant Dizzy Gillespie to fly in from New York. "When I told Diz who was on the date, he said, 'I'll be there,'" Granz recalled. By letting Hubbard call the tunes, Granz challenged Gillespie, Terry, and Peterson as well. Peterson for his part restrained himself to maintaining the rhythm to keep the fire lit under the trumpeters. "Norman was after everybody that day," he said. "Freddie had a tune and so forth and Norman had to send across the street for some manuscript paper, so that he could sketch it out for us. It is amazing that Norman could foresee that we were all going to hunker down and really get into this thing because it had been sprung on us. It was a wonderful date."[14]

The bond between tenor saxophonist Zoot Sims and pianist Jimmy Rowles provides a representative example of Granz's flexibility in accommodating an artist's preferences. Beginning in 1977 and continuing over the next six years the two musicians collaborated on several excellent albums for Pablo. "Jimmy Rowles knows so many old tunes that when I play them people think they're new," Sims said of his musical cohort the day after they completed *Suddenly It's Spring,* their final album together. Granz was disappointed by their albums' low sales, which failed to match the high quality of the music, but this did not prevent him from continuing the series as long as the two men wanted to record together. "Zoot and I sat down one time," Granz noted, "and I said, 'You know, you've done eight or nine albums with Jimmy. Maybe it would be a good idea to try another piano player, Zoot?' I didn't say, 'I'm going to give you this or that piano player.'"[15]

The 1980s marked the inevitable slowdown of Granz's activities as he headed toward final retirement. The fortunes of Pablo can be roughly charted by two measures: the honors his recordings received and the dwindling number he produced. While the significance of the Grammys may be debated, Pablo artists, and by inference Granz's vision, were recognized with a total of eighteen awards. Pablo artists divided the best jazz instrumental solo performance category among themselves for five years running, from 1975 until 1979, with three awards going to Oscar Peterson for *The Giants* (1977), *Montreux '77: Oscar Peterson Jam* (1978), and *Jousts* (outtakes from the Peterson/trumpet duets, 1979); one to Count Basie for *Basie and Zoot* (1976); and one to Dizzy Gillespie for *Oscar Peterson and Dizzy Gillespie* (1975). Peterson received another award for best small-group jazz instrumental performance for *The Trio* (1973), while Basie was honored for *Prime Time* (1977), *On the Road* (1980), *Warm Breeze* (1982), and *88 Basie Street* (1984). The Recording Academy smiled upon Ella Fitzgerald a total of six times during the Pablo years for *Fitzgerald and Pass . . . Again* (1976), *Fine and Mellow* (1979), *A Perfect Match* (with Basie at Montreux 1979, '80), *Digital III at Montreux* (1981), *The Best Is Yet to Come* (1983), and her final release, *All That Jazz* (1990). *The Ellington Suites* received an award for big bands in 1976, while John Coltrane also received a posthumous award for best jazz instrumental performance in *Bye, Bye Blackbird* (1980). In addition, Granz was named jazz producer of the year in 1977 and 1978 by the *Down Beat* International Critics' Poll and stayed close to the top until the mid-1980s, while Pablo was recognized as the top jazz label by the magazine in 1976 and 1977. The numbers of records produced show a reduction attributable to any number of causes, from failing to tend to business to attrition among the label's older artists that accelerated in the 1980s—losses that were rarely compensated by ventures to groom or promote young artists who embraced mainstream jazz traditions.

From 1973 through 1979, Granz released around 128 live and studio recordings, including sixteen in 1979 alone from his last Montreux series, and between 1980 and 1986 he produced around seventy-six albums. But the years 1984 and 1985 yielded only five albums each and the year 1986 yielded two. In 1986 he sold Pablo.

In October 1983, Jazz at the Philharmonic returned to Tokyo, appearing at the city's Yoyogi National Stadium. Granz had been approached the year before by one of the country's most prominent music publishers, Shin Watanabe (who had been a young bassist when JATP first came to Japan), about returning for two concerts to commemorate the thirtieth anniversary. Fitzgerald, Peterson, and other artists associated with Granz had played Japan many times over the years, but Watanabe's invitation was the first time JATP as a unit had been back to perform. Completing the lineup were Joe Pass, Harry Edison, Clark Terry, Zoot Sims, Eddie "Lockjaw" Davis, Louie Bellson, and J. J. Johnson to re-create the spirit of the original tour. "It was with great sadness that I was reminded that Charlie Shavers, Ben Webster, Bill Harris, Gene Krupa and Willie Smith were all dead, and added to that Roy Eldridge was retired," Granz later wrote. It is too much to say that JATP was now an anachronism in a country that was by then a regular stop for American jazz stars. The country had long since begun producing its own jazz musicians and had become a major consumer and producer of jazz records. The differences were telling. "In October 1983 we arrived in Japan, but unlike the tumultuous reception in 1953, we were greeted by two soberly dressed representatives of our impresario, and no one else paid us a second glance," Granz said. "It was an interesting, ironic contrast. Japan now has so many touring jazz artists that JATP to the young fans has no particular significance."[16]

The Japanese concerts were the last under the JATP banner, completing the arc that had begun on July 2, 1944, at the Philharmonic Auditorium nearly forty years before. The dates cover Granz's journey from his beginnings as a struggling college student with an insatiable love for jazz to the end of his career as a jaded if triumphant impresario and record producer.

Another sad milestone occurred shortly thereafter when Count Basie and the orchestra went into the recording studio in December 1983, a few months after Catherine, his wife of forty-one years, died in April. He took only a week off from the road. There is little to distinguish the resulting album *Fancy Pants* apart from its being Basie's final recording before he died of cancer on April 26, 1984 in a Hollywood, Florida, hospital at age seventy-nine. Basie's health had begun to fail with a heart attack in 1976, and pianist Nat Pierce had led the band with occasional guest conductors such as Clark Terry taking up the slack during Basie's six-month recuperation at his home in the Bahamas. Over the ensuing years when the bandleader had difficulty walking, Basie arrived onstage piloting a motorized wheelchair, which in the words of one obituary, "he sometimes drove with joyful abandon."[17]

Granz was not present at the overflow funeral service for Basie held at the Abyssinian Baptist Church in Harlem. He was nonetheless cited by Basie's adopted son Aaron Woodward for special recognition alongside Quincy Jones, Benny Carter, Joe Williams, and trombonist Grover Mitchell as one of those "who made a difference in the life of William James Basie."[18] Nat Hentoff, writing in the *Wall Street Journal* in praise of Basie's *Kansas City 7* album for Pablo, expressed what he thought had made the Basie-Granz chemistry so vital in the final quarter of Basie's professional life. "From 1972 until his death last year, Count Basie recorded only for Pablo," Hentoff wrote. "In part because he knew that Mr. Granz would never try to make him record anything he didn't want to. And Mr. Granz would let Basie record just about anything he did want to because he loved his music so. Another reason was that no other label would have issued so much Basie during the past decade. Basie was not a big seller, but Mr. Granz knew that there would be listeners in generations to come who will never have enough of Basie. Mr. Granz records for the future, as well as anyone in the present who values a perfect jazz recording."[19]

"The reality of not being able to record Basie again after the countless albums that I've produced with him over 40 years (between the early fifties and his death) is numbing," Granz wrote in the liner notes to *Fancy Pants*. "It is difficult for me to accept that never again will I be able to work with this great and lovable man and to have the joy of listening to him play. With all respect to his big band (which with Duke Ellington's were far and away the two greatest bands in the history of jazz), it is in the small groups that one can hear what a great pianist Bill Basie was. One of the running mock-serious arguments during his big band sessions was my insistence that he take more solo space for himself, all of which he would immediately agree, and then slyly not play the additional choruses I wanted, knowing that if we made a master take he would not have to play as much as he promised. But all of that was part of the fun of recording him. . . . But the happiness of talking to him at least once a week no matter where he was, telling each other bad jokes, the latest gossip about other musicians, discussing new releases with him, is gone."[20]

Granz's feelings about his departed friend again became evident when he attended a sale of personal effects of Count and Catherine Basie held December 4, 1984, at New York's William Doyle Galleries. Granz had one competitor for an 18-carat yellow-gold Patek Philippe watch with the inscription "To the Count from Norman" engraved on the back, his gift to Basie sometime in the 1950s. Granz kept raising the bid to keep the watch from leaving his extended professional family, not knowing that his competitor was the film producer Jean Bach, with whom he had been friends since the 1940s. Granz finally outbid Bach at $1,600 and quickly gave the watch to Oscar Peterson. He also purchased a gold identification bracelet given Basie by Ella Fitzgerald and returned it to her.

Granz undertook a delicate mission involving Fitzgerald beginning in the early 1980s. He could not help but shudder when he read the unsparing reviews of two Fitzgerald concerts in 1982 and 1983 by New York Times critics John S. Wilson and Stephen Holden, for they fell in line with his own feelings about the uneven and increasingly ragged quality of her performances. For Wilson, Fitzgerald had sounded "shrill" in her 1982 Kool Jazz Festival appearance with the Basie Orchestra as she tried to hold her own in front of the band's wall of sound. Similarly, Holden wrote of her trio set during a November 1983 Pablo tour that, "not so long ago, the singer could have handled the rapid key changes, dizzying leaps and difficult melismas with aplomb. But while she scored many small victories, her singing was fraught with a continuous sense of struggle. If Miss Fitzgerald's best musical instincts were intact, missing—sometimes painfully so—were the physical resources to carry them out."[21]

Granz's quiet campaign to encourage her to retire challenges critics who believed that this "Svengali" overworked Fitzgerald past her prime. He pursued his aim out of an overriding concern for her health, but also from his knowledge that Fitzgerald had long since passed the point of being financially secure for life. Publicist Virginia Wicks, visiting Granz at his Beverly Hills office around 1981 or 1982, listened as he vented his frustrations. "I have told Ella, 'You don't need the money! You don't need the money!'"[22] Fitzgerald was still traveling six months out of the year, and all of Granz's reasons for wanting her to slow down flew in the face of her unquenchable need to perform and record as long

as she could. Duke Ellington's comment when asked about quitting—
"Retire to what?"—applied equally in Fitzgerald's case, given her rest-
lessness and aimlessness when she was not working. Wicks believed as
well that Granz might have been acting on a belief, however unfounded,
that she should not endanger her standing by remaining in the spotlight
too long. Granz, whatever he thought privately, told Leonard Feather
in a 1983 interview, "She just loves to sing, and nobody's going to stop
her."[23] That included Norman Granz.

Fitzgerald sailed seemingly undeterred through a series of health
problems throughout the 1980s as she entered her sixth decade as a
singer. According to Jimmy Rowles, during the two years he led her trio
beginning in 1980 it was obvious that, no matter how effortless her consistently excellent performances appeared to audiences, the toll was palpable. "She was losing weight and she was getting a little tired," he said.
"Then she'd come back and do four or five encores."[24] Rowles folded
long before Fitzgerald as a result of a touring schedule that once included
a one-nighter from New York to Caracas, Venezuela, and the prospect
of twenty-five one-nighters through Scandinavia. In 1985, Fitzgerald
entered George Washington University Hospital in Washington after
complaining of shortness of breath resulting from fluid in the lungs. She
was hospitalized again in July 1986, this time in Niagara Falls, for what
turned out to be congestive heart failure, giving rise to rumors that she
had suffered a heart attack. Fitzgerald underwent open-heart surgery
two months later at Cedars-Sinai Medical Center in Los Angeles and
took nine months off before resurfacing in concert at a nearby college.
One striking result of the surgery was that for the first time in her life
Ella Fitzgerald was a thin woman, although her voice was virtually unaf-
fected. She was barely back in the saddle before being hospitalized again
to remove a toe as a result of diabetes that would eventually cause the
amputation of both legs below the knee in 1993.

Fitzgerald had two genuine and improbable hits during the 1980s.
The first resulted from a series of commercials, beginning in 1981,
for Memorex tape that featured the famous tagline, "Is it Ella or is it
Memorex?" and showed her shattering a glass with the purity of her
high notes. The ads netted her six figures annually over the life of the
spots and yielded new fans beyond her normal jazz constituency. *Ella
in Rome: The Birthday Concert*, recorded during a 1958 JATP tour,
was salvaged from unmarked tape boxes deep within the Verve Records
vault by jazz historian and record producer Phil Schaap and was issued

in the spring of 1988. The album stayed at number 1 on *Billboard*'s jazz charts throughout the summer, generating favorable publicity that delighted the singer. Granz was not as pleased. "Now I don't know why exactly," Schaap said. "She got her money according to the contract . . . and . . . in the process she got a nice bonus because it went to No. 1. Maybe because it didn't say, 'Produced by Norman Granz.'"

The sale of Pablo to Fantasy Records for just over $2.6 million, completed December 19, 1986, and announced two months later, resulted from a chance meeting Granz had with his onetime protégé Saul Zaentz, Fantasy chairman and film producer, at the Chez l'Amis Louis restaurant in Paris. According to Fantasy president Ralph Kaffel, Zaentz leaned over to Granz and said, "When are you going to sell me your label?" Negotiations proceeded from there. Kaffel confirms Granz's distaste for the distribution and sales ends of the record business, which had changed radically between the Verve and Pablo years, as his major reason for retiring. At the time he started Pablo his decision to run a record company from Switzerland would have been more feasible if he had had a strong second in command like Mo Ostin from the Verve days to tend to the ongoing details and finances Granz so abhorred. Granz also hated dealing with distributors who increasingly had no feeling for the music. As Kaffel pointed out, "Norman used to ask distributors, 'Do you know what's on this album? Have you listened to this? You know, why are you returning this?' He got tired of returns. He got tired of people not paying." Granz was in his element with the creative side of producing recordings and concerts, dealing with musicians, discovering talent, and, within reason, funding anything he found worthy.

The Pablo sale covered approximately 350 albums, which included all the released and unreleased material that had been recorded for the label, as well as hundreds of reels of unreleased concerts and other studio recordings going back to the 1940s not covered in the Verve deal. The latter material has been coming out much more slowly through the years because, while Granz owned the tapes, he did not own the contractual rights for their release. This stipulation meant that Fantasy Records performed a lot of legwork in tracking down sources to provide advances or fees to living artists or their estates or to obtain waivers from record companies with exclusive artist rights before any of these recordings could be issued. Overcoming these hurdles has resulted in a steady stream in recent years of "new" recordings, such as Muddy

Waters in Paris in 1972, JATP at Carnegie Hall in 1949 with previously unheard Charlie Parker and a 1952 concert in Berlin, a Shelly Manne European JATP tour from 1960, and George Shearing and Cannonball Adderley recordings from the 1957 Newport Jazz Festival series.

It was around the time of the sale of Pablo that Granz ceased to manage both Oscar Peterson and Joe Pass and, by telephone from Switzerland, began helping longtime assistant Mary Jane Outwater in managing Ella Fitzgerald for the dwindling number of dates she was performing as the decade came to a close. In March 1989, Granz and Fitzgerald returned to the studio for their final release, *All That Jazz,* in which she was backed up by old friends: Harry Edison and Clark Terry on trumpet; pianist Kenny Barron; Benny Carter, who had first commended her to Chick Webb and whose song gave the album its name; Ray Brown on bass; and her longtime drummer Bobby Durham. For a woman who had sung just about everything worth recording in the standard repertoire, she even tipped her hat to Jimmy Rowles by recording his song "Baby, Don't Quit Now." The album won Fitzgerald her final Grammy, although it was clearly awarded more as a last hurrah for her incomparable career than on the merits of the album itself.

Another especially painful indication that the Granz era had reached its twilight occurred roughly three weeks before the recording of *All That Jazz* when Roy Eldridge died in New York on February 26, 1989, at the age of seventy-eight. Eldridge had been in virtual retirement for the better part of the 1980s following a heart attack that forever silenced his trumpet. Known as "Little Jazz," he was the only jazz giant whose sobriquet was directly tied to the music. Eldridge was always good for spirited singing in his distinctive raspy voice, and occasionally some drum playing, but it taxed physical resources that he carefully shepherded following his illness.

Eldridge touched many lives and many touched his in the days immediately leading up to his death. On January 24, he and Viola, his wife of fifty-three years, celebrated their anniversary. Five days later, Phil Schaap hosted a birthday celebration at Saint Peter's Church, New York's celebrated jazz church, which Viola was able to attend despite her own lengthy illness. She was dead two days later. Eldridge's depression and refusal to eat shortly thereafter landed him in the hospital.

Many who loved Roy Eldridge eulogized him at Saint Peter's on March 1, but not the man who had paid for the funeral. Throughout the years Norman Granz had slipped money to Viola unbeknownst to

Roy and had provided Eldridge with large amounts of work since the late 1940s. On the day of the service he came in late and unannounced and merely stood in silence at the rear of the packed sanctuary.

Pam Allen had seen a range of Granz's moods and circumstances in the course of a ten-year up-and-down relationship since she had first gone to work for Pablo Records in 1977. Toward the end she felt somewhat let down that Granz was so willing to sell Pablo to Fantasy, given that he had been unrelenting in keeping his type of music out there.

"Kind, definitely strong, and a little intimidating," was how Allen described Granz when she first interviewed with him in her late twenties. Granz hired Allen, who had not been raised on jazz; as he told her, her "palate wasn't developed enough." She assisted him with contracts, dealing with artists, scheduling studio time, and getting product to distributors.

Allen normally started work around seven in the morning. She quickly noticed that Granz preferred to be the first in the office before it became something of a contest. The usual routine meant working through the morning, after which Granz might regale her with favorite stories. Then Granz took his a three-hour break to play a set at the Beverly Hills Tennis Club and grab a bite to eat. He might return with gourmet ice cream and get on with the rest of the day. Once, Allen said, Sean Connery called to arrange a game of tennis with Granz at a different club. Beforehand Connery, in a move reminiscent of a scene from *Goldfinger,* had spied on Granz's practice game through a telescope. (Granz learned of Connery's espionage through a spy of his own.) Agent 007's license to kill did not extend to the tennis court when he played Granz.

Granz educated Allen on world affairs by taking her to politically infused message movies and steadily giving her books he wanted her to read. "It was the first time I had heard the word *apartheid,*" she recalled in 2003. "We did not always think the same." At one point, he recounted going on the lam in Mexico in 1956 to avoid being subpoenaed before hearings of the House on Un-American Activities Committee in Los Angeles. He startled her when he confessed that for him being a communist was not a thing of the past. "I was shocked. I thought, 'Oh my Lord, I've never worked for a communist before.' I don't know that he held all those same beliefs down the line, but he could tell I was surprised." Granz, who sometimes opened up about his youth, indicated that growing up poor had not only nurtured his communist sympathies but also led him to grapple with African Americans' plight.

Allen noted that Granz's compassion could be abstract in contrast to the blunt manner he frequently brought to his dealings with individuals. She saw this side of him once when she was working late one night and an intruder almost trapped her inside her office before she escaped down the back stairs. Granz walked in as Allen was being interviewed by the police but angrily left at the point she said the man was black. "That offended Norman deeply," she said. "This is the best way I can sum up Norman, and this is a man I loved and also disliked sometimes. I always felt he was very concerned about the great 'out there'—'out there'—that he did not have to deal with. I'm not saying he wasn't kind to me or failed to show a caring side, but it was all those nameless people 'out there' that his heart went out to."

Over time their relationship cooled, said Allen, who since working for Granz has worked in administration at Central Casting in Burbank for almost twenty years. "With Norman, you're on a pedestal or better be under his heel, and he would grind you down. It didn't bother him that people might be upset with him. I loved the Norman that I started out with—the person he was, the vibrancy, a master in teaching, the storyteller. Norman opened my eyes to so many things, so many things that mattered. He was the best teacher I had and the hardest person I ever worked for. But anyone who knew him had an explanation due. There was hurt, but there was hurt for Norman.

"He was bigger than life . . . and when he made it he didn't necessarily want others looking. Norman was a great man. And he loved the music."[25]

Granz's final recording was done as a favor for his friend Frank Tenot. It completed a half century of recording that began on July 15, 1942, when he recorded Lester Young, Nat Cole, and Red Callender on glass in the backroom of Music City and ended with one of his few experiences in a digital recording studio, although some later Montreux concerts were captured digitally. Granz might as well have walked into the Starship *Enterprise,* the technique and ethic of recording were now so alien to him. The album, *Frank Tenot Presents,* featured trumpeter Snooky Young, saxophonist Curtis Peagler, pianist Mike Wofford, drummer Bobby Durham, and bassist Keter Betts. "I understand the value of computers, but I don't understand computerized engineering," Granz said. "I hadn't been in the studio for a couple of years, and there was a young guy there. He never had the slightest idea about the musicians I brought in, not the slightest, and I don't think he had the slightest interest. Where I used to stand over the engineer and say, 'Listen,

I want more bass at that point, and then I'd like a little less drums at that point,' well, I was talking about horse-and-buggy to him. He said, 'Well, don't worry about it. It's all in the computer.' I knew that it would be mixed the way he thought it should be, and I don't blame him for that. He was telling me that a couple of weeks before he had done Michael Jackson. So under the circumstances I guess I had a 'good' engineer. But I didn't know what to do with him. You can't talk to a computer."[26]

22

"Somewhere There's Music"

The rehearsal for the gala benefit performance at Avery Fisher Hall honoring Ella Fitzgerald on Monday, February 12, 1990, brought together for the last time the largest gathering of Jazz at the Philharmonic alums and other musicians associated with Norman Granz. Benny Carter wrote arrangements and conducted for the all-star orchestra gathered for the Hearts for Ella concert, featuring Stan Getz, Dizzy Gillespie, Hank Jones, Ray Brown, Herb Ellis, Louie Bellson, Clark Terry, Joe Williams, James Moody, and Tommy Flanagan. The evening, hosted by Lena Horne and Itzhak Perlman, also included appearances by Quincy Jones, George Shearing, Bobby McFerrin, Manhattan Transfer, and Cab Calloway.

Oscar Peterson, arthritic and seriously overweight three years before he was felled by a major stroke, lumbered up the stairs to a second-floor rehearsal suite to prepare for duets he performed hours later with Perlman and McFerrin. He had initially resigned himself to missing the Fitzgerald tribute and relented only once he was assured that Norman Granz was *not* going to be there. The two men had had a serious quarrel, and only last-minute persuasion by Ray Brown convinced Peterson that the coast was clear. Peterson and his wife, Kelly, flew from Toronto in time for the occasion.

"Peterson's relationship with Granz had never been as free of friction as outsiders perceived, and it is probable that a period of tension preceded their schism," the pianist's biographer Gene Lees wrote of their estrangement.[1] The two men had not spoken since Granz had delivered an inexplicable tirade to Peterson's assistant and vice president of his recording company Regal Recordings. He had called her shortly before the tribute asking where Peterson was; piqued that she was unable to locate him, he browbeat her mercilessly, hung up, and then almost immediately called back and picked up where he left off. She was in tears when she related the story to Peterson, who was furious. The two men argued heatedly, and when Granz said, "Maybe we ought to end it, right here," Peterson agreed.[2]

Long months passed before they warily undertook their reconciliation, according to Peterson. "Norman wrote me a little note after [Hearts for Ella], which I interpreted as being a door opener to the love and friendship that we had, saying, 'When are you going to lose some weight? People saw you and said you played your can off, but that you were heavier than they'd ever seen you. Are you trying to kill yourself?'" Peterson recalled almost ten years later. He did not respond and shortly thereafter received a call from Grete Granz acting as a go-between. She said Granz was going to be in New York on business and wondered whether they could meet over lunch. "Of course, I agreed," he said. "We had a very emotional reinstatement of our friendship."[3]

Granz's and others' concerns for Peterson's health were not misplaced. A stroke that permanently disabled his left hand caught up with him in the midst of a performance at the Blue Note in New York in May 1993. The ensuing months saw Peterson undergoing physical therapy to regain his strength and left him questioning the driving ambition that had left him a virtual stranger to his family over four marriages. Fifteen months after his stroke, the pianist filled the 3,500-seat venue at the Ravinia Festival near Chicago, with thousands more spilling out onto the lawn. The Peterson magic, as pure a rendition of the music as when he had begun and a continuing draw to jazz fans, remained intact. "I can think of more than a dozen jazz artists who could have done that 30 years ago," wrote John McDonough. "Today, I can think of only one."[4]

Within a month of Peterson's stroke, Ella Fitzgerald entered Cedars-Sinai Hospital for the first of two operations to amputate her legs below the knee on account of diabetes. The immediate years leading up to the disabling surgery had been interrupted by continuing honors and canceled dates due to her deteriorating condition. The amputations put her performing days irrevocably in the past, although possibly because of overmedication she was sometimes disoriented and delusional as well. Her friend the attorney Jim Blackman, who had sporadically managed her on the road around the time of Pete Cavello's death in 1990, heard from one of her nieces that she sometimes woke up in the middle of the night thinking she still had engagements to keep. "They would tell her it wasn't until the following week, and that would usually calm her down," Blackman said. Her beloved bassist Keter Betts flew out to spend part of a day with her, only to find her in a fog. As he drove away from the scene, he stopped the car along the side of the road and wept. Incredibly, news of Fitzgerald's condition went unreported for a full ten months until April 1994, reflecting her ironclad desire for privacy and the respect shown her by the press until word had spread to the point where it could no longer be contained. "It was obvious to anyone who saw her at the back of the driveway or in the yard that her legs were gone," said Blackman. He added that frequent coastal drives in her Rolls Royce, including one outing that took her to the gates of O. J. Simpson's Brentwood estate to view the crush of reporters covering his macabre murder case, and visits from friends and family were the remaining pleasures that filled her time.[5] She died on June 15, 1996, after a series of strokes that allowed her to slip away quietly at the age of seventy-nine.

That day Oscar Peterson received a call from Granz as the pianist was preparing to leave for the recording studio, coincidentally wearing a gold medallion Fitzgerald had given him. According to Kelly Peterson, "She's gone" was all Norman Granz could muster in his spare emotional shorthand, even with her husband, who had become acquainted with Fitzgerald around the same time and had spent the majority of his career with her.[6]

Fitzgerald's friends and family gathered for a private service in the backyard of her mansion on June 20 before her entombment at Inglewood Park Cemetery. Her funeral cortege may have stopped traffic along the freeway on the way to the cemetery, but the event was not enough to draw Granz. He had long had frictions with Fitzgerald over his belief that her family took advantage of her. Possibly as a result, Granz's name and role in her life, her long association with JATP and Verve Records, and even the songbooks were nowhere to be found in the lengthy biography in her funeral program. Yet Granz could be assured that the main memorial to Ella Fitzgerald would be the music they had achieved together as part of their union lasting forty-four years.

Other eulogies for Fitzgerald did credit Granz for what he had done for her personally and as an artist by promoting her music. Jonathan Schwartz, one of the foremost broadcasters, custodians, and celebrants of the Great American Songbook (his father was the composer Arthur Schwartz), wrote, "Norman Granz, a gutsy, narcissistic entrepreneur with a passion for jazz, saw Ella Fitzgerald—the 22-million-seller for Decca Records—not only as a bankable commodity, but also as a jazz artist of originality and purpose. She was, he felt, alive on this earth to make music. She could pick up a tune in the time it took to play it. She was, however, almost entirely unable to negotiate the real world—the airline-ticket-buying, hotel-reservation-making, letter-mailing, doctor-calling, taxi-hailing, musician-firing, contract-reading, dress-altering, interview-giving, wide, wide world of human habitation. Granz took everything on."[7] Similarly, Billy Eckstine, who had toured for Granz in the early 1950s and who more typically expressed a hard-bitten, well-earned cynicism about white managers and black talent, was outspoken in his praise of Granz. "Norman was the greatest thing that happened for Ella, as far as management," Eckstine said. "See, at the time that Ella was with Chick Webb, the black musician was used. He was prostituted. He was robbed . . . There were agents who were absolute mongrels. Then Norman came along. He wanted Ella Fitzgerald to become what she was supposed to be: First Lady of Song. And she had been getting the seventy-fifth lady of song's money. And Norman just broke down these racial barriers . . . He did it out of his heart."[8]

Norman Granz's physical decline in the late 1990s closely tracked an ever-deepening pessimism. His paradoxical attitude about his legacy started with his belief that he had not received timely credit for his accomplishments, a predicament he said applied to jazz musicians as well. Yet Granz made himself largely unavailable to those seeking to honor him, chronicle his career, probe his involvement with a multitude of artists in many fields, or question his views on a range of subjects with which he was conversant. Granz's psychic distance from the jazz scene, matched by his physical remove in Europe, magnified his inability to stay current with the music even if he had wanted to.

But it was impossible for Granz to conceal the anger he had bottled up within him, despite the successes, on his own demanding terms, that he had enjoyed through the course of his career. "There was an increased bitterness at the end of his life," said friend Olivier Berggruen. "A new generation had taken over, he was no longer the center of things, it was already the past."[9] Granz acknowledged in 1976 that he had chosen a lonely path over the long haul, but that realization never deflected his course. "The older you get, the more you're forgotten by the record companies; that's jazz in America," he said. "In classical music, the older you get, the more respected you are. . . . Leonard Bernstein isn't in the Top 40 when he issues a record. I am not going for the short haul. I can't make a hit, and I don't want to. Jazz endures; it's the longevity that counts."[10]

Granz by his own count produced twenty-three Grammy Award–winning records, more than any other record producer. That did not stop him from approaching the 1994 Recording Academy Trustee Award with a sour attitude. He rejected the honor well in advance of the March 1 ceremony. Then in April 1994 he ignored the fiftieth anniversary of Verve Records at Carnegie Hall, a date coinciding with the first Jazz at the Philharmonic concert in 1944 rather than the founding of the label twelve years later.

Around the end of 1997, Oscar Peterson gathered some people to put Granz's name forward for the Presidential Medal of Freedom, according to Virginia Wicks, who received a call from him for the first time in many years. Peterson hoped to get the ball rolling with Quincy Jones, a so-called Friend of Bill, as the intermediary to President Clinton. There were some questions about a Granz nomination: his status as an expatriate (he never became a Swiss citizen) and, more practically, a concern that he might decline this honor as well. That concern might have been well founded, if a handwritten note Granz faxed to Clinton around 1996 is any indicator.

Dear President Clinton,

For someone who professes to love jazz as much as you do, it's sad that you didn't name a jazz musician to your Arts Awards [National Medal of Arts]; especially when Benny Carter, the last of the giants of jazz who, at 88 years of age, is still actively playing beautifully. Moreover, when he is abroad he is the finest representative of the USA that you could possibly hope for. All this talk of jazz being the only truly uniquely American art form apparently has gone right by you. Pity.

Sincerely,
Norman Granz[11]

Granz's complaint may or not have led Clinton to rectify this oversight when he presented Carter with the medal in December 2000, barely a month before leaving office. In any event, Granz himself never received a medal.

Oscar Peterson had to break down Granz's resistance before he agreed to receive Jazz at Lincoln Center's Lifetime Achievement Award in 1999. "I think the only reason he accepted that award was because I said I would go and accept it for him," Peterson recalled early the following year. "And because I raised hell with him by the week. I was really salty with him, and I said, '*I'll* go and get it for you.' He said, 'If you want to get it, you can get it, but I'm not going!'"[12] Granz was so moved by Peterson's remarks, which stressed his commitment to civil rights, that he proudly played a tape of the event for his doctor.

The most fascinating example of Granz's attitude toward awards was the effort he made to receive, or more accurately retrieve almost fifty years later, an award he came to believe was the most meaningful of any ever extended him. Granz had declined the Russwurm Award in 1948 when the National Negro Newspaper Publishers' Association gave an award to President Harry Truman for issuing orders to desegregate the army, since he thought Truman had done so only under pressure from the black union leader and activist A. Philip Randolph. "I was a little arrogant in canceling only because of Truman," Granz later conceded. He looked up the organization's successor, the National Newspaper Association in Washington, to belatedly accept the award but met with frustration: he said the association was clueless about the award and its namesake, John Russwurm, the first black newspaper publisher in the United States. Granz persisted over the next two years until the association located his file and agreed to forward the certificate. Again there was a delay, ended only when Peterson called the association to expedite matters. Granz received the award in 1997. "They should have been proud I even wanted it," Granz said.[13]

Granz was not much happier with various reissues of his Verve recordings. He developed a warm friendship and respect for Michael Lang, then director of catalog development, who oversaw the re-release of much of Granz's legacy in the reissue heyday of the 1990s. Nevertheless, he was testy about the fate of some of his most prominent works, such as *The Jazz Scene,* reissued by PolyGram in 1994, complete with Gjon Mili's gallery of photographs of jazz greats from the late 1940s and a second disc of "additional sides." He considered bonus tracks to be nothing short of "bothersome" and "dishonest." "They've taken my *Jazz Scene,* which specifically was to represent what was happening then, and to pad it, because it was only thirty or forty minutes on an LP, and they wanted to get like sixty or seventy minutes," he said. "Putting some other material in it that was remotely connected with it simply destroyed the concept of the album. You don't know how many hours I used to work, staying up all night when I was going to release an album just to get the programming right, because I was thinking that a disc jockey might hear the first track and if he weren't attracted, he wouldn't even bother with the second or the ending."[14] Granz, acting on the same principle, stipulated in the contract selling Verve to MGM that Ella Fitzgerald's recordings could not be reprogrammed, or "repurposed," for future reissues, although that has occurred in many instances over the years. It doesn't take much to conclude that he would have hated the "Verve Remixed" series in which various hip-hop artists remix such classics as Billie Holiday singing "Strange Fruit."

Granz rejected many requests for interviews, often explicitly professing a hostility to history. For example, he turned aside questions for a 1995 National Public Radio seventy-fifth anniversary tribute to Charlie Parker. He ignored Ken Burns's television documentary *Jazz*, airing in January 2001, despite repeated interview requests. "I will be dead by the time the program is broadcast, and I don't care what people think of me after that," Granz reportedly told one of Burns's producers.[15] They did not come away empty-handed, however: after almost five years of negotiations, Granz finally approved use of his 1950 footage of Parker in one of the show's segments on bebop, which featured a brief overview of the impresario's achievements in music and civil rights.

Granz was suited temperamentally and by his vast experience to bully writers he felt, fairly or not, had ventured out of bounds. British jazz historian Stuart Nicholson found himself on the receiving end of a threatened lawsuit by Granz after the publication in Britain of his 1993 Ella Fitzgerald biography. Specifically, Granz contested Nicholson's account of his relationship with Frank Sinatra, in particular whether Sinatra had had Granz thrown out of a television studio, as well as stories involving Roy Eldridge's time accompanying Fitzgerald in the mid-1960s. Granz was also unhappy with what he viewed as the excessive amount of coverage he received in Nicholson's book, though any Fitzgerald biography would need to give ample coverage to his presence in her life. Granz knew British libel laws well enough to know that he would have a far easier time making a case there, where the onus is on writers to *disprove* libel charges and where factual accuracy is not necessarily a winning defense. In the United States, Granz's status as a public figure alone would have undermined his chances to successfully prosecute a case. "Nicholson was frightened I would file a libel suit, because in England you can really score big," he recalled seven years after the book was first published in 1993.[16] Granz itemized his complaints to Nicholson in what must have been an excruciating phone call lasting some four hours. And Nicholson gave in: a comparison of the 1993 edition with the American edition reveals deleted or revised passages reflecting Granz's two areas of concern. Granz said he was glad to avoid a suit that would have upset Fitzgerald.

Even longtime friends mention a frosty demeanor, sudden mood changes, and a brusqueness that reflected a tendency neither to waste words nor to care much about their consequences. Virginia Wicks observed, "He never said or did anything that was really out of line, but he was terribly abrupt. He never felt he had to explain anything to anyone. I never heard him yell at anyone. I never heard him use bad language. But he could put someone down in two seconds just by saying, 'I think that's enough.' And they knew it was enough."[17]

Yet although Granz's abruptness may have disproportionately affected his reputation, it represents only a part of the story of his final years. In Granz's personal papers were numerous letters from musicians thanking him for financial support during a time of illness or for work they had done for him, including one from Barney Kessel, whose career ended with his stroke in 1992. "It has been six years now since a stroke left me partially paralyzed and unable to play," Kessel wrote in 1998. "All this time I am conscious of how much you've helped me, and I continue to improve a little each year much to my doctor's amazement." Mary Lou Callender, widow of Red Callender, wrote, "I am very grateful to you and for your concern and support. I find myself in a most difficult situation full of unwanted surprises. Your help is appreciated beyond words." Harry "Sweets" Edison, succumbing to cancer a year after he wrote Granz in 1998, thanked him for financial support that had eased his final days as their friendship neared the sixty-year mark. Granz bought a new car for Mrs. Eddie Davis upon hearing that the saxophonist's wife was having car problems shortly after Davis's death in late 1986. He also became a member of the steering committee of a scholarship fund in New York for young musicians named after Zoot Sims, who died in 1985. The arranger Russ Garcia, like many other recipients of his generosity, wrote to express his appreciation for Granz's association with him. A 1997 letter that begins "Dear Friend Norman!" goes on to say, "I appreciate all the wonderful opportunities you have given me to work with all the great geniuses of the jazz world."[18]

In 2000, after Granz learned he had cancer, he began dispersing some his money to longtime friends and associates, in the belief that they might as well have time to enjoy it while they were still alive.

Louie Bellson remembered getting a call from Granz asking him for his address. He subsequently received "a big, big, big check, with a note saying, 'Thanks for all the years.' That's his loyalty. I'll never forget Norman because he opened a new world for me."[19] His lifelong friend Archie Green was also a recipient of Granz's largesse. "He phoned me, and said, 'This is Norm.' Very brusque. 'I have the Big C.' At first, I didn't know what the Big C meant. He told me he was working on his will to distribute his money and he was going to send me some. I said, 'Okay.' He sent me $10,000 and then later he sent $10,000 again. To this day, I don't know why, with his relatives and all and his obligations, he chose me. There were no strings attached, but he said, 'I want you to spend it on caviar.'"[20] A note that accompanied a check to Benny Carter was heartfelt: "As one of the early JATPs, and also since you and I are members of the exclusive 'Ain't but a few of us left' club, I want to give you this in memory of the great times we had and how important you were to me, not only musically, but, more importantly, as a man of spirit and dignity. As ever, Norm."[21]

Granz's philanthropy had other manifestations as well. In 1997 he donated $100,000 under the auspices of the Ella Fitzgerald Charitable Foundation as part of his continuing support for the Harlem Little League. His contribution was the largest single gift in its history.[22] Listed as a team sponsor on the organization's stationery, Granz kept a mounted 1992 photo of one team holding their banner proclaiming themselves "The JATPs," leaving the viewer to wonder whether they had even an inkling of the history behind their name. Grete Granz told me that her husband had read as many as six newspapers a day and been frequently moved by hard-luck stories he tracked to the source by going through reporters who had written the articles. Such was the case with one South Central Los Angeles family whose lives had been upended in the bloody 1992 riots following the verdict supporting the offending officers in the Rodney King police brutality case. A check was quickly forthcoming.

The photographer Herman Leonard, who took incomparable black-and-white pictures of jazz figures from the late 1940s and 1950s, some for Granz, held a 1988 show of his work at the Special Photographers Gallery in London; and as he later recounted, "Norman honored me by coming by the opening of the exhibit. I was so pleased by this gesture, because I knew that he wasn't feeling well. I'd worked for him through the years, but we weren't intimate friends. We didn't hang out together."[23] Granz bought several prints on the spot to send to musicians represented in Leonard's photographs. "He said, 'I want this for Oscar Peterson, I want this for Buddy Rich, I want this for so and so.' It was so nice that he came."[24]

Clark Terry vividly recalls a visit that he and his wife, Gwen, made to the Granzes in London. Terry, ever ebullient, was the ideal icebreaker when it came to getting Granz on the phone and humoring him out of a funk. "When we got to talking, he always started out, like [mumbles], but when we end up he's happy," Terry said. "We'd always talk about fun things." The conversations inevitably turned to fine restaurants where they could meet when the Granzes were free. After dinner one night, Grete raised her husband's legendary eyebrows when she pulled out a short sleek cigar. "Yes, Norman doesn't like me to smoke," she said, lighting up. Gwen said her husband felt the same way about her cigarette habit. The couples went their separate ways after an evening of Terry's jokes and genuine good humor that kept Granz's spirits high. The following day, Grete delivered an expensive Chanel handbag from Harrod's department store to the Terrys' hotel room to replace Gwen's worn designer knock-off. As Terry's eye problems worsened in the 1990s, Granz scrupulously studied up on his condition, arranged for him to visit his doctor in Boston, and frequently peppered Terry with questions about his treatment. He was equally generous in paying Terry $10,000 to recruit the musicians for one of Ella Fitzgerald's final concerts in New York.[25]

Quincy Jones and Granz became close around the time he founded Qwest Records in 1980. "What happens is when you're a sideman, you're a sideman," Jones said. "People don't take you very seriously. When you get your own credentials, it's a different kind of relationship. There are a lot of people who won't let you in. That's the way it works. Norman decided to let me in. He was very, very generous and very gracious. I could feel his enormous capacity for beauty and art—he had the tastes—and just life. He had discriminating tastes for everything in life, music, the packaging of it. Norman was a man from another time. He had the ability to envision, to see around the corner, to imagine what things could be like in a better place. I always admired that in other people—to change conditions. He had the ability to understand the mechanics of change, how do you really make a change come about effectively, because he walked straight into the fire on a lot of stuff. He was fearless. He was the same way musically. He was very dogmatic about his tastes musically, but goddammit, that was what he was about. He was right most of the time. We're still feeling the effect of his role, in pure jazz really."[26]

Granz maintained ties with John McDonough from the late 1970s onward, a rarity given the low opinion he reserved for most jazz writers. Although he had first met McDonough during the 1967 farewell JATP tour, their relationship bloomed during the Pablo years. Granz, at one of his many wits-end junctures with music journalists, had sent out a letter in 1982 announcing that critics would have to pay $50 annually for postage and handling to maintain the privilege of giving him and his recordings a hard time in print. McDonough was the only one to pony up a check, which Granz promptly returned. "Is my face red!!" Granz wrote. "I've just discovered that my office billed you for $50 for the year's Pablo releases. Enclosed is a reimbursement check. You're too good a friend to be charged anything by Pablo."[27] One legacy of their friendship is a series of taped interviews over twenty-two years from 1979 until the year of Granz's death. McDonough, a senior contributing writer for *Down Beat,* a columnist for the *Wall Street Journal,* and a freelance producer for National Public Radio, engaged him on a variety of topics of mutual interest, including their similar tastes in jazz. He thought the timing had a lot to do with their relationship. "I think that everyone wants to be immortal and to be able to talk to the next generation," he said. "Norman knew we shared similar tastes in music and that I had an interest in the social justice issues and his involvement in the Communist Party. In some ways, he had the temperament of a fundamentalist preacher as far as absolute values that governed his tastes in music, art, and even food. I think I caught him at the right time in his life. I think if I had tried to engage him when was at his busiest, he might not have had the time or the inclination."[28]

First among his pleasures was the life he and Grete enjoyed over the thirty-three years since they had first met in September 1968. Grete said that even during the Pablo years business intruded minimally on their time together, such was Granz's skill in managing his affairs by telephone as opposed to time-consuming face-to-face meetings, which he hated. Trips to London or Paris, or even New York on the Concorde, were often spur-of-the-moment decisions to visit friends, such as Benny Green or Ken Glancy in London, or to attend museum shows or the theater, and in Paris, always the food. For several years they got away from the European winters and vacationed four months out of the year in Beverly Hills and Palm Desert, where they perused bookstores and gourmet shops for hours and played tennis every day. Granz assumed many of the domestic chores in Geneva, such as the shopping and most of the cooking. (His array of kitchen utensils that hang on the wall like an array of bells in a clock tower has gone largely untouched since his death.) He wrote daily menus, many interspersed with love notes and humorous messages, such as one from October 1972 that detailed its delectable offerings under the heading "Chez Norman." The Granzes made annual treks to box seats at Wimbledon and French Open tournaments to stoke his nearly insatiable appetite for the game and maintain his acquaintanceship with some leading players such as Jimmy Connors.

Granz also treasured the relationship he had with Christian, Grete's son from a previous marriage, a successful advertising film producer living in Copenhagen, and with Christian's wife, son, and daughter, whom Granz considered as his own grandchildren. A photograph from the late 1990s shows Granz preparing for a visit: waving to the camera, he stands beside his Mercedes 350, holding a sack full of grandfatherly goodies and wearing a rubber gorilla mask. Geneva's cultural life did not particularly appeal to the Granzes, so they stayed pretty much to themselves when they were away from their Tite Street apartment in London, which they maintained until 1999. To avoid incurring social obligations, they declined all but a few invitations, even one from a well-known art historian who lived in their building in Geneva.

Granz's career was the subject of a final major retrospective during his lifetime with the October 1998 release of *The Complete Jazz at the Philharmonic on Verve, 1944–1949*. The ten-disc set covers the vibrant early years from the first concert in July 1944 to the night in September 1949 when he introduced Oscar Peterson and only months after Fitzgerald began to entwine her affairs with JATP and Granz. The recordings are particularly striking for the road map they provide from the era of swing to bop to that of rhythm and blues, prefigured especially by the playing of Illinois Jacquet and T-Bone Walker.

In his final years, Granz battled a host of health problems that sapped his stamina before taking his life. He had successfully treated prostate cancer with hormones and no surgery for nearly a decade. He remained physically active until spinal stenosis resulting from fraying vertebrae pinched nerves in his spine and caused him to curtail his physical activity, although he was still able to bat tennis balls up until March 2000. He considered risky back surgery as late as the spring of 2000, when he and Grete spent two months in Los Angeles so that he could undergo a battery of medical tests. However, Granz, who had pneumonia twice around this time, concluded that he was probably too old and fragile to withstand such a serious operation and decided against it. He left town deeply dissatisfied with his physicians.

In 2000, he received word that cancer had been found in the parotid gland in the head and neck. Granz vacillated in the last year about whether to continue to receive radiation treatment from a London doctor who traveled to Geneva twice a week or to let nature take its course. He chose radiation. He suffered greatly in his last few months: he had difficulty speaking and, in the end, was unable to swallow, a low blow to an epicurean. Grete had his favorite foods pureed so that he could still enjoy the taste as his life ebbed.

"Benny Carter had been filling me in about that time that Norman was getting weaker and weaker," said Virginia Wicks. "I knew that very often his wife would answer the phone when you'd call. This time Norman answered the phone. I said, 'Hi, Norman, this is Virginia.' And he said, 'Goodbye, Virginia,' and hung up. I was devastated. I thought, 'My God, he hung up on me.' I called Benny right away and I was almost in tears. 'Benny, this just happened.' And he said, 'Virginia, don't you realize? He's telling you something. He's saying goodbye.' In looking back on it, of course, I thought it was exactly like what Norman would do. He was gone a couple of days after that."[29]

Granz died in bed in his Geneva apartment in the early hours of November 22, 2001. Word spread quickly among his circle of friends. John McDonough got a call from Oscar Peterson on Thanksgiving Day apprising him of Granz's death. In the best tradition of his trade, Jon Thurber, obituary editor of the *Los Angeles Times,* had begun preparing a lengthy obituary in advance of Granz's death after hearing of his ill health during a concert by Peterson at the Hollywood Bowl in August. He called Granz the man who had "set the business of jazz through most of the twentieth century," "helped end the two-track system in which white players generally earned far more than blacks," and helped integrate jazz on a large commercial scale.[30]

Funeral services were held six days later with a small group of friends at the palatial eighteenth-century Frederiksberg Slotskirke in Copenhagen, also known as the "King's Church," where Norman and Grete had married twenty-seven years earlier. Only one musician, Niels-Henning Ørsted Pedersen, stood in for the hundreds who had dealt with Granz and the millions more who attended his concerts or bought his recordings who may not have even known his name but loved the music. Pedersen's musical farewell began with the bassist playing an excerpt from J.S. Bach's first cello suite, followed by an improvised "Blues for

Norman." The priest remarked to Grete that more flowers bedecked the historic Lutheran church for the funeral than he had ever witnessed for such a service. Grete's brother, the well-known Danish writer and screenwriter Hans Hansen, delivered the eulogy.

Granz's headstone was placed at the beautifully landscaped, lushly green, and secluded gravesite in Copenhagen's Ordiup Kirkegaard. The legend on the brown-and-black rippled marble inlaid with gold reads: "You are the one and only. Norman Granz, 6.8.1918–22.11.2001. I will love you forever." Crowning the stone was the logo of Pablo Records, a beacon for what Granz stood for in music and art.

Epilogue: "My Career, Such As It Is . . ."

If Norman Granz had hoped to be left to rest in peace, the obituaries and tributes that poured forth upon his death would have annoyed him. He had expressed contempt for late honors anyway, and these were as late as they come.

"Granz was a true visionary, plain and simple—as a manager, a producer and a promoter," wrote Jon Thurber in the *Los Angeles Times*. "Today, at a time when marketing and promotion are an intrinsic part of the jazz world, it's hard to contextualize what a visionary he was. Over 60 years ago, when bebop's primary appeal was to a relatively small niche of dedicated fans, Granz dramatically expanded the audience for what was seemingly difficult music, both domestically and internationally, via his Jazz at the Philharmonic concerts."[1] "Many critics and musicians considered JATP sessions crude and circus-like events," said *Chicago Tribune* critic Howard Reich. "And the man's manner—typically called 'surly' and 'arrogant'—earned him countless enemies and may help explain why his mantel was devoid of industry honors. There were legitimate reasons for his disenchantment. . . . His standards were higher than everyone else's, which may explain why he achieved as much as he did."[2]

Two obituaries from Great Britain and another from Brazil demonstrated that the news of Granz's passing resonated far beyond the United States.

In London, the *Independent* writer Steve Voce called Granz a "benign bully, . . . who always got his way and who always had a good reason for exerting his clout. His wealth, generated by his intelligence and his enthusiasm, gained him unpopularity as 'a capitalist,' but he did more for liberal causes than any of his critics."[3] Scottish record producer Elliot Meadow recalled how when he had first met Granz in 1964 and requested an autograph Granz had refused because he could not imagine a teenager having any clue as to who he was. Meadow, in fact, had been listening to JATP on records since the mid-1950s. Even later meetings, wrote Meadow, "more often than not left me with the sense of being tolerated rather than welcomed." He added, "I may not have always liked him, but I did respect him for the implacable belief he had in what he was doing. His achievements between the early 1940s and the late 1980s remain unparalleled. As a label owner, record producer, concert promoter and personal manager he was the perfect middleman in bringing the artist to the public and vice versa on a worldwide basis."[4]

"If there was 'a white with a black soul,' it was Norman Granz," offered the Brazilian Ruy Castro, writing in O Estado de São Paolo. "The phrase is just a cliché because in truth there were many whites like Granz who were decisive to the commercial survival and even the artistic advancement of jazz in the twentieth century. . . . But no one (not even Creed Taylor, to whom bossa nova owes much in the United States) became as well known as Norman Granz."[5]

Granz's legacy of presenting and preserving the music of some of America's leading musicians has been obscured. Even his courageous stand on civil rights, his proudest achievement of all, has to some extent been forgotten, and at the end of his life he himself believed that it probably didn't matter anyway. Although his victories in this arena accomplished something within the jazz world during the peak of Granz's touring days in the United States and may have cracked open the doors to integrated musical events in many cities, they lacked a broader effectiveness and had marginal lasting impact on the nation's attitudes. It is fair to ask how Granz's civil rights struggles, waged in isolation, could be measured against those arising from the NAACP, important federal court cases challenging segregation, and demonstrations during and after World War II that surged in the mid-1950s and into the 1960s, resulting in landmark legislation.

However, few have used the power and symbolism of the arts to hold society accountable more shrewdly, with greater purpose, and with less concern for his bottom line than Granz. Dimming memories allowed many to confront Granz during his lifetime in print and in person with the scurrilous notion that he had done little more than exploit African

American musicians on his way to the top. Pamela Allen, an assistant who worked for Granz during the Pablo years, recalled that once, when Ella Fitzgerald's longtime road manager Pete Cavello accompanied her to the NAACP Image Award dinner in Los Angeles, he was mistaken for Granz by some and got an earful about how he had taken advantage of her and other jazz musicians. "You knew Norman was getting grief for that, too," Allen said, "and it had to hurt."[6] Jealousy cannot be discounted as a motivation for some of the attacks aimed at Granz over the decades. Granz, however, dismissed these attacks as "typical of what many people say discussing the position of someone who has been. very successful." As he saw things, he had merely deployed his energy and intelligence to improve his financial situation over time, as when he had used money from his jazz concerts to purchase a Picasso painting for tens of thousands of dollars and later sold it for millions. "When I worked in jazz, if I never did another thing but stay with jazz, you could properly say that I became a rich man in jazz. The reality is that you save your money in an effort to better yourself."[7]

Quite simply, Norman Granz accomplished everything he set out to do. He presented good music, demonstrated that jazz could be a rewarding commercial venture, and enforced his code of personal integrity and social justice within his far-flung jazz kingdom. He was a lone wolf and could be unpredictably brutal or benevolent. These traits shaped how he presented music, as well as how he fought racism.

The most recent evidence of Granz's promotional talent emerged when Ella Fitzgerald racked up an unqualified runaway hit album, both critically and commercially, in late 2009. *Twelve Nights in Hollywood,* released some thirteen years following her death, contains seventy-six previously unreleased tracks from engagements at the Crescendo nightclub in Los Angeles from 1961 and the following year.[8] Granz held two shows each night to record virtually her entire repertoire from that time. Listeners can hear Granz stoking the fire as he calls tunes from the wings and has other passing exchanges with Fitzgerald. The CD set received a full-page story in the *New York Times* by Fred Kaplan, who commented that it showed Fitzgerald in top form: "more relaxed, swinging and adventurous, across a wider span of rhythms and moods, than on the dozens of other albums that hit the bins in her lifetime."[9]

Any final evaluation of Norman Granz has to consider the privacy he resolutely guarded and managed to maintain despite his very public life. That made it all the more intriguing when Granz invited me to see him in what he knew were his final months in 2001. His wife,

Grete, assured me following his death that it had indeed been his idea to extend the invitation and that she had not nudged him in that direction (something that would have been virtually impossible anyway). Asking about his personal life was risky, as was anything that concerned his developmentally disabled daughter from his first marriage in the early 1950s. Granz once suspended interviews for this book for eight months after an extended phone interview in which he revealed more than he ever had about his early family life. He read the transcript and recoiled.

On May 18, I met with Granz at his Geneva apartment. He was dressed in a light yellow pullover, a pair of white trousers, and sandals. He was thin, but healthier looking than I had been led to believe he would be, given the progress of his cancer. Gone, however, were his distinctive thistle-like eyebrows that had once been so expressive of his powerful personality. Granz asked that I not tape or photograph him. The ban on taping lasted until the following Monday when I persuaded him that only by recording the interview could I get all the detail and focus on what he was saying. He showed me several folders, telling me that I could copy the contents. They included a jumble of papers relating to the sale of Verve Records to MGM in 1960, medical records, documents on art auctions, contracts, and heartfelt letters from musicians. Ultimately, he weeded out much of the personal material as well as anything about his business dealings. Knowing that he had asked Grete to consider writing a separate book on aspects of his life other than jazz, including art, and remembering how he had stopped interviews when I had asked him about his early life, I avoided asking him anything about his art collecting—thereby losing an entrée to an aspect of his life that meant as much to him as music.

Our interviews proceeded variously. Although sometimes a single question could draw out hours' worth of illuminating reminiscences concerning bygone eras, events, and personalities, at other times Granz's responses were dismayingly perfunctory. One afternoon, he cruised through some twenty questions in about half the time we had allotted for the four three-hour interviews. Frustrated, I called Elliot Meadow in Glasgow to help devise new lines of questioning and called Virginia Wicks just to blow off steam. Meadow, whose own irascibility gave him some insight into Granz, correctly assessed my situation. "Well, pal, you're going to get everything you want out of Norman Granz. If you think he's going to make it easy . . . You will pay every last day you're there." Though Granz might have mellowed somewhat, he remained intense and abrasive. He was impressed with my research but could quickly turn critical. In one session, a series of curt answers made me increasingly weary in dealing with him. "You're probably smarter than you present yourself," he said in his chilly flat tone. (This later provoked knowing laughter from those who *really* knew him— "It's so Norman.") During our final meeting, Granz favored me with a generous gesture that was equally characteristic of him. I was aware of Grete slipping out as the interview got under way. Granz said, "She's gone over to the hotel. She will pay your bill there." One afternoon when I left Granz's apartment I found her waiting outside the building. "I know this has been difficult, but he has been in pain and he is afraid," she told me. I understood, and told her that it had been a privilege to come and see him as much as I had. Back in New Jersey, I called to thank him for his and Grete's hospitality. He and I never spoke again.

Granz could be bluntly and almost vengefully honest; the truth was a core value he rarely made time to dress up or redress. Things were right or wrong; he liked something or somebody or he didn't. He forgave few slights, mistakes, or breaches of integrity. Quickly breaking ties and moving on, he left no small amount of hurt in his wake over the years, though many expressed fierce loyalty and admiration for all he had accomplished. His love was expressed in the shadows of his shyness and accompanied by great generosity. That he could be at once so calculatedly entrepreneurial and so staunch an upholder of human welfare and dignity remains the unsolvable riddle of his life. Piecing together his complicated life is a task that fills many pages but leaves many more that can never be written. He wouldn't have had it any other way.

Granz was largely a self-educated and self-made man, a point not lost on musicians. He jammed his way to the top with his integrity intact, along with a vision that has stood the test of time for almost seventy years. If other equally influential economic, political, and cultural leaders had been as willing as he to lead by example, America would have moved far more quickly toward racial equality. But for the most part American business, along with government, implicitly and explicitly supported racism by upholding segregation.

Norman Granz explained how his philosophy had been shaped by watching the spontaneity of jazz musicians. "I happen to like the jam session, because I'm a great believer in the role of the individual in any art. I don't think it's difficult to argue that each day we have more and more conformity in our lives and less and less opportunity for the individual, whether it be in the state politically, or in business economically. And the same with music. I really feel that jazz as I know it will vanish, because where is the young player going to get an apprentice-ship? Where is he going to go sit in? Where is he even going to get a sound playing in a band? There won't even be any bands. It's a question of standards. I'm not looking backwards or being nostalgic. I just don't know how the environment in the future can nurture the individual."[10]

Norman Granz wrote a sort of epitaph for himself around the time of the sale of Pablo Records. His assistant Pamela Allen remembers that he walked into her office, pronounced it deliberately, and left. "When they come to you—and they will come—you give them a message for me: I just wanted it to swing."[11]

It did.

Acknowledgments

In writing this book I have been graced by the generosity and sharing of men and women who thought it long overdue that Norman Granz be acknowledged as the major cultural figure he became in the epic second half of the twentieth century. The vast archive of memories and materials previously unearthed about Granz and long-departed musical colleagues have allowed me to tell his story in as much detail as any biographer could hope for, especially given the broad and eventful arc of his life.

First, I wish to thank Norman Granz, who was genuinely ambivalent about whether a biography should be written but nonetheless took time on countless occasions to answer my questions and provide leads to help track down less obvious aspects of the story.

Several people have been indispensable over the sixteen years from the time of my original master's thesis through the time that it developed into a fuller examination of Granz's life and career. John McDonough was an early colleague. He shared numerous interviews he conducted with Granz between 1978 and 2001, as well as his broad knowledge of the music and history, and read and commented on the earliest drafts of the manuscript. McDonough's rapport and friendship with Granz, and his ability to engage him in many areas of mutual interest, resulted in the most significant body of interviews extant. Granz's publicist in the 1950s, Virginia Wicks, understood him as well as anyone; given his mercurial ways, I routinely vetted letters and ideas with her during his lifetime and have kept doing so in the ten years since his death. Our ongoing conversation and friendship have never stopped. Folklorist and longtime San Franciscan Archie Green was invaluable in revealing Granz's intellectual and social development. In one of our last conversations before his death in 2009, Green told me not to stop until I had "found a press that would be honored to honor Norman." It is a fitting tribute to both Granz and himself that that press was in Green's backyard. Nat Hentoff, who came of age with Granz sharing a commitment to jazz and civil liberties, was a friend of this project from the time that Granz recommended he read the original thesis in the late 1990s. (Nat also cheered me on when I appropriated the title of a 1994 column in his *Sweet Land of Liberty* series for the title of this book.) He opened the door to the University of California Press, publisher of his 2010 book *At the Jazz Band Ball*. Elliot Meadow slogged through the original eight-hundred-page manuscript and trimmed some 250 pages using his immense knowledge of Granz's history, an agile appreciation for language, and a willingness to pull no punches in rendering his judgments. He remains, as he never ceases to remind me, "The Editor."

Those who read earlier drafts of the manuscript sharpened my interpretation and minimized the chance of factual errors slipping by. It was helpful to know both from jazz experts and lay readers whether Granz's story sustained interest on its merits. Among these were Jim Blackman, Betty Colbert, Gary Giddins, Lea Isgur, Jack Isgur, Michael Oliver, Kelly Peterson, Bob Porter, Jacques Muyal, Loren Schoenberg, and Pauline Spinrad. John Richardson, the eminent art historian, curator, and biographer and friend of Pablo Picasso, first shared the names of art dealers in Europe whom Granz dealt with and then reviewed the chapter so that the story of Granz's art collecting and relationship with Picasso might hopefully ring as true as his life in jazz. Nick Low of Demus Productions in Glasgow, who produced the 2003 BBC Radio 2 Granz documentary *Out of the Norm,* used an earlier draft of the manuscript in the program and allowed me to conduct interviews for the programs coast to coast.

My colleagues at the Institute of Jazz Studies—Dan Morgenstern, Ed Berger, Vincent Pelote, Annie Kuebler, and the late John Clement—shared their knowledge, which in tandem with the unparalleled resources available there underscores why the institute remains in the forefront of jazz archives internationally as it has for decades. Lynn Mullins, former director of John Cotton Dana Library, where the

Institute of Jazz Studies is located on the Rutgers-Newark campus, was one of the great advocates for IJS and has followed the progress of this book with interest and encouragement.

Special thanks are due to those who spoke to me about Granz, some on repeated occasions. Interview subjects included Pamela Allen, Vernon Alley, George Avakian, Jean Bach, Louie Bellson, Bill Belmont, Shelley Berman, Heinz Berggruen, Olivier Berggruen, Keter Betts, Bobby Bregman, Buddy Bregman, Ray Brown, Benny Carter, Pete Cavello, Michael Cuscuna, Blossom Dearie, Buddy DeFranco, Herb Ellis, Sandy Elster, Phil Elwood, Tommy Flanagan, Archie Green, Al Grey, Norman Halsey, Nat Hentoff, Bones Howe, Phoebe Jacobs, Hank Jones, Quincy Jones, Ralph Kaffel, Leigh Kamman, Lee Konitz, Michael Lang, Herman Leonard, Lawrence Levine, Peter Levinson, John McDonough, James Moody, Jacques Muyal, Mo Ostin, Richard Palmer, Oscar Peterson, Flip Phillips, Bob Porter, John Richardson, Annie Ross, Lee Rowe, Jimmy Rowles, Arthur Schurgin, Irwin Steinberg, Phil Stern, Chuck Suber, Sheridan Sullivan, Frank Tenot, Clark Terry, Toots Thielemans, George Wein, Margaret Whiting, Virginia Wicks, Gerald Wilson, Ben Young, Saul Zaentz, and Mike Zwerin. (Other interviews relating to Granz came from oral histories and other published and audio sources.)

Among friends who have listened, shared ideas, and aided in many ways have been Henry Anderson, Helen Baer, Ian Behrstock, Wren T. Brown, Jean Bubley, Ben Cawthra, Fred Cohen, Stephen Cohen, Grayson Dantzic, Norman David, Dwight Deason, Frank Driggs, Claudia Driver, Luke Dunlap, Nadine Eckhardt, Brien Engel, Dale Fitzgerald, Will Freidwald, Mary Gilmore, Peter Goldsmith, Leighton Hamilton, David and Ursula Harsheid, Gil Hartman, Louis Harrison, John Edward Hasse, Patrick Hinely, Paul Hoeffler, Ashley Kahn, Dave Keller, Robin D. G. Kelley, Brian Koniarz, Anne Legrand, Alfred Lemmon, Don Maggin, Paula Marks, Tony Martin, Jeanne Mixon, Jim and Aida Murray, Stuart Nicholson, Fr. Peter F. O'Brien, S.J., Michael O'Malley, Hank O'Neal, Richard Palmer, Kelly Peterson, Cordelia Pierce, Brian Priestly, Linda Prince, Bill Reed, Louisa Richardson-Deppe, Bruce Ricker, Bob Ruis, Curtis Sandberg, Steve Schiff and Ana Busto, Cynthia Sesso, Tim Sloan, Bill Smith, Steve Smith and Victoria Lewis, Glenn Strong, Lee Tanner, Jon Thurber, Judith Tick, Terry Trilling-Josephson, Dave Usher, Susan White, Ted Williams, and Dr. Mark D. Winston. Steve Sucher of Houston has provided wise advice and no small amount of footwork over thirty years of adventures in good music, including some associated with this book.

Two pros finalized the details of getting this book into print. My agent Arnold Gosewich of Toronto has been in the music and publishing industries and promotion for half a century. He found a similarly able and enthusiastic counterpart in University of California Press acquisitions editor for music, cinema, and media studies Mary Francis. Mary performed a subsequent edit of the manuscript before passing it along to Eric Schmidt, who confirmed permissions and shepherded it through other preliminary processes. Managing editor Marilyn Schwartz farmed out copyediting duties to the estimable Elisabeth Magnus, who wove silk from matted strands of ill-considered metaphors and other verbal tangles. Alexandra Dahne, publicity director, whom I met in New York last December, further cemented my feeling of the press's commitment to reaching out to the many publics touched by the Norman Granz story. Last year, Nat Hentoff, who helped broker my relationship with the University of California Press, said simply, "They are the best I've ever worked with." Until then, I had never associated Nat with understatement.

It is at this point where writers thank spouses, companions, and children who have long since ducked for cover in the face of an interminable period of research, writing, and editing, and heard too much for too long about the topic. You know, boring. In lieu of such, I look again over the names in this acknowledgment and say thanks for your indulgence, hoping that I receive a measure of mercy, not justice.

I have tried to make this book as error free as possible. In this, I only partially fall back on the sentiments of Norman Granz: "I'm not selling perfection."

Chronology

1918, August 6	Norman Granz born in Los Angeles
1932–35	Attends Theodore Roosevelt High School and meets early influence Archie Green
Late 1930s–early 1940s	Finds job at Los Angeles Stock Exchange, as film editor, and on labor crew at Warner Bros.; considers enrolling in the London School of Economics
1939	Hears Coleman Hawkins's "Body and Soul" and decisively turns toward jazz
1942, June	Begins hanging out at jazz clubs and after-hours music activities in black neighborhoods as UCLA student, beginning his own integrated freelance jam sessions
1942, July 15	Produces first recording session, with Lester Young, Nat Cole, and Red Callender; privately recorded, later commercially released
1944, July 2	Stages first Jazz at the Philharmonic (JATP) concert in support of the Sleepy Lagoon Defense Fund
1944, August–September	Assists *Life* magazine photographer Gjon Mili in producing Oscar-nominated short film *Jammin' the Blues*, still considered a classic
1945, Fall	First national JATP tour
1945, October	Releases *Jazz at the Philharmonic, Volume 1*, one of the first commercially produced "live" concert

	recordings in any musical genre, with the backing of record producer Moe Asch
1945–47	Joins the Musicians Branch of the Communist Party
1946	Semiannual JATP tours begin
1947	Campaigns for antisegregation clauses in contracts for touring bands and musicians
1947	Founds first record label, Clef Records, as a division of Mercury; retains ownership of masters as he plans his future as an independent record producer
1949	Recruits Ella Fitzgerald for JATP; debuts Oscar Peterson at Carnegie Hall and becomes his manager
Late 1940s–early 1950s	Takes advantage of new long-playing record format to display the extended jam sessions that characterized his live and studio recordings
1949	Birth of developmentally challenged daughter, Stormont, by Loretta Sullivan
1950	Marries Loretta Sullivan
1950	Produces *The Jazz Scene* record album, a deluxe compilation of musicians with photographs by Gjon Mili, intended as a snapshot of jazz of the period
1952	Produces *The Astaire Story*
1952, Spring	Tours JATP in Europe for the first time (instantly becoming the most prominent jazz impresario on the Continent)
1953–55	Produces albums of comprehensive Art Tatum solo and small-group sessions
1953, November	Takes JATP to Japan
1954	Becomes Ella Fitzgerald's personal manager
1954	Founds Norgran label
1955	Negotiates with Decca Records for Ella Fitzgerald's recording contract
1956	Founds Verve Records primarily to record Fitzgerald, folding his labels Clef, Norgran, and Down Home into the new enterprise; produces *Ella Fitzgerald Sings the Cole Porter Songbook*, a smash hit for the new label that launches their signal series canonizing the Great American

	Songbook and taking the singer's renown to a level that sustains her for the remainder of her career
1956	Questioned by the FBI about 1940s Communist Party membership
1957	Suspends domestic touring of JATP
1957	Passport canceled by State Department on grounds of previous Communist Party membership; successfully sues for its return
1958–59	Tours Duke Ellington in Europe; helps Ellington to obtain jobs scoring major motion pictures: *Anatomy of a Murder* (1959), *Paris Blues* (1961), and *Assault on a Queen* (1966)
1959	Moves to Lugano, Switzerland
1959	Begins touring Yves Montand with concerts in New York
1960	Organizes concerts for Marlene Dietrich that bring her back to her native Germany (and a dangerously polarized reception) for the first time since she fled Nazi Germany in 1933
1960	Sells Verve Records to MGM
1960s	Builds world-class collection of modern art; befriends Pablo Picasso
1966	Films Duke Ellington and Ella Fitzgerald at the Cote d'Azur
1967	Tours JATP in America for the first time in ten years with shows starring the Duke Ellington Orchestra, Ella Fitzgerald, and Oscar Peterson; vows never to do so again
1968, April 23	Auctions a portion of his Picasso collection; auction broadcast live on BBC
1968	Backs theatrical productions, notably Rolf Hochhuth's controversial play *Soldiers* and *Jacques Brel Is Alive and Well and Living in Paris,* both in London and both financial failures
1972, June 2	Stages Jazz at the Philharmonic reunion concert at the Santa Monica Civic Center
1973	Launches Pablo Records (named for Picasso) to record many artists associated with him who in his opinion were no longer accorded recording and performing opportunities commensurate with their continuing stature

1973	Records some of Duke Ellington's final records
1974	Marries third wife, Danish graphic artist Grete Lyngby
1975–83	Produces extensive series of concerts, spawning recordings and videos, at the Montreux (Switzerland) Jazz Festival
1983	Presents last JATP concerts, Tokyo
1987	Sells Pablo to Fantasy Records and effectively retires; relinquishes managing Ella Fitzgerald and Oscar Peterson after decades
1995	Produces *Improvisation,* a video retrospective of many Granz artists, including first-seen 1950 film of Charlie Parker
1996, June 15	Ella Fitzgerald dies
1999	Receives Lifetime Achievement Award from Jazz at Lincoln Center, accepted by Oscar Peterson
2001, November 22	Dies of cancer in Geneva

Notes

PROLOGUE

1. Norman Granz, telephone interview by author, January 25, 2000, transcript, 8–13, in author's possession; "White Café Owner Prefers Fine to Serving Musicians," *Baltimore Afro-American,* October 25, 1947, 6; "Granz and Five Sue Restaurant," *Down Beat,* November 5, 1947, 3.

2. John McDonough, "George Wein: An Impresario's Life," *Down Beat,* October 2003, 80.

3. Nat Hentoff, "The Man Who Used Jazz for Justice," *Washington Post,* May 7, 1994, 19A.

4. Gene Lees, "Hindsights," *Jazzletter,* May 1993, 5–6.

5. Peter Watrous, "A Label. A Vision. A Golden Anniversary," *New York Times,* April 3, 1994, 2:26.

6. Norman Granz, telephone interview by author, March 12, 2000, transcript, 24, in author's possession.

7. Archie Green, interview by author, San Francisco, April 2003.

8. Gene Lees, "A Farewell to Granz," *Jazzletter,* June 1987, 1.

9. Benny Green, interview by Elliot Meadow, 1987, in *Out of the Norm: The Life and Times of Norman Granz,* by Elliot Meadow (Nick Low/Demus Productions, 2003), broadcast by BBC Radio 2, December 2003–January 2004.

10. Norman Granz, interview by Patricia Willard, Geneva, August 23–24, 1989, transcript, 153–54, Duke Ellington Oral History Project, National Museum of American History, Smithsonian Institution.

11. Sinclair Traill, "In My Opinion: Norman Granz," *Jazz Journal,* November 1963, 17.

1. "ALL I WANTED WAS MY FREEDOM"

1. Norman Granz, telephone interview by author, March 11, 2000, transcript, 3–4, in author's possession.

2. Norman Granz, unpublished, untitled autobiographical writings, ca. 1990s, in Grete Granz's possession.

3. Granz, telephone interview by author, March 11, 2000, 9–10.

4. Ibid., 11–12.

5. Kevin Starr, *Material Dreams: Southern California through the 1920s* (New York: Oxford University Press, 1990), 120, 144.

6. Granz, telephone interview by author, March 11, 2000, 9.

7. Ibid.

8. Norman Granz, telephone interview by author, March 12, 2000, transcript, 5–6, in author's possession.

9. Quoted in Leonard Feather, "Jazz Millionaire," *Esquire,* January 1957, 99+.

10. Granz, autobiographical writings. For an overview of Green's astonishing life and career, see "Archie Green (1917–2009)," *American Folklife Center News,* Winter–Spring 2009, 11–12, www.loc.gov/folklife/.

11. Archie Green, telephone interview by author, July 4, 2001, transcript, 2, in author's possession.

12. Granz, autobiographical writings.

13. Archie Green, telephone interview by author, July 7, 2001, transcript, 11, in author's possession.

14. Granz, telephone interview by author, March 11, 2000, 24–25.

15. Green, telephone interview by author, July 7, 2001, 9–10; Norman Granz, interview by Elliot Meadow, London, February 27, 1987, transcript, 23, in author's possession.

16. Granz, telephone interview by author, March 11, 2000, 12–13.

17. Ibid., 18.

18. Ibid., 21–22.

19. Ibid., 19–20.

20. Ibid., 29.

21. Sandy Elster, telephone interview by author, July 14, 2001.

22. Norman Granz, telephone interview by Nat Hentoff, June 1994, transcript, 2–3, in author's possession.

2. "A MARVELOUS CRUCIBLE"

1. "Blackouts Crimp Coast Niteries; Ray Noble, Nat Brandwynne Hurt," *Down Beat,* February 1, 1942, 12.

2. "West Coast Blackouts Keep Musicians Away from Home," *Down Beat,* March 15, 1942, 12.

3. Red Callender and Elaine Cohen, *Unfinished Dream: The Musical World of Red Callender* (New York: Quartet Books, 1985), 28.

4. Leslie Gourse, *Unforgettable: The Life and Mystique of Nat King Cole* (New York: St. Martin's Press, 1991), 30.

5. Callender and Cohen, *Unfinished Dream,* 27.

6. Ibid.

7. Ibid.

8. Gourse, *Unforgettable,* 29.

9. Ibid., 45, 66.

10. David W. Stowe, *Swing Changes: Big Band Jazz in the New Deal* (Cambridge, MA: Harvard University Press, 1994), 132.

11. "Canteen Heads Have Row over Mixed Dancing," *Down Beat,* April 15, 1943; also see Stowe, *Swing Changes,* 161–62.

12. "Charge Prejudice behind Club Drive," *Down Beat,* March 1, 1945, 6; also see Stowe, *Swing Changes,* 162.

13. Norman Granz, telephone interview by author, March 25, 2001, transcript, 10–11, in author's possession.

14. Norman Granz, interview by Patricia Willard, Geneva, August 23–24, 1989, transcript, 2–3, Duke Ellington Oral History Project, National Museum of American History, Smithsonian Institution.

15. Ibid., 1–3.

16. "Lester Young, Count Basie Part Company," *Down Beat,* January 1, 1941, 14.

17. Lewis Porter, *Lester Young* (Boston: Twayne, 1985), 20.

18. Jimmy Rowles, interview by author, New Orleans, April 25, 1981, transcript, in author's possession.

19. Ibid. In the interview transcript, Rowles adds, "The Trouville is where he got his ideas." But I am presuming here that his physical description of Granz dates from when he first met him at the Capri.

20. Leonard Feather, "Jazz Millionaire," *Esquire,* January 1957, 99+.

21. Norman Granz, interview by Elliot Meadow, London, February 27, 1987, transcript, 79–80, in author's possession.

22. Norman Granz, unpublished, untitled autobiographical writings, ca. 1990s, 22, in Grete Granz's possession.

23. Norman Granz, in David Tarnow, *Norman Granz's Jazz at the Philharmonic,* radio documentary, Canadian Broadcasting Corporation, 1994, Program 1, Tape 1B, Institute of Jazz Studies, Rutgers University.

24. Ibid., Program 1, Tape 1B.

25. Norman Granz, telephone interview by author, March 11, 2000, transcript, 22–23, in author's possession.

26. Ibid., 29.

27. Duke Ellington, *Jump for Joy,* LP, Smithsonian Collection of Recordings R 037 DMM 1–0722, 1988.

28. Bruce Zolotow, "The Duke's 'Forgotten' L.A. Musical," *Los Angeles Magazine,* February 1982, 171.

29. Granz, interview by Willard, August 23–24, 1989, 24.

30. Ibid., 30–31.

31. Ibid., 146.

32. "Movie Dance Director: Marie Bryant Teaches Dancing Routines to Hollywood Stars," *Ebony,* April 1950.

33. Archie Green, interview by author, San Francisco, April 2003.

34. Norman Granz, interview by author, Geneva, May 21, 2001, transcript, 42, in author's possession.

35. Norman Granz, interview by author, Geneva, May 25, 2001, transcript, in author's possession.

36. Granz, telephone interview by author, March 11, 2000, 23; Norman Granz, telephone interview by author, May 9, 2001, transcript, 4, in author's possession.

37. Granz, telephone interviews by author, March 11, 2000, 38–39, and May 9, 2001, 4–5.

38. Granz, interview by author, March 25, 2001, 9, 39.

39. Ibid., 8.

40. Ibid., 5–6.

41. Granz, autobiographical writings, 29.

42. Granz, interview by Willard, August 23–24, 1989, 16.

3. COLE TRAIN

1. Norman Granz, telephone interview by author, March 25, 2001, transcript, 8–9, in author's possession.

2. Freddie Doyle, "Swingtime," *California Eagle,* July 2, 1942, 2B.

3. David Tarnow, *Norman Granz's Jazz at the Philharmonic,* radio documentary, Canadian Broadcasting Corporation, 1994, Program 1, Institute of Jazz Studies, Rutgers University.

4. Norman Granz, interview by Patricia Willard, Geneva, August 23–24, 1989, transcript, 11–12, Duke Ellington Oral History Project, National Museum of American History, Smithsonian Institution.

5. Charles Emge, "How Norman Granz's Flourishing Jazz Empire Started, Expanded," *Down Beat,* December 15, 1954, 3.

6. Leonard Feather, "Jazz Millionaire," *Esquire,* January 1957, 99+.

7. Granz, interview by Willard, August 23, 1989, 12.

8. Norman Granz, interview by Elliot Meadow, London, February 27, 1987, transcript, 17, in author's possession.

9. Jimmy Rowles, interview by author, Dallas, March 1982.

10. Doyle, "Swingtime," 2B.

11. Daniel Mark Epstein, *Nat King Cole* (New York: Farrar, Straus, and Giroux, 1999), 97.

12. Red Callender with Elaine Cohen, *Unfinished Dream: The Musical World of Red Callender* (New York: Quartet Books, 1985), 50.

13. "Night Columning," *Los Angeles Sentinel,* ca. July/August 1942, clipping, in Grete Granz's possession. The *Sentinel,* unfortunately, was not preserved on microfilm.

14. Lee Young, interview by Patricia Willard, Los Angeles, November 8–9, 1977, transcript, 7, in author's possession.

15. Phil Elwood, "Granz Is the Collectors' Collector," Jazz Beat, *San Francisco Examiner,* April 29, 1994, B12. Date confirmed with Elwood on September 10, 2001.

16. Norman Granz, telephone interview by author, March 11, 2000, transcript, 31–34, in author's possession.

17. "Night Columning."

18. Granz, telephone interview by author, March 11, 2000, 48–49.

19. Gunnar Myrdal, *An American Dilemma* (New York: McGraw-Hill, 1964), 924.

20. Carrie Miller, "Backstage," Theater World, *California Eagle,* July 15, 1943, 2B.

21. Granz, interview by Meadow, February 27, 1987, 17.

22. Granz, interview by Willard, August 23–24, 1989, 107.

23. Ibid., 14.

24. Norman Granz, telephone interview by John McDonough, September 12, 1978, transcript, 8, in author's possession.

25. Norman Granz, interview by Elliot Meadow, London, February 27, 1987, in author's possession.

4. "THE OPENER"

1. Scott DeVeaux, "The Emergence of the Jazz Concert, 1935–1945," *American Music* 7 (Spring 1989): 16–17.

2. Paul Eduard Miller, "The Jazz Scene: 1944—Events of the Year," in *Esquire's 1945 Jazz Book* (New York: A.S. Barnes, 1945), 49–51.

3. Archie Green, telephone interview by author, July 7, 2001, transcript, 23, in author's possession.

4. *Variety,* February 2, 1938, 52, quoted in DeVeaux, "Emergence," 17.

5. Sinclair Traill, "Jazz at the Philharmonic," interview with Norman Granz, in *Just Jazz 2,* ed. Sinclair Traill and Gerald Lascelles (London: Peter Davies, 1958), 17.

6. Bill Reed, *Hot from Harlem: Profiles in Classic African-American Entertainment* (Los Angeles: Cellar Door Books, 1998), 197.

7. Charles Emge, "How Norman Granz's Flourishing Jazz Empire Started, Expanded," *Down Beat,* December 15, 1954, 3+.

8. Barney Kessel, interview by Ira Gitler, in the chapter "California," in Ira Gitler's *Swing to Bop: An Oral History of the Transition in Jazz in the 1940s* (New York: Oxford University Press, 1985), 308.

9. David Tarnow, *Norman Granz's Jazz at the Philharmonic,* radio documentary, Canadian Broadcasting Corporation, 1994, Program 1, Tape 1B, Institute of Jazz Studies, Rutgers University.

10. Norman Granz, telephone interview by author, March 11, 2000, transcript, 58, in author's possession.

11. Patricia Willard, liner notes to Duke Ellington's *Jump for Joy,* Smithsonian Collection of Recordings, R 037 DMM 1–0722, 1988, 17–18.

12. Stuart Cosgrove, "The Zoot Suit and Style Warfare," *History Workshop* 18 (Autumn 1984): 80.

13. Nat Shapiro and Bruce Pollock, *Popular Music, 1920–1979* (Detroit: Gale Research, 1985), 1634.

14. Carey McWilliams, *North from Mexico: The Spanish-Speaking People of the United States* (New York: Greenwood Press, 1990), 208.

15. Ibid., 114.

16. Ibid., 220–21.

17. "First Lady Traces Zoot Riots to Discrimination," *Los Angeles Times,* June 17, 1943, 1:2a.

18. "Mrs. Roosevelt Challenged on Zoot Statement," *Los Angeles Times,* June 18, 1943, 1:2a.

19. "Mrs. Roosevelt Blindly Stirs Race Discord," editorial, *Los Angeles Times,* June 18, 1943.

20. "Mexican Press Gives First Zoot Suit View," *Los Angeles Times,* June 18, 1943, 1:2a.

21. Chester B. Himes, "Zoot Riots Are Race Riots," *The Crisis,* July 1943, 222.

22. McWilliams, *North from Mexico,* 230.

23. "Two Beaten in Philadelphia," *New York Times,* June 2, 1943, 1:22a.

24. Gene Lees, "Norman's Conquests," in *Oscar Peterson: The Will to Swing* (New York: Cooper Square Press, 2000), 76.

25. Norman Granz, interview by Danmarks Radio, Copenhagen, 1972, transcript, 1–2, in author's possession.

26. "L.A. Session Heps Kids; Granz to Do Second One," *Down Beat,* August 1, 1944, 12.

27. Tarnow, *Norman Granz's Jazz,* Program 2, Tape 2A.

28. Leslie Gourse, *Unforgettable: The Life and Mystique of Nat King Cole* (New York: St. Martin's Press, 1991), 66.

29. Tarnow, *Norman Granz's Jazz,* Program 2, Tape 2A.

30. Norman Granz, telephone interview by author, March 12, 2000, transcript, 17, in author's possession.

31. Benny Carter had been advertised to play but reportedly backed off at the last minute because of a lip injury. A backstage photograph of Carter, trumpet in hand, alongside Cole, Bryant, and Jacquet gives rise to the possibility that he might have performed after all, but he does not appear on any of the recordings.

32. Jean Bach, interview by author, New York, March 20, 2003, in *Out of the Norm: The Life and Times of Norman Granz,* BBC Radio 2, December 2003–January 2004.

33. Miller, "Jazz Scene," 51.

34. Charles Emge, "Kids," *Down Beat,* August 1, 1944, 12.

35. *People v. Zammora,* 66 Cal. App. 3d 166 (1944).

36. Tarnow, *Norman Granz's Jazz,* Program 2, Tape 2A.

37. Gordon Hollingshead to Jack Warner, interoffice communication, August 2, 1944, in *Jammin' the Blues* Production File, Warner Bros. Historical Archives, University of Southern California.

38. Charles Emge, "On the Set," *Down Beat,* November 1, 1944, 7.

39. Norman Granz, interview by John McDonough, January 12, 1980, notes, 9, in author's possession.

40. Tarnow, *Norman Granz's Jazz,* Program 2, Tape 2A.

41. *Jammin' the Blues,* which has been widely bootlegged through the years, was issued in 2006 by Turner Entertainment Corporation as a special feature with the 1944 film *Passage to Marseille,* with which it was paired when the film was released. The technical brilliance of *Jammin' the Blues* is reproduced from a clean print of the original Warner Bros. short film. Highly recommended.

42. Tarnow, *Norman Granz's Jazz,* Program 2, Tape 2B.

43. Ibid., Program 2, Tape 2A.

44. Gitler, *Swing to Bop,* 308–9.

45. Gordon Hollingshead to Charles Einfeld, interoffice communication, August 28, 1944, in *Jammin' the Blues* Production File, Warner Bros. Historical Archives, University of Southern California.

46. Jackie Lopez, "Is Hollywood Yielding?" *Chicago Defender,* March 24, 1945, 20.

47. "The New Pictures," *Time,* December 25, 1944, 50.

48. James Agee, "Films," *Nation,* December 16, 1944, 753.

49. Arthur Knight, "*Jammin' the Blues,* or the Sight of Jazz, 1944," in *Representing Jazz,* ed. Krin Gabbard (Durham: Duke University Press, 1995), 26–27.

50. Gjon Mili to Charles Einfeld, telegram, January 9, 1945, in *Jammin' the Blues* Production File, Warner Bros. Historical Archives, University of Southern California.

51. "L.A. Session Heps Kids," 12.

52. "Lawsuit Almost Halts L.A. Jam," *Down Beat,* August 15, 1944, 1.

53. Ben Young, "1944–1949 JATP Itinerary," liner notes to *The Complete Jazz at the Philharmonic on Verve, 1944–1949,* 171.

54. Leonard Feather, "Jazz Millionaire," *Esquire,* January 1957, 99+.

55. "Granz Bash Clicks Again," *Down Beat,* January 15, 1945, 6.

56. Granz, interview by McDonough, January 12, 1980, 11–12.

57. Lewis Porter, *Lester Young* (Boston: Twayne, 1985).

58. Granz, interview by McDonough, January 12, 1980, 12.

5. LET FREEDOM SWING

1. Norman Granz, interview by Elliot Meadow, London, February 27, 1987, transcript, 20, in author's possession.

2. Scott DeVeaux, "The Emergence of the Jazz Concert," *American Music* 7 (Spring 1989): 7.

3. Ibid., 8.

4. Albert Murray, *Stomping the Blues* (New York: Da Capo Press, 1977), 183.

5. Ibid.

6. DeVeaux, "Emergence," 9–10.

7. Ibid., 13.

8. Rudi Blesh, "*Esquire* Hangs Jazz on a Radio Hook-Up," *New York Herald Tribune,* January 21, 1945, 5.

9. DeVeaux, "Emergence," 21–22.

10. John Chilton, *The Song of the Hawk: The Life and Recordings of Coleman Hawkins* (Ann Arbor: University of Michigan Press), 221–22.

11. Granz's account of his first encounter with Coleman Hawkins is drawn from two interviews: Norman Granz, telephone interview by Nat Hentoff, June 1994, transcript, 38–40, and Norman Granz, telephone interview by author, March 11, 2000, transcript, 41–43, both in author's possession.

12. Granz, telephone interview by Hentoff, June 1994, 39–40.

13. The information on the Philharmonic budget is from "Shrine Aud(itorium) for Granz Concerto," *Down Beat,* May 15, 1945, 6; the Shrine information is from "Poor Advance Cancels Concert," *Down Beat,* June 15, 1945, 2.

14. "Bowl Fluffs Jazz; But Sinatra, Shore Okay," *Down Beat,* June 15, 1945, 1.

15. "New York Stinks Claims Coast Promoter," *Down Beat,* August 15, 1945, 2.

16. Norman Granz, telephone interview by John McDonough, March 6, 1989, transcript, 56, in author's possession.

17. Peter D. Goldsmith, *Making People's Music: Moe Asch and Folkways Records* (Washington, DC: Smithsonian Institution Press, 1998), 168.

18. "'Jazz at Philharmonic' Plans to Tour on One-Nighter Basis," *Billboard,* September 1, 1945.

19. "Jazz Concerts Set for Tour by MCA-Glaser," *Billboard,* November 17, 1945.

20. Eve Lavelle, press release, October 29, 1945, Asch Records.

21. "Jazz at the Philharmonic [Vol. 1]," review, *Metronome,* December 1945, 42.

22. Leonard Feather, "Jazz Millionaire," *Esquire,* January 1957, 99+.

23. Charlie Menees, interview by Ellie Webb, 1981, quoted in letter to Norman Granz by the author, March 12, 1982, in Grete Granz's possession.

24. Manek Daver, *Jazz Graphics: David Stone Martin* (Tokyo: Graphic-sha, 1991), 6–13.

25. Maine Morris, "The Northwestern Picture," *Clef,* June 1946, 3.

26. Norman Granz, JATP concert program notes, November 26, 1945, collection of Jazz at the Philharmonic concert programs, Institute of Jazz Studies, Rutgers University.

27. "Cheers, Moans at L.A. Concert," *Down Beat,* December 15, 1945, 2.

28. Granz, telephone interview by Hentoff, June 1994, 7.

29. Norman Granz, telephone interview by author, March 25, 2001, transcript, 11, in author's possession.

30. Hilmar Ghrondahl, "Music Critic Turns Cynic," *Oregonian,* December 6, 1945, 14.

31. Granz, interview by Meadow, February 27, 1987, 20–21.

32. "'Jazz at Philharmonic' Folds," *Billboard,* December 24, 1945, 17.

33. Norman Granz, interview by author, Geneva, May 25, 2001, transcript, 8–9, in author's possession.

34. Granz/Young recordings from July 15, 1942, and December 1945, and a third from December 22, 1945, featuring Helen Humes, with liner notes by Leonard Feather, can be heard on *The Complete Aladdin Recordings,* Blue Note CDP7243 8 32787 2 5 (1995).

35. Granz, interview by Meadow, February 27, 1987, 80–81.

36. Granz, interview by author, May 21, 2001, 29.

37. Gerald Wilson, telephone interview by author, April 25, 2001.

38. *Esquire*'s Board of Experts (including Norman Granz), "*Esquire's* All-American Band," in *Esquire's 1946 Jazz Book,* ed. Paul Eduard Miller (New York: Smith and Durrell, 1946), 32.

39. "*Beat* Sponsors Twin Concerts with Ellington," *Down Beat,* January 14, 1946, 1.

40. Phil Schaap, liner notes to *Bird: The Complete Charlie Parker,* Verve Records V 837 141–2, 1988.

41. "All-Star Concert Troupe to Hit Road," *Variety,* April 10, 1946, 52.

42. Bob Blumenthal, liner notes to *Bird at JATP '46,* Verve/Polydor VE-2–2518, 1977, originally released on *Jazz at the Philharmonic, Volumes 1, 2, 4,* and *5.*

43. Chilton, *Song of the Hawk,* 237.

44. Schaap, liner notes to *Bird,* 16.

45. "Duke, Woody for the Bowl," *Metronome,* June 1946, 35.

46. Richard Schickel, *Clint Eastwood: A Biography* (New York: Vintage Books, 1997), 40.

47. "Moore Jive Sends Crowd," *Seattle Times,* April 30, 1946, 12.

48. "Jazz Concert Is Reet Solid Stuff," *Denver Post,* May 3, 1946.

49. "Big House Looms for Philharmonic Jazz Session Monday," "Famed Musicians Booked Here by Pyramid Club," and "Jazz Concert Monday Eve. May 13," advertisement, all in the *Pittsburgh Courier,* May 11, 1946, 25.

50. Leonard Feather, "Jazz at the Philharmonic," *Metronome,* July 1946, 46.

51. "Norman Granz' Jazz at the Philharmonic," advertisement, *Variety,* June 5, 1946, 36–37.

52. Norman Granz, telephone interview by author, March 12, 2000, transcript, 34–35, in author's possession.

53. "Granz Jazz Grabs Good Grosses," *Down Beat,* June 17, 1946, 7.

54. "Duke, Woody for the Bowl," 35.

55. Leonard Feather, "U.S. Jazz Is Europe Bound: Redman, Stuff Smith, Hawkins on Way," *Melody Maker,* July 13, 1946, 3.

56. "Anti-bias Clause Inserted in Jazz Group's Contracts," *Pittsburgh Courier,* August 3, 1946, 19.

57. Cecil W. Boykin, "An Interview with Granz," *Detroit Tribune,* November 9, 1946.

58. "Norman Granz Jazz Unit Disowned in L.A.," *Variety,* August 28, 1946.

59. D. Leon Wolff, "Granz Bash a Caricature on Jazz; Everything Bad in Jazz Found Here," *Down Beat,* November 18, 1946, 3.

60. Norman Granz, "Granz Throws Leon's Words Right Back at Him," *Down Beat,* December 16, 1946, 16.

61. Granz, telephone interview by author, March 11, 2000, 18, 21–22.

6. NORMAN GRANZ VERSUS . . .

1. "Granz and Jazz at the Philharmonic," *The Crisis,* May 1947, 144; August Meier and Elliott Rudwick, *Along the Color Line: Explorations of the Black Experience* (Urbana: University of Illinois Press, 1976), 349–54, 196, 200–201.

2. James Farmer, *Lay Bare the Heart: An Autobiography of the Civil Rights Movement* (New York: Arbor House, 1985), 106.

3. Roy Wilkins, *Standing Fast: The Autobiography of Roy Wilkins* (New York: Viking Press, 1982), 199–200.

4. Leonard Feather, "Goffin, *Esquire,* and the Moldy Figs," in *Reading Jazz: A Gathering of Autobiography, Reportage, and Criticism from 1919 to Now* (New York: Pantheon Books, 1996), 736–37; "Granz Scrams *Esquire* Board, Hits Condon for 'Disservice to Jazz,'" *Variety,* January 22, 1947, 44.

5. Norman Granz, interview by Elliot Meadow, London, February 27, 1987, transcript, 42–43, in author's possession.

6. "Concert Trend May End in Trash Can," *Down Beat,* May 7, 1947, 15.

7. Ralph Gleason, "JATP May Push Concerts to New Marks," *Down Beat,* March 25, 1949, 7.

8. Ralph Gleason, "Bay Area Turns Away 800 at JATP Concerts," *Down Beat,* December 15, 1948, 15.

9. Granz, interview by Meadow, February 27, 1987, 41.

10. Helen Humes, interview by Helen Stanley Dance, May 12, 1981, transcript, 146, 173, Jazz Oral History Project, Institute of Jazz Studies, Rutgers University.

11. Trummy Young, interview by Patricia Willard, September 17–18, 1976, transcript, 107, Jazz Oral History Project, Institute of Jazz Studies, Rutgers University.

12. John S. Wilson, "Band Leaders Mobilize to Beat Jim Crow," *PM,* February 13, 1947, 17.

13. "Bandleaders to Help Fight Bias," *New York Amsterdam News,* February 15, 1947.

14. Wilson, "Band Leaders Mobilize to Beat Jim Crow," 17.

15. Ibid.

16. "Press Told of Musicians' Fight on Discrimination," *Washington Afro-American,* February 15, 1947, 17.

17. Martha Glaser to Franklin Williams, February or March 1947 (date stamped March 6, 1947), Franklin Williams to Walter White, memo, March 3, 1947, Martha Glaser to Franklin Williams, April 7, 1947, and Martha Glaser to Franklin Williams, April 9, 1947, all in Records of the NAACP, Library of Congress, Washington, DC.

18. Norman Granz, interview by Patricia Willard, Geneva, August 23–24, 1989, transcript, 34–35, Duke Ellington Oral History Project, National Museum of American History, Smithsonian Institution.

19. "Jazz Jumps the Color Line," *Negro Digest,* March 1948, 61, reprinted and digested from *Christian Science Monitor,* November 17, 1947.

20. "Off the Cuff," *Capitol News from Hollywood,* May 1947, 12.

21. "'Jazz' Plays Sour Note in Floperoo at L.A. Shrine," *Variety,* March 26, 1947, 48.

22. Charles Emge, "Granz Flops in Home Town," *Down Beat,* April 9, 1947, 2.

23. Neil F. Harrison, editor and publisher of *Record Retailing,* "Record Retailing," mimeographed report, February 1947, 1, Appendix B, William Russell Collection, Historic New Orleans Collection.

24. Bill Gottlieb, "Indies Losing Out in Wax Race," *Down Beat,* May 7, 1947, 1.

25. Peter D. Goldsmith, *Making People's Music: Moe Asch and Folkways Records* (Washington, DC: Smithsonian Institution Press, 1998), 201.

26. "'Philharmonic Jazz' Suit in Complications," *Billboard,* October 22, 1949, 17.

27. Norman Granz, interview by Eliot Meadow, London, 1977, transcript, 8, in author's possession.

28. Archie Green, telephone interview by author, July 21, 2001, transcript, 2–5, in author's possession.

29. Norman Granz, telephone interview by Nat Hentoff, June 1994, transcript, 19–21.

30. "Billie Wants No Part of Testimonial Dough," *Down Beat,* December 17, 1947, 1.

31. "Granz Relates Bias Fight," *Pittsburgh Courier,* November 22, 1947, 11.

32. Norman Granz, "Granz Lashes Back at *Beat* Statements," *Down Beat,* October 28, 1947.

33. "Granz Stanza Cut Short by Unscheduled Musicians," *Down Beat,* October 22, 1947, 16; Marvin Wildstein, comments to author, 2001.

34. Taped conversations between Norman and Grete Granz, ca. 2000, transcript, 159–60, in Grete Granz's possession.

35. John Chilton, *The Song of the Hawk: The Life and Recordings of Coleman Hawkins* (Ann Arbor: University of Michigan Press, 1990), 243.

7. MAMBO JAMBO

1. "Wham Coin for Jazz 'Longhairs,'" *Variety,* October 1, 1947, 1, 2.

2. Paul Eduard Miller, "Concerts Have Failed to Bring Prestige to Jazz," *Down Beat,* November 10, 1947, 11.

3. "Blesh, Granz, and Condon," *Down Beat,* October 8, 1947, 10.

4. "Granz Lashes Back at *Beat* Statements," *Down Beat,* October 28, 1947, 19.

5. Lawrence W. Levine, *Highbrow/Lowbrow: The Emergence of Cultural Hierarchy in America* (Cambridge, MA: Harvard University Press, 1988), 180.

6. Whitney Balliett, "Pandemonium Pays Off," *Saturday Review,* September 25, 1954, 45. A later, slightly revised version of this article is included in Balliet's collection of essays, *The Sound of Surprise: 46 Pieces on Jazz* (New York: E.P. Dutton, 1959).

7. Jack Hirschberg, "6,000 Jitterbugs Riot at Lunceford Date," *Metronome,* April 1940, 10.

8. Levine, *High Brow/Low Brow,* 192. Levine describes how in the early to middle nineteenth century America struggled to define a cultural identity separate from those European influences that the country had rejected. It is barely conceivable today, but Shakespeare and opera were mainstream cultural fare, not only in the emerging East Coast cities of the New World but also in miners' camps on the western frontier. Performers routinely adulterated the Bard's texts with comedy or colloquialisms and mixed them into a type of revue to engage appreciative audiences, which could shower good performances with boisterous applause or bad ones with overripe vegetables. "The theater in the first half of

the nineteenth century played the role that movies played in the first half of the twentieth century," Levine wrote. "It was a kaleidoscopic, democratic institution presenting a widely varying bill of fare to all classes and socioeconomic groups." Likewise, early America had a ravenous appetite for Italian opera, translated into English or pared down to presentations of famous arias, not unlike the repertoire of the much-celebrated Three Tenors (2, 4, 17).

9. Lawrence Levine, telephone interview by author, December 22, 2000, transcript, 4, 6, in author's possession.

10. Norman Granz, telephone interview by Nat Hentoff, June 1994, transcript, 37, in author's possession.

11. Norman Granz, interview by Danmarks Radio, Copenhagen, 1972, transcript, 4, in author's possession.

12. Norman Granz, telephone interview by John McDonough, September 12, 1978, transcript, 76–78, in author's possession.

13. Albert Murray, *Stomping the Blues* (New York: McGraw-Hill, 1976), 183.

14. Ibid.

15. "Jazz Concerts: Ex-speakeasy Music Wins Firm Beachhead in Symphony Halls," *Ebony*, September 1946.

16. Lee Rowe, telephone interview by author, July 21, 2001.

17. "JATP Goes Abroad for Spring Concerts," *Down Beat*, January 14, 1948, 11.

18. Leonard Feather, "U.S. Jazz Is Europe-Bound: Redman, Stuff Smith, Hawkins on the Way," *Melody Maker*, July 13, 1946, 3.

19. Arthur Schurgin, telephone interview by author, February 14, 2004.

20. Sheridan Sullivan, e-mail interview by author, received March 13, 2002; Leonard Feather, "Jazz Millionaire," *Esquire*, January 1957, 109.

21. Sullivan, e-mail interview by author, March 13, 2002.

22. Norman Granz, telephone interview by author, March 11, 2000, transcript, 54–55, in author's possession.

23. Ibid., 54–55.

24. Mike Nevard, "He Carries a Torch for Jazz and Racial Freedoms," *Melody Maker*, April 29, 1950, 3.

25. Harold H. Jensen, "Philharmonic Jazz Music Concert Different," *Deseret News*, November 16, 1948, F3.

26. Billy Reese, "Salt Lake City Jockey Gives JATP Assist," *Down Beat*, December 15, 1948, 15.

27. Gertrude Gibson, "Notes from a Newsgirl's Notebook," *California Eagle*, November 24, 1948, 17; "Bird a Floperoo; Hawk Still Tops," *Down Beat*, December 15, 1948, 7.

28. Granz, telephone interview by Hentoff, June 1994, 63–66.

29. Tom Piazza, "From a Fiery Conga Player, Jazz's Latin Tinge," *New York Times*, January 20, 2002, 32AR.

30. Frank Grillo (Machito), interview by Max Salazar, May 1980, transcript, 160, Jazz Oral History Project, Institute of Jazz Studies, Rutgers University.

31. Ibid., 162.

32. John Storm Roberts, *The Latin Tinge: The Impact of Latin American Music on the United States* (New York: Oxford University Press, 1999), 117.

33. Chico O'Farrill, interview by Ben Young, liner notes to *Cuban Blues*, Verve/PolyGram 314533256–2, 1998.

34. Oscar Huelos, liner notes to *Cuban Blues*, Verve/PolyGram 314533256–2, 1998.

35. "Chico O'Farrill: The Well-Rounded Writer," *Down Beat*, February 23, 1967, 24.

36. Ibid., 24–25.

37. It would be another twenty years before the unassuming O'Farrill again released a recording under his own name, *Pure Emotion*, which received a Grammy nomination in 1995. Two additional recordings in 1999 and 2000 added his name again to the honor roll of Latin jazz giants. He finished out his years on a renewed wave of popularity, leading a big band that included his son, the pianist Arturo O'Farrill Jr., at the reconstituted Birdland in New York; he died in June 2001.

38. Norman Granz, interview by Elliot Meadow, London, February 27, 1987, transcript, 75, in author's possession.

8. ENTER ELLA AND OSCAR

1. "'Jazz at the Philharmonic' Band Makes Its Eighth Tour Here," *Cleveland Plain Dealer*, March 6, 1949.

2. Norman Granz, interview by Patricia Willard, Geneva, August 23–24, 1989, transcript, 78, Duke Ellington Oral History Project, National Museum of American History, Smithsonian Institution.

3. Mike Levin, "Remarkable Album" and "Granz-Mercury Put Out Expensive Album," *Variety*, December 21, 1949, 39.

4. Brian Priestly, liner notes to *The Jazz Scene*, Verve Records 314 521 661–2, reissued by PolyGram, 1994.

5. Levin, "Remarkable Album."

6. Granz, interview by Willard, August 23–24, 1989, 79–80.

7. Phil Schaap, liner notes to *Bird: The Complete Charlie Parker on Verve*, vol. 16, Verve Records V 837 141–2, reissued by PolyGram, 1988.

8. Ibid.

9. Norman Granz, telephone interview by John McDonough, September 12, 1978, transcript, 83; Norman Granz, interview by Elliot Meadow, London, February 27, 1987, transcript, 88–89; and Norman Granz, interview by author, Geneva, May 23, 2001, transcript, 9–10, all in author's possession.

10. John Chilton, *The Song of the Hawk: The Life and Recordings of Coleman Hawkins* (Ann Arbor: University of Michigan Press, 1990), 260.

11. Gunther Schuller, *The Swing Era: The Development of Jazz, 1930–1945* (New York: Oxford University Press, 1989), 448.

12. Mike Levin, "Diggin' the Discs: Calls *Jazz Scene* Most Remarkable Album Ever," *Down Beat*, January 13, 1950, 14.

13. Geoffrey Mark Fidelman, *First Lady of Song: Ella Fitzgerald for the Record* (Secaucus, NJ: Carol Publishing Group, 1994), 55.

14. "With a Hoot and a Howl, JATP Kicks Off Another," *Down Beat*, April 8, 1949, 12; Fidelman, *First Lady*, 59.

15. Ralph Gleason, "JATP Plugging May Push Concerts to New Marks," *Down Beat,* March 29, 1949, 7.

16. Fidelman, *First Lady,* 59.

17. "Granz Plans Movie, Video," *Down Beat,* January 6, 1949, 5.

18. Barry Ulanov, "French Jazz Takes Cool Spins," *Metronome,* October 1953.

19. Mike Nevard, "He Carries a Torch for Jazz and Racial Freedoms," interview, *Melody Maker,* April 29, 1950, 3.

20. *Word and Music: Oscar Peterson,* CBC-TV documentary, February 16, 1983.

21. Claude Carrière, liner notes to *The Complete Young Oscar Peterson (1945–1949),* French RCA 66609–2, reissued by BMG France, 1994.

22. John Gilmore, *Swinging in Paradise: The Story of Jazz in Montreal* (Montreal: Véhicule Press, 1988), 108–9.

23. David Tarnow, *Norman Granz's Jazz at the Philharmonic,* radio documentary, Canadian Broadcasting Corporation, 1994, Program 4, Tape 4A, Institute of Jazz Studies, Rutgers University.

24. Ibid., Program 4, Tape 4A.

25. Oscar Peterson, interview by John McDonough and Matt Watson, Mississanga, Ontario, March 20, 1994, transcript, 4–7, Ella Fitzgerald Oral History Project, National Museum of American History, Smithsonian Institution.

26. Norman Granz, announcement, Carnegie Hall, New York, September 18, 1949, *The Complete Jazz at the Philharmonic on Verve, 1944–1949,* disc 9, track 8.

9. THE CONTINENTAL

1. John McDonough, "Jazz: Revisiting Maverick Norman Granz," *Wall Street Journal,* September 5, 1989, A12.

2. Mike Levin, "'JATP' Kicks Off at Carnegie; Mix Thinks Concert Was a Dandy—For a Change," *Down Beat,* October 21, 1949, 5.

3. Sharon A. Pease, "Oscar Peterson Arrives as a Top Jazzman," *Down Beat,* October 16, 1950, 12.

4. Mike Levin, "Oscar Peterson Is One of the Finest Things in Years: Mix," *Down Beat,* April 21, 1950, 5.

5. Norman Granz, interview by author, Geneva, May 25, 2001, transcript, 62–64, in author's possession.

6. Oscar Peterson, interview by John McDonough and Matt Watson, Mississauga, Ontario, March 20, 1997, transcript, 11–13, Ella Fitzgerald Oral History Project, National Museum of American History, Smithsonian Institution.

7. Oscar Peterson, interview by John McDonough and Matt Watson, Mississauga, Ontario, March 21, 1997, transcript, 12, Ella Fitzgerald Oral History Project, National Museum of American History, Smithsonian Institution.

8. *Oscar Peterson: The Compleat Pianist,* BBC Radio 3, April 12, 1974, quoted in Richard Palmer, *Oscar Peterson* (New York: Hippocrene Books, 1984), 20.

9. Stuart Nicholson, *Ella Fitzgerald* (London: Victor Gollancz, 1993), 37.

10. Ibid., 69.

11. Ibid., 122.

12. George Hoefer, "Singer 'Evelyn Fields' on Tracks Really Fitzgerald," *Down Beat,* February 24, 1950, 15.

13. Nicholson, *Fitzgerald,* 121.

14. "Ella Re-signs with Decca," *Down Beat,* November 16, 1951, 1.

15. Irwin H. Steinberg, telephone interview by author, March 23, 2002.

16. See Oscar Peterson, *Debut: The Clef/Mercury Duo Recordings, 1949–1951,* Verve Records 12950, 2009.

17. "'Jazz at the Phil'—For One Night?" *Melody Maker,* March 25, 1950, 7.

18. "'JATP' to Make European Jaunt," *Down Beat,* June 2, 1950, 1.

19. Ibid.

20. Ibid.

21. "Norman Granz Abandons European 'JATP' Project," *Melody Maker,* March 3, 1951, 1.

22. "Granz to Film 'JATP' Short," *Down Beat,* July 25, 1950, 1; "Granz Sets 'Jazz' Fall Tour, Two-Reeler Film," *Variety,* June 14, 1950, 57.

23. Norman Granz, interview by Elliot Meadow, London, February 27, 1987, transcript, 29–30, in author's possession.

24. "Now! The Tenth National Tour of the World's Greatest Jazz Concert," advertisement, *Down Beat,* October 6, 1950, 13.

25. "'JATP' Racking Up Huge Grosses on Current Tour," *Down Beat,* November 17, 1950, 4.

26. Flip Phillips, telephone interview by author, August 10, 1998.

27. Peterson, interview by McDonough and Watson, March 20, 1997, 30.

28. Don Freeman, "I Still Have a Distance to Go, Says Oscar Peterson," *Down Beat,* January 11, 1952, 12.

29. Oscar Peterson, telephone interview by author, January 10, 2000, transcript, 5–6, in author's possession.

30. Ibid., 6–8.

31. The early Oscar Peterson Trio recordings have been compiled in *The Complete Clef/Mercury Studio Recordings of the Oscar Peterson Trio (1951–1953),* Mosaic Records MD7–241, 2008.

32. James Lincoln Collier, *Duke Ellington* (New York: Oxford University Press, 1987), 258.

33. Jack Chambers, "Sweet as Bear Meat: The Paradox of Johnny Hodges," *Coda,* July–August 2001, 17.

34. Derek Jewell, *Duke* (New York: Norton, 1977), 115.

35. Norman Granz, interview by Patricia Willard, Geneva, August 23–24, 1989, transcript, 106, Duke Ellington Oral History Project, National Museum of American History, Smithsonian Institution.

36. "New Men Continue to Inspire Ellington Band," *Down Beat,* July 27, 1951, 3.

37. Don Freeman, "Krupa Scores Personally, Too, with 'JATP' Troupe," *Down Beat,* June 25, 1952, 7.

38. Granz, interview by Willard, August 23–24, 1989, 106–7.

39. Count Basie and Albert Murray, *Good Morning Blues: The Autobiography of Count Basie* (New York: Random House, 1985), 289–90.

40. Norman Granz, interview by Albert Murray, ca. early 1980s, transcript, II, in author's possession, for *Good Morning Blues: The Autobiography of Count Basie,* by Count Basie with Albert Murray (New York: Random House, 1985),

41. Ibid., 10.

42. "We're All Home—Let's Go Says Basie," *Melody Maker,* November 29, 1952, 4.

43. Oscar Peterson, interview by Joel E. Siegel, liner notes for *The Complete Billie Holiday on Verve, 1945–1959,* 189, Verve Records 314 517 658–2, 1992.

44. Unreleased tape of September 13, 1952, JATP concert, courtesy Fantasy Records.

45. "Oscar Peterson Interview," liner notes to *The Complete Billie Holiday on Verve, 1945–1959,* ten-CD set, Verve Records 314 517 658–2, reissued by PolyGram, 1992.

46. Oscar Peterson, telephone interview by author, March 9, 2000, transcript, 26–27, in author's possession.

47. Granz, interview by author, May 25, 2001, 3–4.

48. "Granz Sets 48 Dates for Big Jazz Safari," *Billboard,* September 15, 1951, 16.

49. "Ella, Oscar Peterson Star as 'JATP' Tour Begins," *Down Beat,* October 19, 1951, 1.

50. Norman Granz, telephone interview by author, March 12, 2000, transcript, 19–20, in author's possession.

51. Mack McCormick, "'JATP' Wins in Houston Tussle with 'Big Show,'" *Down Beat,* December 14, 1951, 2.

52. Ralph Gleason, "'JATP' Outpulls Ringling Brothers in Frisco Area," *Down Beat,* December 28, 1951, 6.

53. "Top Name Jazz Concert Packages Find B.O. Bonanza on Road This Year," *Variety,* December 5, 1951, 50.

54. "Jazz at the Phil for Scandinavia, France and Britain?" *Melody Maker,* March 22, 1952, 12.

55. Norman Granz, "Granz Tells Story of Tour; Lauds European Jazz Fans," *Down Beat,* June 4, 1952, 1+.

56. "Flip Flips French Fans," *Down Beat,* May 9, 1952, 8.

57. Mike Nevard, "JATP Brings Paris Fair to a Glorious End," *Melody Maker,* April 12, 1952, 4.

58. Granz, "Granz Tells Story," 13.

59. "MU Rejects JATP Offer to Play Free for Union Funds," *Melody Maker,* April 12, 1952, 1; "How to Do London in 11 Hours—by the Jazz at the Phil Trio," *Melody Maker,* April 19, 1952, 7.

60. Granz, "Granz Tells Story," 13.

61. Nevard, "JATP," 4.

62. Steve Race, "Picking Up Jazz in Brussels," *Melody Maker,* April 19, 1952, 2.

63. Frank Tenot, interview by author, Paris, May 28, 2001.

64. Granz, "Granz Tells Story," 1.

65. Ibid., 13.

66. "Granz's 'Jazz' in 21G Teeoff," *Variety,* September 17, 1952.

67. Max Salazar, liner notes to *The Original Mambo Kings,* Verve Records, 314–513–876, 1993.

10. "I FEEL MOST AT HOME IN THE STUDIO"

1. Barry Ulanov, "The Record Revolution," *Metronome,* March 1948.

2. Norman Granz, "How the LP Changed Methods of Waxing Jazz Sessions," *Down Beat,* September 23, 1953, 2.

3. "Granz Starts Up New Norgran Jazz Label," *Billboard,* February 13, 1954.

4. Norman Granz, telephone interview by author, March 12, 2000, transcript, 41, in author's possession.

5. Bill Coss, "The Granz Recordings," *Metronome,* October 1955, 24.

6. Ibid., 38.

7. The books in Greenwood Press's discography series provide the number of sessions versus that of discs resulting from sessions by Mercury/Clef/Norgran, Blue Note, Prestige, and Savoy. These numbers do not take into account errors by discographers or those made by the original producers. Accordingly, they are approximations that can still be useful in documenting these companies' level of activity. See Michel Ruppli, *The Clef/Verb Labels: A Discography,* vol. 1, *The Norman Granz Era* (New York: Greenwood Press, 1986), and *The Prestige Labels: A Discography* (Westport, CT: Greenwood Press, 1980); Michel Ruppli with Bob Porter, *The Savoy Label: A Discography* (Westport, CT: Greenwood Press, 1980); and Michael Cuscuna and Michel Ruppli, *The Blue Note Label: A Discography,* rev. and·expanded ed. (Westport, CT: Greenwood Press, 2001).

8. Ray Brown, telephone interview by author, June 12, 2002.

9. Norman Granz, interview by Elliot Meadow, London, February 27, 1987, transcript, 51–52, in author's possession.

10. Leonard Feather, "Jazz Millionaire," *Esquire,* January 1957, 99+.

11. Herman Leonard, interview by author, New Orleans, June 15, 1998.

12. Norman Granz, interview by author, Geneva, May 25, 2001, transcript, 46–47, in author's possession.

13. Norman Granz, telephone interview by Peter Pullman, May 7, 1997, in the liner notes to *Cote D'Azur Concerts on Verve,* eight-disc set, Verve/PolyGram 314 539 033, 1998, 2.

14. Norman Granz, unpublished autobiographical writings, ca. 1990s, 17, in Grete Granz's possession.

15. Leonard Feather, "*The Astaire Story* Another Milestone in Granz's Career," *Down Beat,* January 28, 1953.

16. Fred Astaire, liner notes to *The Astaire Story,* Verve CD 835649, PolyGram Records, 1988, 7–8.

17. Feather, "*The Astaire Story,*" 1+.

18. "In the Studio: The Proving Ground," in *Oscar Peterson Multimedia,* CD-ROM, PG Music, 2000.

19. Taped conversation between Norman and Grete Granz, ca. 2000, transcript, 6, in Grete Granz's possession.

20. Norman Granz, "The Story behind the Records," *Melody Maker,* January 8, 1955, 3.

21. Willis Conover, "An Art Tatum Interview: The Second Interview, November 1955," *Keyboard,* October 1981, 30.

22. Granz, "Story behind the Records," 3.

23. James Lester, *Too Marvelous for Words: The Life and Genius of Art Tatum* (New York: Oxford University Press, 1994), 205.

24. Red Callender and Elaine Cohen, *Unfinished Dream: The Musical World of Red Callender* (London: Quartet Books, 1985), 125.

25. Buddy DeFranco, telephone interview by author, March 18, 2001, transcript, 26–27, in author's possession.

26. Lester, *Too Marvelous for Words,* 210.

27. Callender and Cohen, *Unfinished Dream,* 125.

28. Andre Hodeir, "The Genius of Art Tatum," in *The Art of Jazz: Essays on the Nature and Development of Jazz,* ed. Martin Williams (New York: Oxford University Press, 1959), 176.

29. Gunther Schuller, *The Swing Era: The Development of Jazz, 1930–1945* (New York: Oxford University Press, 1989), 477.

30. Ibid., 498.

31. *The Complete Billie Holiday on Verve, 1945–1949,* Disc 4, Track 29, Verve 314 517 658, reissued by PolyGram Records, 1993.

32. Norman Granz, telephone interview by Nat Hentoff, June 1994, transcript, 57, in author's possession.

33. Norman Granz, interview by author, Geneva, May 30, 2001, transcript, 2, in author's possession.

34. Bones Howe, interview by author, Montecito, CA, April 2003.

35. Leonard, interview by author, June 15, 1998.

36. Carl Woideck, *Charlie Parker: His Life and Music* (Ann Arbor: University of Michigan Press, 1996), 131.

37. Phil Schaap, liner notes to *Bird: The Complete Charlie Parker on Verve,* Verve Records V 837 141–2, reissued by PolyGram Records, 1988, 13.

38. Ibid., 19.

39. Ibid., 21.

40. Ibid., 31–32.

41. Review of *Charlie Parker with Strings, Metronome,* August 1950, 30.

42. "Diggin' the Discs with Mix," *Down Beat,* February 10, 1950, 14.

43. Martin T. Williams, *The Jazz Tradition* (New York: Oxford University Press, 1970), 134; Woideck, *Charlie Parker,* 180–81.

44. Schaap, liner notes to *Bird,* 21.

45. Mike Nevard, "He Carries a Torch for Jazz and Racial Freedoms," *Melody Maker,* April 29, 1950, 3.

46. Schaap, liner notes to *Bird,* 20–21.

47. Nevard, "He Carries a Torch," 3.

48. Norman Granz, interview by Danmarks Radio, Copenhagen, 1972, transcript, 11–12, in author's possession.

49. Woideck, *Charlie Parker,* 196.

50. Nat Hentoff, "Granz Wouldn't Let Me Record with Parker," *Down Beat,* April 4, 1952, 7.

51. Granz, interview by Meadow, February 27, 1987, 100–101.

52. Schaap, liner notes to *Bird,* 30.

53. Woideck, *Charlie Parker,* 190.

54. Ibid., 45–46.

55. Norman Granz, interview by Jimmy Lyons on KFRC Radio, San Francisco, January 28, 1965, Institute of Jazz Studies, Rutgers University.

56. Woideck, *Charlie Parker*, 45.

57. Liner notes to *Diz and Getz*, Verve 422–833559–2, 1990.

58. Ben Young, interview by author, Institute of Jazz Studies, Rutgers University, May 8, 2001.

59. Michael Cuscuna, interview by author, June 19, 2002.

60. George Avakian, interview by author, Institute of Jazz Studies, Rutgers University, June 22, 2001.

11. STARRY NIGHTS

1. "The Jazz Business," *Time*, March 2, 1953, 40.

2. Gilbert Millstein, "Hot Jazz Promoter: Norman Granz Didn't Dig Music at First, But Now He Is Big-Time Impresario," *New York Times*, September 20, 1953, 2, 7.

3. Whitney Balliett, "Pandemonium Pays Off," *Saturday Review*, September 25, 1954, 45+.

4. Norman Granz, telephone interview by author, May 9, 2001, transcript, 15, in author's possession; Whitney Balliett, *The Sound of Surprise: 46 Pieces on Jazz* (New York: E. P. Dutton, 1959).

5. Bruce Frederickson, dir., *Song of the Spirit: The Story of Lester Young*, video, 1988, Institute of Jazz Studies, Rutgers University.

6. Pete Cavello, interview by author, New Orleans, April 26, 1981, transcript, 2, in author's possession.

7. Ibid., 3–4.

8. Louie Bellson, telephone interview by author, August 16, 1999, transcript, 6–7, 18, in author's possession.

9. Herb Ellis, telephone interview by author, April 1, 1996, transcript, 15, in author's possession.

10. Oscar Peterson, telephone interview by author, March 7, 2000, transcript, 11–12, in author's possession.

11. Buddy DeFranco, telephone interview by author, March 18, 2001, transcript, 2–3, in author's possession.

12. Ibid., 33.

13. Ibid., 4.

14. Hank Jones, interview by author, Washington, DC, April 14, 1996, transcript reconstructed from notes, 1–2, in author's possession.

15. Dizzy Gillespie, *To BE, or Not . . . to BOP* (Garden City, NY: Doubleday, 1979), 405–6.

16. John Hammond, "Lester Young," *Jazz: A Quarterly of American Music*, no. 3 (Summer 1959): 191–84, reprinted in *A Lester Young Reader*, ed. Lewis Porter (Washington, DC: Smithsonian Institution Press, 1991), 30.

17. Nat Hentoff, "Lester Young," in *The Jazz Makers*, ed. Nat Shapiro and Nat Hentoff (New York: Rinehart, 1957), 264.

18. Derek Young, "Is Lester Young Still the President?" *Melody Maker,* March 21, 1953, 4.

19. Gene Lees, *You Can't Steal a Gift: Dizzy, Clark, Milt, and Nat* (New Haven: Yale University Press, 2001), 223.

20. Don Freeman, "Rich Is Happy with Harry, Wants No Part of JATP," *Down Beat,* June 17, 1953, 2.

21. "Granz' Beef with B. Rich 'Personal,'" *Down Beat,* July 1, 1953, 3.

22. "Flip Replies to Buddy," *Down Beat,* July 15, 1953, 20.

23. Norman Granz, "Rich Is Great Drummer, but a Boor, Says Norm Granz," *Down Beat,* August 12, 1953, 4.

24. David Tarnow, *Norman Granz's Jazz at the Philharmonic,* radio documentary, Canadian Broadcasting Corporation, 1994, Program 3, Tape 3A, Institute of Jazz Studies, Rutgers University.

25. Oscar Peterson, *A Jazz Odyssey: The Life of Oscar Peterson* (London: Continuum, 2002), 94–95.

26. Ibid., 95.

27. Ibid., 96.

28. Oscar Peterson, telephone interview by author, January 10, 2000, transcript, 21–22, in author's possession.

29. Peterson, *Jazz Odyssey,* 153.

30. Ibid., 132.

31. Ellis, interview by author, April 1, 1996, 23–24.

32. Donald Maggin, *Stan Getz: A Life in Jazz* (New York: William Morrow, 1996), 127–39.

33. Letter, Barney Kessel to Norman Granz, May 25, 1996, in Grete Granz's possession.

34. Nat Hentoff, "Uncompromising Impresario," *Quest,* February–March 1980, 45, 93.

35. Peterson, *Jazz Odyssey,* 124–25.

36. Oscar Peterson, interview by John McDonough and Matt Watson, Mississauga, Ontario, March 21, 1997, transcript, 21–22, Ella Fitzgerald Oral History Project, Jazz Oral History Program Collection, National Museum of American History, Smithsonian Institution.

37. "Jazz at the Phil to Play London! To Appear with British Bands at Flood Fund Concerts," *Melody Maker,* February 28, 1953.

38. "Granz Planes into London as Fans and Musicians Blitz 'State,'" *Melody Maker,* March 7, 1953.

39. "Sensational JATP Shows Raise £4,000 for Flood Fund," *Melody Maker,* March 14, 1953.

40. Peterson, *Jazz Odyssey,* 129.

41. Tony Brown, "This Day Made History," *Melody Maker,* March 14, 1953, 2.

42. Norman Granz, interview by author, Geneva, May 21, 2001, transcript, 21, in author's possession.

43. "Granz Grosses 100G in 5 Weeks in Europe," *Billboard,* April 11, 1953, 16.

44. "Granz Plans Own Disk Distrib Setup in Brit; May Book Heath in U.S.," *Variety,* June 24, 1953, 52.

45. Norman Granz, telephone interview by John McDonough, February 1999, transcript, 20–26, in author's possession; Norman Granz, interview by author, Geneva, May 23, 2001, transcript, 39–43, in author's possession.

46. Granz's account of the pairing of Goodman and Armstrong is inconsistent with John Hammond's. Hammond's autobiography says Goodman made the arrangements with Armstrong's manager, Joe Glaser, which does not preclude Granz making the initial suggestion. Hammond does not mention Granz's role at all in his treatment of the episode, although his participation is documented in contemporary sources. John Hammond and Irving Townsend, *John Hammond on Record* (New York: Summit Books, 1977), 312.

47. Ibid., 315.

48. Granz, interview by McDonough, February 1999, 23–24.

49. Granz, interview by author, May 23, 2001, 40–41.

50. Len Guttridge, "What Happened When BG Left," *Melody Maker,* May 23, 1953, 4.

51. Hammond and Townsend, *John Hammond on Record,* 316.

52. Leonard Feather, "BG-Louis Tour Cited as Bitterest Jazz Hassle Ever," *Down Beat,* June 3, 1953, 1.

53. Granz, interview by author, May 23, 2001, 26.

54. Virginia Wicks, telephone interview by author, July 27, 2002.

55. Peterson, interview by McDonough and Watson, March 21, 1997, transcript, 24–25.

56. Nat Hentoff, "Some Fiery Jazz Heard as JATP Hits Carnegie," *Down Beat,* October 21, 1953, 3.

57. Ellis, interview by author, April 1, 1996.

58. Ibid., 8.

59. Peterson, interview by author, January 10, 2001, 25–27.

60. "Roaring Rhythm of Excitement: JATP's First Appearance in Tokyo," *Yomiuri Shinbun,* November 4, 1953, 7.

61. *J.A.T.P in Tokyo: Live at the Nichigeki Theatre, 1953,* Pablo Live, PACD 2620–104–2, 1953.

62. Ellis, interview by author, April 1, 1996, 5–6.

63. Pete Cavello, interview by author, Dallas, TX, March 1980, notes, in author's possession.

64. Peterson, *Jazz Odyssey,* 121–22.

65. "Americans Berate Disorderly Soldiers," unsourced newspaper clipping, n.d., in Grete Granz's possession.

66. "Granz's Jazz Payoff: Three JATP Tours Gross 600G Total Last Year," *Billboard,* January 9, 1954, 1+.

67. "The Man on Cloud No. 7," *Time,* November 8, 1954.

68. Leonard Feather, "Jazz Millionaire," *Esquire,* January 1957, 99+.

69. John S. Wilson, "Jazz and Mass Audiences," in *Jazz: The Transition Years, 1940–1960* (New York: Appleton-Century-Crofts, 1966), 147.

12. "THAT TALL OLD MAN STANDING NEXT TO ELLA FITZGERALD"

1. Stuart Nicholson, *Ella Fitzgerald* (London: Victor Gollancz, 1993), 37.

2. Leonard Feather, "The Granzwagon," in *From Satchmo to Miles* (1972; repr., New York: Da Capo Press, 1984), 181.

3. Norman Granz, interview by author, Geneva, May 23, 2001, transcript, 23, in author's possession. A copy of a one-year letter contract with annual options from Fitzgerald to Granz about assuming the role of her manager, dated April 1954 and unsigned by Granz, can be found in the Ella Fitzgerald Collection at the Smithsonian Archives Center, although he never wavered in stating that the two never had a formal contract.

4. "Any Style Will Do," *Newsweek,* June 7, 1954, 82.

5. Feather, "Granzwagon," 181.

6. Dominic Priore, "Marilyn Monroe: The Lost Performance," *Jazziz,* July 2002, 82.

7. Ibid.

8. Ibid.

9. Nat Hentoff, "Ella Tells of Trouble in Mind Concerning Discs, Television," *Down Beat,* February 23, 1955, 2.

10. David Tarnow, *Norman Granz's Jazz at the Philharmonic,* radio documentary, Canadian Broadcasting Corporation, 1994, Program 6, Tape 6A, Institute of Jazz Studies, Rutgers University.

11. "Granz Forms Two Labels, Dickers for Mars Masters, Cuts EP Price," *Down Beat,* February 8, 1956, 8.

12. Ibid.

13. Buddy Bregman, telephone interview by author, September 14, 2002.

14. Buddy Bregman, telephone interview by John McDonough, July 8, 1993.

15. Buddy Bregman, telephone interview by author, September 14, 2002.

16. Lee Jeske, "Ask Norman," *Jazziz,* November 1996, 59–60 (interview on the songbooks).

17. Milt Gabler to Norman Granz, December 13, 1954, and Norman Granz to Milt Gabler, July 5, 1955, both transcribed by Ed Berger, in Grete Granz's possession.

18. Norman Granz, telephone interview by John McDonough, July 11, 1993, transcript, 7, in author's possession.

19. Norman Granz, interview by John McDonough in liner notes to *The Complete Ella Fitzgerald Songbooks,* 84–85, Verve Records 314 519 832-2 (1993).

20. Buddy Bregman, telephone interview by author, September 14, 2002.

21. Granz, interview by McDonough, in liner notes to *Complete Ella Fitzgerald Songbooks*, 88–89.

22. Nicholson, *Ella Fitzgerald,* 151.

23. Buddy Bregman, telephone interview by author, September 14, 2002.

24. Granz, telephone interview by McDonough, July 11, 1993, transcript, 5, in author's possession.

25. "Ella Fitzgerald: *Ella Fitzgerald Sings the Cole Porter Song Book,*" *Down Beat,* June 27, 1956, 18.

26. Bill Coss, "Record Review: *Cole Porter Song Book,*" *Metronome,* September 1956, 26.

27. Norman Granz, telephone interview by John McDonough, September 12, 1978, transcript, 38, in author's possession.

28. Norman Granz, telephone interview by William Ruhlman, 1996, in liner notes to *The Complete Ella Fitzgerald and Louis Armstrong on Verve*, Verve Records 314 537 284-2, reissued by PolyGram Records, 1997.

29. "Narrow Escape for Granz in Car Crash," *Down Beat*, September 9, 1956, 28.

30. Granz, interview by McDonough, in liner notes to *Complete Ella Fitzgerald Songbooks*, 93.

31. Granz, telephone interview by McDonough, July 11, 1993, 17.

32. Bobby Bregman, telephone interview by author, September 16, 2002.

33. "Ella Fitzgerald Bookings," August 15, 1956–January 19, 1957, Ella Fitzgerald Collection, National Museum of American History, Smithsonian Institution.

34. Joe Russell, "Night Club Review: Mocambo," *Hollywood Reporter*, October 18, 1956, 16.

35. Norman Granz, interview by Peter Pullman, Geneva, May 7, 1997, 2.

36. Leonard Feather, "The Legend [Ella Fitzgerald]. She never knew her father or even where she was born. And her real ambition was to be a dancer like Snakehips Tucker," Calendar section, *Los Angeles Times*, January 30, 1983, 1+.

37. Norman Granz, interview by author, Geneva, May 23, 2001, transcript, 23, in author's possession.

38. Virginia Wicks, interview by author, Los Angeles, April 2003.

39. Paul Smith, telephone interview by author, August 24, 2002.

40. Mel Tormé, *It Wasn't All Velvet* (New York: Viking Press, 1988), 191–92.

41. Mel Tormé, *My Singing Teachers* (New York: Oxford University Press, 1994), 39–40.

42. Granz, interview by author, May 23, 2001, 22.

43. Norman Granz, interview by Elliot Meadow, London, February 27, 1987, transcript, 6, in author's possession.

44. Ibid., 24.

45. Nicholson, *Ella Fitzgerald*, 164–65.

46. Wicks, interview by author, April 2003.

47. Phoebe Jacobs, interview by author, New York City, March 30, 2001.

13. THE JAZZ HURRICANE

1. "Ella's Fella," *Metronome*, June 1954, 7.

2. Virginia Wicks, telephone interview by author, July 27, 2002.

3. Bobby Bregman, telephone interview by author, September 16, 2002.

4. Leonard Feather, "Jazz Millionaire," *Esquire*, January 1957, 99+.

5. Bob Porter, liner notes to *The Challenges*, Verve Records 815 1541 YM, 1983.

6. Louie Bellson, telephone interview by author, August 16, 1999, transcript, 1–2, in author's possession.

7. Pete Cavello, interview by author, New Orleans, April 26, 1981, transcript, 12, in author's possession.

8. Nat Hentoff, "Writer Underlines Granz's Top Jazz Accomplishment," *Down Beat,* December 15, 1954, 16.

9. Norman Granz, telephone interview by author, March 12, 2000, transcript, 20–21, in author's possession.

10. Peter Leslie, "JATP Special: The Jazz Circus Blows In," *Melody Maker,* February 12, 1955, 3+.

11. Buddy DeFranco, telephone interview by author, March 18, 2001, transcript, 29–30, in author's possession.

12. Feather, "Jazz Millionaire," 99+.

13. DeFranco, interview by author, March 18, 2001.

14. Norman and Grete Granz, taped conversations, ca. 2000, transcript, 136, in Grete Granz's possession.

15. Frank Tenot, interview by author, Paris, May 28, 2001.

16. "Keeper of Giants," *Melody Maker,* February 12, 1955, 2.

17. Mike Nevard, "Norman Granz: He Created a Jazz Empire, He Pays More Than Anyone, He's Made Many Enemies," *Melody Maker,* December 15, 1956, 3.

18. "Granz Reports Big Europe Biz," *Down Beat,* March 23, 1955, 1.

19. "Jazz World Mourns Loss of Charlie Parker," *Down Beat,* April 20, 1955, 6.

20. Dizzy Gillespie, with Al Fraser, *To BE, or Not . . . to BOP* (Garden City, NY: Doubleday, 1979), 394.

21. Leonard Feather, "The Parker Memorial Concert," *Melody Maker,* May 7, 1955, 5.

22. Bob Porter, liner notes to *Blues in Chicago,* Verve Records 815 1551 YM, 1983.

23. "Jazz Buffs Too Rough for Buff., Granz Flips Lid," *Variety,* September 28, 1955, 60.

24. Norman Granz, telephone interview by Nat Hentoff, June 1994, transcript, 22–28, in author's possession; Norman Granz, interview by author, Geneva, May 21, 2001, transcript, 4–9, in author's possession.

25. Granz's account is included in Gillespie, *To BE,* 407–10.

26. "Backstage at Music Hall: Ella Fitzgerald, 4 Others Nabbed on Gaming Charge," *Houston Post,* October 8, 1955, 1+.

27. Gillespie, *To BE,* 409–10.

28. "Houston Drops JATP Rap, Granz Spends $2,000 to Retrieve His $30 Bond," *Variety,* November 2, 1955, 49.

29. Don Freeman, "An Institution," *Down Beat,* December 14, 1955, 10.

30. George Wein, "Music: Symphony Hall, Jazz at the Philharmonic," *Boston Herald,* September 17, 1956.

31. Gene Lees, *Oscar Peterson: The Will to Swing,* updated ed. (New York: Cooper Square Press, 2000).

32. Norman Granz FBI File, #100–422788, April 5, 1956, 5.

33. Norman Granz, telephone interview by author, January 25, 2000, transcript, 16–17, in author's possession.

34. J. Edgar Hoover to Dennis A. Flinn, director, Office of Security, Department of State, April 13, 1956, Norman Granz FBI File, #100–422788, 7–8.

35. FBI memorandum, Los Angeles Office, May 14, 1956, Norman Granz FBI File, #100–422788, 18.

36. Granz, interview by author, January 25, 2000, 21+.

37. FBI Report on October 18, 1956, interview of Norman Granz in Los Angeles, October 30, 1956, Norman Granz FBI File, #100–422788, 43–44.

38. Granz, interview by author, January 25, 2000, 21+.

39. Ibid., 17–20.

40. Norman Granz, telephone interview by author, May 17, 1999, notes, 6–8, in author's possession.

14. "THE LOST GENERATION"

1. Burt Goldblatt, *Newport Jazz Festival: An Illustrated History* (New York: Dial Press, 1977), 5.

2. "13,000 at Newport Show Jazz Concerts Have Come of Age," *Down Beat,* August 25, 1954, 2.

3. "Plans Moving for Huge Summer Jazz Festival," *Down Beat,* June 16, 1954, 1.

4. "13,000 at Newport," 2.

5. George Frazier, "Blue Nights and Blue Stockings," *Esquire,* August 1955, 55–56.

6. Norman Granz, "Frazier versus Jazz at the Philharmonic" (letter to the editor), *Esquire,* November 1955, 14, and Leonard Feather, "Words on Music" (letter to the editor), *Esquire,* October 1955, 11, both in *Esquire*'s "The Sound and the Fury" section of reader letters.

7. Buddy Bregman, telephone interview by author, September 14, 2002.

8. Norman Granz, telephone interview by John McDonough, March 6, 1989, transcript, 23, in author's possession.

9. Norman Granz, interview by author, Geneva, May 21, 2001, transcript, 35, in author's possession.

10. Norman Granz, interview by author, Geneva, May 23, 2001, transcript, 31, in author's possession.

11. For an in-depth account of Duke Ellington's explosive comeback concert, see John Fass Morton's *Backstory in Blue: Ellington at Newport '56* (New Brunswick: Rutgers University Press, 2008).

12. Irving Kolodin, "Duke Ellington and Queen Ella," *Saturday Review,* April 12, 1958, 50.

13. "Ella Resting after Surgery," *Down Beat,* March 6, 1957, 13.

14. "Jazz School's First Session Set at Lenox," *Down Beat,* March 6, 1957, 13.

15. Chuck Suber, telephone interview by author, April 14, 2001.

16. Norman Granz, telephone interview by author, March 12, 2000, transcript, 25–26, in author's possession.

17. George Wein, *Myself among Others: A Life in Music* (Cambridge, MA: Da Capo Press, 2003), 181.

18. Granz, telephone interview by author, March 12, 2000, 25.

19. George Wein, interview by author, New York, April 22, 2001.

20. Norman and Grete Granz, taped conversations, ca. 2000, transcript, 45, 47, in Grete Granz's possession.

21. Ibid.

22. Billy Taylor, "The 'Lost Generation' of Jazz," *Esquire,* October 1958.

23. Nat Hentoff, "New Audiences and Old Jazzmen," *Saturday Review,* September 15, 1956, 30.

24. Russ Wilson, "Granz to Revamp Jazz Tour in '58," *Oakland Tribune,* October 7, 1957.

25. Particulars concerning these two dates, including the as-yet-to-be-resolved identity of the drummer—Connie Kay or Jo Jones—remain controversial, as can be seen in the threads of a discussion among some subscribers to the jazz research listserv in 2008.

26. Wilson, "Granz to Revamp."

27. Norman Granz, telephone interview by John McDonough, September 12, 1978, transcript, 27, in author's possession.

28. Russ Wilson, "World of Jazz: Granz Fit Subject for Alger Tale," *Oakland Tribune,* September 22, 1957, B19.

29. Norman Granz, interview by Albert Murray, ca. early 1980s, transcript, 11, in author's possession, for *Good Morning Blues: The Autobiography of Count Basie,* by Count Basie with Albert Murray (New York: Random House, 1985).

15. DUKE, PREZ, AND BILLIE

1. Norman Granz, interview by Patricia Willard, Geneva, August 23–24, 1989, transcript, 116–18, Duke Ellington Oral History Project, National Museum of American History, Smithsonian Institution.

2. Ibid.

3. Paul Hoeffler, telephone interview by author, January 12, 2003.

4. Duke Ellington, *Music Is My Mistress* (Garden City, NY: Doubleday, 1973), 238.

5. Klaus Stratemann, *Duke Ellington: Day by Day and Film by Film* (Copenhagen: JazzMedia, 1992).

6. Granz, interview by Willard, August 23–24, 1989, 50–51.

7. Ibid., 51–52.

8. Ibid.

9. Nat Hentoff, "The Duke," *Down Beat,* January 9, 1957, 20.

10. Granz, interview by Willard, August 23–24, 1989.

11. Ibid., 47–49.

12. Clark Terry, interview by author, Glen Cove, NY, March 22, 2001, transcript, 15–16, in author's possession.

13. Ibid., 156–58.

14. Bobby Scott, "The House in the Heart," *Jazzletter,* September 1983, 1–8.

15. Frank Büchmann-Møller, *You Just Fight for Your Life: The Story of Lester Young* (New York: Praeger, 1990), 177–78.

16. Norman Granz, telephone interview by John McDonough, January 12, 1980, notes, 17, in author's possession.

17. Büchmann-Møller, *You Just Fight,* 215.

18. Ibid., 218.

19. Lee Young, interview by Patricia Willard, November 9–10, 1977, transcript, 24–25, Jazz Oral History Project, Institute of Jazz Studies, Rutgers University.

20. Ad in *Down Beat,* April 30, 1959.

21. Paul Weston, telephone interview by John McDonough, July 1993, in McDonough's liner notes to *The Complete Ella Fitzgerald Songbooks,* 1, 4, 5, Verve Records 314 519 832 (1993).

22. McDonough, liner notes to *Complete Ella Fitzgerald Songbooks,* 105.

23. Hildegard Handel, telephone interview by author, Frankfurt, Germany, September 21, 2002.

24. Leonard Feather, "Ella: The Legend," Calendar section, *Los Angeles Times,* January 30, 1983, 1+.

25. Leonard Feather, "L.A. Honors the First Lady of Song," Calendar section, *Los Angeles Times,* April 23, 1989, 4+.

26. Benny Green, "The Arrival of Ella Fitzgerald and Norman Granz," liner notes to *The Complete Ella Fitzgerald Song Books on Verve,* Verve 314 519 832 2, 1993, 47–48.

27. John McDonough, "Ella: A Voice We'll Never Forget," *Down Beat,* September 1996, 20.

28. Louie Robinson, "First Lady of Jazz: Ella Fitzgerald Has Won Fame and Fortune but Sometimes When Alone, She Cries," *Ebony,* November 1961, 138–39.

16. JOIE DE VERVE

1. Norman Granz, interview by Elliot Meadow, London, February 27, 1987, transcript, 85–86, in author's possession.

2. Norman Granz, interview by author, Geneva, May 25, 2001, transcript, 39, author's possession.

3. Lee Konitz, telephone interview by author, April 11, 2001.

4. Bones Howe, interview by author, Montecito, CA, April 2003.

5. Leonard Feather, "Gerry Mulligan: Before and After," two-part interview, *Down Beat,* May 26 and June 9, 1960, reprinted in abridged form in *Down Beat,* May 2010, 48.

6. "Verve invites your critical consideration of America's newest musical provocation!" ad, *Down Beat,* October 27, 1960, 39.

7. The band's brief but illustrious career has been compiled as *The Complete Gerry Mulligan Concert Band Sessions,* Mosaic Records MD4–221, 2003.

8. Anita O'Day with George Eells, *High Times, Hard Times* (New York: G.P. Putnam's Sons, 1981), 227–35.

9. Carmen McRae to Norman Granz, Thanksgiving Day, n.d., in Grete Granz's possession.

10. Granz, interview by Meadow, February 27, 1987, 58–59.

11. Laurence Wilkinson, "Granz—Dictator of Jazz," *Melody Maker,* May 3, 1958, 2.

12. Nevil Skirmshire, "On Tour with JATP," *Jazz Journal,* July 1958, 4.

13. Roberto Capasso to author, Spring 2002, in author's possession.

14. Norman Granz, telephone interview by author, March 18, 2001, transcript, 3–5, in author's possession.

15. Capasso to author, spring 2002; Alfred V. Boerner to Clare Booth Luce, June 26, 1958, Foreign Service dispatch, National Archives.

16. Capasso to author, spring 2002.

17. P. E. Schneider, "Formidable M. Montand," *New York Times Sunday Magazine,* September 13, 1959, 76.

18. Simone Signoret, *Nostalgia Isn't What It Used to Be* (New York: Harper and Row, 1978), 228.

19. Ibid., 230–31.

20. Yves Montand, with Hervé Hamon and Patrick Rotman, *You See, I Haven't Forgotten* (New York: Knopf, 1992), 290.

21. Ibid., 292.

22. "Troubadour from France," *Time,* October 5, 1959, 51; Montand, *You See,* 296–98.

23. Montand, *You See,* 297.

24. Oscar Peterson, *A Jazz Odyssey: The Life of Oscar Peterson* (London: Continuum, 2002), 219.

25. Gene Lees, *Oscar Peterson: The Will to Swing* (Rockland, CA: Prima Publishing, 1990), 143.

26. Norman Granz, telephone interview by John McDonough, Geneva, February 1, 1999, transcript, 5–8, in author's possession.

27. Norman Granz, telephone interview by author, March 12, 2000, transcript, 22, in author's possession.

28. Quincy Jones, telephone interview by author, April 16, 2002; also see Quincy Jones, "Remembering a Man Who Was 'One of a Kind,'" Calendar section, *Los Angeles Times,* February 1990, written on the twenty-fifth anniversary of Cole's death.

29. Quincy Jones, interview by author, Beverly Hills, CA, April 2003.

30. Granz, interview by Meadow, February 27, 1987, 34–35.

31. Jones, interview by author, April 2003.

32. Hazel Guild, "Nat King Cole Hits Diskeries' Yen for Rock 'n Roll, but Sez TV Will Kill It," *Variety,* May 25, 1960, 57.

33. Norman Granz, "Norman Granz Rebuts Nat Cole on State of Jazz Here and Abroad," letter to editor, *Variety,* June 8, 1960, 51.

34. Steven Bach, *Marlene Dietrich: Life and Legend* (New York: William Morrow, 1992), 400.

35. Norman Granz, unpublished, untitled autobiographical writings, ca. 1990s, 15, in Grete Granz's possession.

36. Bach, *Marlene Dietrich,* 398.

37. Ibid., 399.

38. Ibid., 402.

39. Ibid., 403.

40. Norman Granz and Grete Granz, taped conversations, ca. 2000, transcript, in Grete Granz's possession.

41. Oscar Levant, *The Unimportance of Being Oscar* (New York: G. P. Putnam's Sons, 1968), 28.

42. Will Friedwald, *Sinatra! The Song Is You: A Singer's Art* (New York: Scribner, 1995), 366–67.

43. Norman Granz, interview by author, Geneva, May 23, 2001, transcript, 29, in author's possession.

17. ACROSS THE SEA

1. Gene Moskowitz, "Granz Digs Europe Where He's an Impresario Instead of a Manager," *Variety,* May 11, 1960, 47.

2. Leonard Feather, "Norman Granz," in *The Pleasures of Jazz* (New York: Horizon Press, 1976), 167.

3. Simone Signoret, *Nostalgia Isn't What It Used to Be* (New York: Harper and Row, 1978), 232.

4. Quincy Jones, interview by author, Los Angeles, April 2003; Mike Zwerin, telephone interview by author, March 2002.

5. Richard S. Ginell, liner notes to Shelly Manne and His Men, *Yesterdays,* Norman Granz' Jazz at the Philharmonic series, Pablo Records, PACD 5318, 2003.

6. Oscar Levant, *The Unimportance of Being Oscar* (New York: G. P. Putnam's Sons, 1968), 28.

7. Bill Belmont, interview by author, Berkeley, April 2003.

8. Norman Halsey, telephone interview by author, February 5, 2004.

9. Sue Arnold, "My First Love: 'You've Looked at Every Pair of Alligator Shoes on Bond Street,' He Said. 'Let Me Buy You Some,'" *London Daily Mail,* May 18, 1996, 39.

10. Grete Granz, interview by author, Geneva, October 2003, notes, in author's possession.

11. Recordings from two of Adderley's concerts at the Salle Pleyel in Paris were issued on Pablo Records as *The Cannonball Adderley Quintet: JATP, Paris, 1960,* Pablo Records 5303, 1997.

12. Ella Fitzgerald to Norman Granz at Hotel Saga, Reykjavik, Iceland, telegram, 1962, in Grete Granz's possession.

13. James Moody, telephone interview by author, April 28, 2001.

14. Michael Zwerin, "Keeping Up with Norman Granz," interview, *International Herald Tribune,* December 19, 1980.

15. Ibid.

16. Norman Granz and Grete Granz, taped conversations, ca. 2000, transcript, in Grete Granz's possession.

17. Ibid., 152.

18. Belmont, interview by author, April 2003.

19. Ibid.

20. "Granz acha Tom maior nome sa musica popular no mundo," *O Globo* (Rio de Janeiro), February 13, 1969, in Grete Granz's possession.

21. Granz and Granz, taped conversations, 56.

22. Clive Barnes, "Churchill Examined in Hochhuth's 'Soldiers,'" *New York Times,* May 2, 1968, 58.

23. Norman and Grete Granz, taped conversations, 137.

24. Norman Granz, interview by author, Geneva, May 23, 2001, transcript, 33, in author's possession.

18. "MUSICIANS DON'T WANT TO JAM"

1. Nat Hentoff, "Paying the New Jazz Dues," *Nation,* June 22, 1964, 635.
2. Ibid.; Gene Bach, interview by author, New York, March 20, 2003.
3. "AFM, Agencies Back Granz Plan for Jazzmen's Non-Segregation Clause," *Variety,* November 8, 1961, 55.
4. Dan Morgenstern, conversation with author, 2001.
5. Norman Granz, interview by Elliot Meadow, London, February 27, 1987, transcript, 77–78, in author's possession.
6. Dave Jampel, "Almost Nothing Left of Jazz in U.S., Complains Impresario Norman Granz," *Variety,* January 29, 1964, 53.
7. Dave Jampel, "Things Aren't Too Bad in Jazz Today, Goodman Sez; Raps Norman Granz," *Variety,* April 8, 1964, 67.
8. Norman Granz, "Granz Denies BG's Allegation That He Deserted Jazz in Hour of Need," letter to the editor, *Variety,* April 29, 1964, 173.
9. Max Jones, "The Jam Session Is Dead," *Melody Maker,* March 21, 1964, 13.
10. Norman Granz, telephone interview by author, March 11, 2000, transcript, 58–59, in author's possession.
11. Leonard Feather, "Jazz Beat: Message from Granz: Yank, Get Hip!" *New York Post,* October 31, 1965.
12. Norman Granz, telephone interview by John McDonough, March 6, 1989, transcript, 23, in author's possession.
13. Leonard Feather, "Jazz Today as Seen by Norman Granz," *Down Beat,* December 30, 1965, 26–30.
14. Nat Hentoff, "Second Chorus: Raising Waxing Criteria," *Down Beat,* October 20, 1966, 10.
15. Norman Granz, "A Reply to Nat Hentoff," *Down Beat,* November 17, 1966, 14.
16. Hentoff, "A Reply to a Reply," *Down Beat,* November 17, 1966, 14.
17. Bones Howe, interview by author, Montecito, CA, April 2003.
18. Norman Granz, interview by Patricia Willard, Geneva, August 23–24, 1989, transcript, 89, Duke Ellington Oral History Project, National Museum of American History, Smithsonian Institution.
19. Ibid., 90–91.
20. Ibid., 153–54.
21. J. Wilfred Johnson, *Ella Fitzgerald: An Annotated Discography* (Jefferson, NC: McFarland, 2001).
22. Klaus Stratemann, *Duke Ellington: Day by Day and Film by Film* (Copenhagen: JazzMedia, 1992), 530.
23. The result of the filming, produced by Jacques Muyal, was released in 2007 by LaserSwing Productions/Eagle Eye Media as a two-DVD set: *Duke Ellington at the Cote d'Azur with Ella Fitzgerald and Joan Miro* and *Duke: The Last Jam Session.* The concerts were released on Verve Records as *Duke*

Ellington and Ella Fitzgerald: The Complete Cote d'Azur Concerts on Verve, Verve/PolyGram 314 539 033, 1998.

24. Derek Jewell, *Duke: A Portrait of Duke Ellington* (New York: Norton, 1977), 164–65.

25. Ibid., 166.

26. Ibid.

27. Norman Granz to Duke Ellington, April 10, 1967, Institute of Jazz Studies, Rutgers University.

28. Norman Granz to Duke Ellington, April 11, 1967, Institute of Jazz Studies, Rutgers University.

29. Jewell, *Duke,* 166.

30. Patrick Scott, "Can JATP Turn Back the Clock?" *Toronto Daily Star,* April 1, 1967, 26.

31. D.W., "At the Academy: Ella and Duke Return Jazz to Old Stand," *Philadelphia Daily News,* April 1, 1967.

32. Whitney Balliett, "Jazz Concerts: Heaven and Earth," *New Yorker,* April 8, 1967, 163.

33. Clark Terry, interview by author, Glen Cove, NY, March 22, 2001, transcript, 64–65, in author's possession.

34. Norman Granz, telephone interview by author, January 25, 2000, transcript, 5–7, 28.

35. Granz, interview by Willard, August 23–24, 1989, 38–40.

36. Ibid., 40.

37. Harvey Siders, "Monterey Montage," *Down Beat,* November 25, 1971, 30. Sarah Vaughan's set was finally released in 2007 as *Sarah Vaughan: Live at the 1971 Monterey Jazz Festival,* Concord/MJF Records MJFR 30351.

38. Leonard Feather, "Monterey Jazz Festival," *International Musician,* November 1971, 4.

39. Norman Granz, interview by John S. Wilson, March 14, 1975, notes, John S. Wilson Papers, Institute of Jazz Studies, Rutgers University.

19. PICASSO ON THE BEACH

1. Norman Granz and Grete Granz, taped conversations, ca. 2000, transcript, 172, in Grete Granz's possession.

2. Norman Granz, unpublished, untitled autobiographical writings, ca. 1990s, in Grete Granz's possession.

3. Granz and Granz, taped conversations, 113.

4. Norman Granz, telephone interview by John McDonough, March 6, 1989, transcript, 25, in author's possession.

5. Olivier Berggruen, interview by author, New York, April 25, 2003.

6. *Tomorrow Show,* Tom Snyder, host, with Norman Granz, Oscar Peterson, George Benson, and Leonard Feather, National Broadcasting Corporation, ca. 1978.

7. Berggruen, interview by author, April 25, 2003.

8. Granz and Granz, taped conversations, 127–28.

9. Clark Terry, interview by author, Glen Cove, NY, March 22, 2001, transcript, 8–9, in author's possession.

10. Ray Brown, telephone interview by author, June 12, 2002.

11. John Richardson, interview by author, New York, March 4, 2004.

12. Granz and Granz, taped conversations, 99.

13. Ibid., 95–96.

14. Ibid., 95.

15. John Richardson, telephone interview by author, January 25, 2003; Berggruen, interview by author, April 25, 2003.

16. Day book, April 23, 1969, Anderson and Sheppard, London, courtesy of Anderson and Sheppard.

17. Granz and Granz, taped conversations, 104.

18. Ibid., 107–8.

19. Ibid., 83.

20. Ibid.

21. Ibid., 112.

22. *Picassos for Sale,* BBC Television, April 23, 1968, DVD, in author's possession.

23. Bevis Hillier, "Colour TV Makes £813,000 Art Sale Debut," *Times* (London), April 24, 1968.

24. Norman Granz FBI File, #100–422788, September 6, 1968.

25. Norman Granz, telephone interview by Nat Hentoff, June 1994, 76.

26. Granz, autobiographical writings.

27. Berggruen, interview by author, April 25, 2003.

28. Ibid., 106.

20. "ONE MORE ONCE"

1. Benny Green, interview by Elliot Meadow, 1987, in *Out of the Norm: The Life and Times of Norman Granz,* by Elliot Meadow (Nick Low/Demus Productions, 2003), broadcast on BBC Radio 2, December 2003–January 2004.

2. Norman Granz, introduction for Santa Monica Civic Center concert, June 2, 1972, on *Jazz at the Santa Monica Civic '72,* Pablo Records PACD-2625-701, 1972, reissued 1989, disc 1, track 1.

3. Norman Granz, interview by author, Geneva, May 21, 2001, transcript, 18–20, in author's possession.

4. Leonard Feather, "The Granzwagon," in *From Satchmo to Miles* (1972; repr., New York: Da Capo Press, 1984), 184–85.

5. Norman Granz, interview by John S. Wilson, March 14, 1975, notes, 2, John S. Wilson Papers, Institute of Jazz Studies, Rutgers University.

6. Christian Renninger, "Joe Pass," *Radio Free Jazz,* May 1978, 11.

7. Norman Granz, telephone interview by Nat Hentoff, June 1994, transcript, 55–56, in author's possession.

8. Ibid., 10.

9. John McDonough, "Count Basie: A Hard Look at an Old Softie," *Down Beat,* September 11, 1975, 17+.

10. Norman Granz, telephone interview by John McDonough, March 6, 1989, transcript, 4–7, in author's possession.

11. Norman Granz, liner notes for *Satch and Josh,* Pablo Records 2310–722, 1975.

12. Bob Porter, interview by Elliot Meadow, January 2003, Institute of Jazz Studies, Rutgers University.

13. Norman Granz, interview by Patricia Willard, Geneva, August 23–24, 1989, transcript, 59, Duke Ellington Oral History Project, National Museum of American History, Smithsonian Institution.

14. Released as *Duke: The Last Jam Session* on LaserSwing Productions/Eagle Eye Media (2007), a two-DVD set also containing the 1966 Duke Ellington/Ella Fitzgerald Cote d'Azur concerts.

15. Granz, interview by Willard, August 26, 1989, 159–61.

16. Ibid., 123.

17. Derek Jewell, *Duke: A Portrait of Duke Ellington* (New York: Norton, 1977), 211–12.

18. Ibid., 212.

19. Duke Ellington, *Music Is My Mistress* (Garden City, NY: Doubleday, 1973), 237.

20. Norman Granz, telephone interview by author, September 27, 1998.

21. Although Granz said in a November 1999 interview that he had only heard about Pass and read about him in jazz magazines, Eric Miller, his assistant in the Pablo years, said Granz had been a fan of Pass's even before 1970.

22. Oscar Peterson, telephone interview by author, March 7, 2000, transcript, 23–24, in author's possession.

23. Joe Pass, interview by Fred Woodruff, 1978, for Pablo Records promotional tape including interview and examples of his Pablo recordings, Institute of Jazz Studies, Rutgers University, courtesy of Ella Fitzgerald Charitable Foundation.

24. Joe Pass, interview by Martin Clarke, Hong Kong, n.d., Institute of Jazz Studies, Rutgers University, courtesy of Ella Fitzgerald Charitable Foundation.

25. Review of Joe Pass, *Virtuoso, Down Beat,* October 10, 1974, 21. See also Lee Underwood's praise for *Virtuoso* as "a gold mine of guitar artistry" in "Life on the Other Side of the Hour Glass," *Down Beat,* March 13, 1975.

26. Stuart Nicholson, *Ella Fitzgerald* (London: Victor Gollancz, 1993), 203.

27. *Take Love Easy,* record review, *Down Beat,* October 10, 1974, 22.

28. Gene Lees, *Oscar Peterson: The Will to Swing,* updated ed. (New York: Cooper Square Press, 2000), 218.

29. Ibid., 219.

30. Ibid., 20.

31. Norman Granz, unpublished letter to the editor of *Jazz Forum,* September 2, 1975.

32. Vadim Yurchenko, "Oscar Peterson in the Soviet Union," *Jazz Forum,* January 1975, 47+.

33. Granz, unpublished letter, September 2, 1975.

34. Oscar Peterson, interview by John McDonough and Matt Watson, March 21, 1997, transcript, 27–28, Ella Fitzgerald Oral History Project, National Museum of American History, Smithsonian Institution.

35. Ibid., 26–27.

36. Frank Tenot, interview by author, Paris, May 28, 2001.

21. TAKIN' IT ON OUT—FOR GOOD

1. *Tomorrow Show,* Tom Snyder, host, with Norman Granz, Oscar Peterson, George Benson, and Leonard Feather, National Broadcasting Corporation, ca. 1978, videotape, in author's possession.

2. Ed Berger, conversation with author, 2009.

3. Video recordings of several Montreux Jazz Festival concerts from 1975, 1977, and 1979 have been issued by Laser Swing Productions, the company founded by Norman Granz, Frank Tenot, and Jacques Muyal and Eagle Vision. Artists include such Pablo Records mainstays as Ella Fitzgerald, Oscar Peterson, Count Basie, Dizzy Gillespie, and Joe Pass. The twenty DVDs parallel multivolume sets from Montreux that Granz released in the late 1970s.

4. John S. Wilson, "Sinatra, Basie and Ella Fitzgerald Appear to an Audience of Old Admirers," *New York Times,* September 10, 1975.

5. Letter, Norman Granz to John S. Wilson, September 12, 1975, John S. Wilson Papers, Institute of Jazz Studies, Rutgers University.

6. James Gavin, *Stormy Weather: The Life of Lena Horne* (New York: Atria, 2009).

7. Mo Ostin, telephone interview by author, November 16, 2004.

8. Stuart Nicholson, *Ella Fitzgerald* (London: Gollancz, 1993), 168–69.

9. Norman Granz, telephone interview by author, March 12, 2000, 3–4.

10. Gary Giddins, "Soulfully, Sarah Vaughan," *Village Voice,* October 1978.

11. Oscar Peterson, telephone interview by author, March 9, 2000, transcript, 4–5, in author's possession.

12. Norman Granz, interview by author, Geneva, May 21, 2001, transcript, 53, in author's possession.

13. Norman Granz, liner notes to *The Trumpet Kings Meet the Oscar Peterson Big Four,* Pablo/OJC OJCCD-603, 1980.

14. Peterson, telephone interview by author, March 9, 2000, 23.

15. Norman Granz, interview by Elliot Meadow, London, February 27, 1987, transcript, 102, in author's possession.

16. Norman Granz, liner notes to *JATP: Return to Happiness, Tokyo, 1983,* Pablo Live PACD 2620–117, 1987.

17. John S. Wilson, "Count Basie, 79, Band Leader and Master of Swing, Dead," *New York Times,* April 27, 1984, A1+.

18. Stuart Troup, "Count Basie: One More Time," *Newsday,* May 1, 1984, 4/Part 2.

19. Nat Hentoff, "The Perfect Jazz Recording," review of *Count Basie/Kansas City 7, Wall Street Journal,* March 4, 1985, 24.

20. Norman Granz, liner notes to *Fancy Pants,* Pablo Records PACD 2310–920, 1983.

21. John S. Wilson, "Count Basie's Orchestra and Ella Fitzgerald," *New York Times,* July 4, 1982; Stephen Holden, "Jazz: Ella Fitzgerald Sings with Count Basie Group," *New York Times,* November 27, 1983.

22. Virginia Wicks, telephone interview by author, May 2001.

23. Leonard Feather, "Ella," Calendar section, *Los Angeles Times,* January 30, 1983, 1.

24. Nicholson, *Ella Fitzgerald,* 214.

25. Pamela Allen, interview by Elliot Meadow, January 2007.

26. Norman Granz, telephone interview by Nat Hentoff, June 1994, transcript, 50–53, in author's possession.

22. "SOMEWHERE THERE'S MUSIC"

1. Gene Lees, *Oscar Peterson: The Will to Swing,* updated ed. (New York: Cooper Square Press, 2000), 285.

2. Ibid.

3. Oscar Peterson, telephone interview by author, March 9, 2000, transcript, 14, in author's possession.

4. John McDonough, "He Draws Fire—and Crowds," *Wall Street Journal,* January 11, 1995.

5. Jim Blackman, conversation with author, 1996.

6. Kelly Peterson, conversation with author, 2010.

7. Jonathan Schwartz, "The Divine Pleasures of an 'Absent Genius,'" *New York Times,* June 23, 1996.

8. Billy Eckstine, in Elliot Meadow's *Out of the Norm: The Life and Times of Norman Granz,* Program 4, BBC Radio 2, December 2003–January 2004.

9. Olivier Berggruen, interview by author, New York, April 25, 2003.

10. "In the Recording Biz, Norman Is Best," *Leisure,* May 2, 1976, 8.

11. Norman Granz file, Benny Carter Collection, Institute of Jazz Studies, Rutgers University.

12. Peterson, telephone interview by author, March 9, 2000, 12–13.

13. Norman Granz, telephone interview by author, September 27, 1999, transcript, 5, in author's possession.

14. Norman Granz, telephone interview by John McDonough, Geneva, ca. January 1999, transcript, 3, in author's possession.

15. Peter Miller, conversation with author, 2000.

16. Norman Granz, telephone interview by author, May 9, 2001, transcript, 12–14, in author's possession.

17. Virginia Wicks, interview by author, Los Angeles, April 2003.

18. Russ Garcia to Norman Granz, May 15, 1997; Barney Kessel to Norman Granz, January 29, 1999; Mary Lou Callender to Norman Granz, n.d.; and Harry Edison to Norman Granz, ca. 1999, all in Grete Granz's possession.

19. Louie Bellson, telephone interview by author, August 16, 1999.

20. Archie Green, interview by author, San Francisco, April 2003.

21. Norman Granz file, Benny Carter Collection, Institute of Jazz Studies, Rutgers University.

22. Dwight Raiford, member of the board of directors of Harlem Little League, to Norman Granz, May 26, 1997, in Grete Granz's possession.

23. Herman Leonard, interview by author, June 15, 1998, New Orleans.

24. Ibid.

25. Clark Terry, interview by author, Glen Cove, NY, March 22, 2001, transcript, 9–11, in author's possession.

26. Quincy Jones, interview by author, Los Angeles, April 2003.

27. Norman Granz to John McDonough, June 1, 1982, in author's possession.

28. John McDonough, conversation with author, September 22, 2003.

29. Wicks, interview by author, April 2003.

30. Jon Thurber, "Norman Granz, 83; Visionary of the Jazz World Was Producer, Promoter, and Social Conscience," *Los Angeles Times,* November 24, 2001, B18.

EPILOGUE

1. Jon Thurber, "Norman Granz, 83; Visionary of the Jazz World Was Producer, Promoter, and Social Conscience," *Los Angeles Times,* November 24, 2001, B18.

2. Howard Reich, "Granz a Champion of Jazz, Race Relations," *Chicago Tribune,* December 2, 2001.

3. Steve Voce, "Norman Granz," *Independent* (London), November 25, 2001.

4. Elliot Meadow, "Norman Granz: Impresario Who Promoted Ella Fitzgerald and Duke Ellington," *Herald* (UK), November 27, 2001.

5. Ruy Castro, "Norman Granz Gave Life and Survival to Jazz," *O Estado de São Paolo,* December 1, 2001 (trans. Gil Hartman).

6. Pam Allen, interview by Elliot Meadow, Los Angeles, January 2007, in author's possession.

7. Norman and Grete Granz, taped conversations, ca. 2000, transcript, 234–45, in Grete Granz's possession.

8. *Ella Fitzgerald: Twelve Nights in Hollywood,* Verve Records, 80012920-2, 2009. Some of the songs were released in 1965 as *Ella in Hollywood,* which added stadium-level applause, was poorly received, and went out of print.

9. Fred Kaplan, "Intimate Ella Fitzgerald, Rediscovered," Arts and Leisure section, *New York Times,* November 29, 2009, 1+.

10. Norman Granz, interview by Elliot Meadow, London, 1977, transcript, 20–21, in author's possession.

11. Pamela Allen, interview by Elliot Meadow, Los Angeles, January 2007.

Selected Bibliography

ARCHIVAL SOURCES

Fantasy Records (Pablo Records): Fantasy Records vault, unissued concert recordings, 1940s–80s

Federal Bureau of Investigation: Norman Granz FBI file

Historic New Orleans Collection: William Russell Collection, newspaper clippings on Norman Granz and Jazz at the Philharmonic

Institute of Jazz Studies, Rutgers University: Jazz at the Philharmonic concert programs, recordings, and radio and video documentaries; Jazz Oral History Project; Benny Carter Collection; John S. Wilson Collection; other artist and photo files; books, periodicals, memorabilia, and ephemera

Library of Congress, Division of Maps

Library of Congress, Division of Music and Division of Newspapers and Periodicals: national and international music periodicals, African American and general-interest newspapers

Library of Congress, Records of the NAACP: National Office Files (New York), correspondence files

Smithsonian Archives Center, National Museum of American History, Smithsonian Institution: Duke Ellington Collection, Ella Fitzgerald Collection

U.S. Department of State: files on Norman Granz, Yves Montand, and Simone Signoret

Universal Music (Verve Records): research file, newspaper clippings, discography, and itinerary for *The Complete Jazz at the Philharmonic on Verve, 1944–1949*

University of California at Los Angeles, Special Collections: Norman Granz registration summary

Warner Bros. Corporate Archives, Los Angeles: Norman Granz work documents and time sheets
Warner Bros. Historical Archives, University of Southern California: production file, *Jammin' the Blues*

NEWSPAPERS, MAGAZINES, AND TRADE PUBLICATIONS
Atlantic Monthly
Baltimore Afro-American
Bass Player
Bergen (NJ) Record
Billboard
Blues & Rhythm
Boston Globe
Boston Herald
Boston Phoenix
Cadence
California Eagle
Capitol [Records] News of Hollywood
Chicago Daily News
Chicago Defender
Chicago Herald-American
Chicago Sun
Chicago Tribune
Christian Science Monitor
Chronicle of Higher Education
Cincinnati Enquirer
Clef
Cleveland Call and Post
Cleveland Plain Dealer
Coda
Collier's
Congressional Record
Crisis
Dallas Morning News
Denver Post
Deseret News
Detroit Free Press
Detroit Tribune
Different Drummer
Down Beat
Ebony
Esquire
Götesborgs-Tidningen
Guardian
Herald (United Kingdom)

Hollywood Reporter
Home News (New Brunswick, NJ)
Houston Post
Houston Press
Independent (London)
Indianapolis Times
International Herald Tribune
International Musician
Interview
Investor's Business Daily
Jazz Forum
Jazz Hot
Jazziz
Jazz Journal
Jazzletter
Jazz Monthly
Jazz Record
Jazz Report
Jazz Tempo
JazzTimes
Kansas City Star
Kansas City Times
Keyboard
Latin Beat
Leisure
Le Monde (Paris)
Le Samedi Culturel
Life
London Daily Mail
London Telegraph
Los Angeles Mirror-News
Los Angeles Sentinel
Los Angeles Times
Melody Maker
Metronome
Michigan Chronicle
Minneapolis Tribune
Mississippi Rag
Montreal Star
Musica Jazz
Musician
Nation
Negro Digest
Newark Star-Ledger
New Musical Express
New Republic

Newsday
New Statesman
New York Amsterdam News
New Yorker
New York Herald Tribune
New York News World
New York Post
New York Times
New York Times Sunday Magazine
Oakland Tribune
Observer (London)
Observer Review
O Estado de São Paolo
O Globo (Rio de Janeiro)
Oregonian (Portland)
Pageant
Palm Beach Post
Philadelphia Daily News
Pittsburgh Courier
P.M. (New York City)
Podium
Progressive
Pulse
Radio Free Jazz
Record Changer
Record Retailing
Redlands (CA) Facts
Rolling Stone
San Francisco Chronicle
San Francisco Examiner
Saturday Review
Seattle Post-Intelligencer
Seattle Times
Senior Scholastic
Stereo Review
Swing Journal
Time
Times of London
Toronto Daily Star
Toronto Evening Star
Toronto Globe and Mail
Toronto Telegram
Vanity Fair
Variety
Village Voice
Wall Street Journal
Washington Afro-American

PRIMARY PUBLISHED SOURCES

Anderson, J. Lee. "Lee and Lester, Part I: Marching to a Different Drummer." Interview with Lee Young. *Mississippi Rag,* December 1992, 1+.

"Backstage at Music Hall: Ella Fitzgerald, 4 Others Nabbed on Gaming Charge." *Houston Post,* October 8, 1955, A1.

Balliett, Whitney. "Pandemonium Pays Off." *Saturday Review,* September 25, 1954, 45. Reprinted in *The Sound of Surprise: 46 Pieces on Jazz.* New York: E. P. Dutton, 1959.

Basie, Count, and Albert Murray. *Good Morning Blues: The Autobiography of Count Basie.* New York: Random House, 1985.

Blumenthal, Bob. "Influential Producer Brought Jazz to the Concert Stage." *Boston Globe,* November 26, 2001, E3.

"Career Girl Press Agent." *Look,* January 26, 1954, 31+. [Feature on Virginia Wicks, JATP press agent.]

Cohen, Fred. Letter to editor [on Gene Lees's "A Farewell to Granz," June 1987]. *Jazzletter,* December 1987.

Conover, Willis. "An Art Tatum Interview: The Second Interview, November 1955." *Keyboard,* October 1981.

Coss, Bill. "Ella! Everybody Thinks She's the Greatest, Except Maybe Miss Fitzgerald Herself." *Metronome,* October 1953, 13+.

———. "The Norman Granz Story." *Metronome,* October 1955, 19+.

Crow, Bill. Letter to editor [on Gene Lees's "A Farewell to Granz," June 1987]. *Jazzletter,* December 1987.

Elwood, Philip. "Granz a Modern Jazz Dynamo." *San Francisco Chronicle,* December 1, 2001.

———. "Granz Is the Collectors' Collector." Jazz Beat. *San Francisco Examiner,* April 29, 1994, B12.

———. "Record Everything." *San Francisco Examiner,* November 25, 1977.

———. "Remarkable 'Jazz Scene' out on CD." *San Francisco Examiner,* November 24, 1994, C12.

Emge, Charles. "How Norman Granz's Flourishing Empire Started, Expanded." *Down Beat,* December 15, 1954, 3.

Feather, Leonard. "'The Astaire Story' Another Milestone in Granz' Career." *Down Beat,* January 28, 1953, 1+.

———. "BG-Louis Tour Cited as Bitterest Jazz Hassle Ever." *Down Beat,* June 3, 1953, 1.

———. "(Ella Fitzgerald) The Legend. She never knew her father or even where she was born. And her real ambition was to be a dancer like Snakehips Tucker." Calendar section, *Los Angeles Times,* January 30, 1983, 1+.

———. "Goffin, *Esquire,* and the Moldy Figs." In *Reading Jazz: A Gathering of Autobiography, Reportage, and Criticism from 1919 to Now.* New York: Pantheon Books, 1996.

———. "The Granzwagon." In *From Satchmo to Miles.* 1972. Reprint, New York: Da Capo Press, 1984.

———. "Jazz Millionaire." *Esquire,* January 1957, 99+.

———. "Jazz Today as Seen by Norman Granz," *Down Beat,* December 30, 1965, 26.

————. "Norman Granz." In *The Pleasures of Jazz.* New York: Horizon Press, 1976.

Fega, Mort. Letter to editor [on Gene Lees's "A Farewell to Granz," June 1987]. *Jazzletter,* December 1987.

Filene, Benjamin. "'Our Singing Country': John and Alan Lomax, Leadbelly, and the Construction of an American Past." *American Quarterly* 43 (December 1991): 602–24.

Gillespie, Dizzy. *To BE, or Not . . . to BOP.* Garden City, NY: Doubleday, 1979.

Gitler, Ira. "Norman Granz: One of Jazz's Leading Iconoclasts." Interview. *Radio Free Jazz,* November 1977, 10+; December 1977, 5+.

Granz, Norman. "A Divergent View from Norman Granz: The Brubeck Stand." *Down Beat,* July 21, 1960, 24.

————. "Esquire's All-American Band." In *Esquire's 1945 Jazz Book,* 27. New York: A.S. Barnes, 1945.

————. "Granz Denies BG's Allegation That He Deserted Jazz in Hour of Need." Letter to the editor. *Variety,* April 29, 1964, 173.

————. "Granz Tells Story of Tour; Lauds European Jazz Fans." *Down Beat,* June 4, 1952, 1+.

————. "How LP Changed Methods of Waxing Jazz Sessions." *Down Beat,* September 23, 1953, 2.

————. "I'm Still Human." *Melody Maker,* May 10, 1958, 6.

————. "Norman Granz Rebuts Nat Cole on State of Jazz Here and Abroad." Letter to editor. *Variety,* June 8, 1960, 51.

————. "A Reply to Nat Hentoff." *Down Beat,* November 17, 1966, 14.

"Granz Captures Ella for Verve and Clef." *Melody Maker,* January 7, 1956, 1.

"Granz Glad 'New Yorker' Panned His Astaire Album." *Down Beat,* February 11, 1953, 8.

"Granz Inaugurates LA Sunday Swing Shows." *Down Beat,* March 1, 1944, 6.

"Granz Lines Up Bandleaders v. Discrimination." *Variety,* February 12, 1947, 3.

"Granz Mapping Big Strides in Jazz Disc Field." *Billboard,* January 17, 1953, 28.

"Granz: No One Wants to Jam for Their Bread." The Jazz Scene. *Melody Maker,* December 4, 1965, 6.

"Granz Prepares Big LA Session." *Down Beat,* July 1, 1944, 11.

"Granz Relates Bias Fight." *Pittsburgh Courier,* November 22, 1947, 11.

"The Granz Stand." *Metronome,* November 1953, 21+.

Hammond, John, and Irving Townsend. *John Hammond on Record.* New York: Summit Books, 1977.

Hentoff, Nat. "The Impresario Who Brought Civil Rights to Jazz." In *Listen to the Stories.* New York: Harper Perennial, 1995.

————. "JATP Sells Democracy." *Down Beat,* May 7, 1952, 9.

————. "The Man Who 'Conserves' Jazz Artistry: After Four Decades, Norman Granz Still Provides a Forum for Our 'Indigenous Classical Musicians.'" *Chronicle of Higher Education,* March 5, 1979, 24.

————. "The Man Who Used Jazz for Justice." *Washington Post,* May 7, 1994, 19A.

————. "Norman Granz: Impresario of Recorded Jazz." *New York Times,* February 8, 1976, 24.

————. "The Perfect Jazz Recording." Review of *Count Basie/Kansas City 7. Wall Street Journal,* March 4, 1985.

————. "Raising Waxing Criteria." *Down Beat,* October 20, 1966, 10.

————. "A Reply to a Reply." *Down Beat,* December 20, 1966, 10.

————. "Uncompromising Impresario." *Quest/80,* February–March 1980, 43+.

"An Institution: That's What Years of Touring Have Made JATP; Even Price Boost Doesn't Deter the Big Crowds." *Down Beat,* December 14, 1955, 10.

"Jam Sessions Begin in Hollywood." *Down Beat,* July 1, 1942, 7.

Jampel, Dave. "Almost Nothing Left of Jazz in U.S., Complains Impresario Norman Granz." *Variety,* January 29, 1964, 53.

"'JATP' Kicks Off at Carnegie." *Down Beat,* October 21, 1949, 5.

"Jazz at the Philharmonic Attuned to Racial Amity." *Christian Science Monitor,* November 17, 1947, 2, 19.

"'Jazz at the Philharmonic' Head to Be Cited at Freedom Rally." *Pittsburgh Courier,* May 17, 1947, 17.

"'Jazz at the Philharmonic' Plans to Tour on One-Nighter Basis." *Billboard,* September 1, 1945.

"Jazz Audiences More Specialized: Granz." *Variety,* March 31, 1965.

"Jazz in Clover." *Newsweek,* September 27, 1954, 60+.

"Jazz Jumps the Color Line." *Baltimore Afro-American,* February 14, 1948, 8.

Jeske, Lee. "Ask Norman." *Jazziz,* November 1996, 58+.

"Keeper of Giants." *Melody Maker,* February 12, 1955, 2.

"L.A. Jam Session Attracts Crowd." *Down Beat,* July 15, 1944, 6.

Lees, Gene. "A Farewell to Granz." *Jazzletter,* June 1987, 1+.

————. "Hindsights." *Jazzletter,* May 1993, 4+.

Levin, Michael. "Calls 'Jazz Scene' Most Remarkable Album Ever." *Down Beat,* January 13, 1950, 14.

————. "'JATP' Kicks Off at Carnegie; Mix Thinks Concert Was a Dandy— For a Change." *Down Beat,* October 21, 1949, 5.

McDonough, John. "Jazz: Revisiting Maverick Norman Granz." *Wall Street Journal,* September 5, 1989, A12.

————. "Norman Granz: JATP Pilot." *Down Beat,* October 1979, 30.

———— "Pablo Patriarch: The Norman Granz Story, Part II." *Down Beat,* November 1979, 35+.

McWilliams, Carey. *North from Mexico: The Spanish-Speaking People of the United States.* New ed. New York: Greenwood Press, 1990. Originally published 1948.

————. "What We Did about Racial Minorities." In *While You Were Gone: A Report on Wartime Life in the United States.* New York: Simon and Schuster, 1946.

Meadow, Elliot. "Norman Granz: Impresario Who Promoted Ella Fitzgerald and Duke Ellington." *Herald* (United Kingdom), November 27, 2001.

Miller, Paul Eduard. "The Jazz Scene: 1944—Events of the Year." In *Esquire's 1945 Jazz Book,* 49–51. New York: A.S. Barnes, 1945.

Millstein, Gilbert. "Hot Jazz Promoter: Norman Granz Didn't Dig Music at First, but Now He Is Big-Time Impresario." *New York Times,* September 20, 1953, 2, 7.

Morgenstern, Dan. "Granz Back in Record Biz on Modest Scale." *Down Beat,* September 14, 1972, 9.

Nevard, Mike. "He Carries a Torch for Jazz and Racial Freedoms." Interview. *Melody Maker,* April 29, 1950, 3.

———. "I Offered JATP to the Musicians' Union for Nothing—and Heard No More." Interview with Granz. *Melody Maker,* December 22, 1951, 11.

O'Day, Anita, with George Eells. *High Times, Hard Times.* New York: G. P. Putnam's Sons, 1981.

Peterson, Oscar. "Coming to Grips." *Oscar Peterson Journal,* November 29, 2001, www.oscarpeterson.som/op/journal12.html.

"Press Told of Musicians' Fight on Discrimination." *Washington Afro-American,* February 15, 1947, 17.

Reich, Howard. "Granz a Champion of Jazz, Race Relations." *Chicago Tribune,* December 2, 2001.

Schwartz, Jonathan. "The Divine Pleasures of an 'Absent Genius.'" *New York Times,* June 23, 1996, 2, 3.

"Speaking of Pictures: Mili's First Movie Is Skillfully Lighted Jam Session." *Life,* January 22, 1945.

Thurber, Jon. "Norman Granz, 83; Visionary of the Jazz World Was Producer, Promoter, and Social Conscience." *Los Angeles Times,* November 24, 2001, B18.

"Tours, Disks Build Millions for Granz." *Billboard,* June 9, 1951, 10+.

Watrous, Peter. "A Label. A Vision. A Golden Anniversary." *New York Times,* April 3, 1994.

Wein, George. *Myself among Others: A Life in Music.* Cambridge, MA: Da Capo Press, 2003.

Wilkinson, Laurence. "Granz—Dictator of Jazz." *Melody Maker,* May 3, 1958, 2.

Yanon, Scott. "Ella on Record: The Most Logical Way through Ella's Life Is through Her Music." *Jazziz,* November 1996, 65+. [Fitzgerald tribute]

Zwerin, Michael. "Keeping Up with Norman Granz." Interview. *International Herald Tribune,* December 19, 1980.

SECONDARY SOURCES

Bach, Steven. *Marlene Dietrich: Life and Legend.* New York: William Morrow, 1992.

Berger, Morroe, Edward Berger, and James Patrick. *Benny Carter: A Life in American Music.* 2nd ed. Studies in Jazz 40. Lanham, MD: Scarecrow Press and Institute of Jazz Studies, Rutgers University, 2001.

Bubley, Esther, and Hank O'Neal. *The Norman Granz Jam Sessions.* Levallois-Perret Cedex, France: Filipacchi, 1995.

Chilton, John. *Billie's Blues: A Survey of Billie Holiday's Career, 1933–1959.* London: Quartet Books, 1975.

————. *Roy Eldridge: Little Jazz Giant.* London: Continuum, 2002.

————. *The Song of the Hawk: The Life and Recordings of Coleman Hawkins.* Ann Arbor: University of Michigan Press, 1990.

Clarke, Donald. *Wishing on the Moon: The Life and Times of Billie Holiday.* New York: Penguin Books, 1994.

Clayton, Buck, and Nancy Miller Elliott. *Buck Clayton's Jazz World.* New York: Macmillan, 1986.

Cosgrove, Stuart. "The Zoot Suit and Style Warfare." *History Workshop* 18 (Autumn 1984): 77–91.

Dalfiume, Richard M. "The 'Forgotten Years' of the Negro Revolution." *Journal of American History* 55 (March 1986): 90–106.

Dance, Helen Oakley. *Stormy Monday: The T-Bone Walker Story.* Baton Rouge: Louisiana State University Press, 1987.

Delannoy, Luc. *Pres: The Story of Lester Young.* Translated by Elena B. Odio. Fayetteville: University of Arkansas Press, 1993.

DeVeaux, Scott. "The Emergence of the Jazz Concert." *American Music* 7 (Spring 1989): 6–29.

Epstein, Daniel Mark. *Nat King Cole.* New York: Farrar, Straus, and Giroux, 1999.

Farmer, James. *Lay Bare the Heart: An Autobiography of the Civil Rights Movement.* New York: Arbor House, 1985.

Faulker, Scott David. "Norman and Duke: A Look at the Relationship between Norman Granz and Duke Ellington." MA thesis, University of Nevada at Reno, 1996.

Friedwald, Will. *Jazz Singing: America's Great Voices from Bessie Smith to Bebop and Beyond.* New York: Charles Scribner's Sons, 1990.

————. "Lady Day . . . Billie Holiday." In *The Billie Holiday Companion: Seven Decades of Commentary,* edited by Leslie Gourse. New York: Schirmer Books, 1997.

————. *Sinatra! The Song Is You: A Singer's Art.* New York: Scribner, 1995.

Gendron, Bernard. "'Moldy Figs' and Modernists: Jazz at War (1942–1942)." In *Jazz among the Discourses,* edited by Krin Gabbard. Durham: Duke University Press, 1995.

Gennari, John R. "The Politics of Culture and Identity in American Jazz Criticism." PhD diss., University of Pennsylvania, 1993.

Giddins, Gary. *Rhythm-a-ning: Jazz Tradition and Innovation in the '80s.* New York: Oxford University Press, 1985.

————. *Riding a Blue Note: Jazz and American Pop.* New York: Oxford University Press, 1981.

————. *Satchmo.* New York: Doubleday, 1988.

Gitler, Ira. *Jazz Masters of the Forties.* New York: Macmillan, 1962.

———— *Swing to Bop: An Oral History of the Transition of Jazz in the 1940s.* New York: Oxford University Press, 1985.

Goldsmith, Peter D. *Making People's Music: Moe Asch and Folkways Records.* Washington, DC: Smithsonian Institution Press, 1998.

Gourse, Leslie. *The Billie Holiday Companion: Seven Decades of Commentary.* New York: Schirmer Books, 1997.

————. *Unforgettable: The Life and Mystique of Nat King Cole.* New York: St. Martin's Press, 1991.

Green, Archie. *Torching the Fink Books and Other Essays on Vernacular Culture.* Durham: North Carolina University Press, 2001.

Hobsbawm, Eric. "Jazz Concerts." In *This Is Jazz,* edited by Ken Williamson. London: Newnes, 1960.

————. *The Jazz Scene.* New York: Pantheon Books, 1993.

Klein, Norman J. "The Sunshine Strategy." In *20th Century Los Angeles: Power, Promotion and Social Promotion,* edited by Norman J. Klein and Martin J. Schiesl. Claremont, CA: Regina Books, 1990.

Knight, Arthur. "*Jammin' the Blues,* or the Sight of Jazz, 1944." In *Representing Jazz,* edited by Krin Gabbard. Durham: Duke University Press, 1995.

Lees, Gene. *Cats of Any Color: Jazz in Black and White.* New York: Oxford University Press, 1994.

————. *Oscar Peterson: The Will to Swing.* Updated ed. New York: Cooper Square Press, 2000.

Lester, James. *Too Marvelous for Words: The Life and Genius of Art Tatum.* New York: Oxford University Press, 1994.

Levine, Lawrence. *Highbrow/Lowbrow: The Emergence of Hierarchy in American Culture.* Cambridge, MA: Harvard University Press, 1988.

Lippincott, Bruce. "Aspects of the Jam Session." In *Jam Session: An Anthology of Jazz,* edited by Ralph J. Gleason. New York: G.P. Putnam's Sons, 1958.

Lipsitz, George. *Rainbow at Midnight: Labor and Culture in the 1940s.* Urbana: University of Illinois Press, 1994.

Maggin, Donald L. *Dizzy: The Life and Times of John Birks Gillespie.* New York: HarperEntertainment, 2005.

————. *Stan Getz: A Life in Jazz.* New York: William Morrow, 1996.

Mazon, Mauricio. *The Zoot Suit Riots: The Psychology of Symbolic Annihilation.* Austin: University of Texas Press, 1984.

Meriwether, Doug. *Mister, I Am the Band! Buddy Rich, His Life and Travels.* North Bellmore, NY: National Drum Association, 1995.

Modell, John, Marc Goulden, and Sigurder Magnussen. "World War II in the Lives of Black Americans: Some Findings and an Interpretation." *Journal of American History* 76 (December 1989): 838–48.

Murray, Albert. *The Blue Devils of Nada: A Contemporary American Approach to Aesthetic Statement.* New York: Pantheon Books, 1996.

————. *Stomping the Blues.* New York: McGraw-Hill, 1976. Reprint, New York: Da Capo Press, 1977.

Nash, Gerald D. *The American West Transformed: The Impact of the Second World War.* Bloomington: Indiana University Press, 1985.

————. *World War II and the West: Reshaping the Economy.* Lincoln: University of Nebraska Press, 1990.

Nicholson, Stuart. *Billie Holiday.* Boston: Northeastern University Press, 1995.

————. *Ella Fitzgerald.* London: Gollancz, 1993.

O'Neil, Thomas. *The Grammys: For the Record.* New York: Penguin Books, 1993–.

Palmer, Richard. *Oscar Peterson.* New York: Hippocrene Books, 1984.

Peterson, Oscar. *A Jazz Odyssey: The Life of Oscar Peterson*. London: Continuum, 2002.

Pfeffer, Paula. *A. Philip Randolph, Pioneer of the Civil Rights Movement*. Baton Rouge: University of Louisiana Press, 1990.

Porter, Lewis. *Lester Young*. Boston: Twayne, 1985.

———, ed. *A Lester Young Reader*. Washington, DC: Smithsonian Institution Press, 1991.

Rowan, Carl T. *Dream Makers, Dream Breakers: The World of Justice Thurgood Marshall*. Boston: Little, Brown, 1993.

Ruppli, Michael, ed. *The Clef/Verve Labels: A Discography*. Vol. 1. *The Norman Granz Era*. New York: Greenwood Press, 1986.

Schickel, Richard. *Clint Eastwood: A Biography*. New York: Vintage Books, 1997.

Schuller, Gunther. *The Swing Era: The Development of Jazz, 1930–1945*. New York: Oxford University Press, 1989.

Shaughnessy, Mary Alice. *Les Paul: An American Original*. New York: William Morrow, 1993.

Shipton, Alyn. *Groovin' High: The Life of Dizzy Gillespie*. New York: Oxford University Press, 1999.

Sitkoff, Harvard. "Racial Militancy and Interracial Violence in the Second World War." *Journal of American History* 58 (December 1979): 661–81.

Stratemann, Klaus. *Duke Ellington: Day by Day and Film by Film*. Copenhagen: JazzMedia, 1992.

Vail, Ken. *Bird's Diary: The Life of Charlie Parker, 1945–1955*. Chessington, Surrey: Castle Communications, 1996.

Verge, Arthur. *Paradise Transformed: Los Angeles during the Second World War*. Dubuque, IA: Kendell/Hunt, 1993.

Wilson, John S. *Jazz: The Transition Years, 1940–1960*. New York: Appleton-Century-Crofts, 1966.

Woideck, Carl. *Charlie Parker: His Life and Music*. Ann Arbor: University of Michigan Press, 1996.

LINER NOTES

Dance, Stanley. Liner notes to *The Complete Anita O'Day Clef/Verve Sessions*. Mosaic Records MD9 188, 2000.

———. Liner notes to *The Complete Johnny Hodges Sessions, 1951–1955* [on Verve Records]. Reissue, Mosaic Records MD 6 126, 1989.

Green, Bennie. Liner notes to *Count Basie: The Golden Years*. Pablo Records, PACD 4419–2, 1996.

Hershorn, Tad. "Biography of a Philosophy." Liner notes to *The Complete Norman Granz Jam Sessions*. Verve Records 3252, 2004.

Morgenstern, Dan, James Gavin, Milt Gabler, and Bud Katzel. Liner notes to *Ella Fitzgerald: The 75th Birthday Celebration. The Original Decca Recordings*. Decca GRD-2–619, 1993.

Mosaic Records. Liner notes to *The Complete Verve/Clef Charlie Ventura and Flip Phillips Studio Sessions*. 6-CD set. Mosaic Records MD6 182, 1999.

Schaap, Phil. Liner notes to *Bird: The Complete Charlie Parker on Verve*. Verve Records V 837 141–2. Copyright 1998 PolyGram Records.

Verve Records. Liner notes to *The Complete Billie Holiday on Verve, 1945–1959*. Originally produced by Norman Granz. Executive producers, Michael Lang and Richard Seidel. Verve Records 314 517 658–2. 10 CD Set. Copyright 1993/PolyGram Records.

————. *The Complete Jazz at the Philharmonic on Verve Records, 1944–1949*. Originally produced by Norman Granz. Supervised by Michael Land and Ben Young. Verve Records 314 523 893–2. Copyright 1998 PolyGram Records.

————. Liner notes to *The Complete Lester Young Studio Sessions on Verve*. Originally produced by Norman Granz. Supervised by Michael Lang and Ben Young. Verve Records 314 547 087–2. Copyright 1999 PolyGram Records.

Willard, Patricia. Liner notes to Duke Ellington, *Jump for Joy*. Smithsonian Collection of Recordings, R 037 DMM 1–0722, 1988.

Young, Ben. "1944–1949 JATP Itinerary." Liner notes for *The Complete Jazz at the Philharmonic on Verve, 1944–1949*. Verve 314 523 893–2, 1998.

Index

TEXT
10/13 Sabon

DISPLAY
Din

COMPOSITOR
BookComp, Inc.

INDEXER
Ruth Elwell

PRINTER AND BINDER
Thompson-Shore, Inc.